9.20.10

To Becci –

Born the day
Warsaw ghetto
fell.

Thank you for being a
nice sister

L, F

NATALIE Scott

NATALIE Scott

A Magnificent Life

John W. Scott

PELICAN PUBLISHING COMPANY
GRETNA 2008

The word "Pelican" and the depiction of a pelican are trademarks
of Pelican Publishing Company, Inc., and are registered in the
U.S. Patent and Trademark Office.

Library of Congress Cataloging-in-Publication Data

Scott, John W., 1947-
  Natalie Scott : a magnificent life / by John W. Scott.
     p. cm.
  Includes bibliographical references and index.
  ISBN 978-1-58980-580-4 (hardcover : alk. paper) 1. Scott, Natalie
Vivian, 1890- 2. Journalists—United States—Biography. I. Title.
  PN4874.S364S36 2008
  070.92—dc22
  [B]
                           2008011584

Printed in the United States of America
Published by Pelican Publishing Company, Inc.
1000 Burmaster Street, Gretna, Louisiana 70053

For Cyndy

For Wyeth, William, and Samantha

Yea, Life Spells Strife,
Passion and Pride,
Love and Desire and Dreams.
May these things never be denied
While yet there's breath!
Oh! Not I trust,
Till Death,
Shall striving cease
In Peace!

Basil Thompson, *Peace*

There is something sublime in calm endurance, something sublime in the resolute fixed purpose of suffering without complaining, which makes disappointment often times better than success.

Author unknown
(Found in Natalie's mother's scrapbook)

Verily I say unto you, as ye have done it for one of the least of these my brethren, ye have done it unto me.

Matt. 25.40

Contents

Acknowledgments

Natalie Vivian Scott was my great-aunt. This book is as auto-biographical as narrative storytelling and the availability of first-hand accounts would allow, particularly in the war chapters.

Since Natalie was a professional writer, her own accounts were often too good to omit here: so full of feeling and color of the moment; people and events of both world wars; Mexico; the New Orleans French Quarter; Paris; the indomitable spirit of refugees and war wounded; companions such as Sherwood Anderson, William Spratling, William Faulkner, and Hart Crane; the bevy of New Orleans and Mexican writers, artists, and friends; the characters with whom she shared her great struggles. My hope is that the technique of blending Natalie's words into the narrative enables the reader to become closer to this very unique individual.

So the first person I have to thank is Natalie Vivian Scott, whose journalism, prolific letter writing, vast array of important friendships, and life of pure adventure made this book possible.

Two key personalities in Natalie's life must be acknowledged, though both died many years ago: Natalie's mother, Muddie (Martha Fauver Scott), and Martha Gilmore Robinson. Both Muddie and Martha possessed the wisdom to recognize the unique and lasting value of Natalie's life and her portrayals of war. Both stored her keepsakes and many letters (Natalie dubbed them her "outpourings" because each typically numbered more than thirty pages), finally amounting to more than fifteen oversized boxes in Martha's New Orleans attic. These she turned over in 1966 to Newcomb College and Tulane University, who already possessed a sizable Natalie Scott collection. There were many other places and sources that produced the fragments of Natalie's life, but none as valuable as this archival

9

collection supervised by Lee Miller, to whom I can never offer adequate thanks for his time, interest, and assistance.

I am deeply indebted to the Louisiana Endowment for the Humanities, particularly John R. Kemp who took an immediate active interest in the project, and to Milburn Calhoun and Pelican Publishing Company for their untiring interest over the years in the characters of the French Quarter, the many creative personalities who have graced the cultural history of New Orleans. Thank you for causing this book to be published.

Dr. Stan Hilton, of Louisiana State University, is another who has earned my deepest gratitude. He is merciless in his critiques. One difficulty for a historian who is fascinated by his subject is excluding any compelling episode from the text. My first manuscript exceeded twelve hundred pages. My self-editing hit a wall at half that length. Thereafter, I bled with every deletion. I put the project down innumerable times, weary of the endless revisions. I sometimes abandoned it for months, rationalizing that it was good enough to publish as is. Stan disagreed as he read my successive drafts. I thank him for challenging me to create a better book.

Dr. Chuck Shindo and Dr. John Rodrique were instrumental at the formative stages of this project. Chuck's help became extremely important in the New Orleans phase of the story. I thank them both.

Dr. Penny Chittim Morrill, an expert in Mexican antiquities and the leading biographer of Natalie's supremely talented friend William Spratling, graciously shared with me her wealth of knowledge and the fruits of her own years of research on Natalie's life in Taxco, Mexico, particularly in the 1930s. With great kindness, she has done much to promote and encourage my work. Thanks also to David Read for his hospitality in Taxco, his wonderful Natalie Scott-William Spratling memories, and his suggestions on drafts of several chapters.

Special thanks are owed to Antonio Gallegos, of Taxco, for revealing to me the beauty of Mexican culture and arranging interviews while guiding me for a month through the Taxco region of Guerrero, including spots Natalie frequented on her wilderness horseback journeys. My times with the Gallegos family are perhaps my best memories of this venture.

Debbie Harper's word-processing and computer skills, wonderful temperament, and willingness to sacrifice untold hours have made this book possible. She deserves special thanks for sticking with me from the beginning through the completion of this project. Likewise, I thank Lee Brewer, who helped me put together the index, an act of true friendship.

I am indebted to many others. Susan Tucker, of the Newcomb College Center for Research on Women, provided factual gems from Natalie's school days. Prof. John Shelton Reed, of the University of North Carolina, read the manuscript, liked it, and recommended the book to publishers. Thanks also to Gibert Joseph of Beauvais, France for his assistance during my visit there to research the World War I phase of the book; also to Henri Jean Renaud (and his wife, Yvette) for extending warm hospitality in Sainte-Mère Eglise, France, and for his noteworthy manuscript correction regarding his family.

I am grateful to my daughters, Natalie and Elizabeth, for their critiques and technical corrections. My sister, Ashley, my brother Hammond, my son, John, Irma and Jim Henderson, and my father, now deceased, Judge Nauman Scott, have each been quiet inspirations for this book. My mother, Blanche Scott, a journalist, died several years before this project began, but her keepsakes, her correspondence with her mother, Hilda Phelps Hammond (a key figure in Natalie's life), and a recorded interview made a valuable contribution.

Two vital figures on this project are no longer here to celebrate the book's publication: my brother Nauman and my aunt Bé (Sidonie) Scott Thomas. Nauman and I began the project together. His death prevented us from completing it together. The French Quarter and Mexican portions of this book particularly reflect Nauman's influence.

My graceful, beautiful, and courageous aunt, Bé Scott Thomas, died in August 2005. She enjoyed a special relationship with Natalie, her godmother. Her vivid memories, her collection of letters, photographs, and mementoes, and our innumerable (often hilarious) discussions were a personal joy for me. They were also of enormous practical benefit to my efforts to reconstruct Natalie's life and to gain deeper insight into her nature/personality.

Beyond everyone else, my wife, Cyndy, has been my partner in this endeavor. We have enjoyed the pleasure of discoveries and new friendships and the thrill of pure satisfaction when valuable facts emerged from research, old newspapers, and our travels.

Our joint mission has been to preserve the important story of Natalie Scott, a life that not only entertains and fascinates, but inspires and ingrains eternal lessons. Her biography has been long overdue. Our hope is that the reader will benefit, as we have, from Natalie's unique blend of love for humanity and the seldom overt but deeply spiritual nature of her magnificent journey.

NATALIE *Scott*

Chapter One

The Winds of Time

The old hearse brought her body home to Taxco on the rough colonial stone road from Mexico City. She had first traveled the old Taxco road three decades earlier as a passenger in a dilapidated station wagon stuffed with native Mexicans, their chickens and baskets upon their laps. In this small mountain village, she entered a new life. Now Natalie Scott lay in a simple wooden coffin, the hearse following a car driven by her Taxco friend, gifted silver designer Héctor Aguilar, his wife, Lois, beside him. The lonely caravan slowly climbed through the mountains beneath a pale November sun.

They passed beneath the ancient stone aqueduct, then rolled to a stop below the village. A Catholic padre robed in black and a crowd of golden-skinned townspeople awaited them, the men attired simply in white trousers and shirts. They removed the coffin, the women draping a blanket of bright white lilies over it, the men then lifting the oblong box onto their shoulders. They began the long uphill walk to the *zócalo* (plaza), the same stone earth Natalie had so often climbed upon returns from her horseback expeditions through Mexico's mysterious Tierra Caliente, deep jungles, and soaring mountains, from Matamoros on the Texas border to Chiapas in Central America.

Villagers crowded the edges of the narrow, winding road, moving behind the coffin bearers as they passed. They quietly formed a procession, led by the padre and diminutive dark-haired women carrying an enormous wreath of colorful flowers— brilliant in oranges, yellows, pinks, lavenders, and whites. At one point, they passed within sight of Natalie's peasant school, her *guardería de niños* for impoverished children where she had been happily at work only four days earlier, unaware of anything amiss, of the death that would suddenly visit her. The crowd thickened as the procession reached the ancient plaza. The coffin passed between long lines of flower-bearing children, many her godchildren, many born in her bed with Natalie and her housekeeper as midwives, her home offered for clean safety during childbirth.

Priests emerged from the grand pink-stoned church, a dozen townsmen behind them carrying the enormous silver crucifix of Jesus, removed for the first time in two centuries from its imposing position above the altar. Immediately opposite the great church, the Bar Paco patrons, notable artists and writers among them—Natalie's friends—descended from the second-level veranda to join the crowd. They placed flowers on the moving coffin as the bearers approached the arched opening into the Borda Palace. From the broad building's balconies, those preparing the great room watched the coffin's progress. The bearers, once inside, rose up the twisting staircase, careful with their burden, and entered the splendid flower-filled ballroom. The bier for Natalie's coffin awaited in the room's center. On the far wall, the priests and their helpers affixed the great crucifix.

Here Natalie would lie ceremoniously for two nights before burial. The townsmen would serve as her honor guard in shifts around the clock, enabling continuous visitations.

A middle-aged member of the honor guard, a Taxqueñian named Luis Reyes who had been a *mozo* (young helper) in the telegraph office the day Natalie first settled in the village, completed final preparations before opening the broad doors for the people of Taxco to have their time with Natalie. Spreading a blue felt cloth over the head of the casket, he placed upon it a large framed photograph of Natalie, seated and surrounded by the little ones of Taxco. Also upon the felt, he placed her war medals from the two world wars, the most imposing being the one awarded her by the French nation for her valor, the Croix de Guerre. Few in Taxco, other than old friends such as Bill Spratling who knew her from their French Quarter days in New Orleans, possessed knowledge of Natalie's war heroism. She was the only American woman to earn this greatest French medal in the Great War.

With all in place, the first shift of the eight honor guards at their stations, Luis Reyes opened the doors and the people of Taxco began their emotional visitation. Gentle guitar music and soft voices offering Mexican serenades rose on the cool evening breeze from the *zócalo,* over the open balcony, and into the large room.[1]

The Gulf Coast

Natalie Scott's first view of Bay St. Louis, Mississippi came in December 1896 from the interior of the popular Louisville and Nashville train that ran from New Orleans through a series of gulf-coast resorts. At six years old, she had seen many new sights during her family's long move from Ashland, Kentucky. Ashland had been small and remote along the Ohio River, on the rough, sparsely populated coal-mining plateau near the West Virginia border. Instead of the mud, country folk, and small cabins she was accustomed to, Natalie had encountered the crowded sights, smells, and sounds of New Orleans. The train paused briefly in Gulfview and Waveland, both summer retreats for well-to-do New Orleanians, before finally chugging into the sleepy hamlet of Bay St. Louis.

The bay was not always so sleepy. Each spring the town's population would swell, its splendid summer houses filled with seasonal residents escaping the oppressive humidity, semi-tropical rains, and mosquitoes of New Orleans, the town's merchants, gardeners, hoteliers, coachmen, winemakers, and resort keepers suddenly very busy for five profitable months. New Orleans newspapers, particularly the society pages, kept track of daily activities on the bay. The big city's elite—her political, social, and business leaders—were all mainstays of the quaint bay's summer society, attracted there by the mixture of cooling waters, gentle breezes, and shady lanes. Their rambling coastal houses were surrounded by profuse gardens and wrapped with long porches for lounging under fans, playing cards, and socializing.[2]

The Scotts were a family of five: Natalie, her parents, Boss and Muddie, and her brothers Wyeth and Nauman, nine and eight years old respectively. Boss had headquartered his small railway-construction business in New Orleans since 1879, though he spent little time there. His railroad jobs were in Sheffield, Alabama; Cave Springs, Georgia; Bristol, Tennessee; and Ashland, Kentucky. The children were born in these scattered places, close to his work. Boss was usually gone, living in tent

"Muddie," Martha Vivian Fauver Scott (New Orleans, ca. 1918). *Courtesy of Special Collections, Tulane University Libraries*

"Boss," Nathaniel Graves Scott (New Orleans, ca. 1918). *Courtesy of the Kay Gunn-Rev. Pike Thomas Collection*

encampments and supervising his construction crews. Several successive jobs in the Kentucky-Indiana region made it possible to settle in Ashland for six peaceful years after Natalie's birth in Bristol, Tennessee on July 18, 1890. Bay St. Louis's reputation as a health resort and its rural setting probably accounted for the decision to reside there instead of New Orleans, especially since Muddie and Boss had been raised in small villages in Louisiana and Alabama, respectively.

They settled in an old white house, a lease, facing the bay. It was fronted by magnolias and oak trees and encircled by a broad porch. The property behind the house allowed ample space for a large vegetable garden, persimmon and pecan orchards, an arbor where scuppernong grapevines thrived, a carriage and horse barn, an outdoor privy, a brick water well, and wide grounds for horseback riding, picnics, and lightning-bug hunts. The home itself, although without plumbing or electricity, boasted coal-burning fireplaces in two of the four bedrooms, and the interior was easily cooled in the summertime by opening the tall, shuttered windows to the refreshing gulf winds. The Scotts would spend almost six years in this comfortable house.

Natalie remained home for tutoring sessions with Muddie in January 1897, while her brothers attended the Bay St. Louis Public School. Muddie was teaching literature at the Silliman College for Women in East Feliciana Parish, Louisiana, when she met and married Boss. This home tutoring continued for several years, for Muddie was convinced that her daughter needed more attention than could be offered in a school of 100 older students with three instructors. Under Muddie's strong influence, Natalie acquired a deep love for reading and an early understanding of government and music. She mastered the piano and her academics with equal ease. Later, in school events, she often played accompaniment on the piano. Not surprisingly, by the time she finally enrolled at the public school, Natalie had decided to become a schoolteacher, following in Muddie's footsteps.[3]

With one important exception, Natalie's six years in Bay St. Louis were a delight. The enormous exception arrived abruptly in late August 1897, right after Natalie turned seven. A horrendous yellow fever epidemic gripped the gulf coast from Mobile to New Orleans until December, victimizing thousands of families. In an initial effort to fend off the plague, Bay St.

Louis leaders closed down the summer season and imposed a strict quarantine system, using at least 120 volunteers to guard against any entry, with everyone considered a possible disease carrier. Anyone leaving could not return either. The town required that all buildings be disinfected. A siege mentality prevailed throughout the community. Fear of the dreaded "Yellow Jack" permeated every household, including the Scotts'. As the local paper, the *Seacoast Echo,* reported, "There is no use for our absent friends to apply for passes, none will be given, and we trust the people outside of the city will appreciate the situation, and not ask for them, as it is not pleasant to refuse permission to come back." All public entertainment was canceled, all persons were prohibited from going on the depot grounds, and no trains were permitted to stop, as "mail is thrown off and received in true pioneer style."

In late September, Muddie Scott suddenly collapsed with severe headaches, chills, and nausea. The doctor ordered quarantine. He gave Boss instructions for Muddie's care, but she experienced vomiting, constipation, abdominal cramps, and muscle pains for four days before a break mercifully occurred. Although the children were not allowed near their mother, they could see from a safe distance the pain and suffering in her flushed face and sunken eyes, and they were frightened. They took on all chores, but only Wyeth (the oldest) was allowed to leave the premises when errands became necessary. Then Muddie relapsed after a few days, the fever and symptoms striking her harder than before: jaundice, black vomit, wracking epigastric pain, and the hemorrhaging of her mucous membranes. Strictly quarantined and diagnosed with yellow fever, Muddie became critically dehydrated with a faint pulse and high fever, mentally confused, then virtually comatose.

Muddie's illness came at the height of the epidemic. The *Seacoast Echo* published a "Fever and Death" summary each day, with reports of new yellow fever cases, hopeful accounts of some doing better, and the mounting lists of victims. Illness and death struck the Scotts' neighbors and friends, the poor and the prominent. The state health board issued a new ordinance for Bay St. Louis: "The remains of parties dying of yellow fever shall be wrapped in a sheet, with solution of bichloride of mercury, . . . and burned within four hours after death. Rooms in which persons have died of yellow fever shall be fumigated as soon as the remains are removed therefrom."

The death announcements finally began to dwindle by the second week of November. The *Echo* reported the epidemic to be "ebbing" in New Orleans, where health officials "declared the quarantine off" and announced full train service would be restored the following week. An editorial on the back page reflected upon the disease's grim democracy. "The yellow fever is no respecter of persons. We have had Uncle Sam's chief postal deputy away from the exigencies of his duty. In addition to several colonels, majors, judges, captains, honorables, and many of the other prominent citizens with their names figuring on the victims list, we have had one of our spiritual directors stricken, the railroad agent, the secretary of the board of health, one of the town editors and not forgetting the undertaker."

The long vigil in the Scott home finally gained reward on October 21, a Monday night, when Muddie's fever eased. Her vomiting stopped, and she held down some thin soup. The worst of the terrible ordeal had finally passed, though the ravages of yellow fever often left permanent physical consequences. In Muddie's case, perhaps due to damage to her liver, heart, or lungs, she remained a semi-invalid—rail thin and frequently ill for the balance of her life. Through her convalescence, the children served as her eager nurses. The public school finally resumed its regular classes the first week of December, so Natalie became the only youngster in the house during the day. Normalcy returned in stages. By Christmas, the terror began receding into memory. But the children had learned firsthand the fragility of life. The family would also fear for Muddie's fragile health with every subsequent illness.

The yellow fever epidemic created a major landmark on the otherwise gentle landscape of Natalie's childhood, the only moment of great fear, family desperation, and helplessness. This early encounter with death inflicted an indelible mark upon the seven-year-old, as stricken families about her were losing loved ones, the bodies soaked in chemicals, burned, and quickly buried. The fact that there are only a handful of indirect references to this episode in her lifetime of writing underscores its profound impact upon her. Although Muddie survived, she became thereafter, as the daughter grew to adulthood, the object of Natalie's unusual vigilance.[4]

Mr. and Mrs. Scott

Natalie's father, Boss, was born Nathaniel Graves Scott and was raised a merchant's son in Guntersville, a tiny north Alabama town. As a boy of thirteen, with no more than a primitive elementary education when the Civil War broke out in 1861, he enlisted in Company B of the Confederacy's First Kentucky Regiment. This unit was under the command of Lt. Gen. Nathan Bedford Forrest, arguably the most unique and instinctively able of all Southern commanders. Disapproving and worried, the boy-soldier's parents wanted their oldest son home, and, after his first year in combat, they secured his discharge due to his tender age. But after a brief period in Guntersville, Boss ran off and rejoined the bloody fight with his old unit. His youth enabled Boss to serve Forrest as an effective spy, unsuspected as he walked the streets of enemy-occupied towns and encampments.

Boss's closest boyhood friend in Guntersville was John Allan Wyeth, a fellow Confederate soldier who would achieve national prominence as a pioneering surgeon and successful author. He later became an important friend to Natalie, taking a personal interest in her Red Cross work in World War I. Dr. Wyeth became president of the American Medical Association, New York's leading physician, and the author of authoritative medical textbooks and an autobiography. His definitive biography of General Forrest, which remains today the best work on the subject, acknowledged the boyhood awe he shared with Boss for this larger-than-life Civil War hero.

The Civil War marked the most exciting, monumental experience of Boss's long life. His war record distinguished him, a lifelong badge of honor. The first world war would serve much the same purpose for his daughter, Natalie, who wrote home in one war letter that she and her compatriots realized that "this is the time of our lives," the experience that would complete their character, never to be forgotten.

Boss came home after the war to abject poverty. Guntersville had been burned by the Yankees and his father's small business was destroyed. Not yet seventeen when the war ended, Boss met more heartbreak in 1865 when his mother died during childbirth at age forty-two. His father struggled to rebuild his mercantile business but died in 1873.

Boss became a construction worker for the Selma, Rome, and Dalton Railroad, one of many small companies trying to restore the South's decimated railroad system. He advanced to skilled positions, eventually earning supervisory responsibilities. He became the superintendent of construction for the Texas and Pacific Railroad, driving piles, grading, and laying tracks in Texas and Louisiana. By 1879, at age thirty-one, he established his own small firm in New Orleans, an independent contractor doing work for numerous railroads and the Army Corps of Engineers.

Boss and Muddie were thirty-seven and twenty-five, respectively, when they met during the summer of 1885 in Clinton, Louisiana, where Muddie was teaching school. The two were married six months later on December 17, 1885. Of Irish descent, blue eyed, and with a thick moustache and playful personality, Boss enjoyed Irish legends and holidays, particularly St. Patrick's Day, which, he explained to his delighted children, always magically restored him to age seventeen. He created far-fetched tales about leprechauns, the miraculous creation of Ireland, eternal youth, and the adventures of an Irish character named "Big Mike on the Levee," all told in Irish brogue. Natalie loved these stories and the boisterous interplay, when Boss became "Boss McGinty McGee O'Flynn McGaw" and Natalie was nicknamed "Peggy Moriarity."[5]

Muddie was born Martha Vivian Fauver in 1860 and was only eight when her mother died. Her father (a farmer and blacksmith) was unable to care for the nine children, so Muddie was taken in by a family named Nauman. She attended school at Feliciana Female Institute, then graduated from Silliman Female College in Jackson, Louisiana. This was the earliest female school in Louisiana, its beautiful campus spread over twenty wooded acres in the Feliciana hills. Muddie excelled as a student, her love of literature leading her to a teaching career at Silliman. In contrast to Boss, a fundamentally practical man, Muddie exuded idealism. She adored the literary classics, as well as the novels, poems, and essays of the great Romantics and post-Romantics. Her greatest impact on her children, particularly Natalie and Nauman, came in this realm. She would read aloud nightly while standing in the door of their adjoining bedrooms. Natalie reminisced in a letter to Nauman from the war zone in 1918 how it had always been Muddie who fell asleep, on her feet on those evenings, her weary voice trailing off as the children remained wide awake.[6]

Muddie was a keeper of scrapbooks. One of them she filled almost completely with clippings of poems, literary quotations, and romantic keepsakes, such as roses, clovers, and locks of hair memorializing special moments. She meant this scrapbook for her children, as her handwritten inscription confirms: "I hope the children will read these and realize by what lights of idealism she breathed the way of spirit beautified." Natalie would preserve the scrapbook throughout her life. It was filled with page after page of quotations by literary greats from every age: Lord Byron, Shelley, Longfellow, Homer, Dante, Goethe, Shakespeare, Kipling, Swift, Tennyson, ancient Greek and Roman writers, French political thinkers, and an array of obscure authors. This special volume, informally collected over decades, became Muddie's book of wisdom. It was in essence her compilation of the best thoughts and expressions of history dealing with every circumstance and test of character, addressing kindness, bravery, poverty and wealth, motherhood, friendship, prayer, ethics, innocence, adversity, laughter, manhood, feminism, sex, death, and much more.

Many of her treasures were funny. "An ordinary woman's waist is 30 inches around. An ordinary man's arm is about 30 inches long." Others were more stirring. "No amount of training can make a gentleman or gentlewoman unless the gentle spirit be within." "Do not dare to live without some clear intentions towards which your living shall be bent. Mean to be something with all your might." "The nation without sentiment is a nation without virtue, without character, without aspiration or self-respect." "We must get honesty, directness and lofty purpose wrought into the fibre of our being. We must fix right standards of judgment. We must be taught and be willing to learn the way that we should choose." "God will put up with a great many things in the human heart, but there is one thing that He will not put up with in it—a second place. He who offers God a second place offers Him no place." "The soul has a duty to itself and a duty to others. A human being is compelled to educate itself. It is obliged and bound by a most imperative duty to develop itself to the utmost of its natural resources, and make the most of what God has designed and made possible of it. But his duty does not rest here. It has another duty to its fellow beings, and one must help his brothers. So mankind has a double duty of self-culture and self-sacrifice." "There is something sublime in calm endurance, something sublime in the resolute fixed purpose of suffering without complaining, which makes disappointment often times better than success."

Muddie seldom missed an opportunity to share her love of literature with her children. If Natalie or her brothers misbehaved, Muddie imposed the perfect punishment. The wrongdoer would sit and copy, repeatedly, verses of great poetry selected by Muddie. The following punishment verses from *The Building of the Ship* by Longfellow were copied by nine-year-old Natalie and eleven-year-old Nauman Scott in 1899:

> Build me straight
> O worthy Master!
> Staunch and strong,
> A goodly vessel,
> That shall laugh
> At all disaster,
> And with wave and
> whirlwind wrestle.

This particular punishment goes on for pages. Muddie's nature amused even her children. Commenting on a chattering group around a dinner table two decades after Muddie's death, Natalie wrote, "It reminds me of Muddie, when we used to start, as children (or even, perhaps, as adults?), all talking at once. She would suddenly put her hands to her ears with a distressed expression, and exclaim, 'I am conscious of a din.'" Even under distress, Muddie's gentle nature prevailed, tempered and understated.

Boss and Muddie were in modest, but sound, financial condition. In 1898, they owned a horse, two carriages, an expensive piano, a high-quality watch, and two pistols, according to tax records. Boss's business apparently did reasonably well. The fact that Boss leased instead of purchased a home may indicate that he viewed Bay St. Louis as a temporary domicile. At fifty years old, he was just beginning his best years in business. But money would never be plentiful.

The Scotts were familiar, well-liked figures in Bay St. Louis.

Wyeth, the oldest but physically the smallest of the children, discovered a love of fishing, sailing, and hunting. Nauman, sturdy and athletic, enjoyed rough sports and, like his sister, was a voracious reader. Natalie spent much of her time on horseback, clomping over the white shell streets of Bay St. Louis. The family became active members of Christ Episcopal Church. Muddie joined organized charity work and was informally active among the needy families in the community. Muddie would regularly send Natalie out with baskets of bread, meats, jams, outgrown clothing, and other helpful items for the ill and the less fortunate.[7]

A fair assessment is that, as parents, Muddie and Boss each stood in contrast with one another but together balanced rather well. Where Boss could be gruffly direct, perhaps profane, Muddie's approach was more formal, yet understanding. Where Muddie imposed academic standards and lofty thinking, Boss

Natalie Scott with her brothers, Wyeth (left) and Nauman (right) (Bay St. Louis, ca. 1898). *Courtesy of Special Collections, Tulane University Libraries*

provided practical and useful skills. Where Muddie offered calm, tenderness, gentleness, Boss brought noise to the household with his loud emotions and boisterous laughter. A mixture of their personalities found its way into Natalie's nature. In the final analysis, largely because Boss's work took him away so often, Muddie was the more significant influence on her children, particularly Natalie and Nauman.

School Days

Ten-year-old Natalie joined her brother Nauman at the Bay St. Louis Public School for the 1900-1901 term, where they would be classmates for two years. Their curriculum included Latin, English, literature, elocution, geography, algebra, and math. Wyeth, a contented but indifferent student, had been sent off to the University of the South preparatory school in Sewanee, where his schoolwork did not improve. Natalie and Nauman were close in age, fifteen months apart. They became top students, participated together in typical school activities, and shared many of the same friends. Both were named to the honor roll, with Natalie earning honors in Latin, geography, algebra, and math. The small school would have no graduates until 1905. In early June 1902, Natalie received the school's highest recognition for academics when the faculty chose her to give the valedictory address at the term's closing exercises. She was not yet twelve years old.

With her new status as star pupil, and her ambition to someday become a teacher, Natalie and her teachers became enthusiastic about her future. When the Mississippi teachers' Summer Normal opened on the coast in mid-June, Natalie attended the sessions with her teacher Minnie Lou Bowers. The annual Normal was a conference for the state's schoolteachers that included a training course to prepare new teachers for their licensure exam. These prospective teachers also submitted academic papers for grading by the state board of examiners. Passing grades meant a teaching license good in any county in Mississippi. Exceptionally promising secondary-school pupils, including Natalie, were honored by being allowed to take the teacher exams. Natalie's photograph appeared in the local newspaper with an article proclaiming the

Natalie, age eleven, in a local news-
paper clipping (Bay St. Louis, 1902).
*Courtesy of Special Collections, Tulane
University Libraries*

eleven-year-old's success.
"She came out with flying
colors. Her composition,
on 'Our Trade Relations
with Cuba', is a master-
piece," read the photo cap-
tion.

The Scotts maintained
their residence in Bay St.
Louis through the summer
of 1903, moving to New
Orleans shortly after
Natalie's thirteenth birthday. The *Seacoast Echo*
reported their departure,
referring to Natalie as the
Scotts' "bright and gifted
daughter." "Ms. Natalie will
become one of Newcomb's
girls," it continued. "The
departure of this highly
esteemed family from the
bay is deeply regretted not
only in social circles, but in the schools, where the children
ranked among the brightest, and in the humbler walks of life,
where Mrs. Scott was known and loved for her unbounded char-
ities, the dispenser of which was her sweet daughter, Natalie."
Their new address became 4907 Carondelet. Natalie entered
Newcomb High School, and Wyeth and Nauman were enrolled in
Ferrell's School for Boys.[8]

Newcomb High School prepared young women for Newcomb
College, an institution affiliated with Tulane University. The
campuses were at opposite ends of St. Charles Avenue, with
Newcomb located on Washington Avenue in the heart of the
Garden District. Natalie adapted well, making friends easily.
There were skating and tennis invitations and horseback riding
in Audubon Park. Natalie helped organize the school's
"Sophomore Class Night." The family acquired season tickets for
the French Opera House on Bourbon Street. Muddie and Natalie
were regularly in attendance, as were many of her school

companions. She found herself among talented, academically motivated young women with whom she cemented permanent friendships. A floor of Newcomb's College Hall was devoted to the high school, which reached its highest enrollment—almost two hundred students—during Natalie's years there. She performed well and earned a Newcomb College scholarship with her high score on a competitive entrance exam. At the age of fifteen, Natalie became a college freshman in September 1905. Her brothers were enrolled by this time in the civil engineering school at Tulane, both being groomed to enter their father's business.

Newcomb College enormously influenced Natalie's formative years. It offered an odd combination of Victorian conservatism and progressive-era liberalism, stiff propriety and broad-minded tolerance. It provided a deep foundation of literary and artistic learning and fostered a compelling interest in public affairs, social ills, history, and political action. At Newcomb, Natalie became one of a formidable band of women. Their minds were sharpened by academic interests, and they were committed to individuality and creativity, finding joy in all art forms. These attributes would be preserved in their "1909 Prize," created upon their graduation. This award would go to the graduate in each succeeding Newcomb class who best personified the values that the 1909ers identified in the daring creativity of the ancient Greeks and the Renaissance intellectuals.[9]

Completing its second decade of existence and at last achieving its goal of seriously educating New Orleans women, Newcomb College had hit its stride. The uphill struggle of building a campus and gaining acceptance for the school's work had been accomplished, enabling it to assemble a superb faculty. A sense of freedom to experiment with new ideas, in the best spirit of the progressive era, prevailed among the students. Here's how Hilda Phelps Hammond, Natalie's best friend at college, looked back upon Newcomb three decades later.

> Domiciled in an old New Orleans home of great architectural beauty, with friendly oaks touching their branches over the paths of the one-block campus, Newcomb had none of the modern buildings and equipment which it possesses today, yet there emanated from that small college a certain mellow flavor of culture and ideals which left a permanent impression on those who studied there.

Intellectually, we were afforded every opportunity: a faculty whose degrees had been obtained from the finest universities of Europe and America gave us the intellectual run of the thoughts and emotions of the writers and thinkers of history. There was no censorship, no casting aside of certain books as being unfit for the feminine mind—we read freely the lives and passions of great men and women; in the pages of Balzac, George Sand, Victor Hugo and Voltaire we browsed without restriction. Yet side by side with the intellectual freedom there existed a quaint code of decorum, as though the ledger must be balanced in favor of Garden District standards. . . . Sports found us arrayed in long skirts over voluminous bloomers, while Dramatics insisted upon Orlandos, Petrucchios and Romeos wearing men's apparel from the waist up and skirts from the waist down![10]

Natalie's own recognition of the impact of Newcomb upon her is evidenced by the inscription she wrote two decades later in the anthology of plays she donated to Newcomb, which included her own award-winning play, *Grand Zombi*. She was perhaps reflecting (as she wrote) on the internal fires that had compelled her political activism when World War I broke out, her war service in Paris and the war zone, her literary and artistic pursuits in the 1920s French Quarter, the fires that were still compelling her in new directions: "To Newcomb,—'guiding goddess of my harmful deeds',—and stimulus towards better. Natalie Vivian Scott,—1909. June 11, 1929."[11]

Natalie as a freshman became a sub-editor of the *Jambalaya*, the school yearbook, and joined the YWCA and the freshman basketball team. Misbehavior provoked Dr. James Lyon, her physics professor, to bring her name before the faculty meeting on March 19, 1906, as the minutes reflect. "Mr. Lyon called the attention of the faculty to Miss Scott's boisterousness, although her class standing is very good in his branch. In all branches both her conduct and standing is very good." She was the only freshman chosen by the Newcomb Drama Circle to perform in the May school play. By then, she was labeling her friends with nicknames that later appeared in her missives from the war zones of World Wars I and II: Whilda for Hilda Phelps, Kmarfoonie for Martha Gilmore, Wagness for Agnes George. Natalie became Knat or Snatta.

Natalie exemplified the sense of independence and class unity permeating the campus, yet few students displayed as much

Class of 1909 basketball team, Newcomb College. Hilda Phelps is holding the ball. Natalie, second row on far left in light jersey, played center. *Courtesy of Special Collections, Tulane University Libraries*

leadership. Hilda Phelps, her close friend, became one clear
exception. Her father was president of the New Orleans *Times-
Democrat,* the leading morning newspaper in the South, and was
soon to become president of the *Times-Picayune.* Hilda was the
class and student body president, the school's debating champion, and the most evident innovator on campus. During the
1930s, Hilda would create and lead the Louisiana Women's
Committee to fight Huey P. Long in its crusade for honest elections. They carried their challenge to the U.S. Senate, a breakthrough for women in Louisiana politics. Another best friend,
Martha Gilmore, the first editor of *The Newcomb Arcade* (the
school's new quarterly magazine), was a top student and a sorority organizer. She would later join Hilda in the Huey Long fight.
Thereafter she organized World War II volunteerism in Louisiana
and led the state's women in demands for political reform
through the 1940s and early 1950s.

Though very social, Natalie did not join a sorority. She served
in only minor posts: class historian for one year and class poet
for another, which gave her the opportunity to write a comical

history and poem in two successive Tulane yearbooks. Her history in the 1907 yearbook extolled the "unprecedented éclat" that marked the '09's "debut" on campus in 1905 and the "uncontested sovereignty" and "prosperous reign . . . surrendered" by all other classes since. As for that class's accomplishments, Natalie wrote: "They made chemical discoveries wonderful and important; they handed in mathematical quizzes undeniably perfect; they gave vent to glorious outbursts of Spenserian songs; their history essays have served as models for all succeeding classes. In fact, they showered welcome gifts of perfect work upon the astonished and delighted professors."

Yet, on a far more serious note, Natalie founded and was first president of the Student Club, the purpose of which she explained in the 1909 Tulane yearbook. "In the complicated college life there is a natural tendency to the submerging of the individual. This tendency, especially the last year or so at Newcomb, has been accentuated. It is just a few girls who run things and the mass of students are unknown, as well as unacquainted. Now the duty of the college is to bring out such girls—girls who are wanting not in real fineness, but perhaps in aggressiveness. The Student Club is a place where all students meet on an equal footing, where the spirit of good-fellowship is predominant. It is a delightful rendezvous during study hours, meetings, parties and receptions."

Tulane and Newcomb were under the same organizational umbrella, but Tulane, being the older, larger institution, dominated extracurricular activities, the *Jambalaya* yearbook, and the *Tulane Weekly* newspaper. Tulane maintained a broad assortment of varsity sports and clubs—language, social, musical, literary, and otherwise. Newcomb offered few of these. The Newcomb class of 1909 would completely reverse this situation, preparing a strategy to attack the imbalance so that, by the time they graduated, Newcomb's campus life matched, and in some ways exceeded, the Tulane program.

Their campus crusade began the summer of 1908, when the twenty-nine class members, as new seniors, decided to overhaul the school's campus life. Ideas had been percolating in their heads for three years. Under Hilda Phelps' leadership, they conducted meeting after meeting in the Scott home to filter the good ideas from the bad and to formulate a specific action plan. Muddie Scott encouraged the activity, donating the parlor, dining room, and kitchen to the cause. Natalie's brothers were occasional observers. Jack (Wyeth's nickname) was engaged in construction work for Boss, and Nauman, tall, dark haired, and blue eyed, was destined for stardom on the Tulane gridiron that fall. By September, the 1909 reform platform was ready for execution, and the campaign was launched when classes began.

Natalie became the newspaper writer of their campaign, their Newcomb proposals dominating the *Tulane Weekly* that autumn as well as receiving substantial attention from the city's daily newspapers. A variety of articles, all written by Natalie, filled the October 7 *Tulane Weekly,* proposing a new Newcomb Athletic Association, a new Newcomb debate program, a new literary club, a new track team, a new tennis team, and a Newcomb Glee Club, together with a Banjo, Mandolin and Guitar Club. Another of Natalie's articles "deplored" the dissolution of *The Tulanian* magazine several years earlier and announced that the Newcomb girls were going to establish their own magazine, to be named *The Newcomb Quarterly.* "Now the Newcomb girls had a very small share in the management of the Tulanian and so they have not really had a chance to see what they can do. There is great literary ability at Newcomb, a capacity for work and there is enthusiasm," she wrote. "Why cannot Newcomb publish a magazine and manage it herself?"

The students conducted a series of public meetings presided over by Hilda Phelps, finally culminating in a mass outdoor reform rally on campus on Friday, November 13. Muddie was there amidst the large crowd cheering their speeches, later putting away the rally's program in a scrapbook. In reaction to the Newcomb women establishing their own magazine, the Tulane administration resurrected the defunct *Tulanian.* Natalie was named the managing editor, though a Tulane student became editor-in-chief, and the new eleven-member editorial board included just five Newcomb students. Thus a rival magazine, *The Newcomb Arcade,* came into being, with Martha Gilmore as editor-in-chief, featuring articles, book reviews, essays, short stories, poetry, and art all created by Newcomb students, together with campus and alumnae news.

The first edition of *The Newcomb Arcade,* in January 1909, featured a short story by Natalie dramatizing the eternal struggle between Man and Nature. The tale told of a desperate wanderer in the Western wilderness, hallucinating over his lost comrades and his lover awaiting him back home. Gradually succumbing to his thirst and starvation, he finally died, unknowingly within reach of a sparkling stream. The tall forest and the day's receding sunlight, both beautiful but unfeeling, were the only witnesses to his struggle. The power of the piece, entitled "The Forest Primeval," immediately established a high standard for the new magazine. *The Newcomb Arcade* published its first three editions between January and June 1909, with Natalie being the most prolific contributor to both the *Arcade* and *The Tulanian.*

Meanwhile, Martha Gilmore and Natalie jointly wrote additional articles in the *Tulane Weekly* proposing a new debate program and Literary Society, and both ideas were promptly implemented. The class also inaugurated a season of English, French, and German plays. George Bernard Shaw's *You Never Can Tell* became the first production. The French Circle, another new organization, gave its first soiree in March featuring scenes from Molière's *Les Femmes Savantes.* They concluded the year with a senior class play, their own adaptation of Plantur's *The Menaechin.* The plot concerns the search of Menaechus Sasocle (classmate Louise Westfelt) for his twin brother, Menaechun (Natalie), but the students filled the classical script with hilarious modern slang.

More reforms were accomplished. Newcomb got its first female member of the Tulane Board of Administration. The Newcomb girls also gained parity in the production of the 1909 *Jambalaya,* with three of six board members being Newcomb students. The impact upon the yearbook was obvious in its wide coverage of Newcomb affairs and campus life. The new Newcomb Athletic Association also established a new system of teams in basketball, crew, tennis, and track.

The basketball program competed against outside teams as well as within the school. A favorite memory was the senior class basketball team's victories over all rivals, particularly the humiliation they inflicted upon the juniors by a score of 72 to 26, with Hilda the team captain and Natalie playing center for the victors. The games were played on an outdoor court at Newcomb, the girls attired in ankle-length dresses and the goalposts decorated with red and white wrapping. Cheering crowds surrounded the court for each game, some standing and some sitting on the ground among the oak trees and lovely Garden District residences. An occasional horse-drawn carriage or early-style automobile passed by, providing a sedate setting for the fierce competition. The contrast underscored the many changes under way at Newcomb College.

The Newcomb administration had announced that a large tract of land away from the Garden District had been purchased beside Tulane University for the purpose of building a new Newcomb campus, abandoning the old school. The students, though upset by the news, conducted a ceremony in January so each could plant seedlings at the new site from the oak trees on the Washington Avenue campus. The actual relocation did not occur for another ten years.

An entertaining poem entitled "A Student Body Meeting," published in the June 1909 graduation edition of *The Newcomb Arcade,* preserves a hint of the heated turmoil, passion, and sense of humor typical of the campus reform politics that year and leaves an impression of the personalities of the leading players.

A Student Body Meeting

In a student-body meeting, recreation moments fleeting,
Arguments were growing wilder—each one had been used before,
Hilda on the plat-form walking, tired-out with useless "squawking",
Natalie was hoarse from talking, Sara's voice was heard no more,
Justine rose to move adjournment—each girl started for the door,
Quoth Miss Gilmore, "Please, the floor!"

Down we sat with resignation, even muttered indignation,
Some to think of ways of leaving, some of epithets galore,
All had gloomy looks to scatter, none had interest in the matter,
Suddenly there was a clatter, Bertha rose and sought the door,
Up spoke Hilda, gently sighing, looking at the fast-closed door,
"But Miss Gilmore has the floor!"

Onward still with simple reason, on from season into season,
Martha talked upon her subject, talked and talked from boundless
   store.
Not a single sigh was uttered, not a single threat was muttered,
Not a single eye-lid fluttered, on the eyes which saw no more—
For each girl was slumbering softly, seeming to avoid a snore,
While Miss Gilmore held the floor.[12]

Natalie had entered Newcomb as a fifteen-year-old freshman during the fall of 1905, the youngest, except for Hilda, in her class. Both were eighteen upon graduation, their friend Martha two years older. As a freshman, Natalie earned As in English, French, history, math, physics, and physical education, with a B in Greek and a C in Latin. With few exceptions, Natalie's grades were strong throughout her four years. Her advanced-mathematics teacher, after the summer session of 1908, wrote this note to Muddie: "My dear Mrs. Scott: This is to briefly acknowledge receipt of your very, very kind note of a few days ago, and to enclose for Miss Scott the results of her work during the summer. If Miss Scott's exam paper had fallen below 100 I would have been disappointed for the reason that she does mathematics more quickly and with less exertion than any student I've ever instructed. It is peculiarly refreshing to direct the work of such a student."

Natalie was chosen at graduation to present the senior cap and gown to the representative of the new senior class. Hilda, as student president, and Natalie, as the cap and gown honoree, gave speeches. Natalie's mother was given special recognition and made an honorary member of the class of 1909. Muddie responded with a warm congratulatory talk before the audience.[13]

As she passed this stage of her life, Natalie, clearly a success socially, seemed on track to follow the course of most well-educated, middle-class Southern girls of that era—to marry well and raise a family. She also seemed likely to achieve the career in teaching that had been predicted for her since her days as an eleven-year-old overachiever in Bay St. Louis. Her aptitude, interest, and now her close connections with Newcomb College seemed to guarantee these ambitions. The next few years made such a life in education more certain than ever. But Natalie, though only eighteen, had also displayed during these Newcomb years the high passion for a cause, the individualism, and the sensitivity that would lead her into an entirely unexpected future.

Explorations

A long-standing invitation from her Steele cousins led Natalie to the heart of historic and social Washington, D.C. during the summer of 1909 to begin two semesters of studies at Fairmont

Seminary in the field of ancient Greek drama. Lee Steele, the associate principal, and her younger sister, Fannie, lived in a three-story mansion owned by Fairmont that was used for many school activities. Located on the 1700 block of Massachusetts Avenue, Fairmont was described by one publication as "one of the finest 'cultural schools' in the country." Natalie developed an affection for the school, referring to it in letters during World War I as "dear old Fairmont." The city proved to be an education in itself, offering exposure to a larger world of politics, culture, people, and attitudes.

Fairmont shared this block with the Finnish, Belgian, and Canadian legations, as well as the Force School, where Pres. Teddy Roosevelt's three sons had attended public school. One neighbor was Mrs. Frances Hodgson Burnett, the author of the book *The Secret Garden*. The homes of numerous luminaries were within a stone's throw, including James G. Blaine (former presidential candidate and secretary of state), Gifford Pinchot (who resigned in controversy as chief of the Forest Service under William Taft), Reginald De Koven (composer), Massachusetts senator Henry Cabot, and Melville W. Fuller, chief justice of the Supreme Court. The next nine months were jammed with sightseeing trips to Baltimore, Philadelphia, and New York; visits to Mount Vernon, Monticello, the U.S. Capitol, and the White House; outings to the huge pier at Bay Shore Park on Chesapeake Bay; and football games, parties, and student plays at Princeton. America's most rich, famous, and powerful became familiar names to Natalie, who even met a few of the prominent figures.

Fairmont's activities frequently made the Washington society pages, the social column of Daisy Fitzhugh Ayres of particular interest in New Orleans since it was published locally in the *Times-Democrat*. Natalie was mentioned in this column on at least three occasions during the 1909-10 term, once in early December being described, after her appearance in a Christmas benefit performance, as "a charming girl, with artistic talent, from New Orleans." On May 25, Natalie acted in an elaborate Greek production entitled *A Festival Day in the Temple Apollo* presented by Fairmont's class of 1910. The "distinguished" audience included Mrs. James Sherman, the wife of the vice-president, and a reception in Mrs. Sherman's honor was held afterwards.[14]

Nauman, by then a Tulane law student, came to Washington to

represent the family at the Greek performance and later for Natalie's June graduation. After two weeks of sightseeing and packing Natalie's bags, the two siblings boarded a train for New Orleans. The journey home was marked by lost luggage, socializing in Roanoke with family friends, and spontaneous changes of plans, ultimately leading the two on an entirely unplanned riverboat trip down the Mississippi River.

The social whirl of New Orleans quickly captured Natalie. Many of her old Newcomb friends, including her best friend, Hilda Phelps, had completed their society debuts the previous winter. Natalie's turn arrived that first winter back in New Orleans. The debutante season—a glittering panorama of parties—allowed the new maidens on the marriage market to make their official bow to the social world. The climax of the season each year was the Rex and Comus Mardi Gras balls.

This debutante season proved to be far more important for Natalie's brother Nauman. He fell deeply in love with a dark-haired girl from Pointe Coupee Parish. Her father, a French Creole named Albin Provosty, was a lawyer, farmer, and country newspaperman, and her uncle, Justice Olivier Provosty, was a member of the Louisiana Supreme Court. Nauman finished law school in 1912 and soon began practicing law in Alexandria, Louisiana with a well-established lawyer named L. J. Hakenyos, later Judge Hakenyos. Nauman proposed marriage to Sidonie, the two setting the wedding date for November 1914. Jack would serve as Nauman's best man, Natalie as Sidonie's first maid.

Natalie became a teacher at Newcomb High School in June 1911, fulfilling her long-presumed destiny. Her teaching career spanned from 1911 until 1917, when she shipped out on her Red Cross mission to Europe during World War I. She taught French, Greek, and literature courses, meanwhile working her way, for four years, towards a master's degree at Tulane in ancient Greek literature. Her friend Hilda joined her in this effort in 1912, perhaps pushing Natalie to move more quickly through the curriculum. Earnestly tackling her teaching duties at Newcomb, she became a faculty sponsor of journalism projects and athletics, as well as a regular competitor each spring in the Newcomb-Alumnae basketball game. Hilda and Carmelite Janvier, another former classmate, joined her on the faculty in 1913. The three veterans of the 1909 reform year soon initiated another innovation: they

Natalie (left) and Hilda Phelps, in costume for a play (New
Orleans, ca. 1911). *Courtesy of Special Collections, Tulane
University Libraries*

Natalie Vivian Scott (ca. 1912). *Courtesy of Special Collections, Tulane University Libraries*

created the Newcomb "coaching school," to provide summer tutoring, testing, and course credits for marginal students to qualify for admission to Newcomb College. The threesome served as the coaches.

Natalie enrolled in journalism and Spanish courses in 1913. Already fluent in French, with a working knowledge of Spanish, Greek, Italian, and German, Natalie began a personal project to master Spanish. It was part of her plan to take Muddie on an extended trip through Guatemala in June 1914. They would depart when she earned her master's degree. Natalie's master's thesis was entitled "A Comparison of Certain Plays of Euripides with Later Plays on the Same Subject." Composed of four chapters, it analyzed the Phaedra plays, comparing works of Euripides in ancient Greece to Seneca of Rome in the first century A.D. and Corneille in the seventeenth century. Her research required virtuosity in Greek, Spanish, French, and Italian, her thesis peppered with quotations and citations in each of these languages. Natalie received her master's degree two months before her twenty-fourth birthday. Hilda Phelps simultaneously earned her master's in English and philosophy.[15]

A week later Natalie and Muddie boarded a ship in New Orleans that took them to Guatemala, where they traveled for much of the summer. The trip proved memorable, both impressed by the great natural beauty of this Central American country, the Mayan ruins of the pre-Conquest civilization, and the simple courtesy and lifestyle of the Guatemalan people. Natalie made numerous references to specific Guatemalan friends and activities there in her World War I correspondence. She referred on one occasion to the enormous poverty and despair they had witnessed among the "warm-hearted people," expressing sorrow over the devastating 1918 earthquake, which added to their hardships.

During this 1914 trip, the two travelers followed in the press the disturbing news of assassinations and ultimatums that threatened war between Austria-Hungary and Serbia in the Balkans of eastern Europe. By the time they boarded their ship for the return voyage, Germany had invaded neutral Belgium and the great nations of Europe were at war. Natalie immediately began volunteer work in New Orleans aimed at Belgian refugee relief.

Natalie and Muddie took off on another long trip the next summer, traveling west by train to tour Southern California and Colorado. Hilda Phelps and her mother, Blanche, joined them for the Colorado phase of the journey. The Elkhorn, among the towering peaks surrounding Estes Park, became their primary destination. The train deposited them at a stone depot in the tiny mountain community of Lyons, north of Boulder. There the foursome boarded a nine-passenger, steam-powered automobile called a Stanley Steamer, which took them on a spectacular five-hour climb up a rocky, narrow road through the mountains to the front door of the Elkhorn. They were each assigned a horse, a room, and a table in the broad dining room, which was heated by a large, deep fireplace and adorned with mounted elk, deer, and bear trophies. From here, their base camp, the two young women explored the newly created, entirely wild Rocky Mountains National Park on horseback for six adventurous weeks. Back at the lodge, Muddie and Blanche Phelps relaxed with books.

Natalie would recall their mountain adventures a decade later as a columnist for the *New Orleans States* when she wrote of the horseback explorations of archeologists-anthropologists Frans Blom and Oliver La Farge into the mountains of Chiapas: ". . . the trip done on horseback, in the heart-lifting benediction of great solitudes. Even fatigue is a delight under these conditions. Haven't we ranged the Rockies together, got lost above timberline, ridden twenty-six hours on a stretch with a ten-minute stop; there is something delicious in the impersonal brutality of nature in the raw. Its oblivion of your very existence makes it seem a wild Nirvana in which you fling yourself with a shuddering joy." Natalie would again seek out this "delicious" wild sensation amidst nature "in the raw" during the 1930s, when she settled in the mountain village of Taxco, southwest Mexico, and explored much of that country on long horseback journeys.[16]

Chapter Two

America Goes to War

In contrast to the United States' hesitation, Natalie and Hilda immediately declared themselves for the Allied cause, particularly on behalf of beleaguered Belgium, hammered by the Germans despite its neutrality. Mass executions of Belgian civilians occurred in Linsmeau, Seilles, Tamines, Andenne, Dinant, and Louvain. Germany's Zeppelin bombing raids on Antwerp brought more horrors. These reports shocked the Western public. They galvanized Hilda and Natalie in faraway New Orleans, prompting both to volunteer for Belgium relief and Red Cross work. Natalie read the appeals for help from a British nurse in Brussels named Edith Cavell. When the Germans entered Brussels, Cavell, along with other British nurses, were given the opportunity to go safely to Holland, out of harm's way. Most, including Cavell, stayed. With her hospital overflowing with casualties, Cavell sent an urgent appeal to the *London Times* seeking public donations to cover the mounting medical needs. She wrote other publicized letters informing the world of Belgian suffering. These accounts hardened Natalie and Hilda's determination to raise funds for the thousands of Belgians pouring across the French border into refugee camps, facing a severe winter without essential clothing, food, and medical supplies.[1]

Their leadership began modestly. They presented to the Belgian consul in New Orleans, Leon de Waele, an idea for a large fundraiser: a play performance. Natalie and Hilda secured the support of two of the city's prominent society leaders, with Mrs. Paul F. Jahncke agreeing to become the event's chairman and Mrs. Joseph Friend the treasurer. By October, seventy-five New Orleans families had made cash contributions. Natalie and Hilda scheduled this "Benefit Performance for the Women and Children of Belgium" for late November at Antoine's Restaurant, its owner, Jules Alciatore, agreeing to their use of his elegant French Quarter establishment as a dinner theater for the evening. Natalie, Hilda, and Mrs. Jahncke performed the leading roles in the two-act production, entitled *Christmas Boxes,* followed by dancing and orchestra music in the grand ballroom. As the *New Orleans Item* reported the next day, "The benefit performance given Friday night at Antoine's was a great success. Major T. E. Davis and Mr. Leon de Waele, the Belgian Consul, were guests of honor. It is hoped that the winter will be made easier for each destitute Belgian woman and child by a pair of made-in-New Orleans shoes."

The war in Europe settled into a fierce stalemate on a long battlefront reaching across northern France. Through 1915, Natalie followed with growing dread a side drama to the bloody war, the German court martial of the British nurse Edith Cavell in Brussels, charged by the Germans with helping British and French war prisoners escape into neutral Holland. Cavell admitted her guilt; the Germans convicted and sentenced her to die by firing squad. American diplomats intervened, but their protests fell on deaf ears. The head of the German Political Department in Belgium refused to contact the kaiser on Cavell's behalf, declaring that it was too late even for the kaiser to prevent her death. At the execution post in October 1915, Cavell requested large pins. In a final act of Victorian modesty, she used them to secure the hem of her long skirt tightly around her ankles so the dress would not fly up when she was shot. Four firing-squad bullets hit Cavell, killing her instantly. Her martyrdom fanned the already heated anti-German sentiment in America. Natalie's commitment to her war work deepened, eventually taking her to the French battlefront.[2]

Natalie joined fellow Newcomb graduates in establishing the Newcomb Unit for war relief. She also joined the YWCA refugee assistance program and the Allied Liberty Bond campaign, while organizing canned-food and clothing drives with 1909 classmates. The Red Cross relied upon her as a public speaker, not only because of her passion for the cause, but for her understanding of the local relief effort.

On Thanksgiving day 1916, her speech rallied 246 volunteers gathered for a holiday dinner at the YWCA headquarters. Here she met Dr. Tom A. Williams, a national Red Cross leader visiting

New Orleans. Natalie had informed the Red Cross of her willingness to serve in Europe. She had prepared herself by improving her multilingual skills and in early 1916 enrolling in a Red Cross Special Nursing Course taught by the U.S. Army Medical Corps, receiving her nurse's aide certification in July. America entering the war seemed unlikely. American isolationism remained an entrenched sentiment even after the sinking of the *Lusitania*. Woodrow Wilson won reelection by reminding the American people that he had kept the nation out of the war. But events transformed America's neutrality. In February 1917, the Germans began unrestricted U-boat attacks on all ships, whether flying the American flag or not. President Wilson broke off diplomatic relations with Germany. As the specter of U.S. involvement became more ominous, Natalie's family began to worry.

Muddie and Boss were more frightened than disapproving of their daughter's interest in overseas service. Her brother Jack wrote Natalie a three-page letter from his National Guard camp in New York urging her not to go too far with her patriotism. "There is one thing that I want to ask you not to do, if I may? That is if war is really declaired [*sic*] with Germany, and we have to send troops over, will you please promise not to join the Red Cross. I would hate to have to think of you thrown among so many soldiers, and the work you would have to do." The family preferred that Natalie do her part, as she had for the past three years, from home. Yet the question simply simmered, unresolved, as no opportunity to serve abroad had yet materialized. Muddie offered no opinion, realizing she had conditioned Natalie for such a cause since infancy, with a steady diet of literature and personal guidance celebrating the most heroic attributes of the human spirit. Natalie pressed forward, honing her French language skills and taking more Spanish and Italian courses during 1916 and 1917, preparing to go overseas as a translator. On April 16, Natalie enrolled in a wireless telegraphy course at Loyola University, acquiring one more skill for war service.

The U.S. had declared war on Germany on April 6, 1917. In June, Hilda Phelps was appointed by Gov. Ruffin Pleasant as state chairman of the Louisiana Woman's Committee of the Council of National Defense, and Natalie was named state secretary. Their job was to mobilize the involvement of women in the war effort, coordinating both volunteers and those who wanted wartime employment. The Woman's Committee became a full-time operation that summer in a tiny office, Room 206 of the St. Charles Hotel. They began a volunteer registry for virtually every wartime cause. The leaders of the local Liberty Bond drives relied upon them for volunteers. The Red Cross needed help finding more nurses, plus women to answer phones, raise funds, collect clothing, and form special knitting committees across the state. Even tasks such as placing food conservation posters and pamphlets in store windows were done by Woman's Committee volunteers. They organized a fundraising dance to supply a local artillery battery preparing for training camp. They also organized a large train station reception to meet New Orleans soldiers returning from boot camp at Fort Logan H. Root. Hilda, Natalie, Martha, and many others of their 1909 class were there to applaud the speech by Mayor Martin Behrman, serve the refreshments, and welcome home the war-destined troops.

Dr. Tom Williams, the New York physician who had heard Natalie's Red Cross speech the previous November, had brought Natalie's application for overseas work to the attention of Dr. Alexander Lambert, the new director of the American Red Cross Medical Operations in France and Belgium. Impressed by her leadership on the home front and the practical skills she had acquired for war service, Lambert decided to recruit Natalie for his staff in Paris. This news would not reach her until mid-August.

New Orleans, like the rest of the country, was not unified over America's entry into the war. Due to organizational and training delays, American troops were unable to engage in European fighting until the final months of 1917, not entering combat en masse until the late spring of 1918. Also unprepared in spirit, the nation was troubled by dissent and protest. The 1917 compulsory draft met strong opposition, with many draftees claiming exemptions or failing to report at all. Litigation challenged the draft law as unconstitutional. Many Louisiana draftees hired lawyers to make technical exemption arguments on their behalf, causing delays. Frustrated draft officials were falling short of their quotas.

One meeting of the New Orleans second district exemption board was reported under the following headline in the *New Orleans Item:*

Dr. Alexander Lambert of New York. Director of Red Cross Medical Operations in France and Belgium through World War I. President of the American Medical Association (1919-20). Teddy Roosevelt's physician and hunting companion, he was Natalie's boss and mentor in Paris (1917-18). *Courtesy AMA Archives*

HISSES AND CALLS FOR POLICE MINGLE AS 2ND DISTRICT
BOARD HEARS CLAIMS FOR EXEMPTIONS

Crowd Hoots Announcement Of Only Six More Cases To Be Heard
After Eight Hours Settle 40 Of 150 Pleas—Women Faint And
Children Frolic On Gymnasium Apparatus—"When You Interfere
With Us You Help The Kaiser," Shouted By Chairman, Subdues
Near Riot; Verbal Clashes Between Officials Caused By Course Of
Questioning And Delays."[3]

Hilda Phelps, Natalie Scott, and the Woman's Committee
found themselves caught in the middle of the compulsory draft
controversy. The key to the committee's success rested upon
recruiting women, then putting them to work. But the massive
war demands overwhelmed their numbers. Many thousands of
volunteer workers were needed, but most women failed to register. Hilda and Natalie went to Governor Pleasant, proposing that
the legislature enact a new law compelling every woman in
Louisiana to register, even though actual work would remain
strictly optional. The governor and the legislature complied and
passed the law, mandating that every female "age of 16 up" register with the Woman's Committee.

In a two-pronged strategy to energize Louisiana's women,
Hilda published a letter in the state's newspapers while Natalie
undertook an August speaking tour across the state to explain
the law's purpose and appeal for help. Most papers published
Hilda's letter on page one.

Our aim is to have at once complete statistics as to the women
who are trained to take up the work of the men, or who wish to
train, along lines of work needed by their country, and also to
obtain a list of the women who will volunteer their services for
philanthropic work. From the patriotic standpoint every woman
wishing to serve her country in this crisis will be placed where she
will be of most use. . . . Every effort will be made to cooperate with
business houses and government offices so that women who need
employment, now or later, may secure employment. . . .
Emergency training classes will be organized, free or for the smallest possible fee, and many women who register for training may
thus have the opportunity to better themselves financially.

The names of those women who refuse to register will be sent by the Woman's committee to the state council, in whose power it lies to take such action as it may deem necessary. . . . It must be distinctly understood, that although the registration is required, the offer of service is purely voluntary. No woman need offer any assistance unless she so desires. . . .

Cordially
Hilda Phelps, Chairman[4]

Natalie's public meetings were arranged by local Woman's Committee leaders. The last stop was Alexandria, where the newspaper announced "a mass meeting of the women of Alexandria" for the morning of August 13, 1917, with Natalie Scott as the featured speaker. The newspaper emphasized the meeting's importance: "All heads of organizations or their proxies are urged to be present, and each woman in the city who is interested in war work is earnestly requested to attend." Mayor William W. Whittington hosted the crowded meeting in city hall. Natalie's speech became the front-page story the next day, emphasizing the tasks to be performed locally, especially work with military camps in the area. The audience selected officers and organized committees.

Behind the scenes, two important developments occurred in the Scott family. Having joined the army, Nauman received orders to report to Camp Stanley in Leon Springs, Texas for infantry training to become an officer. His army service would leave Sidonie alone with the couple's one-year-old son, Nauman, Jr., born in June 1916. Sidonie was expecting their second child that fall.

Natalie had big news too: a surprise letter from Dr. Alexander Lambert asking her to join his Red Cross staff as quickly as possible in Paris. Natalie accepted by wire, also writing Lambert a letter the same day. She would leave immediately for Paris. Though she had mixed feelings, especially due to Muddie's uncertain health, she sensed that a great adventure for a great purpose lay before her. The news rapidly spread among her New Orleans friends and through the Woman's Committee network around the state. Natalie's Paris appointment made newspaper headlines in New Orleans, unexpectedly influencing the military draft controversy. On August 19, local newspapers reported a shift in public opinion, crediting as a factor the publicity over Natalie going to war. The front-page headline and subheadline of the New Orleans States, beside Natalie's large photograph, declared:

ORLEANS WOMAN'S CALL TO FRANCE
STIMULATES REGISTRATION INTEREST

Miss Natalie Scott, Former Secretary Of State Branch Of National Defense To Go To Paris At Call Of Red Cross—Example Proves Service Is Not To Be Confined To Men And Diffidence Among Louisiana Girls Is Transformed Into Eagerness

Natalie served as useful local propaganda for Wilson's war mobilization, her example publicized as a fresh breeze of patriotism in the midst of so much dissension. A newspaper survey of Woman's Committee leaders across Louisiana confirmed that registrations had suddenly increased everywhere.

> The example of one Louisiana woman in offering herself to the government and being assigned to service in Paris is turning the opposition and defiance of the young women of the state toward registration into a willingness to do anything the government demands.
> Miss Natalie Scott who has been secretary of the Louisiana branch of the women's committee, Council of National Defense—the official body organized to serve as a clearing house for women's war service—is the one who has wrought the transformation among the women of this state. She goes at the call of the Red Cross to serve as secretary to Dr. Lambert, head of the hospital division of the American Red Cross in Paris, and is the first called on from this state.
> 'Young women felt that they would obligate themselves by registering,' says Miss Bertha Wolbrette, who succeeded Miss Scott as secretary of the state committee. . . . 'Miss Scott's being called on to go across the water serves as a concrete example of what any girl may be called upon to do. All her co-workers are frankly jealous of her opportunity and a new interest in the registration is noticed on all hands. When it is explained what opportunities this registration offers for a girl to better herself, by taking the training the government will give to those who volunteer, if it needs them, then they are eager to put down their names.'[5]

Another article about Natalie appeared on August 26, this time in a popular Sunday social column written in the form of a letter to a fictitious "Peggy" from a fictitious "Cynthia St. Charles."

I've just been talking to Natalie Scott, Peggy. She, as of course you know, has been selected by Dr. Lambert, a distinguished New York physician now doing war relief work in Paris, as his secretary. Natalie does not know Dr. Lambert at all, but he has asked for her on the very strong recommendation of Dr. Williams, another well known American doctor now working somewhere in France.

Dr. Williams met Miss Scott while he was in New Orleans last winter. So impressed was he, as everybody is, with her extraordinary combination of intellect, charm and wonderful efficiency that Dr. Lambert, through Dr. Williams' description and account of her, has sent her, a perfect stranger to him, a most urgent request to cross the perilous high seas and come to Paris to do secretary work for him. Did you ever know of one young woman being more greatly complimented, really more honored?

Of course we are not surprised, Peggy, are we? For we together with most of New Orleans admire Natalie so immensely that we believe her deserving of everything and capable of everything. We are very glad to have New Orleans and Louisiana womanhood represented in important places by such a very splendid young woman. She herself makes very light of the whole thing. But we, her friends who love her and know her, do not make light of it. The way before her, while probably full of excitements and thrills, will also be filled with much hard work and with the ever-present knowledge that she's a long, long way from home.

And so, Peggy, while we bid her Au Revoir and God speed, let us pray that her fine doing of her duty, her splendid patriotism may be rewarded and bring her much happiness.[6]

So Natalie not only went to war, she went off with great fanfare. Bewildered by so much attention, and tremendously preoccupied with the sudden task of packing for perhaps years overseas, she spent the final week before departure at home with her family and friends.

The Road to Paris

The road to Paris began with a farewell party at 4907 Carondelet, then continued at the train depot until the ten-o'clock train whisked Natalie from New Orleans. Her departure on the night of September 4 capped an exhausting week of packing, while also cramming a steady stream of visitors into each day.

The party arrived en masse at the train depot around nine. Natalie gave final hugs to everyone, while Hilda and Agnes both shoved letters into her purse to be read later. When she kissed Jack, who had been so quietly helpful all week, Natalie found herself crying. Boss made her laugh when he asked, loud enough for others to hear, whether her money was safely pinned in her girdle. Muddie gently held her face and kissed her, then pressed her forefinger over Natalie's heart, making the small gesture of a cross, the Lover's Cross as Muddie called it. Natalie returned the gesture and they embraced. Stepping aboard, Natalie waved, laughed, and threw kisses to her entourage as the train gained speed, pulled away from the brightly lighted station, then entered the night.

Muddie and Natalie had similar reactions to this sudden, indefinite separation, though each expressed her feelings differently. Muddie showered her daughter with gifts—a diamond ring, new clothes, a new hat, a mechanical pencil, an umbrella, framed photographs, and a miniature combination dresser and washstand. Subsequently, in New York, another box of gifts arrived from her mother, along with a spate of letters. Natalie likewise overreacted, sending Muddie sixteen letters plus a plethora of telegrams between her departure and September 13, when she boarded her ship in New York.

The trip from New Orleans to Washington, D.C. consumed two nights, delivering Natalie early Thursday morning, along with her companion, Mr. Leigh Carroll, a New Orleanian just appointed manager of the Gulf Division of the Red Cross. Upon arrival at 8:00 A.M., they ate breakfast at the Shoreham Hotel, which Natalie found to be *simply jammed with people on various war business.* She encountered passport problems, finally having success with an official named Mr. Hamblin. *Mr. Hamblin was most agreeable. Entre nous, he really liked me very well! He knows Arthur Derby, Louis Stouffer, Mary Elise Whitney and all the idle rich very well,—so I suppose that accounts for his pleasantness to me. Several people rang up while I was there, waiting for some papers to fix up for me but he told them that he was "occupied." I started to ask him to call, but I decided he might have a wife somewhere,—and then he uses "O dear" as an exclamation, and that has no charm for me.*

I wandered around for an age looking for the passport place, the

Bureau of Citizenship, because, of course, I was too stingy to take a taxi. I met a very nice man named Scott who is a very high up apparently. Mr. Carroll introduced him and I liked him tremendously. He was very gay. He said, "You have a very nice name." And I said, "And so have you. Aren't we lucky?" so we smiled upon each other and took up many minutes of the government's time.

Natalie stayed two nights at Fairmont Place with cousin Lee and Fannie. She was fascinated with the colorful crowds in Washington due to the government's frantic war mobilization effort. *They say it has now 40,000 people more than normal, and service of every kind is absolutely demoralized. The Shoreham almost ruined my nerves, for everybody there seemed poised for instant flight. When you addressed one, he would pause as tho ready instantly to dart away, as soon as you finished, and really hardly able to wait till then. The phone service is the same way. A new exchange had to be installed and, even so, it is a matter almost past patience to get a number. And the cars! They are packed always as ours are at Mardi Gras. And uniforms, uniforms everywhere, every sort, kind and description. I hear, à propos of uniforms, that Chattanooga has sold several hundred thousand dollars worth of swagger sticks since the training camps started!*

Her train trip to New York on September 8 began miserably because of the cold weather and the crowds, but the mood soon brightened as they passed two different trainloads of troops. She wrote of the unity and optimism of the soldiers. *Poor fellows! They were in awful-looking old day-coaches, but they were a jolly crowd on the whole. One from our train called out to a car on theirs, while it was standing still, "Hey, you fellows! Goodbye." They called back, "Where you going, Pinky?" "Home," he yelled joyfully. And they came back, ungrammatically but delightedly with "Where's that at?" It was in Georgia. It was a foolish dialogue, and it sounds inane when written, but to hear it, it was full of such good-feeling and comraderie [sic] that it was really a pleasure to listen. Lots of the boys had handkerchiefs tied on their heads, and one had on a lavender real boudoir cap! They all crowded out of the window when the car stopped and called to each other, and teased the various vendors and baggage men. And once, when a certain captain walked down their line, they all cheered.*

Natalie went directly to the Vanderbilt Hotel in New York, that same afternoon contacting a former Fairmont teacher, a playwright named Wright. She took Natalie *down in Greenwich Village, just off Washington Square, to a delightful Italian restaurant for dinner. Afterwards, we wandered around the square, and through the village. It reminds me somewhat of New Orleans, tho the houses are brick; but there is lots of ironwork. . . . Miss Wright hasn't changed a bit, and is so interesting! She has a play to be produced by the Washington players this fall.* She enjoyed two other excursions before her departure, one with Sara Stern, a 1909 Newcomb classmate whose family owned a summer cottage on the ocean in nearby Allanhurst, the other an invitation to see Mary Smithers, a friend who lived in Garden City, New Jersey. Rushing out of the Vanderbilt, Natalie just made the eleven-o'clock train to Mary's home. *I have had a lovely day over here. Mary had a wonderful dinner. By the way, for supper to-night, she had peppers stuffed with spaghetti and they were delicious. I thought you might like the suggestion. We had a fine golf match with two men from here.*

And Long Island! *The number of lovely little towns and summer houses along it! And now the encampment! We drove thru Camp Mills to day, where there are said to be 12,000 men. It is beautifully in order, and the great expanse of tents, and the groups of men, all so busy and always so busy in so orderly a way—really, like numbers worked by one brain—makes an ensemble that makes me draw a deep breath, and realize that we are at war,—and that I am going to France.*

Natalie spent her final day, Wednesday, September 12, with Sara Stern in Allanhurst, going and returning by train. *I had a lovely day, really wonderful. Mr. and Mrs. Stern, and Mr. Blanc, Sara's uncle, were all there, and they were as sweet as they could be. The Sterns have a very pretty house, and its location is perfect, with the Atlantic stretching out before it, and wonderful show places all around. Of course, in the innocence of my unsophisticated soul, Allanhurst meant nothing to me; but I noticed that the clerk at the Vanderbilt looked impressed. Shadowlawn, the place where "our Mr. Wilson" spent last summer, is there, and is really worthy of the honor. It is magnificent. Sara says that the New Jersey people are thinking of buying it and presenting it as a summer house to the President.*

The Sterns' car is a beauty,—so elegant and comfortable; Sara and I drove all around in it. It is quite an advantage to the poor. All these wealthy people spend so much thought and worry over these homes, to get those beautiful effects, and I simply go along . . . without an effort or spending a cent, get the benefit of it all.

Mrs. Stern outdid herself in cordiality. She ordered luncheon expressly for me, and had grillards [sic] and small hot biscuits, because she said she knew I would not have any more! And she really got tearful when telling me goodbye. The day is really at hand! I wish you could see the alluring soldiers in the hotel,— French aviators who kiss ladies' hands, Scotch Highlanders, Canadians, and always our dear old khaki fellows.[7]

The wharf seemed alive Thursday morning with other passengers and well-wishers at shipside. Natalie was transfixed by the tumultuous shouting, the penetrating ship whistle followed by *the howl of a fearsome siren* as the ship, the *Touraine*, cast off, and the hawsers splashing into the water. The view of the city in one direction, and the open harbor and Statue of Liberty in the other, was enhanced by the clear, sunny day. A fellow passenger, a *Boston Globe* journalist named Frank P. Sibley, kept a diary during the voyage and described their vessel.

> The first thing I noticed about the ship was a certain sloppiness. Her two funnels were stubby; her boat deck is crowded; and there is an uncomfortable suggestion in the number of lifecrafts carried in addition to the boats. Forward, a small caliber gun is mounted; aft, there is a 65 millimeter. She is gray, of course, and not at all too big. We are limited practically to the promenades, to the salle de conversation, whose chairs are bolted at deck, and whose green and gold and white decorations do not go at all well with the red carpet, to the fumoir de la premier class, and to our state rooms.

Natalie wrote a letter that morning aboard the *Touraine*, which she was able to send back to shore for mailing. She was far more satisfied with the vessel than Mr. Sibley. *On—and off! I am really started at last. The boat is lovely. Mr. Carroll came to the dock, and I got off with no trouble. It was much better that none of you all were there; for I walked out with hardly a qualm. There are many charming looking people on board. I have met my cabin mate, who is the wife of a correspondent on Pershing's*

Natalie (hand on head) with new friends aboard the *Touraine*, crossing to France and World War I (September 1917). *Courtesy of Special Collections, Tulane University Libraries*

staff, young, pretty, and attractive. So, comparatively, I am happy. There are fetching looking uniforms on board, in Field Services; and many trained nurses. So we are all in the same boat, in all senses of the word. Have to rush. I am going to send just a line to Nauman, and one to Hilda. Kiss Sidney, and Boss, and Wyeth, and Mrs. (Albin) Provosty, and my Precious Child all for me once more. . . . And you and Sidney must exchange the Lover's Cross for me. My love, and my love, and my love, as broad and huge and profound as this old ocean I am now on.

Natalie wrote Muddie a single letter covering the nine-day crossing, which amounted to a twenty-page diary. *My room-mate is a very, very nice girl and we are delighted with each other. She* (Mrs. Tom Johnson, also referred to as "Johnny") *is going to join her husband, who is with the N.Y. Sun and a syndicate of newspapers, is with Pershing, and one of sixteen accredited correspondents abroad.*

Next to us in the steamer chairs is an odd assemblage, going for canteen work. Their uniforms are attractive, dark grayish tailored suits, with brown stiff military belts, and tailored hats with a Red Cross on the band. Mrs. Belmont Tiffany is with them, and in command,—very much so! She is pleasant enough, but so efficient: she simply bristles with efficiency, and has what is, in my humble opinion, a disproportionately great pleasure in her own conversation!

Yesterday afternoon, at three, we had a lifeboat drill, and had all to don our life preservers, and take our places near our boats. It was then that I met the Globe correspondent. He is a tall, slim man, really journalistic-looking. We were all joking about the life preservers, submarines,—in short, "joking with Davy Jones, sir", as sailors should. He said no people but Americans, in rehearsing for such a grim drama as we, could be so jolly over it. He is entertaining and well-read and loves chess; sometimes, I think he is very nice. Then, sometimes, I don't like him.

Natalie and Mrs. Johnson, her roommate, got to know the captain. He showed them the ship's course, explaining they would travel north near Halifax, then across the ocean directly to the French coast, then south to the Garonne River, which would carry them to Bordeaux. The German U-boat warfare had persisted relentlessly since America's April entry into the war, sinking almost six hundred Allied and neutral ships in May and June. Though convoys with warships discouraged German attacks, the *Touraine* was not in a convoy. Therefore, precautions against German U-boats were strictly enforced. *It is so eerie here. We have no lights outside at night, and have to close every hatch in the staterooms, if we have lights. That makes it so hot, that we sleep out on deck almost altogether. We enter the danger zone to-night, and everybody is cracking jokes, and making friends with their life-preservers. There is one man who is really scared, and everyone unites in teasing him.*

Mr. Sibley's diary included a humorous account of Natalie's first encounter with the aggressive personality of Mrs. Belmont Tiffany.

Miss Scott, a New Orleans young woman, who was going over to be secretary to Dr. Lambert, is very amusing, very feminine. She sat down by Mrs. Tiffany one afternoon, and Mrs. T. tore into her right away. By direct questions she found that Miss Scott doesn't even know shorthand, and doesn't know why she was chosen for the position. Mrs. Tiffany asked if she were familiar with medicine and surgical terms and in general showed a most amusing belief that Ms. Scott, like the son in the "Walrus and the Carpenter", had got no business to be there.

Miss Scott finds time to practice shorthand for perhaps an hour a day. She shows signs, however, of giving up the book system in favor of an abbreviation system like mine, which can be devised by anyone. Meanwhile, she was ruling odd scraps of paper for practice sheets so I gave her one of my precious notebooks.

Mr. Sibley even composed a little poem in his diary, the last refrain revealing how amused he was by Natalie Scott. Here is an extract of two verses.

> I went on a journey by sea
> To France, and there traveled with me
> Folks of many conditions
> And sorts, and positions,
> Beat on setting democracy free. . . .
>
> The funniest one, on the level,
> Was a young southern girl in a rebel,
> To a shorthand she would stick,
> For an hour at a lick,
> And the rest of the time raise the devil.[8]

Mr. Sibley had his own problems with Mrs. Tiffany, as he reported after a political discussion with her. "She thinks the I.W.W. is composed of riotous thugs with no program beyond a general ruckus, and told some of the women in her unit this morning that I was a Socialist and member of the I.W.W.!" But, as Natalie noted, Mrs. Tiffany gradually softened. *It is rough to-day, and many have succumbed, including the efficient Mrs. Tiffany. Everyone predicts that I should, too, because I have studied and written so much; but—knocking on wood—I haven't yet had a qualm. The Y.M.C.A. is singing* Old Black Joe *in the distance.* By midvoyage, relations with Mrs. Tiffany decidedly improved. *This is Thursday! I have been really working! You will see about my encounter with Mrs. Belmont Tiffany in Mr. Sibley's journal. We have all rubbed it in, till she is really embarrassed. And she has really been very sweet to me since; so I have forgiven her. Meanwhile, I announced that I would fit myself for my position by practicing with a typewriter, belonging to Mr. Vibbert, Prof. of Psychology for the U. Of Michigan. He is going over for the American University Union. . . . There is a*

*Pittsburgh millionaire going over for the Red Cross (married)
and he asked me if I would do some letters for him. I took 13
and typed them in the afternoon, on a strange typewriter. And
some of these were 2 pages! Mrs. Tiffany was impressed.*

Time passed with a series of shuffleboard and bridge games, in
which Mrs. Johnson and Natalie, as partners, were continuously
in demand by the ambulancers and soldiers on board. *Mr. Fowler
and Mr. Miller, two ambulance men, one Yale, the other
Nebraska, played bridge with Mrs. Johnson and me last night,—
while criticism and advice as to the game was showered by a
shifting audience,—Mr. Sibley, Mr. Walker, Mr. Eyer, Mr. Wyley,
Mr. Shellinglaw, etc. etc. We had many bids for games to-day.
There are two really wonderful looking men in the corps: Mr. de
Forest, who is a real blond Canadian type, and Mr. Benedict,
whose grey-blue eyes fairly startle you from his good-looking
bronzed face! We play shuffleboard everyday, de Forest being my
favorite partner. He is rather serious, and has a face of an idealist. I am delighted with him. Mr. Vibbert and I are also the best
of friends, and everyone laughs at me for my high-brow friends,
for he and Mr. Sibley spend lots of time with me, and go with no
other girls.* She reported a contingent of fellow Episcopalians on
board, including Bishop Wall of Detroit with his companion, Dr.
Finches. She wrote of the YWCA and Salvation Army groups on
board who would gather at night to sing patriotic songs.

A final highlight of the voyage was a concert, including a min-
strel show, many songs and stunts, and an auction organized by
the Ambulance Corps to raise funds for the French orphans. The
auction raised over a thousand dollars. Natalie donated a bottle
of Houbigaut perfume, which Sara had given her in New York,
and a box of Havana cigars. She also made the high bid of three
dollars for etchings donated by a French artist, which she sent to
Muddie from Paris, noting that *Mr. Sibley was auctioneer, [and]
with his saturnine expression, and impressive length of
appearance, combined with an unceasing stream of clever sayings, kept the audience convulsed, and cheerful, as their coin
was thus painlessly extracted.*

Her last entry on ship appeared on Saturday, September 22,
the day before their arrival at Bordeaux. *This is our last day on
board. We are supposed to reach the mouth of the river by midnight. Meanwhile, everyone is supposed to have life-preservers*

and themselves prepared. I am upstairs. The air below is very bad; but the port-holes may not be opened for fear of the water rushing in quickly should the ship strike a mine. All about, fore and aft, the sailors stand with glasses scanning the horizon. I have often heard of an horizon being scanned, but now I have really seen it! The boat zig-zags constantly so that it will be difficult for a submarine to get our range.

Then, on September 23, her first night in France, she wrote from the Hotel de Bordeaux of the past two days' danger and the feelings on board when land was finally sighted. *Yesterday and last night were the most dangerous times of all. Everywhere the French sailors, tense and abnormally quiet, strained their gaze out on the horizon. The captain left the bridge hardly a moment . . . no portholes were opened and the air below was stifling. No matches could be struck, and even the smoking room and salle de conversation were locked and black. Between 12 and 1 the light was sighted. Soon, in a hushed voice, the lookout called something in French, then, "Land ahoy." I was with George de Forest, and there were many others around the deck. We strained to catch an almost imperceptible point of light in the stretch of faintly starlight darkness. Gradually it was clearer, and in time we could see a soft play of light from the distant lighthouse. The sailors began calling to each other, cheerily. We were inside the net! . . . We were safe. France was there before us. We had not been frightened, and yet, I think there was not one of us who was not stirred. You know I am not emotional, but the tears come to my eyes when I think of it. All the significance of it,—hands across-the-sea, danger, service, wonder at nautical science, everything swells indistinguishably in one big emotional heave. . . .*

When we first saw the light, Mr. de Forest and I called out, softly, at the same time, without thinking even, Vive la France! And the others, standing near, took it up, softly, too. And when we were inside the net, there began, still in hushed voices, thru the dark, La Marseillaise. *But there is no use telling about it. I can't give you an idea of it.*

With the danger past, the travelers were able to retire to their berths for the night with the portholes opened. Natalie awoke early, immediately looked outside, and saw yellow land and a white lighthouse as they entered the Garonne River of southern

France. Minutes later, on deck, she watched the riverbank glide by. *Close enough to see the peasants in their beautiful blue blouses, and all their absurd but harmonious touches of color in bright belts, brilliant skirts. . . . Many of them waved to us. At one place, a crowd of American soldiers gathered. We passed a German prison camp, the prisoners were working in the fields.*

The ship arrived at midday on Sunday. Natalie then described *the din, the Bedlam, the Babel of amateur French, of English, of real French,* as the chaos of unloading luggage ensued. Finally, she reached the hotel, then explored parts of the city. Many of the men on board asked for her Paris address so they could reach her there, and Johnny, her cabin mate, rode the train with her to Paris. With these familiar faces nearby, she reasoned, *it won't seem so cold and cheerless,—even tho I tremble at the thought of Dr. Lambert!*

The immediate signs of war made a deep impression upon her, though they were still far away from the battlefields. *But I must pause to remark that I have never seen such variety of uniforms in my life as there are here. It gives the town a superficial effect of gayety, with all the mingling colors. But, looking more close-ly, it is to be seen that the bandages and the wounds are almost as many and varied as the uniforms. And, also, it seems that mourning is almost half of the costumes here for women.*

The train for Paris left early on Monday morning and Natalie finally arrived in the French capital that night. She checked into the Hotel St. James, on Rue St. Honore. It was not far from the Red Cross office of Dr. Lambert at 4 Place de la Concorde, where she reported Tuesday morning for work.

Chapter Three

Paris

I went, bright and early, to report. The office is in a beautiful location, 4 Place de la Concorde. To reach it, I had to pass the Tuileries gardens. When I reached the office, there was a light fog over everything,—enough to make the vast stretch of the Place de la Concorde and the tremendous bridge beyond take on even more majestic proportions. The statues are of heroic size, and a large obelisk rises up in the midst of it all. My own modest proportions seemed those of some audacious figure, an affront to the great scene. But I soon blossomed out after meeting Dr. Lambert. He is a great man and a lovable man. He is burdened almost past endurance with the organization of this work; and yet he was as affable, as unhurried, and kind to see as tho he were possessed of the utmost leisure.[1]

Dr. Lambert was indeed an affable man, confident in his work and professional relationships. He was above average in height, fifty-six years old, and dark haired with a bearded chin and a moustache peppered with grey whiskers. His father and brothers were also physicians, one brother serving as the dean of Columbia's medical faculty. Lambert had been Pres. Teddy Roosevelt's personal physician. During the 1890s, he had undertaken groundbreaking research in bacteriology, particularly dealing with tetanus and diphtheria antitoxin. He had been the attending physician at Bellevue Hospital since 1894 and a clinical professor of medicine at Cornell University Medical College. He was also renowned in medical circles as a pioneer heart specialist and as creator of the Lambert Method for treatment of alcohol and narcotic addiction. In April 1917, Major Lambert had been ordered to active duty in France as chief medical adviser of all American Red Cross activities in France and Belgium, and in June he was among the first three Red Cross officials to arrive in Paris.[2]

63

Natalie's war work began modestly in safe surroundings, with little hint of the tumultuous events the war had in store for her. She began under the guidance of Dr. Tom A. Williams, the same physician who had recommended her, with a temporary assignment to complete an enormous report on war neurosis. Natalie's job was to translate and make digests of French war reports while touring hospitals with Dr. Williams, observing patients and assessing the effectiveness of medical techniques. *I have no track of time. This morning I sorted Dr. Williams' notes, then corrected some of the typewritten parts and wrote some others myself. He took me to luncheon and then to Neuilly, to see the American hospital there. It was intended as a school before the war began; but was taken over as a hospital by the French and recently, only about a month ago, turned over to the Americans.*

There was one man with a doubly fractured leg done up in peculiar apparatus with weights and pulleys, holding his leg in a position slanting upwards. It seems that only in that position could he move without injuring his leg. Dr. Williams says the war has brought out many devices of the kind. I happened to encounter the gaze of a young fellow of about twenty-three, who had one leg cut off just below the hip. Many were out in the large open grounds, in the sun. They were laughing and talking, singing, and playing games. One was laughing delightedly at the speed with which he could run his rolling-chair.[3]

Initial impressions of war-worn Paris were shared in her early letters, such as this introduction to a Frenchman she encountered when she obtained her *carte d'identité. The clerk was the sweetest Frenchman you ever saw; he had one of those delightful loose blouses, a black one, dark, upstanding dark hair, and soft dark eyes, and a face that was heavy, but very alert, if you can picture the combination. And so French. In a flash, up, out of his chair, thru the door, vanished; in the instant, in again, down again, writing busily; then down with the pen, and sorting papers, and humming, "da-da-da-de-da-de"—"la-la-la-la"; then a sentence muttered half aloud, and a laugh to himself. He was my heart entirely.*

He spoke no English, but was most cordial in French. I asked if he had been in the war. "If I have been in the war? La-la, Mademoiselle, I have been in eight months from the start. Then they send me back. They send back all the old."

I said, "but why did they send you?"

He laughed delightedly at my flattery—tho it was very well-justified at that—and said, "Because I am old. I am fifty. Did you not think I was so old? La-la!" I have never heard anything more attractive than his way of saying "La-la." It doesn't sound at all finicky; but just hearty, and boyish, and altogether attractive.

He added, after a pause, with a sigh—a characteristically quick change from gay to grave,—"Ah, yes, I am old. I have grown sons."

I said, "And are they in the war?"

"Are they in the war? But what should I say? One sick, one prisoner, and one dead."

And the cheery little fellow was quiet a few minutes. So was I. After a while, I asked him if he had seen General Joffre, and he said "yes," delightedly, and spoke with praise of him. He was loquacious in a way; but not about himself. He had been in the retreat, and in the Battle of Marne he and his sons had all fought—"nous quatre," he said. His son had been an interpreter in the army and then a courier for Gen. (Joseph Jacques) Joffre, and was killed at Verdun. Another son had been in Belgium, and in the trenches when the snow was several feet deep all around. He has bronchitis and had had pneumonia, and is so weak he "cannot lift 5 kilogrammes". The old fellow was not complaining at all; on the contrary, he was cheerful. I think of him as a "little fellow," because he was so simple and cheery and true-hearted; but he is strong and stalwart, too. Of such is the Republic of France.[4]

One by one, Natalie's friends from the *Touraine* began leaving Paris on their separate war assignments. Mr. Wyley and Mr. Fowler were being shipped out by the ambulance service to either Soisson or Verdun, and Mr. Morris to London. Then George de Forest, Mr. Miller, and Mr. Shipley, all with the ambulance service, were abruptly sent to Verdun. But she made new acquaintances and even occasionally encountered old friends from home. *I told you, I am sure, about running into Alfred Chapman on the Grand Boulevard the other day. He came this morning and brought a friend. I took them into the courtyard garden to take their pictures. We saw a group of good-looking American officers, with a Canadian and one French over with them, just sitting down across the garden. Alfred discovered he knew one. Soon, the whole group had come over to be introduced!*

One of them was a Mr. Jesse, whose father used to teach at Tulane. Another, Mr. Hicks, was from San Antonio, and knows Ettinger Legendre. They are stationed at Fontainebleau about an hour from here; and invited Johnny and me out for next Sunday. And we are going to ride in the morning and golf in the afternoon, with a canoe-ride and a tour of Fontainebleau in between. Isn't that alluring?

The Canadian wore a most alluring costume, khaki, with a touch of green on the sleeve, and the cockiest, jauntiest little taru, caught up on one side, and tilted,—he was very attractive with twinkling gay eyes, and the jolliest laugh. He was at Verdun and Vimy Ridge.

Natalie further commented on the Canadian in a later entry of the same letter. *To-night is just a scrawl; because I am in need of sleep! The nice little Scotch-Canadian I told you of, Captain Clark, arrived last night, as scheduled, and his little Scotch cap was as Scotch and cute and cocky as ever. He took Johnny and me to dinner at the Café Prouant, and afterwards we went to the Olympia theatre, where there is vaudeville.*

The dinner was delicious. Of course, I put Capt. Clark thru a perfect cross-examination. I made him tell me lots of slang. One thing is, a "blighty", which is a wound sufficient to cause a man to be sent back to England. He says the men are perfectly elated when they get one.

Then I began asking him about the trenches; but I soon changed the subject. He was not eager to talk of it, nor I to listen, after a minute. He told me of one man whose overcoat weighed 150 lbs. with the mud. He told us of seeing a whole battalion of men cut down in a twinkling, absolutely to a man, by machine guns. Of his best friend, who was killed six months ago in a charge. Before leaving, his friend had waked him up to shake hands, and apologized for doing so. The Captain's leave is up to-morrow, alas, and back he goes. He came by to say goodbye. I never told you how he shocked me, by what he said about the attitude of the Canadians. Of course, I have heard that they are the fiercest fighters on the side of the Allies. Well, Capt. Clark says that time after time they go in and take no prisoners. He said that the Germans crucified one of their men, and gave no quarter, and they had to get even. Somehow, I couldn't enjoy talking to him after that. I would rather be killed than to think I should ever come to such a condition of mind.[5]

On October 14, a Sunday, Natalie and Johnny took the ninety-minute train trip to Fontainebleau as the guests of Mr. Jesse and Mr. Hicks, the two soldiers from the garden of the St. James Hotel. *The boys met us at the train with a carriage and took us to the hotel, the Savoie.*

In the morning, we went to see the Palace. It is a huge, rambling building, with several courts, and many beautiful gardens, with beautiful lakes, flowers and woods. We were shown thru by a guide who could win any tongue marathon. The boys wanted me to tell them what he was saying, so I would be christening Louis XIII as Napoleon was getting married, and would still be revoking the Edict of Nantes when Napoleon was abdicating. The place is, of course, a hot-bed of history.

After the Palace we prepared to ride. You can imagine with what joy on my part! And the boys were perfectly charmed with my riding-clothes, especially with the hat! Poor Johnny was very jealous of me, for she, since she does not ride, had to go for a drive in a carriage.

And then,—I can't believe it, can you,—we rode thru the forests of Fontainebleau, where kings have chased the wild boar. It is a royal forest, really. The trees stretched away, old, and endlessly. The dead leaves so thick beneath them seem to be the droppings of ages. It reminds me of a description of the woods, by Yeats, in which he speaks of 'Dropping, a murmurous dropping; Old silence and that one sound.' There are all sorts of alluring bridle paths. Many led to vantage points of wonderful views, with a clear sweep of valley and hill-side below; and sometimes even huge boulders. The woods were beautiful in color. I pulled some rich gold-looking leaves to send you one; but when I got off at the hotel, my horse appropriated them![6]

During October, in the push to complete Dr. Williams' report, the office work grew demanding, claiming late evenings and weekends. Natalie occasionally carried out hospital surveys alone. She traveled by train through the Vincennes forest to St. Maurice Hospital, and her notes on its apparatus and techniques, based upon the explanations of the physicians, pleased Dr.

Williams. She also made the survey of the Grand Palais hospital, a reeducational school. *All the different trades are in different rooms, of course. I went to the first, and saw groups of men polishing some sort of heavy metal clamping instrument. They seemed very busy. And I could not notice one disfigurement. Of course, I didn't want to look at the men too closely: I have a horror of that aggressive, prying disregard of all the men's sensibilities: I've seen samples of the attitude at the Charity. So I would always pretend to be most interested in the work, then looking at the men themselves out of the corner of my eye.*

They have learned to use their instruments so skillfully. I saw three men leaning over a table, pressing out some designs for book-binding. It was not till I passed them again that I noticed that all three of them were armless on one side! There are vocations for every degree of intelligence,—harness making, glass-blowing, book-binding, architecture and interior decoration; soap-making; hair dressing; accounting; and a class in English for all who wish it. My guide had studied only 5 months and he spoke to me in English altogether. It is fine to see what an interest those men have in their work. I couldn't help but remember that poor young boy I saw at the hospital at Neuilly, the one who had lost his right leg, and kept staring so hopelessly ahead, and looked so listless. I suppose they all go thru that stage; they must. And this work is like new life to them. I bought some of the tiny little memorandum books they make and will send you one.[7]

Work and Play

Natalie's workload increased when another translator suddenly abandoned her job to return to the United States. Dr. Burlingame, one of Dr. Lambert's assistants, needed a secretary so she helped him while beginning work on two other reports, one of which dealt with rehabilitation innovations developed during the war. This once again took Natalie to various hospitals to observe new techniques. *I was working busily over the translation, but had to stop and go over, at 11 to No. 5, rue Francois Premier, to aid Dr. Williams in having some pictures taken of some new varieties of apparatus for nerve injuries. "No. 5" is the Headquarters of the Woman's War Relief Corps, of which Mrs. Lambert is the hard-working head.*

When I arrived, there were several soldiers waiting, five or six in all. But the apparatus is very simple and wonderfully effective. One man had his hand hanging limp, with a helpless thumb without the apparatus. With it, he could lift a chair, move his thumb and use his hand, in fact, almost as well as tho there were nothing wrong with it. I saw the men with paralyzed feet walking and thought they were the helpers,—they got along so well. Then I noticed a slight limp. The apparatus itself is of fine steel bars and springs, the bars about twice as thick as a hat-pin. When it is adjusted on the shoe, it is hardly noticeable. Of course, there is a different variety to fit each case, with special adaptations. At last, the Williams neuro-psychopathology report was submitted.[8]

Natalie's letters were filled with names of those who stepped briefly into her life until the war took them elsewhere. *While I was in the midst of my labors, Pierre Charbonnet's card was brought in. I always liked him, anyway, even though everyone made fun of his slight tendency toward dandyism. He is on Colonel Winters' staff and you know he is the Chief Surgeon of the Army here. Pierre and I went and had a really Parisian dinner at the Café Prouant, and afterwards we went to the Be La Chane. I'll send you the program, just for fun. The costumes and scenery were very clever, but rather daring.*

When I came in with Pierre, Mr. (Dick) Matheson, Mr. Stone and Mr. McKain were sitting there. Mr. Matheson is in aviation; the latter two are ambulancers, but Mr. Stone is going up for a commission in the artillery. They assured me that I could cheer them, especially if I were constrained with the fire, a bottle of beer, and cheese. We tried it, and we were all cheered. It is now, by the way, Wednesday night. I am sitting in my room with Hilda's brown coat on, and swathed in a very handsome automobile rug lent to me by Mr. Matheson. His rug is a joy, and he is rather nice, himself, rather serious, young, and good-looking, too. I would be quite charmed with him, if I weren't so busy and hadn't met so many "young men". I haven't tried to keep you informed of them all, as they pass in review.

Mr. Stone and Mr. Matheson are both manly, fine fellows. Mr. Matheson has an extremely flattering opportunity for office work here,—he evidently has pull!,—but he is going into active service instead. I asked him, just to see what he would say, why he didn't stay here, that he would be useful here too. He said, "Maybe so. But I can't get to feel that way. I know that when I saw the other fellows coming in from the front, and the field, I'd feel like a quitter, if I'd been just sitting here keeping my feet warm on an office window." So then I told him I thought he was right.[9]

Amidst her horseback rides at Fontainebleau and the Bois de Boulogne, her dinner dates, and her occasional visits to the Folies Bergères (*the atmosphere was too smoky, in every significance of the phrase*), Natalie sent home vignettes about her outings. One example was an after-dinner trip with Johnny and Mr. McLean to the Ritz, where she was much amused by an Englishman who had lost his dog. *We were three hours at dinner, and immediately thereafter, we went to the Ritz for tea. A very good time watching the crowd. An English officer, of the type so much caricatured, was a constant delight in his unceasing solicitude for "pee-tah", his dog, a retired animal, who had a trick of vanishing under various pieces of furniture; and immediately his master would miss him, fix a monocle, look about in blasé alarm (if you can imagine it!), call a waiter, and enunciate (I mean it!) "I say you know. I wish you'd have a look about for Peeta-a-ah."*

Natalie's social whirl reached new heights on a Sunday late in October. Eight different men engaged her company during the course of the day and evening. She was awakened that morning by the delivery of Mr. Hicks' card to her room. Then, while they were visiting, Alfred Chapman arrived to take her to lunch. So Mr. Hicks was invited to join them. Then John Ervin, a Yale graduate and Chicago attorney working for the Red Cross, came to visit. So all three men escorted her to the University Club Hotel, which, Natalie wrote, *is on par with the Ritz,—what appears on the table is equally perfect, tho less authentic! Instead of taking dessert there, we went for cakes, with chocolate, to a tea-room.*

Pierre (an afternoon date) and I went for a walk in the Bois de Boulogne. Just as we arrived, the sun burst thru, to set in a splendid, fiery haze. The leaves in Bois were its match for gorgeousness, in truly brilliant yellows and reds, and de Maupassant's Paris-on-Sunday swarmed by in winter's garb. Major Clark, of the Medical Division of the regular army, met us when we came back, by appointment. And he and Pierre and I went to Maxim's! Stoney was here when I got in and insisted that I should have a sandwich with him. He had told Dick [Matheson] that he would get me to! So I did. Stoney is taking me to the movies tonight.

Sometimes I think I shouldn't have such good times, when there is so much that is terrible that is at hand. But then, on the other hand, there is always some 'nice American' involved, and if they enjoy being with me, it's sure to do no harm, anyway, which is more than can be said for some of the pleasures of Paris. And, anyway, it doesn't interfere with my work at all. So I have decided that it is really all right.[10]

The fast-paced social life finally began to take its toll. She found an inexpensive pension owned by an elderly lady, the Baronne, and her daughter Mademoiselle Hélèna (also referred to as Alice). This new home would remove her from the bustle and flow of new acquaintances in the hotel. There was no central heating, no electricity, and no running water in her fourth-floor room, but she liked the family, noting that *they are very cultural and speak excellent French.* The address was 13, rue Léon Cogniat, a long walk to the office.

By November 13, Natalie was finally working directly for Dr. Lambert. She was placed in charge of examining all reports, correspondence, and records, then organizing and maintaining an effective filing and record-keeping system. Equipment inventories, supply requests and orders, and medical and scientific records all passed through her hands. *He could never have managed with a secretary. As it is, two assistants and five stenographers are swamped with his work. And tho filing has not a romantic sound, the work affords an opportunity I could have no other way of understanding thoroughly the tremendous work of the A.R.C. and of seeing Dr. Lambert's brain at work. And it is really a great brain, too. And I get the report of all the research work, the trips of investigation, accounts of conditions through all the war-zone—all the best that some of our best men have to offer.*

To-day for instance, there were reports on a visit to the French front by Lieut.-Col. Ashford, or rather, a survey of the treatment of burns; a paper on the prevention and treatment of gas gangrene, which is a condition peculiarly worked in this war; and a wonderfully interesting one on orthopaedic surgery, a good account of scientific miracles, in the incredible work that is being done in replacing bones, and regenerating bone tissue. So much stress is laid now on prompt treatment,— under normal conditions,—horribly normal! This promptness is one of the great preventions of gas gangrene, which was responsible for many amputations at the beginning of the war. But the amputations are enormously decreased now.

Major Lambert writes extremely well, with touches of acrid, brusque humor, and at times of inspiration. And it is fun, in the course of all these records, to see what big things we have in hand, as well as the big ones we have done.[11]

Evelyn Preston, nicknamed Pressy, a co-worker in Dr. Lambert's office, became Natalie's best friend in Paris. From a well-connected New York family, as were a number of others in the Red Cross headquarters, Pressy had known Dr. Lambert long before the war. She was bright and well informed, for her father, Major Ralph Preston, was the deputy commissioner of the Red Cross for Europe. Another co-worker was Ruth Morgan, a New Yorker, Pressy's cousin and the director of the Dietetic Service section for France. As the holiday season approached, Natalie joined with Miss Morgan to organize a Red Cross Club and Christmas program for the hospitalized soldiers. *I suggested a Xmas carol chorus as a simple way of bringing people together. Miss Morgan was delighted and the idea has taken very quickly.*

Natalie received the long-awaited news that Sidonie had given birth to a daughter; Natalie became the godmother. Muddie sent photographs, which Natalie passed around the office. Her letter home expressed her joy and, unlike the humorous messages to Boss that typically appeared in the final paragraph of her letters, contained an emotional closing. *I certainly hate to say good-night: you have seemed so near all day and soon you'll be drawing back across the ocean until the next boat comes forth with another letter. Again, my very best love, best love to everybody—Boss, Nauman, Wyeth, Sidney, and the 'jewels', and Mrs. Provosty. I think your name for the Sweetest-Dearest children, "the little editions of Nauman and Sidonie", is very cute; and I am so glad it is Sidonie Scott! It's certainly been a joyful day for me, thanks to you and Providence,—and I know I'll be spared for putting you first!*[12]

Two outings prior to Thanksgiving were notable. One was an excursion to Versailles with a French soldier named Jean

Millescamp, whom she would continue to see throughout the war. Even through 1918, when she was a nurse in a war-zone evacuation hospital, he visited whenever possible. Jean would become a highly decorated French war hero. This young officer may well have been in love with Natalie, though the war would suppress the potential for their romance.

Their trip to Versailles occurred on a very cold day, so Natalie and Jean had the grounds to themselves. She described him in her letter home as a handsome, hazel-eyed French soldier who spoke English with a charming British accent. He was the son of a lady Natalie recruited to teach French to her friend Stoney. A first lieutenant in the French cavalry, he had served since the war's beginning and would soon return from his leave to the front. They stood in the frigid wind before the statue of Louis XIV, chatting about the monarch's magnificent excesses and those of his successors. Jean showed her around, reflecting on the French Revolution of the eighteenth century and the events that led to the beheading of the king and queen. *"That wide avenue to Paris is rather a fine street, isn't it? It was there that the mob came all the way from Paris, to take the king and queen back to the city."* Then we went around the back,—and I gasped as I got a full view of the sunken gardens. I do love sumptuousness! My democratic soul says *"You were a crime";* my artistic soul says, *"You are not true beauty"* but my story-book soul, my chin-in-hand, wide-eyed listening soul says, *"You are as a tale that is told,—and the proof of the tale!"*

I saw an old well, covered with moss and foliage, and admired it. Jean said, "Yes, it is a fine old well, isn't it? They buried parts in it for the guns, when the Germans were so near to Paris,"—which gave me an appreciation of modern history! Jean pointed out, too, the road at the side of the Chateau down which they marched to start for the front. "We saluted the chateau and bade it au revoir, as we passed," he said.

Natalie also attended the Grand Opera for a performance of *Jeanne d'Arc*, which she described as *magnificent,* as the guest of Mr. Barbour, the secretary-general of the Red Cross. *Jeanne d'Arc was there, with beauty of music,—enraptured, enthralled and entranced, I sat back in my seat and never stirred a muscle!*

France's great operatic soloist, Mlle. Martha Chenal, performed the lead role. Natalie described her *as one of the great singers in*

France. If her voice is not so great as it was, she is all the greater; for she has certainly given it freely for her country. It is her great gift, and she has not spared it. She has sung the 'Marseillaise', *again and again, every where, at benefits, on the streets, for the soldiers, often and often in the open air and even in bad weather, till her voice is seriously impaired. But it is still great, I think. You can imagine that, with such devotion, she was the ideal person to portray Jeanne d'Arc.*

Thanksgiving was spent quietly at the pension, with the elderly, good-natured Baronne and her daughter, the other residents, and Natalie's guest, Jean Millescamp. Natalie raised her glass of Bordeaux in a toast *to the health, and wealth, and happiness of 'my people—hearts across the sea,'* and imagined the turkey, the brown gravy, the mince-pie with almonds, the plum-pudding, the sherry, and the nuts that she knew were gracing the Scotts' dining table in New Orleans. Then she toasted her brother Nauman, who, she assured the table, was also thinking of home from his army training camp in Texas.

Christmas 1917 did not disappoint Natalie. The temperature was breathtakingly cold throughout December, and Paris was beautiful in the snow. Her participation with the Red Cross chorus and her volunteer service among refugee children made the holiday season particularly meaningful. By necessity, her season began during November, as the family presents would need almost a month to make their way across the Atlantic to arrive in New Orleans on time. *It's bitterly cold. I left the office at 4:15 yesterday, and rushed about desperately, trying to get things for Xmas. Already nearly dark, and darkness, the chill, the bundles, my wild rushes, inspirations, heightened hopes, and dissatisfied selections made me think so much of our annual Xmas eve turmoil. The chains I got for Sidney are made by the mutilés* (amputees in the war); *similar ones are worn by all the 'rich and great' here, so I thought only appropriate that the 'rich and great' there should have some.*[13]

Companions and Co-Workers

Natalie wrote neat introductions for Muddie of her companions, co-workers, and hangouts. Here is a handful of pertinent ones.

Mr. Stone: *Stoney came to dinner. He came by the office and walked home with me. I had told him it was a twenty minutes' walk; but I forgot that I am more than usually strenuous. And Stoney was breathless when he arrived, and in gales of laughter at the same time over my idea of a twenty minutes' walk, and also, over my ability to look in shop-windows as I rushed past, without running into other pedestrians. I left him bubbling in the salon, while I went to comb my hair. The Baronne and Mademoiselle Dalesme discovered him there, and soon I heard the most remarkable sounds issuing forth, outlandish speech on Stoney's part, staccato French interjections, explanations, and interpretations, punctuated by bursts of laughter. Stoney, as usual, attempting Herculean feats in conversation.*

Stoney said he always had wanted to know French anyway, and now more than ever, just so he could talk to that old lady. He'd 'like to talk to her by the hour; she has such a lovely, sweet old face,'—a remark which is typical of the nice boy Stoney is. He is full of fun, tho, and is always ready to laugh. I imagine he is very well off. I know that his father was on the Belgian commission.

Mrs. W. K. Vanderbilt: *I met Mrs. Vanderbilt formally this morning. She has frequently and elegantly been in our office. This morning she came in as I was talking to Miss Morgan, and I was duly presented. Having no other inspiration as to how to be effective, I bestowed upon her some of Major Young's chocolates, which was a most successful maneuver. She is really a distinguished looking woman. I have thought before that it was surely the clothes. But to-day she had on a uniform and she was just as distingué. The manners often proclaim the millions! Another thing about her which is proclaimed is years of skin massage, her face is lined, and a second glance shows the years, but her skin has the creamy, 'milk-fed' (my coinage of application of that adjective!) look which can result only from perfect care, suggesting long vistas of cold-cream bottles through the years. She is very pleasant. At least, she says, "O thank you. How perfectly delicious" with a very agreeable inflection!*

Miss Lovejoy: *She is really very attractive, with really gray eyes, and dark hair, and a pretty, prim little mouth,—a Puritan type she is.* (Natalie nicknamed her Lovey.)

Dr. Wright: *Dr. Wright is at the head of the Dispensary, now, a very responsible position. He takes it most seriously, too, of course. Yesterday, Major Lambert went out just as we did, and he stopped to speak to me and then he talked to Dr. Wright on some medical topic. Dr. Wright was so funny, for he immediately assumed his judicial, elderly manner, which amuses me immensely. He has it on nearly all the time for the world at large, feeling that it goes with his position; but with me he is very jolly and full of fun.*

Miss O'Gorman: *Always more attractive. That combination of quiet refinement and irresistible humor perfectly delights me. She eggs me on with all sorts of extravagances and we carry on the most frivolous conversations ever descended to by two sedate ladies. She has rather gray hair, and slightly prominent kind eyes, with a twinkle that is a worthy supplement to the humorous twist of mouth.*

Maj. Richard Clarke Cabot: *By no means handsome,—a blond Don Quixote in appearance—but he is one of the most thoroughly lovable men I have ever seen. He has a wife in Boston. Those who know him well say he is much finer than his books* (which, Natalie noted, *are highly rated*). *We often meet in the Cave for luncheon. The other day, I was in the depths of woe, when Major Brent's friend failed me as a Santa Klaus. And Major Cabot insisted that I should be consoled, and, with that cheerful optimism that makes warm blood freeze, insisted on pointing out points of advantage and cheering aspects of the situation. But I was Rachel, and would not be comforted. My tea was brought; I tasted it, sighed, and remarked in the tone of final desolation, "I find now my tea is cold,"—as tho it were the last straw. Major Cabot considered, and finally said, "Well, if it was hot, you might burn your tongue." I looked at him defiantly, and said, "I love to burn my tongue." He roared (after his manner of roaring, which is as 'guilty as any sucking dove'), and says I have furnished him with a perfect example of pessimism. He eats, by preference, as do many of the other men, in the 'Cave'. There is an officer's dining-room upstairs.*

Evelyn Preston: *Pressy is rather an extraordinary girl. She has had everything all her life, and yet she is quite fresh and unspoiled. She has three brothers and they have lived out of doors a great deal. I suppose that accounts for her resistance to all insidious influences which wealth and social prominence must have subjected her to (Isn't that a pompous sentence?!).*

She is taller than I am, by several inches, but very well built, so well-proportioned that she doesn't seem tall. She is nineteen and girlish,—with the distressing effect, sometimes, of making me feel old, a thing which rarely happens to me. She has a very young, golden idealism,—it plays about freely on all great people over here, many of whom she knows personally. On Thanksgiving Day, she went to a wonderful dinner at the Ritz, where there were a hundred guests, and almost everybody distinguished here,—Gen. Pershing, Major Perkins, Mr. Endicott, Ambassador and Mrs. Sharp, Admiral Jellico. And her frank enthusiasm was certainly refreshing. Everybody, or, at least, so many people are, so fond of pulling down idols nowadays, that it is a pleasure to have someone put a prop under their pedestals!

Pressy's mother died when she was two years old, and her father has been really rather remarkable in his devotion to his children.

Dorothy Cheney (nicknamed "the gentle Che"): *She is a connection of Mrs. Lambert's and she came over to work for the French orphans, but got discontented with that work, because they sent the children to institutions. So she asked Major Lambert for a job and, obliging as he always is, took her in, but she hasn't really got set yet. She has been with us now about two weeks. Major Lambert really needs someone to help him since Dr. Ward left, and, of course, I am tied to the files absolutely. Miss Cheney is a slim, plain thing. She is 37, she told me; but I would never have thought it for she is so small that it makes her look younger. She is one of twelve and has a sister canteening. I hear that they are the Cheneys of the Cheney silk and are immensely wealthy. She lives at the Hotel France et Choiseul. Major Lambert married a Cheney, it seems, and so did Major Hugh Bogan. (This I get from Pressy!) She asked me to brunch with her the other day. She is really painfully quiet, but talks quite a bit in her quiet way when she gets started, and sometimes says some very funny things.*

Florence Johnson: *There was a nice girl [at Pressy's] from New York, named Florence Johnson. She has lovely red hair and a very good figure, and is quite smart looking, in a trim, lithe way that reminds me of Alice. She came over with some relief work, very much in earnest to work. Miss Johnson had just arrived and Pressy was eager for news of their mutual friends, and it was amusing to hear the names. I felt as tho the N.Y. social register had come to life on their tongues.*

Ethel Harriman Russell: *Meanwhile, I began to suspect Mrs. Russell of being one of that group whom we know of as the 'rich-and-great', because I noticed her refer to Mrs. Vanderbilt with calm familiarity as "Aunt Something". Her name, too seemed vaguely familiar. After she departed, which she did in an hour or so, Pres told me that she was Ethel Harriman. You remember, I wrote you not long ago about Pres having been to her wedding. So I was much impressed.*

Dr. Gwathmey: *Dr. Gwathmey is, I think, a widower. He has lived in New York for years, but talks as tho he was fresh from Virginia. Anyway, he has a grown son in the army. I don't know when I have seen a more attractive figure than those two soldierly, well-knit figures, as they stood there talking, so interested in each other. The son came over more than two years ago, without a word to his father, in the steerage, on the* Arabic, *just two or three trips before she was sunk. He was in the French army for a while as lieutenant; then took six months training, and is a lieutenant now in the British Army. Now that we have gone into the war, tho, he wants to join our army. And I must say that I think he will be an acquisition.*

He was shot—badly wounded last spring. Captain Gwathmey came over immediately. The message he received was that his son had been shot in the face. Imagine making the slow, tedious ocean voyage with that message ringing through your brain! Anyway, he found when he got here that the blow had been a glancing one, and "When I walked in, there was the boy sittin' on the edge of the bed, smokin' his pipe."

Dr. Burlingame: *Dr. Gwathmey and Dr. Burlingame and I were the only ones in the office about one. They got into an argument, Dr. B taking the stand, apparently seriously but really in fun, that exercise was bad for a man whose occupation is sedentary. Dr. G. championed exercise. Finally, Dr. B., to uphold his side, challenged his antagonist to stand on his head. I closed the door, to safeguard the dignity of the office; they carefully and solemnly removed everything from their pockets, and then those two big boys calmly proceeded to stand on their heads! That led to walking on their hands, and all sorts of fantastic things, challenging each other to new contests like a pair of school-boys, while I sat up and looked on and laughed till the tears ran down my cheeks. And in five minutes, presto, change, Dr. Burlingame discussed matters of policy with the Director of Surgery, A.E.F., and Captain Gwathmey, in another corner of the room, in grave converse with Dr. Brewer and several others of the most distinguished surgeons of America. And I sedately filing!*

Ms. Vivian: *The khaki clad stenographer in our office, which is so addicted to slang. Pressy and I could scarcely endure her when she first came. She is really not bad looking, khaki-colored soft straight hair, khaki-colored eyes, and high color, very slim of face and figure. Her one defect is a slightly overshot jaw. Really, now, Pressy and I have both become quite attached to her, for she is quite amusing. A sample of Ms. Viv's diction is this, uttered as she breezed into the lavatory while I was washing my hands yesterday afternoon. 'Gee girls, I'm shriekin': who's snitched the soap?' But she is a good hearted soul, and has groundrock ideas that would do credit to one a great deal more finished,—besides a keen sense of humor.*

Mme. du Chemin: *I must introduce you to another one of my Parisian friends. Don't raise your eyes to the mountain-tops of aristocracy, but rather descend with me to the basement kitchen-dining room,—the Cave, as we call it,—and meet my good, mothering dear Mme. du Chemin. I am sure that there was never such another. She is generously proportioned, and fairly revels in preparing food; and she is perfect satisfaction when she sees anyone enjoying her productions. Of course, I give her much pleasure of that kind!*

The Cave: *Can eat in the cave for 2 francs fifty, or even less. It has so much atmosphere! There is a long board table, with some benches and some chairs. The whole room is tiled, and the long range is just back of a very low partition, above which Mme. du Chemin's head can constantly be seen, bobbing busily about, and dominating the bustle and confusion of her busy, awkward helpers and presiding skillfully over sizzling pots and pans, and a various rattling, noisy din of the operation of onions and spoons. I love to stand on tip-toe and peer over at the scene, and exchange a word with my friend, who is never too busy to toss me a sentence of welcome, as she stoops for a glimpse in the oven, or critically stirs and tastes some savory-looking dish.*[14]

A Wartime Christmas

Meanwhile, more friends left Paris for war duty. *Mr. Jesse came in Tuesday morning then again on Friday, to say au revoir.* She went out with Mr. Hicks at the end of November for a farewell luncheon at Larue's, *an extremely elegant and criminally expensive spot, delicious, tho—especially the mushroom omelet!* Then, as Christmas approached, Stoney visited to say goodbye before he reported for combat duty. *He has received his commission as second lieutenant in the artillery. He was calm but really quite excited, as is only natural. He was rather subdued over it all. I tried to cheer him up a little and he promised to write to me, but he was really rather sorry to go, I think. He had made his little niche here and had his little circle. And there is something appalling in knowing yourself bound for a war. I shall miss him.*

Jean Millescamp departed for combat with his French unit. He and Natalie spent his last night in Paris together, sharing dinner in a quiet restaurant. The following day a friend from New Orleans, an army doctor named Alex Ficklin, visited briefly, on leave after having been under German shelling near the front. Natalie cautioned Muddie not to breathe a word of this news to Trixie, Alex's fiancée in New Orleans.

One particularly pleasing event at work had been Natalie's opportunity to meet Maj. Grayson M-P. Murphy, the highest-ranking officer of the American Red Cross in Europe. *But yesterday was a great, great day: I heard Major Murphy, R.C. Commissioner for Europe, speak. And I spoke to him! He addressed the R.C. employees on the subject of the Italian situation.*

The way I met him was quite droll. I was busy and went up only at the last minute, expecting to stand. But my friend, Mr. Pace, the large and affable general of activities upstairs, deferential and decorous, but only too audible, summoned me up the aisle to the one vacant chair just placed in the aisle. As I reached it, he picked it up, and said, "Better forward, Miss Scott," and sedately proceeded with the chair. For me, there was a choice of following Mr. Pace, sitting on the floor, or ignominiously retreating. I followed Mr. Pace. That misguided, well-intentioned soul strode straight on past the first line of chairs and planted my chair facing the audience, just back of a single other chair with a soldierly-looking figure already seated in it. I sank into the chair in great relief, much rejoiced at the broad, shapely pair of shoulders which afforded protection from the gaze of the general public.

Mrs. Copp, chief of stenographers and mistress of furniture ceremonies, came over and said, "I'm afraid you haven't a good place, Miss Scott." I said, "Why?" "Why because you won't be able to see Major Murphy's face when he's speaking," she answered. The soldierly figure turned about and gave me a full view of a face handsomer than should have ever been allowed to one man, if he is to have any other grace from Providence, with a boyish smile, and in a rich, pleasant voice, he said, "That is really not worth regretting." I was astounded. Of course, it couldn't possibly be Major Murphy, in the logical nature of things, because I was sitting back of him, but who else? "You must be Major Murphy," I thought aloud. Mrs. Copp said, "Why it is Major Murphy, of course,"—while he laughed spontaneously and very heartily and said, "Now you see how little you have to regret." And he rose, took his place and addressed the audience.

Would anyone but my foolish self ever be put in so ludicrous a position. The shelter of those broad, shapely shoulders was gone,—when I needed it most! I looked like the president of a suffrage club.[15]

Natalie's work included compiling reports of wartime heroism among medical workers. The opportunity to meet, incidentally, a few of the people she read about in these reports brought the stories to life. In particular, the work of Maj. Hugh Young impressed her. Already a famous surgeon, Dr. Young of Johns Hopkins would be America's preeminent physician of the 1930s. *One of the big celebrities, I think, whom I admire tremendously, but know only slightly, is Major Young of the American Medical Service for Civil Population, or the A.M.S. for C.P., as we affectionately abbreviate it. I developed a great admiration for Major Young thru the files. The doctors under him all write of him with such mingled admiration and love that I know he must be really a remarkable man. The object of the Service is to prevent the spread of disease among the civilian population with which the soldiers come in contact, and, thereby, of course, the health of the soldiers is safeguarded. But the side of*

Dr. Hugh J. Young (center) of Johns Hopkins Hospital, Baltimore, founder of the Brady Urology Institute. A pioneer surgeon who saved the life of "Diamond Jim" Brady, he directed war refugee social medicine in France. He was greatly admired by Natalie, and they were often dinner and social companions. Dr. Young appears here with Marshall Ferdinand Foch (left) in Paris in 1918. *Courtesy AMA Archives*

Major Young's work which interests me most is the general medical care of the civilian population. To read of it in its beginnings is like reading some dramatic piece of fiction, their wholly inadequate instruments, their great hardships, bad weather, inadequate transportation facilities, and everything to combat, and yet doing much to alleviate the unspeakable conditions in which the peasants live.

I admired him so much that I dreaded seeing him. I have had some dis-illusionments in my existence. But he was not one. He is not handsome at all; but that is an afterthought when you see him: he is of medium height, compactly built, and has the kindliest, pleasantest, strongest face you can imagine. When he smiles, his blue eyes twinkle and gather pleasant lines about them. I think of all these men as so inseparable from their work.

Most of them are middle-aged, or more, and married; so that there are no romances imminent. Things seem too intense just now for the lighter fancies; and I'm not material for a grand passion. During the Christmas holidays, Natalie and Major Young would begin a warm and permanent friendship.

Paris stood under an ever-deepening blanket of snow. Natalie partitioned her fourth-floor room in the pension into a two-room salon opening onto her small balcony, enabling her to occasionally entertain friends. She purchased a small oil stove for warmth and to prepare cinnamon toast, hot chocolate, and tea.[16]

A number of Christmas activities attracted Natalie. Staff gathered in *a long barn-looking basement hall* to pack Red Cross bags for refugees with soap, a toothbrush, toothpaste, towel, candy, handkerchief, and shoestrings. She organized with Lovey a Christmas-tree party for 300 refugee children and orphans, finding sources for toys and refreshments. *I think it will be lots of fun. Our Xmas carol chorus is so in demand for songs (in spite of my association with it!) that it is really a hard matter. Major Cabot said it was harder to arrange one program than to run all of his refugee work!* Major Cabot served as their choir director.

The Christmas activity suffered an interruption on December 20, when a German bombing raid descended upon the city. To Natalie, the raid and cannon fire seemed like a dramatic scene on stage. *For, quite suddenly, the long, eerie wail of the siren curdled the quiet night. Automatically, my eyes swept the sky,— as much of it as I could see for the buildings that shut it out. Afterwards, boo-oom, a dull, slow thud, muffled by the distance: the cannon! Very strange that it should seem so impossible and unreal, when there is everything here to make it seem real. At the theatre, often, I have heard just the same sound. They make it by striking a leather cushion with strips of rattan. I shuddered and felt apprehension. The dining-room was really a very theatrical setting,—old French. Mlle. Dalesme and Mlle. Broussois sitting and rising and looking, and sitting again. The only thing that broke the thread of zeppelin talk was my pin* (a Christmas present received that day by mail from Muddie). *They couldn't look at it, and admire, and exclaim enough. Madame even rose, slowly and laboriously from her chair, half leaning on me and half leading me, drew me over by the table under the light where she could see it well. Then more zeppelin talk.*

We heard the whir of the engines of our sirens just a few minutes after the first cannons. It seems that bright nights are favorites for raids: it seems a sacrilege to plan anything cruel 'on such a night as this.' I feel so sorry for the poor Londoners to whom there can be no joy in the beautiful moonlight night. For them now it means, I suppose, dread. They are 'game', though, I hear, and have their parties and keep up high courage. Well, I'll set an example, and forget the Zeppelins,— pretend I am at the sea-side, and the purring I hear is that of a passing motor boat with a pleasure party on board, who have 'gone aboard her for the land of heart's desire'.[17]

Major Cabot had arranged numerous Christmas performances for the Red Cross chorus. In their first appearance, the choir performed in a canteen that was so packed with nurses and war workers that they were literally standing amidst the crowd, many choir members unable to see their director. Things did not go well. Natalie also described the Christmas-tree party organized for local orphans and refugee children. *Grown people were with the children, and the poor things were all so starved for pretty things that they were wild with fear of getting left out, and pushed and crowded fearfully. They stormed the tree, and Major Cabot and Dr. Wright, who were to take down the presents, soon had not even elbow room. Finally, we managed, so arranged that the children had to pass one by one.*

The majority were plain peasant stock apparently, some sturdy and rosy-cheeked, some gaunt and hollow-eyed and worse; and some few looked really rather aristocratic. There was a quiet refined sweet-faced little woman, who sat with two handsome little boys, gently at the side of the room. The little boys looked wistfully at the other children pushing and struggling for toys; but she would not let them join the contest; so finally I went over and asked her to let me see that they got something. The little boys brightened instantly; she consented, and off I went with a warm, eager little hand in each of mine. Soon we had acquired a gun and a wagon. And when I left, I had a glimpse of a caisson driver and a soldier, happily oblivious of everything around them,—my two little friends.

One big store here had a distribution for refugee children, too, and I passed by and saw throngs waiting, and throngs leaving happily a lovely red Santa Klaus, waving from their show-window. It is marvelous to see what the French still manage to accomplish; when I think of the decorations and all the carefully planned, well-carried out festivities at these canteens and hospitals, and all the provisions made for the refugees and the poor children, I wonder how the people have the money and the energy. One would think they were bled past endurance, both of money and strength. I think I told you of Mlle. Broussois, who stays here part of the time. She goes to a canteen hospital, in a portable, made of a sort of papier-maché compound. It was captured from the Boche (the Germans). *Anyway, it is cold in winter and hot in summer. There is heat only for the patients. The attendants eat and sleep without any fire at all, and they do all the menial work of the hospital. They sleep, three nights a week, each. Mlle. Broussois always comes back looking wretchedly. She has been doing that steadily since the beginning of the war.*[18]

Then on Monday, Christmas Eve, the choir presented a late-afternoon performance in the great hospital, Val-de-Grace, before a vast assemblage of wounded soldiers. *We went up a broad long stairway and came at last to the room where our chorus was. It was a sort of assembly room. Our chorus was in one corner, just ready to start. And all the rest of the room was filled with wounded soldiers, and a few blue robed, white capped nurses.*

You have seen pictures of groups of soldiers in the hospitals,—every sort of injury and bandage and scar, looking as tho they had come surely out of the jaws of death, out of the mouth of hell! Perhaps it's imagination, but there seem to me always to be a certain wistful expression in the eyes of the soldiers who have been wounded,—even when they are smiling and happy, a reminiscence of pains, or perhaps surprise at finding themselves still on the old familiar earth. They suggest, each one, vistas of the most stirring, varied kinds,—families distressed, battle-fields, suffering, heroic acts,—each one of these would have roused the deepest interest in whole communities in normal times. Now there are thousands, or, literally, millions of them. It seemed very dramatic to me when I walked in. It was the largest group of wounded I have seen.

They were French, of course, and in the corner, in front of them was grouped our American Chorus,—America meeting France. We sang better than we had ever sung before. And the soldiers were delighted. They applauded and applauded. And they begged us to sing one quaint little old English carol, "Bring a Torch, Jeannette, Isabella", over again, and of course, we were delighted to do it. When we finished, they stood up,—those who could,—and all shouted, "Vive l'Amérique! Vive l'Amérique!" And, of course, we shouted back, "Vive la France! Vive la France!" And then great exchanges of Xmas greetings, and many, many compliments from the French Chief Surgeon to Major Cabot[19]

Natalie talked with many of the patients, until she realized that everyone in the chorus had gone. She rushed back for the office's Christmas dinner, then on to the Gare du Nord, where the chorus would sing that evening. *That is one of the greatest centers of arrival and departure of soldiers. Monday night, it was swarming with them,—all nationalities.*

I found the "Pavillion" where we were to sing. It was a very large hall, larger than any of the banquet rooms in our hotels at home. Long tables, decorated for Xmas, and with a huge tree in the middle. And soldiers! You never saw so many. Every available place at the tables was taken, and there were lots standing. They kept perfectly quiet and attentive the whole time we were singing; and you couldn't hear even a whisper from them. The whole spectacle was tremendously impressive,—all those sturdy fighters, some just going to, some just back from all the suffering and hardship of the trenches, and we complacently singing carols to them. Any sort of celebration of Xmas is bound to have a touch of grim irony right now, when all the Christian nations are flying at each other's throats. But I did wish from the bottom of my heart for feeling of peace and love, or any sort of source of inner strength, would grow in the hearts of those poor soldiers. How worn out thoroughly, soul and body, they must be with it all. After three years, and after seeing more than a million of their men killed.

They applauded us violently. And then afterwards some man made a speech. He was the kind that says, "La France" as tho it were a prayer. The soldiers were full of enthusiasm and applauded him intently and called out "Bravo! Bravo!" again

*and again. It was really wonderful to watch the expressions on
their alert faces. I could hardly tear myself away.*

*I was so anxious to write you about it, while all the panorama
was fresh in my mind. I stood and watched the mass of people,
crowded about the entrances, waiting to speed or to receive
some soldier. Those who were expecting friends were in great
spirits, chatting and calling out things to each other, and
always with an eye on the crowd of soldiers streaming out. And
then, spying the friend, "Hey, mon diable" and "Hay mon
vieux"—or some other such gay greeting. But then there were
many little groups of two, a soldier and his wife, or his mother,
standing silently side by side, in a docile misery of parting.
Sometimes there was a whole little family together, with a soldier father, he always with the youngest in his arms of course.
And there was an old, old couple there who met a boy who
seemed not a day over seventeen and how they did revel in seeing him! I could have watched it all for hours. Xmas afternoon
we sang at another French hospital.*

On Christmas day the choir sang before a large banquet for Red
Cross workers of the American Mission, then listened to other performers. Natalie sat with Major Perkins (the Red Cross commissioner for France), Major and Mrs. Lambert, Major Cabot, Miss
O'Gorman, Dr. Manning, Dr. Wright, and Miss Lovejoy. That
evening, Natalie joined the Lamberts for Christmas dinner and
was seated between Dr. Lambert and Maj. Hugh Young. *Major
Young is considered the best surgeon at Johns Hopkins. It was he
who operated on 'Diamond Jim' Brady, and was the cause of
Johns Hopkins receiving that great gift of money. And it is so nice
to find Major Young, who is so able and skillful and successful,
so human and lovable. He told me about his two little girls, one
three and one seven, and of how they had written him. Major
Young answered it with a cable. He laughed and said, "I've supposed she was the youngest American who had received a cable."
And I was so proud to be ahead of him with my niece!*

*I was sorry the evening ever had to come to an end. Dr.
Burlingame offered to take me home. Major Young a second
afterwards announced that he was going to take me home. Not
that I like Dr. Burlingame less, but . . . ! It was snowing when
we went in search of a taxi, and we wandered for some time
vainly, two or three chauffeurs refusing us, in the high-handed*

way they have here. So then, in front of the Hotel Continental, when a taxi drew up and some people got out, I got in without asking the driver, while the other people were paying him. Major Young gave him my number. He said he couldn't take us,—Major Young looked at me, expecting me to get out. Not at all! I told the man the number again, pleasantly. He got down and explained that he couldn't take us, he had a 'client', etc. I let him talk and then I beamed upon him pleasantly and told him he had to take us, because I wasn't going to get out! He argued some more, and I smiled all the time, and told him I would die if I got out, because I had a cold; and I was not ready for death. Major Young simply stood by, amused as he could be. Finally the chauffeur shrugged in despair, and asked meekly, 'how to go'! So Major Young got in and we drove off happily.

But it is luck, isn't it, to see intimately people who are doing the big things that are being done now? I thought so, as I sat at dinner that evening.

The holidays brought friends who had Christmas leave time. Dick Matheson reappeared with a friend, so Natalie called Johnny for a bridge game in her room. On another evening, Juno West, a New Orleans friend, and his companion Lieutenant Newton surprised her, taking her to dinner at Voisin's and to the opera. Natalie suffered from an acute case of *enterite* (diarrhea) throughout the holidays but, despite its *crescendo,* she *treated it contemptuously, going on as usual.* Alfred Chapman came again, with a group of friends, and they went one evening to Prussier's. *Prussier has the best food and best caviar of any place, I think, and is less expensive. We had lobster mayonnaise and a wonderful confection, filet Boston,—filet of beef, cooked to perfection, with oysters. And you can imagine how I, with my malady, felt when confronted by them. Of course, I partook! And, of course, I paid the price.*

Our boys are showing up magnificently. There is not a word of complaint from any of them, nothing but good-fellowship and good cheer and enthusiasm. And they have had their hardships. This boy who was with Juno apologized for shivering, and explained that he was more susceptible since he had had his feet frozen,—and then apologized for speaking of that! And he and Juno laughed in the greatest amusement over how cold they had been at different times and the expedients they had adopted for warmth!

Before closing her holiday letter to Muddie, Natalie commented on her plans for New Year's Eve. *To-morrow night will be New Year's Eve. I am going to sit up to see the New Year come in. I have been inquiring about a copy of Tennyson, so that I shall be able to read our old pieces as usual, and I do hope I can get a copy. My greatest hope is Miss Morgan. Anyway, even if I should not get a copy, I know the poems nearly by heart and will say them over anyway, and think of 4907 and all its inmates, and the Alexandria branch and all its inmates and be wishing every one of you a Happy, Happy New Year. And I know we will all be joined in hoping 1918 will be a year of Victory and Peace.*[20]

German Air Raids Increase

As 1918 began, Natalie was enjoying her work and friends in the Red Cross headquarters, unaware that deadly events would radically transform her role in the war. Her Parisian social pursuits gradually receded before the growing intensity of German air raids and bombardments of the city, a foreshadowing of the great attack.

The American Red Cross in France had matured and grown as war demands increased. The director of military affairs informed them that the office would again expand by another 500 people. Rumors about reorganization were flying through headquarters, including word that Natalie's unit would change. Dr. Lambert planned to focus more precisely on medical and scientific work. He envisioned a new library system for Natalie to supervise, and he decided to place Dr. Burlingame in charge of administrative, supply, and distribution operations. These plans were not revealed to Natalie until February.

For her part, Natalie considered her present work quite worthwhile. *Sometimes I can just get along with all my wits about me, keeping up with all my work, and answering all the thousands and one questions that are fired at me all day long. "Miss Information" is Dr. Baer's name for me. He is very funny. He said his key-word is "Just ask Miss Scott. She'll tell you." Thus I often get requested to see people, and dispose of them. Sometimes they are very amusing. Yesterday, there was the most ceremonious old French gentleman, who knew not a word of English. He came with requests for various and sundry articles for a French hospital, and I took up his mission for him, and put it through, greatly to his satisfaction. He promised to send me some picture post-cards of the wounded! And he bowed so many times, and paid me so many compliments that I was horribly embarrassed. I bowed till I began to feel like a Chinese mandarin. He finally bowed himself backward into an entering gentleman, and nearly made me disgrace myself and soil all my excellent impression by losing my gravity![21]*

News arrived by cable the third week of January informing Natalie that her closest friend, Hilda Phelps—her cohort in mischief, politics, academics, theater, and all her beliefs and causes—would soon be married to someone unknown to Natalie. *You may imagine how stunned I was to get Hilda's cable. I was simply thunderstruck, and I know she would be gratified if she could know how thoroughly surprised I was, and what a dramatic thing her cable was to me. It certainly seems a change in New Orleans for Hilda to be married, and I can't imagine it. It presupposes a something 'still steadfast, still unchangeable' which I can't associate with Hilda, whom I think of always as restless, seeking new fields and pastures green, in things and people. Hammond is certainly a 'pasture green' to me. Her cablegram said simply, "Marry Hammond January twenty-fourth-Love-Hilda Phelps". I can't place any Hammond for the life of me; and I have certainly tried.*

A week passed before the riddle of Hammond's identity was finally solved. *I had a letter from Hilda, too, in which she mentioned Lieutenant Hammond in a galaxy of beaux, and so, at last, I know who he is. It was certainly a whirlwind affair, wasn't it, and an evidence once more of the decisive nature of her mind. It sounds like real romance, and is, I hope.*

Descriptions of intense German bombing raids on Paris crept into Natalie's letters. *Every time there is a full moon, and everything is especially pretty and fine, some kill-joy predicts a zeppelin raid. But tonight a fog has come up and that makes it less likely. There is a French plane up, tho, and I can hear its motor plainly.* On February 2, enemy air raids pounded Paris. *Here it is, after eleven, and I mortally sleepy, and what must happen, but the Zeps must come and rouse me up. The siren has blown, and the cannons are booming away constantly. I have been writing to Juno (West) and just telling him, after hearing the gruesome serenade begin, and the siren, that nothing short of a bomb at the window could wake me up, when la Mlle. Alice, in curl papers at my door, telling me that 'il faut descendre.' I have just been arguing with her and telling her that I prefer a very, very remote chance of misfortune up above to a certain death of cold in the frigid underground (I've never been there, but I know it's cold!). The cannons are very plainly to be heard and more constant than last time.*

I had an awful scare. I had forgot to close my "persons" (my heavy shutters) and the light shone thru. Suddenly, there was a call from the street, "La lumière en haut. La lumière en haut" (the light upstairs!). *In a second, several other voices joined, and what sounded to me like a mob of men's voices calling angrily, "La lumière en haut." Needless to say, I blew out my light in a second! A woman in the street is excited just now, and calling, "Mais non. Mais non. Mais non," quite hysterically, which sounds really exciting.*

The gentleman across the way has just knocked and offered to escort us down. Mme. Delasme is joining her voice with mine now, because we are both too comfortable to go down and Mlle. Broussois and Mlle. Alice insist and so it goes; but I think I'll cut the Gordian-knot by turning in. Mme. Delasme is arguing all the time, even while giving in. There is an officer across from us just back on leave. He says he has no luck—"pas de chance". He is going down and says that I should; but I think I shan't, unless the others get insulted by my staying. The officer has left us to our fate, in wrath. Mlle. Alice and Mlle. Broussois are disgusted with me; but to morrow morning they will envy me! They have all gone.

Good night. Pleasant dreams. And don't mind the Zeps any more than I do. And don't say I am fool hardy. There are so many alarms. They give the alarm the minute the Boche planes are sighted within a certain zone and they may never get to Paris. The cannons are getting really "furieux". Still I don't know.

Well, good night.

The next day, Natalie wrote the rest of the story. *Things got hotter and hotter after I wrote you last night. I went out on the balcony and had a lovely view of a perfect night, and lovely stars flying prettily through the dark spaces up above. It all looked quite peaceful and like 'the heavens declare the glory of God, the firmament showeth his handiwork' but unfortunately* the 'children of men' are otherwise minded, as the Poom-poom of the cannons, quite close they seemed, very plainly indicated. There were some planes lighted all the time, steadily, some lighted for a moment and then were dark. The motors purring like big beasts of prey, some that were steady and some that broke and blurred. This morning, I was told that the steadily lighted, steadily purring were French, and the others Boches.

Last night, I would try to feel which were the French motors, and sent my prayers after them, and felt quite sentimentally inclined toward them, as though they knew that I was down there watching them, and they had my safety specially in mind. I thought of my dear Keats, as I watched the star-like lights of the busy planes, and reveled, as I couldn't help doing, in the beauty of the night: being alone and privileged to indulge myself, I shouted to myself,

> Away! Away! For I will fly to thee,
> Not charioted by Bacchus and his pards,
> But on the viewless wings of poesy, -
> Though the dull brain perplexes and retards,
> Already with thee! Hapley the queen moon is on her
>   throne clustered about by all her starry fays.

And then to Wordsworth, "the moon doth with delight, Look round her when the heavens are bare". But the constantly growing din of the cannonading spoiled the lines.

Across the stretch of sky which I could see, planes would dart, sometimes four or five in succession, straight and fast. I saw several signal rockets drop, and once I saw something drop and then a splash of flame flare up. Finally, I got my lamp and went down to join the Baronne. I found a funny group assembled in the drawing room: Madame Delasme sitting complacently in the most comfortable chair with a thin black scarf over the white hair, much the most distinguished figure in a group in which curl papers and overcoats grotesquely humped were the prevailing notes. When I decided to go down, I had searched about with my trusty glimmer (Marfoonie's gift) till I found the boudoir cap Mrs. Provosty sent me Xmas and had tucked up my hair and put it on. It was the first appearance of Mrs. Provosty's boudoir cap, so I have decided to christen it my shrapnel-helmet.

It was really droll to see us all humped up together. There we were, our group, with Madame looking like Sunday-at-Church, Mlle. Broussois and Mlle. Alice both in curl papers, and the other family, an old lady as old as the Baronne, but tall and angular in contrast to the Baronne's much more gracious lines, a daughter of about 40, thin and nervous in curl papers and alarm, with a stoical, apathetic husband hidden behind in a mass of black whiskers, and several attractive children from 4 to 14, all drowsy with sleep except the oldest, a pretty little slip of a girl, who laughed quietly at everything I said. Of course, I thought her very intelligent!

I stayed with them about half an hour. We would point out to each other the passing lights,—then back to the fire and discuss the probable location of the bombs we heard drop. If all of us had been correct in our theories, Paris would now be off the map. So I bid a retreat and left the gathering, so sleepy that I do not even remember tumbling in!

This morning, Dr. Wright told me his vague gleanings of news. Bombs had fallen in Paris: and a French plane had fallen in the Place de la Concorde. Sure enough, there was a great crowd around there looking. The plane looked very tiny, much too small to brave all of space as it had done. The aviator had made an abrupt descent. It would have been successful, except that he struck one of the lamp columns, breaking the top of it and smashing his machine. He was thrown out backwards and his skull was fractured, but he has a chance still of getting over it. It seems that many people went out in the Place and on the streets, and almost all those who were killed were of its number. The reports this evening were 109 killed and from 275 to 300 injured. The figures have been mounting steadily. Of those total number of killed, only one had an occupation of a military kind, so that the noble Germans have not lost the glory which is theirs uniquely in history of warring on women and children, and a peaceful population. What will ever wipe out the shameful stains on their name in the page of history?

There were said to be 4 squadrons of 15 planes each last night, and six squadrons of 15 planes each are expected tonight. Two bombs fell about 12 blocks from us. They were aimed at the Arc de Triomphe and it was by no means a bad aim. The top two stories of the house had been smashed in as tho by a large hammer. It looked so odd to me, all the interior exposed to view,—it seemed almost indecent! Or like a stage interior! And the trunks and wardrobes were lying in the ruins, perfectly intact! Window panes were smashed in from the shock, for several blocks around. Two blocks away, another bomb had fallen. The rue Quatre Septembre back of the Crédit Lyonnais (my financier) represents a very gruesome spectacle, with human flesh and blood in a red plaster on the walls.[22]

These raids went on relentlessly through March and April, with almost everyone believing they were a prelude to a massive German ground offensive.

Unexpectedly, Natalie received a visit from a prominent Parisian lady, a Provosty (Nauman Scott's in-laws) family cousin, the Marquise de Valori. *She is lovely. She stayed only a few minutes, as she glanced in the office while waiting for me and saw that I was occupied with several people. But she talked of New Orleans, the Ledouxs, Weindahls, and Provostys, and asked me for luncheon with her and her sister, the Baronne Brin, to-morrow Thursday. Of course, I accepted immediately. It was perfectly lovely of Tante Mizette to write to her. So I'll be lunching with a Marquise and a Baronne to-morrow.*

The luncheon solidified a new friendship with these generous ladies. *The Marquise de Valori lives in a handsome apartment house, with immense wrought iron gates, handsome doors, a wide, spacious entrance corridor. A perfection of a maid admitted me to a den, large hall, and showed me to a huge drawing room, very rich, and very French. While I waited, a diminutive, frisky little dog came in, a tiny little fellow, with fuzzy, yellowish grey hair, and dancing brown eyes. He promptly ran up to me, and then stood on his hind legs and began to dance! As I was watching him, delighted, the Marquise came in. She looked like a French picture, in a quiet purple dress, with an old piece of jewelry, three large pearls, with a heavy gold chain going thru, pinned, down the front of it. We sat easily and talked till the Baronne Brin came in. The Baronne Brin reminds me somewhat of Tante Mimi, and is a shade more vivacious,—or, perhaps, I had better say, less reposeful than the Marquise.*

They had invited a friend to come to luncheon, with her two sons, officers in the French aviation. They came soon, and you should have seen my eyes, how busy they were not to miss anything of the scene of the arrival,—the ladies ceremoniously greeting each other, then the young men, in their smart French uniforms, stepping up and kissing the hands of the two ladies,—and I feeling most fearfully modern and an anachronism! The Marquise brought me into it by presenting the young men. They both stood at attention and bowed most correctly, and I did my best. They were very different and both attractive. One was much taller and more vivacious than the other.

We had a most elaborate and perfectly-cooked luncheon. There were several different courses,—six, I think, or seven. We spoke of Americans, and their probable showing in the fighting, and the Baronne said she was afraid they were too unused to fighting. The Tall Officer said, "Do not be so deceived." Then he went on to speak of the esprit de corps in the regiments, of the men's pride in them, and of several occasions when little contests had got their blood up. "Never fear for the Americans," he said. And he said he had never seen men so built,—"not one, not two, but regiments of them, broad-shouldered, and tall, and strong." He was quite sincere, not at all speaking in flattery but, on the contrary, rather apologetically for seeming to differ with the Baronne. I was proud, as I always am, of our men, and pleased with the generous Frenchman.[23]

Blessings Brighten as They Take Their Flight

Natalie received another visit from her New Orleans friend Alex Ficklin. They went to the Gaumont Palace, *the largest moving-picture in the world. Alex came in the office to say farewell today, and also because I had told him I would present him to Major Cabot, whom he admires very much. He had read one of the Major's books as a text-book when he was at college. The Major was very sweet and said he would be charmed to see Alex. We had a very funny conversation. I explained Alex, and I said, "It seems you wrote a book,—Diagnostic Something or Something Diagnostic. I am sure that diagnosis appears, but whether in the role of an adjective or a noun I don't remember."*

So he said, "We'll look and see." And he dived down into a heap of papers at the side of his desk, and produced the book. It was in two volumes, a gorgeous affair all done up in purple and gold (just like the Assyrians) and of royal proportions. So that I might not appear too impressed, I remarked, "Well, I may talk a great deal, but I wouldn't put it down in writing. I wouldn't commit myself."

I took Alex up. Alex talks very well, and he and the Major and Dr. Wright seemed to get along very well. I think his regiment must be somewhere near the front, for he was extremely secretive about it.

Mr. Fowler, one of Natalie's friends from her Atlantic crossing, surprised her with a visit while on leave from his ambulance duties. Her time with him drew her closer to the real war. He was an ambulancer in the Rheims area, mainly carrying gassed cases. *We sat and ate toast and butter and apricot confiture and drank chocolate quite contentedly. Meanwhile, Mr. Fowler talked. I wish I could have taken down some of his description of Rheims in short-hand. He says it is really a ghostly city to live in.*

It is a large city, you know, and there are now only about a thousand people living in it. He says you walk down the streets, where grass is growing up between the cobble-stones, and you get 'conscious of yourself' and it gives you the queerest feeling, for you hear your own foot-falls, and sometimes hardly another sound anywhere near you for blocks and blocks. He has several very good pictures of the cathedral, showing the big hole in the center, and one which shows even the details of the havoc wrought on all the statuary in front. Just the shell of it is left. He says its like a skeleton. And the city, for that matter, is like the city of the dead. Lots of pipes are broken, the drainage is bad, the houses deserted; and from one or all of those causes, there is a musty odor in the city and he says that after anyone is in it for a little while, he inevitably finds himself thinking of it as an odor of tombs.

Natalie, within her comfortable Parisian world, felt the contrast presented by Mr. Fowler's words. She thought of the plight of others, especially the French civilians. *But I look at poor little Léontine (the house maid), so trim and chic, and fresh-looking, only twenty-six, with a husband to whom she is devoted and who is wasting away very, very gradually as a result of his wounds. She saw him go away, a firmly built, fine looking young fellow (so Mlle. Alice says), strong, and full of life,—now she is watching him die a death which may drag through years.*

He will leave her, of course, with nothing except a child to support. It seems too hard.

Mr. Fowler stayed a long time and seemed in high spirits, and I was delighted. He vowed he had had a wonderful time, and certainly wished he wasn't leaving to-morrow. He said, "And, I say. I guess you won't mind if I write you a letter once in a while, will you?" Of course, I told him how pleased I would be if he would, and waved him good-bye and good luck.[24]

As Natalie was writing her letter to Muddie, the Germans interrupted her, the alarm sounding and the sky filling with attacking airplanes. *The "alerte", the avions, and the cannons! They have come with the moon, the wicked Boche, and to-night such a cold night, too. I have been hearing the cannons for some time, but they have been distant, and I hoped would not get more boisterous. The people are running down stairs already. It is no way for the Boches to behave! Mlle. Alice is calling me already. Mlle. Broussois has been in, with her hair down her back, but all dressed. She had just started to undress when the "alerte" sounded. The cannons are heavy and the avions sound purposeful,—and plentiful. The serenade is quite lively.*

February 23 marked Natalie's fifth full month in France. She noted that for the first time in her life, contrary to her perennial reputation of lacking punctuality, she had not been labeled in Paris as *the late Miss Scott*. Furthermore, the filing system she had created to organize the diverse and voluminous demands of the Red Cross office proved to be clean, neat, and effective. Perhaps this was not a major achievement, but she felt surprised and pleased with her own performance. *Have I told you, by the way, that I have the record for being the only one in our office who hasn't missed a day since the start, even and all? And I have been here longer than anyone except Miss Buchanon. No, I haven't. Dr. Burlingame and Miss Preston were here a week before I was, and Miss B about a month before. And Major Lambert almost two months. However, they have all missed at times through illness and most of them have gone on vacations. In fact, all, except me, have been on vacation. It's just as well that I don't want it, for I can't have it anyhow, because no one can take my place at the dear old files. I really hate to leave my wearing, tearing and always interesting present job. I can never really believe I haven't made a mess of filing,—it's so opposed to my whole nature, that I can't believe I have managed to do it at all. I have never seen so many I's in anyone's letters as in mine!*

Unknowingly, Natalie became an absent participant in the Hilda Phelps-Arthur Hammond wedding in New Orleans. When the moment arrived at the reception for the bride and groom to slice the wedding cake, Hilda, in a short and emotional tribute, dedicated the first piece to her friend Natalie, off at war, and set it aside to be shipped overseas to her. It arrived at the Red Cross office on a Thursday in late February, almost a month after it was sent, Natalie sharing the sweet treat with everyone in the office. *I think that nothing that Hilda has ever done for me,—and she has done many sweet and thoughtful things, as you know—I think nothing else quite "touched the spot" as this did, sending me the first slice of her wedding-cake. To think that in all the excitement, with the crowds around, the crowd of people and of things, in all the surprises and the happiness, that she could remember me is something that I cannot forget. Heaven knows I could never, never deserve the friends I have. So that is past. Time bears us forward on a swift flood, so it seems at times. I do hope that the union is sterling and that Hilda is going to be really happy.*

Though matters were settled that Natalie would take over the medical library, she felt doubtful about her new job as she prepared to train her replacement, expressing feelings that perhaps she really belonged in social service work. *She-who-is-to-replace-me will be here March first, next Friday, and I start instructing her in the gentle art of filing, as developed by one Natalie Vivian Scott. I'll have this "job" three weeks at most, I should say. Meanwhile, the Red Cross has started a new thing which bids fair to be one of the biggest things it is going to do,— that is, Social Service in the hospitals, for the wounded. The idea is to divert the men, make them cheerful, write letters for them, talk to them, and read to them, and so on. Then, too, to make recommendations as to their convalescence, where it should be spent and how. The personnel for this work is going to be chosen with the greatest care, they say, and will be the choice of the services.*

Miss Morgan has been put at the head of it, and she is almost worn out with working on it, already, but she is getting things well under way. The other day Pressy said, "You know, Scotty, if Tuts (her undignified name for Miss Morgan) had her way, and you weren't tied up to Major Lambert, she'd grab you like a shot for the Social Services." I thought this was some of Pressy's enthusiasm, and smiled agreeably.

Yesterday, Miss Morgan told me that she would give anything to have me in it, and that she was going to make efforts in that direction after I had started off a little with the Medical Center. Of course, if Major Lambert thinks it better that I should stay in the Medical Center, I'll do that. He is not here now. But he thinks so very highly of the Social Services work, that, I think, that if Miss Morgan thinks I'll suit them, he will be very likely to turn me over to that service. It is under him, too, of course, tho not so directly.[25]

From the moment she heard of it, Natalie wanted to go to work with Ruth Morgan in the new Social Services program, though her loyalty to Dr. Lambert restrained her from proclaiming her preference. Miss Morgan insisted on pressing the matter. She and Pressy envisioned Natalie assisting Miss Morgan in her administrative labors or taking a hospital assignment in the field. The Social Services program seemed as close to the war, to the actual soldiers in combat, as Natalie could hope to get. *I am going to leave the whole thing in Major Lambert's hands, for he knows the whole situation, the value of the work, and the comparative importance of the two positions, and he knows me. Of course, it will mean hard work, and a wholly unsparing devotion. I shall certainly think it is the greatest privilege in the world to be allowed to have a share in it. Major Lambert is away still, but will be back in a few days and then it will all be settled. My substitute for filing comes Friday. And so things change.*

The struggle to hold off the Germans in France suffered a serious setback due to the Russian military collapse and the fall of the czar's government to the revolution in 1917. The Allies had done their best to bolster the Russian war effort, but the bad situation worsened in February 1918 with a formal peace pact that Russia's Bolshevik government signed with Germany. Natalie commented on this turn of events. *Certainly, it has thrown a blacker line than ever on the somber shadow of war-clouds. For the first time, I feel depressed over it all,—not uncertain as to the issue, for we can admit only one, but as to the tremendous cost. However, time will tell, and may yet have some unexpected good tidings for us.*

Many people here are looking for a raid to-night. The moon is full to-night, the weather clear and cold, and everything propitious for the "power of evil." There is a new alarm signal now. It is three shots from the cannon at regular intervals, and then the siren. May we not hear it soon!

In early March, the time came to say goodbye to Major Cabot and Miss O'Gorman. Both were leaving Paris to return to their posts in Bordeaux, disappointed that their six-month assignments in Paris had not been extended. A farewell party was held for them at Pressy's hotel. *We were all a little quieter than usual, though, to think that the Major and Miss O'Gorman were going away. We went upstairs after dinner, and Lovey made coffee and I lounged in the chaise lounge which is tacitly now assigned me when I go there; and we talked. Major Cabot thinks the Social Service work a great opportunity, fraught with many difficulties but more than worth the trouble.*

After a while, Major Cabot read They. *He reads very well. His style of reading grows on one. At first, I didn't like it, but soon I found that I was getting every one of the points of the story, which is rare when a thing is read aloud. I never enjoyed it so much before. It is one of the best things that Kipling has ever done. It is a gem. It has an exquisitely poignant quality. What with it and the thought of the approaching departure of those two whom I have grown so fond of, I felt really dismal when the story was done. Then, too, there is something about hearing music or a book that is familiar that takes me home instantly, so I had a momentary feeling of mingled woes that was really forlorn. However, it soon vanished as Dr. Wright and I walked home in the light drizzle and let the cool air blow on our faces.*

There is no such thing as stability on earth anywhere, but the void of it is more aching here than anywhere. Everyone is here to-day and gone to-morrow,—but true to the saying, blessings brighten as they take their flight—it is a charm as well as a sorrow, and keeps things interesting. I shall miss Miss O'Gorman and the Major more than I like to think of, though; but still it has certainly been a pleasure to know them both, and though their presence here was fleeting, they have an abiding place in my memory and friendship.[26]

Then came an unexpected setback: Dr. Lambert flatly rejected the Social Services idea. *And speaking of Miss Morgan, she said that she spoke to Major Lambert about taking me for social services and he 'turned the proposition down cold.' She said she had not wholly given up hope of me. But for the present, at any rate, I am certainly to remain in Paris. My 'supplanter',— the "vampire", as Pressy calls her, has not yet arrived. She is being delayed by sinus trouble, it seems. I am not in a hurry to leave my present job anyway.*

Natalie learned from Dr. Lambert of a letter he had received from Dr. John Wyeth, Boss's prominent New York friend. A feeling of protective responsibility for Natalie stood at the heart of Dr. Lambert's attitude. *I have just had my little conversation with Dr. Lambert. I didn't tell you how sweet he was about Dr. Wyeth's letter. He read me the passage about 'asking for me the same care that he would for his own daughter', and then looked at me in a quizzically inquisitive way he has sometimes. I said, "Well, you can certainly say that you forestalled his request,— you granted it before it was made." Major Lambert laughed his jolly laugh.* But Dr. Lambert took seriously the requests from home to look after Natalie.[27]

Air Raids Continue

As the fear of a new German offensive spread through the city, Natalie wrote on March 3 of mixed predictions of a full-scale attack. *When I have a chance, I read the articles in the* Petit-Parisian *by some French officer, which generally give a sane, conservative estimate of the situation, and he's very much in doubt as to whether these present attacks are really prefaces to the great offensive which everybody has been predicting for so long, or are merely feints. By the time this letter reaches you, it will all be settled one way or the other,—the offensive will or won't have been. Here everyone is telling of it, and opinions are most divided. Many people think that there is a great German offensive imminent, and have been duly expecting it for weeks. If the soldiers are in the same state, their nerves must be taut to breaking by now.*

Meanwhile, the Red Cross work from Dr. Lambert's office continued for homeless refugees and the soldiers in the field. *It is growing with marvelous rapidity and is intertwined now throughout all of France. Dispensaries, hospitals, infirmaries, convalescent homes spring into existence almost over-night it seems. I am wrapped up in it all and am never more pleased than when I can follow the workings of some phase of it. Our work, you see, deals with Military Affairs. This includes, of course, all the Base hospitals, since they are all under Army supervision and control. For example, if a Base Hospital is in need of supplies, the request is made by its commanding officer to the Chief Surgeon's Office, A.E.F., and, if it is approved there, it is filled either from the army stores or is passed on to us and we fill it. Such a request comes to our office for approval, and if we approve it, we pass it on to the Hospital Supply Service, who make out a requisition to fill it, on the Stores or the Purchasing Department, depending on whether or not we have it in stock. The routine is really simple.*

The work of Civil Affairs is, of course, along different lines from ours,—tho we touch it at many points. They do wonderful work for the refugees and the invalided, and for the civil population, in fighting tuberculosis, in the reeducation of mutilés. We come in touch with them chiefly when it is a question of medical care. Every day, as I go to our office, I pass thru the outer-room of the Bureau of Mutilés, and there are always a group of men, with missing limbs, sitting there waiting. The Red Cross gives them artificial limbs. I seldom enter a Metro where there is not at least one blessé (one wounded in the war) and we never go down the street without seeing some. But, tragic as each individual case seems, I cannot realize the significance of them somehow, and the war still seems a distant nightmare.

An important promotion for Miss Morgan occurred in early March: an appointment to the Red Cross Finance Committee for France. She became the only woman to hold such a position. More honors followed within the Red Cross family. Pressy's father was awarded the Legion of Honor for his services. Natalie congratulated Mr. Preston during a visit with Dr. and Mrs. Lambert at their apartment at the Hotel France et Choiseul. *We sat in front of the fire and had lots of fun. Mr. and Mrs. Barbour came in for call, too; he is the Secretary General, you know, and he has just received the Legion of Honor, too,—at the same time with Mr. Preston. Mr. Preston brought his in to give to Pres the other day, and I took it and looked at it, and was very much excited, because it was the very first Legion of Honor that I had ever touched. So then, suddenly, I took Mr. Barbour's and handled it, and so I said that I was getting very blasé about them, after so much familiarity. Then I even had the nerve to try it on, and I found it so becoming that I asked Mr. Barbour to tell the President how well it looked on me, so that he might be tempted to send me one, too.*

It really is quite a compliment to Mr. Barbour and Mr. Preston. They were over here in the service of the Clearing House for a long time before we declared war, so, of course, their service is more particularly for France. The Legion of Honor is the queen of all medals, naturally.[28]

We have just agreed on a fine plan of Pres's, which is to go to a show to-night, she, Florence Johnson, and I. I should go to dinner with them at the hotel, and then afterwards to the show, and spend the night with Pres.

They joined a French audience to see a very *snappy* and risqué play, which, they all agreed, *would not have been performed on an American stage. I enjoyed ever so much spending the night. It is such a sociable sort of thing to do, and Miss Morgan and Pres are such thoughtful, perfect hostesses. I ended up in Pres's nighty and Miss Morgan's kimono and the combination was marvelous, indeed, when you consider that Pres is half a head taller and Miss Morgan half a head shorter than I! However, both garments were very elegant. Pressy has all her "undies" made at Giraud's. So I felt very swell, even tho any elegance was of such a hybrid sort! I luxuriated in a real porcelain bath-tub, which we don't boast of possessing in our pension, and I felt quite civilized and spoiled, as I had my chocolate, bread and confitures in bed.*[29]

The mixture of war and pleasure reached almost comic, surreal proportions on an evening Natalie spent with Dr. Young during a German aerial bombardment. With an entire restaurant to themselves, they pleasantly ignored the bomb blasts and air raid outside that threatened their safety. *I answered the phone in the office, and Major Young said over the phone that there was an American officer eager for my company at dinner, if I had nothing amusing to do. Of course, I didn't! So he came by for me. We had planned to go to Fagot's. It was a quiet unpretentious place, not very large, very aristocratic. The food was worthy of royalty. Meanwhile, I forgot to say, that as we sat down to dinner and were discussing the relative merits of Vermouth Cassis and cocktails, the uncaring wail of the siren curdled through the air. It was the alarm signal. The guests departed hastily. We had beautiful service, of course, for there was nothing to rival us in the waiters' attentions. The doors and windows were all closed tight, so that the cannonading and the bombs were muffled and did not disturb us at all hardly.*

Well, we began with Vermouth Cassis. And I inquired of the head-waiter who hovered solicitously above, as to the quality of the hors d'oeuvres. "Madam, we have here Napoléon, the king of hors d'oeuvres", and he waved his hand grandly, and a little waiter stepped forward, who was, sure-enough, most absurdly like Napoleon. He smiled upon us condescendingly and struck a Napoleonic attitude. And I assure you that he is the king of hors d'oeuvres. I philosophically reflected that he had probably made more people happy in his sphere of royalty than his more famous namesake in his!

Then we had lobster, broiled live, with one of those divine mysteries which are French sauces. Then chicken with "truffles and champignons" and green peas. Meanwhile, we had a champagne that was simply perfect. I think he just wanted to give me a treat, like the child from the boarding school. So we drank to "Muddie". And then we drank to "everybody who was around our tables on Xmas Day". When we were ready to leave, the waiter said there was not a taxi to be had, because of the raid, which was in full swing, and, of course, the Metro had stopped running, as it always does during a raid. I was aghast and alarmed. "But not so our indomitable Major", as one of Major Young's doctors said about him in a report. He said, as tho he had it all arranged, with perfect serenity, "I'll get you home all right." So we started.

When the waiter opened the door to the street, I stepped back: it was so dark, I thought it was a cellar! We went out, tho, and started on foot. A heavy old wagon rumbled by and we called to ask the man if he would take us home, but he ignored us. The cannonading, which had been muffled in the restaurant, was now plain and constant, and air-planes darted across the sky, and on one side of the sky there were constant flashes, from the cannons, or shrapnel.

Major Young's idea was to go down to the Boulevard St. Germain, where, if anywhere, we could get a taxi. We passed several Abris (bomb shelters), and we had an inspiration to investigate one. So in we went. A little boy met us at the door and guided us down three long flights of narrow, narrow steps, underground. I shuddered, and said, in French, "This is worse than the bombs." And he laughed, with the little boy's wicked enjoyment of everyone's fright, and he said, "These are the cat-acombs." The steps ended in a long, dim passage barely wider than the steps, and intersected by another passage equally nar-row,—and both crowded with a stoically waiting crowd. The air was damp. The people were very quiet, talking hardly at all,—think of it, and they French!—little children, old ladies, every sort, even quite a few nondescript sort of men. We had only a hasty look and left at once for the upper air, which seemed safer, bombs and all. We found a taxi just after we left the abris and he took us home. The last thing I heard as I tucked myself sleepily in was the pounding of the cannons.[30]

Another of the deadly air raids struck the city as Natalie hosted a cinnamon toast party. This time Lovey, Mr. Field, Dr. Wright, and Dr. Hardy were her guests. The Germans struck just as every-one arrived, that now familiar siren screaming its warning across the city. *The excitement in the street climbed up to our loft apartment very quickly. We put out the light, and stepped out on the balcony to see. The busting shrapnel flashed very pretti-ly, like fireflies, a lazy flash here, there, and everywhere, and then there were big, dim sheets of fire flashing up,—from the cannon, the 'barage', I suppose. From out of the void excited voices would rise, asking where were abris, sometimes pitched high and suddenly in a shriek of excitement.*

It all seemed like a stage somehow. We had gone on after the alarm and made the toast, too. There were Miss Lovejoy and Dr. Hardy leaning over the grate, toasting the bread on long forks. I toasted on my burner. They pressed Mr. Field into service to 'butter'. And outside the cannons boomed, and the bombs 'boomed', and the shrapnel 'busted'. Finally we wolved deli-cious cinnamon toast. We heated the chocolate and had a real feast. And I thought of Fairmont, and felt the same age and the same spirit. You know when the conversation takes that anec-dotal turn,—Carm, Gwen and Louisiana would say it always does with me. Every time one would start a story, he would see that watchful waiting glint in the other fellow's eye that Mark Twain has made famous. And the tales went on, went on—So the party was a great success.

About 11:15 we stopped talking, listened, and heard no cannons. So I let them depart. I am sure they had not gone half a block when the cannonading began with "renewed vigor", so I rushed out once more on the balcony, hoping to call them back. The cannonading had shifted by this time and the excitement was all across the river. So I went in to bed. This raid was worse than the last, doing much more damage in lives and property than the others. Worst of all was a panic in the metro station. Sixty in all were killed, some dying of wounds, others stifled. Then, an American Y.M.C.A. worker was killed when a bomb struck a contiguous hospital, and two nurses, and a doctor and three patients were killed.[31]

Another disaster struck Paris when a large ammunition depot exploded, destroying a populated section of the city. Natalie was taking a lunch break in the cave with two co-workers at the moment of the explosion. *Suddenly I felt a strange surging in my head, so violent that I clapped my hands to my head. The next instant, there was a tremendous detonation, and the windows rattled and shook violently, a sudden strong gush of air. We rushed out on the street to where it* (the bomb) *had fallen. Then over one whole quarter of the sky hung a gigantic, beautiful, but sinister white cloud. Everyone knew there was disaster of some sort near us. The first cry, of course, was "Les Sales Boches" (the Dirty Huns). Then a Frenchman near us said that the cloud was by St. Denis, in the direction of the powder magazines, as time showed, the correct theory, awful as it was to think of.*

Dr. Clark was sent out to represent our office and he took me along with him. We drove thru an old, old poor quarter of Paris. Many ambulances passed by us, going in both directions. Window-panes were broken miles away by the force of the air-current started by the explosion. There was a hole there big enough to put our whole building in, which is almost a block by itself! Small explosions went on all afternoon.

An American ambulance was the first on the scene and the Red Cross has rented 200 rooms to take care of those who are left homeless as a result of the explosion. Red Cross doctors and nurses worked busily and steadily with the wounded. I suppose there is no doubt that everyone who was in the building was killed outright. The fire continued steadily, the firemen fighting it desperately all the time. That night, about eleven, Mlle. Alice tapped on my door and told me to go to the window and look. And there all across the corner of the sky was a fitful glow, flaring up brightly sometimes, destruction was still having its way.

Poor Paris! It seems a city of disaster just now. Mlle. Broussois' hospital is near the magazine which exploded. It was nearly entirely destroyed. Afterwards, they worked desperately for hours with the wounded, and all day yesterday, too.

The Mighty German Offensive

By March 11, Natalie's replacement had arrived. The new filer, Miss Cairns, struggled to learn the filing system, overwhelmed by the constant interruptions that Natalie had accepted as part of the job and delaying Natalie's move to her new library assignment. With the medical library installed at the Place Vendome, Natalie began to shuttle back and forth, going there to receive physicians who had made appointments.[32]

Then Natalie encountered a well-known young man she liked immediately, the son of Teddy Roosevelt. *When I went up to tell Major Lambert about the stenographer, I found him talking to a young aviation officer and started not to go in. But he saw me and beckoned for me to come. So I did, and told him of my luck, and then started out. And he called me back, and said he wanted me to meet Quentin Roosevelt. And the officer,—the very young officer, for I suppose he is not over twenty—stood up, very slim and very boyish, and bowed. I thought he was Archie, who is wounded and tactfully told him we had been worried about him. So he laughed, delighted at my mistake and said, "O no. I get up high, so I can keep out of all those dangerous things." And I beamed, and said, "Yes. That's the charm about aviation, isn't it? That and the officers (very killingly)."*

Of course, he and Major Lambert were delighted with this foolishness, and he bowed, and giggled, ran and hid behind the drawn red curtains and said he couldn't let his blushes be seen! He was really refreshingly boyish and I enjoyed him a lot. He talked to Major Lambert just as though they were the same age. One fine sally was where he told Major Lambert and me about two "corking good-looking French girls who were working in the Red Cross." We had been talking about the Library and how to make it popular. So when he said that, I said to Major Lambert that I thought the best way to make the library popular would be to make a card-index of all the pretty girls, graded according to looks. I left them still beaming and guffawing over the idea like a pair of boys—as they were!

The pounding by German air raids pressed on. Natalie wrote on March 19 that the raids had become all-day and all-night affairs. She described bombardments of the Gare de l'Este, the Place de la Republique, and the Tuileries, the last witnessed by Natalie as she stepped from her office and took cover.

By this time Paris was under bombardment both by air and by shelling, a surprise to the city's population because the big guns had limited range. *There is a rumor afloat that the Germans have broken thru the British lines. I suppose the two are connected. Imagining that new and more powerful guns have been invented by the Boches, it hardly stands to reason that, when the utmost limit so far has been 22 miles, they should suddenly invent something to carry 40 miles. 18 miles is a tremendous jump. So I suppose the upholders of the "shell" theory have to bring the Boche through the lines to get his shells here!*

This morning, my deep and innocent and very sweet Sunday morning slumbers were rudely interrupted, and I came suddenly and rebelliously out of them to hear—oo-om, which you may recognize as the tail-end of a boo-oo-om. The papers are most discouraging this morning. They say the English have retreated. Of course, they still say that this bombardment is from long range guns, and from the depths of my soul I pray that this is so, and it does not mean what I fear more than anything else in the world,—that the English have retreated considerably, so that the Germans are quite close. There have been shells bursting at intervals sometimes of five, sometimes fifteen or twenty minutes, all morning. I think it really must be bombardment, for the detonations come now at regular intervals of about fifteen minutes.

From across the street, as she wrote, lovely musical notes lilted through the air as someone played the piano *quite well,* amidst the rhythm of German cannons bombarding the city. *It fits the morning, for if ever there was a bright, fresh, cheerful spring morning, it is this, it is this. It would seem like peace, perfect peace, if only we could be blind to the significance of the dull recurrent booms (one just as I write that!). They shatter the smooth surface of the morning's calm, and break it, like the crack of doom. Or, rather, the threat of doom. It is a dull, heavy sound, that slowly surges thru the whole air it seems, and recedes reluctantly. Just now, an avion came so low that, for the sound of its engines, it might have been on the roof.*

I have always known that I was everything that was antipathetic to the Germans, and now another very marked point stands out,—their punctuality! Just on the dot, in fifteen minutes, they have sent another shot.

Will you stand it, if I speak of shells again. I know you must be exhausted with them,—the thing and the theme are just as preponderating at present. It is interesting because probably the bombardment of Paris (if this is a bombardment and not a raid) will be an important element in the history of the war. The Boche is livening up, and the last shell came after an interval of only ten minutes!

Natalie tried her best to report the events as the shells continued to fall, interrupting her train of thought. She described one pleasant diversion, a trip to an interesting little cafe that brought her in contact with a group of war correspondents. *I dined with Johnny. Had a real lark. We went to a tiny little place called the Café des Alpes just about a block and a half from the hotel. It is tiny, very plain, presided over by a pretty, kindly domineering culinary genius, whose autocratic ways have won for her the title of the "General". If she takes a dislike to people, she won't let them go in at all! If she likes anyone, her attention is embarrassing.*

There was a correspondent (the place is almost turned over to them, this real haunt) named Orr, who is quite an Important Person, it seems, in the world of correspondents, and she was charmed with him. She would step and pat him on the shoulder, or even smooth his hair, and announce to the world, "C'est mon fils, vous savez. C'est mon petit poilu." (It's my boy, you know. It's my little trench soldier.) *He smoked away on a pipe, tranquilly and made no return to these demonstrations, but she was not discouraged. We had a delicious dinner, soup, chicken,*

*potatoes, salad and cheese, with a deep red wine, all for eleven
francs. Extraordinary these days.*

*There was one table of seven, all Americans, four men and three
women; the men were all correspondents (Orr was one) and they
began singing and swinging, a rollicking "correspondents' song".
I wish I could remember the words. Something about their typical
rut of the correspondents; and then a rousing chorus demanding
to know when they would get to Paris, to Paris, to Paris! The next
table joined in with them, happy-hearted and American, there in
the heart of Paris. They smiled at us sociably, and we smiled back
pleasantly, and soon left,—the sad duty of discretion.*

As Natalie continued her letter, she chronicled a break in the
bombardment's rhythm. *Twenty-five minutes without a detonation. I have heard that they stop always for luncheon, and I
suppose it is true.* She used the interval to mention her lunch
two days earlier with Captain Gwathmey. *He had news that his
son was at Rouen, slightly wounded, so he was leaving that
night to see him. He was quite tranquil and undisturbed and
when he heard of the offensive, he said he was glad his son was
wounded, because that kept him out of the offensive!* When she
realized that the Germans had indeed stilled the cannons to have
lunch, Natalie stopped writing and ate lunch, too.[33]

There were nervously amusing interludes in the shelling. One
evening, seeking a distraction from the bombardment, they
played piquant at the pension. *Mme. has not played for years,
and it was too amusing to watch her. I wish it were not so
impossible to describe her. She would bend over the cards, very
interested and very amused at herself for being so, and make her
slow, fumbling, but finally successful efforts to arrange them. If
they were good, she would chuckle delightedly, and say, "Ah-ah-
ah," and if they were bad, she would say "Ach", impatiently, and
play any which way to get rid of the ugly hand, and laugh at herself for doing it. Then she would look up at me (I was sitting on
the arm of her chair) and say, "je n'ai pas de patience, moi", so
comically that I couldn't help laughing, and she would join in.*

Then, suddenly, all changed for Natalie in Paris. The sudden
massive German ground attacks brought wild confusion. Natalie's
March 25 letter to Muddie described a frenzied, tumultuous week.[34]

The mighty German offensive began during the early hours of
Monday, March 21, 1918, sending the Allied troops reeling in

retreat from their front-line trenches. The capture of Paris and immediate victory to end the war was the goal of this all-out German air and land assault. The news electrified the city; conditions in the Red Cross office approached chaos.

Natalie tried to get an overseas cable through to New Orleans to let Muddie and Boss know she was safe. *If you read about the shells falling in Paris, the cable would be one way of letting you know all's well. Things are so tense now, with this tremendous offensive on, and so much, lives and the ideals which make life worth living, at stake just now that my mind is scattered. When you think of your harmless, pleasant fellow-citizens swept in an instant from their peaceful occupations to eternity, it makes you forget everything else in a sort of rage. Last night, I was waked up,—as was the rest of Paris—at one o'clock by the cannons. It startled me from my sleep so violently that I had jumped clear out of the bed. Then the siren! There was never such a blood curdling sound since the screech-owl that screeched at four in the morning when Judge Pyncheon had just died for us, "member"? And you can imagine that the combination of midnight and a brain clogged with sleep intensified its effect—"the Zeppelins'll git you,—if you—don't—look—out. . . . " The thing goes, "woo-oo-oo."* Johnny is going to Dijon. The raids and bombardment were too much for her and so Tom decided to take her down to Dijon. They leave in the morning. Pres leaves tonight for Italy, but she is not leaving because of the excitement. In fact, she regrets, she says, going where it will be hard to get direct news of the offensive.

Natalie spent the next three days in the Red Cross headquarters dealing with the overwhelming flood of demands. *And while all of that is going on, the fate of all of us, of all the civilized world, is hanging in the balance, being fought out bitterly, and bloodily, with untold sacrifice and heroism not many miles from here. The news seemed dark this morning. Retreats here, and retreats there, and all the hard-won territory gone. But no one is down cast or discouraged. No one speaks of failure, even to say or to imply it is possible. Captain Gwathmey tells us that one of the long-range guns has been silenced. Paris goes her way and trusts her armies. Major Young told me something this afternoon that encourages me tremendously, that the English have retreated and the Germans advanced, leaving the French in strongly entrenched positions on the German flank.*

Meanwhile, towns and hospitals are being evacuated. The office is abustle and astir with rushed supplies, rushed orders, changing doctors, sending nurses, preparing beds and equipment here. Not a moment, I suppose, does the thought of this offensive vanish from anyone's consciousness. Our reconstructed villages, the work of so much thought, and love, and labor are lost to us; the roads to Amiens are being fought over desperately, Péronne taken,—but those things you know. Dr. Burlingame is wild to go to the front. He slipped off today but they caught him and made him stay. It is really his duty, for he has to handle the supplies and the assignment of officers, doctors and nurses, and so on. But, of course, it is hard, for anyone whose blood runs in sanguine shade in his veins must want to be there and lose the whole world, and life, and everything in adding his effort to stop the course of the Germans. Major Young told me this afternoon that he is going. I think I told you before that he said he would like to be a regimental surgeon, that he felt he simply had to be in it. Tomorrow, he is coming to see me. By that time, how will things stand?[35]

The last entries were scrawled, barely legible and obviously hurried.

Friday—Have been so busy working with refugees, wrenching them thru and from Paris that I haven't had and haven't a second. Am here only for clean clothes now. Will leave this to be mailed Monday in case I don't come back before. I am at one of the stations, sleep there. Was never better and am useful for once, therefore happy as any one can be in the midst of misery. The French are wonderful. My dearest, dearest, dearest love to each and everyone of both families and a thousand L.C.'s to you. Devotedly, Natalie

They are mostly old women and dirty babies and children and as brave and loveable and heartbreakingly funny as ever you could imagine. Love and love.

Mon. A.M. Back at the office. The mail is going so I won't hold this. I hate to send this skimpy letter, but it was all I could do this week. All is well. I am top-notch in health, and my spirits vary with the Allied line! Except that they're always a good bit in advance. No one is discouraged, altho some are impatient. More and more and more love, Natalie[36]

Chapter Four

Heroism in Air Attacks

Natalie had written her last hurried letter entry in Paris on Monday, April 1, a week after she had abruptly been thrown into refugee relief work. The furious pace had precluded any opportunity for Natalie to write. That afternoon she finally composed a coherent explanation of how she had become a refugee relief worker, recording the events since the previous Wednesday, March 27. *I spent the afternoon at the Place de la Concorde. The atmosphere was tense with the excitement of the German offensive. We were rushing busily, dictating, telephoning on a scale such as we have never known before. Of course, I was tingling with it all. I was simply on fire to do anything, anything in the world to help! You can imagine.*

In the next office, the Department of Military Affairs, Mr. Fosburgh, Mr. France, Mr. Van Schasile and several others were gathered together singling out men for investigations, sending for reports, and planning. The most pressing question was that of the refugees who were pouring in from the tortured North at all stations. Nurses and doctors were sent to look over conditions and report back to headquarters. I went down to Miss Russell and offered my services for the night as a Nurse's Aid, bringing proudly to the foregoing my once scorned diploma. She assigned me to the Gare d'Austerlitz (train station). The Gare d'Austerlitz was urgently needing some French speaking people, and so they told me to go. Meanwhile, two men were being dispatched to make a report on the Gare de l'Est and the Gare du Nord, so we decided to combine on a taxi.

A long, long ride brought me to the Gare du Nord and my first sight of refugees,—vague forms of all shapes except that of human beings, in the dim light outside the Gare du Nord, where they were huddled silently and patiently, dropped down on

113

boxes, benches, the ground, anywhere, waiting for the right thing to happen. We found Schuyler Parsons in charge and getting along quite well, except that there wasn't enough sleeping space. There was a long, low-ceiling basement room, dimly lighted, with a cement floor. Then mattresses, sent by the Red Cross, had been stretched out all along the sides, with two blankets for each, and every mattress filled up with a half-indistinguishable form. There were some refugees gathered together in a little group, waiting for their places, and an old woman of 93, who was looking about her quite cheerfully.

I discovered that the two men knew very, very little French, and they seemed very glad of my assistance, so I went with them to the Gare de l'Est as interpreter. I discovered several things about the official attitude, one of which was that the refugees were not to stay in Paris, but were to be sent on just as quickly as possible, and they were not to be allowed to sleep outside of the stations, so that was why we had to arrange to have the soldiers move out of the station. You can't imagine the forlorn, sad crowd of refugees always in the background, and everything abnormal in the dim light, sometimes of the moon, sometimes of the ghastly blue lights.

Then the Gare d'Austerlitz. That was a small station, and packed with people. Poor things women and children, almost entirely, with sometimes an old man, or a wounded soldier who has been evacuated with his family. And with them are bundles of every description,—boxes, sacks, bags, big handkerchiefs, bolsters, all bulging, all grotesque with abnormal knots and bumps, and giving glimpses of a pathetic medley of sordid little belongings. And how they guard them! Sometimes they would steadfastly refuse to be tempted by the offer of food, tho they looked cold and hungry, and, at first, I was puzzled, but soon found that generally the reason was the fear of losing their baggage. So then, I would arrange to have it watched and shoo them in to the comforts of hot coffee, hot chocolate, bouillon, bread, cheese, corned beef, crackers, figs, chocolate, etc. At Austerlitz, there was a very orderly and well-managed, tho small canteen, and they helped us with the food, cooking the chocolate, coffee, etc., and helping us serve it. Of course we supplied it.

Well, at Austerlitz, the mattresses had just come, so we went to work in another long, stuffy, chill room, laying them down with as much economy of space as possible. They were so good, so amiable, and so grateful for every least little thing, that I was glad I was too busy to let my mind take it all in,—their utter destitution, their homelessness, and their courage.

Of course, the children were the most cheerful of all. I expected they would be fitful with fatigue. But not at all. They were quite cheerful. As I made the rounds, I stopped to pull the blanket over two pairs of small feet which stuck out over the edge of one mattress. As I did, I heard a sleepy "pluck-chick" at the side, and I started when I saw a white hen settled comfortably there. Two delighted giggles came from the dim upper regions of the mattress. I peered up to see two pairs of wide awake brown eyes, shining and bright, and two round little boys' faces beaming at me. Of course, we had a conversation. I wanted to know whether the hen had pulled their camion (wagon). And then I wanted to know the hen's name. And both of these humorous remarks made a great hit,—or, at least, they brought out quantities of giggles. And soon I was hearing all the details of their very hurried trip. I was introduced to the dog, what was dragged out unceremoniously from some retreat at the end of a string. Then heads popped up from all about, and contributions to the conversation came in from all sides. It turned out that I had started a family of twenty-five. It was the third time that they had been evacuated. In the course of the next few days, I had many long, personal talks with various ones of the refugees and some of them I shall never forget.

As Natalie told her story of the refugee stations, an assortment of personalities emerged in the narration, one who proved very troublesome. *I must speak of Dr. Mosher. She is a "lady doctor", but, entre nous, I feel about her as Bishop Dudley did about the Christian Lequitists,—neither appellation is very appropriate. However, I don't like to say anything about her, because she afterward tried to do me an ill turn. I haven't feeling toward her at all, but regard her rather as one of the paths we run across. Somehow or another, she has been taken into Civil Affairs. She looks like a Buddha, minus his benignity, and she strides through the world masterfully, in a service hat and a khaki suit. She was the doctor in charge that night, but all of the work was in charge of Military Affairs, and various ones of the men were down there helping, all of us working like slaves. There were two trained nurses there in attendance on Dr. Mosher and they worked with us very well.*

It was about half-past one when word came that a man had fainted just outside of the door of the refugee "doctor". Dr. Mosher was gazing down at him. He began to revive, opened his eyes and moaned. I lifted his head just a little from the cold stones and we got him on a mattress. He seemed to be suffering horribly. I looked at Dr. Mosher, who stood there like a stone. I asked her what to do, and she said she had nothing to do anything with? A soldier came. Then several more. One of them pulled out a piece of sugar, ran and got some ether from the infirmary, and insisted on giving the man the sugar with ether on it. It seemed to revive him, but only to greater suffering. He was very shabby, gaunt, and unshaven, and he had a scar just above his ear and one on his head, and wore on his shabby coat the decoration for the Croix de Guerre (France's great medal for combat heroism).

We decided to get him to the Infirmary so that Dr. Mosher would have facilities at hand, so the men shouldered the mattress, I helped as much as I could. A nurse received us there but she had no help to offer us. And Dr. Mosher gazed at the man and said, "He is a very sick man. I don't know what's the matter with him, but he is a very sick man." Meanwhile, the poor fellow was looking from one to the other of us pitifully. Sometimes he would claw at the collar of his shirt and say, "Ça brule, Ça brule." ("It burns, It burns.") The throat was open. I thought perhaps he was thirsty, so we gave him some milk. He drank it greedily, but swallowed with the greatest difficulty. He talked brokenly, and I pieced out gradually his story. It hurts now in my memory like a burn. Almost always, I can see some gleam of happiness, some little ray of brightness in any life. But I cannot see what ever the most determined optimism can do in this man's case.

He was a laborer in Belgium, married, and had three children. The invasion of Belgium came and never again did he see or hear word of his wife and three children, whom he adored. His three brothers were killed in the war. He was wounded in the leg, in the arm, and twice in the head. Now, he is epileptic as a result of one of his head wounds, and is not really sound mentally at all. He has no relatives, no home, not a plan in the world. And he was discharged from the hospital as cured. He was not lucid most of the time, restless and threw himself about on the mattress. I knelt by it and stroked his head, helplessly. It did really seem to calm him and gradually came through his senses as a friendly act. He would turn to me agonizing, and say "Morts?—Tous?—Tous les trois?—Mes frères sont tous morts?" ("Dead? All? All three? My brothers are all dead?") And I would try to reassure him. Then he would say their names. Finally, one of the men said to take the man to the hospital. The great hospitals of La Pitié and Salpetrière, which are like miniature cities, are fairly near.

The change from the cool outside air to the close air of the room made the man restless again. He tossed about. He talked of his children, his voice soft and gentle, coaxing. "Viens, petite. C'est papá." ("Come, little girl. It's Papa.") And on and on. You know I am not emotional or easily affected, but it simply tore through me more horribly than a physical pain. I can never, never forget it. It was last Wednesday night. I have dreamed of him, thought of him in the midst of all the stress and turmoil ever since. It simply seems too hard. A poor, good man, happy in his work, unoffending,—torn, hurled, crammed into this horrible war, and spit out again a wreck, a half-man, with no one in the world to turn to, unable to work, not sick enough for the hospital, not well enough for the world, and no one to care. I don't dare think of it. It haunts my mind; but I will not think of it.

The men slipped fifty francs into his pocket-book. I found that the Belgian Relief Committee would probably look after him and went to the hospital to say so. He had gone early the morning after we had taken him there. Thousands of men have died in this war and some sort of tomb stone marks the place for many of them. If only this poor simple tortured soul might have been one of them. He has a tombstone, if not more lasting than bronze, at least warmer, and as lasting as I, in my memory, where he will have a lasting place as one of the saddest martyrs of the war.[1]

Natalie was making up for lost time. After six months in France, she now moved inwards from the margins of the war towards its epicenter, its realities. Instead of experiencing the war's brutalities vicariously through soldiers such as Jean

Millescamp and ambulancers such as George de Forest and Mr. Fowler, she was becoming a participant in the conflict, leaving behind pleasant diversions at the Bois, the Theatre Guignol, the opera, or the elegant restaurants of the city. Her enthusiasm for the cause, now that she had touched the face of the war, required total immersion. *All the succeeding days, as I spent every store of my energy in doing whatever I could to make things a little less hard and bleak for the refugees, there was a sort of feeling of atonement,—as tho I, part of a world which had treated him so cruelly, were making up to him for it in just an infinitesimal way when I did things for others who were in sorrow, need, sickness and affliction. It was unreasonable, unreasoning, but persistent.*

Natalie slept with the refugees that night and during the days that followed. *It was about 3:30 a.m. Mr. Ober fixed a mattress for me, and I tumbled down and slept until nearly six. The next morning, we had to have all the refugees fed before 7:30, when the soldiers were due at the Canteen; so we were wildly busy getting them into the tiny canteen in turns and serving them,— just one trained nurse and Mr. Ober and myself. At eight, two other trained nurses came on to relieve the night one, who departed.*

Many of our night group got off on a morning train, but others kept drifting in, and there wasn't a second when I wasn't flying about getting them settled. About noon, the Commissaire Militaire, a French captain, came. He told me that orders had been received to march all the refugees through Ivry, the shipping station of the Gare d'Austerlitz, and asked if the Red Cross would like to do anything over there. I phoned Headquarters and they said for me to go over and look things over and report. Mr. Ober turned up. So he and I set out for Ivry. I was suffering from my shoes as they were new and stiff, not the ideal footwear in which to rush to and from unceasingly for chores. I acquired several blisters. We made arrangements with the station officials about a place to house the refugees.

There was a huge warehouse sort of structure, the bottom floor of which was all taken up with boxes, barrels to be shipped; the top floor was a great bare barn of a place, walled with canvas. Downstairs, a small room had been walled in as a kitchen. It had four small gas jets for cooking and a faucet for water, and a long table. The refugees had begun to assemble. The afternoon was damp and chilly and they huddled together miserably while the wind cut thru the building sharply. I went over to talk to them, shivering myself in my light suit, while Mr. Ober went to the Gare d'Austerlitz in a camion to get some of the supplies there. He came back soon with mattresses and boxes of cheese, sardines, crackers, canned beef, and so on; and, after depositing these, rushed to town to get some cooking utensils and some helpers. So I was left alone, with much food, no utensils, not a knife, or a fork, or an instrument of any kind,—and some three hundred cold and hungry refugees!

Me and some of the refugees put the mattresses about upstairs. I found that they hadn't had anything to eat since early morning, when they had had a cup of coffee so I impressed one of the amiable agents de ville into service, and he and I opened a case of sardines and a case of crackers, and then the tins of sardines. I took a hat-pin and 'sterilized' it with water and a few jabs thru a handkerchief. Down that line of refugees we started. I made the refugees stretch out a hand, then the agent would place the cracker sidewise in the hand, and I would fish for sardines, and put the 'haut' on the cracker! It was great sport.

Of course, it was a very light meal and in itself not worth much; but, aside from the fact that some of the people were really hungry, so that even a morsel was welcome, I concluded that it was a little diversion for all of them anyway. We all took it like a game, and I would laugh and talk as I went, and they all joined it and it was really very sociable. The little accidents that befell, the excuse for talking. Meanwhile, I was taking the whole of the plucky forlorn crowd right into the depths of my affection. There were women who had walked twelve miles on a stretch, carrying heavy baskets and a baby, families with tiny children who had been as much as five days on foot on their way, old people who had had to leave at a minute's notice, without being able to take a thing.

But they were cheerful, for the most part, or, at worst, stoical. I could count on my fingers the number of people I saw in tears. Mr. Ober came back with many supplies and utensils, and some assistance, so we soon had hot chocolate, coffee, bouillon, and milk going, and there was bread, crackers, cold sliced corn *beef, sliced cheese, dried figs, and some chocolate. We had a little fence put up around two long tables, and we would have them go in a few at a time and sit at the table. It was such a relief to find ready, heavy service to do to appease just a little the demands of the great, throbbing sympathy the situation of these wretched people demanded. I felt as tho I could never exhaust the energy to do things for them.*

Because Natalie had been working among the refugees around the clock, day after day, Dr. Mosher and a few other older workers urged her to go home. *My old friend, Mrs. Belmont Tiffany was there, presiding in the kitchen, stirring chocolate, and sloshing pans about in her aggressive efficient way. She really was quite agreeable to me anyway, even tho she joined the ranks of the enemy and said I should go home. Mr. Ober, however, was in charge, and he gave me permission to stay; he couldn't very well do otherwise, for he had been on the go as long as I had, and he was staying. I had to swallow my rage! I know you can sympathize with my attitude; in fact, I inherited it from you, you know. You know how you are when you are interested in things. And I was bound up in heart and soul in that work, almost more than I have ever been in anything in my life.*

After I had burrowed happily under four blankets on a nice, clean mattress, next to two nice clean refugee sisters, and was just about to go off into the sleep of the weary, I heard a stern voice calling, and just pulled my eyes open wide enough to catch a glimpse of the generous shadow of Dr. Mosher, with a trained nurse, a ministering angel of darkness, in attendance. I registered deep slumber. She called my name again. I sighed, and muttered sleepily. But she wouldn't desert the call. So I answered. I will spare you the details, but she had brought up some sort of medicine which she insisted I should take, because I needed it! As I was quite comfortable and reasonably sure of continued existence without this draught (and doubtful of existence with it!), I thanked her most pleasantly, and most politely, but declined. Mr. Ober, making the rounds and hearing the argument, came up and took my part, but I shooed him away, as he had no patience with the doctor anyway.

As a climax, she said, "I am your doctor, and I order you to drink it." So I answered in my sweetest tones, "There must be a mistake somewhere, for I haven't asked for a doctor at all. I feel quite well, and I think it wiser to let well enough alone. So there's really no use urging me. I thank you very much for your interest, but I'd rather go to sleep."

She insisted again, so I said, as tho making a great concession, "I'll tell you what I'll do: you leave it there, and if I feel badly in the night, I'll drink it." She said, "Indeed not. You'll drink it now or not at all."

I grinned, the friendly luck at this opportune dilemma, I said, "I couldn't drink it now." She snorted, and left in a rage. I overwhelmed her with attention the next morning, not really obviously. I hate unpleasantness in the atmosphere. But apparently I couldn't have chosen a better way to enrage her. She has gone about with a tar-brush after me ever since, so everybody tells me. Fortunately, her methods are so violent that they are not effective, and everyone comes to me laughing. I am really sorry, though. I hated to ruffle the poor old soul. I would cheerfully have let her bully me in some ways, but I had to draw the line at that medicine.

I must just speak of my dear old couple. She was 73 and he was 76, the dearest, cleanest old toil-worn people. I found her sitting on a pile of hay guarding her bundles, while he walked up and down. She had on a little white frilled cap, tied under her chin, as neat and immaculate as tho she had just put it on, black wool scarf over the shoulders, as erect as tho she were in a chair in the salon. She had the sweetest face, all tiny little pleasant lines. I sat down and started talking. The more I talked, she talked. She couldn't say a sentence without mentioning her husband,—how good he was, how hard he had always worked. They had had a farm and animals. The Germans had taken most of them before. Then the field of battle moved away again, and they had started once more. And now they had to leave everything. They were going to live with their son in Bordeaux. Most of their bundles were little presents for the grandchildren,—apples, some feathers, a knitted cap, and so on.

"He" came and joined us soon, tall and muscular, and had hardly yielded even a slightest stoop to age. He assured me that she 'always ate very little and that was why she was so delicate'. I discovered that they had had nothing to eat. Neither

wanted to go down without the other, and they didn't want to leave their baggage unguarded. So I promised to guard their things and sent them both down happy.

Imagine me on the haystack, with all the handy little array of bags and baskets and sacks at my feet, my various refugee friends coming up to talk. There was one cute little boy just about four, with a bright, round face, and sparkling dark eyes. I asked him if he was a Boche. His mother smiled, and asked him "eh, Pierre? Tu es Boche, toi?" He looked at her, turned his head on one side, and his eyes simply danced, as he said, "Non. Prussian." Then he buried his head in the hay, overcome by his boldness.

An old man told me that he would always pray for me. Then he thought a minute, to make it more definite, and added, he would pray that I would 'escape the German bombs and get a good husband.' Of course, I answered that I would try hard to do both, and he and all of his party were highly amused at my great wit. When the trains would be made up and the people got aboard, we would go through, giving a loaf of bread to each family, and a franc and a piece of chocolate to all of the children. They were most gratified and appreciative. Ever so many told me that the first thing they would speak of in their new homes would be the Croix Rouge Americaine.[2]

Gisors

Natalie's entry describing the refugees abruptly stopped, not to be picked up again until Saturday, April 6. Back in the Place de la Concorde office, she wrote, in a very large scrawl: *Saturday— leaving now as Nurse's Aid. Write later. Love and love—N.*

Her explanation followed days later in a new note, this one written on both sides of a mangled old envelope, the only paper she could find. She announced, in a tiny script that filled every available space of the envelope, that she had just arrived at a "lovely chateau" not far from the battlefront. She had traveled for several days with American troops from Paris, riding on the hood of an overloaded Red Cross truck.

This is all the paper I have. I left, going from the office by home, packing and to the other end of Paris in 30 minutes. This is one of the best things that I have done. I feel as tho I am a book,—pictures of old walls, castles, parks, camions, quaint cities, camouflaged cannons, purple-shadowed valleys, and American soldiers.

More details as to the wild journey: this is a temporary mission. We are to have a Field Kitchen for the American soldiers. The kitchen will be permanent, but I am a transitory attachment to it. Each kitchen has two R.C., a nurse and an aide, and the aide who was to go on this particular party did not appear. So, when Mr. Rice rushed into the office and said, "Do you want to go as nurse's aid to _____ (for security reasons, Natalie could not disclose her location, so she left a blank space)? If you do, get your hat and coat",—I was up before he finished the sentence. A rush, and we found Major Lambert. At first, he said, "No." He was afraid I would want to get away from him. "You know your mother's depending on me to look after you." So I told him nothing would make me leave him.

I'll wager that there were never any R.C. papers so quickly ready. The camion was ready to start and waiting for me. I was wild for fear that they would leave me. You never saw such a stir,—then a wild taxi-ride home and Léontine and the concierge so excited that they were almost helpless, wild ride to the end of Paris—plunged out of the taxi into a long courtyard. And it wasn't ready. I found I had left my passport. So I had to go back. Mr. Balthus said to make the best time I could. So there was more rushing. 90 rue de Chasson Vert is the headquarters of the Red Cross Camions. All of them are under Mr. Douglas, the multi-millionaire copper-miner of Douglas, Arizona. He was just as nice as he could be. We talked to him for some time. He couldn't be better done on the stage as the drawling, kindly westerner, big and genial.

We left at four o'clock. We were a picture. We have a big camion loaded to its utmost. The chauffeur, Miss Bergan and one of the nurses sat on a duffel-bag on the floor, and I on the hood, with my back to the front, and my feet hanging over inside. My seat sounds odd, but it has proved the best, because the hood gets hot, and I am sitting on a real radiator. The extremely fresh air made that a blessing.

We made our first stop at 7:15, still light, a very old, quaint French city. There is an old 17th century covered bridge there, and the walls of a chateau built in the time of Saint Louis.

It was so comical but so interesting, too,—for we came in, heaped up in the front of the camion and were brought to a stop right in front of the railroad station, the center of all things. A tiny town, it certainly seemed very illogical to find a group of slim, tall young Americans in khaki in front of that station! The American boys gathered about our camion in a swarm. They were pathetically glad to see American girls. They were anti-air-craft.[3]

Natalie's group drove all the next day through the French countryside, skirting the battlefront. They lodged the evening of April 9 in a village she later identified as Gisors, seventy miles northwest of Paris. Her work here would prove her value as a translator, soon moving forward to greater responsibility, ultimately becoming ward nurse and the translator at a Beauvais evacuation hospital in the Picardy war zone. By April 11, a Thursday, she was earnestly at work in Gisors.

To-day, for the first time, I was a nurse's aid,—in name; in reality, I was a semi-nurse and interpreter. Our men are now with the French, some sent to French hospitals. Down here in the village, there is a little French hospital, and there were about thirty patients from our American army and only one nurse who speaks any English. All the treatment was from the French. Things were pretty difficult. They called Miss Bergan and me. She goes at night and I go in the day, from 7:30 to 7:30. I was constantly up and down the three flights of steps as interpreter. I made the rounds with the doctor, of all patients, and hardest of all, I helped at an operation, the amputation of a finger. The poor boy was only 20. He was just about to take the chloroform when I came in and had been rebellious. When I spoke to him, he was as docile as he could be. He told me this afternoon that the last thing he heard as "it got him" was my saying, "breathe deep".

It seems to me I have lived a year in the day and still it was short. To-day, I have learned to read French thermometers, to change every sort of compress, keep temperature charts, and a great many other useful, confusing things. So, till to-morrow![4]

The next letter entry identified her location as Hospital Auxiliare #25. *I am sitting here where I have been most of the day, by the bed of a strong, fine American boy, who is fighting for his life, with a bad case of pneumonia. There is not much to* do for him,—too little, just his medicines and things to make him comfortable. And the nurse gives him a hypodermic at intervals. The doctor has given up, but I can't. All day he has been struggling with that horrible oedema—the death rattle. It hurts me to hear it. Just a plain fellow, only 22 or so, but very strong, wonderfully good. He is not suffering so much as he was.

He is from South Carolina and has that southern bur that I love. Sister said just now that he was a good patient, and I told him so, translating her French. He tried to smile, and said, "Yes'm. Thank her for me, ma'am. And tell her I want to thank her anyway for all she's done for me." Sister Ste. Eugénie has been nursing for years, but her eyes filled with tears when I gave her the message.

This overcrowded French hospital was short of nurses and badly needed a translator, so the Red Cross unit was doubly welcome. War wounds, amputations, pneumonia, meningitis, and psychiatric issues all numbered among Natalie's cases. She worked a regular twelve-hour day as a nurse's assistant. But the doctor made his rounds after dark, so Natalie's presence as a translator became essential at odd hours. She rarely made the one-mile walk to the chateau, where she resided, before 10:30 at night.

It is 6:30 and I am sitting down for the first time to-day. I am perched on the front seat of an ambulance, guarding it, so that the drivers couldn't get away. I am so pleased with myself, because I have just fixed up four of my pets. They wanted to rejoin their regiments, and the doctor said they should be sent to the American Base Hospital and there to the regiment which is a sort of clearing house of convalescents. They would lose their own regiments. So I busied myself with their troubles. I asked this ambulance to take them, but the drivers said they weren't going near enough to the regiments in question. So, I slipped over to a French military post across the street and calmly proceeded to call the Headquarters, Administrative Section, and I got orders to send my protegés to their regiments by this ambulance. So here I sit and watch for the ambulancers, who will probably be in a temper! I have some cigarettes in my pocket to appease them.

The Red Cross sends us cigarettes and we give them out to

the boys. Every morning I go all thru the wards French and Americans both. They are lots of fun. The French are much more deferential, the Americans are very funny. The French are much more patient than our old boys, who are wild to be up, to eat, to do everything the minute they are better. But our boys are fresh to the war and the French are worn by it. They take what comes, extravagantly appreciative if it is good and just quiescent if it is bad. Our boys call out the minute I come in the room. They love to tell me foolish things to tell the doctor. And often I do tell him and he enjoys them. He (the doctor) is very nice in a quietly breezy, business like manner, and a thin face with rather rosy cheeks and a moustache that looks as tho a stiff breeze was blowing it all the time. He and I get along beautifully, he assuring me that he would have to give up if it weren't for me as his tongue, and also that I look beautifully in my coif and white clothes (borrowed glory from a nurse).

Natalie's critically ill pneumonia patient *pulled through after all. He took a turn for the better late in the afternoon. Late in the evening, the doctor looked up and said it was extraordinary, but he was better. Yesterday, I was dancing with the news.*[5]

A backlog of five letters from Muddie arrived, along with a note from Pres:

> Dearest Scottie—We hear such wonderful things about you and are so proud! A little curious, too. I miss you like hell and long to hear what you do in detail. The office goes on very leisurely now that you are not here. If ever you should see one noble youth called Harry Reynolds, give him my love. Your devoted and admiring Presti[6]

The crowded conditions and extraordinary demands served as a source of inspiration. As the only interpreter, Natalie had to be in many places. *We have had a wild time yesterday and to-day crowded to its utmost capacity and far past. Patients have slept about everywhere. There were two officers on the floor in the bathroom, more sprawled along a corridor, two more slept on a table in the laundry room. They said it was the most comfortable room they had had in months!*

I have never even said how, on the cold, misty afternoon after our arrival here, we went on the porch and saw five American officers on horses. They were delighted to find that we spoke English. One evening, I went for a ride with Lt. Taylor, from Texas, in the wild, wet woods, and then on a path about six inches wide (it seemed!) which clung to the ancient wall of the Prisoner's Tower. We had a wonderful gallop back, as hard as the horses could tear. These boys were an interesting crowd, for they were in the first group of Americans to hold a sector of the front. When these troops arrived here, it was a most impressive sight to stand on the top of the hill in front of the chateau and look down at the succession of camions and fine, khaki-clad soldiers, on foot, or horseback, quietly, seriously and busily moving. I couldn't have said a word as I watched them. The boys joke each other in the most appalling way. "Gibson's going to go out on a shrapnel boat, because I want to get those putters of his", announced Lt. Davis at the table. They were gay and happy and business-like, too. There were 150 men quartered here.

I have met lots of interesting people here. Col. Shaw and Major Beale are probably my choice. Then Col. Shaw's aide, Captain Sinclair, Captain Edmundson, Major Philips. When Captain Prichett came by, he had Captain Edmundson of the Army with him. I told them how seriously we needed a certain serum. Captain Prichett turned to Captain E., and said, "Can't you get some over to-morrow." Captain E. looked at me a minute and laughed, and said, unwaveringly, "Under the circumstances, I think I might find some and bring it over." They all laughed. It is a standing joke how they love to see American women.

Captain Edmundson and Mr. Montâque came over early in the morning with the serum. And it has saved the boy's life, I think. Captain E. brought four boxes, and he and Mr. Montâque stayed and talked quietly a while. That afternoon, they came back again with four more boxes and talked some more. When they left, they both started laughing like children and finally explained that they had saved the four boxes purposely as an excuse for an extra visit.

The hospital couldn't feed all the people, and the Red Cross came to the fore, as always. I hastily went for Mr. Balthus and asked him for our rolling kitchen. So it is installed in the back yard of the hospital, working away merrily.

One dear boy of 21, who looks like Geoffrey Marshall etheri-alized, has acute T.B. and there is no hope for him, they say. He is the finest little fellow you ever saw. I call him Geoffrey Loyal Ford, which amuses him immensely. He was so interested to know that he looks like someone I know. He never complains. He can't see why they sent him to the hospital, tho every after-noon he coughs himself weak. He told me, earnestly, "Wasn't anything the matter, only the full pack and my wind. And on the last hike, I hadn't been long out of the hospital with bronchitis, and the lieutenant gave me a light load the first day. But then the second day he thought he could break me in again to a full pack, but we had to climb a hill, and I couldn't make it, because I lost my wind. I could'a made it, tho, if it hadn't been for the full pack." I won't let myself think of that boy.[7]

Closer to the Front

Though Natalie had heard rumors that her Red Cross unit might be moved, she knew not where or when. Her translation services were in more demand closer to the battlefront. *To-day I moved with our men. I am the only woman attached to this body of troops! This morning, I went down with dear, good Miss Bergan to the hospital, as usual when in walked Mr. Lowery. He looked at us and said, dramatically, "Good-bye." I said "good-bye", too, just to be agreeable. Then he told me that Col. Shaw has sent for me to go along with the troops to act as interpreter in various French hospitals "further up".*

After a rush through the hospital to exchange goodbyes with the staff and her patients, she moved out in a vehicle, accompa-nied by Lt. Montâque and Captain Prichett. *We overtook our army. Oh, how I wish you could see them, the steadily march-ing khaki line. By we would go, past cannons, past groups of men on foot, officers on horseback, or in big gray or khaki motors, or motor-cycles, past lines of ambulances,—all moving forward.*

Natalie had been attached to the U.S. Army's First Division, America's most decorated combat force of World War I, as an emergency interpreter in French hospitals. After reporting to regiment headquarters, where Colonel Shaw and Colonel Mabie welcomed her, Natalie went immediately to work with the wounded. *We saw the blessés coming in,—men just direct from the front, wounded only a few hours before, with the dirt of the trenches still on them. And I saw my first Boche wounded. The Boche prisoners say that their officers all tell them that this is the last month of the war,—that the Germans will win this month! My first Boche blessé, a poor, sickly looking boy, had been shot in the foot.*

There was an alerte that first night but nothing happened, just a lone Boche plane on its wicked way to poor harassed Paris. In the middle of the night, I was awakened by a barrage, very plain, and the flash of the guns and of the shrapnel is quite bright, all night long boomed away in the distance like pounding surf.

Natalie had arrived in Beauvais, much nearer the German big guns. It was an ancient Picardy town thirty-five miles northeast of Gisors. The first morning she made the rounds of all the wards of the French hospital as interpreter with the doctors. She met Father Hammick, a Red Cross priest in a khaki uniform, very nice and *most good-looking,* who introduced her around. He took her to the Red Cross Club, managed by Smith College workers to entertain the soldiers. *It was quite nice and sociable—a*

Natalie, front row, in Beauvais (1918). *Courtesy of Special Collections, Tulane University Libraries*

piano, magazines and an open fire. We met the head of the Smith College Unit and some of the girls, who seemed a very good sort. The head left us breathless. She said, "Now, suppose you just tell me who you are and what you do. You know that's the only way we can ever get anywhere, isn't it?" Father Hammick and I escaped to the hall a few minutes later and laughed together. It is always embarrassing to ask a Red Cross person who they are and what they do, anyway, for often they are in doubt about it themselves![8]

For security reasons, Natalie did not identify Beauvais in her letters, though she explained there were fifteen military hospitals in town, and a large military airfield. The administrative office relied upon her to keep all records on the English and Americans and to prepare daily reports to the Red Cross. Natalie made the rounds of all American patients at least twice daily with the various physicians, and the nurses needed her as well. She also dealt with visitors who wanted to see patients. On April 25, she reported her patients to be improving with one exception.

The one who really hurts me is a fine, strong boy, barely twenty-one, with meningitis. He suffers a great deal. I sit and talk to him, when he can't sleep to keep him from being so restless. Yesterday, I wrote a letter for him to his older married sister as the nurse brought some flowers in. I asked her to bring them over for him to see and he was delighted and wanted to smell them. Then, of course, I asked him if he would like to send one to his sister, and he said, "sure". He kissed it. He followed the flower with his eyes as I put it in the letter; then he said, "Tell her, 'Flowers from France'." He didn't know how nearly a dozen or so tears from France came to going with the flowers. There is so much tragedy over here that the weight of it all is far deeper than tears,—even for an un-tearful person like me. You must either go crazy, or be heartless, or extremely strong-minded. My ambition is the last. I have never lost my nerve except once, and that was when they made the lumbar puncture for this boy. They had to run the needle in five times. I got along all right until it was over,—then I subsided for an hour or so, but have been all right again ever since.

The diagnosis of Natalie's meningitis patient was changed to typhus and he was further isolated for his treatment. Another soldier, a pneumonia patient under the nursing care of Miss

Cleveland, died. Miss Cleveland went to pieces over it, a reaction that disturbed Natalie. *She is a fine girl, full of energy and enthusiasm and high ideals, but much too temperamental and not self-controlled. There was never any place where self-control was more needed than here at present. It takes a real deliberate effort to keep in a cheerful mood. When I find myself getting black, I do something foolish such as reciting Shakespeare to Henrietta, the French maid,—she presents a new reaction to it every time, to indulge in some French slang. It doesn't require much to bolster my spirits,—pleased with a rattle, tickled with a straw!*

We get the gassed cases, and they are pitiful, indeed. It does seem a cowardly weapon somehow,—a thing you can't meet and fight with outright! I look at the poor fellows and sometimes you can only feel a perfect storm and agony of pity. Of course, you know the effects of gas. It effects all the most sensitive parts of the body, causing deeper burns, inside-out. And their eyes, and linings of the throat and chest suffer most.

We haven't very many Americans here,—just about 35, three very serious cases. Mumps is the most popular complaint. I also call them mumpsies, and they think I am very witty! It is ridiculous to see these rows of moon-round faces coming out from covers. Young Americans are not likely to let such an opportunity for "ragging" go by. They tease each other unmercifully about their looks.

As a rare American female in those parts, Natalie received much attention from both patients and officers. *They take me out to dinner, they come by to see me just to talk, and they send all sorts of foolish things. I have been out to dinner every day. To-day, I had luncheon with Captain Francis, Captain Prichett, and Mr. Carroll, a journalist. We really have just as amusing times as tho things were quite normal and calm. In fact, I suppose we are much gayer. Because there's no escaping the reality, and the sometimes slight, but always unremitting strain. The journalist is a nice, round person. He improves on acquaintance and I like him quite well.*

The Smith Unit are here, and they have been extremely nice to me. Mrs. Andrews, the head of it, wife of Captain (I think!) Barnett Andrews of the Army, has asked me to dinner, and to luncheon with her. I did lunch with Dr. Greenough (a female physician with the Smith Unit). *I have met Gertrude Ely (Y.M.C.A.) and Miss Arrowsmith, also Miss Cleveland, an extremely tall and good-looking brunette, very temperamental, has taken me up and the world is full of a number of people.*

The Médecin-Chef here has given me a large, sunny office all to myself, and has been lovely to me. The Smith Unit, and, in fact, all the Americans had found him most unapproachable, so I am doubly pleased. The various doctors couldn't be nicer.

I must tell you that I met an interesting person today. The Colonel sent for me, he rarely asks for anything. I rushed to see what he wanted,—and found that Mr. Cobb, of the Saturday Evening Post, and other fame, was there and the Colonel had sent for me to introduce him! Wasn't that nice? He knows Dr. Wyeth quite well, it seems, and had the loveliest things to say about him. Mr. Carroll, the N. Y. Tribune journalist, was there, too, and they made me (without much difficulty!) sit down and talk for some time. [9]

Hospital Temporaire #15 would be Natalie's home for the next

Irvin S. Cobb, war correspondent for the *Saturday Evening Post* (ca. 1915). He was Natalie's favorite among war correspondents in Beauvais. *Courtesy of University of Kentucky*

Natalie (second from left) in Beauvais, with unidentified companions (1918). *Courtesy of Special Collections, Tulane University Libraries*

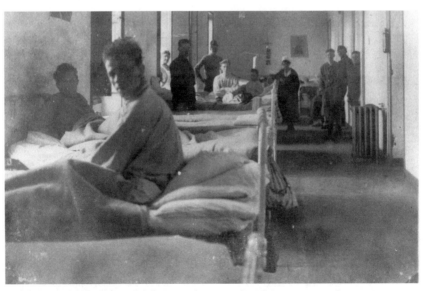

A military hospital ward (Beauvais, 1918). The nurse at the center-rear of the photograph may be Natalie. *Courtesy of Special Collections, Tulane University Libraries*

A watercolor portrait of Natalie painted by a patient (Beauvais, 1918).
Courtesy of Special Collections, Tulane University Libraries

Natalie teases a soldier with his pistol (Beauvais or Nantes, 1918).
Courtesy of Special Collections, Tulane University Libraries

six months. Beauvais boasted several hotels, including the Hotel de France et d'Angleterre, where Major Busby took her for lunch in late April. Here she again encountered the *Saturday Evening Post* writer Irvin S. Cobb, America's best-known war correspondent at the time. Cobb was a unique character whose postwar books, intellectually folksy, would enhance his reputation as the nation's favorite humorist. His mantel would be eventually inherited by his friend Will Rogers, with whom he occasionally appeared in popular movies during the 1920s.

Mr. Cobb was there, and he rose from his chair to bow as we came in. Afterwards, he came over and sat at our table to talk. He said he was sorry he had not been able to get to the hospital. I said I hoped that he would come soon. And he gallantly said, "I will." Then, with a bow,—"Hospitals have taken on an added attraction for me." And do you know I had nothing to say! I regarded him speechlessly. I was so annoyed! I told Major Busby so, and he just laughed. Afterwards, Mr. Cobb came and sat down with us.

I saw Miss Cleveland and Miss Justice having luncheon together. I left our table to run and speak to them. I pointed out Mr.Cobb to them, thinking they would be interested, and they were, but Miss Cleveland added, "but for real charm, what is really winning my heart is the one who is opposite you." Of course, Mr. Cobb is not charming to look at, for he is quite heavily built, with an impassive sort of face,—it is expressionless, which makes his droll sayings droller!

Dr. Samphor, a French physician, invited Natalie to be his guest for dinner at the Continental Hotel. *There we saw Captain Prichett, Mr. Montâque, Mr. Balthus, Mr. Lowery and a captain who bowed to me cordially saying he knew me from Gisors. Also, there was a Colonel and a Lt. Col. of the general staff and quantities of French aviation officers at dinner, not a word of English at all, and quick, most amusing conversation. Dr. Samphor is very funny and quite clever, and he takes pleasure in trying to lose me in French, so, of course, that inspires me. You would have loved the picture the hotel dining-room presented, with all the smart uniforms,—and just a few women. It looked very military, and very, very smart. The aviators are very dashing, and one Belgian officer was a sight divine. The dim lights, the white napery and wines, the mirrors and the uniforms, looked like a stage picture. It is the mise en scène, unfortunately, of some real tragedies.*[10]

In an April letter to Major Lambert, Natalie joked that she was doing her duty for his medical library as a missionary among the doctors at the front. Her letter brought replies from both Dorothy Cheney and Major Lambert. Miss Cheney let her know she was missed, she envied her adventure, and "I have my doubts of your settling down with your little files again." Dr. Lambert assured her she would be free awhile longer.

> I am going home and shall be gone till the middle of June, so there is no danger from me within the next few weeks and I think you can enjoy your roving spirit to its full extent. I notice that you carefully leave out all date, address or postal sector as to where you are or where you might possibly be. I have an idea though, and hope to be able to get this to you.
>
> Stay where you are, take care of yourself. I think you are really doing a very valuable piece of work as an interpreter up there for the men and the doctors. If you meet Major Roosevelt, give him my love and tell him you are my assistant here but are on a temporary aberration of duty. Wear your tin hat and look after your reckless self and when I come back in the middle of June, I shall look after you again. Miss Cheney and Mrs. Lambert send their love to you. I haven't asked any permission but I send mine too!
>
> Faithfully yours,
Alexander Lambert[11]

Dr. Greenough, the female physician associated with the Smith College Unit, worked occasionally in the wards of the hospital; she and Natalie became friends. This relationship would become important that summer when the American Club faced closure. Dr. Greenough would recruit Natalie to entertain the soldiers during off-duty hours. *This afternoon late, I had promised to take tea with Dr. Samphor and Mme. Casteran du Rais (the directrice). So I asked them to go with me to take tea at the American Club, the habitat of the Smith Unit. Dr. Greenough, the 'lady doctor', as the boys call her, received us and gave us chocolate confitures, and chocolate tablets. Afterwards, three American lieutenants from here came in and we had a very gay time,—tho I was hard-pressed in my job as interpreter,—especially since both sides began telling jokes! Neither side, the*

Doctor and Mme. C.R. on the one, and Dr. Greenough, and the three boys on the other, understanding a word of the other's language. We had lots of fun, tho. Mr. Sarles insisted that I should try on his shrapnel helmet, and I did, tilting it smartly to one side, so that it looked very rakish. They all found it very smart.

I never did tell you much about the Smith Unit. They have been lovely to me. They asked me to make this "club" my headquarters. They are doing some good work. They have a canteen from which they feed the wounded passing through. They visit the Americans in the hospital, have taken them books and magazines; and they run this American Club. They are under the Red Cross. [12]

Expanding Duties

On May 2, Natalie was surprised by a very large package from home containing two boxes. One offered an assortment of female garments, and the second, a gift from Boss, was packed with an enormous variety and volume of candies. *As for Boss's candy, besides the whole immense family of thanks that I send him, there are a whole lot of other starved-for-candy-war-workers and fighters that send their thanks along with mine. It is just like the "foine Oirish gentleman" I have always had such a crush on. Some of that candy is going to have the distinction of going to some very fine and brave Americans a few miles from here, who are doing constant hard and dangerous work, very cheerfully. I know some of them pretty well. They have a field hospital which enjoys the distinction of being shelled at flattering intervals; and know that this will be a "bomb" most startling of all, certainly most welcome!* [13]

Natalie also received a letter from Pressy, delivered through Dr. Clark, who supervised American medical operations in Beauvais. It brought welcome news from Paris.

My Dearest Scottie: More compliments to you!!! Dr. Clark has given the latest and most flattering reports. I hear you have everyone eating out of your hand, have an office of your own and countless nurses under you, and of course all the fellahs have fallen. What care I!!! Last week, *HE* came to town for the day and took me to lunch. I suppose you see him constantly and I hear the whole Daly Unit is in love with him, but still, I am happy. Nothing much has been happening here. There was a big Red Cross male dinner Thursday night and Tuts [Ruth Morgan] and I went and heard all the speeches through a crack in the door. Puckins [their private nickname for Dr. Perkins, the new head of the Red Cross operations] made a very good speech and Davison made some thrilling points, although, of course, they cannot help putting in phrases that humiliate yours truly, such as "Women, girls, *even* stenographers, are doing a tremendous service, etc." It hurts my pride somethin' terrible. I met the Director of the Tulane Univ. Unit the other night. Some talker! Are they all like that from N.O.? Doc Lambert left for "Marika" this A.M. He and Ma [Mrs. Lambert] came for dinner last night, and she seemed quite brave. Before she had been harping on the subs, etc. and was sure of his demise.

I am some speed Queen on this machine. You ought to see me go now. Record breaking. I am outrageously happy, not jealous of you a bit. This P.M. I am taking the evening train to Fontainebleau and have engaged two horses for Sunday. Don't think you I am going with someone, not on your life; the two horses are so I can ride morn and eve. Ain't it grand? My Pa made me promise to take a groom, but am not going to, and am going to read Musset and think of Scottie, and let off some of the steam that is giving me spring fever so badly. We have moved from the F. & C. [Hotel France et Choiseul] and are now living in luxury at the Castiglione. When you come in on your perm, we will give you a party.

Don't forget to let me know if you run across Harry Reynolds, a phoney lookin' fellah but a great friend of Bill's. Wal, goodbye, Scottie old scout. Good luck to you and a huge hug from your devoted, Prestie[14]

As the German offensive pressed on, the large Beauvais airfield sent its aviators daily to combat. The local anti-aircraft guns did their best to down German planes flying past, en route to raids on Paris and elsewhere. The battlefields each day fed heavy numbers of wounded soldiers into the fifteen local hospitals.

Natalie's job duties expanded to addressing the needs, recommendations, complaints, and supply requests of the nurses. She liked the very busy work. *I wrote the above few lines in twenty minutes, because, just after I sat down, Miss Justice came in my office and started proposing various impossible things to be done, and I had to argue with her. Then, when I had just finished the sentence, in came a Red Cross Major to go around the hospital. And now, after half-past-two, I have just finished the tour of inspection.* She completed only three brief paragraphs on the letter that day but finally made a more substantial entry the next morning.

This is May 6, early, early morn. As I started your letter once more, Mr. Lowery came by to tell me that our American boys at another hospital were without an interpreter and were having a bad time of it. As all my crowd here is getting along swimmingly, I got myself in on the front seat of Mr. Lowery's camion and went over to the other hospital, the Jeanne Hachette,— named for a lady who figures largely in the town's history. It is much, much brighter and cleaner than my old 15, which has that dusty, bare-boards expression which is characteristic of many old school-houses. Natalie's #15 was an old agricultural school converted for wartime use as a hospital.

J. H. is for the grand blessés. It takes only wounded, and especially fractures. We have about 14 there of our boys. There were six Americans in a row in one ward. They were lying there quietly when I went in. Soon, the one in the next bed chimed in and soon they were all in, first one head and then another (two of them swathed in bandages) would bob up to contribute a remark. Often, I can tell them about friends in the hospital over here, and I brought messages over, and will take some back to-day. These boys were telling me their various "incidents,"—how they happened, etc. One said, happily, "I got my souvenir, all right," and held up a piece of shell. "The old doc had me on the table, and that's the first thing I saw afterwards. And, believe me, she's going to stay with me now."

The next fellow looked at him enviously, and said, with evident regret, "Mine went right on through. Just took a piece out o' my leg and kept on going." One very young and delicate looking little fellow was carrying a stretcher when he got hit. "I was just taking out another fellow when I got mine," he said. "If it hadn't been for the strap over my shoulder he would'a fell." The big bone of the forearm was shattered. I said, "What did you do? It must have hurt you horribly." He said, "No. I didn't know what it was. My arm just went limp. And I said to the fellow at the other end, 'Gee. Somethin' must 'a happened here.' And he came back and looked, and said, 'I reckon somethin' has happened!' But it didn't hurt much,—not to speak of. Didn't even keep me from carrying' the stretcher. We went a kilometer and a half. Of course, I had the strap on my shoulder to carry it with.—But she's making up for lost time now, hurting," he added, looking at it with a twisted grin. He hadn't slept for several nights, the nurse told me.

I was there to receive several new arrivals. They were so glad to hear my voice speaking English to them! One had just been lying there with his eyes closed, making no reply to the Frenchman who kept asking him questions. When I spoke to him, he answered immediately. Another, with his head all bandaged up (I can't bring myself to say or write their injuries,—it seems to tear the dressings off, somehow), was so pleased at the chance to talk that I finally had to stop him, for his own sake, with a promise to see him to-morrow! He told me he thought I was a sister, but he didn't care what I was since I was American. He said he hadn't talked to any girls since he left Trenton.

The Médecin-Chef took me all over the hospital himself. He said he would like very, very much to have me stay there as interpreter, and said they certainly needed one. So I promised to go there in the afternoon until they can get someone. The doctors want to ask the history of wounds, and their treatment; the boys want to ask all the little thousand and one things that make hospital life a little less miserable, and the French officials want to make out records.

Natalie was to take a survey trip to other medical facilities with Colonel Hutton, a medical general staff officer whose position was liaison between the French and American officials. Colonel Hutton first made a stop at the Continental Hotel, Natalie waiting while he completed his business there. The wait became extended when Colonel Hutton had to hurry back to the hospital.

Meanwhile, several newspaper correspondents entertained Natalie. *At the Continental were Mr. Cobb ("Irv"), Mr. Carroll (of the Philadelphia Ledger, I think), and asked me, as I waited for Col. Hutton, if I wouldn't have coffee with them. I sat in the courtyard of the Continental at a table, sipping tea and talking and having a great time with Mr. Cobb and Mr. Carroll, Will Grimes (of the Chicago Tribune, I believe), and one other quite well-known journalist whose name I can't think of just now to save my life* [probably Morton Green of the *New York Tribune*, as reported by Cobb in his *Saturday Evening Post* article, May 25, 1918].

There is no doubt about it,—journalists are just about as interesting as any group of men from any profession,—by which remark I mean to imply that they are really more interesting. Gradually, we accumulated other people. Father Hammick, chaplain in our Red Cross, who had been acting as temporary chaplain for a regiment of our infantry, came in just back from the front, worn looking and showing the stresses of the great strain. He had lived in a shell-hole with seven other men for a week. They crawled out at night, for food, getting only one meal a day.

Anyway, Father Hammick told us, half-serious and half-comically, the story of his leaving,—and it was not a calm departure. I think that one of the men went off to write it up. Mr. Cobb was at his best and told some delightful stories. No one else could make them sound so funny. Such was the story of Sarah Bernhardt's performance of Anthony and Cleopatra. *I laughed this time until I was ashamed. Captain Prichett came and joined us, and a Major whose name I have forgot. Then came two most delightful Frenchmen, Jean Hugo (grandson of Victor) and a very good-looking aviator in the smartest uniform, scarlet brushes with a black stripe, black coat, black boots, and a chasseurs black capote!*

And I just sat there, happy. Mr. Cobb gave me a lovely little silver medallion to hang on my identification bracelet. He is much amused, because I bought it and have never yet had it marked. He accuses me of conceit, and says that I take the attitude of being so well-known as not to need identification; whereas, I defend myself, my point of view is that my disc is identification as it is, because a perfect blank will naturally suggest me! Captain Prichett took pictures of us. Mr. Cobb said that he and I should represent an Italian bride and groom, and Father Hammick stood back of us to give us his blessing, and everyone else laughed!

Ironically, this mock marriage to Irvin Cobb—performed during a pleasant break from the horrors that had brought all of them to this obscure French town—would be Natalie's only occasion ever to be a bride.

Natalie's narrative returned to the subject of her trip to the field hospitals at the front with Colonel Hutton. *We spun along thru this beautiful French landscape thru several little towns with glimpses of old houses, and villages, and American soldiers, and past a Field Hospital, and finally we pulled up at Crèvecoeur, where there is a big French hospital, which serves as an evacuation station. A nurse, the daughter of Clemenceau, took us through. The hospital is very well-equipped, much, much better than my poor #15.* Crèvecoeur (approximately twenty miles north of Beauvais, with the battlefront just to the east) *is just a group of business-like looking brick buildings, not at all French in appearance. There is no town near, but it is a busy one, in itself with a big autochir attached to it. Do you know what an autochir is? It is a movable dressings-station or hospital, with baraques* (barracks) *that can be carried about on a motor and then dismounted and set up. There was an operation just in progress in this one.*

We went from there over to another hospital, an American Field Hospital in a tiny little town. There is a huge chateau there which is a French hospital,—the Americans are just across the road, in tents. They take gassed cases there,—the very severe ones, give them treatment and evacuate them as soon as they are transportable. They are comparatively near the front, and near an ammunition dump, which is constantly being shelled by Germans. Things were rather calm when we arrived, then gradually the big guns opened up. They sounded so close and loud. It was the beginning of a big bombardment. Anyway, I took my candy there, and the men were as delighted as children with it.

Captain Prichett and Captain Edmundson took Natalie to Field Hospital #2, composed of a group of brown tents. Here, gas cases and eye injuries were treated. Nearby, Natalie gathered some fruit from a wild plum tree to take to one of her seriously ill patients, a Wisconsin native who spoke often of the fruit trees near his home. *Then up came two horses, with Major Ford, the C.O., on one and Captain Cole, a Gisors acquaintance, on the other. They dismounted, and Major Ford was presented. Of course, I enthused over the horses. And he insisted I should* mount one. *Secluded road, nice horses, and a very pleasant Major. Bliss! We had a lovely time. He was most agreeable, and insisted I should come and have a long ride with him and luncheon at the camp. I said I had no way to get there. So he said he would send his side-car any day I said. I named Wednesday and was agreed.*

They also stopped at the aviation field. *There were endless numbers of planes up. There were several esquadrilles and several smaller groups, and a few lone ones too. Your imagination soars with the planes. I get perfectly exhilarated with watching. Then three planes held our attention. They kept so close together that they seemed almost to be touching at times. They stayed dangerously close to the ground, and performed all sorts of maneuvers in the most perfect union. They looped the loop, and circled, and dived, with a beauty of motion as perfect as a bird's. They would dive straight down for the road apparently, then just recover in time to swoop barely above the tree tops. A delight to watch. Once, they swooped so close to us that I instinctively cowered down feeling that they were going to hit us. We stayed there craning and gaping till they finally alighted. But it was the most beautiful exhibition of flying that I have ever seen.*

Tuesday, Captain Prichett told me that one of the three men who were in that group went that same night on a flight for real business. He engaged three Boche planes, and sank two, but the third sank him. He fell inside our lines and was killed. He was buried today. Captain Prichett knows a lot of the aviators. They were all very much distressed, as the aviator in question was very popular, as well as a good air-man. He had twenty German planes to his credit. I feel as tho I knew him, after watching, and loving, his flight. One of the officers who was billeted with us at Gisors has been killed. He was one of the two who came a few days after the others. I try not to let myself think of it. [15]

Losses and Gains

Natalie was surprised to learn from one of her patients that her friend Alex Ficklin, from New Orleans, was on the medical staff of Field Hospital #3, one of the facilities she had recently visited. She sent word to him. Alex appeared the next morning, spending much of the day observing her work and making rounds with her. After Alex left, Major Ford, with whom she had ridden horseback during her battlefront hospital visit, took her to dinner at the Continental. Despite two subsequent invitations from Major Ford to come horseback riding, including one occasion when he sent Lieutenant Nettles and Captain Bird in his car to bring her, she declined both opportunities. She was swamped with work.

Saturday afternoon we received a large number of patients, some of them gassed. There were over sixty patients all at once. The French custom is that the name, regiment, and diagnosis of each patient must be obtained before he is given a bed. The officials spoke no English, and the patients no French! Imagine a square, merry court-yard in France, with an excited little French sergeant in one room, writing records and talking all the while,—and in the courtyard many American boys, all tired, and quite a few suffering a great deal,—with French orderlies running about, with no apparent purpose, among them; the boys themselves changing places every minute,— such of them as could walk. Finally, we did got them all placed. I took the sickest ones first. Afterwards I would call out three names at a time, in stentorian tones,—band together the owners of said names, and hold them while I got the details necessary to French requirements, and turned it over, in my best French, to the sergeant.

Afterwards, there were a lot of questions to be asked of them and a dozen things to be arranged. These boys were all in the Annex, which is a block away. There was only one French nurse there, and the new little American, Miss Cook. We got two other nurses immediately from the Red Cross. The Red Cross has just done miracles in keeping up with this protracted emergency; especially valuable have been their nurses and supplies. Then, of course, I was involved again, as the connecting link between them and the French doctors and nurses. Meanwhile, there were all my boys over there to look after. Sunday was the busiest day you ever saw. The nurses worked like Trojans.[16]

We had an alarm—a heavy barrage last night with little mistrailleuses peppering away and the big guns booming angrily. The avions don't notice us tho. They ignore us and save their attitude! The gossip this afternoon is that they bombarded a town about twenty kilos from here in broad day this morning. We heard quite a cannonading, but, of course, could not tell where, except that it was near. We are beautifully interested, though, as far as safety goes, for there is nothing here the Boche want. I tell the boys that, and add, "they don't know that I am here." And it passes for great wit!

One gas patient died in the afternoon and then another boy that night. *The gassed boy was named Walcott. He was a good, quiet, patient fellow, and I am unalterably thankful to say he didn't seem to suffer much except, of course, for the dressings. The sight sears into your brain. You can never forget it. I am back to my old self once more, and I am determined not to let all the "horrors" get possession of me. Just now the lights went out as is their ugly habit at nine-fifteen. It is so unceremonious! We are not supposed to have any lights afterwards, but I light a candle with my beautiful briquet that Captain Prichett gave me. It reminds me of old Fairmont days.*[17]

Natalie rose before six the next morning to finish the letter and rush it to Mr. Lowery, who was boarding a train for Paris, where the mail would move out faster. Her final entry told of another raid the night before. *I washed my hair last night, after lights out. I despaired of getting it done in the day-time. Then there was an alerte, while I was drying it. Everybody got up, and several of us went out on the balcony and watched the rocket signals, the shrapnel, and the flare of the cannons. It was a lovely, starry night, and the air was cool and fresh after a long, oppressive day. We hoped our guns stopped them. We could hear Boche engines.*

One man did die last night. He was delirious most of the time. One of the nurses asked him, just before the end, if there was anything he would like and he said, impatiently, "Yes. I want to go home." Wednesday was the funeral of the two who had gone home, Sunday. It was very beautiful. It reminded me of the day of Mrs. Phelps' funeral. There was a short service in front of the mortuary chapel. The hearse (I know you will shudder at the word) was drawn up in front. A squad of American soldiers and a squad of French made up the guard of honor, drawn up on each side. They presented arms as each of the plain pine coffins was brought out. The sharp, quick order would come first to the French; then, in English, to the Americans. The simple caskets were covered first with the tri-color and then with the American flags,—which lent them a splendor of color and symbol. Many of the French nurses were there and several American nurses. Our officers convalescent in the hospital, the French Médecin Chef and several other offi-cials were just behind the Red Cross chaplain. There was a squad, too, of the convalescent gas patients and many of the men from this hospital. The sunlight sent shafts of light through the trees onto the little gathering, and, as the minister intoned part of our simple, impressive service, it was all peaceful and beautiful and solemn,—but not at all sad.

Afterwards, we followed the hearse, all of us on foot, through the old, narrow, winding sunlit streets of this ancient little French town to the country, a garden spot, with tall, cool trees, and a mass of bright flowers everywhere. I thought of the Blue Bird. The diamond seemed to turn, and the two wooden boxes to glow already with the rich hue of new and different forms, and all the flowers, the quiet, peaceful calm of the place seemed to say, with the children, "There is no death". There was anoth-er short service and prayer at the cemetery. And then four bent old Frenchmen let the caskets down into the narrow opening in the rocky earth. Four old veterans of the war of '71 were there with their flag, tied with crèpe. They dipped it in salute. The minister threw in the first clod of earth. And that was the first funeral of an American soldier that I have seen. I took a flower from each casket for their mothers,—and I thought of their mothers through it all.[18]

Natalie received the same day, May 17, a box and note from her friend Harold Ober, who had directed her refugee work dur-ing the evacuation crisis in Paris. He was answering her request for various Red Cross supplies for the hospital, including a load of old phonograph records so her patients could hear music: "Mr. France told me the other day how you left on half an hour's notice with only the things you happened to have with you. I'm afraid our Refugee assistants, the A.F.F.W's, would not have been able to do that. I hear that you are doing wonderful work at Beauvais but it is not a surprise to me after the week at Ivry. Please remember me to Mrs. Clark and let Dr. Clark know anything else you need that I can send you. Sincerely Yours, Harold Ober"[19]

The next week, the volume of patients continued to rise at Hospital #15, now called Hospital Complementaire Auxiliare de l'Armée #42. *We have 66 patients, and so I patter about constantly from one to another of them,—the bee flitting from flower to flower! There is a ripple of trouble, just at present, though, because the powers in Paris are, as usual, putting a hand in. I love the Red Cross so much that I hate even to admit that it makes mistakes, but occasionally it really does,—just to show that it is human after all!—the Paris office always tries to manage all the details about everything. They are afraid to trust anything to their representatives, and they make rules and regulations without sufficient knowledge of conditions. Now, they are making a rule that there shall be no more interpreters, but that all interpreters shall be Nurses' Aids first and interpreters afterwards,—the height of common sense for hospitals where there are ten or twenty patients all in one ward; but it is very, very hard for this particular hospital.*

We take lots of contagious cases, and the wards are highly specialized even for general cases, so sixty-six patients scattered over the length and breadth of a rambling four-story building which encloses three sides of a large square. By the time I make the rounds of all, getting their complaints and symptoms straightened out, it takes a great deal of time. And then I have to keep their records up to date and make out a report each day, and then a weekly report at the end of the week.

They say just to go ahead and do a little of anything Nurses' Aid-ish(!) to comply with the letter of the law. So I have told the Médecin-Chef about it and he laughed and said he would take me in his service in the officers' division, and that he would be very severe with me! He is very, very nice. We get along beautifully. He is a tall, slim, grey-haired silent man. He reminds me of Mr. Phelps.

Natalie developed an infection on the bottom of her foot that would plague her all summer. Lieutenant Nettles brought three cans of medicine called "foot-ease." Finally, Dr. Clark examined the infection. *He insisted on looking at it, and told me two things to do for it, and I acquiesced meekly,—having none of the things necessary to do any one of them! And, of course, he told me not to use it and not to go to the contagious wards! I have been using it constantly and it is much better anyway. I have been using a cane. It is quite a good-looking one that Captain Prichett gave me, and it looks very smart. I think I shall carry it as a swagger stick afterwards!*

As Natalie struggled with her foot, her work produced more anecdotes for her letters. *There was a big old Texan here, named Booty, who had been cook (much to his discontent they shoved him into that, because one evenin' the cook was sick, and he fixed up a mess for the fellows like he used to do campin', and they made him cook). Anyway, he was one of the most lovable giants you have ever seen, as gentle, and strong, and kind-hearted a gentleman as ever was,—even with all his disregard of the king's English. He and several others almost as nice left to-day. Eight left together. I gave them cigarettes and figs, as I always do, and shook hands all around, and they all had the nicest things to say. One little old eighteen year older didn't know whether he should shake hands or not, because of his warts! Of course, I shook warts and all. His warts are the sorrow of his life, and more than for anything else he thanks me for getting aid for them from the doctor! I watched them swing-ing down the walk, some in helmets, some in caps, all in khaki,—a group of men to be proud of. They turned and waved good-bye several times.*

In the next room, a victrola is playing. There is a poor fellow in there who is mildly insane. I sit with him often. To-day, he has been 'talking to God' all day, he says. As it is a less painful delusion than the one he has been having, I don't discourage him. His poor mind is topsy-turvy.

A boy came in to-day with mumps. A shell had exploded near him and killed four men near him and wounded several; it had thrown him against a tree, knocking him senseless. And when the surgeons examined him they found he had mumps. I said, "But weren't you lucky not to have any worse injury than mumps?" "Yes", he said without conviction. And then he added, bitterly, "But I almost wish it'd got me instead of the little fellow next to me. He was the finest little fellow you ever did see. He was a man, if there ever was one. And he wasn't but just sev-enteen." I wander along and tell you all these little scraps in the hope that they may just suggest our every day atmosphere.[20]

May 28 brought elation to Beauvais as word spread of a solid

victory won by the U.S. troops at Cantigny, a village on the
Somme not far from Beauvais. The Germans were overrun and a
hundred German prisoners taken. Natalie, thrilled with the
unexpected American gain, felt surprised by the subdued reactions from her American and French patients. *Such a great,
great day for us! I am so proud of our men! All the town knows
about our gain, and the French are ecstatic. As for me, I could
simply cry with joy. Major Ruineur told us the news. I rushed
immediately and told all of the boys everywhere, and the dear
old fellows simply beamed. But almost unfailingly would come
a fallen countenance, and the lament, "And just think. I wasn't
there." I told Captain Garrett, too. He is in the engineer corps
and his usually happy face was a study. He was ashamed not
to be delighted, but he was so sad over missing it that he couldn't
be happy over the gain. I was dying to say something to the
French, too; but I felt that it was more "delicate" not to. So I
restrained myself. Soon, tho, the news got to them, too. They are
the dearest people in the world. They came and shook hands
with me, every so many of them, the médecin-chef, ever so many
of the doctors, the nurses, and all, and said, "Félicitations",
again and again. And then they would say how they had always
known we would do it, and how the French loved the
Americans. And I would say that all we asked was to do as well
as the French,—that no one could hope to do more. So we all had
a lovely, most polite time!*[21]

Shattered Calm

Then came a sudden shattering of the calm, making the elation over the American combat victory short-lived. Beauvais was
all at once in the middle of the furious German response. That
same night, a devastating German air raid rained bombs upon
Beauvais; Hospital #42 was hit hard in the attack.

*Last night we had a raid, and a pretty bad one. I had no
intention of writing you about it, but Mr. Ford and some other
journalists came by this morning and had already all the
names of the nurses (American) here, and said they were sending the story at once. And anyway, I decided that it would not
be so bad, because by the time you get this letter, things will be*

settled more. Perhaps the "sales Boches" may be in Berlin by that time, with our men behind them!

Last night, I went to bed rather late, after dressing my game foot and pampering it a little with compresses, hot foot-bath, and the like. I was tired and turned in with a grateful sigh.

The next thing I knew, was a tremendous crash thru the universe. I came out of a heavy sleep to face black darkness and lesser sounds. Another reverberating crash, and the cannons. After my old Paris habit, I tucked my head under the bolster. But then came the rush of nurses, and hushed, excited voices and knocking on my door.

Then someone mentioned the patients, which cleared my brain like cold water with a sudden realization of where I was, and my responsibility as the only American woman in the hospital. I slipped into a shirt and waist and slippers, someone found a helmet for me, and off we went. The moon was bright and peaceful. There was hardly any barage, in marked contrast to the usual procedure, when there are few bombs and many cannons. Last night there were many bombs and few cannons. One bomb had fallen in the court-yard, right in the pathway under the trees, leading from the pavilion to the hospital. The distance is not quite 200 yards, I should say, and the bomb had fallen half-way between and right on the pathway. We did not pause to consider the matter.

Even at the time, tho, I had a humorous flash of the picture we presented, in the moonlight, with poilus's helmets, streaming hair, and all sorts of nondescript costumes. We looked like Boadiceas in comedy! I was hobbling painfully, wincing at the stones and debris. The bomb had knocked a tree across our path. This morning, one of the nurses solemnly remarked that I had "saved the lives of all of them." I gulped inquiringly, eager to be a heroine and believing that I might have been, but just not able to place it. I said, "How?" She said, "Why, by being so late and so much trouble to awaken", because, if I hadn't delayed them, they would have all been on the pathway when the bomb fell! "The late Miss Scott" has at last had her failing appreciated!

We came over here to a confused scene. It was quite dark inside and slivered glass was under foot thickly, and debris of every sort as well, for things had been hurtled from shelves, pieces of the bomb had splintered the wood-work, as it seemed a black Bedlam at first. Then, my eyes and ears grew accustomed quite soon. I found two of my Americans just getting down. They were very sick, so I rushed up and got stretchers and covers for them.

There was a little French nurse, an Algerian, Mme. Florio, who was perfectly fine. She is a little burnt dip of a thing, but she had nerve and self-possession both. After getting those two men settled, I hurried off to make the rounds of "my" men, of course, to see if there was any way to help any of them down. Just two were hurt very slightly with little slivers of glass. Almost all of them were already downstairs. I had a time getting a "diphtheria boy", who had had burns from gas, downstairs. We couldn't find any stretcher-bearers, so I held one arm across my shoulder and almost carried him down. He was very sick and miserable. Mme. Florio was very dramatic about him. As I started up to get him, she said, "Nurse! Where are you going?" I said, "For a patient." She said, "I will go with you." I tried to make her go back, as I was sure I could get him down all right by myself; but she got quite excited, caught my arm and trotted up with me, crying, "Ah non! If you die, I will die with you. We are allies. In my country, we are like that. If we are together, it is till death." I told her I hoped we would still have a long way to go! As a matter of fact, we had had our share of bombs already by then, one at the back and one just at the side (about forty feet from my office window) so I didn't really expect any more bombs.

One of the French nurses received a wound which is going to be fatal, it is feared. A morsel of shell came thru the window and wounded her in the stomach. She was here on a stretcher for some time and then taken to a surgical hospital. She was on the table for an hour and a half. The nurse (Mme. Loren) is not expected to live thru the night. She is quite conscious. She received the Croix de Guerre this afternoon. A French general presented it to her. He made her a little speech, saying that she had been a devoted and unselfish nurse, and that her courage had not failed her, and that it gave him pleasure to present her with that token of appreciation of her services, as felt by the President of France. She turned her head aside, and said, "Ah, mon général, pour quoi me donnez-vous ça? Je ne l'ai pas mérité." ("My general, why are you giving me this? I've not deserved it.") *She was very weak and white-looking, Mme Casteran said, and her little speech sounded very pathetic. The General looked at her and could say nothing for a minute, and tears streamed down his cheeks. He said, "Mais oui. Vous l'avez bien mérité."* ("But yes. You did well earn it.") *She said "Ça sera pour ma petite fille alors."* ("It will be for my little girl then.") *She has a little girl and she is leaving her almost alone in the world.*

They say there were a number of children killed in the town, too. But I have not heard that confirmed and the damage seems small compared with the number of bombs dropping.

The attack began a full month of German air raids on Beauvais. The second night (May 29) would be far more serious, more devastating. German bombs reduced the four-story hospital to a one-and-a-half-story facility. Natalie's reflexive acts of bravery in climbing four times during the deadly raid into the smashed upper floors to carry disabled patients to the basement would make her a war hero. She would become the only American woman to win the French Croix de Guerre in the Great War. Her gallantry would be widely reported by the French and American press. The distinction would earn her celebrity status in New Orleans after the war, whether or not she wanted it. Natalie never foresaw such recognition, her letter home offering only a brief account of the second raid. *We are evacuating all our patients to-day and are busy, busy, busy, as you can guess.*

We had another party last night, worse than before even, and there were two of them. All of the nurses from the pavilion decided to sleep in the hospital, thereby eliminating the time and risk of coming over . . . to the hospital. We had mattresses on the ground floor, and we kept our clothes on. We were all rather tired, but we didn't get turned in till about ten-thirty. And then, with fifteen women in a room, fourteen of them French and one of them I, you can imagine that silence was slow to spread its wings above us!

Just as I forgot the world, the flesh, and the devil, and sank into heavenly slumber, I heard that wicked, now familiar crash announcing our friends, the enemy. Mme. Florio, at my side, shook me, and I grumbled sleepily, "Déja!" Then I shook myself, got on my helmet and old brown coat (do tell Hilda!) and rushed out. The crashes were thick by then. I rushed up the steps to get my boys down. My sickest patients are on the top floor. As I reached the second landing, there was a perfectly deafening crash and I was thrown against the wall. Glass splintered everywhere and plastering, too. Someone called that a bomb had struck the officers' quarters which started me up again instantly, from a second's daze. The boy who was worst off of all was just above the officers' quarters. The top floor was black. Men rushing downstairs for shelter almost swept me along, but I made the top floor, which was black. I rushed along the corridor, feeling the wall as I ran.

The boy, a gas patient, badly burned and with diphtheria, was on a side corridor. Doors and part of the wall (just a little, it turned out) had fallen across it. I got down then to find him safe, but everything tumbled and mashed about him. I got two Americans, whom I caught on their way down, and they took him down for me, while I went for others. There were only four who could not get themselves down. Those four I almost carried, holding a hand with their arm across my shoulder. It was quite the most exciting time I have ever had, for there was a deafening din and crash of bombs all the time, and flashes, too. Even our eminently respectable parson was moved to the soulful utterance that "Hell had broken loose", so I suppose I can quote him.

Natalie's letter omitted the fact that she had ascended the four flights of stairs, alone, four times during the attack, each time carrying another wounded soldier down to the cellar, where everyone else had settled. The subsequent reports of the Médecin-Chef recorded the full story of her heroism.

Emergencies went on through the night. *Of course, there were the busy times of getting stretchers and blankets and gargles and other necessities. Fortunately, we had evacuated the three stomach cases that afternoon, so we were spared mustard plasters. Three Americans came in, two wounded and the Ambulance driver. A house had been bombed and fallen on their ambulance, crushing it to pieces, and they had escaped with just the most minor injuries. A little boy, a dear little fellow of just about eight, was brought in wounded.*

By the time I had made all my rounds to see that all of my boys were down, things had calmed down. I slipped out for the

Annex, because I was worried about our nurses and boys there. I found the street blocked with ruins,—the remains of several houses simply pulverized to fine dust, almost, piled up in the street higher than I am. I climbed over (especially difficult because of my game foot, and because I had no slippers on, having rashly bestowed mine on a patient). I stepped on something I thought was a sack. But several who were working busily to pull away the ruins and get to the victims, turned their lanterns there just then and I saw that it was what had once been a horse. It was quite flat. I went on quickly. I knew that there were people just like that and it is a grim thought. Of course, as a matter of fact, like that they are killed quickly and mercifully and do not suffer, but it gives you a physical shudder somehow to think of it.

The annex was all right. They had received two Americans wounded, too, from another Ambulance which had had a house tumbled on it. The Ambulance was torn to shreds above, and the litters were even cut, but the men were not hurt. I looked at it, with the driver. Neither of us could understand how it possibly happened; but we were just thankful. Two other Americans were not so fortunate. They were crushed to death under the house that was torpedoed next to us.

There was another alert at two; but in between I stretched out for a minute's relaxation, and then again at three-thirty. At five, I went the rounds of my patients again, and left the stretcher ones sleeping peacefully. Several journalists have been here and so has Major Murphy, and everyone is busy as can be. The Boche plane came over at noon, I suppose to take pictures, and we expect a worse raid than ever (if possible) to-night. I don't know where I'll be transferred to. I am sorry to see H.C.A. #42 break up, but it is obviously the only thing to do.

I think things will calm down here probably, as soon as we begin evacuating the hospitals, so, whatever you do, don't worry. And, if anything should happen (and I assure you I don't in the least expect it), remember that I have had a share of happiness enough for several lives anyway,—that my little group of family and friends, and especially Muddie,—is enough and more than enough for anyone. I can't think of anyone who has lived more happily and fully than I have. This life over here gives just a little suggestion of being useful, too, so that I have everything that anyone can have. Eternity is mirrored in such a happy present.[22]

Then Natalie hurried off to help Captain Garrett, who was *appalled by a prospect of going off in a pair of brown flannel pajamas, which are all the clothes he has just now . . . mild despair, very comically.* She added a final postscript. *We are making great precautions and are going to get our patients in the cellar to-night* before *the raid begins, which is, I'll admit, a relief to me. It took more determination last night for me to skip up those steps than it had for me to jump off the end of the wharf the first few times!*

The idea to move everyone into the cellars originated, in part, with Natalie, who realized the certainty of more German bombing raids. *I asked the Médecin-Chef to have the stretcher-cases taken downstairs at the beginning of the evening, and he said it was a good idea. I thought that he would have them left on the first floor. He had them all taken to the cellar and ordered all the other patients down there, too. Many of the men, French and Americans, who were able to walk, went out to the woods. Every one expected an awful night.*

One of the doctors, who is French Protestant and very proud of it, and is most serious minded besides, hunted me up to say a last farewell. He held my hand and recited the second chapter of St. John (I think) in French to me. I was terribly embarrassed. I didn't really enjoy having him hold my hand all the while, but I didn't at the same time like to interrupt St. John. So I stood and looked foolish, wondering idly what sort of expression would be the proper one for the occasion. As a matter of fact, the passage was beautiful, and I suppose I should blush to laugh about it; but it was ridiculous.

The Médecin-Chef told me that he was glad I was not nervous. "You know, this will be a diabolical night. They took pictures to-day at noon. To-night is the last night of _____! To-night, _____ will go up in smoke, in ash, in blood. To-morrow, there will not be a stone left standing on another." The poor man has been constantly harassed the last few days and, while he is so cool and calm, the strains had made him take the gloomy view of things. I didn't answer him for a second. Then I suddenly said, "Why, I thought you said you were going to evacuate your patients to-morrow. How can you if there is not a stone left standing?" He laughed and laughed, and it really did him good.

Natalie worked until 10:30 that night getting the patients settled on their mattresses in the cellar, then was ordered into an adjacent cellar where more mattresses had been packed in for nurses and staff. Two American officers were also there, including Captain Garrett, an engineer and former Cornell professor described by Natalie as *one of those cheerful people, who have nice crinkly laughter lines at the corners of their eyes.*

I had my French helmet and gas-mask, as ordered, and a pitcher of milk besides, for luck. Several steps took us to where a square patch of light shone across our expanse of utter darkness. We stumbled toward the light and found a wide, square chamber (it was about the center from which four narrow passages led off into darkness). The nurses were already ensconced. Unfortunately, one of them, the fattest, insisted I should sleep by her in one of the radiating corridors, which were about 3 feet wide. I managed to squeeze in,—but such a squeeze! I lay on my side and could move only my upper arm and one foot. Captain Garrett took up his place with his mattress at my foot, a poilu and a little French nurse were at my head. We were all so turned and so glad to lie down, we made foolish remarks and went off into gales of laughter.

An alerte sounded and a barage followed dulled by the thick brick walls about us. I went to sleep in the middle of it till three-o'clock. Then I waked up with a start, half paralyzed on my nether side and not able to move a muscle. You know how I hate being underground anyway. Mme. Martin waked up, but even together we couldn't get me up, and we had to call the poilu for help. The three of us extricated me. I saw my pitcher of milk. So I sat on a big stone, and took a sip, eating all the cheese and a sandwich one of the girls had, in the meanwhile!

So the 'fire, and ashes and blood' didn't materialize. Delayed anyway.

Later in the day, Natalie received terrible news and added a paragraph before the letter was taken by her friend Bishop McCormick to be mailed in Paris. *I am horribly shaken up, bewildered. I have heard that my friends of Major Ford's outfit have been killed. I am trying to hope it may not be so. But sometimes nothing seems too horrible to believe. I haven't got myself adjusted yet.*

One of our pneumonia cases has suddenly got worse. I'll be up with him all night. He doesn't want me to leave for an instant, poor fellow.

Do notice the rose-leaves. There are kisses in each of them for all of you and my very dearest love, and for you always and always L.C.'s.[23]

Chapter Five

The War Nurse

In his 1940 autobiography, Dr. Hugh Young (by then America's best-known surgeon), who visited Natalie in Beauvais shortly after the bombings, wrote that the hospital's roof "had been blown off" and that Natalie made daring rescues of disabled soldiers, dashing repeatedly to the fourth floor through the wreckage and bombing fury after the rest of the "staff had taken to the cellars." Internal Red Cross reports during early June 1918 cited her valor: "Major Murphy reported to the Chief Nurse what he considered to be a very stunning piece of bravery on the part of Miss Natalie Scott at No. 42. A few days later, Ms. Scott showed great devotion to duty and forgetfulness of self at the time of another raid when, although completely worn out, she remained day and night at the side of a dying American patient."[1]

The war in France had reached its decisive phase in June. The same American newspaper editions that reported Natalie's heroism also headlined successes of the German offensive. Rheims was falling, and the Germans were reaching the Marne and taking the Paris-Chalôns railway as the Allied forces retreated another eighteen miles. As the Germans swept forward northwest of Soissons, the Allies fell back to the Ailette River; in the salient between the Somme River and the Aisne battlefields, the Allies were in retreat. To the east, the German wedge, with its flanks below Soissons and Rheims, seemed poised to drive down the Oise valley to Paris. Beauvais lay deep within the perimeter of this furious, bloody storm.[2]

The summer of 1918 would complete the transformation of Natalie Scott into a veteran war nurse, as she, the doctors, and nurses of Beauvais tended the needs that overwhelmed the fifteen local hospitals. Such work would test the endurance of the human spirit.

Natalie knew nothing of the American newspaper accounts or Red Cross reports. She would not realize she had made news across the country back home until July, when clippings arrived from her mother. Meanwhile, the demands upon her at the hospital remained incessant as the Germans persisted with their air attacks on Beauvais. *Such frantic times! There has not been an instant to get my breath. Just now, I am sitting in the meningitis ward where there is an English boy very sick.*

These days have been so busy. After the raids, we began evacuating patients very rapidly. Then one nice, dear old country boy who had been gassed and then had measles, developed pneumonia. He was very sick and I stayed with him constantly almost. He was a great big strong fellow, very good and plain and sweet. He always wanted to be up, and I would scold him, just pleasantly. Then the Red Cross sent and asked me to stay with a lieutenant at Hospital #14.

Major Murphy had gone by #14 and decided that I was tired and had insisted that I should dine with him. I refused, because I had to get my patients stowed away, some in the cellar and some on the first floor, and, most of all, I wanted to see how Nolan, my sick boy, was. But Major Murphy said I could have an hour to do that and then dine with him. So I agreed.

We went out to dinner, and, even with an undercurrent of worry, I relaxed and was happy. When I stopped by here, on my way back to staying up that night with Lt. Arnold, I found that Nolan was dead. It nearly killed me to think that I hadn't been with him. I stood and looked at him, and looked at him. I couldn't believe there wasn't life still there. Only a little while before, he had been telling me his troubles, looking at me with those trustful eyes of his. I couldn't take it in. For a minute, all my thoughts went wild. But some of the boys, who didn't even know that Nolan had gone, came and called me for another patient so I went one to the other, with the momentum of habit till gradually my equilibrium came back.

Not that I should ever forget the boy, or lose the horrible poignant regret that I wasn't with him. Major Murphy was wonderfully good. He insisted on sending the ambulance to take me up to No. 14 and he went up with me. It was sadness again. My patient was the most lovable boy, just a youngster of 22, shot through the lung,—a touch of boyish arrogance, which seemed painfully touching in all of this suffering, half petulant one minute, and then the next apologizing ever so sweetly. I thought of Albin and Ledoux (the brothers of Sidonie Provosty Scott) *and all of those youngsters of ours. I just waited on him hand and foot every instant. He said, "I wish I had had a sister who could come over here like you." Such remarks are my treasures. "These are my jewels."*

He had a lazy old Southern drawl. He asked if I was a Southern girl,—when I said, "yes", he sighed and said "I am glad you are Southern." He called me nothing but honey *and* dear, *in his poor old tired voice. I said, "Isn't there any nice girl back in America you want me to write to for you?" He said, "I'll think." In a few minutes he said, with his eyes closed, "You ready to write, dear?" And I said, "Yes". He said, "All right, begin. 'Dear Aunt and Folks.'" I would just imagine how, "Dear Aunt and Folks" would feel about that letter,—just a few lines as it was.*

Once, he was propped up in bed, he pushed the covers back and saw a big circle of blood, where his wound had bled. He looked at it distastefully and said, "Looks like an awful lot of blood wasted, doesn't it, honey?" I said, "Not wasted." He looked at me and smiled. Another time, he said, apologetically, "You must be awfully tired. I suppose you think I am pretty cross." I told him how sweet and good he was, and how we knew his Aunt and grandmother must just think the world of him and miss him horribly. He said, "They do. They do." Then he thought a minute and added, sadly, "This will break their hearts." He said that he wasn't lonesome at all; and added, very proudly, "I'm never lonesome. Poor fellows! I was company commander. I had 150 men under me. That's a lot for a kid, you know."

Natalie had stayed with him all night the first Saturday in June and, on Sunday, he was weak and delirious but recognized her. *I took him some fruit and eggs and the sweetest little flowering red geranium all in my nice old basket which all of the boys know. He watched the things come out of the basket, as interested as a child at Xmas. Now I must hurry and go to his funeral this morning. Somehow, it seems the saddest one of all. And he was so young and did so well. I had a huge spray of roses sent him. I feel as tho I should like to bury him in roses.*[3]

Natalie apologized for the gloominess of her letters, assuring Muddie of her steady cheerfulness with *the boys. I found that soon I felt as cheerful as I acted! It is curious, too, how often these days I think of my old Horatius. "To every man upon this earth death cometh soon or late, . . . how can man die better than by facing fearful odds, For glory of his country and the honor of his God."—Do you remember how I used to ring it out, and how excited I used to get over it. I still love its bold spirit and its buoyant virility. And I think of it often as I look at our boys who have found 'best death'.*

The hospital had been badly damaged, especially the upper floors and roof. Inside walls had collapsed, and windows throughout the hospital were blown out. Forced to house the entire patient population downstairs on the first one and a half floors, Natalie and her fellow nurses stayed in the hospital around the clock.

Here it is, six in the morning. We had a hot and heavy raid last night, served in three courses. I sent them all to the cellar, except the cerebro-spinal meningitis. We have him in his place on the first floor, but I have to stick to his side. He is the most restless, doesn't keep still an instant. I stay in here at night, too, because sometimes the night nurses can't do anything with him. Last night you would have thought from the racket that there wouldn't be a stone left standing—it was going up in smoke, and flame, and blood—as the Médecin-Chef said. We have raids almost every night now. Lots of people leave town every night, tho, and go to sleep in the woods. The Red Cross expedites its nurses to a chateau six miles out, but I don't go, as I am the only American in this hospital. A great many casualties are prevented in that way. A bomb tumbled on top of a little orphan asylum and all of the inmates would have been killed.[4]

Twelve of Natalie's favorite patients left in mid-June. *One was Palmer, a gassed boy who came to us with diphtheria and very bad gas burns on his legs. He was one of those who couldn't walk, and whom I got down with such difficulty during the first raids. I would think of raids every time I looked at him. He was the most comical fellow. He makes capital of his infirmities. His voice is a whisper as a result of the gas, and, because of his burns he has to walk with his legs crooked apart, in the most gingerly manner, so that he looks like a big crawfish. He is not more than thirty but his face has deep quizzical lines on it, and his long, thick straight hair is always in disorder. He has a great big mouth and several gold teeth. He will get up and shuffle*

about, then stop, and say something funny in this hoarse whis-
per of his, and everybody is convulsed.

He is a floor-walker in a millinery establishment! In the same
ward with him is a plasterer. He can discuss modern literature
and modern authors with a thoroughness and discernment
which keeps you on the Qui-vive. I used to be a little skeptical
about Kipling's remarks on our stenographers who discuss
Ibsen with such ease, but he knows whereof he spoke. The plas-
terer has his own opinion of Conrad, Burnett, Chesterton, and
Tarkington, and Rex Beach, and he supports them ably and log-
ically. He has done cement work, too, and he loves out-of-doors
and lots of exercise. "But there's more money in plastering." He
enjoyed Palmer tremendously. Palmer said he didn't like any
out-of-door exercise "except", he added as an afterthought,
"driving a car". They were always referring delightedly to
Palmer's 'automobile muscle'.

In that ward was Hymes, who seldom spoke, and always
grinned, and Jim Kelly, whom Boss would love,—home in
Kildane, Ireland, and his birth right still intact, a brogue as
thick as Boss's best, and a solemn face that gets positively sad
when he makes a joke. Then there's a youngster of nineteen,
who listens to them all impartially, and never talks unless the
conversation hits one of a choice number of themes, where he is
eloquent. I feel as tho the Shamrocks should spring into bloom
wherever the feet of Jim Kelly touch the soil. He looks the soul of
gloom and makes no remark for several minutes. Then forth
into the world he launches an Irish-ism in its native garb of
brogue that sets the ward rocking with laughter. Tell Boss I
know he's related to Big Mike on the Levee.

I enjoy them so much. There is the scarlatina boy, nineteen,
the oldest of a family of seven. I went to see him last night after
ten and found him still awake. I said, "Why, you should have
been asleep long ago. What have you been doing?" He said, "I
have just been thinking." "And what about? How do you make
your fortune after the war? Or how to win the next battle?" He
said, "No'm. I was just thinkin' how nice it would be when I did
get home." Poor little fellow. I sat down and talked to him a
good little while, and when I left he was telling me that, "after
the war there'd be two kinds of men, those who was in this
thing and those that wasn't." The crowd that left yesterday was

a combination, too. There was one, Mr. Stiffen, the happiest-hearted little Italian Jew you ever saw. He was always in a good humor, always talking and playing foolish jokes. He would give away anything in the world. And everyday he would spend from thirty to forty francs (six or seven dollars!) on cokes, and treat everyone in the hospital to them.[5]

There was a convalescing patient named McDonald, one of three soldiers who had come in from town drunk. *The next evening, I got permission for the other boys to go out; but not for the three black sheep. I was really afraid they would sulk. So I told them perfectly, frankly and pleasantly, too, why I didn't get permission for them, that I was sorry I couldn't. I brought the graphaphone up for them, and tried to make things pleasant for them in the ward. And they were sweet as they could be.*

The next day I got permission for all of them to go out. When they were gone about a half an hour, one of the sergeants here called me to go and get one of 'my Americans',—that he was drunk, and quarreling with a Frenchman and had threatened him with his revolver. I thought immediately and with a sinking heart of McDonald, Irish and hot-tempered, tall, and dark, and strong. I ran out, and saw him, as I thought. The crowd opened for me, and I said to him very quietly, "come with me at once, McDonald. Don't say another word to any of these people. You are disgracing your uniform." I turned and he came with me without a word. It was plain that he was very drunk. I could really have wept with disappointment. I said, "When did you have the rum, McDonald?" He looked at me, smiled sheepishly, and said, "My name's not McDonald, Ma'am." And it wasn't he! He looked rather like him, and I had dreaded it so much that I had taken it for granted. Anyway, when my boys all came in, as sober as judges, about ten minutes before their time was up, I could have embraced old McDonald.

A French captain invited several at the hospital, including Natalie, for an excursion outside of town to examine the mistrailleuse gun placements, which were used to combat the German air raids. *Mme. Hüch, Mme. Casteran du Rais, and I went. First of all, we had coffee with the Captain and his lieutenant in their tiny quarters. He had made for us a most delicious crème. And afterwards, we had coffee with cognac. But we had to climb the hill to see the mistrailleuse, quite deep down in a round hole gorged into the hill-side and camouflaged with green boughs. I went down with the lieutenant following. We must have made an amusing picture, down in that hole in the ground, I listening solemnly and the lieutenant launching volumes of enthusiastic technical details at me! The others simultaneously burst out laughing,—which didn't daunt the lieutenant in the least. He suggested I should go up the first clear evening and stay there for a raid! I took him seriously, of course, and was all for doing it. But the Captain was horrified at the suggestion.*

The hill itself was lovely and gave a wonderful view for miles about. The old city, setting for the great cathedral which dominates it entirely, was just below. The English aviators say we have 'the Hun's number', that he is afraid of our fire and tumbles his bombs anywhere. This looked like it. Everything looked so fresh and spring-like that the ugly bomb holes seemed an unreality,—like the blotch of Prussianism on the face of civilization. Two gorgeous rainbows spanned the whole sky from horizon to horizon,—and one end lay where our troops were fighting. We could hear the muffled roaring of their guns. As we watched the whole wonderful scene, in the glory of a sunset with its colors all freshened and more vivid after the rain, avions circled over us. Suddenly, we saw a signal-rocket go up. The men said they were Boche signals. Many followed the first.

We are all in ecstasies over our good news today,—a thousand prisoners, and an advance which is almost general. We are simply jubilant. An English plane has just dived down low over us and I could even see the pilot wave. An English brigade has been here just since the 3rd and has "got" fifty "Huns". This news I just heard to-day from another aviation lieutenant I met. Isn't that cheering. Fifty blotches removed from the fair face of the earth.[6]

Headlines for Heroism

Natalie's foot problem nagged her through June, compounded by a finger infection on her left hand that, despite treatment, worsened until Dr. Clark caught a glimpse of it, examined it, and ordered her to immediately see the surgeon at the American Hospital. *He* (Dr. Clark) *picked me up on the spot in spite of all remonstrances and took me off. Dr. Clark had just got his car from the Red Cross and was elated with it. I told him I thought it was more for the chance of showing off his car than for caring for my finger that he made me go.* The surgeon, Dr. Moorehead, excised the wound, removing dead skin, and repeated the minor surgery over and over again during the next few days, redressing the finger each time.

Muddie's letters from home informed Natalie that she had been headlined as "Air Raid Heroine" in newspaper accounts of events in Gisors and Beauvais. Natalie discounted all of it. *Reports to Paris have done me a good turn again about work here, referring especially to the bombardments I believe. Miss Stimson, who is Chief Something or other, and a very nice woman, was here the other day and told us this. That sort of thing is really foolish, that is, as far as personalities are concerned, because anyone who has the luck to be on the spot, would do the same thing,—or more![7]*

Waves of changes in the medical hierarchy occurred in Beauvais, with many of Natalie's friends receiving promotions. Most pleasing to Natalie was the promotion of Major Murphy. *I am perfectly delighted. He is so good and so able. I saw him the night he received his promotion, and he did not even mention it. I was dining with Mr. Telstead and he came over to speak to us. I think really he would have told me, if there had not been someone else there. A propos of him, you know he was here 'the morning after' one of our first bombardments and got all of the lurid details fresh from various ones of the French nurses, and from us. He saw all the débris and asked about everything. Out of the accumulation of these things, it seems he has concocted a most exciting story which he tells, and Miss Stimson embodied it in her report to Paris. Dr. Clark saw it when he was there.*

Then, with the line of combat moving farther away from Beauvais, the aviation camp was to be broken up, the pilots reassigned. Natalie spent an evening of revelry with a large aviation group. At an impromptu farewell party at the Hotel de France et Angleterre, she was the dinner guest of Mr. Carlson and Mr. Telstead, her Australian patient (an aviator).

The place was smart as a whip with uniforms, and full of good-looking men who wore them, with an almost insolent ease the English have,—so stalwart and trim and well-groomed they are. There were various French uniforms, too, more dashing, still. "There's so-and-so," Mr. Telstead would say. "He fell (so-many) thousand feet out of control a few days ago, and recovered just four hundred feet from the ground." "And see that slim blond fellow, the second from the end. He has just got the D.F.C. (Distinguished Flying Cross). He went for five Huns single-handed and got three of them and made his get-away." "And there's so-and-so. He got lost over Hun-land, and he got four Huns before he found himself, all in one afternoon. He has the D.F.C. and the M.C. (Military Cross), too." And so on, indefinitely.

Major Murray-Jones and I had met before, and he came up to speak to me, feeling very badly because of the beginnings of "Flu", as they call Influenza (I tell them it is no wonder that, with such a name, it has so invaded the Flying Corps!). Major Bell came up to him as he talked to me, and stood laughingly waiting to be introduced. He thought I was French, and tried to speak to me in French. Just for fun, I answered him in very rapid French, and, of course, the others were delighted at his dismay, as well as his mistake. Each of these officers had decorations. Captain Phillips, who couldn't have been a day over twenty-five, came up, too. He had two decorations, and when I told him to be really gallant and tell me how he won them, he said they were for eating strawberry jam.

You can never realize that just a few hours makes a difference for these men, a difference between doing things that the world stops to admire and chatting like school-boys on a holiday. So many of them are almost school-boys, too.

The aviators were all to leave the next day, their field to close. *Many did. But others! Major Murray-Jones succumbed to Flu in camp and two others fell before it in town. The doctor had gone on ahead, and poor Mr. Telstead, who was by no means recovered, was the healthiest of the lot. There was the Major ill at the deserted camp, with no food and absolutely refusing to come to the hospital or even to town,—and Telstead with no French to meet the exigencies of the occasion. Meanwhile, Capt. Forrest, who had stayed to fly one of the planes over, fell ill, too. He refused to come to the Hospital, and yet he had to have treatment.*

Behold us, a troubled pair, in consultation. The Médecin-Chef is always a present help in time of trouble. He prescribed, giving "absent treatment" to the ailing heroes. Then a tour of the whole of this town in a tender, a perfectly enormous prairie-wagon (horse-drawn) *structure, with Mr. Telstead and me perched sedately on the front seat, I quite demure in my nurse's veil. Milk, and oranges, and lemons, and sugar, and vichy water, and gimming [lime],—you will never know how much time and conversation can be expended in getting these things in small quantities! But it was finally done.*[8]

More wounded German prisoners became patients at the hospital, a situation governed by strict rules against fraternizing. *We have a little Boche prisoner here now, with a wound and scarlatina combined. I dutifully stayed away from him when he first came, knowing the rules. He was quite young and pitiful-looking and I would have liked to say just 'good morning' in my poor German. I said just enough to find out how he slept and what hurt him. He was very grateful. The French men are quite good to him, give him his drink, and help him in lots of ways, because he is almost helpless. They are certainly the kindest race in the world.*

Yesterday, I helped dress his wound. Afterwards, he asked if he might have some lemonade to drink. They give it a great deal here; so I went and asked the old orderly,—the homeliest, best old soul you ever saw, if he might have the lemonade. He said, severely, "No. All the care they need, these Boches, yes. But no whims. No whims." And he turned and went off. I knew this was the accepted attitude, so I said nothing. An instant later, he was at my side. "It is true", he said, "that they are Boche. But, after all, it is not their fault. It is a great misfortune. And this, when the man is suffering. And when he is just a boy." And he was gone, and then back in a minute with a big bottle of lemonade.

Then came a visit from Dr. Hugh Young, the heroic physician Natalie and Pressy had admired so much in Paris, recently promoted to colonel. He brought news of Major Lambert. *As I came up to the hospital, from the American Hospital, I saw a big U.S. touring car in front of the gate. I wondered what distinguished visitor could have come in it. And out came Major,—Colonel Young! I was so pleased to see him and so surprised! He was just as full of fun and jolly and entertaining as ever. He insisted on seeing all our ruins and took my picture in front of them. He said he was going on thru, and just stopped to see me for an instant. He brought me greetings from Major Lambert, who had just returned from America, after being made president of the American Medical Association.*

And soon he was asking me to dinner! I was delighted, of course, but I said, "I thought you were going on through." He laughed and said, "O, I've changed my mind." I was so pleased that I simply chattered all the time. And afterwards I was disconsolate! There was no telling when he will ever be back here again, for this is quite a way from his beaten track, and I shall never forgive myself for talking so much, instead of making him talk![9]

In early July as Natalie opened a letter from Muddie, a number of newspaper clippings tumbled out in front of several English aviators. They noticed Natalie's photographs and name in headlines about her heroism during the Beauvais bombings, which left her horrified and embarrassed. *And they were as sweet and impressed as they could be. Dr. Greenough came in at the time, and she read, and she was just as nice as she could be. And I wanted devoutly to crawl under the bed. Think of those men, who run tremendous risks every day of their normal lives almost seeing all of the headlines about me,—and all because I trotted some soldier-boys down some steps! I went to dinner at the A.C. [American Club] the other night, and they all teased me to death, calling me the "heroine of Beauvais" and threatening to set my statue up opposite that of the lady who is the Heroine. It seems that the Paris newspaper had various stories about me. I never saw them, but Colonel Young told me about them and so have various others. I asked the newspaper men here not to use my name at all, but they are not answerable, apparently.*

However, Muddie, I could see that you enjoyed my ill-gotten fame, so I don't care. And I am delighted that Newcomb was pleased, too. I only wish I could do something to deserve the local opinion. Natalie made another letter entry a couple of days later on the same subject. *A propos of the newspaper articles you sent, tho, I must tell you that I heard something just as worrisome, but pleasant anyway (since I have no conscience, and don't mind ill-gotten glory!—or, perhaps, just undeserved glory). Mr. Lowery tells me to-day that Miss Stimson sent in a report both to Paris and to Washington in which she gave a glowing account of yours-truly! He says it sounds like a moving-picture story and he just came around again to make sure that he did know me. There were, in all, five really exciting nights, and they seem distant memories now; so you can imagine what a jar it is*

*to have one of them brought up again with me figuring in it,—
especially in such an unnatural light!*

A farewell party was held at the American Club for four of
Natalie's aviation patients who were returning to combat duty.
*Mr. Collins, one of the officers, played the piano very well. The
boys call him Paddy. Mr. Paxton plays the mandolin, all of them
sing. And they would sing everything southern for me,*
Kentucky, *and* Alabama, Tennessee, *and I want to see My Home
in Dixie,—and, of course, I would applaud enthusiastically.
Finally the boys sang* Cheerio, *as farewell. You must know*
Cheerio *at home by now: we all love it. The chorus goes, "Bon
soir, old thing, Cheerio, chim-chim, N'a pas (Il n'ya plus!) Too-
ra-loo, Good-bye—ee." The boys always sing it, and their
favorite part is "Well, bon soir, old thing. Cheeri-o",—this even
to me! Curley took lots of pictures of me with a little Kodak,
some of me dressed up in some of his aviation togs, the big
leather coat, the leather fur helmet, the goggles and boots. I
hated to see all of those boys go,—and break up the 'squadron'.*

*Everyone is leaving here now, it would seem. Colonel
Murphy came by yesterday to say good-bye. I thought it was
very sweet of him, because he had received orders to go to
Headquarters and to leave in an awful hurry. I hate to see them
all leaving. But I am getting rather philosophical about it; for
there always seems to be a compensation some-where,—someone else nice turns up.*[10]

They celebrated the Fourth of July at the American Club with
a party for all the Beauvais hospitals hosted by Colonel Besson
and the First Engineers Regiment. The evening featured dancing,
vaudeville acts, skits, and performances concocted by patients
and staff. On July 14, the French national holiday, the big event
of the evening was a special theater program in town. *The Théâtre
des Armées was in town to give a show! We got there just in time
for a lovely selection from Tosca, sung by one of the artists from
the Opéra Comique and from the Opéra in Paris. The program
was given entirely by the very best of French artists, from all the
best theatres of Paris. There was a very clever comedy, some
Alsatian dancers, a comedian (who sang the most unspeakable
songs) and then a comedy of Molière's, which was very funny
indeed. My poor gallant escorts, tho, were bored to grief and suffering. Mr. Van Fleet never before realized how tired he was of*

hearing the French language! They were very funny. You can imagine Nauman under the circumstances!

One very effective touch, very French of course, was the presentation of a lovely bouquet of flowers to the prima donna in La Tosca, *by a poilu. He was a real poilu, just fresh from the trenches, and wounded in the arm, and just an ordinary, good old soul. The prima donna kissed him on both cheeks, and, of course, the audience stormed applause. Later, an American soldier presented a bouquet to the Alsatian dancer. Of course, he, a patient from one of the hospitals, too—was embarrassed and delightfully awkward and a ripple of friendly laughter spread through the audience. It swelled to a real surge of merriment when the dancer kissed* him, *too, on both cheeks; for he, unaccustomed to such demonstrations, made a tentative effort to return the salute! You can imagine how we all enjoyed that!*

On the same row with us were eight or ten with every conceivable sort of head-wound,—lots of them with various pieces of apparatus on for holding their jaws in place and so on. And

An audience of wounded, photograph taken by Natalie on stage (Beauvais or Nantes, 1918). *Courtesy of Special Collections, Tulane University Libraries*

*all through the audience, bandages, splints, and all sorts of
such evidence of war. But the audience was a very gay one, just
the same.*[11]

Natalie had been late for the concert because she gave a party
for patients who could not leave the hospital, the French and
Americans together enjoying the occasion. *We borrowed the big
graphaphone from the American Club. Some of the French
nurses heard all the gaiety and came to investigate so I asked
them to stay. I tried my best to get some of the Frenchmen to
sing, but it couldn't be done. Then I began on the Americans.
Finally, I found an earnest-looking little red-haired fellow with
a pug-nose, who said that, altho he didn't have any voice at all,
he'd try. But he squared his shoulders and threw his head back
and did his best. Afterwards, it was easy to find other people to
sing, French and Americans. The party was a great success,
tho,—so great that it had to be broken up finally, in order that
the patients might get some sleep.*

*I couldn't love these plain, fine old fellows any more no mat-
ter what happened, all so different, and yet all indefinably alike
in their Americanism. It seems to be, I think, their common
standard of ideals,—a simple, "this is right, and that's wrong"
which they just accept with a perfect faith. Of course, they don't
put these ideals into words or reason about it in that way; but
it is amusing and beautiful to see how they are always there,
the pivot, immovable, on which their arguments turn. Our
politicians and 'higher minds' may argue as to whether or not
we are really fighting for democracy, but our men never doubt
it, nor do they argue as to what democracy really is. They feel
it as something as holy and perhaps as mysterious as the Holy
Grail. And I find them as fine as the knights of old,—
Launcelots, and Tristans, and Galahads, too.*

Transformation

As Natalie's birthday approached, she purposely opened no
letters from home for the last week, saving each delivery for July
18. When the day arrived, she privately buried herself in the
world of New Orleans, brought forth by letters from classmates
Carm Janvier and Adèle Drouet, Sidonie, her brother Nauman,

her parents, and many others. *It meant a trip home for me and then your letter, yourself. Of course, there were my dear* little *blue flowers of big happiness. And Boss, with all those gr-r-rand Irish messages of his, and perfectly enormous donation.* Dr. Clark surprised Natalie by putting her on the telephone with the Paris Red Cross headquarters so she could speak to Pressy. *I was certainly delighted to hear the old girl's voice again, just as buoyant and delighted and pleased as ever, and as cordial. She wants me to go to Paris for a rest and visit her and 'Aunt Ruth' in their new quarters in the Hotel Castiglione. Some time or other, perhaps I shall.*

Natalie's patients managed to host a party for her, featuring fruit juice. *When I went to my room that night, what should I find but a perfectly enormous bouquet of all sorts of flowers, from 'Madame Florio et les infirmières amies de Miss Scott'. I had told them all about how we used the blue flowers for our birthdays and how they meant happiness.*

And yesterday morning, I came into my office to find a magnificent 'gerbe' (bouquet or sheaf, rather) of flowers, sweat peas and lovely carnations,—les ocilets de poète, they are called, because they are so sweet. It was tied with a great rosette of American and French ribbons intertwined. And it was from one of the French sergeants here. One of the nurses told me he had walked four kilometers out into the country to have it made! Don't you think I had a happy birthday?

The same letter reported the sensational news from the front lines. Large numbers of wounded arrived with fresh word. *And then, yesterday, the wonderful news.* Thousands *of prisoners, twenty villages, and the plateau overlooking Soissons! But think of the news! And followed this morning by the report that Soissons itself is recaptured! We are all rejoicing immeasurably. Yesterday afternoon we had some of them, seven, who had been in the attack that morning only. Think of it. Fresh news of it all. The boys we received from the offensive say they were packed in trucks one afternoon about four; they rode all that night until three in the morning, when they lay down an hour. Then they marched all that day and that night until two in the morning when they had two hours rest. Some of the troops got in just in time for the zero hour which was 4:35. They say the Germans were wholly surprised and the Americans took so many prisoners they didn't know what to do.*

*I saw a man who said he had talked to a lot of Boche prison-
ers who, as he said, were "sitting down there grinning and
swilling Red Cross chocolate",—as they were quite content to be
taken prisoner. I could write a book of the stories they all have
to tell. We are expecting lots of wounded to be evacuated here.
They sent for me to help out, because they were terribly
rushed.*[12]

As the Allied victories mounted, Natalie learned that Quentin
Roosevelt, Teddy's son whom she had enjoyed so much in Major
Lambert's office in Paris, had been shot down and killed. *I am so
sorry to see that Quentin Roosevelt is reported down in flames;
because, for one thing, he was really quite a fine little
American, as far as I could judge. You remember I wrote you
about him? And then Major Lambert liked him so much. I hope
perhaps it isn't true.*

News of another well-known soldier among the war dead
reached Natalie. She did not know the poet Joyce Kilmer, though
she admired his work. Like that of the young Roosevelt, Kilmer's
battlefield death seemed very personal to Natalie. *Have you read
of the death of Joyce Kilmer? It really gave me quite a shock
when I saw a poem signed by him, and printed underneath,
Killed July—(I forgot the date). I almost felt as tho it was someone I knew.—And I did, in a measure: By your works shall ye
be known. There were no particulars about his death, his regiment, or anything like that. I should like to know. If you have
seen anything about it, I would like to know.*[13]

It was Sunday, July 20, when the overcrowded American
Hospital sent for Natalie to come help. She was, for the first time,
put to work as a surgical nurse. Too busy, she did not write again
for a week. *We had stirring times. I was assigned to Ward I, on
the first floor, in the far wing of the building, filtering my way
in between the rows of stretchers. There were nurses moving
about quickly among them. Doctors were turning back the
blankets and making hurried examinations to determine the
order of operations, girls and orderlies were giving out hot soup
and hot chocolate. Very busy, very rushed, but there was
method and order in it all. For the most part, they were sleeping really passionately, anywhere they could get, simply overcome with fatigue.*

I found Ward I, a long, sunny room with twenty-four beds

and twenty patients in it. And, also, I found my nurse, Miss Wormwood, a small, round, and severe person, of thirty, I suppose, tho her slickly smoothed-back hair and glasses proclaimed indifference to the question. She had a tight, thin mouth that looked as tho its habitual action was snapping. I discovered afterwards that she is famous in the hospital for just that. However, I felt peacefully inclined, and made up my mind at once that I would be so meek that she couldn't find a rough edge anywhere to take hold of to start a fuss.

To a man, these patients had suffered major wounds. *There was a young soldier who had both legs shot up with machine-gun bullets. In one, the nerve had been injured and he had no feeling in it; while the other had only too much feeling. He called one Eliza and the other Jane, and the whole ward had accepted the appellations and used them quite complacently. He referred to Jane also as the "dead member".*

He came back from the dressing-room exhausted with pain. His face was twisted with pain, and as I went to help him from the stretcher, he said, thru his jutted teeth, "I can manage Eliza all right, if you'll just follow up with the 'dead member'. Keep her comin'." I grew very attached to Tolleffson. He is from Wisconsin. The doctors made every effort to save the leg, but had finally been compelled to amputate it. It was awfully hard on the poor fellow, after all the suffering to lose it after all. Natalie had assisted in the surgery. *I looked at the hideous wound, all ugly and old and diseased, and at the foot swollen and distorted with gangrene. The physical stress left me quite spent.*

Though her sensibilities were tested, circumstances transformed Natalie into a full nurse. Her amputation patient, Mr. Tolleffson, provided another example of her medical work. *You see, I had nothing to do with the dressings, which were really the most gruesome part of the work there. I would get the patients ready. Miss Wormwood would then 'assist' the doctor. Miss Wormwood was very jealous of this process and never had me near at all,—which just suited me. One day, I went up in the ward alone to borrow some sheets and found Captain Peck just about to dress an amputation. He had sent out for an orderly to hold the leg. As I arrived, he glanced up and saw me. He said to the orderly, "Have you ever done this before?" The orderly said, "No, sir." So Captain Peck called to me and said, "Miss Scott, I'd rather have you do it." I gazed at him for a second, and then I said, "O, but I haven't done it before, either."—and smiled pleasantly, and went on!*

A little while later he came in our ward. He came over to me, and said, in an aggrieved tone, "I should say you were a very independent nurse." I said, "But you didn't want the orderly, because he hadn't done it before." He said, "Well, but I asked you." I said, "But I didn't think you wanted me. Why didn't you ask me again?" He looked at me and burst out laughing. "How many times," he demanded, "do you require to be asked?" "That depends," I said. "But never mind. The next time I'll do what you ask me the very first thing." He said, "Agreed."

In one minute afterwards, he was calling me. I had thought I was safe in my ward, because Miss Wormwood was so jealous of her dressings. I went over to Tolleffson's bed where the doctor was. He ignored Miss Wormwood and said, "Miss Scott, will you please hold this leg?"

I did it. And I suppose I looked dismal, for the doctor thought I was going to faint. But I didn't faint. Poor old Tolleffson! He was as good as he could be.[14]

Natalie's work hours began before daybreak in order *to see my patients and be at the other hospital by 7:30.* After lunch, Natalie returned to HCA 42 to again make rounds and tend to paperwork, then it was back to the American Hospital as quickly as possible. *Then, at night, when I left there about a quarter of nine, back over here and around for a last look in on my little family here, which would get me turned in about eleven. I was thoroughly happy in it all and enjoyed every bit of it. But it would have me tired. And one of my patients here had to have an operation on his throat. He wanted me with him. I was helping the doctor, and was standing by the table. When he opened his eyes after, he looked right at me and smiled and said, "Hello".*

We got 20 Americans in the evening. I laughed and told them just to pretend they were millionaires or debutantes and to sleep late and have their coffee in bed, and read. None are very badly gassed. I took them the Stars and Stripes, tooth brushes and tooth-paste, writing-paper, chewing-gum, and tobacco. I was perfectly delighted to find one of my old patients over there among them. He grinned and said, as he shook hands cordially,

"Well, Miss Scott, it sure is good to see you. I was just tellin' the fellows that I bet we wouldn't be here long before we seen you."
I get letters every day from various patients. They pile up simply alarmingly. But I'll finish them up yet!

I had just finished writing a letter in answer to one from a very nice little fellow, Paul Webb, who was an aviator patient of mine, English, and had written me a very nice letter after he left. Mr. McDonnell came into the office and said, "Was there a Mr. Webb who was a patient here after you came." I said, "Yes", and "Why". Dr. Cowens had just received a letter saying that he had been killed. He was killed two days after he wrote to me. He was a young, young fellow, just about nineteen, an only son. I think his family is very distinguished. His father, or his uncle, I forget which, is a Duke. It was certainly a shock. I had just put the letter down after addressing it, and the name seemed to stare up at me as tho it had eyes. I shall try to write a note to his father and mother.[15]

In early August, Natalie was called upon to work a portion of each day in a third local hospital, this time to lift the spirits of blind soldiers isolated by the language barrier in a French facility. *Captain Hull told me about two English officers who are in an 'eye' hospital just a block from me (I told you we were a city of hospitals). Both of these poor fellows are in bed, wounded in legs and one eye, and they cannot read, or write, or play games, or do anything but lie there and think of their troubles. So Captain Hull suggested that I should go to visit them with him.*

I've been to that hospital before. It is the abode of dull sound and gloom. The sound is the awful one of making caskets, as there is an undertaking establishment next door. It reminds me of David Copperfield, *hearing the coffins made! The hospital is run by some of the towns people here, and it is an effort. The financial strain, after four years, is making itself very evident. So there are no little luxuries, nor even little comforts. The most dismal place you can think of.*

I found our officers. They were a lieutenant and a captain, both of the tanks, and in the room with them was a French officer, of the French tanks. He spoke English, too, and had the Croix de Guerre, two citations and a palm, and the Legion of Honor. One of the Englishmen, the lieutenant, was a cheerful soul. The captain was more refined, but less cheerful by far, the combination of an eye-wound, a French hospital and gloom. I soon found myself writing letters for the Captain. The poor fellow heaved such a sigh of relief and pleasure to think that they were written, that I was more than glad I had stayed on.

In the "eye hospital," Natalie also met a wounded French officer, Lt. Trurault, who struggled with depression over his loss of vision. She described a Sunday visit. *I saw his nurse on the street and she asked me to go to see him again and try to cheer him up a little. So I ran in to-day. Every time I would start to go he, and a little lieutenant of the Alpine Chasseurs would insist that I should stay. I wanted to finish my letter to you; so they said they would give me pen, ink, and paper, and would promise to be good and not disturb me, if only I would stay. So, here I am.*

It is a nice little ward, just six beds, all wounded officers. Poor Mr. Trurault is blind in both eyes just now. He has lost one, but the doctor thinks that he will regain the sight of the other. However, it was much better and is now bad again, so he, poor fellow, gets simply savagely blue, at times. Then he makes a great effort and is cheerful and gay. But it must be maddening not to know whether you will ever see again. Two Frenchmen out of French tanks have been in to "pay their respects" to Lt. Trurault. They were wounded by the new German anti-tank gun of which you may have read. In the room, besides, are a staff captain and lieutenant (all French) who were wounded by a bomb.

There was one who spoke Spanish quite well, and he and I teased the others by speaking Spanish. Then another spoke German, so he was charmed to have revenge on the "Spanish" by speaking Boche with me. Afterwards, my brain felt like a wet cloth wrung out! We didn't talk for just a few sentences, but for a long time on a stretch. It is quite wearing. And then they all started rapid French,—all teasing me, and I had to keep my poor brain on the qui vive to keep up some sort of repartee.[16]

War Work Deepens

Natalie wrote Muddie about a controversial but fascinating French nurse. The woman had scandalously left her husband, a prominent commandant in the French army, years earlier *in the company of another gentleman* and subsequently had numerous other affairs. *She is attractive in a bold sort of way; but she is not really vulgar, at all. Her hair is dyed, but cleverly and she makes up cleverly, too. She's a queer combination, for she has lots of good qualities, too. She is very kind-hearted, in a way, and always carries sugar in her pockets for her patients (and that is entirely a luxury). And yet sometimes she seems to be without feeling. She called me the other day and said she wanted to show me something very, very funny. She laughed all the way. It was a black, black Senegalese, who is dying with gas pneumonia. He doesn't speak any French or English, and he suffers constantly. The poor little thing can't be more than 18 or 19. She found his little black, black face, round pink tongue, white little round teeth, and yellow-white eyeballs very funny. The suffering in his poor little old black face made him seem much more tragic than a comic figure. I couldn't understand. So heartless about the little fellow. She is surely a queer character and I am fascinated watching her. She is perfectly crazy about American men; and pursues them and flirts. I am afraid you would be less tolerant of her than I am.*[17]

An English boy has been brought in, at noon, very sick with dysentery, and I am writing here just by the side of his bed. He is in a very bad way, and I am terribly afraid for him. He has a delicate face, and large, dark eyes; and he manages a suggestion of a smile for each little tiny thing I do for him, and sometimes 'thank you', in a whisper. I write five minutes, and fan him thirty. This is the first very bad case of dysentery I have seen, and it's certainly dismal. This boy's hands and feet are ice-cold and purple, the nails nearly black and the skin wrinkled on his fingers as tho he had been a long time in the water. I fan him, and have him smell ether, and give him a rice-water concoction the doctor ordered, also a hypodermic of caffeine, and that's all we can do for the present. It is now 6:15 Monday morning. I have been over here all night with the English boy. He has been having a very bad time.

Natalie took the opportunity, during the long hours, to complete the letter for that day's mail, informing Muddie of the August operational changes under way in Beauvais. *The Smith College Unit left yesterday for somewhere near Chateau-Thierry. They are taking their trucks and are going to transport refugees for the present and then, I believe, go back into 'reconstruction' work. They have left three members here for a week to keep the Club open, and after that, the Club may close,—which would be a great pity. Also, the work of delivering the daily papers to the hospitals has been theirs. There are not so many patients— Americans, that is to say,—as there were. Still, it seems a pity for them to be without an American to go to see them. I think I shall try to take some of it on.*

Natalie's friend, Dr. Greenough, remained behind to operate the Club. She sent a note asking Natalie to come to the Club around 6:30 for something important. Though occupied with her nursing duties, Natalie managed to arrive a little late. *My boy got quieter, and the doctor said there was no probability of a change in his condition for many hours yet. So I slipped down to the Club for seven. The important thing was a dinner for the boys of a certain Ambulance company.*

Dr. Greenough wanted me to "liven them up"! I was some- what perturbed at the order, as I felt I rather needed livening myself; but I found myself being very gay. There is no alterna- tive when one has a chair placed in the center of a ring of twen- ty-odd boys, the only feminine fixture. We had lots of fun. I started the boys teasing each other about their sections of their state. They soon had me laughing away as hard as I could at their violent onslaught. There were a lot of Canadian English and Scotch in; and one English lieutenant and a private sang some duets beautifully, tenor and bass duets. A Scotchman sang some Scotch songs and he soon had the whole room full of men in the raging chorus. It was great to listen to; but I had to run away, like Cinderella, in the midst of it.[18]

Each day seemed a mix of Beauvais's grim world of illness, wounds, and death balanced by lives being saved and the cama- raderie of the war effort. *I didn't tell you of the time I had the other evening. It was lots of fun: as you see, the War Zone is full of it! Well, Dr. Greenough, who is getting to be quite my chum and is certainly a dear good soul,—Dr. Greenough asked me to go with her to give out tobacco to some departing Canadians. We took a perfectly huge basket and filled it with Bull Durham and Tuxedo tobacco and off we went merrily to the train. It was the usual palatial equipage of the soldier en voyage,—the "chevaux quarante hommes", as they called them.*

The soldiers were lolling in the door-ways, or gathered about in little knots talking, in some cases rather noisily. I think some few (alas, not too few!) had hobnobbed at too great length with John Barleycorn. They are more given to that, as a whole. The difference between their troops and ours is very noticeable always, for they are in general an older type. Four years has drained many of their best men. And how glad they were to see us!

One of the men called my name, to my surprise. I had seen him at the Club once, a trim, good-looking boy. Another friend I encountered was none other than the Irish-American-Canadian of whom I wrote you, who went to Mashburn's funeral with me. He recognized me immediately. The men were trying to persuade him to play the flute, as I came up and he was refusing. I joined in with the men in urging him to play. He consented immediately. "Anything to please you, sister", he said, in his funny Irish brogue. "What will ye have?" I considered a minute and said, laughingly, "Dixie," without an idea that he knew it. He started it at once and I, of course, was delighted and applauded, all the men laughed. Soon he went into Yankee Doodle. *I said to Dr. Greenough, for the men to hear, "Ah, that's you." And they all bursted out laughing. And my old friend immediately changed off to* The Bonnie Blue Flag, *etc.*

It was a spectacular sort of scene, in the heart of France, this whole group of weary soldiers in their worn uniforms, two women only, and this old weather-beaten fellow playing with all the abandon of an artist, while the others listened admiringly. The light was fading rapidly, and it seemed very pathetic to see them, tired and worn-looking, setting out for new labors. And when I noticed those who had imbibed too freely, I felt inclined to follow our dictum in regard to old Mr. Galan,—I was glad they had got drunk and forgot their troubles![19]

Then another pleasant episode occurred that suddenly, briefly, memorably presented Natalie with the attention of an entire boxcar of soldiers. *I didn't tell you, did I, about the train loads of Americans going through. We heard shoutings at various times during the day. It was Americans passing thru. Of course, I wanted very much to go down and wave to them. I thought they had all gone. Just as I reached the Club, tho, I heard the shouting begin again. Miss Wood was there, and I caught her by the hand and said, "Come! Now! Let's go wave to the Americans. Is there anything that we can take them?"*

Dr. Greenough was there, beaming approval, for anything for "the boys" appeals to her. She caught up some boxes of chewing gum and thrust two into the hands of each of us and off we flew. We raced as hard as we could go and got there as the last two box-car transports were rolling slowly by. We called, "Hello, Americans. Good luck! Good luck boys!" and threw the packages. They answered with a wild whoop and the door already full of khaki forms, was at once swarming twice as thickly, all waving, all grinning and most shouting. Then, as the train was going slowly, we ran after it down the rough cinders of the track for fully two blocks, where it really stopped. The boys were out in an instant, crowded about us. I said, as 'the hosts' advanced, "Where are you all coming from?" Whereupon there was a general shout, and "Hello, Virginia", "are you from Dixie?" and so on, on all sides. And then, "Wait a minute, we've got a Virginia fellow for you. Where are you, Virginia?" Virginia stepped out promptly, a tall, fine-looking fellow, and smiled, and drawled "Here I am. You don't think I'd miss that, do you? Might miss music, but not any good old Southern talk."

Then, of course, we all talked at once. There is nothing like coming to France to be appreciated! The boys were largely from Pennsylvania, had just come over in May and had been with the English in active service already. I said, "O, you're rookies. I've been over eleven months." One answered immediately, "That's nothing. I've been over here seven years since May,"— and was greeted with a chorus of approval. I caused pandemonium by asking my usual cruel question as to whether or not they had butter-cakes and maple syrup for breakfast.

So our conversation went. I tell you about it, not because it was brilliant, but to give you an idea of their light-hearted boyishness. As for me, all the while, as I laughed and joked with them, the pathos of it pried insistently at the portals of my consciousness. It was nearly nine and quite dusky. The moon lay huge and round and flat as if blown there, against a dull sky,— like a big round port hole with light streaming thru it. There was not the peace of silence and not the chaos of sound. It was a drab hour. And there were these fellows, just from hard-ship, danger, and discomfort, with the prospect of a wretched night in those box-cars, stopping for a minute at this strange little French town, as delighted to see two American girls, as tho it were a show, and yet taking it in a way for granted,—and joking as tho they had not a care in the world.

I told them about the town and the cathedral, and the clock and they asked all kinds of questions and were especially interested in the clock. They asked all sorts of details about it, all said "Gee!" and "Lord!" and "Some clock", and so on. And then for a second they fell silent, pondering the moment. Suddenly one asked, "Well, say, does it tell when the war's goin' to end?" And, of course, he was applauded.

They were just here a few minutes. Soon, they were all asking the number of my hospital, how they could get there, and so on. And, as the train left and they ran to jump up, they called back various promises to get the mumps, to get gassed, and so on, till their laughing voices were drowned by distance and the roar of the train, and we could just see them still waving goodbye,—Just an instant, out of the unknown, and into it again and my blessings.[20]

Events had settled the question of Dr. Lambert possibly recalling Natalie to Paris. Dr. Lambert had been elected president of the American Medical Association, perhaps submerging his concerns about Natalie's safety beneath his added responsibility. Natalie had become a seasoned veteran of war-zone medical work and she was much needed where she was. His sense of guardianship had become inappropriate. *He wrote me a very sweet letter in which he told me that he thought I had 'found my work.' Really, I do love it. Working in Paris in an ordered bureau seems so cold and distant and detached, though the work is quite as important, quite as useful. In fact, as I must admit in honesty, while I was in it, I did really find it inspiring. It is just a case of 'I am I' and so I love this work.*

Despite the departure of the Smith College Unit, the American Club did not close. Dr. Greenough dedicated herself to its survival. *They left only three members, Dr. Greenough, Miss Walton, and Miss Wood. Dr. Greenough and Miss Wood are running the club with enthusiasm, and much labor. They have requested my assistance now, so I plod over,—it's just three blocks or so—every evening now, and dispense chocolate, cheer, and conversation. There is always an eager group of khaki boys, relaxing happily in a homely American atmosphere. The Scotch amuse me more than any other almost.*

Everybody calls them Jock quite as a matter of fact. They call each other Jock. And they can always sing, or do something amusing; and those little Toms of theirs are so jaunty and when they have kilts! We had a 'Hie-lander' in a 'Hie-ly' exultant humor the other day who gave a spirited rendition of "My Hieland Lassie". We have not had any trouble with drunkenness so far. Someone wickedly suggested to poor Jock that he should sing "Just a wee Jock and Jois". You know the 'wee Jock and Jois' is a 'sign o' liquor', and there is a line in there, "if you can say it's a braw, bricht, moonlicht nicht, It's all right, ye can." So of course everyone held their breath as Jock came to that part. And he went thru it triumphantly! Everyone applauded violently, and Jock was innocently pleased.[21]

The dichotomy of Natalie's activities took her from the task of stimulating laughter and good times in the American Club every evening to tragic news in the hospital ward every day. *I just had a charming letter from Jack Collier, one of my English aviation lieutenants. He essayed to be cheerful, but he was rather cast down, it was plain: his two tent mates, his most intimate friends, had just been killed that day, and he had been to the funeral of another the day before. Little Carlson, of whom I wrote you, also a former patient, is badly wounded in the leg. Since I am telling you all of the cheerless news, I'll tell you of another letter just received from Lt. Taylor of the Machine Gun Company (you remember: the officers who were billeted with us at Gisors). He is wounded in the arm (a scratch, he says, of course) and Lt. Blecker was killed. So it goes. There is nothing to do but to say "well done" and to keep a green place in some untrodden region of my mind "for those who have gone West". Poor boys! It is certainly the trial by fire. But they stand transfigured and glorified in the test.*

There are still a few Americans and English in the hospital; but I am very busy just the same, because I am helping now with the French. The hospital is full of dysentery. The nurses have all that they can do, as several are away on leave, and we are shorthanded. So I go about, helping to give piqûres (shots), sponging the patients, giving them various potions, and so on. Yesterday, tho, was the funniest thing of all, and shows how versatile we can get to be. There were two Frenchmen, much weakened with their malady, so that their hands trembled so much that they couldn't shave. They were miserable. I laughed and said, "Do you want me to shave you?" I was joking; but they took it very seriously and were perfectly delighted. I hated to disappoint the poor things. I have never shaved anyone before. They said they didn't care, and so it ended by my shaving them. One had a beard, and I had to cut it with bandage scissors before I could go ahead! There is certainly no monotony in this life!

Night before last, I volunteered for night duty again in a pinch. I had a ward of twenty-two, of whom two were grand malades, so I didn't sleep a wink all night long. I was on the third floor, and looked out on soft, dark masses of tree-tops flooded with moonlight. Inside, the varied sounds of the patients' breathing,—one of them in difficult, painful gasps. I would sit quietly for a second and wonder could it be true that these were soldiers of the Great War, sick, all about me, two of them fighting a losing fight with death. It was real enough. At ten-thirty and again at one-thirty there was a distant sound of bombs and of a barrage. The Germans had been over two towns near here and dropped a perfect wealth of bombs. One of my grand malades of that night has just 'gone west' a few minutes ago. There has been little hope for him. He is a young fellow, strikingly handsome, in a bold, sullen way, full of strength, puzzled, and resentful of his illness.

That same night, a funny thing happened, tho. Funny is a queer thing to call it, but it seems funny to me as I look back at it and see my own feelings. There was another grand malade on the same floor, and he had been moved in the office with a serum before him, for quiet. I went to ask his nurse for something, and finding the door ajar, walked right in,—to find the nurse in the midst of a fervent kiss, the party of the second part being a sergeant, a patient. I was so irritated; I took it almost as a personal insult, somehow. It seemed so shocking to find her "carrying on" in that fashion with a man dying under her care. I was so disgusted I could hardly speak and I have hated to look at her ever since. It is just her temperament, I suppose. These poor French girls,—they are brought up in such a disastrous fashion! That one is a merry, kind-hearted little thing and I hate to think of her cheapening herself so.

An Anniversary Approaches

Then Natalie had another unexpected visitor, Jean Millescamp, the attractive Frenchman who had taken her to the theater, to Versailles, horseback riding, and on other outings the previous autumn in Paris before returning to the front with his regiment. *Yesterday, I came down to my office, just en passant, and came face to face with Jean Millescamp! I was simply stunned! He is twenty-five kilometers from here and had come in by train. He looks rather older and not quite so splendidly well as he did, you know, but good-looking anyway. He has remarkable eyes, very large and almost green, very, very fine and quite dark. He has an olive skin with just a flash of red in the cheeks, and black straight hair always sleek and neat,—he himself is immaculate. His manner is so quiet and reserved, even when he is joking, laughing, as he generally is. He was in town only four hours. It took him nearly an hour to find the hospital. And we were almost two hours at luncheon. He has cousins in the town somewhere, and saw them just a second. So I felt quite flattered to have so much of his time. His regiment will leave probably to-day for other parts of France so, I suppose that will be his only visit.*[22]

Natalie made almost daily trips to the "eye hospital" to see Lt. Trurault and the other blinded officers in his ward. These patients enjoyed teaching her new French phrases, a sort of ongoing course of instruction amidst playful fun. *They give me all sorts of phrases to practice "R's" on. At the same time, they are teaching me a lot of slang, which is very useful often, especially in reading the comic papers. I go over to see them as often as possible because they do really seem pleased to see me, and all shout greetings at once when I come in. They generally have thought up some words and written them down for me when I get there. One is an Alpine Chasseur and he made me promise to wear my beret over there. I did yesterday and they all made quite a fuss over it and said I should have my picture taken in it.*

These officers asked me how soon after the war I was going to get married. Of course I said "Never." Then I told them I would go to Serbia and adopt seven little Serbians. They were all horrified at the idea. Then they suddenly discovered that they were seven, and insisted that I should adopt them instead.

So they now call themselves the "seven little Serbs". They are really very amusing.

Most of them have lost one eye. Sometimes they get blue over it. They were all laughing and talking about types of beauty in women the other day, and one said suddenly, "Why should we speak of that? No one would look at a one-eyed man. He is grotesque." He laughed, but he meant it and they all fell silent. It hurt me so. I laughed though and said at once, "Now don't pretend. There's no use trying to fool me. You know perfectly well that there's nothing so irresistibly romantic. Don't you remember that queen,—you should know, for she was your queen—whose greatest love was a man who wore a black patch over one of his eyes." They say sympathy, except very, very rarely, is disastrous for the blind.

It is two-thirty at night. Mme. Florio has three grand malades to-night, who are in a very, very bad way, and one quite delirious so I am staying over to help her out. Anyway, I had quite a busy and exciting day. I had some English come in as patients. And I gave a great many hypodermics among the French. I went back to my office for something, and found Jean Millescamp just coming out. He had managed to get off again! I was perfectly delighted to see him and he was quite pleased like a little boy on a holiday from school. He had on his brand new Croix de Guerre. Lt. Gallet had told me that he had been decorated. I didn't really understand the details of his service. He was supposed to take a machine gun in a certain position. They got there and found that the gun had been removed; so they had to do quite a risky piece of business finding out where it was and taking it, as they did finally. Jean, of course, was quite silent about it and gave me no details, this conventional (and very provoking) course of action in such regards, it seems.

Jean arrived at eleven and had to leave a little after two but I enjoyed it. He is the picture of health, and full of fun, and I always feel refreshed after his visits, as tho I had been on a pleasant party. He has never forgot how fond I was of the Parisian pastries and still teases me about them. I had written him that I had been trying to cook and was doing wonderfully; I felt I had to prove it, so I made him some coffee on my little burner in my office, and he made me extremely cross by being much more practical about it than I was.[23]

Dr. Greenough, in her determination to make the American Club a success, daily recruited Natalie to stir fun among the men, while Dr. Greenough and Miss Wood did the practical work. It proved an effective formula. *Yesterday evening, tho, I really had quite a dilly of a time. Dr. Greenough had told me that she was going to have a certain ambulance company in for dinner and asked me to go down. I was still humming busily about the hospital; someone brought me word that there was an American waiting to see me. So I rushed down,—to find George de Forest!* De Forest had been among Natalie's favorite friends on the 1917 ship crossing that had brought her to France.

It was his Ambulance Section that was invited to dinner! They are a long distance from here and their lieutenant won't let them come in as a rule, but he made an exception for the Red Cross dinner! He escorted me to the Club, after I had kept him waiting awhile,—of course! I found the Club swarming with boys, thirty Ambulance men. George presented each one individually to me. I found myself between George and a very attractive young Mr. Pratt. Six of the boys were Cornell products. Two of them played musical instruments, one the ukalali and one the mandolin. They got me on the piano and we all played together and they sang. And it carried me back to the days of my childhood (it seems almost) and the K.A. meetings, and, earlier still, those of Delta Tau Upsilon. War was not.

We all enjoyed ourselves so much that we overstayed our time and didn't leave till after nine, which is very late. It is sprinkling, so the whole thirty took me home in the white truck in which they had come down. It was quite pitch black and I got an idea, from the little drive, how difficult it must be to drive near the front in the dark with no lights. One of the boys was hanging out on the fender on each side to give directions and guidance, but even so we bumped once and took a corner of curbing with a grand bump.

Upon her return from the Club that night, Natalie went for a final round of her hospital patients and encountered Mme. Florio, whose day had been very difficult. *She had had one death in the afternoon and was rather nervous. So I stayed with her awhile to console her. I made her some hot chocolate with some milk then I stayed on with her till half-past two, when all the patients quieted down. One had had a very violent delirium.*

Then came the departure of Natalie's "seven little Serbs," the blinded soldiers she had become very close to. *Two of my seven little Serbs are gone, to my great sorrow. Anyway, they had their pictures taken together and ordered two for me, so that will be some consolation. I'll send you one. They have asked me to go to-morrow and have my picture taken with the five remaining. They all have the Legion of Honor. So you see, I shall be quite distinguished.*

I had word yesterday that Jimmy, my blind boy, would be going away soon, so I went over to take him out for a farewell walk. He seems to enjoy it tho it is a bitter humiliation for him to be so dependent as he is. I try to make it as little conspicuous as possible. To-day the other boys took him down to the Club and were coming by here. I went to the window and talked to them. All of them are minus at least one eye, and Jimmy blind, of course. The French nurses were all at the table and were much touched at the appearance of the poor old fellows, all disfigured (to outward sight and transfigured in our imagination with the halo of heroism) as they were. After I promised to go to see them off, the nurses called to me to give them "nos compliments et notre admiration." I delivered the message, and the boys were very pleased.

Afterwards, I went over to see them. They were really rather sad about leaving, but consoled themselves with the thought that it was a first step towards home. They gave me a picture of the five of them together, and each wrote his name on the back,—except Jimmy, of course; some one wrote his for him. The last of my seven little Serbians were going. I told them all good-bye and waved farewell and good luck to them, with the same old 'sinking sensation' of parting.[24]

September 4 would mark the one-year anniversary of Natalie's departure from New Orleans. Her life, and her perception of life, had been deeply altered. As the anniversary approached, Natalie pondered with Muddie her fateful decision to come to the war. *Sometimes I wonder if, had I known how hard it would be at the last minute, I would have screwed my courage to the striking point. However that may be, I am glad, glad as I can be that I did decide as I did. And that you helped me. For you did. I could never have brought myself to go, if I had not known that you were sincerely willing. It is another of the infinite number of debts that I.O.U.! It has meant more things to me than I dreamed were possible.*

When I think of all of the varied experiences that I have had in this year,—And never at any time have you played a bigger part in my life than during this time. And at no time have you been as constantly and wholly present with me as now. Your letters, with all the faith, which is so far from justified but which is sweet all the same to me. So that this year which has kept me away from you has brought me closer to you in reality. It has been a great year for me, and I can never, never cease to be grateful for it. I certainly have never done anything to deserve such a privilege. The 'virtues of the mother are being visited unto the second generation' in this case, and I am reaping all the rewards which you have earned!

What the next year will bring we don't know. I sincerely hope and believe the end of the war,—that next year on the 4 of Sept.—I'll be at home talking it all over, and other things as well, with you and everybody.[25]

Chapter Six

Armistice and the Croix de Guerre

September began for Natalie with an impromptu train trip to Paris to finally close down her room in the boardinghouse there. *It will mean packing my trunk, leaving rue León Cogniat and having my trunk stored, at the Oxford and Cambridge probably. You know how I hate that when I am alone. However, it has to be done.* Natalie arrived in Paris by morning train on September 2, spending the first night in her old room. *Here I am! I have to write to you, a line anyway, just because I am back in the old place.*

Well, I had such a day! I saw everyone I knew almost. I went to see Col. Murphy and he was just fine, so sweet and cordial and good, as always. As I was leaving, he said, in his earnest way, "You don't know how good it is to see someone you really want to see." What could I say but, "Yes, I do, because I've just seen you,"—with a smile to seal it. Major Lambert was out of town, and will be till Friday. I think I'll wait to see him. Natalie's exploits during the Beauvais raids were well known in the Red Cross headquarters and the topic, with enthusiastic congratulations, was raised repeatedly by the friends she encountered. *It is really ridiculous how seriously these people take those raids; but it is lovely of them at the same time.*

Press is just fine, just the same old girl as ever, and cordial beyond expression. When I entered the office, there were over a dozen serious-minded business people in the office, and old Pres simply whooped like a boy,—and startled them all to death! She is the most boyish, whole souled person in the world. Of course, she asked me to dinner immediately, for a 'long talk'.

I've just come back. They have the most sumptuous apartment you ever saw in the Castiglione Hotel, with a private dining room, drawing-room and four bed-rooms! The next best thing to being rich yourself is to have friends who are. We had the most elaborate dinner and served with a warm elegance. And Miss Givner-Wilson came in. She is the one who is making such a success of her canteen at Issondun, for the aviators.

Natalie and Pressy had dinner one night at Henri's, a popular restaurant, and afterwards went to the Opera Comique for the *Contes d'Hoffman*. Natalie declared the performance "magnificent." *I spent the night with Prest afterwards at the Castiglione, in the L.L., as I call it,—the Lap of Luxury! I take to it just as naturally! However, that's no indication of my temperament, because I take quite as naturally to the other extreme, which is service at our hospital.*[1]

Natalie returned by train to Beauvais on Friday night, September 7, bringing back with her a small typewriter, which she named "Cora," a *Corona, borrowed from the gentle Chee. I know that all of my friends will rejoice with me at this piece of good fortune of mine. Which reminds me that I saw Major Gregory in Paris. He asked me if I had ever got a certain picture that he had sent me, and I said, "Why yes. I wrote and thanked you for it long ago." He said seriously, "That must have been in some of the parts that I couldn't read." I pretended to be scandalized at the implication.*

Major Lambert came back and I saw him several times. He was just as cordial as he could be. I went to see him at the Library and he saw me coming in and called out, Hello. There was someone with him, so I asked the secretary, who is a stranger to me, if the Major was very busy indeed, and she said yes, that it was an important conference. So, terribly disappointed, I wrote just a little note and left. A little while later I saw him flying along down the street. He arraigned me severely for not having gone in. I explained that I had been told that it was an important conference. He said, "It was; but it wasn't any more important than seeing you",—which I thought a beautiful speech. He told me that he had been through Beauvais the day before and had stopped by the hospital to see me and was very disappointed not to find me. So that pleased me, too. He wanted me for dinner, but, as I was going he told me that my invitation was extended at that moment for my next trip to Paris and that he wanted me to come and tell him all about my work.

Natalie saw Dr. Lambert again that same day when she paid a

visit to Dr. Burlingame, who had learned that Mr. Desoil, her Médecin-Chef in Beauvais, had recommended that the French government decorate Natalie for her heroism. *Dr. Burlingame has an idea (I don't know where he got it) that I have always an endless string of admirers about and he never lets an occasion go by without trying to tease me about them. Generally, it doesn't worry me at all; but yesterday, with Major Lambert there, I was really rather teased, I have to admit, and they saw it and were delighted. As they were pleased, I supposed it was all right! I don't know whether or not I told you that the Médecin-Chef here has proposed me for something or other in the kindness of his heart. I told Dr. Lowery about it and made him promise not to tell a soul, but of course he immediately told most of the Red Cross of Paris. The decoration has not arrived yet and may never arrive, but everyone was as interested as though it were already pinned upon me. They didn't even act as though they thought it was absurd, which was very nice of them under the circumstances! Dr. Burlingame had heard of it, too, and wanted to give me a luncheon in honor of it and vowed that he would.*

After only four days in Paris, her home away from home, Natalie's old friendships felt reestablished. *I told everyone good-bye and they were all so sweet that I felt as though I were leaving home. I saw Miss Stimson several times and she was very cordial, too. I have never known her well. I admire her very much, though; really about as much as any of the women I have seen over here in Red Cross work. She has a face that is at once strong and sweet and intelligent. I should really enjoy knowing her better, and hope that some day perhaps I shall. She showed me some of the clippings taken from her report, the same that you had sent me. I told her that I was glad she had mentioned the name, because otherwise I should never have recognized myself!*

I have become accustomed to the quietness of a comparatively small town and it really amused me to notice how bewildered and wearied I was by the noise and crowds of Paris. That old city, by the way, is quite cheery. You can not call it really gay, for everyone has the air of having something to do; but it is quite plain that all is going well. The cafes and the theatres and all of the restaurants have crowds all the time and everyone seems cheerful.

The news continues to be too wonderful. It does seem incredible. The doctors from one of the surgical hospitals here told me this morning that they had wounded in last night who left the front past Ham at three in the afternoon, and that their troops, after having gained eleven kilometers, were still going forward and meeting only mild resistance. Such news is like an elixir![2]

The hospital is a dismal place just at present. We have had as many as ten deaths a day from dysentery; and also from grippe, infectious. None of these have been Americans. But it is terribly sad and really depressing. The worst of all is when the families arrive, too late, as is nearly always the case. The night I came in, there was a poor woman who arrived after ten and her son had just died that afternoon. If she had caught the morning train, she would have seen him. As it was, she was too late, and it was heart-rending to see her. There are always several every day, and I find it one of the saddest things in all of the life at the hospital.

Last night, I resumed my old Club habit, and Dr. Greenough was delighted. She had four Ambulance boys in to dinner, and she wanted me to sit down and talk to them. I don't know when I have seen a happier crowd, laughing and swapping yarns, and finding nothing in the world more amusing than some joke on themselves, especially about being scared. They all agreed that air-raids were undoubtedly the worst things in the war, and that pleased me a great deal, because I know what they were like. It always distresses me to think that I as a woman will never see some aspect of the war: it is tantalizing to curiosity and to pride as well. So I like to think that I have been in part of the war,—in the past! Candidly, I prefer it as a past view!

Natalie listened as several of the ambulancers swapped stories of air raids, machine-gun ambushes, and other brushes with death. They found humor in their most frightening experiences. But with one grisly story, the mirth vanished from the room. *Once, they got quite gruesome. One of the boys said that before he went into the army he had never been able to stand the sight of blood. He was broken in first by having to hold the light through a whole night for operations, when he would be so sick sometimes that the light would sway in his hands, and the nurses would call him sharply to order. After the last attack, he got permission to look about in what had been No Man's Land.*

He said that he was quite unconcerned before the most horrible sights, and even amused himself by changing the positions of some of the men. And once he sat a dead German up, cocked a hat over one eye, and put all sorts of paraphernalia about him in fantastic positions. He said that he was very much amused over it all the time. And then the next day, as he remembered it, it made him quite ill.

All the others looked thoughtful and quiet as he talked. It was evident that their minds were busy with the sights that they had seen. Of course, I made a hurried change of subject, as gracefully as possible.[3]

Just as her brother Nauman had written Natalie a long birthday letter in July, Natalie returned the favor in time for his October birthday, informing him of a possible change in her work. *We have a hospital full of French just now, but few Americans, and I am not pleased. I made myself obnoxious in Paris and was promised the first opening in the War Zone. I shall be in the French hospitals still, even if I am changed. It makes me sad to leave here though, for I have so many pleasant memories and associations here. And I have a little office that would make you green with envy,—even though it has no law books in it. I have a big window full of bright red geraniums looking out on long avenues of trees. I have a desk, and two tables, the one in the center with books and flowers on it always, and a chaise longue and a nice easy chair, two, in fact, and then two silk American flags crossed over a picture of our three Generals, with President Wilson just at the side. Those are over my desk. My patients love my office, and when they are convalescent, they stroll in all the time, and take a book, and lounge and read and wait for me here. Wouldn't you like to be one of my patients?*

Then Natalie wrote more to Muddie. *These are sad times at the hospital, with all of the sickness that is prevalent. Monday, I went to the cemetery to the interment of a young Frenchman, just twenty-one years old. His mother and sister arrived late one evening to find that he had died that afternoon at two. His father and his other sister, a volunteer nurse, came the next day. He was an only son, and it was all terribly sad. Mme. Casteran went to the funeral and asked me to go, too, with the nurse they were all well-controlled, though completely crushed with grief. This girl, the idea that seemed to possess her, above every other one, was that she had cared for so many strangers and done everything for them in her power, but that she had been unable to do anything for her own brother. The boy was the center of everything for them.*

I went to see our boys while I was out there, and I am so glad I did, for you cannot imagine anything lovelier than the place where they lie. They are on a slope a little above the main part of the cemetery, which is full of flowers, but thickly wooded with cedar trees. From the slope, you look over the trees to the quiet little town below, which clusters about the cathedral. And the slope itself is a mass of brilliant flowers, a riotous garden of them. It is more than a peaceful place: it is happy and even the white crosses seem a strange flower, too, the richest France has produced! I am so glad that I saw it. I went to the places of my different boys, and greeted them once more, in spirit, and thought of all their mothers, and wished that they could have just one glimpse of that beautiful spot.

One of the nurses is off on permission, and I am taking her place in the Officers' Division, so I am quite occupied, having my own 'family' as well to look after. One of the first things I had to do was to 'special' a French major of engineers, who was dying of infectious pneumonia. He was a fine, strong man; and he has a lovely wife and four little children. It was very hard to see him die, and only strangers about him. He died with his head on my arm.[4]

Yet on the battlefield the news was good. *We are all exultant, jubilant, even in the midst of the sadness and the quantity of work that surrounds us here. Last night, at dinner after all the news of St. Mihiel, the nurses all complimented me extravagantly, till I felt as tho I were the General 'himself'. And they ended by a violent attempt at "Hurray for Amerique et les Americains!"—and all applauded vociferously. And the French are so generous with their praise. One remarked yesterday to a crowd, "Et on dirait que St. Mihiel était impregnable!" ("And they said St. Mihiel was impregnable!") And the others agreed, and laughingly said that 'nothing was impregnable for the Americans.' I am too happy for anything in the world.*

Only I wish I were near! I talked it over with the Médecin-Chef and he was lovely wanting me to stay, and then argued that soon there would be Americans here, and so on. But I told him I know it wasn't so, and that I ought to go. So finally he said, "Well, stay one month more, anyway." And then he added, laughingly, "I'll offer you a bribe",—and went to get a box of chocolates and offered me some. There is work, work, work. Piqûres, ventouses, mustard plasters, etc., etc., etc.,—massage even (imagine me!), but all are interesting, and I'm glad to do them. Every ward is full.

Then there was another death, a French major. Natalie had nursed him throughout his illness, so his death was traumatic. *This morning, I had a terrible time. The family of the French Major who died, arrived, and they wanted to see and talk to me. It was his wife, and his brother, and sister. They were simply overwhelmed with grief, poor things, and I felt simply sick with sympathy for them. The poor wife kissed me about a dozen times. I was so glad to be able to tell her that he had smiled quite happily before he died. I had to see them twice, and it really exhausted me. A more cheering visit was five ambulance men with their lieutenant to see some of their comrades. The lieutenant invited me to dinner at the Club to-morrow night. Dr. Greenough had invited the section to dinner, and so he said that I was appointed an honorary member immediately of Ambulance Unit 637, and he is coming to-morrow night to get me.*

A German Ruse?

On September 13, several letters reached Natalie, including the first in awhile from her mother, others from Hilda, whose father was gravely ill, and one from Carm. Natalie responded to her mother almost immediately. *I had a delightful note from Col. Young. He wants me to go to Neufchateau for headquarters; but it is too retired from activities for me. Anyway, it was very nice to have all those nice letters. I have another one, too, from Lt. Taylor of the Machine Gun Company. Just think,—of those seven officers who were there, billeted with us in Gisors, 2 have been killed and five wounded. Lt. Taylor is getting along nicely and his wound is healed. He is back in the company in command.*[5]

Yesterday, we received from another hospital a meningitis case, an American. He was in a terrible way, and wild with pain. Meanwhile, I sponged his head constantly with cold water. Even so, he would cry out every minute or so. I have never seen anyone suffer more. He turned towards me, and put his hand in my lap, and would look up at me helplessly, just like a suffering animal, as close to me as possible. Sometimes he would toss about, but he always returned to that position.

Just now, they have brought in a French-boy, very sick, too, with meningitis. I've given him medicines and sponged his head and he is asleep. Otto, the American is sleeping, too, now, after a piqûre of morphine. It is a horrible disease. I don't even know the address of Otto's family, for he hasn't been conscious long enough to give it to me.

Natalie's meningitis patients struggled on for days. *The French boy was conscious just a few minutes and I tried to get him to tell about home, so that I would have a message to send his family. But, the poor fellow, between pain and the drugs, was only half coherent. Here I am, once more with Otto. He is much better to-day, I am thankful to say. The poor little French boy gave up to-day at half past one while I was here. There was hardly ever much hope for him. He was still under the morphine, and never spoke at all. He was just a boy.*[6]

Later Natalie added a lighter note to the letter to her mother, writing of two patients whom she had nicknamed 'les enfants gatés' (the spoiled children). *There are two very nice young Frenchmen. They are from the same regiment and are good friends. They always want something and have such an appealing way of asking for it, that Mlle. Bonnet and I cannot resist them. Of course, when they started, they were really so ill, that it was really necessary to humor them, and now that they are better, they confidently expect the same indulgence. Finally, I began to tease them about it, and gave them the name of 'les enfants gatés'. Far from being discouraged by it, though, they seem to think that it gave them a license and title to be spoiled, and enjoy it tremendously. They say that they are called that and have all the odium, so they might as well have the pleasure, too,—all of the pain, why not the profit! Very well-bred and very well-educated. The maid remarked that M. de la Motte was writing to his mother, who was a Countess.*

Anyway, he is the nicest kind of boy. In the morning, when I come in with the thermometers, he tucks his head under the covers like a little boy, and says, pleadingly, "Ah, please don't wake me up. It is much too early." And then he pretends to be asleep. Yesterday, I went in and found them both bounding up and down on the springs as though they were about five years old, in sheer pleasure at being better. They will leave in a day or so now. Another very nice patient is M. Manoni. He is a friend of 'les enfants'. To-day he did a sketch of me, which I shall duly preserve. I made them all a crème this afternoon, which is the first food les enfants have had.

Then came the death of Otto, Natalie's meningitis patient. *Monday, at noon . . . , I stayed with Otto, as usual, until seven-forty-five that night. He was much, much worse, and by evening I saw plainly that there was no hope for him at all. Sure enough, that night Miss McCandlish came knocking at my door. She had been on night duty with him, and he died very quietly about one o'clock. She came to spend the rest of the night with me. It was very strange to think of Otto, it seems so now, for he was never conscious the whole time he was here, for more than perhaps a minute. He seemed to lapse from a living, breathing death to one more quiet and peaceful. The peace is his. But back in America, in Wisconsin, where he came from,—there is where the pain will be. I hate to think of that.*

The funeral followed in the morning. *To-day was cloudy. The casket was brought out and the chaplain read the burial service, which is so beautiful and dignified and impressive that it seems to build cathedral walls, altars, and candles, and long dim aisles,—its tremendous significance suggests all the visible symbols. Many of Otto's friends from his own regiment were there, patients from the American Hospital. Four of them were pall-bearers. They all stood at attention before the casket, draped with our flag and with a beautiful wreath of flowers on it. Just as the chaplain finished the service, the sun broke through the clouds, and fell in a flood of brightness and warmth like a benediction on the colors, and their bearer.*

It was very odd that I should have had a letter from the mother of one of my boys just at the time that Otto died. A dear old grey-blue-eyed lad of about nineteen, who reminded me quite a bit of Wyeth. He had had spinal meningitis and recovered; but there were days when the chances seemed slim, and I wrote to his mother for him. She is evidently a plain sort of woman, but devoted to her boy! Her letter would bring tears to your eyes, for worship of him glowed in every line. She had given my letter to the paper in her home town, and wanted to know all about me, and so on. She is from Texas,—a neighbor, you see! She is sending me a handkerchief! And she wants to send his picture, so I won't forget him! It makes me feel terribly embarrassed. But I'll show you the letter some day, among others.

The overcrowding of the hospital and the steady stream of dying patients persisted through early October. *Really, it is almost overwhelming here at times. And the hospital continues to be very crowded. Mr. Desoil looks quite worn out. I feel very sorry for him. He passed me to-day on the steps and stopped a second. He looked at me and smiled and said, in his funny way, "Let me look at you a minute. I need the sunshine. There is much work and I am tired." He said it in English. He does look very worn.*

M. de la Motte, the playful aristocratic patient Natalie had nicknamed "the Child," interrupted her one evening as she wrote to Muddie, so she turned the fountain pen over to him to add an entry. He proceeded in his heavy, large-lettered script. "A charming Nurse overwhelmed me with care: it is, I confess, your daughter. I beg you to permit me to thank you of all that and to lay at your feet my homage. M. de la Motte." Natalie went on: *The Child came wandering down the corridor just then, looking too amusing in his big blue dressing gown. He is much better now, and full of life. He is about as big as a minute, but quite strong. His arm is bigger than mine, and every bit iron muscle. He is just about fifteen in spirit, being twenty-three in reality. He takes his cane, and walks down the corridor putting on all sorts of airs, and loves to astonish me by doing tricks with coins. When various dishes come in, he sniffs at them delightedly, and says, "Ooff-f", like a puppy. He is the sweetest boy you ever saw. Someone asked me to-day when I would take a vacation. He exclaimed, "Now, Miss, I will not approve that you go a-way before that I depart."*

It is foolish to write you all these foolish little things, but they are the charm of hospital life,—a novel with the characters living and breathing. And I like to write about M. de la Motte, or "Monsieur L'Enfant", because he is a type you would love.

Yesterday afternoon, I had such a busy time. The day being

*Sunday, I decided to make a crème for my malades, every one
of them. You can't imagine what an undertaking it was, with all
the regular medical regime and that besides. But, really, the
crème was fine. We haven't any oven, of course, so I made the
custard on our jets and then I put the meringue on oiled paper
and skipped down and put it in the oven separately. Brown as
they could be, and delicious, and I dabbled them about on top
of the little cups of custard, pretty and very good. I know Boss
would get himself hospitalized immediately and come over
here, if he could see my cooking! I had to make some omelets,
too, and oeufs au plat, and some lait de poule* (nonalcoholic egg
nog), *besides toast for the Child and oatmeal. My little family
was perfectly delighted, especially the Child, who made me the
prettiest speech in his naive English.*

*Afterwards, I went to the American Hospital to the evening
service, expecting repose. And I had to play the hymns* (on the
piano). *So it was not repose. However, I had on my new uniform
for the first time, and everyone paid me compliments. I went up
to show it to my oldest patients, as they had asked me to.*

A letter arrived from the Marquise de Valori and Madame Brin,
the elderly aristocratic ladies who had befriended Natalie in
Paris, inviting her to visit them in their chateau near Nantes. An
early October visit she had planned with Pressy had been postponed, as the Red Cross headquarters was moving several blocks
from the Place de la Concorde to the Hotel de Guise. Natalie
quickly made arrangements to visit her friends' chateau the week
of October 6, then to join Pressy in Fontainebleau for ten days.[7]

The Marquise de Valori's place, the Chateau Beausoleil, lay
beside the Loire-Inférieure, seven kilometers from the town of
Mauves, not far from the Atlantic Ocean. No carriage awaited
Natalie at the Mauves station when she arrived Monday night,
confirming her fear that the ladies had never received her
telegram. So she checked into a small hotel, ate a "petit omelet,"
and wrote a long letter to Muddie reporting the details of her train
trip and her stopovers in Paris and Angers. Starting at eight o'clock
the next morning, she traveled in the carriage of a "courier" to La
Chapelle-Basse-Mer and, finally, to the nearby chateau. *Here I am,
really installed. And delightfully! Beausoleil is certainly* beau,
and I am just as spoiled and wrapped in luxury as I can be.

I got up early yesterday morning and came over with the

courier,—a sad-eyed man, 'bearded like the pard'. On the front seat, the courier himself sank to insignificance, beside, beneath, between and among, casks, kegs, sacks, bottles,—an imposing dis-array of things. We went over two bridges with long flat vistas of the Loire. And peasants passed us by from time to time, the women with their little fresh white caps of Brittany. As we climbed one hill, the old horse trudging, suddenly came past the carriage curtains a more than life-size image of the Crucifixion. It quite startled me at the side of the road, at the top of the hill, looking over the whole country-side,—the cross high up on a mound and the white figure of Christ gleaming in the morning light. At the foot were little straight stones and grouped about, which gave quite well the effect of people kneeling,—certainly a very French and I suppose very Briton idea, for they say the Britons are the most simple and pious of the French these days. The house is square and white, covered with ivy and Virginia creeper, with wrought-iron work about the windows and doors, and a big entrance enclosed in glass. The hedge about the place is all gay with hedge roses, at regular intervals. It is entirely pretty.

Mme. de Valori came down at once, Madame Brin a little later, as she had not been feeling well. Everything is so fine,— tapestries and old pictures everywhere; the silver, and china, and linens perfect, and the servants so well-trained. I have a huge bed, with exquisitely embroidered, faintly scented linens, and a great canopy and curtain of rich silk tapestry. The maid serves me hand and foot. We had others yesterday afternoon,— two Comtesses, a Viscountesse, and a Viscount, the latter very, very young. One reminded me a great deal of Olivier Provosty, and one very much of the manner of Adèle Drouet. The latter was the Comtesse de Bellelièvre, and she is pretty and bright and animated; she has a husband and son both in the war.

They enjoyed walks through the gardens, quaint conversations about family over delicious meals, and spirited contests of bridge for harmless sums of money. They traveled by carriage to an enormous chateau, La Solleraye, where they were received ceremoniously by the owner, the Comtesse de Solarye, her husband (a baron), and their granddaughter, Mlle. De Cainlis (a baroness). On Saturday, the ladies took Natalie to Nantes in their carriage. *Their motors have been requisitioned, and most of their horses, as is the case with everyone in that part of the country; but they still have a very smart carriage horse, and an eminently correct coachman. There were some perfectly delightful glimpses of the Loire, a broad expanse of silver, with bare rocks jutting out over it in places.*[8]

Natalie bade her hostesses farewell and boarded the crowded train for Fontainebleau. She was met by Evelyn Preston and Ruth Morgan and then joined them as Major Preston's guest at the Hotel France et Angleterre, the most luxurious in Fontainebleau. *I had scarcely arrived when Pres was wanting to head me to the golf course. She and I took on Miss Morgan and Mr. Preston and beat them, which made us feel very fine and haughty.*

They celebrated Miss Morgan's birthday Saturday night, then awoke Sunday morning to news that the war might actually be ending. *To-day is Sunday, October thirteenth! What news! What news! Mr. Preston came in while Pres and I were still in bed and gave us the papers, and we shrieked, and Miss Morgan rushed in, and we all shrieked. Pres bounced up and down and almost out of bed, and then wept from sheer excitement. I was too happy for words or tears or anything. Pres and I, who had been singing, "Rejoice, rejoice" last night, sang it over again lustily, and afterward, sang the* Star Spangled Banner *with enthusiasm and inaccuracy, and then* America. *I said I had to go to Services. So we all went for a little while to a Roman Catholic Church, which was all that we could find.*

The news that created so much excitement was an announcement by the German government that seemed to accept President Woodrow Wilson's condition for negotiations, the complete withdrawal of their troops from France and Belgium. Natalie immediately wrote a four-page letter entry to Muddie, describing the utter joy of people everywhere on the streets, as they threw hats in the air, waved newspapers, and shouted admiration for the American president. Then, almost as an afterthought, she voiced skepticism. *We still have qualms even so. We fear the Boche, even bearing peace treaties. The French, too, think that there may be trouble about the terms of evacuation. They are by no means willing that the Boche should retire with arms and supplies, and they fear that it is a ruse and a trick. I wonder if we could bear the disappointment.* The suspicions proved accurate. By Monday, it became clear that Germany would not quit.

Back to Beauvais

Natalie rode horses every day during her visit. *Long, exhilarating canters that seemed to relax and refresh my whole being. We passed thru the significant group of trees known as the "Bosquet du Roi". We wound and twisted, always up, till we came out on a bare hilltop, with a rock jutting out for a magnificent view. It is so good to feel that you can ride and ride and still have the forest about you. It is like the great lovely Rockies for that, and you know how I love them.* They went on an excursion in Major Preston's "big motor" through the French countryside, finally stopping in Moret, a Renaissance-era village where Natalie felt she was stepping back centuries into the past. Pres and Natalie shopped and then chatted through informal suppers by the fire in Pres's room. They rode their horses to the picturesque villages of Rielos and Burron and took a buggy ride to explore Barbizon, another village ten kilometers away.

At the end of the week, Natalie became Pres's guest at the Castiglione in Paris. She arose early the first morning to meet with Miss Fitzgerald, a Red Cross official who proposed several options for a new assignment. Natalie suggested that her translation skills would be of best use where both French and Americans were together. *Of course, I said I wanted most of all to go to where I could be the most useful, but I couldn't resist adding, with a grin, that if I could be equally useful in the War Zone near the front as out of it, I would prefer the War Zone! So she decided on Mlle. St. Paul's unit, and I am charmed.*[9]

Upon Natalie's return to Beauvais on Wednesday, October 23, she found only one American patient in the hospital, and she resolved to leave Beauvais the following Monday. Her new unit would be *the Ambulance St. Paul, as it's popularly called. It is a French Surgical Ambulance,—ambulance being used not in the service of a vehicle for transporting the wounded, but a small front mobile hospital. It is very much like an autochir only generally nearer the front more consistently, as I understand it. This particular one is quite well-known. It was equipped completely at the outset of the war by a young French lady, Mlle. St. Paul, and she has continued to operate it and she directs it personally. I hear that she is very charming, quite young, and has beaux yeux* (pretty eyes),—*that with her beaux yeux (this is distinctly gossip and I have discreetly forgot the sources, which are many and various) she manages always to have a very interesting position for her ambulance. I don't mean to imply even a suggestion of scandal; but the mildest gossip. I hear that she demands a great deal of work. So I won't mind that.*

The six months Natalie served in Beauvais had been the most significant period of her life, and she began to ponder how much she would miss the Beauvais medical community, her friends, and her work there. *Everyone here is lovely about my leaving and vow they are distressed. My greatest grief is that Mr. Desoil is away on his vacation and will not be back until after I leave. I have a very sweet card from him to-day. I am going to send some things home to you,—all my letters, some few of my helmets, some Boche money, pieces of shrapnel and of bombs which fell near here. Tell Boss he can wear that Boche helmet on Sundays.*

I feel quite sad about leaving dear old Beauvais. I love the old place, and love the hospital, and it touches me a great deal to see how sweet everyone, even the least of the servants, are about my leaving. Mr. Jovis, Médecin-Chef of the Centre (all of the hospitals here) came by yesterday and told me good-bye, and made me all kinds of nice speeches. I feel as tho I have friends all about here, and it is quite sad to be going into the midst of unknown things,—except that they'll be very interesting! I am as two-faced as Janus,—my backward eyes are weeping, and my forward ones are already alight with the interests of the future. Mme. Casteran du Rais is going to celebrate in honor of my departure by making some chocolate for some of the officers and me at ten o'clock! and it has just struck.

When the moment arrived for Natalie's departure, there was a sad scene with her hospital friends. *The Directrice wept. Mlle. Bonnet told me that, whatever happened, she wanted me to remember that she loved me. Each one of the nurses kissed me several times on both cheeks, and so on. I really was quite distressed myself. I felt like singing, "adieu la petit table", in a tragic manner, as in Marion. But, of course, I was rushed,*

rushed, rushed till the last instant. Captain Jackson sent me to the train, and I had two Red Cross men and a French orderly with my things, as well as the Directrice and Mme. Florio.[10]

After traveling two days, Natalie settled into a tiny room with Mlle. St. Paul's unit in the war-ravaged village of Resson-e-Long, then wrote of the desolation she witnessed during her journey. *We passed through a beautiful, very old forest, the forest of Compiègne, for miles and miles. Then we would whirl through antiquated little villages, past groups of soldiers, camions on the move, and so on. Then we came to old trenches, barbed wire entanglements, camouflaged cannons, and all the sorry panoply of war. We came to the little town which we thought our destination. Not a house. I couldn't realize that it had once been a happy gay little village. It is all ruins. It was desolate. The most pathetic thing was to see one or two children (I think we saw five, three in one family, and two lone ones). They looked so puzzled and lost. Childhood seemed so out of place. The* Comité Americain *(the work of which Miss Anne Morgan is the moving factor) is installed, having just arrived yesterday. Lots of people laugh about her, but her committee seems to arrive just the same. And already on the outskirts of the town we saw two fields being plowed.*

Finally, we found a soldier who knew where the Ambulance was,—in another little town, three kilometers away. So off we went. The 'town' is a little group of about twenty houses, with ours the largest at the end of the street and on a hill. We passed by a number of American soldiers (colored!) on the way. It seems there is a colored replacement camp near here. Mlle. St. Paul was not here, will be gone till to-morrow. And there are no Americans here now, it seems. The Médecin-Chef received me, and was quite charming and pleasant. He took me about and showed me how the chateau (a tiny one) had been mended and put in order, and he showed me the operating rooms and the salle des entresante (recovery room). I am writing in a little tiny room with just space for my bed and night table, and a chair against the wall. I am sitting on the bed writing on a board on my knee, with a candle on the chair by me. I must stop for my candle is quite half gone, and it has to last three nights.

The next day, Natalie added to her letter. *I am now in charge for the afternoon of a salle of 24 beds, all wounded cases, of course. I must get up in a few minutes to take temperatures. The patients are all French, except two little black Singali,—I bathed one of them this morning. We, the nurses, the doctors, and the operating room are in the house. The patients are in big tents outside, big Bossoman tents. They are huge, and hold fifty beds each. The work is rather new to me, tho not entirely so, and I like it very much. There is one who has been given up as hopeless. He is just about twenty and a delicate, refined looking boy. He has a bad hip-wound. He is delirious nearly always, but he knows me now. Of course, I do every slightest thing I can for him. He talks about home. When I give him something to drink (as I have to every few minutes), he says, almost always, "Ah, that's good. That does me good. It's like what I have at home." Then he is always talking of going on permission and having his father and mother meet him at the station with the automobile.*

There is a cute little Singali, who is not very badly wounded, and who never says a word, but sometimes flashes a sudden grin, and is apathetic again so quickly that you can hardly believe it happened. There is another little fellow of 20 who suffers a great deal with his foot. Next to him is a big heavy man about 40 who fell from a great height and is horribly bruised and has some dislocations. He is a perfect stoic. He tries to encourage or divert the young fellow. He explains to me confidentially that the little fellow is having a hard time, and it's too bad.

We have several Boche orderlies and they are excellent workers. One is really as tender as a woman (and tenderer than some!) with the patients. Especially with Jean, my poor little hip boy, he is kindness itself. Sometimes, Jean, in his delirium, seeing a Boche, starts back, and it hurts the poor fellow terribly. I feel sorry for him,—if that's not traitorous.

It is not far from here to Soissons. I do wish you could see Ambleny, the most pitifully dilapidated place you can imagine. All a ruin. But the stones have been piled neatly in place, and with a touching faith, some of the returned inhabitants set to work to build again. There was one old fellow on what was left of his roof, putting shingles on that corner, evidently intending to make that part habitable first. The courage of such undertakings is pathetic. Poor little fellow, I felt like applauding him.

At night here we can hear the cannon from the front, but they are quite distant, not so near by far as they were when I first went to Beauvais. The Médecin-Chef here says that we are just forty kilometers from the front, but I am sure that we are more. Did I tell you that Mrs. Harriman came by yesterday to see the autochir? She is a very pleasant-looking grey-haired woman, of 'comfortable-looking proportions'. She came by with Mrs. House (wife unto Colonel) and Colonel Mott. He brought the party by here to see the Ambulance though poor Mrs. House was afraid to get out, because she was afraid of the 'contagion'! I never before met the idea that a wound was contagious! Mrs. Harriman braved the danger and came happily in. She was very interested in the cases, and I was going to show her ours, as I was the only person in the ward at the time, but poor Jean just at the moment had an idea that he wanted to get out of bed. So I had abruptly to turn my back on Mrs. Harriman, much as I regret it. But Jean would have precedence over royalty just now, as would any of those poor fellows. I was sorry, though, especially as I am not sure that Mrs. Harriman understood.

Mlle. St. Paul is not much in evidence. They say that she had not been well. She made to-day at luncheon the first appearance at the table since I have been here. She seems quite agreeable and attractive in the French vivacious way. She has a delightful smile and a very merry laugh.[11]

Natalie served with this surgical mobile unit for approximately three weeks, through the end of the war. Her work with the wounded, in the desolation of this recent battleground near the Aisne River, was accompanied by almost constant rumors and reports of armistice. Natalie wrote after her first week with the St. Paul unit, on the first of November, of the rumors she had heard in Paris. *Paris was rife with rumors when I was there. The Emperor and Empress of Austria had arrived in Switzerland and some members of the Hohenzollerns with all of the 'little H's' and the Kaiser was expected any day, having already abdicated in favor of his six-year old grandson. So ran one of the rumors. Then another said that hostilities had already ceased at one front. And so on. Then when I got up here, I heard the cannons going not at all peacefully, so I decided that I would wait a little while yet!*

Then on November 9, word reached them that an armistice had indeed been signed. *I am sitting on the bed with Cora* (Natalie's recently acquired typewriter) *in my lap and an inadequate candle in the distance sputtering and guttering away, but I have to write to you, for the great news has just reached us that the armistice has been signed, and I have to tell you that I am thinking of you. I can hardly believe it. When I was told, it made no impression on me at all hardly. Since then, the idea is taking hold of me more and more, till I feel that I can hardly sit still here and write, but must do something. The Frenchmen have been singing and singing all evening, playing all of the national airs, and are as hilarious as happy children. I love them. They know how to laugh. I sometimes think that it is the greatest boon in the world. Perhaps the poor old misguided Boche will learn it some day.*

But anyway, over and above all, THE NEWS. I know that America is ringing with it. Though there will be only too many hearts that will be still too heavy with the price they have paid to rejoice wholly. But it is great! The human butchery of the last four years is at an end. As I think of it, the armistice, though, sometimes a sort of vista of torn, mangled suffering, worn-out human flesh comes before me, glimpses into the memories of the last year, and it sickens me in a way that it has never done before. I wonder how the nations have stood it all this while. The very fact that I am suddenly more than ever before horrified at it all, now that it is over, shows me, in a way. Under the strain, we have not let ourselves feel or think beyond the present actuality of time and place. No one could have stood an envisaging of the whole situation with no knowing when there was to be an end to it.

To-night, the war seems to me horrible in a way that I have never felt before. Little wizened faces of men, torn flesh, mutilated limbs, faces twisted with suffering,—as though I had never been in a hospital before. I hope that the sun will shine to-morrow and do away with the picture. I can't be rid of it to-night.[12]

The truth was that the armistice had not yet been signed, so once again their celebration proved premature. But the end was truly only days away. Meanwhile, they continued packing to move the St. Paul Ambulance forward to a new, uncertain place, Bavaria according to one rumor. *It is a grey and dismal morning, but I am feeling much more cheerful than last night anyway. Gruesome last night. We shall have some work still at Chantilly. I'll go to Paris probably for two days next week, and there I'll hear everything from Miss Morgan about Red Cross plans.*

Then, on November 11, the day that would become known to history as Armistice Day, Natalie made this letter entry while awaiting her Paris train in Chantilly. *This is Monday morning now. Our train arrives soon, and I am sitting on the side-table in the dining-room, my things all ready. The latest is that we may be going not to Bavaria, but to the Vosges. Nothing is really certain about it. Miss Brass is engaged to an officer in the French Press Section, and last night he asked me to dine with them and all the Press here who are with the French État Major (French General Staff). There is a Mr. Mowrer, of the Chicago Daily News, Mr. Laurence, of Reuters, Mr. Knox, of the Illustrated London News (I think that's it) and one of the Associated Press, whose name I forgot. Quite interesting. We had a great discussion as to whether or not the armistice would be signed this time. They all, with one accord, said yes, whereas I still say no. We shall see!*

The German delegates meeting in Compiègne, not far from where Natalie was sitting, had signed the armistice papers that morning at ten minutes past five. By agreement, the fighting would cease and the armistice would begin at eleven that morning. The German army still occupied French and Belgian territory and had not yet been forced back into their own country. At eleven the German army surrendered their arms and the evacuation began. Allied troops moved into German territory and, by terms of the agreement, assumed the occupation of western Germany.

Red Cross Work Continues

Natalie learned the war was over when she stepped off the train in Paris. The armistice celebration had exploded everywhere. She proceeded to the Red Cross headquarters to join Pres and other friends for a day and evening of celebration. *Thursday I returned again to Chantilly once more, all primed, set and cocked for Germany. That night came a telegram from the Service de Santé saying that the force of nurses should be cut down and that only those who were militarized with the French should be taken! I really could have wept. The whole Ambulance left*

Friday morning. I rose up in the cold and dark and packed my things, between shivering and wishing that I were going to Strasbourg. And then I went to Paris on the nine o'clock.[13]

Old friends from New Orleans highlighted Natalie's stay in Paris, some having just arrived as volunteers while others were soldiers in town on leave. She and Johnny were taken by three officers to a military dance, and, on another evening, she had dinner with a close family friend from New Orleans, Rosalie Nixon, who had been in Paris a month doing volunteer work. Muddie had given Rosalie a rose to hand deliver to Natalie.

Others had arrived that summer, including Sadie Downman and Marion Monroe, who came with the Newcomb Unit; Natalie joined them for dinner one night with a crowd of other Louisianians. She also enjoyed tea at Rumplemyers with Mme. Casteran du Rais, in for a day from Beauvais. *Then I had a most happy time when Colonel Murphy came to see me, for I admire him more than almost any man I have seen since I came to France. He was full of fun, and we had a gay time. I felt foolish and frivolous and he encouraged me, so you can imagine what a degree I reached. Sometimes I think that these men who have so much responsibility really enjoy letting themselves go into just a little session of nonsense. And I always enjoy it.*

Natalie also ran into John Wogan, an old family friend. *I was in the Red Cross building, rushing as usual, when I heard someone call my name. I looked up and saw a strange but handsome major speaking to me. I smiled cordially, but questioningly. He said, "Well, you don't even know me. John Wogan." We went to a delightful little restaurant in Montmartre and had a delicious luncheon and quite a pleasant time. John had been in lots of excitement and I dragged out details from him. Afterwards, we went in and had our pictures taken just for fun, in a funny little French studio. I do hope they will be good. We posed killingly on an old wall.*[14]

Natalie attended a special Sunday-afternoon church service, the "Military Service of Thanksgiving for Victory," at the American Church of the Holy Trinity in Paris on November 17. Bishop Brent, the senior chaplain of the American Expeditionary Forces, gave a special address towards the end of the service. The final hymn, as they left the church, began with this refrain:

Ten thousand times ten thousand
   In sparkling raiment bright,
The armies of the ransomed saints
   Throng up the steeps of light:
'Tis finished! All is finished,
   Their fight with death and sin:
Fling open wide the golden gates,
   And let the victors in.[15]

Natalie received new orders directing her to the American Hospital in Nantes. The atmosphere of a postwar hospital, she expected, would be different; already, so many soldiers and Red Cross workers were going home. Her last day in Paris, Natalie shared a farewell lunch with Pres. *She is going back to America on the second of December, and you can imagine how that will make me feel. Paris will not be the same place for me at all. I always feel that there is one place at least where I will find a warm welcome and friends. But anyway that is a sure sign that the war is over! Pres and I were both dismal with the thought of her approaching departure. She insisted on giving me a perfectly lovely afternoon dress of a soft blue velvet, a Cheruit model. Think of it. It was too short for her and she had hardly even worn it. I tried it on and it looks perfectly fine, and is quite becoming to me. It makes me feel like an heiress, when I put it on. Then she gave me, too, a very handsome coat. It is really too big for me, but I can easily have it fixed. Pres is the most generous person in the world and it really seemed to give her almost as much pleasure to give me the things as it did me to receive them.*

We had a cozy and delicious luncheon by the fire in the drawing-room, and then Pres lay down again and asked me to read to her, some poetry, and I stayed and had such a peaceful, pleasant time, all afternoon. I hate to think that it is the last of that kind for me over here. But in a way it is nice, for it means that before so very long I can be thinking of taking a boat home, too. If I let myself think of it too much, I would take the boat right away. I'll tell you what is going on here in the course of time and then you can tell me what you think of my going home. I went by the office to tell Major Preston good-bye, and he was perfectly lovely to me. His eyes filled with tears and he couldn't say a word. So, of course, I felt the same way, and gulped dismally

*and said, "Good-bye". And he said, "Good-bye", and we
squeezed each other's hands and I fled. So endeth the first lesson. A pleasant chapter closed. And no matter where or how
agreeably another opens, it will never be quite the same.*

Many on the train were going to Le Havre to board ship for
home, including a large number of soldiers and naval aviators.
Natalie reached Nantes at four in the morning, slept on a straw
mattress at the YMCA until nine, and arrived in the office of the
American Expeditionary Forces Base Hospital 34 an hour later.
The hospital occupied a school building; there were seven or
eight rectangular barracks. *I was taken to Judge Fead, the
Hospital Representative here for the R.C. He is a Circuit Judge
in Michigan, extremely agreeable, and attractive, too. He is
rather a heavily built, middle-aged man, with pleasant very
brown eyes, which crinkle with fun, very often. He was telling
me that he was falling in love with me already; so you can see
we get along quite well.*[16]

Judge Fead put her to work on the typewriter at his desk,
which was located in the middle of an intersection of hallways.
The consequence was that everyone stopped to talk, a fact that
Judge Fead thoroughly enjoyed. *There is the Directrice, Miss
Strickling. She is a good, kind soul, and seems to be very fond
of the boys,—She has a great habit of saying something about
the boys, as though they were puppies, or kittens, and then saying soulfully, "Lord love 'em." Also, she is always eager to get
the room 'swep out'! She is from Texas originally and has long
been a business woman in New York, a buyer, I believe. She is
really sincerely kind-hearted. She is about forty, tall, big-boned,
but with good features, and nice dark hair, and brown, troubled eyes and lips a trifle tight.*

Natalie received news from home of the November birth of
Hilda's first baby, a healthy son, Arthur Jr. Hilda had confidentially informed Natalie by letter months earlier, before the news
was generally known, that she was pregnant. *And Hilda! Our
ways ran side by each for a long, long time, but when they did
begin to diverge, they spread a long way apart. But I am very
happy to hear about the baby and so glad that he is a son.*[17]
Natalie learned after New Year's that Arthur and Hilda had chosen
her to be the infant's godmother.

I have been busy all day long writing letters for the soldiers.

My main job so far seems to be talking and you know that that is one thing that I am equal to. We have a big hall sort of place that we are supposed to make attractive looking. So far the only thing that we have done in that line has been to put up two silk American flags of mine. Today, though, I put out a lot of pens, ink and paper. And those tables were simply crowded with boys writing home. I went in some of the wards where the boys were too sick to write themselves and wrote letters for them. I took Cora with me, and she and I had a busy time. She made a great hit with the boys. Some of them want me to write letters for them, even though they could write themselves. They thought that Dad would be so impressed.[18]

When Natalie first arrived at Hospital 34 in late November, no Red Cross personnel were there other than the directrice. Natalie became a social worker, counselor, and activities director. She converted the hospital's big, empty, unused hut into a Recreational Hut, distributing "the donation stock," including cigarettes, tobacco, candy, handkerchiefs, and toiletry items. She also obtained boxing gloves and basketball and tennis equipment for the recovering patients and organized a baseball team. *The main point is that we are to make the boys happy. So that when they come and want to spend half of the evening telling about how their best girl went back on them, how they lost their best chance in business, how they don't know whether to finish school or not, and on and on, you feel not only inclined by natural sympathy to listen and advise and sympathize, but you feel, too, that it is part of your job.*

Natalie organized a new hospital library. *The boys are delighted and come in droves all the time. The shelves are all up, there are bright cretonne curtains, and a rag on the floor. I have some very attractive prints up, pictures of the President, of Maréchal Foch, of Lloyd George, and of Clemenceau, and my two little silk flags that stayed so cheerily through all the raids in Beauvais. I love the little library, because it makes me think of ours at home. It is just about the same size and it is snug and cozy, attractive chairs, of a little wicker, brown tones. We were given a lot of books. In fact, people are constantly bringing them in. I have had to have cards printed and now I have to typewrite the titles of the books on the cards. I have a good assistant. His name is Jack Jones. I have called him Jack*

Natalie, after the armistice, making hospital rounds with books for patients (Nantes, ca. 1919). *Courtesy of Special Collections, Tulane University Libraries*

Library Jones and everyone has taken it up. He is a quiet, handsome boy, with a sensitive face, the face of an artist, and with fine grey eyes. He is very well read and well-informed, invaluable to the Library and we are the best of friends.

When I see the boys still here, I feel that I ought to stay a little while longer perhaps. I don't want to be a quitter when the monotonous humdrum begins. I don't want to forget the old song I have hummed along with the boys, but with great feeling and earnestness, "And we won't be back till it's over over there." I would certainly like to get a peep into Germany with no matter what organization. I should like to see a little of Italy, too, since I'm near it. I spoke of it to Rosalie and she seemed quite in line for going, too. So did Johnny.

When the armistice was first spoken of, I began to dread 'the horrors of peace', as I think that I wrote you. Miss Stimson, the Chief Nurse of the Army was here to-day and addressed the nurses. Among other things, she told them not to think that because the war was over, the effort was over, or rather, the need for it. She used a very good phrase, quoting it from someone else, she said, 'the indomitable spirit that no monotony can quell.' I thought it very good and very apt for these times. I know that I have never since I have been here felt less spontaneity about my work. And I am determined to get it back. Now![19]

Natalie became concerned about Jean Millescamp because she had not heard from him since receiving a short message in Paris. *I have had no word from Jean Millescamp since his shaky note saying he had Flu and I am worried about him.* This would be the final mention of Jean Millescamp in Natalie's letters, though very few of her 1919 letters now exist. Natalie would remain in France through most of 1919 and during the next decade would often settle in Paris for months at a time, but he never reappeared in her life. Jean also disappeared from French military records. He may have died in the deadly influenza epidemic.

From the moment Natalie informed her mother that the Médecin-Chef had submitted her name for a decoration by the French government, Muddie asked pressingly about the medal in each letter. *I am distressed for your sake. I should never have written you about it at all, because I wanted to save it as a surprise. I really never doubted that it would arrive, for the Médecin-Chef did ask for it. So I don't know that I should ever get it, on the other hand that I shan't, because they are sometimes, in fact, generally, long in coming. I am so sorry about it for your sake. Not that any decoration should be coming my way, because I am just one of very many, and all of that. I really am sorry, for your sake, though, for I know you would have liked it, and so would Boss.*

As Christmas approached, everyone—patients and staff—became deeply absorbed in a long list of holiday projects: making Christmas bags for every soldier, decorating the hut and all the wards, planning the Christmas Show and dance. *Everyone, especially of the boys, is bursting with importance as to his part in the Xmas festivities. I just wish you could see our stage. The indefatigable Klein has been working away day after day, and we have a drop that looks as professional as anything you ever saw, with a very attractive design around the edge, with a motif in rose, and there are rose draw curtains. The boys are perfectly enchanted with it. The scenery is now in process of construction as we have grown a whole oak to-day and built the foundation of a castle. I feel as you used to say you did about the electric light man. I am really in awe. These performances are not all amateur, though. We have people from Keith's and the Orpheum, and all such abodes of the élite of Vaudeville. They are all young, though. It reminds me of the old days at college, but the results here are somewhat better. We have the vaudeville planned for Xmas and then, at the end of January, we expect to have our crowning success of the theatrical season of the Hut, a musical play the whole score of which has been composed by our own talent. I wrote you about our musical genius, who composed the finale for the* Follies *the year before he went into the army. He says that he is going to compose a song for me.*[20]

Gift packets were prepared for each soldier. *You know there are over twelve hundred patients in the hospital, besides the nurses and the corps men necessary to care for them. And we are having a Xmas, too, for the Motor Transport Corps who are stationed across the street from us. Over three hundred of them. You can imagine the prospect of dividing up candy, nuts, Xmas cards, socks, handkerchiefs, razors. There is to be a Xmas tree for each of the wards. As I dip up candy, endlessly, count cigarettes, and all of those things, I am still as touched as I can be by the greatness, the shining spirit of the Red Cross.*

Natalie did not write again until the day after Christmas, when she, and everyone else, was exhausted from the Christmas festivities. *We gave them (the patients) trees and ornaments, but they decorated their own wards. The boys did almost all the work, and it was really wonderful to see the pleasure and the cleverness. Some of their ideas were very original, too.*

One of the wards, 414, had a most elaborate tree. They made a tent, a first aid dressing station, with a wounded sergeant just outside, and a Red Cross flag flying over the tent. The Piece D., tho, was the automobile for Santa Claus, which was a marvel of ingenuity. It was constructed entirely of hospital furnishings. The body was splints, with khaki-colored blankets stretched tightly about it, the color seemed quite automobileistic to us, the steering wheel was the top of a Thomas splint. Candy tins made stunning headlights, and the rubber-ring air cushions were the extra tires. And the whole thing was decorated in holly and mistletoe. A big Santa Klaus presided over everything on the ward. In another ward, 329,—(one of my pets) they have a 'town Boche', as I call him (and they do, too, now). He is an older man. He is quite clever at making things. The old Boche took a great interest in Xmas, and the boys brought him paper, strings, and tinsel, and he made the most delightful little trinkets and ornaments of all kinds with which they proudly loaded on the tree. One of them, clever with the brush, made a huge jolly old Santa Klaus portrait for the wall. And then,—crowning glory—a fire-place! They took sheets, somehow stretched them taut, sloping about all the way to the ceiling, like a real old-fashioned chimney, and lined it to make it look like stones. They took thin red gauze and made a little cage. On top of that they put real wood, underneath was a light, and the effect was most realistic,—exactly like a fire.

Every ward had some idea of its own. Even 130, which is the saddest ward of all. All the depressing paraphernalia of fractures and splints were decorated. The orderlies and the very few of the patients who are able to be up had done their best. Even the ropes of the pulleys on the fracture apparatus had been wound with tin-foil. It seemed so brave. Thin, thin, wasted, pallid faces of boys who had spent months in bed, looked up with renewed interest of the Xmas gaiety. I spent a great part of the afternoon of Xmas day in the ward with them, and one of the boys came in and took a picture of the ward with me in it.

There were ever so many visitors in all the wards, mostly French, of course. They were all amazed and touched at the great display. There was a Negro quartette which went thru. It was hard to decide whether they themselves or the patients enjoyed the performance more. They sang rag-time songs in the raggiest way, led by the short, coal-black, fat, perspiring bass, who was a show in himself. The boys were wild about it. The Y. sent a woman singer, too. A chorus which the chaplain got up here in the hospital, went in all the wards, singing carols.

Captain Fead dressed himself up like Santa Claus and went thru the wards to deliver the sacks. There was Communion Service in the Hut at ten, a splendid sight to see the fine clean earnest faces, and the straight, fine figures kneeling, in single reverence, side by side. It was as much an inspiration as the service. Our tree reached to just within inches of the top of the hut, a perfect tree, straight, shapely, and symmetrical, aglow with color, lanterns, toys, every kind of ornament, and aglitter with tinsel and 'almoux d'ange' (angel hair). The realization of the ideal Xmas tree. Xmas night, we had a big old fashion party. A howling *success. There was a dance after the party. I haven't told you yet about the vaudeville performance of Xmas eve. I told you Woody (familiar for Woodworth, Acting First Sergeant, formerly of Something and Woodworth, Keith's Vaudeville Circuit) was the chief factor. I enjoyed it immensely and the audience, they were simply wild with enthusiasm and roared with laughter.*[21]

Home at Last

From March 2 through March 15, Natalie traveled with a girl-friend and two officers through many parts of France and Spain, passing through the Pyrenees and visiting Carcassonne, Narbonne, Perpignan, Nimes, Arles, Marseilles, Cannes, Nice, and Monte Carlo, among other places. Natalie then resumed operating the Red Cross hut and library at Nantes. That spring, she had been assigned the task of writing a history of the Red Cross work at Nantes, which she did in May. In mid-June 1919, the hospitalized Americans finally went home, and the Nantes operations closed. Natalie obtained a pass to travel in the northern war zones of France, Belgium, and Germany, visiting battlefields and military cemeteries. She returned to Paris in time for the Fourth of July and Fourteenth of July celebrations in the city, a time when Pres. Woodrow Wilson and other world leaders were struggling with the treaty of Versailles and Wilson's League of Nations. Natalie went to work for the Red Cross Hospital Supply Services, categorizing and disposing of hospital stock. Her talents as a translator were useful in dealing with French purchasers of surplus materials.

Natalie wrote Muddie that she would stay a short while longer in France for an unexpected but necessary purpose, which, rather mysteriously, she could not divulge. She assured Muddie there should be no worry—she would explain later. Natalie had been officially notified that the French government was citing her for heroism. She would soon become the only American woman in the war to be awarded France's highest medal given for bravery in combat, the Croix de Guerre. This time she saved the news as a surprise.

Meanwhile, Natalie enjoyed life in an optimistic, postwar Paris. She attended the international track and field competition held to celebrate the peace and to honor Gen. John J. Pershing. The new Paris Olympic stadium was being named for him. *Two very nice naval ensigns took me out to the Stadium to see the games. I had the greatest luck and got into the Tribune d'Honneur. John Wogan had promised me tickets. I was in the same grandstand with General Pershing, and all of the other dignitaries.*

The grandstand is an enormous place, and it was packed full to a great overflowing. Lots of amusing things happened. There was one very well-dressed, aggressive lady, apparently American, with a nice-looking French couple. She bustled up to every officer in sight, and deluged them all with information, that she was with the Comte and Comtesse d'Ardigne, and that the Countess supported out of her own pocket a whole hospital,—and I don't know what else besides. But it was really funny to hear her. She finally got seated quite near us, and she attempted to domineer everyone in sight, telling them to move, to get up, to sit down, and so on. I named her the Duchess, and every one took up the name, and we became quite sociable in our mutual amusement over her.

But the games were really fine. I felt very proud of "us" for continuing such an occasion. The stadium seats, I think it is 40,000, and it's made very solidly. There were, of course, many uniforms, and the massing of colors gave a barbarically joyous effect. There was one grandstand occupied principally by French soldiers, and it was lovely to see the ensemble of their blue uniforms, with a touch of bright colors in women's hats and dresses, and in a few artillery uniforms that were mingled with them. It would have been great to go there just to see the crowd.[22]

Natalie celebrated her second French birthday with presents and letters from home and some from her Parisian friends. She paid a farewell visit to Madame Brin and the Marquise de Valori, who were leaving for Switzerland, and both gave her gifts to bring back to America. She went to Montmartre with an officer that evening and saw Paris by moonlight, a very stimulating night out.

There is an awfully nice boy here from Saratoga, New York, a Yale man, Captain Finley. And we went out for dinner together. He is quite nice-looking, well-groomed, and very, very nice. We sat down to dinner in a very nice café near here and ordered dinner. And then we regretted that we had gone there, and wished we had gone to the Boeuf à la Mode. So I laughed and said, "Let's get up and run." So we did nearly, except that he made me tell an awful fib to the head-waiter in order to cover our escape. He made me say that he had left a thousand francs in the hotel and that he had to go back and look for it! Naturally, that put us in the best of humors for the Boeuf à la Mode, where we had a leisurely and delicious dinner of sole meunière and cauliflower au gratin and other sundries,— including ice-cream, to make a combination worthy of Boss!

Then Captain Finley told me about a queer little "box" of Montmartre, a little Bohemian restaurant, which he described most alluringly. I said, "Give me the address. I must surely go there some evening." And he said, "Let's go now." And we did.

You can't imagine what fun we had. We went quite a long way on the Metro, and got off on one side of the big hill which pushes up in one corner of Paris, and which is Montmartre. It looked very wild-looking and forbidding, and we had to climb quite a steep, dark, very narrow little street. In the middle of the ascent, when I thought a house had fallen down on the side of the road, Capt. Finley said, "Here's Freddy's." I gasped, and said, "I'm sure we'll be robbed." But in we went, under the little tumble-down arbor where barely discernible non-descript figures were sitting silently about at a few rough tables crowded together, to a veritable shanty of a place. We entered a dark, dirty little entrance-hall, hardly as big as our side-porch, and the maid there spoke to us very sharply, saying, "Tas-st!" most reproachfully. I dutifully sank my voice to a whisper and said, "Qu'est-ce qu'il y a?" ("What is it?") And she whispered back, impressively, "On récite" ("They are reciting"),—and pointed us to the doorway. There was a short flight of steps, just about four, looking up to a little dingy, dark room about the size of our dining-room, and we slipped in.

Such a scene! Rough, round board tables, with a color that age only had given them. Rough seats about the wall, and the queerest medley of people sitting about on the benches or on rough wooden boxes, at the tables. They were mainly eccentric looking in one way or another,—girls with short hair, and some with long, some dreamy looking French officer, an American man in civvies, and one American officer. Some of the 'wild ones' would be leaning back pensively, absorbed in visions apparently; others would be gathered together in groups, leaning excitedly over the tables discussing something so intensely that they seemed on the verge of tilting off their wooden boxes.

A huge crucifix, as high as the room, hung over us out of the obscurity of dim light and tobacco smoke. It was a clever imitation of much corroded stone, and the feeling of the figure, the lines of it and the pose were really impressive. In another corner of the tiny room was an old Greek goddess, quite close to the crucifix,—in the aesthetic sociability! Pictures, sketches, were hung about the dingy walls, where there was not even light enough to see them, and at one end of the room, heavily framed, was a good portrait of Freddy,—Freddy, who rushed us all with uncompromising firmness. A short figure of a sturdy, strong old man, with a thick white beard, his shirt turned in at the neck, in his shirt-sleeves, with the sleeves cut short, and a heavy black belt above his corduroy trousers, at least five inches wide! He cried, "Hark", to us surprisingly whenever he was egging on a pet 'artist' to perform, and should any rash person venture to talk thereafter, he glared simply ferociously.

We sipped cherry brandy contentedly, and simply enjoyed it every bit. One emaciated, dreamy-looking gentleman, whose vitality seemed to have been wholly to hair, of which he had a great deal, was reciting when we came in. And he was really fine. It was well-done, with a very evident ability. He recited several things, with more feeling, and, at the same time, finish and delicacy than you find often on the stage. When he finished, everyone applauded vociferously, while a nervous wooly dog, like a poodle many times magnified, barked vociferously. Then someone sang. And then another made verses,—very quickly and badly. Then old Freddy played the guitar and sang some old-fashioned French folk-songs that were quite delightful. After each performance they would pass around a white saucer, where the guests 'chipped in' contributions for the artists! And then the "poet express" insisted on composing one to Captain Finley and me. It was certainly an occasion!

Finally, everything began breaking up, so we left. We climbed on up and over the hill to go back that way to my hotel. And to do it, we had to pass by the great new church of Montmartre, Sacré Coeur, all white stone in the light of the moon, and looking down silently on moonlight Paris, studded with electric lights. The air below had been close and warm—There we breathed. And everything was quiet and still in the moonlight. It was wonderful,—the kind of scene you could never forget.[23]

Natalie received her Croix de Guerre with Bronze Star, a citation to the Order of the Regiment, in a Paris ceremony on September 6, 1919. The order was signed by the French marshal Henri Philippe Pétain, commanding chief of the French Armies of the East. By then, Natalie had decided not to inform anyone

Croix de Guerre ceremony (Paris, September 1919). The French officer with Natalie is probably Mr. Desoil, the Médecin-Chef of her Beauvais hospital who recommended that she be decorated for heroism. *Courtesy of Special Collections, Tulane University Libraries*

Natalie wearing her Croix de Guerre (Paris, 1919). *Courtesy of Special Collections, Tulane University Libraries*

in New Orleans of this honor until she arrived home. She took a final trip before setting sail for New York in October, first traveling across the French Pyrenees, visiting Biarritz and Bayonne on the Bay of Biscay, then Pau. On the Mediterranean coast at Marseilles, she boarded ship, visiting Florence, Rome, Pompeii, and Naples.

Sophisticated Biarritz impressed her, particularly the extravagant people there and *the elegance of my very elegant hotel. It is a most palatial spot, and we sat in a big center lounge, all glass paned almost, which gives into the spacious, glass-paned, terraced dining-room, which looks down on a sloping lawn and the sea. It is most amusing, sitting there. Every sort of person (except the poor!) was represented,—Spanish, Italian, Jap, Chinese, English, and a few Americans in civvies, all rather elegant. It was amusing to see the Japs and Chinese especially in all of the height of European finery. The gowns were simply overwhelming, all quality, but of quantity a great scarcity. There were actresses, nouveau riches, and some people of refinement! Next to my room was a well-known Parisian actress who promenaded the corridors in pajamas, and left the door open wide where her exquisite attire was of such slight extent that I had to turn away my eyes! The maid confided in me that the said actress ran yesterday wearing her* dress only!

Natalie described a Europeanized Japanese family she had befriended; *the girls (for they were only that) wore the most exquisite gowns, and were really bewitching, quite European and very finished in manner, and seemed equally at home in English and French.* There was an American woman whose American husband kissed the hands of the ladies while *he smoked a cigar in a tortoise shell holder with the snappiness of a ward-boss. But he wore morning gowns and exquisite waistcoats!*

All the men exhibited great originality, many low colors, colored handkerchiefs, extraordinary waistcoats, picturesque sweaters. Natalie cited as an example one *who wore a red tie, a red-striped waistcoat in the morning, and a red carnation (with a tuxedo!) in the evening. And women! Such costumes! At dinner, really there was no limit to the 'undress'. One woman who sat at the table next to us had a single strip of tulle about half an inch wide supporting the front of her dress. I say the front because there wasn't any back! And jewels! Diamonds are big as eggs, it seemed. One woman had a magnificent jewelled cross that made me remark to Jimmy, "And on her breast a sparkling cross she wore" . . . etc! It is tempting to go and tell you more but I can't, as it is train time.*

In Rome, Natalie toured relentlessly for more than a week, visiting favorite places several times: the Colosseum, the Pantheon, the Sistine Chapel, the Raphael rooms of the Vatican, the Church of St. Mary Maggiore. She enjoyed *La Tosca* sung under the stars, *and in the last set, my heart simply throbbed with emotion to see the outline of the scene, the Castella di Angelo, with St. Peter's and the Vatican in the distance, a scene the original of which in all its grandeur is burnt eternally into my memory, for I have seen it again and again these last few days.*

There are beggars everywhere over there. You never saw anything to equal it. As we were having dinner in front of the little 'ristorante' on the Piazza Venezia, along came an old woman, bent over almost double and hardly higher than my waist, leading a blind man! They show you horrible sores, or stumps of limbs. Even the babies beg. They will run, and kiss your hand and they hold out their hands for a penny!

Accompanied by friends from the ship, including a young New Orleanian named Buddy Shields, Natalie also visited *the Scala Sancto, or Holy Stairs, supposed to be those by which the Saviour mounted to the Justice Hall of Pilate, brought to Rome by Helena, the mother of Constantine! You have to go up on your knees, and so Mr. Shields and I did dutifully. I must say, I could not muster a serious thought. There were two old ladies going up just ahead of me by means of the most elaborate gymnastics, and they looked perfectly ridiculous. At the same time, I looked equally absurd, for the steps were broad, and you would have to give a wiggle each time you mounted one, in order to get forward enough to mount the next one.*

There was one old soul, though, who really wrung my heart with sympathy. She was so poverty stricken, so care-worn and used-up-looking, and so lost in fervent ardor, praying devoutly for a long while and then pressing her lips to the steps. I felt ashamed to look at her, for I have had so much that is good and she looked so utterly dead to any suggestion of happiness. Perhaps her fanaticism is a joy to her!

Natalie described her days in Rome as magical. *Horace is in my mind all the while, not of an age but for all times seems to express the individuality and spirit of the Romans. And of course the shadows of my old school-friends, Cicero, and Seneca, and Pliny, and Caesar attend me constantly, a truly royal cortege. All along the Appian way, the little boys run beside the carriage and turn hand-springs as everyone throws them pennies.* Natalie's Italian proved sufficiently fluent during their stay. They finally departed for Mt. Vesuvius, Pompeii, and Naples, where they boarded ship and stayed over in Palermo before setting course for the Straits of Gibraltar.

As the cross-Atlantic voyage approached the final day at sea, New York City drawing near, a growing sense of excitement possessed the passengers. *I am simply numb with the thought that the land which is there veiled by the fog is America. I don't know why,—on a voyage, I always think of Columbus for some reason when he first saw land. Each time it has an excitement of discovery.*

The same seemed true for the large number of European immigrants who crowded aboard ship with her, all seeing the New World, their new home, for the first time. *And as for the refugee-immigrants, it was thrilling to see them. They shrieked, and shouted, and embraced each other, and the children seemed never to stop shouting. They would reach to one side of the deck, look, and call to each other, and point. Then a few minutes later to the other side some would go and soon the others would follow. And sometimes they would all group together, and stand there gazing earnestly and steadily, as tho they could not take their eyes off 'the promised land'.*

Such variety of types—huddled old women who had waited stoically, little children, in non-descript garments, who could make themselves at home anywhere, but found even the novelty of the boat experience eclipsed by this stupendous new thing; there were several young married couples, clean but shabby. They stood near each other, rather silently, each couple linked together, looking and looking. There were several young girls, the most simply dressed, with always some piece of finery, a ribbon or a flower, or a gay scarf. And sometimes there was a whole family, father, mother, poor-looking and patient, with children passing about them full of eager questions. Most interesting of all to me was an American soldier, bringing back his old mother and his grandfather to America. He was really fine-looking, tall and straight, with brilliant black eyes, and very intelligent. I often spoke to him in passing and he seemed pleased. And on the dock, I saw him again, managing everything for his little group and helping others. As he left, leading his old mother, I went over and spoke to them, and told the mother that I hoped she would be happy in her new home. She overwhelmed me with Italian thanks.

But seeing land! You can't imagine the thrill of it,—it was 'half akin to pain.' I think there was no 'man with soul so dead' on the Patria, *that didn't say 'this is my home, my native land.'*

The harbor is magnificent. You have to be proud when you look at it. And then the Statue of Liberty. It seems so to epitomize all America, the fulfillment of the hope that burns in the tense, earnest eyes of the immigrants. The whole sky was softly flaming in rose color and the gigantic buildings cut sharply into it in massive lines of real beauty. I felt busting with pride and wanted to say, "This is my own country."[24]

In New York, Natalie visited Dr. Wyeth, Evelyn Preston, Dr. Lambert, and many of her other wartime friends. The families of several of her deceased patients were in the New York area, and she paid visits to their homes. After a stopover with her cousins in Washington, Natalie boarded the train for New Orleans and arrived home on Saturday evening, October 25, 1919. She was met at the station by Muddie, Boss, Jack, Sidonie and Nauman, her niece and nephew, and a large gathering of her New Orleans friends and press reporters.

The next morning, Natalie's photograph appeared on the newspaper's front page, with the story of her arrival home.

Orleans Girl Home With Croix de Guerre
Miss Natalie Scott Honored for Bravery;
Throng Welcomes Her

Seldom has a conquering hero received the reception tendered Miss Natalie Scott, New Orleans war nurse heroine and Red Cross worker overseas for more than two years, as she arrived at the Louisville and Nashville station late Saturday night. Her mother and father, Mr. and Mrs. Nat G. Scott, were there. They had been waiting in the station more than an hour. Her friends, too were unwilling to miss the opportunity of being the first Orleanians to welcome the girl heroine.

They glimpsed her face as the coach passed slowly by, preparatory to stopping. Unable to restrain themselves, they started cheering. Miss Scott herself seemed overcome with joy. She returned the greeting with a hearty, "Hello folks. Glad to see you again!" She was attired in her uniform, epaulets were intact, and she carried a riding whip in her hand. On her coat, but pinned inconspicuously, she wore the Croix de Guerre. It was the expression of the French government for the valor she displayed.

"I'm glad to be back," Miss Scott said, the center of an admiring group. "It was a wonderful experience. It has taught me some things, too, that degrees in every university in the country would fail to impart."

Of her feats, Miss Scott declined to talk.[25]

Chapter Seven

The French Quarter Renaissance

Thus the curtain fell upon Natalie's early life, and a new one lifted immediately. A fresh drama would lead her through a wondrous New Orleans decade, the French Quarter Renaissance of the 1920s. That first Sunday morning in the city, Natalie was invited by an old Drama League colleague to help start a theater organization in the French Quarter. She had returned from Europe with a new appreciation for the old town, its narrow streets and Old World architecture now reminding her of Montmartre and Beauvais. Understanding the intrinsic beauty and value of the Quarter, Natalie eagerly embraced the idea of a new French Quarter theater, with the broader cause of historic preservation and restoration. Their new organization would become Le Petit Théâtre du Vieux Carré. While spending her early weeks unpacking, visiting with loved ones, giving speeches for the Red Cross, and marching in the Armistice Day parade, Natalie became a founder of the new theater.[1]

The French Quarter, a century earlier the finest section of a prospering city, had declined disastrously by 1919. Almost all the elite Creole families had long ago abandoned the Vieux Carré for more favored uptown neighborhoods. The deteriorating Quarter was a downtrodden mixture of immigrants, tramps, prostitutes, peddlers pulling their wagons, and itinerants seeking a cheap place to lay their heads. These hard-luck inhabitants shared the Quarter with a scattered handful of actors, obscure intellectuals, artists, and journalists. Here, without visible sign of law enforcement or city services, neglect seemed superimposed upon the ancient architecture, assaulting the senses. Streets and sidewalks lay broken and unimproved; stagnant water stood in drainage ditches. Delicate wrought-iron balconies served as improvised clotheslines; and chickens, pigs, scrawny cows, and old horses were stalled within ruins of once-elegant courtyards, even in broken-down sections of the old Pontalba buildings. Abandoned mansions, barely recognizable, housed cheap dives, flophouses, and tenements.[2]

All civic efforts towards restoration had failed. Yet this new drama group, Le Petit Théâtre du Vieux Carré, recognized the old town's underlying beauty. Despite its drawbacks, they chose the French Quarter as their home. They found its authentic and offbeat unpretentiousness an appropriate backdrop for creativity. They invited uptowners there, exposing them to its Old World charm. These creative people, who appreciated the Quarter's faded beauty and bohemian atmosphere, gave birth to a natural restoration movement.

Natalie became one of Le Petit Théâtre's twenty founders. Their leader, the elderly society and theatrical figure Mrs. Oscar Nixon, with fellow organizer Helen Schertz, a local author, searched the Quarter for a suitable playhouse. They chose a second-floor space in the lower Pontalba building, on the corner of St. Ann and Decatur streets. It was an abandoned tramp's hotel that had become too filthy even for the tramps, and the rental price was seventeen dollars per month. Ambitiously scheduling their first performance for late November, only a month away, this band of theater-lovers faced three formidable tasks: attracting uptowners to the Quarter for amateur theater, transforming their leased space into a playhouse, and producing their first play.

Natalie plunged into the first two, organizing luncheons and French Quarter tours to recruit dues-paying members, selling tickets, and joining fellow organizers to clean, paint, and prepare the place. By opening night, a remarkable transformation had occurred. The walls were a fresh gold, with life-sized green peacocks painted near the ceiling upon a gilded panel. Rows of black-and-gold-painted kitchen chairs awaited the audience. Candles were mounted upon a large wooden wheel hung as a handsome chandelier. Finally, a handcrafted stage, twenty-four feet wide with a proscenium opening, was festive with flowers and green plants.[3]

The November performances attracted curious capacity crowds to the tiny second-floor theater. During intermissions, the audiences flowed onto the long balcony overlooking Jackson Square and the Mississippi River. The successful debut inspired

Le Petit Théâtre organizers to proceed with rehearsals for the December bill.

Only weeks earlier, a far more noteworthy theater opening had occurred a few blocks away, a moment long anticipated, attracting vastly larger crowds and front-page headlines. On November 11, in celebration of Armistice Day, the freshly renovated French Opera House on Bourbon Street had reopened after a two-year wartime hiatus. The city's elite, in sparkling evening attire, packed the place. But the daily performances by international celebrities ended abruptly within a month. Disaster struck the nation's oldest opera house early on December 4. A three-o'clock fire alarm sounded at Toulouse and Bourbon streets, bringing fire trucks through the narrow streets, the sirens awakening inhabitants to the fact of a major emergency. Hundreds gathered that awful night, watching as firefighters fought the flames. The Toulouse street wall, sixty feet high, collapsed on one of the fire trucks as firemen ran to safety. One of the Vieux Carré's most beloved structures burned to the ground, never to be rebuilt. This was an aesthetic disaster that seemed to toll the final collapse of the French Quarter itself, far overshadowing the small gain made by the opening of Le Petit Théâtre. The loss to the Vieux Carré could hardly be exaggerated.[4]

The fire occurred a week after Le Petit Théâtre's opening performances. Their December bill bravely went on as scheduled. It was another modest success, providing the Quarter, in the aftermath of tragedy, with a faint pulse, as another round of capacity audiences applauded their work. They expanded the format in January to three one-act plays, including *Le Passant* by François Coppee, entirely in French. Le Petit Théâtre's selections displayed throughout the season a commitment to variety, experimentation, and originality. Natalie's Newcomb friend Martha Gilmore Robinson and her brother Samuel Louis Gilmore performed in *The Land of Heart's Desire* by William Butler Yeats in January 1920; Natalie played a lead role in *Two Crooks and a Lady* by Eugene Pillot during March.

With their membership exploding from 20 to 500 by May, the end of their first season, the troupe reengineered the cramped Pontalba playhouse over the summer. They tripled the seating, a stopgap that could not accommodate ticket demands. So Le Petit Théâtre proceeded with plans to build a large permanent theater across Jackson Square on the corner of Chartres and St. Peter streets. By the time this beautiful new playhouse opened in November 1922, Le Petit Théâtre's membership had grown to 3,000, making it arguably the most successful amateur theater in America. Membership doubled by 1927.[5]

Le Petit Théâtre's success sparked a modest but steady migration to the Quarter. Early French Quarter pioneers such as journalist Lyle Saxon and painter Alberta Kinsey gradually were joined by increasing numbers of artists, musicians, and writers. The curious from many prominent uptown families cleaned and moved into old properties. New arrivals were attracted not only by architectural aesthetics and cheap rents but also, oddly enough, by the Quarter's offbeat inhabitants and the sense of escape to a quiet refuge.

These ingredients produced a bohemian flavor that was creatively stimulating. A sense of liberation from society's rules resulted in a colony of kindred spirits passionately pursuing their artistic work. The old town's increasing appeal then spurred small restorations from Jackson Square to Canal Street, between Chartres and Bourbon, as modest shops, bookstores, and coffeehouses opened throughout the 1920s. The Louisiana State Museum, headquartered in the Cabildo beside St. Louis Cathedral, and the Louisiana Historical Society, led by novelist Grace King, capitalized on the new momentum by raising monies to preserve major landmarks.[6]

Natalie became a newspaperwoman in early 1920, as a feature writer and columnist for the *New Orleans States*. She covered hard news stories, such as the sensational Andrew J. Whitfield trial in March, the murder victim being the Honduran diplomatic consul. Natalie also regularly wrote feature stories and a popular Sunday column that traced every type of interesting activity in the city—social, artistic, and political.

Using the Irish nickname Boss had playfully given her during childhood, Natalie entitled her newspaper column *"Peggy Passe Partout,"* or "Peggy Who Goes Everywhere." Natalie's more philosophical interpretation was "Peggy's Magic Key," her providential gift that opened to her a world of adventure and discovery. Her primary focus was New Orleans and the pursuits of New Orleanians, but in a couple of years, she was also traveling extensively overseas to write columns and feature articles.

d In First

NIGHT EDITION RACING, LATEST SPORTS

TES

L 17, 1920.   IN CITY HOTELS AND ON TRAINS. 5 CENTS; SUNDAY, 10 CENTS   PRICE THREE CENTS.

Miss Scott's Story Of Whitfield And Wife

All the Incidents of Murder Trial Pictured In Detail With Dramatic Shadings So You May Visualize Court Scenes.

BY NATALIE VIVIAN SCOTT.

THE FOURTH DAY of the Whitfield trial. For three days the old red brick courthouse has been the goal of a swarm of curious people, a swarm that grows constantly larger, though each day it seems that the last limit of capacity has been reached. For three days, the long, high-ceiled room on the second floor has been the scene of a drama of constantly increasing intensity, of an infinitely varied play of personality, of a series of emotional climaxes. For three days, a searchlight of never-ceasing questions has played on every incident of the night of November eleventh that could be fitted into what is known as the doings of Andrew J. Whitfield and of Dr. and Mrs. Cordova on that night.

The story of that night, of the way in which the paths of these three people met for the first time and crossed so tragically, has been told and retold by one person after another. And always, from the long slow process of selecting the jurors, through all the play and interplay of questioning and argument that has gone on unceasingly, there has been the fascinating, absorbing spectacle of the clash of mind, of intellects trained, and keen, pitted against one another, the thrust and parry of question and counter-question.

Of the actors who played more or less important roles in the drama that is being unfolded, only one of the principal figures has yet spoken, Señora Cordova. The other two will be heard in the court-room for the first time today.

The court-room, which packed crowded Thursday, today is packed with spectators jammed solidly in every available inch of space in the aisles. There is every class among

CARRANZA ARMY IS MURDEROUS, SENATE TOLD

(By United Press)

WASHINGTON, April 17.—Lively debate broke out in the senate today over the Mexican request that Carranza soldiers be permitted to cross American territory to attack Sonora rebels.

During the debate, Senator Knox announced that the permission had been refused. Later, however, he said he based this on an article in a morning newspaper.

Mr. Knox made the statement dur

WITNESS FOR WHITFIELD IN ROGUES GALLERY

Exclude Evidence of U. S. Agents That Cordova Feared Death

After Argument lasting nearly an hour, District Attorney Luzenberg won his point when Judge Landry excluded the evidence of Mr. Pendleton and Mr. Tolvar. Immediately after the defense rested its case. A brief recess will be taken by the State before its rebuttal witnesses are placed on the stand, for the recess at 3:55. The case may possibly go to the jury late tonight.

Testimony late Saturday by Department of Justice officials in the trial of Andrew J. Whitfield tended to show that Dr. Leopoldo Cordova, former Honduran consul, man be, if accused of murdering, was deeply involved in political complications and lived in fear of his life from intrigue.

J. M. "Doc" Tolvar, government agent, said

Natalie's newspaper writing introduced her to many of the noteworthy personalities visiting the city. Her personal interviews during her first year alone included Gen. John J. Pershing, Enrico Caruso, William Butler Yeats, Eamonn de Valera, president-elect and Mrs. Warren G. Harding, Franklin D. Roosevelt, and Anne Morgan, to name only a few. Some became permanent friends; Pershing dined with Natalie on a subsequent visit, and his sister later stayed for several days in the Scott home. Many were not yet famous but destined for accomplishment—for example, George C. Marshall, who accompanied Pershing to the city in February 1921, and her friend Harry Hopkins, director of the New Orleans Red Cross, later to become Franklin Roosevelt's New Deal relief strategist. Jane Addams, the great American social worker who would win the Nobel Peace Prize in 1931, began her friendship with Natalie at the National Conference of Welfare Workers in April 1920. Also in April, the American Medical Association, with her former Paris Red Cross chief Dr. Alexander Lambert as its president, met in New Orleans, reuniting Natalie with many medical friends from the war.[7]

There were troubles too. Cancer struck Natalie's parents in 1920. Boss lost part of his tongue in two operations, permanently impeding his speech. Muddie underwent painful radium treatments, leaving her with deep burns. She was hospitalized from August until November in Baltimore, with Natalie at her side. Here Natalie visited several military hospitals. In a later newspaper column promoting a New Orleans charity concert by French performers named the Neckelsons, she commented on the forgotten victims of the war. *You remember there was a war? Some strange things happened. For instance, in front hospitals, cramped, hastily erected, within range of shelling, frequently bombarded, it was often possible to hear vaudeville songs, the latest and best that Paris afforded, or to catch strains of operatic music which were the pride of the Opera National, swelling from a rough baraque, where lay wounded soldiers. Such was the work of the Theatre des Armees. The artists of France of every class supported it; many of them gave much of their time and much of their money in this way. And the Neckelsons were among the number.*

Their war-work is not over. A large percentage of the proceeds of their concert goes to the blind of the Allied Armies. When I hear people remark jauntily that "the war is over" I think of a visit I made recently to Evergreen, a school for blind soldiers, near Baltimore. Down the long line of the boardwalk in the beautiful grounds, I met at intervals fine young fellows, tapping along hesitantly, and feeling their way as slowly as old men. They talked gaily enough, but when they thought themselves alone, their figures slumped listlessly. The memory of them makes me think that the Neckelson performance would be worth while, even if it had something less interesting to offer than the unfailing charm of wizardry and the magic of a lovely voice.[8]

International politics became an occasional topic in Natalie's writings. The consequences of America's isolation, she feared, would be another war. She interviewed English author and poet Coningsby Dawson, then attended his lecture that evening. *His lecture Monday night was beautiful in its idealism. But he proposed an inexorable question: "Are we going to make the world safe for peace?"* Then Natalie asked her readers: *Does the war sometimes haunt you at inopportune moments? As you are about to lift a cup of tea to your lips, do you suddenly, for no reason, see an ugly gaping wound before you? On the golf course, does the stretch of pleasant green suddenly contract to dingy walls, with rows of white beds, and pain-twisted faces? Does what during the war seemed glorious seem sometimes now only horrible? It happens to all of us.*

Coningsby Dawson gave back the old glory of the hardly vindicated ideals of the war, sloughed over so often now by egotism. He gave back the power to look with pride and not shuddering on the memories of agony and supreme sacrifice. He had his own share of suffering, though naturally he did not mention it in his lecture. Coningsby had suffered arm wounds and *gas gangrene, one of the most exquisite tortures of this civilized warfare of ours. But for himself, and those who suffered and gave with him and beyond him, he answers that it was "worthwhile". And he asks, as those have most right to ask, whether those hard-won ideals are to be lost now by after the war political squabbles and international jealousies.*

Natalie's commentary was usually laced with wit, her writings on women's suffrage being a typical example as she followed the debates in the Louisiana legislature. One of her Sunday columns painted a vivid picture of disapproving husbands. *There are some Burning Questions which engage us greatly. Chief among them still is woman suffrage. Up at the suffrage front, in Baton Rouge, it is especially burning. And every day, as some of the valiant contestants return, others from here of our beauty and our eloquence (feminine gender) go up to take their places. The effort is heart-felt and strenuous, but logical and orderly, to get the right answer to the ever-present interrogation: to vote, or not to vote.*

Entre nous, one of the most interesting "features of the case", as the lawyers say, is the Husband. I think that the Little Theatre expounded, in one of its plays, that there was only one genus or species or class of that being; but really there are some differentiations to be made.

For instance, there is the husband of independent mind. He tells his wife that it is plainly her duty, since she started helping the cause and since things are going well at home, to run up to the storm-center and help her side. Yes, indeed, this did happen,—it is no vision of centuries hence. Then, there is the opposite extreme, the husband of day before yesterday, who thinks (or would you say "think"?) that woman's place is in the home. He is often kind-hearted; he would love to see his wife run across the Lake for a week, leaving the children with her mother, or to have her go off for a few months in the summer; but speak of Baton Rouge to him, and he thunders in St. Elmo style of oratory, "There's the modern woman for you; leaves her home and her children to go to rack and ruin, while she plunges into the filthy swirl of politics." Then there's middle man, as it were; he doesn't really care, but the fellows at the club start teasing him, and, hang it all, he doesn't want to be made a fool of, and have people laughing at him; so he veers over to the extreme position and asserts himself "like a man," and tells his wife: "Thou shalt stay at home; thou shalt not go to Baton Rouge"—and then feels very comfortable when she obeys him, with an injured air!

So it goes. And, meanwhile, the day of reckoning and decision is at hand, and we shall soon know where Louisiana stands; and cheer ourselves with the thought that, whichever way things go here, we shall yet vote, whether thanks to ourselves or another state. But, as for those three styles in husbands, don't think that I invented them. I am not that clever. That's the work of providence, and there's a prototype for each instance![9]

A New Magazine

Natalie ushered in 1921 by performing in a comedy called *Game of Hearts* with three other Le Petit Théâtre regulars, before a large New Year's Eve dinner-dance audience at the New Orleans Country Club. The play kicked off a series of parties that moved to two downtown restaurants (with drinks she called New Orleans Volsteads) and a place named Child's, followed by French Market pastries and coffee at daybreak. During January and February 1921, Natalie performed the lead role in Le Petit Théâtre's production of *Joint Owners in Spain*. In May, a farcical play she wrote with Sam Gilmore entitled *What, Again?* became the featured production. Lyle Saxon gave the comedy a glowing review in the *Times-Picayune,* as did the enthusiastic *New Orleans Illustrated News,* spicing their critiques with photographs from the production.[10]

Post-play parties added social gaiety to the productions. The usual gathering spot was the nearby Quartier Club on St. Peter Street, formed in the autumn of 1920 to celebrate the beaux arts. During one after-theater rendezvous that was preserved in Natalie's column, actress Jessie Tharp stood in the midst of the crowded party to read aloud a humorous poem, inspiring a series of spirited encores. *The Little Theatre had yielded up its audience and actors; the studios, which have sprung up everywhere in the Vieux Carré were well-represented: Musicians, artists, actors, authors. Mrs. Kahn played the violin delightfully with Mrs. Schertz accompanying her; Mrs. Castellannos was pushed up to the center of the table, where she gave a perfect imitation of a French Opera ballet girl; Harry Loeb followed, with his puns and a burlesque recitation. Mrs. Schertz rendered a touching ballad concerning gum; Mr. Blood, a well-known English actor, who was guest of the club for the evening, gave some finished pieces of impersonation in Scotch and cockney dialect. Harry Loeb went to the piano and played and everyone sang; and, finally, as though to prove that we have a right to the French Quarter, he played the "Marseillaise," and everyone sang it. An evening in care-free and clever Bohemia, that was, the magic land is our door on St. Peter Street!*[11]

Still another organization, one that would play a vital role in the French Quarter's artistic revival, opened in 1921 and was introduced to the city via Natalie's column in May. *June 1 will mark the coming out party of the latest debutante, the Arts and Crafts Club of New Orleans. She is quite the modern type—with a serious purpose in life, a purpose with a dual nature, artistic and practical. Artistically, she means to foster, diversify, and raise the standards of arts and crafts in New Orleans, and practically, she means to bring the creative artist closer to his public. The plans are comprehensive, and include the luxuries of club, exhibition, and sales room, an assemblage of current literature on arts and crafts; classes in different branches, and so on. The headquarters for the present are at 913 St. Charles Street, but that's merely till they are formally introduced.* The Arts and Crafts Club found a permanent home in December 1921, the old Brulatour Mansion, 520 Royal Street, offered by art patron William Irby. The club was well settled and in full swing by January 1922.[12]

In 1920, Natalie had leased a small apartment in a tall house on Orleans Alley, just behind St. Louis Cathedral. In June 1921, she made her first financial investment in the French Quarter, when she and John McClure, a poet and neighbor, purchased the building. McClure had just begun editing the city's new *Double Dealer* literary magazine while he and his wife also operated the Olde Book Shop on Royal Street. Their aim for the apartment house was to provide inexpensive lodgings for serious artists and writers in the center of the Vieux Carré.

Local newspapers made note of the transaction: "For Natalie Vivian Scott, society and feature writer of the *States,* Newcomb alumna and war service worker, and John McClure have bought an old home at 626 Orleans Alley and they intend to convert the building into studios at the first order. Lack of studios is said by those who are in the know on that sort of thing to be one of the obstacles in the way of art's development in New Orleans. So the announcement brings joy to the gay little Vieux Carré and its inmates." They soon filled their old mansion with creative people, productive artists and writers, while Natalie and the McClures also maintained their apartments there.[13]

The French Quarter Renaissance would owe much to the magnetic appeal and groundbreaking quality of *The Double Dealer* magazine. The first edition of this pioneering literary publication appeared in January 1921. This most important of Southern "little magazines" eventually attracted an intellectual audience of 18,000 subscribers across the United States and overseas. It achieved the reputation of having a remarkable eye for raw talent, providing many young authors with their first opportunity to have their work published. Though the founder was a talented New Orleanian named Julius Friend, two others deserve equal credit for its literary success, Basil Thompson and John McClure. A fourth, Natalie's old friend and prolific literary contributor Samuel Louis Gilmore , eventually became an editor as well. But there were other key participants, Natalie Scott among them, whose collective literary and operational involvement throughout the magazine's five-and-a-half-year life assured *The Double Dealer*'s literary importance. While strongly supporting the magazine from its start in her newspaper column, Natalie did not formally join its staff until August 1921.

In concept, Julius Friend wanted *The Double Dealer* to be brazenly original, irreverently funny, unrestrained, shocking, full of zest, and intellectually thoughtful. It was to be a forum for free thinkers to throw off the straitjacket of conformity, to ignore political, social, or literary correctness. The magazine declared as its motto, "Honesty is our policy," and Friend's editorial in the first issue proclaimed its audacious mission:

> But, heigh-ho, you say, what has all this to do with *The Double Dealer,* this unchanging depravity and this timorousness of human nature? Here is the answer. *The Double Dealer* is concerned with this human nature, the raw stuff, cleared of the myths of glamor-throwers and Utopia-weavers, casting off the spell of "all the drowsy syrups of the world." We mean to deal double, to show the other side, to throw open the back windows stuck in their sills from disuse, smuttered over long since against even a dim beam's penetration. To myopics we desire to indicate the hills, to visionaries the unwashed dishes...the pathos of a fop in an orphan asylum, the absurdity of an unselfish reformer. We expect to be called Radical by Tory and Reactionary by Red. But we remain only ourselves who can "deceive them both by speaking the truth," and, as the honest soul amongst you, we ask you in the mysteries of your subterranean retorts to drain a beaker of the forbidden juice of the fruit to—THE DOUBLE DEALER.[14]

A Harvard graduate six years younger than Natalie, Julius

Friend joined with Basil Thompson as the most determined of the magazine's leadership to emphasize the rebellious personality of *The Double Dealer*. Thompson, also a New Orleanian, had achieved recognition as a prolific young poet, published in two small books and many literary journals. Three years younger than Natalie, Thompson as an editor proved so sensitive to the appearance of self-promotion that he excluded his own material from *The Double Dealer*'s pages, except for his biting editorials written under humorous pen names. One chronicler offered this description: "Basil knew he was like Shelley, that he would not live long; and he did everything in his power, apparently indirectly, to hasten the end. He was charming, lovable, witty, dramatic in his own way, the spark of the joint undertaking; and *The Double Dealer* group fizzed and effervesced under his influence." He would die in April 1924, midway through the magazine's life, after writing a series of poems about his own death. At age thirty, he was a victim of his own lifestyle, having contracted pneumonia as a complication of his excessive drinking.[15]

The steady hand that proved to be most responsible for the editorial genius of the magazine belonged to John ("Jack") McClure, a widely published poet and experienced editor. As co-editor and a prolific contributor, he took over as the chief editor after Basil Thompson's death. McClure, a modest Oklahoman, once described himself as "a physical weakling who somehow always got along fairly well in a world of strong men." He and his wife, Grace, were gentle, thoughtful people, among Natalie's favorite friends.[16]

With the editors being part time, unpaid, and short-handed, there was a monthly struggle in *The Double Dealer*'s Baronne Street office to pull together each issue, but Natalie enjoyed it. As a staff member, publicist, and investor, Natalie gave time and money to the cause. Her small donations eventually made her one of the four largest stockholders in the never-profitable enterprise. The artistic value of the unique magazine served as their reward, and it attracted national notice and intellectual curiosity to the Quarter. The literati who came to the Vieux Carré found ample opportunities to publish locally, as William Faulkner did. The magazine also carried the work of new authors into the great publishing centers—New York and elsewhere. It served as a magnetic advertisement to writers everywhere that the Quarter was the place to be.[17]

The Double Dealer's unsung, unpaid staff was composed of four women and one man: Natalie Scott, Flo Field, Olive Boullemet Lyons, Marguerite Samuels, and Gideon Stanton. Yet it remained intact throughout the magazine's existence, providing crucial stability, literary judgment, and work capacity. Meanwhile, the editorial leadership changed many times. Julius Friend took leave of his editorship after Thompson's death; McClure began his long writing and editing career with the *Times-Picayune* while serving as the magazine's chief editor.

Everyone in *The Double Dealer* family, editors and staff alike, shared responsibilities. The magazine stopped listing the editors and staff in a hierarchal way, a quiet acknowledgment that everyone's roles overlapped in the monthly drive to produce each issue. The staff labored on in obscurity, enjoying the challenge and providing a backup system for one another's periods of unavailability.[18]

Rising and prominent writers whose work appeared in *The Double Dealer* the first year included Benjamin de Casseres, Vincent Starrett, Alfred Kreyemborg, Lord Dunsany, Louis Untermeyer, William Alexander Percy, Hart Crane, Arthur Symons, Howard Mumford Jones, Carl Van Vechten, and Oscar Williams—not an imposing list but a very good beginning. The cast improved dramatically in 1922, when contributors included Ernest Hemingway, Sherwood Anderson, William Faulkner, Ezra Pound, Maxwell Bodenheim, Allen Tate, Edmund Wilson, Jr., Elizabeth Coatsworth, and Thornton Wilder. A host of young authors was given the first opportunity to publish. James Fiebleman, Hamilton Basso, and Robert Penn Warren were teenagers and Hemingway and Faulkner entirely unknown when their work first appeared here.

The breakthrough had occurred when Sherwood Anderson, arguably America's premier short-story writer and novelist at the time, pleased with a review of his work written by Hart Crane for the July 1921 issue, strolled into *The Double Dealer* office in mid-January 1922. Immediately embracing the group with his effusive personality, Anderson proceeded to write for the magazine's February, March, April, and June issues. All the while, he lodged in the LaBranche building at Royal and St. Peter streets and was a frequent visitor at the nearby Scott-McClure House. Anderson returned irregularly over the next two years, finally making his home on Jackson Square during the summer of 1924 after marrying his third wife, Elizabeth. New Orleans remained their residence through 1926.[19]

Natalie was among those who welcomed Sherwood Anderson to *The Double Dealer* office that first day. She preserved the occasion in her January 22 column the following Sunday with poetry and gentle teasing of her new friend.

> "I met a writer in their midst,
> full beautiful, a muse's child,
> His eyes were fine, his step was firm
> And his hair was wild.
>
> And there I talked, ah joy betide,
> The strangest talk I ever talked,
> By the warm fireside."

I admit it's an informal introduction for Mr. Sherwood Anderson, author of "Winesburg, Ohio," "Poor White," and most recently "The Triumph of the Egg." Mr. Sherwood Anderson, whom Mencken, of the unequivocal pen, has just pronounced in the latest issue of Smart Set, the foremost writer of fiction in America. Mencken further remarks that Mr. Anderson has no forerunners and no followers, but stands alone. He has been in touch with "The Double Dealer" for some time and his first visit here was to the editorial rooms. He is comfortably ensconced in Royal street now, just around the corner from the McClures, where he "drops in of an evening" not infrequently. And he has some agreeable things to say about the Quarter. He is distinctly a feather in our artistic cap—and distinctly that is the only feather-like suggestion about him!

As for the girls, my dear, perhaps this will show you. In two days he was "Sherry" to them, and now I hear it is Cheri. Quite typical. Natalie and Anderson became close friends from their first meeting, Anderson becoming a regular topic and reader of her articles. Six years later in a New York newspaper, Anderson declared Natalie to be "the best newspaperwoman in America."[20]

Natalie's mother died in January 1922, the first of three devastating personal losses Natalie would suffer over the next four years. In the aftermath, Natalie planned a summer trip abroad, to write her column and feature articles as she went. Thereafter she traveled extensively each year, living in France, New York, and Mexico for months at a time through the 1920s.

Natalie made her second French Quarter restoration during February 1922, after purchasing a century-old, double-level, Creole-style cottage at 714 St. Peter. She cleaned, repaired, and repainted the place, again inexpensively leasing space to artists and writers and leaving it to her tenants to decorate their abodes as they pleased. Sam Gilmore became one of her lodgers here; years later he purchased the place from her. Oliver La Farge became another tenant, living here from 1925 until he left New Orleans in 1929 after finishing his Pulitzer Prize-winning novel, *Laughing Boy*.[21]

For her 1922 summer tour, Natalie led nine Newcomb college girls across a turbulent Europe, where the French army soon entered Germany's Ruhr valley to enforce delinquent Versailles treaty reparations payments. Internal political dissensions and financial chaos rocked numerous countries, particularly Germany and Russia. Naming the group "Natalie Scott and Her Nine Muses," the New Orleans press followed the trip. Her reports of their exploits regularly appeared in her "Peggy Passe Partout" column, with occasional feature articles. Natalie took these Newcomb women to see Europe's cultural highlights but also the war's battlegrounds, frontline trenches where the rude panoply of war (destroyed tanks, guns, other remnants) remained, and war cemeteries where she shared memories of soldiers—her patients—who lay there.

In a front-page interview upon her return, Natalie succinctly summarized the trip. *"Oh, it was a lovely summer," said Miss Scott. "We had a splendid time. Adventures? Scores of them, but the only dangerous one when we went for a swim in Genoa and for bathing suits they gave us Mother Hubbards in which we nearly drowned. Ever try to swim in one?"*[22]

Enter Spratling and Faulkner

William Spratling, age twenty-two, stepped into Natalie's life that September, destined to become the father of Mexico's modern silver industry and America's finest silver designer. She leased to the young artist-architect a second-floor apartment at

Natalie Vivian Scott, a charcoal drawing by William Spratling (1922). *Courtesy of the Bé Scott Thomas Collection*

the Scott-McClure House overlooking the garden behind St. Louis Cathedral. She had no idea that this thin, dark-haired, long-jawed man would exert a remarkable influence upon her future, and she upon his. Though he was an odd combination of temperamental loner and gregarious party-giver, the two had much in common, particularly their love of wit and their creative interests. Spratling, who possessed little experience with the performing arts, allowed Natalie to introduce him to Le Petit Théâtre. She eventually cast him in bit parts and enlisted his talents for stage designs and programs.

In New Orleans to teach architecture at Tulane University, Spratling had already become an exceptional artist. Orphaned at age thirteen, at age fifteen he attended the excellent Art Students League in New York. The next year he moved into his grandfather's Alabama home, subsequently attending nearby Auburn University during the war years. Here the architecture faculty and just about everyone else utilized his artistic talents, enabling Spratling to support himself, an early sign of his entrepreneurial instincts. Decades later, Spratling recalled in his memoirs his early New Orleans days.

> The owner of my apartment was Natalie Scott, a very social newspaperwoman of great charm and vast popularity. Thanks to Natalie the young professor of architecture was, in a very short time, "integrated" and in immediate contact with many people. A little later Natalie and I traveled the length and breadth of Louisiana in her old Buick to prepare our *Plantation Houses of Louisiana,* the writing of which caused Natalie, the gadabout, three years of suffering. This was published by the Architectural Book Publishing Company in New York in 1926.
>
> New Orleans in the twenties was a lively and colorful new world. It presented broad horizons to a young man fresh from

Auburn. The people there, many of them destined to become great, Roark Bradford, Caroline Durieux, Sherwood Anderson, Hermann Deutsch, Oliver La Farge, Frans Blom and many writers, painters and musicians, European and American, who came and went, formed a stimulating background. . . .

Of the writers, Sherwood [Anderson] of course was our star performer, a sort of magnet who attracted luminaries from afar. Freddie Oechsner and Hamilton Basso, students then, also sat at Sherwood's feet. We were all very close. We saw each other every day, almost every evening. If it wasn't Lyle Saxon's house, it was at Sherwood and Elizabeth's or my own, and there would be John Dos Passos, or perhaps Carl Sandburg or Carl Van Doren or a great publisher from New York, Horace Liveright or Ben Huebsh, all people we were proud to know.[23]

Beginning in October 1922, Spratling's art, published works, and occasional parties were often reported in Natalie's Sunday

Artist-architect-author William Spratling stands in the attic apartment he shared with William Faulkner at 621 St. Peter Street (ca. 1926). Future novelist Hamilton Basso sits beside him. *Courtesy of Special Collections, Tulane University Libraries*

columns. She recruited him to teach at the Arts and Crafts Club, his Saturday-afternoon outdoor sketching class becoming particularly popular. The French Quarter entered a golden age during 1922. The versatile Paul Swan, portrait painter, sculptor, and exquisite dancer, thrived there, building a career that would be acclaimed from New York to Paris; novelist Lucille Rutland returned home to New Orleans in late September 1922. *The Double Dealer* gained wide attention. One editorial was republished in the *London Mercury* in September and another critiqued in the *Manchester Guardian*. Basil Thompson's article on the French Quarter's rebirth appeared during November in *Nation* magazine.

The Quartier Club continued its Lyceum series, with London literary figure Hugh Walpole appearing as its December speaker. Genevieve Pitot, a New Orleans concert pianist touring Europe for two years, settled in the French Quarter, presented a December concert, and became a regular at Quarter parties. Dancers Elizabeth Lyons and Josephine Mostler, after performances with Isadora Duncan, returned to New Orleans, where they taught classes in the Vieux Carré. By December, over four hundred members were enrolled in Arts and Crafts Club classes. It offered voice lessons by concert soloist Isabel Kline and held a variety of exhibits that winter—woodblock prints by Marjorie Callendar, beautifully designed rugs by Marc Antony, and paintings by Will Stevens, Caroline Durieux, and Alberta Kinsey, among others. The Green Shutter coffeehouse displayed Newcomb pottery.[24]

November marked the grand opening of Le Petit Théâtre's spacious new theater, and the inaugural performance packed the house. Natalie attended with a crowd of friends, including Spratling, Martha Robinson, and Sherwood Anderson, who was briefly in the Quarter that winter. Basil Thompson's talented wife, Becky, a Chicago dancer who owned a studio on St. Peter Street, played a lead role that night.

Through 1923, this creative atmosphere inspired artists of all persuasions. The French Quarter Renaissance had arrived, its evolution uniquely recorded in Natalie's newspaper column.

Spratling and Natalie traveled separately in Europe during the 1923 summer, meeting briefly in Paris, Natalie's home base as she explored and reported on Spain, Morocco, Germany, and Russia. Spratling's first two publications appeared during that fall, in time for Christmas gift buying. The first was *Pencil Drawing,* an instructive book illustrated with his 1923 European renderings. Almost simultaneously, the Tulane Press sponsored *Picturesque New Orleans,* ten Spratling French Quarter prints enclosed in a historical folio, all of which was printed through Spratling's labor at the Arts and Crafts Club.

John Dos Passos arrived in early 1924 and enjoyed the French Quarter camaraderie. He completed his novel *Manhattan Transfer* in his Esplanade Avenue studio and thereafter became an occasional Quarter resident.[25]

Sketch of Orleans Alley (location of Scott-McClure House) from *Picturesque New Orleans,* by William Spratling. *Courtesy of Special Collections, Tulane University Libraries*

Basil Thompson's death on April 7, 1924, was a severe shock to the Quarter's artistic enclave and almost caused the closure of *The Double Dealer*. Its April edition did not appear until June. Its contents were entirely devoted to Basil Thompson, his poetry, and his essays. The May and June editions were canceled entirely. In grief, Julius Friend stepped away from the magazine for a year.

While Spratling went traveling abroad on a shoestring budget, Natalie canceled her summer travel plans to spend time with Basil's widow and assume some heavy duties for *The Double Dealer*. Her summer brightened upon Sherwood Anderson's unexpected arrival with his new wife, Elizabeth, the couple settling in their new Pontalba lodgings overlooking Jackson Square. Natalie became their close companion, introducing the couple around and acclimating Elizabeth to her new surroundings. At summer's end, a grateful Anderson gave Natalie a copy of his book of short stories, *The Triumph of the Egg*, inscribed "to

express some slight appreciation for her gracious help to me in knowing a little of the Pleasure of New Orleans." Another of Anderson's books appeared that fall, *The Story Teller's Story;* another would soon go to press. His productivity had been stirred by life in the Quarter.[26]

Natalie left New Orleans at the end of September for Greenwich Village, living there until the Christmas holidays. Frequenting the Gamut Club, she regularly attended productions of the Provincetown Theater Players, the Neighborhood Playhouse, and The Triangle, which she explained *was a unique experimental theater with, for habitat, a*

Elizabeth Prall Anderson and Sherwood Anderson (ca. 1923). *Courtesy of Special Collections, Tulane University Libraries large triangular cellar under the Chinaman's laundry on the outskirts of Greenwich Village, a magnet for New York's intellectuals. It is an original, enterprising, alert organization of undaunted open-mindedness, and it is quite fascinating.*

Le Petit Théâtre was well represented on the Broadway stages during this period, Jessie Tharp, Walter Ellis, Cora Witherspoon, and Elizabeth Lyons all cast in major productions. Tharp's performance in *The Last of the Lowries,* according to the *New York Morning Telegraph,* "ranks with the finest performances in our commercial theatres this season." Tharp also played five weeks with the Theater Guild in *Masse Mensch,* working with director Lee Simonson, and performed before packed audiences at the Waldorf. Natalie enjoyed the success of her French Quarter cohorts: Charles Bein's painting exhibit was scheduled for winter at the New Galleries, and Tommy Farrar gained recognition for his stage-scene designs. Here Natalie also entered the social circles of writer-literary critic Edmund Wilson, who began irregular visits to New Orleans; Mississippi novelist Stark Young; publisher Horace Liveright; author Anita Loos; playwright John Emerson; and H. L. Mencken, all friends of Sherwood Anderson.[27]

During 1925, William Faulkner moved into the French Quarter, a major addition to the creative circle. Faulkner, an unknown, who viewed himself as a poet, having worked earlier with Elizabeth Anderson in a New York bookstore, came to meet Sherwood Anderson in November 1924. Faulkner returned to New Orleans early in January, becoming a guest in the Andersons' apartment while Sherwood traveled on his cross-country book tour. Faulkner passed his mornings writing, "the afternoons plowing about, meeting strange people" in the streets around Jackson Square. He wrote short sketches, which the *Times-Picayune* began publishing at five dollars per column, a significant sum to Faulkner. He became friends with Natalie and *The Double Dealer* family, getting to know, according to his letters, the "beggars, people following the races . . . painters and writers, John McClure, a poet and literary editor of the *Times-Picayune,* . . . bums and cops and strange people, and in the evening we gather somewhere and discuss the world and politics and art and death."

By March 5, Faulkner moved into Spratling's new apartment, a larger place next door to the Scott-McClure House. Natalie saw

WS 1925

William Faulkner, by William Spratling (1925). *Courtesy of Special Collections, Tulane University Libraries*

much of him through the spring and summer as she and Spratling collaborated on their *Old Plantation Houses in Louisiana.* During 1926 and 1927, Faulkner lived in the attic apartment of Natalie's building at the corner of St. Peter and Cabildo Alley. Influenced by the Quarter's writers, particularly Sherwood Anderson, Faulkner was transformed from poet to prose writer, publishing his first two novels, *Soldiers' Pay* and *Mosquitoes.* He began other novels, developing many of the characters and conceiving the Mississippi settings for future work, while producing a stream of essays, poems, short stories, and sketches for *The Double Dealer* and the *Times-Picayune.*[28]

The mentoring and sponsorship of Sherwood Anderson proved crucial to Faulkner's effort to write his first novel. Sherwood and Elizabeth critiqued each chapter (so Faulkner reported in letters home to his mother that spring) as drafts emerged from Faulkner's all-morning writing sessions on the balcony of Spratling's apartment. Anderson placed this first novel, *Soldiers' Pay,* in his publisher's hands. Meanwhile, Anderson inadvertently inspired the plot and lead character for Faulkner's second novel, *Mosquitoes,* by chartering a yacht for a mid-March weekend escapade with a handful of French Quarter companions, including Faulkner and Spratling, to explore Lake Pontchartrain and the Tchefuncte River. Natalie's column the week before noted her plans, a "wild schedule," to make a trip across Lake Pontchartrain to Mandeville during the coming week. The next week she reported that the vessel was the *Josephine* and that they swam in the middle of Lake Pontchartrain with "Spartan indifference" to the chill March winds, fished on the Tchefuncte, and explored the banks in a skiff—"everything from aquatic sports to high literary pursuits."[29]

The year 1925 also welcomed to the city's intellectual life Tulane's Department of Middle American Research, created in February. It brought two important figures to the city, archeologist-anthropologists Frans Blom, age thirty-one, and Oliver La Farge, twenty-four, both men trained under famed anthropologist A. M. Tozzer of Harvard. La Farge had completed his undergraduate work the year before, after participating in two Harvard expeditions among the Navaho and Hopi Indians of the American Southwest. He would return there after 1930, the year his Indian-themed novel, *Laughing Boy,* won the Pulitzer Prize. Blom had discovered important Mayan ruins in 1919 while working for a Mexican oil company. Using his artistic training to make detailed drawings, he gained the attention of archeologists such as Sylvanus Morley of the Carnegie Institution. This led to Blom working under Manuel Gamio at the Palenque ruins, then for Carnegie's excavations in Guatemala. When the Tulane program was created, Blom was chosen to lead its first field expedition. These two men immediately established for Tulane a high international reputation in pre-Columbian studies.

Natalie's first encounter with Blom occurred on February 17, 1925, during his first brief visit to New Orleans before sailing for Mexico. Putting aside Carnival festivities, Natalie disciplined herself to attend Blom's faculty presentation on the Mayans, an occasion she found entirely fascinating. At a tea, she interviewed Blom before his departure, chatting about the Mayan calendar, rulers, religion, and astronomy. She devoted her next Sunday column to him and his intrepid expedition with Oliver La Farge.[30]

La Farge arrived for a brief stay-over at Tulane a week later. Natalie, who knew his family, introduced him around. The annual crescendo of Mardi Gras arrived simultaneously with the studious, rather innocent La Farge. Firmly in Natalie's grasp, he enjoyed social outings and even was placed on a Mardi Gras float all duly preserved in Natalie's post-Carnival column. *One of the last members of the expedition to depart was Mr. Oliver La Farge, of New York, Saunderstown, New Jersey, Harvard, and other where. He is the one of whom Mr. Blom spoke, the only other white man who will accompany him on his daring jaunt through untried wilds in Yucatan.* According to Natalie's newspaper description, the young La Farge *was dark-skinned, tawny-eyed, suggesting the tale of the Pocahontas heritage of the La Farge family, an excellent rider, an enthusiasm over Carnival trucks and Mardi Gras in general. Spectators of an informal contest on the Waldo lawn assert that he does an excellent handspring, and is quite gifted as to standing on his head. Such is versatility!*

Just after Carnival he took ship as blithely as he had taken the Carnival truck, and set out to join Mr. Blom. They go from Vera Cruz to Mexico City, and then they start on the journey which puts an ugly furrow of envy in my soul, unbroken months of the wilds, the "raw bush" as the phrase is, on mule-back, with native guides, rare Indian villages, unknown to white men, with all the while the thrill of the new and strange haunted by the ghosts of a rich, dead past, the thought that through the towering virgin forest, beneath the tangle of matted vines, may be the carcass of a perished city, may wait a stone which, like the Rosetta Stone, will unravel the mysteries of unknown "Glyphs". The wild joy of the adventurer with the steady purpose of the scientist to give it meaning; mind unleashed to hob-nob with the centuries.[31]

Sailing for Mexico

From the jungle depths of Chiapas six months later, Blom and La Farge brought back an intelligent Mayan Indian leader, known as the "Wise One" to his people, to spend intensive weeks explaining Mayan customs, rituals, and oral history in his ancient Indian dialect, which La Farge was rapidly mastering. His name was Tata of the Yokotan tribe. Their ship's arrival attracted national press attention, Blom and La Farge attired in their stained, worn jungle outfits, with bright scarlet sashes of the Backajon tribe. Their expedition had made startling discoveries of twenty-four buried cities, the tomb of a pre-Columbian Mayan king, seventy-three great Mayan monuments, and twenty-two Mayan inscriptions, information vital to the history of this vanquished civilization. Present for the spectacle, Natalie offered Tata, La Farge, and Blom an apartment in her 714 St. Peter Street property for their weeks of study. This became La Farge's permanent New Orleans home. Frans Blom found his own place in the St. Ann Street Pontalba building before the year's end.

Tulane explorers Oliver La Farge (left) and Frans Blom pose with Prince
Tata prior to their expedition's return to New Orleans (August 1925).
Courtesy of Middle American Research Institute, Tulane University

Natalie befriended Tata, even bringing him to her father's
home, along with Blom, La Farge, and a few others, for a memorable dinner. Prince Tata, as he became nicknamed, knew nothing about dining tables, silverware, and such formalities. But he
enjoyed the occasion, sitting attentively in his native garb, entertained by Natalie's efforts to learn words of his Mayan dialect.[32]

Bill Spratling and Bill Faulkner were absent during the excitement of the Tulane expedition's brilliant return, as the two were
off in Italy together. Natalie had joined well-wishers at dockside
in July to see them sail away. She received an early August postcard from Faulkner informing her they had safely arrived in
Italy, their first destination being Rapallo. *Bill Faulkner's card,
written in his fastidiously perfect, small characters, tells the
reason of their choice: they went to see Ezra Pound. Teasingly,
he makes no comment on that interesting literary figure after
having found him. He has bought a knapsack—baggage "pour*

le sport," and plans to walk from Genoa to Paris. Bill Spratling, however, more limited in time, is going directly on by more usual means of travel, to Spain, where he intends to visit the cities in the northern part, rather a hasty glimpse, before he goes on to Paris, and thence to New York and home.

Back in the city by September, Spratling joined Natalie at Frans Blom's October lectures. First learning from his new friends and then living in Mexico himself, Spratling would become an expert in Mexican colonial architecture and in pre-Columbian designs. His insatiable search for ancient artifacts would enable him to gather over his lifetime one of the finest private collections anywhere of pre-Columbian objects. Likewise, Natalie would attain in the next decade expertise in native Mexican anthropology, crafts, and folkways. During the 1930s, she explored much of Mexico on horseback for months at a time, often alone. She would guide museum expeditions and achieve modest proficiency in numerous native languages.[33]

With the addition of Faulkner, La Farge, and Blom to the St. Peter Street neighborhood, the Vieux Carré Renaissance reached its literary high point in 1925-26. Both La Farge and Blom were soon writing important books, among many local writers making their mark. Roark Bradford, who would be a co-winner of the Pulitzer Prize for drama in 1930 for the play *Green Pastures,* an adaptation of his book *Ol' Man Adam an' His Chillun* (1928), worked at the *Times-Picayune* with John McClure, Lyle Saxon, and Hamilton Basso; Meigs Frost and Natalie Scott were featured writers for the *States.* All were successfully publishing. Anita Loos visited during the spring of 1925, writing *Gentlemen Prefer Blondes* during her stay. John Dos Passos and Edmund Wilson by then were occasional lodgers in the French Quarter. Sherwood Anderson remained the Quarter's leading figure, publishing two more books, the bestseller *Dark Laughter* (1925) and *Tar: A Midwestern Childhood* (1926).[34]

Meanwhile Natalie purchased the run-down and empty Court of Two Sisters, in July 1925, and the French Quarter landmark became another restoration project. Though the building possessed potential, Natalie faced substantial financial risk with her limited means. She declared this to be the "most beautiful courtyard in the French Quarter." She made improvements, then leased apartments. One tenant, Mrs. W. B. Gregory, implemented

States Star Writers Romance On Latin America

MEIGS O. FROST and MISS NATALIE VIVIAN SCOTT, brilliant members of The States editorial staff, from drawings by Prof. William Spratling, New Orleans artist and head of the architectural department of Tulane University. Mr. Frost dips into Honduras and Miss Scott into Mexico for fascinating stories today.

New Orleans States promotes its feature writers Meigs Frost and Natalie Scott, with drawings by Spratling. (*New Orleans States,* December 1926)

an imaginative idea on the ground floor: a tearoom/catering establishment. It evolved quickly into a profitable restaurant, featuring the attractive courtyard and pretty Newcomb girls as servers.

Natalie had acquired in April 1925 the tall building on the corner of St. Peter and Cabildo Alley, 621 St. Peter Street. Her friends Marc and Lucille Antony lived here, both artistically successful while operating their interior-decorating shop downstairs. Spratling loved the view from the attic so, upon his return from Europe, he converted the space into an apartment (Faulkner joining him by December 1925); Spratling occupied this studio until 1929. Here Faulkner would write *Mosquitoes* and Spratling, in addition to his art and architectural publishing, would conceive, illustrate, and produce the small book of caricatures of French Quarter personalities, *Sherwood Anderson and Other Famous Creoles,* with Faulkner writing the introduction in caricature of Anderson's writing style. Natalie tripled her investment when

William Philip Spratling (1929). *Courtesy of Special Collections, Tulane University Libraries*

THE LOCALE, WHICH INCLUDES MRS. FLO FIELD

"The Locale" from *Sherwood Anderson and Other Famous Creoles* is a caricature drawing of the French Quarter by Spratling (1926). Natalie's building at bottom left housed the attic apartment of Spratling and Faulkner. At the upper left ("Literature & Less") is the Scott-McClure House. *Courtesy of Special Collections, Tulane University Libraries* she resold the Cabildo Alley building sixteen months later, investing her profits in other property and the stock market.[35]

By mid-1926, Natalie and Spratling had visited approximately one hundred plantations, their illustrated manuscript of *Old Plantation Houses in Louisiana* nearing completion. Their plan was to publish the book in time for the Christmas buying season. The two also planned extensive Mexico travels that summer. These plans changed abruptly when a double tragedy struck the Scott family in June. Natalie's brother Nauman, at home with his family in Alexandria, lost his life to an accidental pistol shot on June 15, the eve of his oldest son's tenth birthday. Visiting friends in Galveston when the tragedy occurred, Natalie rushed to Alexandria while her brother Jack remained with her father, whose health, already poor, worsened. The Alexandria funeral in the Scott home was followed by a memorial service in New Orleans, then burial in the family plot in Metairie Cemetery. Boss never recovered from the shock of his son's death. He died on July 6 from heart complications, the last three weeks the saddest of his life and also the worst for Natalie. Distraught over the deaths, she and Jack struggled to bring comfort to Sidonie and help care for the five children.

The loss of both parents and her brother, all between 1922 and 1926, changed the course of Natalie's life. Initially she went into seclusion. But her gentle friend Lyle Saxon coaxed her out with a quiet invitation for breakfast in his apartment, while her best friend Hilda Phelps Hammond provided comfortable companionship. A recklessness, a thirst for change, emerged. Natalie's connections with New Orleans were drastically altered, a severing process that, influenced by other factors as well, would lead by 1930 to her new life in Mexico. She did not go to Mexico the summer of 1926. Instead, she traveled back and forth to Alexandria, helping Sidonie with her children. Bill Spratling departed alone by ship for Mexico the last Friday in June. Following his return in August, he exhibited his summer's artwork and published illustrated articles on Mexican architecture.[36]

Nothing was done to produce another issue of *The Double Dealer*. The May issue, which appeared in June just before Nauman's death, proved to be the last. H. L. Mencken, publisher, author, and the nation's best-known social critic, became concerned enough about *The Double Dealer*'s demise to visit the city in October to try to revive it. John McClure hosted a party on his behalf at the Scott-McClure House. But the magazine was not resurrected. Natalie left for a long journey in Mexico during October, then on to Europe for virtually all of 1927. Three decades later, in 1953, John McClure and Julius Friend explained to an interviewer that "lack of time on the part of the staff was the sole cause" of *The Double Dealer*'s discontinuance, though the interviewer chose to disregard this information, assuming finances must have been the real reason. Actually, the magazine possessed ample guarantors and contributors to make up monthly deficits for the foreseeable future. The true reason, as Friend and McClure said, was the lack of staff time. Changing priorities in everyone's personal lives, as in Natalie's case, culminated in the close of the publication's colorful career in June 1926.[37]

Natalie sailed in October for Mexico, then took a train through the mountains from Vera Cruz to Mexico City. *The trip up from the coast defies superlatives,—a climb in twelve hours from sea level to ten thousand feet; mad vegetation most of the way, with flowers weird and brilliant beyond the dreams of futurist artists. There are deep gulches, hair-raising sheer drops, thread-like bridges over dizzy space, and always the natives. White haciendas, flat-roofed, with deep colonnaded galleries. Mexico City is in the midst of a fantastic landscape.*

Natalie arrived with a supply of names from Frans Blom and Spratling, people with whom she would form permanent friendships: Fred Davis of the Sonora News Company, magazine publisher Frances Toor, painter Diego Rivera, among others. She began doing translations and editing, free of charge, for Toor's magazine *Mexican Folkways,* each article appearing in both Spanish and English. She gained friendships among its staff and regular contributors, including Rivera (art director), author Anita Brenner, anthropologist Manuel Gamio, artist Jean Charlot, the remarkable statesman, artist, and scholar Dr. Atl, social reformer Moises Saénz, photographer Tina Modotti, artist-caricaturist Miguel Covarrubias, antiquities expert René d'Harnoncourt, and artist Roberto Montenegro. All were creative and intellectual leaders of their generation in Mexico. Natalie also knew Louisianians there, such as artist Caroline Durieux, her husband, Pierre, and son, Charlie, and she wrote about many of them in the articles she sent back to the *New Orleans States.*[38]

Only five years had passed since the bloody Mexican Revolution, and Natalie arrived in the midst of the new Mexican government's battle with the Catholic Church. The government condemned the Church as exploitive of the peasants and as an enemy of the revolution. A prolonged religious war was under way, the bloody Cristero Rebellion, which saw the Catholic peasants of western Mexico forming their own armies to fight for the Church. Violence raged in the countryside, but conditions were calmer in Mexico City. The clergy there refused compliance with the government's licensure laws and other regulations; the government retaliated by prohibiting those priests from officiating in churches. One of Natalie's feature articles, "The Crucible of Insolubles," presented a thoughtful analysis of the cultural contradictions and challenges facing Mexico, why this beautiful country posed such a strange riddle to all foreigners.

Addressing the Catholic Church question, she cited the charges of vast wealth that *poured out of the country through ecclesiastical channels, and of the vast proportion of land and wealth that remained in its power even with laws against it. In communities of want and poverty rise magnificent convents and churches.* Yet Natalie questioned the validity of these charges, noting that most such churches had been built centuries earlier during colonial times. The Catholic Church, she wrote, seemed to be the institution closest to the peasant.

Natalie traveled to Tepotzotlán, admiring its magnificent sixteenth-century church and monastery, and Cholula, *a town of some ten thousand where there are three hundred and sixty-five churches, and Puebla, also rich with churches. Not a priest is in any of them now, but the churches are open, and always there are candles burning. Two Sundays ago in the evening, I went to the great shrine of Guadeloupe. The church was filled, almost entirely with Indians in their shapeless, faded and colorless garments; filled, too, with the sweet monotony of their prayers, which were led by one and then another of them, many among the closely crowded kneeling figures held candles, which etched out an earnest face here and there. There was a matchless, moving beauty in the scene. Women moved on their knees painfully on the cold flooring towards the altar. One man prayed with his arms held out in the sign of the cross, a ragged old man with a lined face and patient eyes.*

She wrote of the many *infused elements,* such as the foreigners who spend their lives there but do not consider Mexico their home. *Rarely do they seem to love the land.* She wrote of Frances Toor, an exception, *an American woman of cleverness and enterprise* who was publishing an interesting magazine, *Mexican Folkways,* yet cultured, well-educated foreigners in Mexico were unaware of its existence.

Natalie made horseback rides away from the city and settled areas. Among the native Mexicans in the multitude of Indian villages, there were inexplicable barriers; *dialects remain distinct for generations and show no sign of merging. You may ride on horseback from Mexico City a few hours and find Indians who speak no Spanish, and at your next stop you will find a dialect yet different from theirs.*

Mexico City deeply impressed her, so *resplendent, with wide avenues, with buildings of colonial architecture, a park that would be an ornament to any capital in the world, graced with magnificent trees, fountains and bridle paths, plazas, bustling with life, it has train cars of expensive make. As sophisticated a setting as you can find in America or even in Europe.* Yet the contrasts remained profound; *all along the Alameda there spring up 'puestos,' little Indian booths, and Indians squat on their haunches, or on the ground, selling wares. Their costumes are a thing distinctive. The women wear full skirted, full-bloused dresses, often of some deep color, lavender, or rose, or blue, and always shawls, a most useful article. A deft flick of the hands, and it is holding the ubiquitous, serious baby, or a basket of oranges, or even a water jar, leaving the two hands of the wearer free!*

In the sweet peace of Cuernavaca the soft-voiced maids are called by such names as Trinida, Nativida, and Geronima. One realizes that the picturesque ruins on the outskirts are the ruins of the sugar-houses pulled down by the Zapatistas. The country is often so lovely, so colorful, so fantastic, and picturesque, that all else fades into sheer enjoyment. And in its quiet suburbs, its beautiful old monasteries, its gardens, the illusion of peace and beauty prevails.

Deeply impressed by the distinct, complex culture of these people, yet touched by their earnest simplicity, Natalie realized that her comprehension of Mexico's contradictions only scratched the surface, that a great deal remained to be learned. Her first venture into Mexico ended after three months, her ship bringing her home in time for Christmas with Sidonie and the children.[39]

Sherwood Anderson had acquired in mid-1925 a small property in mountainous western Virginia near the quaint town of Marion. Spratling designed a new house for him there; construction got under way that autumn. After five productive years in the Quarter, Anderson decided the time for change had finally arrived. By the end of 1926, the Andersons completed their move to Virginia's Appalachia. Here Sherwood acquired the only two newspapers in Smyth County, one Republican and one Democrat. He enjoyed himself immensely until his death in 1941, writing books while filling these newspapers with short stories, unique editorials, and local news and lore as well as offering the opposing political views of the two parties. Natalie stayed in touch, visiting Anderson in August 1928 and also seeing him on rare occasions in New Orleans and New York.[40]

Transitions

The year 1926 brought many changes to the Quarter: closure of *The Double Dealer;* Sherwood Anderson's move to Virginia; Natalie's departure for Mexico, then Europe. Lyle Saxon, eager to move from journalism to fiction, ended his association with the *Times-Picayune,* relocating to Greenwich Village to be near national book publishers. Roark Bradford also left the *Times-Picayune* to focus on writing fiction. Faulkner, after he and Spratling published *Sherwood Anderson and Other Famous Creoles,* would soon return home to Mississippi, fully focused on his career as a novelist.

Sherwood Anderson and Other Famous Creoles appeared in December. The little book of caricatures memorialized their Vieux Carré companions including Natalie, the city's equestrian champion each year of the 1920s. Captioned "Peggy Passe Partout Takes a Hurdle," her caricature depicted her on horseback jumping over the Court of Two Sisters, the financial risk Natalie had successfully hurdled. The book poked gentle fun at everyone, with Sherwood Anderson as its centerpiece, as he had been of their literary and

MISS NATALIE SCOTT,
Winner of "Horse Show" first honors.

The perennial New Orleans equestrian champion during the 1920s, Natalie was a founder of the New Orleans Equestrian Club (1923). *New Orleans Illustrated News*

artistic coterie since 1922. As much as anything, the book honored him and the good times in the French Quarter during his residence, when the entire neighborhood really was one happy family. Spratling remembered and wrote of it in 1966, the year before his death.

There were casual parties with wonderful conversation and with plenty of grand, or later to be grand, people. Ben Huebsch would be down from New York to visit his writer Sherwood Anderson, and Horace Liveright and Carl Van Doren and Carl Sandburg and John Dos Passos and many others were there from time to time and there was constant stimulation of ideas. Roark Bradford worked the city desk of the *Times-Picayune* along with poet John McClure, and Oliver La Farge was with Frans Blom in archeology at Tulane while he shared cooking expenses with me and Faulkner. . . . Our wonderful Lyle Saxon would arrive at his house in the quarter from slaving at the *Picayune* until midnight and one could always find there a dozen or so writers and painters or musicians and actresses or caricaturists and a pitcher of absinthe and good conversation.

Tellers of stories, like Natalie Scott and our dear Flo Field, were at their best there and Bill Faulkner and Sherwood Anderson would like as not be off on an interminable chapter in the life of a legendary person named Al Jackson, which was sheer nonsense. . . . The absinthe helped us to swallow their continuing anecdotes about the life of Al Jackson. These kept up from party to party, just humbug. But, after all, both Sherwood and Bill were, I suppose, congenital leg-pullers.[41]

At this midpoint of the 1920s, Natalie and Spratling may have become romantically involved, despite the ten-year gap in their ages. Spratling's leading biographer believes this to have been the case. Blessed with a perceptive nature and great talent, no one proved more entrepreneurially productive in his artistic pursuits; Spratling possessed a rare gift for turning his art into income. Anderson's celebrity gatherings virtually always included both Natalie and Spratling, the two rubbing elbows and sharing illegal alcohol with visiting figures from the American literary scene: Carl Sandburg, Frederick O'Brien, John Dos Passos, Edmund Wilson, John Emerson, Anita Loos, and numerous leading publishers of the day.

Spratling seized these opportunities, nurturing friendships with publishers introduced by Anderson and N. C. Curtiss (Spratling's mentor in the Tulane School of Architecture). He departed each summer for Europe or Mexico, painting, sketching, and writing as he traveled abroad. Upon his return, his illustrated articles and magazine covers would appear in a variety of publications (*Architectural Forum, Architecture, Southern Architecture and Building News, Travel,* among others). Natalie secured for him the opportunity to write a weekly architectural column in the *New Orleans States;* and she occasionally published Spratling pencil portraits of personalities being discussed in her column. If the two were romantically linked, which remains to be confirmed, the years would mellow their feelings into something quite different—a deep but platonic friendship, with the tugs of a sibling relationship.

Before Natalie left for Europe in early 1927, where she would travel and write for a year, she and Spratling submitted their plantation book to their New York publisher. She also wrote another play, called *Grand Zombi,* a romantic tragedy in one act based on the nineteenth-century, semi-legendary Voodoo Queen of New Orleans, Marie Laveau. She entered this creation into a national playwriting contest sponsored locally by Le Petit Théâtre. The plot dramatized the racial plight of young mulatto women in Old New Orleans. The young Marie is rejected by her wealthy white lover; she discovers her mysterious powers in an act of revenge. However, the contest was forgotten as Natalie left suddenly for her European and North African travels.

During Christmas 1926, Natalie had proposed to Sidonie Scott, Nauman's widow, the one thing she believed would simultaneously raise everyone's spirits: travel abroad that summer. But in February, upon learning one afternoon of an inexpensive Spanish steamship voyage leaving immediately from New Orleans, Natalie sailed away that night, thereafter sending her newspaper articles from Europe. In Spain, her itinerary took her to Cádiz, Gibraltar, Málaga, Cartagena, Valencia, Seville, Majorca, then Barcelona. She traveled on to Aliento, flying in a small plane to the North African city of Oran and going on to Fez, back to Oran, then Algiers and Tunis. She traveled across the Gulf of Tunis to Sicily, Naples, Trieste, then Vienna, before proceeding to Paris. There she went to work writing feature stories for a Parisian newspaper and free-lance pieces for the Associated Press and the International News Agency.

Sidonie, with her mother and the children, arrived in Le Havre the first of June. Natalie took the entire family on an excursion to Paris, then delivered the children to a summer camp on the Normandy coast. In an automobile acquired by Natalie, the three adults visited Gisors and Beauvais, where Natalie had been stationed during World War I. In Paris, they were entertained by friends, enjoying leisurely days in the Latin Quarter with excursions to Versailles, Fontainebleau, and the chateau of the elegant Madame Chaffroix, a generous hostess who spent her winters in her New Orleans home on St. Charles Avenue. The travelers explored the Loire valley, southwestern France, and the coast of Brittany, then worked their way back to Normandy to visit the children. Afterwards, the threesome toured England and Scotland until the end of August, when Natalie saw the family set sail from Le Havre.

The Hotel Danube in the Latin Quarter became Natalie's Parisian home for the next four months. She enjoyed her newspaper work and seriously contemplated a permanent move to France. She was not in America during November for the publication of *Old Plantation Houses in Louisiana,* thereby missing the favorable reviews and Christmas sales that greeted this first serious study of Louisiana's antebellum architecture. Natalie stepped off her ship in New Orleans just before Christmas. She visited a few friends before heading upstate to spend Christmas with Sidonie and the Scott children, accompanied by her brother Jack.[42]

Natalie decided in early 1928, after eight years writing her

"Peggy Passe Partout" column, to resign her position with the *New Orleans States*. Her journalistic success in Paris and her book with Spratling gave evidence that she could earn her living writing independently. Her one-act play, *Grand Zombi*, written so quickly the previous Christmas, won the national contest. Le Petit Théâtre performed it in Natalie's honor during April. Esther Dupuy, the dark-haired dancer with whom Spratling enjoyed a pleasant romance, performed the role of Marie Laveau. *Theatre Arts Monthly* selected *Zombi* as its best play of 1928 and copyrighted it in December, with Natalie earning performance royalties. *Zombi* won the magazine's international contest and thereafter was published in an anthology of eighteen best plays entitled *Plays of American Life and Fantasy* (1929), collected by Edith J. R. Isaacs, editor of *Theatre Arts Monthly*. Other playwrights recognized in the book included Eugene O'Neill, Stark Young, Harold Chapin, Alfred Kreyemborg, and Zoe Akins. Natalie donated a copy of *Plays of American Life and Fantasy* to the library of Newcomb College, writing this inscription: *To Newcomb,—"guiding goddess of my harmful deeds",—and stimulus towards better. Natalie Vivian Scott,—1909. June 11, 1929.*[43]

Yet Natalie possessed no great desire to succeed as a writer or playwright. The deaths of her brother and parents left her restless for change; she decided to put the world of newspaper deadlines behind her, freeing her energy for new projects. She had sold the Court of Two Sisters several months after Nauman's death for a substantial profit, most of which she invested in the stock market. She also profitably sold her St. Peter Street cottage to Sam Gilmore and acquired two rental properties in uptown New Orleans. In May 1928, she purchased her new home near Audubon Park, 439 Lowerline, only a block from the home of Arthur and Hilda Phelps Hammond. Leasing the upstairs to a tenant, Natalie lived downstairs peacefully for the next two years, continuing her free-lance journalism while writing her first two New Orleans cookbooks. By the end of the first year, however, she and Bill Spratling were already discussing a relocation to lovely Taxco, Mexico.[44]

Spratling had spent his 1926, 1927, and 1928 summers in Mexico, traveling, sketching, and occasionally lecturing on colonial architecture at the National University in Mexico City. He became an insider of the Mexican art world, prolifically publishing illustrated articles in prominent American magazines on such topics as Mexico's architectural treasures and its magnificent new generation of artists: Diego Rivera, David Alfero Siqueiros, Roberto Montenegro, Miguel Covarrubias, Rufino Tamayo, Jose Clemente Orozco, among others. He also wrote an occasional article for Frances Toor's *Mexican Folkways*. In June 1928, Spratling resigned from the Tulane faculty before leaving again for Mexico, apparently confident he could make a living with his art and illustrated journalism.

This became a period of transition for Natalie and her French Quarter circle, all seeking to find new levels of accomplishment in their fields. Frans Blom and Oliver La Farge began writing books and magazine articles. La Farge even pursued fiction writing, publishing numerous short stories before the appearance of his 1929 novel, *Laughing Boy*. Blom turned to scholarly writing, his two-volume *Tribes and Temples* released in December 1927. Blom's work became authoritative in the Mayan field, and he continued his long career with Tulane as chairman of the Middle American Research Department. Lyle Saxon published his short story "Cane River" in *Dial* in 1926, which became an O. Henry Award finalist the next year. He published *Fabulous New Orleans* and *Old Louisiana* in 1928, then *Lafitte the Pirate* in 1930, which was adapted in Cecile B. DeMille's 1938 film *The Buccaneer*. He finally published a novel, *Children of Strangers* (1937), during his directorship of the WPA Federal Writers Project in Louisiana. Roark Bradford's 1927 short story, "Child of God," won the O. Henry Memorial Award, then his *Ol' Man Adam an' His Chillun* (1928), adapted with Marc Connelly into the play *The Green Pastures,* won the Pulitzer Prize. Of course, William Faulkner's subsequent success overshadowed that of his French Quarter cohorts. He won two Pulitzer Prizes, for *A Fable* in 1955 and *The Reivers* in 1963, after already winning the 1949 Nobel Prize for Literature.[45]

Sherwood Anderson reached his commercial peak during his New Orleans years, his best-selling *Dark Laughter* providing the money to settle in western Virginia and to acquire two newspapers. He did not live in the French Quarter again, remaining, however, a Midwesterner-turned-Southerner for the rest of his life. Elizabeth Anderson returned to California after the couple's 1929 separation; their divorce was complete by 1932. She worked at the Stanford University bookstore until Natalie invited her to come to Taxco in 1935. Mexico became Elizabeth's permanent home. Sherwood remarried, happily and permanently, and in the 1930s wrote prolifically in his newspapers and published numerous books and short stories, including *Puzzled America* and *Kit Brandon.* Natalie enjoyed visits there, the first time in August 1928 while writing for the International News Agency. Anderson's last published work was an editorial entitled "Chance Rules Us All" published in the Marion College newspaper in 1939; it reflected on his adopted South. He mentioned Natalie Scott as he meditated affectionately upon New Orleans.

> It is like all America, a changing thing. In New Orleans and Mobile the river packets have almost completely disappeared. When I first began going South, twenty years ago now, the little packets and some of the big ones still loaded . . . at the foot of Canal Street in New Orleans. There were the singing ragged Negroes. You got Negro song, not as you hear it in northern concert halls, but against background of river, rain and woods. Oh what I owe to the South, the months . . . the aggregate years . . . spent loitering there. Friends made, Julius Friend, Jack McClure, Weeks Hall, in that strange old house he brought back to life up on Bayou Teche, Natalie Scott, Wharton Esherick, a Yank like myself. . . . Bill Faulkner, the talented one . . .[46]

Natalie enjoyed her Lowerline home. It was roomy with large screen porches, and she and Hilda Hammond regularly made the short walk between their homes (Natalie being the godmother of two Hammond children). The two influenced each other in creative ways. Both regularly contributed articles to the *New Orleans Illustrated News* and the *New Orleanian.* Hilda, emerging from ten years of child-rearing, worked for the *Times-Picayune* while creating a children's section of the Pelican Bookshop in the Quarter and conducting book parties with refreshments, puppet shows, and story readings. Natalie wrote two unique, profitable New Orleans cookbooks, while Hilda wrote a national-prizewinning children's play based on Jean Lafitte and the Battle of New Orleans, later publishing a children's book, *Pierre and Ninette in Old New Orleans.* Natalie's social life remained active. Lyle Saxon and Oliver La Farge were in the city most of 1929, as was Frans Blom. Bill Spratling's return from New York, where he had been commissioned to draw portraits of the Theater Guild's fifty top stage performers, was brief, however—just a few weeks in March before he sailed back to Mexico.

Natalie remained in New Orleans through 1929, managing her modest properties and her nicely growing nest egg from prior stock-market investments. She also organized and rode in horse shows, continuing her reign as the city's perennial equestrian champion. In mid-April, Natalie and ten other New Orleanians, including opera impresario Harry Loeb and writers Grace King, Dorothy Dix, Lyle Saxon, and Roark Bradford, were honored at a banquet of entertainment entitled "New Orleans in Song and Story." She returned to Mexico City, Cuernavaca, and Taxco for several months in the autumn, once again writing for *Mexican Folkways* and exploring Guerrero villages by horseback.[47]

In November, Natalie's first cookbook surprised New Orleans. Entitled *Mirations and Miracles of Mandy: Some Favorite Louisiana Recipes,* it was favorably reviewed by local newspapers as the "perfect Christmas present." The cover featured a smiling image of the fictitious black "Mandy," a red tignon over her hair. Dedicated to her cook, Pearl Sideboard, the volume was full of Mandy's kitchen wisdom, one-liners expressed in black vernacular such as this one from the dessert section: *"dey talks erbout a sweet toof lak dey's on'y one; huh! by de end o' dinnah dey's all o' 'em sweet."* Among the soup dishes was another: *"many ez dey got cooks in de kitchen, da's how many ways you kin ster up a gumbo."*

Though seldom a cook, Natalie was a devoted gourmet, intensely interested in the art of cooking. She appreciated the black culinary artists, as she made clear in her introduction. *There are the Mandys of all my friends,—Mammy Lou, and Phrosine, and Tante Celeste, Venida, Felicie, Mande, Titine, Elvy, Mona, Relie. It is said that the witch doctors of North Africa have a mastery of mental telepathy. These Mandys, too, have some such subtle sense. In the various cuisines of which they are the muses, mysterious rites go on, heritage of many countries, heritage of many years. I have peeped here, watched there, borrowed and begged, and doubtless, inadvertently stolen, to offer in these scant pages a few of these local treasures. Wanting a more worthy token, I offer them this little tribute,*

*with, fittingly, echoes of their homely wisdom and reflections of
their homely but true art.*

The *Mirations and Miracles of Mandy* became the first of five
very successful Louisiana and Mexican cookbooks Natalie wrote.
All went through subsequent editions. *Mandy* is still being republished today, year after year, by Pelican Publishing Company in
Gretna, Louisiana, near New Orleans. *Gourmet's Guide to New
Orleans: Creole Cookbook,* first published in 1933, is also
offered by the company. A new printing of Natalie's *200 Years of
New Orleans Cooking* appeared in 1999, nearly seventy years
after it was first published with Bill Spratling's French Quarter
"decorations." All share a flavor of good will and humor, along
with a unique selection of sound recipes. Each has an added
touch, such as Mandy's "wisdoms," celebrity recipes, and
Spratling's etchings, to make them even more interesting.[48]

Natalie and Martha Robinson finished 1929 by performing the
two lead roles in Le Petit Théâtre's production of *The Devil's
Disciple,* by George Bernard Shaw. Then Natalie and brother
Jack again spent Christmas with the Scotts. Though the stock
market had crashed in October, it took time to realize that it
would not recover. By January, the reality set in. Natalie lost virtually all of her savings and the $5,000 she had invested from her
father's life insurance and her past real-estate profits. She did
manage to maintain her modest uptown rental properties and
the French Quarter house she owned with John McClure. Still,
rental rates plummeted during the long depression.[49]

Meanwhile, Spratling moved in important artistic circles in
Mexico, busy with numerous projects but struggling financially.
He planned a book, *Little Mexico,* and accepted a $200 advance
from his publisher to go "native"—to isolate himself in a Mexican
village. He wanted *Little Mexico* to be written from within, by an
inhabitant, so the reader could feel the rhythms of a native
Mexican world. He chose Taxco for its isolation and mountainous
beauty. The peasant village seemed preserved from an earlier
century, uncorrupted and yet within a day of Mexico City. Other
demands postponed Spratling's book: organizing art exhibits for
the Escuela de Bellas Artes, marketing Weyhe Gallery paintings,
and trying to sell to the New York gallery works of Diego Rivera
and Carlos Merida, among others. Then U.S. Ambassador Dwight
Morrow entrusted Spratling with another project, to arrange a

lasting gift from Morrow to Cuernavaca "which would add importance to that village." Spratling convinced him to retain Diego Rivera, the nation's most acclaimed artist, to paint a mural in the Cortés Palace of Cuernavaca. The $12,000 fee that Spratling negotiated shocked Rivera, who gratefully promised him a $2,000 commission. With the money, Spratling settled comfortably during February 1930 into a unique home he renovated in Taxco. It was in a beautiful spot above the *zócalo,* with a view of the Church de la Santa Prisca, the red-tiled roofs of the village, and the mountains beyond.[50]

Natalie, planning another extended visit, became a resident of Taxco during the summer of 1930, leaving New Orleans in May. By the end of July, she had settled into a small three-room Taxco *casita,* blessed by a patio fountain and lovely view, just below the Church de la Santa Prisca and an uphill walk to Spratling's much larger abode. A report from Natalie appeared in the July 20 *States* society section. *I have taken an infinitesimal, wholly adorable cottage here, with a big garden, full of everything, and a superb view. I have a cute little maid, who all but pays to work for me, and feeds me magnificently on chayotes, and*

Taxco, Mexico, with the Iglesia de la Santa Prisca. The trees in front indicate the *zócalo.* This photograph is taken from near Casa Scott, home of Natalie Scott (ca. 1930). *Postcard in the Collection of Penny C. Morrill*

camotes, and ejotes, and calabasos and such delicacies. There are several Americans scattered about. Bill Spratling lives about eight blocks away—when he is here; but he has been in Mexico City most of the time, involved in getting up the exhibit of Mexican arts and crafts which the Carnegie is taking on tour in America next winter. He has a grand collection of Mexican stuff himself.

The town, Taxco, is incredibly charming, set precariously on a mountain in the midst of mountains, houses and innumerable churches of Mexican colonial trend, for it has been here since not long after Cortez. Little white houses with colonnaded galleries and red tiled roofs, with a gay pink church looking down on everything and little white churches scattered all about. Too sweet, I tell you.

I am too kind to speak of how deliciously cool it is, and how I shiver under my two blankets when a wind blows up at night. I had a grand swim in a mountain pool yesterday in the midst of the woods, cupped into solid rock and icy cold.[51]

Chapter Eight

Mexico

The first silver the Conquistadores sent to Spain from Mexico had been mined in Taxco four centuries before Natalie arrived there. The pink-stoned church rising in the middle of the village is an astonishing monument built over a mine still rich with silver. The mine made its owner, nobleman and devout Catholic José de la Borda, wealthy beyond his prayers. So early in the eighteenth century he closed the mine, sealed it, and built the unique church that would be just a short walk from where Natalie and Spratling made their homes.

According to local legend, as the Indian builders were working high above the church roof, putting the tall towers in place about the massive dome, a terrific thunderstorm burst upon them and sent long jagged lances of lightning at them from heaven's blackness. They knelt and prayed. Later they told a miraculous story of the divine angel Santa Prisca suddenly appearing in a glory of light, her shining hand seizing a great bolt of lightning that would have slain them. The grand edifice had found its new name: Iglesia de la Santa Prisca, the miracle preserved in ancient paintings within its ancient walls. The little community in 1930 numbered several hundred. Even its streets reflected the artistry and mining history of the people: the roads near the church were paved with strange cobblestones of black basalt, white marble, and a native stone green with copper ore, forming Indian mosaics of bulls and deer and stars. By 1930, Mexican artists were rediscovering the village, many of them friends of Natalie and Spratling.[1]

A month after Natalie's May 8 departure by ship for Vera Cruz, New Orleans newspapers printed reports that she had settled down to serious writing in Cuernavaca, with Bill Spratling preparing illustrations for her work. More accurately, she had arrived in Taxco on a shoestring budget, traveling from Mexico

City over the rough old stone road built by de la Borda two centuries before, a passenger in a dilapidated Studebaker loaded with nine people, their bundles, and a few chickens. Natalie described this bouncing full-day journey as *100 miles horizontal and 600 vertical.*

She did have numerous projects under way, writing several magazine articles that were arranged before leaving home, as well as her cookbook *200 Years of New Orleans Cooking.* By mid-July, she had moved into her small Taxco *casita,* at Callejón de la Luz, Number 1. There she also worked informally for *Mexican Folkways,* her unpaid translations and editing reminiscent of her earlier role with *The Double Dealer.* Natalie began exploring on horseback, getting to know the neighboring Indian villages tucked among the mountains.[2]

Spratling and Natalie made their first wilderness journey together in late August and early September 1930. Planned as a ten-day trip into the Tierra Caliente, "the hot country" to the west, the adventure consumed three weeks. They dropped down through the jungle to the spectacular Balsas River, which threaded through the states of Guerrero and Michoacán. At the Balsas, they boarded a small native vessel, negotiating enormous rapids during the first leg of the journey. Traveling by boat and horseback, they visited Meacacingo, Teloloapan, Acapetlaluaya, Arcelia, Totoloapan, Pungarabato, and other points on the river. They descended deep into Michoacán, to villages within plunging valleys, and returned overland by horseback. Spratling had become consumed by his interest in pre-Columbian designs and artifacts. He rapidly gained expertise in the subtleties of the ancient artistry, searching among villages for figurines, masks, pottery, sculptures, and other relics.

Spratling, no horseman or outdoorsman, had expressed misgivings in a letter to his friend Carl Zigrosser, of New York's Weyhe Gallery, about the hardships they would encounter on this long wilderness expedition. He added a wry note about Natalie's eagerness for the adventure: "It should be a highly interesting trip and Natalie's crazy to do it." Spratling dramatized their journey in his 1932 book, *Little Mexico,* describing the precipitous descents and climbs, the wild river rapids, the native inhabitants with their mysterious practices, and the search for treasures and artifacts.[3]

Beyond the capital of Mexico, they say, all is Cuantitlán—small town stuff. It is not true. Because beyond, and below Mexico all is "Tierra Caliente"—the hot country. . . . Here in Mexico one says "Tierra Caliente" as though speaking of another land. And it takes on the quality of another land in people's thoughts. It is a Mexico unknown even to Mexicans. In the same sense it is the country's physical subconscious. It is vast and fecund; forbidding and promising; it is practically unexplored and difficult to access. Allá en tierra caliente! Yes, there is supposed to be much gold there but it is wild country, and also it is infernally hot. Then too there is the pinto. What if one goes and comes back with the pinto? Only imagine such a disease!—a disease which affects and discolours an entire people, about which practically nothing is known. White men have killed themselves from sheer disgust of the thing. There isn't even a name for it, only "the Dis-colour." Through all the region traced by the river Balsas there is pinto; but there is much more besides. There are great sierras; rich valleys. There is gold and silver and petroleum, untouched; sugar, ajonjoli and coffee grow abundantly. There are ancient cities, temples, pyramids— vestiges vastly significant of antique culture and the most ancient races of the continent. In open country and in huts of the poor exist sculptured gods in marble, in jade, in exquisitely wrought clay. It is all pregnant with what has been, and what will be Mexico. Tierra Caliente, seen from the mountains of Guerrero or Oaxaca or Vera Cruz, quivers in a distant blue heat. It appears somewhat unreal, fantastically impregnable, like Indo-China, or Africa.[4]

Every year during the 1930s, between her fortieth and fiftieth birthdays, Natalie made such wilderness trips on horseback, often alone and often for months at a time. Between these long explorations, she frequently visited Guerrero villages and became a well-known guest. She gradually learned to communicate in their dialects and gained sophisticated knowledge of their folkways, religion, food, festivals, dances, art, handicrafts, and history.

Natalie purchased the small *casita* on Callejón de la Luz, returning to New Orleans only occasionally over the next two years, usually for a holiday. Though Natalie did not realize it, the New Orleans chapter of her life was over, with a very different one under way in Mexico, a vastly different world from the others she had known so intimately—New Orleans, Paris, New York. Her life seemed to fit into a series of clear-cut stages: the Bay St.

Louis period, idyllic and structured except for the horror of the yellow fever epidemic; the Newcomb period, the happiest of times; World War I and the Red Cross period, the joys and tragedies of war-torn France defining her as a woman; the French Quarter and "Peggy Passe Partout" period, with its intellectual growth, frivolity, and the lasting wounds of losing her dearest loved ones. Her Mexican life of the 1930s would be the next period, the structures of her life—her parents, her status in New Orleans, her career, specific goals—all removed. Unexpectedly, due to the Great Depression, she had lost much of her financial security. At first blush, the change in her environment seemed drastic, radical.

Yet Taxco was a relic of the past, just as was the French Quarter, which Natalie had championed for restoration as a place to live, invest, and work. Taxco possessed the same prospects. Spratling's house on Calle de las Delicias and hers on Callejón de la Luz, comparatively primitive, had proven to be charming dwellings. By November 1930, they had formed a "Friends of Taxco" organization devoted to protecting Taxco's ancient beauty from modern intrusions. Later Natalie recruited a physician for the town, the first step towards creation of the Hospital Adolpho Prieto. She also instigated local efforts to bring water/sanitation/electrical systems to Taxco. Moisés Saénz, the former assistant secretary of the Mexican Department of Education and by then the president of the government's Beneficiencia Pública, commissioned Spratling that autumn to build a

William Spratling on horseback, with the spires of Santa Prisca beyond (ca. 1933). This photograph was taken by Natalie Scott. *Courtesy of Special Collections, Tulane University Libraries*

Taxco house for him beside one Natalie had overhauled for Hubert Herring. The next year Natalie prepared a small cottage for artist Caroline Durieux, who had moved to Mexico City with her family in 1930. She renovated another house, a much larger one above the Santa Prisca *zócalo,* for photographer Gordon Abbott and Arnold Tempest (an American mining engineer) during 1931.⁵

Natalie lived in two Mexican worlds, one being the Guerrero world of the campesinos, the quiet country folk, illiterate villagers living in poverty conditions much as their ancestors had lived for centuries. She found them gentle, laboring, and modest in outlook and expectations; this was a world of no vehicles, no electricity, no plumbing. Yet the Taxqueñian world also offered sophisticated, brilliant talents. Her accomplished friends included artists Diego Rivera, Frida Kahlo, Roberto Montenegro, and transplanted Japanese artist Tamaji Kitigawa; Frances Toor; musician Carlos Chavez; Rufino Tamayo; authors Anita Brenner and Katherine Anne Porter; historians Carleton Beal and Stuart Chase; Miguel and Rosa Covarrubias; antiquities experts/dealers Fred Davis and René d'Harnoncourt; and the scholarly author-anthropologist Hubert Herring. Taxco friends Chiltipin and Johnny Sutherland opened the Hotel Taxqueño, and Charles (Carlos) and Elsa Nibbi took over the old Hotel Portillo, then with only three bedrooms, creating the much larger Hotel Victoria, its broad veranda and balconied rooms overlooking the quiet peasant town.⁶

The most passionate, the most controversial, and perhaps the most talented of the remarkable Revolution-era generation of Mexican painters soon moved into a small cottage beside Natalie. The radical David Alfaro Siqueiros repeatedly created conflict with the ruling Mexican Party of the Revolution with his political activism for agrarian reform, labor unionism, and the outlawed Mexican Communist Party. He and Natalie became trusted friends.

A soldier in the Revolution, Siqueiros saw the indigenous Mexicans, the landless campesinos, as the inspirational heart of the Revolution but betrayed and forgotten by those in power. He became an international figure as much for his radical politics as for his magnificent painting. During the late 1920s, Siqueiros ran afoul of the Communist Party with his controversial marriage to the beautiful Uruguayan poet Blanca Luz Blum, whom the party considered a security risk. This led to his expulsion, and he found himself hunted by both police and the party. The police

Natalie with David Alfaro Siqueiros (right, Mexico City, January 1932).
Courtesy of Special Collections, Tulane University Libraries

captured him on May Day 1930 outside the Uruguayan consulate, imprisoning him in the notorious Lucemberri Prison.

On November 5, 1930, after the government failed to win the prisoner's loyalty, Siqueiros was released and placed under house arrest in the town of Taxco. He would be subject to the authority of the district's military commander, only able to travel outside of town with special permission. Siqueiros had virtually abandoned his painting for his politics during the years before his imprisonment, but in prison he began using a pocket knife to etch scenes on cheap crate boards. He made plain and candid depictions of prison life: peasant families visiting imprisoned loved ones, the religious fervor of the poor, scenes of brutality and hardship. Slipping simple pieces of artwork out of prison to Blanca Luz, Siqueiros instructed her to try to get some money by selling these to his old, prominent friends. She had little luck.

In Taxco, Spratling had just opened his silver and handicraft workshop, Taller de las Delicias. He collaborated with the artist to publish a booklet of the Siqueiros prison woodcuts. Spratling would write in the preface, "This little group of engravings by Siqueiros reveals none of the hysteria or selfish rancor of the ordinary sufferer of social injustice. Rather they form detached but pointed commentaries on what the artist saw and felt there. They are the result of a sensitive and finely interpretive mind . . . pregnant with deep emotional conviction." This small publication, *13 Grabados,* put some much needed money into Siqueiros's hands and represented a small but important move towards reentry into the art world. It also sealed the Spratling-Siqueiros friendship.

Natalie had opened her home to the proud couple, befriending Blanca Luz and quietly helping with her household needs. Siqueiros and Blanca Luz came to know well the small New Orleans colony in Taxco: Spratling, Natalie, and Caroline Durieux (often Natalie's guest). The little Siqueiros house, with a large, red, paper star lantern hanging on the porch as a silent testament to David's unshakeable Communist commitment, stood adjacent to Natalie's *casita.*[7]

During 1931, a New Orleans friend, July Brazeale Waters, then in her midthirties, enjoyed an extended visit with Natalie. She shared her vivid memories in a 1982 interview, providing a rare glimpse of Natalie's Taxco world.

I went on down to Taxco—I hardly know where to begin. From Natalie's old house on the side of a mountain—there were no windows on the street side—you could see where the road wound around the mountains. But it was private. I insisted on hot water to take a bath in the morning and María Luisa, the little Mexican girl who slept on a pallet in the kitchen,—the happiest little person you ever knew. And she would go across to the ice factory and bring a big kettle of hot water and pour it into a little tub that Natalie happened to have and I would take my bath. Natalie and Carrie [Durieux] would go out and bathe in the fountain outside of the house on the mountainside. They laughed about me being so particular with that hot water.

A priest was forbidden. Religion at that time and to practice in a Catholic church was forbidden. So they had a hidden convent. It being Easter week it was very, very important. All of the people had come to Taxco for the celebrations. They were sleeping out in the square with little tent things over them, under the sky and just enjoying themselves thoroughly. Fireworks at night, celebrations. The Good Friday service was really one of the most remarkable things that I have ever experienced in my life. I went with Natalie and some friends of hers from Mexico City. María Luisa had to go up several times to find out when it would take place because all of the services were forbidden at that time by the government. Finally the priest had arrived. María Luisa came back breathless to tell us so we went up to the service. They had all of the way of the cross. Then they had the crucifixion. A life-size figure of the Christ on a cross straight up with the crown of thorns, with his head bowed down. The most realistic thing and when Christ actually died, when he gave up the ghost, Beelzebub, who was right at the foot of the cross, arose with a great shriek and fell down. So then they put the Christ figure in a glass coffin. Then all of the women lighted the candles; the men bore the big coffin above their heads so that everybody in the church could see Christ in the glass coffin. The women with their black rebozos on their heads, chanting around the whole church. It really got shivers up and down my spine, and all of a sudden I was separated from Natalie. I was all alone and there was this enormous crowd. Everybody was standing. When suddenly I looked up, right next to me there was a woman standing and had her face all,—this awful disease. I ran all the way back to the house. When I got in,

Carrie laughed. She said, "Gracious, you look like you have seen a ghost." I said, "Well, I certainly have."

One of our entourage was Tamayo, the painter, and he was just beginning to make any kind of reputation. We were all dancing. I remember dancing with Tamayo, which I was very proud of later now that he is very famous. Natalie and Tamayo,—they decided they would go serenade different people in Taxco. The musicians came with us to serenade. They called it singing little monetas,— little morning songs. So we went from place to place serenading and the donkeys would start braying when we started singing. We went on to Natalie's house and danced some more. They drank something like our bourbon. Very, very potent. We had quite a little party.

Questioner: Tell me a little bit about Bill Spratling. He must have been on the scene.

July Waters: He was an odd kind of a person. Rather an introvert. I brought butter from the city when I went down because that was the hardest for them to have, always rancid when they got it in Taxco. Anyway, I brought some butter. So Natalie sent up a half a pound to Bill by María Luisa, and Bill sent back something by his *mozo* later on; they communicated that way and he sent down his *mozo* to invite us to dinner one night. Oh, there was a very interesting thing I forgot I have to tell about.

Questioner: Please do.

July Waters: I went with Natalie and another artist that Natalie knew very well. They both knew this other artist well and his wife. I went with them and had lunch at their house. He was David Siqueiros, one of the most famous: Orozco, Diego Rivera, and David Siqueiros. A big revolutionary painter. He and his wife, Blanca Luz, or White Light. She was a niece of the president of Uruguay, who was violently opposed to her having anything to do with this revolutionary. The girl ran away with him [Siqueiros]. And she took one box of her possessions; they had that box at their house and they showed us some of the things. They were her treasures. Somebody sat on the bed and somebody sat on the box and there were two or three chairs and we just made the best of it. She cooked a Uruguayan dish in this big pot and they didn't have enough plates for everybody but they managed. Everybody just ate the best they could. They didn't have enough forks, though there were only five of us, the three of us and the two of them.

Questioner: And they lived in Taxco?

July Waters: They lived right there in Taxco and they had this little house up on the mountainside. It was very, very interesting and they were very, very attractive. He was beautiful. He looked like one of the Italian frescos with the angels. The face, he had black, black curly hair and it was very pretty. They were beautiful. And she was perfectly beautiful. They were later on divorced. They came to America, they weren't happy. He got married again.

We didn't see them anymore and Natalie inquired, they couldn't communicate somehow. Natalie found out they had been shut up together in that house, wouldn't let anybody in and just had the door barred. You would go outside of Natalie's house and the Siqueiros house, this little doorway in the fence would let you in. Natalie was worried about them. Well, what happened is they were confined by themselves fighting it out. Everybody was worried to death. They thought one of them would be dead. But when they opened up and saw everybody, everything was nice. It was just as calm as if nothing had ever happened. They had very violent tempers, both of them. So they just shut themselves up and battled it out.

Questioner: You said Natalie Scott was very attractive?

July Waters: She was, I always remember her later with gray hair. But she never spent anything to speak of. She didn't always have enough. She could see the humorous side of everything; it always came to her rescue, her sense of humor. She had a quick repartee.[8]

By December 1931, the Siqueiros couple and Natalie had been neighbors for more than a year, companions on excursions to Guerrero villages and longer leisure trips to Acapulco and Mexico City (Siqueiros having received government permission). On one such occasion, David made a gift to Natalie of a lithograph, a reclining nude of Blanca Luz, with this inscription: A su gran amiga Natalie Scott, Acapulco, Mexico, 16th de Oct. 1931." Siqueiros shared several small paintings with her during the year. Having taken notice of the striking photograph in Natalie's *sala* of a handsome, dark-haired man, Siqueiros learned from her the story of her brother's death. He etched a portrait of Nauman from the photograph, making prints that Natalie gave as Christmas presents to Sidonie and her children in Alexandria. Meanwhile, Natalie made arrangements with the Arts and Crafts Club to exhibit and sell some Siqueiros lithographs in the French Quarter during February 1932, an opportunity for Siqueiros to gain income.[9]

Natalie with an unidentified man and Blanca Luz Blum (left), wife of David Siqueiros (Mexico City, January 1932). David took this photograph. *Courtesy of Special Collections, Tulane University Libraries*

His career on the rise again, Siqueiros was featured in a one-man show of his Taxco artwork in the Spanish Casino, Spain's cultural center in Mexico City. The event was arranged by Alvarez del Volle, the Spanish ambassador. Siqueiros went into the city several days early; Natalie and Blanca Luz followed the day before the exhibit and spent the afternoon with Siqueiros and the ambassador. The Siqueiros show reestablished the artist as Diego Rivera's rival, exhibiting over one hundred works: sixty oil paintings (many of monumental size) plus lithographs, xylographs, and drawings, including paintings such as *Mine Accident, Peasant Mother, Proletarian Mother,* and *Portrait of a Dead Child.* These startling works made a powerful statement of the artist's exhaustive output in Taxco.[10]

Gaining permission from Mexican authorities to exhibit, paint, and teach in Los Angeles, Siqueiros left Taxco the spring of 1932. In a letter to Carl Zigrosser in New York a year later, Natalie asked how David and Blanca Luz were getting on. *Lots has drifted down here as to Diego's visit in the States, very conflicting in trend. I'd love to hear details about it. I wonder, as to the effect of the exhibit of Mexican painters which David Siqueiros took to Los Angeles, above all the impressions made by his own work. He and Blanca Luz promised to write me, but of course they have not. I am genuinely fond of that colorful, dynamic, impossible, and loveable pair. For me (O so confidentially!) they are more sincere artistically and personally than our great Diego.*[11]

In the Wilderness

Natalie acquired and renovated a new home, this one larger with a spacious *sala,* bedroom, and kitchen, a picturesque veranda, and a *casita* for guests perched on a high cliff across a narrow chasm from Spratling, the *zócalo* far below. Spratling reported to Carl Zigrosser in late September, "Natalie has a new house, across the barranca from mine, and it's pretty swell. She sends her best to you, and she and I both wish you were down here again with us." This pair amused visitors with their primitive means of communication, hollering across the *barranca* (ravine).

Natalie earned small commissions, roughly five dollars per month per property, as leasing agent/caretaker for the properties of friends such as Carrie Durieux, Gordon Abbott, and Hubert Herring. She leased and renovated dilapidated cottages, then began subletting them to writers and artists coming for long stays. She published in New York in 1931 her new cookbook, *200 Years of New Orleans Cooking.* Natalie's first Mexican cookbook, *Your Mexican Kitchen,* appeared in 1935, published in New York by Putnam. Meanwhile, she steadily translated Mexican literature into English and carried on her modest rentals, managing ten properties by 1936. Natalie would open her *pensión,* the Kitigawa House, in 1937, then her school for peasant children in 1939.[12]

Caricature of Natalie Scott, by Caroline Durieux (Taxco, ca. 1933). *Courtesy of the Bé Scott Thomas Collection*

Hart Crane, the famous but troubled New York poet, had come to Mexico in 1931 on a Guggenheim fellowship to write an epic poem on the Conquest, but the project floundered amidst the chaos of his drinking binges. Natalie and Spratling had known Crane in New York, Spratling even writing a letter that helped Crane win the Guggenheim grant. The extroverted Crane's best poem,

A luncheon celebrating Natalie's renovation of Caroline Durieux's Taxco home (Chavarietta 9). Natalie at center, Spratling partially visible seated at right. Durieux took the photograph (1931). *Courtesy of the Collection of Charles Durieux*

"The Bridge," had been hailed by some as a masterpiece, bringing him considerable respect in Mexico. Siqueiros painted his portrait in Taxco. Yet Crane's drinking produced serious problems. His nightly carousing in Taxco exhausted Spratling, his host, who wrote in his autobiography: "His conversations tended to become too long-winded and sometimes, say around nine o'clock in the evening, I would have to tell him to go. Find some other listener." Hours later, as Spratling struggled to sleep, "I could hear, from just across the barranca, every word of Hart's sonorous yet rollicking voice from Natalie Scott's house. Their words floated to me as though across a lake, accompanied by Natalie's enthusiastic laughter." Spratling finally allowed him in his home only during daylight hours.[13]

Meanwhile, Natalie leased her new house to Peggy Cowley (the estranged wife of publisher-critic Malcolm Cowley) for December and January, as Natalie planned to be in Louisiana for the holiday season. In her absence, Peggy and Crane struck up an affair. With Natalie away in New Orleans and her Mexican servant at the couple's disposal, her home became their love nest. Crane and Peggy

Peggy Cowley and Hart Crane seated on the step of Natalie's porch in Taxco (ca. 1932). *Courtesy of Special Collections, Tulane University Libraries*

made sudden and surprising plans to marry upon their return to New York. Also in Natalie's house, during the sober days the lovers enjoyed together, Crane accomplished his only quality writing in Mexico, creating his poem "The Broken Tower" and finishing much of it before his return to Mexico City. Upon her return to Taxco, Natalie learned all that had transpired. Though worried about Crane's stability, she could do nothing more than hope for their happiness. Crane and Peggy boarded ship for New York in April. Tragically, their affair ended at sea when the unbalanced Crane, after an altercation with sailors, leaped overboard to his death, his body never recovered.[14]

Though Natalie's life in Taxco had gained a measure of permanence, and tenants occupied her Lowerline Street house, New Orleans remained her home. Yet to friends and visitors, she had become a Taxco institution. Her evolving role those early days was remembered in a 1960s letter written to Spratling by author and Mexico historian Lesley Simpson, reminiscing about the day the two men met in 1931.

> Brownie Aquirre took me to Taxco and put me up in the house you had built for Moisés Saénz. There I inevitably met Natalie Scott, the *grande dame* of Taxco, with whom I fell in love, as did everyone who knew her. Natalie, who had a passion for taking care of lost gringos, had me up to her funny little house perched on the edge of a barranca. While we were having tea and habanera (a gruesome combination), we were interrupted by a barking of dogs and a clumping of boots, and a character in blue jeans, followed by his dogs, strode across the verandah. He greeted Natalie briefly, dismissed me with a glance, and walked off. I must have looked puzzled, for Natalie said "Oh, don't mind him. It's only Bill. He thinks you're a tourist. I'll fix it up." Which she did that afternoon at Doña Berta's Bar . . . I made the great breakthrough.[15]

Simpson remembered in his letter the magical atmosphere in 1931 Mexico: "Shoals of refugees, fleeing the Great Depression, were coming to Mexico, the New Land of Promise, advertised by Stuart Chase, in his *Mexico: A Study of the Two Americas,* as a country that had solved the problem of living with itself. Painters, writers, and scholars swarmed to breathe the invigorating air. . . . We were all writing, or intending to write; painting, or intending to paint." That same year, a narrow new road connected Taxco to Cuernavaca and the capital, easing Taxco's isolation. Spratling's workshop prospered with the new tourist trade. There he trained a new generation of Mexican silversmiths, many graduating to fame in their own shops.

During 1933, perhaps weary of her struggle for money, Natalie seriously contemplated newspaper and publishing opportunities in New Orleans and New York. A return home seemed promising. She sold her Taxco house, abandoned her struggling rental business, and went to New Orleans. Her Mexico friends believed she had gone for good. She joined the anti-Huey Long crusade

Birthday party at home of Bill Spratling, which included Spratling's silversmiths. The two embracing silversmiths in foreground are Antonio Castillo (left) and Antonio de Pineda. Natalie appears in the background, center right (Taxco, September 1939). *Courtesy of the Antonio Castillo Collection*

of her old Newcomb classmates, led by Hilda Phelps Hammond. Their Louisiana Women's Committee doggedly fought Long's corruption—seeking to overturn illegal elections, provoking U.S. Senate investigations, and trying to defeat Long's presidential ambitions. By July 1934, after eight months writing again in New Orleans, Natalie yearned for her abandoned life in Taxco. She decided to make a surprise visit. And she decided to make the trip by horseback.[16]

Numerous books and stories about the creative American expatriates who gathered in Mexico during the 1930s refer with astonishment to Natalie Scott's memorable return to Taxco. She returned to embrace Taxco, without doubt or reservation, as her permanent home. Alone for all but the first week, Natalie began the journey in Brownsville, Texas, this 900-mile adventure occurring between August and October 1934. In New Orleans, she managed to enlist two young men to drive her to the border then join her for the first phase of the trek: Mexican sculptor Enrique Alferez and *New Orleans Item* reporter Austin Boyle, a Chicago native just graduated from Notre Dame. The horseback route took the threesome south along the gulf coast through the thorny snake- and tarantula-infested wilds of the Mexican state of Tamaulipas. There they forded flooded rivers, finally turning west to Ciudad Victoria, at which point both men returned to New Orleans.[17]

Their one week in the wilderness made a lifetime impression upon Natalie's two companions. Both lived long lives, into the 1990s, never forgetting the hilarity and hardship of their horseback trip with Natalie. They told of rock formations rising above a cool Tamaulipas river, with holes in the soft stone where they bathed joyously after days of riding. They recalled being stuck in forests of towering, thick thorn bushes for days, the large thorns like small knives. They carefully worked their way south, making their campsites each night within the dense thorny forest. They settled in another campsite near the gulf shoreline, a wide plain where the grass stood above their heads. They were awakened very early the next morning by the earth's puzzling movement under their sleeping bags. Scrambling to their feet, they discovered a carpet of sea snails moving en masse, making their migration to the sea.

Oversized spiders and rattlesnakes plagued them; flooded rivers ran so deep and swift that ropes stretched across, tied to

Natalie with her Buick. This photograph appeared in the *New Orleans Times-Picayune* after Natalie won a bet on how fast she could drive from Alexandria to New Orleans (New Orleans, 1934). *Courtesy of the New Orleans Times-Picayune*

trees, were necessary to cross with the horses. One morning the men awoke, hungry and low on food, to find no sign of Natalie at the campsite. Hearing distant laughter, they discovered her enjoying a visit with a peasant woman, both casually eating apples and chatting comfortably as they sat before the woman's modest adobe house, surrounded by an apple orchard. The woman was generous, offering more apples for their journey. Natalie climbed into a nearby tree and began dropping the tasty fruit to her hungry companions, who then abandoned the trip in Ciudad Victoria.

Alone, Natalie struck on, heading southwest over the high mountains of the Sierra Madre Oriental range, making camp in Indian villages where possible. She sent postcards as best she could, a rare opportunity in these remote lands. One to Martha Robinson dated September 13, 1934, came from the mountain village of Cerritos, northeast of San Luis Potosi. Its photograph depicted the narrow, winding dirt trail outside of town, with Cerritos visible in the near distance, backed by a dark mountain. Thrilled to reach the town, Natalie spent the night at the Hotel Potosi. *Electric lights and post-cards, as I live! Rode up that road in foreground yesterday—glorious scenery, with marvelous birds and flowers, very kindly people. Cactus in these parts stupendous. My hotel is the building with arches (see arrow). The town is small and quaint and full of color, lots of character,—charming buildings, drop me a line in Taxco. Love, Nat.*

High in the Sierra Madres, in an Indian village where Natalie was made welcome, the tribe had outdoor bathroom facilities consisting of side-by-side holes over a pit. As she was engaged, expecting privacy, the village chief joined her on the hole beside her—which was the regular tribal practice, as she soon realized. She and the chief amiably conversed, even laughing together as they answered the call of nature. Natalie, with her talent for languages, had acquired broken proficiency in several Indian dialects, though the Indians' "pigeon Spanish" often became the means of communication. She reached an isolated ranchero, where the sole occupant, a kindly Mexican, extended her every courtesy and, apparently lonely, invited her to stay on if she wished.[18]

By the time Natalie arrived at the Rio Lerma northwest of

Mexico City on September 28, 1934, several friendly Mexican travelers were riding along with her. Due to heavy rain and rushing floodwaters, the Rio Lerma became impossibly treacherous to cross. All attempts failed, with several horses being swept off the wooden bridge into the swift river. Later, when the trip was finally over in October 1934, Natalie hired a Taxco native to paint a *retablo* for her as a souvenir of the dangerous incident. The small painting served as a wry expression of thanks to the Taxco goddess Santa Prisca for miraculously protecting her. Such small miracle paintings are common in Mexican churches, placed by parishioners to memorialize an act of God in their lives. Natalie's colorful painting illustrated the rushing floodwaters washing two horses off the bridge but—with Santa Prisca hovering above, grasping lightning bolts—Natalie and her companions being

Natalie Scott *retablo* (October 1934) of her horseback adventure from Brownsville to Taxco. Santa Prisca, Taxco's patron saint, hovers above, protecting Natalie as she crosses the flooded river. *Courtesy of the Collection of Natalie Vivian Scott (Natalie's great-niece)*

granted safe passage through the turbulent river. The Spanish words on the *retablo* explained: "Miss Scott, guided by a man from San Bartolo, of name Julio Corea and having come out of the crossing without casualty, thanks are given by Miss Natalie Scott to the miraculous image of Santa Prisca who is venerated as Patroness of the Mineral Town of Taxco, Guerrero and to whom this is dedicated."[19]

Natalie rode into Taxco on the centuries-old Borda road in October 1934 covered by trail grime from the long ride, her old broad-brimmed African safari hat on her head. Surprised Taxqueñians began recognizing her and greeting her. A laughing crowd surrounded her horse as she climbed towards the *zócalo*, and children scattered to spread the word up ahead. Friends appeared from all directions; the Sutherland family emerged from their Hotel Taxqueño, witnessing her grand arrival. As the

Natalie on one of her horseback expeditions (Mexico, ca. 1935). *Courtesy of Special Collections, Tulane University Libraries*

laughing traveler tipped her hat, shouting her greetings to surprised friends, her exhausted horse suddenly collapsed beneath her. Natalie's trip had concluded with the memorable affirmation that she had outlasted her weary horse.[20] One version of the story appeared decades later in Elizabeth Anderson's autobiography. Incredulous when she learned of Natalie's adventure, she asked Natalie if what she had heard was true. Natalie added a humorous twist with her reply:

> A local legend had grown up around her fantastic trip of over eight hundred miles through wild territory. Everyone in Taxco believed that she had come riding triumphantly into the Borda Plaza and that her horse had promptly dropped dead of sheer exhaustion. It was a legend I would not find hard to believe, considering her sturdy frame. I asked her if it was true.
>
> "Of course not!" she said. "Not more than two weeks after I got here, Caroline Durieux and I wanted to go see an old hacienda in the country. Caroline offered to supply me with a horse but I said, 'That's foolish. I've got a perfectly good horse that I rode here from Brownsville.'
>
> "So I had the horse saddled and brought out. It took one long, sad look at me. *That's* when it dropped dead!" Natalie rocked with laughter. "The poor thing thought I was headed back to the border!"[21]

A Mexican Guide

A year later, in an exchange of letters with novelist Katherine Anne Porter, who had left Mexico in 1931, Natalie explained how she too had left Mexico. *Yes, I went back to the States, stayed nearly a year, became reimbued with the sacredness of lucre in mass psychology, but at the same time such a loathing of Huey Long,—not personally but of Huey Long-ism, because it showed up in such strong and hideous light the failing moral stamina of my own people. Didn't know how to balance the two, so compromised as I always do: planned to take a good job in the U.S. but first to cleanse my soul of Huey Long for one brief while at least.*

So I bought me a hoss in Matamoros and rode down for six and a half heavenly hard weeks thru grand country, quite alone except for the first week. And so of course I stayed in Mexico. And perhaps the tricky old sub-conscious knew all the time that I would.

So now I have bought back my charming little house, done lots of happy things to it, and the garden is a delight. And in a week from tomorrow, I set off on a two or three months riding trip thru Guerrero, Michoacan, Jalisco, and up into Nayarit,— if the curley headed young lad who represents a museum and is paying all the gastos does not fall by the wayside somewhere. Elizabeth Anderson has been visiting me, and is due back tonight. She is renting my house for the 'duration of the trip' and is going to care for my garden, too.

Katherine Anne wrote back, wanting more details on the horseback trip, asking if she had written it up. In her reply, Natalie explained that *Putnam (in person of Earle Balch) expresses an interest in a book about my riding trips, but I don't seem to get around to doing it; and yesterday I had a letter from the editor of Cosmopolitan asking for a long article thereon, but I fear that my old journalistic flair has deserted me.*[22]

The "curley headed young lad" in Natalie's letter was Donald Cordry, an ethnographer representing the Heye Foundation and the Southwest Museum in Los Angeles. Natalie would guide Cordry over the next few years on several anthropological expeditions over much of western and southern Mexico. She would often share artifacts, native weavings, and rare collectibles that she found with Frans Blom, enhancing the Tulane Middle American Anthropological Museum.

This first Cordry trip, from November 13, 1935, until March 1936, ended in Acapulco, where they received a five-day-old message by wire informing them of the death of Donald's father. Out of contact with any cable service for over a month, they had not known of his illness. Natalie wrote to Martha Robinson: *Don is a curly-headed amiable young man, strange as possible, and his reaction really was chiefly annoyance that the trip couldn't go on. That distressed me, too, for it was magnificent, but naturally I was more concerned about Don's poor mother, alone at such a time: he is an only child. Anyway, I finally got him off, and came on back here. Of course I haven't told you anything about my riding trip. You can't imagine how liberating it is to the old psyche, the hard going and the stupendous views, and the rhythm of the horse's going, which seems to set one's spirit moving rhythmically, too. One of the most pleasant feelings I know is climbing, climbing and feeling the horse's muscles straining under you. Extraordinary country, crossing the Sierra Madre at the highest crossable spot, with a view that squeezed your heart. But a trail that was pretty bad, hung up sky-high and dropped off down and down. One man told me that he had taken a trail twice as long in order to avoid this one!*

One section of the trip lay thru grand sugar country that reminded me vaguely of Louisiana. They make a dish there,—if it should be called a dish—that reminded me of Louisiana, too: a round squash has holes gouged in the top and is then suspended in boiling syrup, in the great kettles. To eat that, with a glass of cool milk, is a treat, after days of eggs and tortillas.

Along the coast, there were lots of Indian mounds, ayacates: you could walk out on them and find bits of pre-Conquest pottery, and even little clay idols, a great quickener for the imagination. I fell terribly in love with a little town, Zihuatenejo, to which we clambered down a mountain, finally thru cocoa palms, to the loveliest seeming lake, which was really a harbor, almost completely encircled by low mountains. Only about fifty houses, most of them thatched huts, and lots of fine beaches. Our last day was a good fifty miles, between a long narrow lake and the sea, with worlds of beautiful water-birds, cranes, and egrets, water-hens, gulls. I miss that traveling tremendously.

Later in the letter Natalie mentioned a few of the trip's leisurely moments. *I felt like spending the rest of my life in a little haciendita, that had the most charming mauve adobe annex to it, and an inexhaustible (so it seemed) supply of those grand "calabazos". Then, in another instance very gay in an Indian village, staying in the house with the priest, an ex-nun, and sacristan, sacristan's brother, and an ex-friar, a most Chaucerian assemblage. There were charming local observances of the day, and we had a Xmas tree at Xmas Eve supper, and a grand exchange of presents. And on January 31 while you were freezing in New Orleans, I was mopping my brow in the midday sun in the mountains![23]*

A less romantic view of Natalie's lifestyle traveling through mountain villages was experienced by twenty-year-old Celeste Lyons (Frierson), the daughter of Natalie's New Orleans friend Empsie Lyons. When Celeste visited Taxco in 1935, Natalie took her on a mountain excursion. Empsie had forbidden such a journey, but Celeste goaded Natalie into taking her anyway. They rode over the top of the mountain behind Taxco and descended into a great valley, arriving at a village at nightfall and sleeping that night in a one-room, low-ceilinged adobe hut. They shared a crude, flea-infested bed, Natalie against the wall and Celeste on the very edge. Celeste scratched all night, but Natalie seemed not to notice the pests. Remembering the occasion sixty years later, Celeste laughed thinking of the horse she bounced on from Taxco. Hers was no larger than a burro, while Natalie rode a very large horse that took huge, comfortable strides—a scene from Don Quixote and Pancho. The village was no more than a dozen huts. They ate with the villagers, and Celeste awoke at four o'clock, sick as a dog with vomiting and diarrhea. It took her several days to recover, which caused Natalie great worry that her friend Empsie would find out her orders had been violated.[24]

Natalie and Spratling lived with occasional bouts of dysentery, accepted among their colony as a fair price for life in Taxco. In a letter to Katherine Anne Porter, she jokingly referred to the period of Katherine Anne's absence from Mexico as the author's post-dysentery period. *Only mine, alas, isn't post nor past but very present. It's all settled in my system, which means that the system in question is by no means settled ever. However, we seem to hit it off well enough together on the whole, the bugs and I, and only at intervals do they demand bit of notice.*[25]

In 1936, the famed journalist-future World War II war correspondent Ernie Pyle visited with Natalie, then published a syndicated feature newspaper story that appeared across America and abroad in numerous languages. Pyle later republished the popular article. The opening recalled Natalie's apprehension in September 1917 when she left New Orleans for France and World War I. Here is how Ernie Pyle perceived her.

THE STORY OF A GIRL WHO WAS AFRAID, AND WHO WON A HERO'S CROSS IN FRANCE, AND NOW RIDES ALONE ALL OVER MEXICO

TAXCO, Mexico, April—Natalie Scott grew up to be afraid of everything. She got over it all right. She got over it plenty. I'd hate to see anything she's afraid of now.

Natalie Scott's childhood was spent at Pass Christian, on the Mississippi coast, the garden spot of the New Orleans territory. I judge that she was a daughter of considerable means. She has a culture that comes usually only from an early start along paths of velvet. She learned English and French simultaneously, as New Orleans' daughters do. She started riding a horse when she was five. But she was afraid. She was also afraid to make her debut.

I forgot just how Natalie Scott got into the war. It had something to do with her ability to speak French. She served through the whole thing in French hospitals. When she went in, she would faint at the sight of blood. When she came out she had the Croix de Guerre, and no fear of anything that walks, flies, crawls, or slinks through the night.

Natalie Scott probably knows Mexico better than any of the 15,000 Americans who live in Mexico. In two years she has ridden horseback, mostly alone, over a good many thousand miles of Mexico. She has ridden from Texas to Taxco—took six weeks.

She has ridden all over primitive Oaxaca in the south—two months.

She travels light. She wears riding pants and boots, but takes one dress to put on in the evenings if she's in a village. Mexican women don't like women who dress as men. She carries a serape (heavy blanket) to wrap around her when she has to sleep on the ground. She carries a canteen of water, and one change of underclothes, and a small toilet kit, and that is all. It's all on her saddle.

She's had some weird times. Once, down south, she was met outside a village and taken before the town council—assembled bare-footed on a dirt-floor hut. One by one the councilmen rose and made speeches in the Mixtec Indian dialect. She couldn't understand—but she suspected. Finally the town "secretary", who always knows Spanish, got up and said they had got along all right without any outsiders, and what was she doing there, but it didn't matter anyhow for she wasn't welcome, and to GET OUT.

She had to think fast. She thought of crops, the key to any Indian's heart. It worked. She said: "See, you don't know what they raise in Michoacan, and they don't know what you raise here. That's what I came up for, to see your crops." The first thing she knew they were producing special dishes of food for her. She stayed and talked all day and all night. They begged her to stay longer, but she had to go.

Another place they didn't beg her to stay, they told her. The village was run by an old, old man, who got it into his head this woman on horseback knew about a treasure in the pyramid ruins. He told her that if she'd tell him, he'd split with her. She couldn't tell him, for she didn't know. When she rode away, she was followed and brought back. Next day she left again, and rode between lines of silent men holding shotguns—and was brought back. Then the old man kept her in a hut for three days, thinking she'd tell. Finally he gave up, and told her to get out and stay out. She got, and stayed.

Natalie Scott's longest day's ride was 15 hours, starting at 3 in the morning. She has forded rivers deep as her waist. She bathed in rivers, in secluded spots. Her house stands behind a maze of foliage, way up on the mountain. You can sit on her cool stone veranda and look down at Taxco. The rooms are full of weird Indian fiesta masks, and French books, and native art, and old, old furniture on a bare stone floor.

Natalie Scott came to Mexico six years ago, because her yearly trip to Europe was too much for a depression income. She came to Taxco, and she stayed here because it was the first place for years where she could sleep at night. She will live here for the rest of her life.

She is a handsome woman, neither young nor middle aged. Her bobbed hair is graying. A New York literary tea or a Paris drawing room would be (and has been) graced by her presence. She lives on a slight income from New Orleans. She has worked on newspapers in New Orleans and Paris. She has written three cook-books—two on New Orleans foods, one on Mexican. She is proud of these.

She expects to take more horseback trips. She'd like to do an expedition for a museum. She has already mapped and stepped off several buried pyramids. "Are you going to make a book of your experiences?" I asked.

"I'd like to, but I'm too busy now," she said.

"Busy doing what?"

She laughed. "Busy walking up and down these hills," she said.[26]

In November 1936, Natalie was interviewed by WWL radio in New Orleans about her travels, her pre-Conquest collecting for Tulane's museum, and Mexico's native peoples. Here is an extract.

Question: Tell us something of these dance masks and what material they are made of.

Natalie: You understand that the dances are not social nor aesthetic in purpose, though often they are aesthetic in effect, because of the Indians' natural feeling for the beautiful. And they are social, because the performers are villagers and a whole village and people from nearby villages as well look on. But the intent is religious. The dances are given in honor of some patron saint. They represent drama to the natives. The dance is most often a pantomime representing a story, and usually there are words as well. Sometimes the masks are made of alternating layers of cloth and paste, so that they look like a crude paper-mâché. Usually, they are made of wood, often a very light wood called Zempantle. But sometimes, as in the dance of the Tlaceleres, where the dancers whip each other with heavy quirts, the masks are thick and heavy. The Tulane Museum of Middle American Research has some fine examples. Some of the dances date obviously from after the Conquest, but some few, like the beautiful Deer Dance of the Yaquis, or the Tehuanes, the Tiger Dance, of my own state, Guerrero, are of pre-Conquest origin.

Question: What do you take on these trips and what conveniences do you have in traveling?

Natalie: On most of my trips, I have taken only what I can carry on my horse. A bolster-shaped pack with zippers down it, with a change of shirt and underclothes. And a dress. I always change into a dress when I arrive in a village, for the Indians don't like ladies in trousers. And a gourd of water—a gourd keeps water deliciously fresh. And a manga, which I believe is called a poncho up here. And a blanket. My horse looks like a hat rack with all these things strung on. I sleep where the natives sleep, often on the floor with the family; sometimes in hammocks in the hot country; or on cots made of cane tied together. I eat what they eat, tortillas, sometimes cheese and honey, and an occasional chicken. I find that if you demand things of Indians, you get little. If you ask hospitality as a courtesy, you get all the best they have. For graciously formal dignified courtesy, no courtier in the world can equal the Indian. And his generosity is limitless.

Question: What has impressed you most in taking these trips into the interior of Mexico?

Natalie: For one thing, the superb beauty of the country, ranging from seaside and cocoa palm of the lowlands, or virgin forest hung with orchids and starred with giant begonias, to the austere grandeur of the mountains. For another, the graciousness of the people, as I have said. But most of all, the achievements of the present government in education and hygiene. The smallest, most remote villages have schools. The teachers are devoted: they teach until four, then supervise play, and frequently have night school as well. And they instill into the people elements of hygiene. In parts of Mexico, there are villages where the adults speak only an old Indian language: now the children all speak school-learnt Spanish. These people who were formerly economic slaves are living in constantly improving conditions. The government has changed from a government for the few to a government for the many. I'm incurably a lover of people. So all this delights me even more than the majestic archeological ruins, the fantastically beautiful foliage and flowers, and the strange animals—tigers, and tapirs, snakes, monkeys, and gorgeous birds. It's a great country. Always when I go back to it, I want to shout, "*Viva Mexico.*"[27]

Natalie continued to guide Donald Cordry, the Heye Foundation ethnographer, on very productive expeditions, though the odd young man was not her favorite. He infuriated her in mid-1937 when he absconded with artifacts she had put aside for Tulane, as she explained in a July letter to Frans Blom. *I've had a bad taste in my psychic mouth ever since dealing with that little rat Cordry! The latest is that he annexed some of my things, sending me a few pesos in return, fixing his own price. Things that I had sent on by mule-back. One was a composture of parrot feathers; I had painstakingly got him one of the same sort so that I could stay with mine. He wrote me that he had kept it, because he "needed it for the museum"! And he kept some other things as well. What a man.*

The rest of the letter was much happier, giving an account to Blom of expeditions, expenses, and objects being sent to the Tulane collection. *Certainly I wouldn't take more than $100, which is very slightly under what I spent; and wouldn't even think of taking the 30% plus. And if $100 makes a large hole in what you have for such collections, send any part thereof.*

It makes me very sad to take anything for the things, because I had counted very much on giving them as an out and out present. Natalie then explained that she had returned from the expedition to find her houses unrented, and *all sorts of things had been stolen or broken, which had to be replaced. If I emerge from it, as I optimistically hope, I'll spend your money to buy more 'things'.* To the goods sent to Blom, Natalie added *a mask, rather unusual, that I got on my trip last year, bought in Choopan but made in Yalalag,—Sapotec serrano; also a huipil [blouse], Chinanteca Serrano, quite handsome. So these at least will be presents.* She described handsome regional costumes, fajas, and quiscomes from the State of Mexico, Tamaulipas villages, and Ixthahuaca (near Toluca). She explained to Blom that in October she planned a ride to Olinala and Oaxaca, *where there are some marvelous huipiles, having seen them previously on a ride to Tlaxiaco, thru Zocatepec and Amsugos.*[28]

Blom wrote back, pleased with the new acquisitions:

> We are specially interested in complete costumes. The complete ones are rare. You will be a great help to build up our southern Mexico collection. Dance costumes are also welcome. Drums, chrirmias, etc. all that kind of family life gadgets are up our alley. Be sure each piece has a note with exact location of where you get it from, also a note what language the particular bearer speaks. If any pieces are of limited use, as fiesta, church, baptism, wedding etc. state this also. Don't worry about liking these things you send. We have a craving for textiles, of all kinds, before the textile art becomes swamped with aniline dyes, and decay through tourist taste.

He sent her $100, adding, "Let me know if you need cash. We haven't got so much, but things are clearing up."[29]

The Guardería

In late August, Natalie sent another large shipment to Tulane. *I had a show of them here in my house, displayed all the things, to friends. A tea party of about 70, quite successful. There were many suggestions that I should keep the things on display for awhile and charge tourists to see them! So they must have thought them interesting. I went to Topeltepec, an Aztec village and about 7 hours on horseback from Teleloapan, last weekend and got three rather unusual masks, a tecolete, a quite entrancing gallo, and a viejo. A friend going to New Orleans will take them up for me. Soon, I am going to Chilapa to spend a few days, some villages with very nice regional dress. And the huipil from the Chinantola Alta should be along at any moment now.*

Some day that may be a really nice collection! Some day. Totoltepec was fine,—all the people speak a pigeon Spanish and the older ones are much more at home in Aztec. . . . Do let me know what you think when you see the collection.

When Blom encountered problems getting the collection through U.S. customs, Natalie prepared a detailed itemization of values required by the customs agents. She expressed some concerns to Blom. *I hope the lovely arrows won't be ruined by so much delay. The woolen bags and fajas wash beautifully. The cotton embroidered things are liable to fade, and should be washed very, very carefully. That's why I didn't have it done here. I hope that I shall soon have news that these things are reposing in the museum.*[30]

Natalie followed this shipment with more donations to Tulane. She also submitted to Tulane's Latin American Library her various translations of Mexican literature, including her *Book of Verses for the Dance of the Companions of Santiago*. Simultaneously she shipped off new short stories to her literary agent, but she was not proud of them. She wrote to Martha Robinson, *The agent, quite a good one, writes enthusiastically about them—and doubtless will fail to sell them. They are deliberately "tripe", so would probably have more chance than two somewhat better ones I've done, but am holding.*[31]

On another mountain adventure in the summer of 1939, Natalie caught a lift in a 1926 Chrysler for the rough ride to Chilpancingo, then Chilapa. She arrived there on a colorful market day, with men and women gathering from nearby Aztec villages in their bright regional clothing. *The Square was packed solidly with these gorgeous creatures, a magnificent show in the sunlight. I had been told the horses in Chilapa were not good, so I had to go mule-hunting. Bound, you see, for Olinala, where the best lacquer-work in the country is made. The mule was difficult. The stirrups were too short, one much shorter than the other. But the country was beautiful. And then the mountains began. Mountains that riz up most awfully from narrow valleys,—and over one after the other.*

My mozo was pure Aztec. He grew quite excited as we began climbing a sky-scraper mountain. On top we shall see the 'folcanos', he kept telling me. On top was pretty grand: we looked out over an array of harried peaks, and saw in the angle between two dark mountain shoulders, Popo and Izta all white and glistening in the sunset light. Something one could never forget.

After which we got lost, but finally found our village at dark. All little huts of twigs in the dark. A 'bed' of lashed bamboo with a clean mat. We had brought hard boiled eggs and coffee, fortunately; there were only tortillas to be had. An 11½ hour day, the next day, ten hours in the saddle, one for luncheon, and half-hour for 'tea'. Tremendous climbs: from tropical foliage up to the scrub-oak heights in half an hour sometimes so mercilessly steep were the climbs. But it was grand country. We followed a river part of the way, beautiful, but rough and full of boulders.

Ahuacetzingo was charming. It is set up on a high founded knell, all red clay, with fresh green trees shooting up out of it. All the houses were made of stout bamboo lashed neatly with thorns of palm fibre, and then plastered with the russet clay; and they were topped with a thick neatly cut thatch of warm brown grass. Nearby were storerooms of golden tan bamboo. The 'streets' were red clay,—so the color effect was lovely. Beyond the town was a little stream lined with magnificent ahe-huebe (cypress) trees. Reached Olinala at seven that evening,— a sad little hushed town with poverty overhanging it. Visited all the lacquer-work (well, all the best). Practically every house in the town works at it, and it is something to watch. Each object is painted completely over with a heavy enamel-like paint, and the designs scratched out with a pigeon-quill, the feather used to brush off the 'dust',—all with quick deft twists of the hand.

They are so far from transportation that they do not know how to market their goods. My expenses were being paid by an exporter in Mexico who wanted their work. I found no one fam-ily produced enough so I promptly organized a 'cooperative'. You would have grinned could you have seen me presiding over the meeting of the 16 best workmen. I hope it will help the little town, anyhow.

They ran into heavy rains after leaving Olinala. *The river was swollen to a raging torrent. Two little Aztec men who lived on the cliff above told us it was impossible to cross. The wife of one came down and stood on a rock that jutted low into the furious current. And as she stood there, the river hurled a two-foot fish against the rocks, threw it up, bruised to death, at her feet!*

After hours my patience waned; so I coaxed and tipped the two men, who finally agreed to try to get us over. Quite excit-ing, and you nearly lost your friend, when the mule lost his foot-ing. Only the nimble limbs and wit of the Aztec saved us. We had to take the upper trail instead of the river bed. I looked back at some of the cliffs that we had clambered down and couldn't believe my own eyes: they looked as flat as a wall; and the trail down them so steep that one looked directly at the bottom, over the mule's ears.[32]

The work of both Natalie and Spratling received featured attention in the May issue of *Modern Mexico,* describing them as co-leaders of the literary and artistic set that followed them to Taxco. The article declared Spratling's silver and serape shop "the most artistic headquarters for handicrafts in all the Republic." It continued, "Spratling taught the Guerrero craftsmen to improve on their own designs, his success due to his own innate genius as well as his deep regard and admiration of the Indians. Natalie Scott has the same profound affection for her native neighbors." Describing Natalie as "a writer of distinction," the article focused on back-country horseback expeditions "where she collects curios for museums and increases her knowledge of Indian tribes."

> She has crossed the mountains from Matamoros to Mexico City; she has spent months in the Nayirit mountains with the Coras and the Huicholes; she has penetrated into the fastness of the Oaxaca forests; she knows every little hamlet in the state of Guerrero . . . long trips without guides or pack animal. A gourd of water, a bolster with a zipper of clothes, a string bag, a raincoat, a zarape comprise her equipment . . . bathing in rushing rivers. Her worst experience was six days in the Cora Indian country without a bath.
>
> When not on horseback, she is at her typewriter or engaged in renting Taxco houses to visiting artists or overseeing her pension, the Kitigawa House. Here, if she likes you, you can obtain food and lodging for four pesos daily. If you are rich enough to afford a hotel, you may pay her $4.[33]

During 1937 Natalie had taken on another major project in Taxco, a *pensión* for artists that she named the Kitigawa House. Tamaji Kitigawa, the magnificent Japanese painter who arrived in Mexico during the 1920s, had operated since 1931 an open-air art school for children in his two-level Taxco home up the hill from Spratling's Las Delicias workshop, a spot with a panoramic view over the Hotel Victoria. Natalie had promoted the school, eager to get the peasant children off the streets. She sponsored art shows and fundraising for supplies, even utilizing two of

Natalie Scott (ca. 1937). *Courtesy of the New Orleans Times-Picayune*

Natalie Scott (left), Martha Gilmore Robinson, and Sidonie Provosty Scott at floating gardens of Xochimilco (1937). *Courtesy of Special Collections, Tulane University Libraries*

Kitigawa House, Natalie's boarding house or *pensión* for artists and writers (Taxco, ca. 1937). *John W. Scott Collection*

Kitigawa's student painters to illustrate her 1935 cookbook, *Your Mexican Kitchen*. With Japanese militarism in the Pacific endangering relations with the United States, the Japanese government issued an order for its nationals abroad, including Kitigawa, to return to Japan. The sad occasion in 1937 of the Kitigawa family's departure led to Natalie taking over the school, ultimately converting the place into a popular *pensión* for serious artists and writers to reside inexpensively, a throwback to her Scott-McClure House for French Quarter artists during the 1920s. The Kitigawa became a headquarters for creative people in Taxco.[34]

Easily the most important, most lasting project Natalie pursued in Taxco was her peasant school for young children, the Guardería de Niños Sor Juana Inez de la Cruz de Taxco, named for Mexico's great eighteenth-century poet. As a first step in December 1938, Natalie invited a large mixture of leading Taxco families to her home to discuss *over tea the child problems in Taxco,* problems due to poverty, disease, malnutrition, and neglect. Her solution was the Guardería de Niños, a project that required funds for suitable housing, equipment, meals, and operating expenses.

The school/kindergarten idea had evolved in Natalie's mind for several years, her concern mounting as she witnessed the high local death rate among children from malnutrition, dysentery, tuberculosis, occasional outbreaks of typhoid, and other health problems. Poverty was the primary culprit, with the efforts to teach sanitation difficult, *as bathing is a revolutionary thing.* By 1938, Natalie was bringing Dr. Alberto Curiel in to treat the acutely sick, paying the cost herself or finding donors to pay. *The doctor is really very good: he charges only a peso a visit which is now, twenty cents! But of course some of the medicines and injections are expensive.*

As a solution to risky childbirth in unclean hutches, Natalie brought pregnant mothers into her home to deliver in her bed. She and her helpers, María Luisa and Luz, served as midwives, in close touch with Dr. Curiel. Not surprisingly, Natalie found herself the godmother of a steadily rising number of Mexican children. Her concern extended to the unfortunates, particularly the many fatherless families where infants and youngsters were left unattended daily, their mothers absent as they eked out a living. Thus was born the Guardería de Niños. At first aimed at the youngest children, the program also included elementary-age children expected to help the younger ones. It also served as an early-morning and afternoon depot for older schoolchildren—feeding them, getting them to school, and keeping them busy after school until their mothers came for them. Aside from being kept off the streets, these Taxqueñian children were well fed, clean, healthy, and in a supervised program.[35]

When Natalie hosted the first organizational meeting in her Taxco home, inviting dozens of leading locals, Mexican and American, to hear her plan, the crowd overflowed from her *sala* and porch, many observing through the windows. *The obvious solution was a Guardería de Niños, which would as far as possible take the place of the mother during her working hours. To do this, it would be necessary to accumulate sufficient funds to buy necessary equipment, install a suitable house and for insuring in advance at least several months operation.*

For the first ten months of 1939, Natalie led an intense fundraising effort. Monthly parties were held in various homes, and pledges for fixed monthly donations were sought. *The parties were the social centers of the period,* she recalled in a 1950s fundraising speech. *Many American residents entertaining privately, acquired the habit of suggesting to their guests that they contribute to the Guardería.* Natalie's many trips to the government's Asistencia Infantile de Mexico in Mexico City resulted in a modest monthly stipend, 145 pesos. She persuaded several leading locals—Carlos Nibbi and the Castrejón family, among others—to make similar pledges. Dr. Alberto Curiel agreed to become the facility's physician. Years later Natalie referred to him as *the guardian angel of the Day Nursery,* who *treats the children free of charge whenever necessary, usually even donating the medicines.*[36]

The original all-female board of directors, the Mesa Directiva, had eleven members, all Mexican except for four. Natalie was the president; Elizabeth Anderson was the assistant treasurer; Russian dancer Tamara Schee and Chiltipin Sutherland were members. Among their fundraising efforts was a grand August

Natalie (second from right) with (from left) Marie Curiel, Conchita Castrejón, and Sofia Giles. These Mexican friends were board members and valuable supporters of the Taxco school founded by Natalie (Taxco, ca. 1939). *John W. Scott Collection*

1939 concert featuring Waldeen, a popular dancer-choreographer in Mexico City. Regional dancers were also provided for the show by the Artes de Mexico, along with an array of singers and musical entertainers, and a raffle offered the prize of a Valentín Vidaurreta painting donated by the artist. Natalie wrote to Martha Robinson, *A week ago, we had our mammoth benefit, quite the most exciting show that Taxco has witnessed. A very good dancer, Waldeen, and her assistant Elizabeth Waters, came down and danced for us for nothing. The huge if unsightly Hotel de la Borda lent itself to us. It was packed and jammed. After that program, tables were brought in, and we had a 'cabaret' with various* numbers. *It was a great success financially.*[37]

The Guardería opened its doors in December 1939 with a small celebration, the occasion not easily accomplished. The project dominated Natalie's busy days throughout the autumn. *I don't think that ever in my life, except during the war, have I been so busy. Morning, noon, and night, all too literally. The Day Nursery began to seem a Sisyphus stone: no sooner was one difficulty dealt with than ten others popped up. I almost lost hope, but kept struggling desperately, and now, lo and behold, we are going to start on Monday. We are tremendously fortunate in a woman doctor of the Rockefeller Foundation. She had an appointment in Campeche. Impossible to come. So I invented an excuse for writing again, finally got her interested.* The purpose of having this temporary Rockefeller Foundation social worker, Dr. Erica Hinton, a specialist in childhood diseases, was to get the Guardería off to a good start addressing health needs. *Her appointment was with the Asistencia Pública (Public Welfare), so then I had to go to work on them to get her appointment changed to Taxco. It's just succeeded! But I interviewed all sorts of people, spent hours on end in offices (one day ten hours in Asistencia Pública!), pulled wires such as I could. And now it is done.*

But that was only one detail: a huge house, the furnishings; lots of things that had to come from Mexico [City], all on my own expense. So you can see why I am so flat broke. And one million details. We had the Inauguration on the 20th. Very funny to inaugurate before being ready for work, no? The 20th is the Day of the Revolution, a holiday. Seemed apt. Moreover, we invited the Secretary of the Asistencia Pública, the Governor, Ambassador Daniels. The former sent representatives and a glowing letter to be read aloud (he gave us a hundred pesos, too, which wasn't bad). Asistencia Pública sent the head of the Child Welfare Department, which was just what I had hoped. I got him off in a corner, told him of our progress, our projects, and so on. The results were really very good. Very nice man he is, too.

Well, that's my big baby. Wish you could see the house. It is central, quite large, has a grand porch full of sunshine, and a big room with high ceilings. We had it all fixed up with baths, electricity, paint, and so on. It is most attractive.

Simultaneously, Natalie earned fees directing renovations for

María Estrada, manager of Natalie's Guardería for peasant children (Taxco, ca. 1940). *John W. Scott Collection*

another Taxco property owner. *A large house, it is really three houses hooked together. I am there now, in fact, all the time that I am not with the Guardería or the Kitigawa House, I am here.* Meanwhile, Natalie also helped a new business open. Her next-door neighbor, Héctor Aguilar, the manager of Bill Spratling's operations, decided with his wife, Lois, to launch a silver business, backed financially by Kim and Tamara Schee. Aguilar's silver career would rank second in Taxco only to Spratling himself.

The Guardería was busy immediately, Natalie's Dr. Hinton assisting her the first four months. *A devoted worker, María Estrada, was employed full time as general worker, cook and laundress. Dr. Hinton outlined a routine: an affordable diet of nutritive value. The children would arrive, clean at 7:30 a.m.; have three meals a day, a rest period after lunch, to be called for after merienda (snack), at six o'clock. Meetings were organized with the mothers of Taxco, Dr. Hinton offering advice on diet and child care, every one being introduced to the services of the Guardería.*

Sra. Estrada, with her close and sympathetic knowledge of the problems of the poor in Taxco and of the individuals concerned, guided the committee decisions on which children to admit. *The children accepted are those who are most in need of help.*

The Guardería opened with twelve children enrolled but quickly grew to twenty-five, the maximum allowed by funds on hand. A small monthly fee of one peso per child was charged, the purpose *not for the small financial help but to keep the mother aware of her obligation, to maintain her self-respect so that she was to some small extent paying for their welfare. Criticisms and comments by the mothers* were *invited and heeded with interest.* Assisting Natalie and María Estrada, the directors shared responsibility for organizing recreational activities, education programs, fundraising, and toy donations. A steady stream of donations came from American tourists *who have heard of the Guardería and visited it.*

Music and dancing were emphasized. *There is a record player with many records, some in Spanish and children's songs in English; constructive educational toys. Tinker Toys, drawing-books and crayons; a black-board, dolls and many books.* The children learned a number of American songs, *the idea being that they will early learn pronunciation of English. One of their most dearly-loved games is one to an English song called Farmer in the Dell. Also teaching regional dances. The children know a simple version of the jarabe and love it.*

A tradition of Christmas parties began in 1939. Natalie's friend Alice Crouch, a new Taxco resident, took responsibility for two events, *one the day after Christmas and the other on the Day of the Kings,—piñatas and simple toys, chocolates and sweet buns.* Each child received clothes, underclothes, and shoes, *a joy to the children. Much hard work is involved in securing the necessary donations for these parties. The children of the mining-engineers come to visit the children bringing a Christmas tree and a present for each child. The children of the Guardería are taught they may 'corresponder' by singing a Xmas hymn in English to their visitors. So they practice with enthusiasm.*

Natalie expanded the school's operations into medical and surgical care of *children whose mothers could not possibly meet the need, even to children not enrolled in the Guardería.* For example, in 1939 one child was found to have a dangerous mouth infection. Natalie

Natalie Scott's Christmas card (ca. 1939). *Courtesy of Special Collections, Tulane University Libraries*

The Scott-Provosty family at the Scott home in Alexandria, Louisiana. Natalie appears on the back row (fourth from left), with nephew Nauman beside her (fifth from left). The younger nephew, Bino, appears against the column (far right). Both would serve in World War II (Christmas 1939). *John W. Scott Collection*

took her to Mexico City to a dental surgeon, saving the child's life. The Guardería paid the dental bill. Another was Fernando, a five-year-old deaf mute abandoned by his father, and his mother desperately poor. The Guardería took in Fernando, his seven-year-old brother, and his nine-year-old sister, all malnourished and with no education whatsoever. They were able to attend school, with the Guardería taking care of them. The sister won academic honors in her class two years later.

Meanwhile, Natalie made persistent efforts to find help for Fernando. *At the age of six, he was admitted to the Government's school for deaf mutes.* Subsequently she wrote, *He has been there for several years. He is learning to talk, and to read and write. He will be taught a trade, and to read lips.*

This was the beginning of two decades of schooling and care by Natalie for Taxco's peasant children, a Taxco generation provided with hope, love, and opportunity. It would be Natalie's permanent legacy in Taxco.[38]

Celebrities Galore

Meanwhile, the procession of odd new Taxco residents, visiting celebrities, and tourists bearing letters of introduction kept Natalie busy leasing properties and entertaining. She took writer John Van Druten, author of *Cabaret,* into the mountains during 1936 on horseback; *I egged Johnny on to riding, and the poor fellow was thrown and had his arm broken.*

John Dos Passos came often, while Russian dancer Tamara Schee and husband Kim Schee, *a well-set-up young American full of psychic kinks,* settled in Taxco in 1935. *A deliciously amusing English painter named Edward Wolfe (Teddy Wolfe)* and *some ex-Hollywood people turned painter and writer and various other such* were among the constant stream of new residents and visitors. Natalie's Taxco letters through the decade are filled with people and occasions, *including a couple named Lincoln who are unusual, intelligent and super-educated and merrily human. Yesterday I fled with them to the mountains, out to my favorite Tetipec. Today the Norman Bel-Geddes have arrived, and a cocktail party is starting them off, and luncheon tomorrow. The Davis house (around the hill from mine) has been taken by a charming young couple, the Grafs. Very important dancers of the modern school, who have danced all over the continent, before assorted royalties, and with*

Natalie (left) with Elizabeth Anderson and author John Van Druten (Taxco, ca. 1935). *Courtesy of Special Collections, Tulane University Libraries*

the best orchestras, including Stakowski's. But they are very genuine, seem almost naifs and shy, and very likeable. He's quite handsome. The Arthur Calder Marshalls are here,—he's an English writer.[39]

The steady flow of new arrivals led to awkward moments and amusing anecdotes. *I was expecting two girls whom I had come to know quite well, so when Luz came in, as I was changing my clothes, and told me that two senoritas were there, I called out merrily to them. And continued to toss flippant remarks thru the window and I sailed merrily out onto the porch,—to confront two eminently sedate ultra-ladylike ladies! One was the wife of the new American Consul General in Mexico, the other lady-plus presented an introduction to me from some person whom I can't place at all. I meanwhile tried to pretend that I was an entirely different personality from the one who had just been casting airly persiflage thru the window. I did rather well, and was just regaining composure, when I escorted them down my walk. And then I glanced with pleasure at my little fountain,— only to find that Luz had adorned it with two POTS DE CHAM-BRES! Ay de mi.*[40]

Another guest in 1939, Walt Disney, was still so early in his career that Natalie did not remember his name as she reviewed new arrivals in a letter to Martha Robinson. *The people who are staying on for the moment include a couple named Tenggrin. The Tenggrin male was with,—O dear, the man who makes the movies, Snow White and so on: can't imagine why his name has slipped my mind for the moment. His wife tells me that he works at such high tension in the studio that it made a nervous wreck of him. So he expects to spend a quiet time here.*[41]

The diversity of accomplished Taxqueñians and distinguished visitors complemented Natalie's picturesque, challenging Mexican world. Her weekends were typically graced with sparkling personalities and occasional celebrity surprises. One July Sunday in 1938, for example, Natalie (with her friend Bob Griffith) met *the two very nice López-Figueroa sisters at the Telva, and Miguel and Rosa Covarrubias. I had supper with all of them, and later went to a very swagger party that Valentín Vidaurreta was giving. The same little crowd of the Rancho Telva plus several men were drinking at the Bar Paco. I lunched with them all afterwards. At the Bar Paco, everybody was autographing a book, laughingly, and saying it was for Tyrone Powers, whose picture has been in the paper as a recent arrival in Mexico. Later, at the hotel after luncheon, I chatted with some of the men, whose names I had not caught. Afterwards, I asked Bob who they were. "Why, that's Tyrone Powers and his crowd," he said. "I thought you knew." One of them really was Tyrone Powers, a nice-looking (not exceptionally) young man with quite charming manners. And his movie-director,—or something.*[42]

Natalie's niece, Bé Scott, visited for the 1939 summer, driving down from Louisiana with two young friends. Natalie took her on horseback excursions to surrounding villages, and also introduced her to the local colony of creative people and misfits. *Bé has acquired a beau, very nice one,—professor at Cornell, with a lot of charm. They've been inseparable all week. Adrian, the Hollywood designer, has been here all week, with the actress Janet Gaynor, his new wife. Adrian was here before, some years back, came to a party at my house, and was quite nice, and he looked me up again this time. Had them up for dinner, with Waldeen (the dancer) and the Schees.*

Silver designer Héctor Aguilar, his wife, Lois, and Bé Scott were there too. *Adrian promptly sat in my best chair, and it collapsed under him. Then he went to close a door, and the glass fell out!* Natalie's houseboy, Rosendo, proudly served the famous Hollywood honeymooning couple. His first appearance took them by surprise. The golden-skinned boy emerged beaming from the kitchen, decked out like some movie director in sunglasses and beret. Rosendo efficiently carried trays of food and drink throughout the evening, and all immensely enjoyed his nod to Hollywood. Following dinner, the guests played charades late into the night.[43]

War Clouds Gather

War clouds were gathering over Europe, clearly discernable to Natalie by mid-decade. She was appalled that great Western nations, collectively frozen by their foreign policy of isolationism, were turning their backs to grave dangers in Europe and Asia by ignoring aggression against innocent countries. The fear of war actually made war more likely, she told Martha Robinson in a March 1936 letter, deeply offended by the Nazis and the Fascists.

The European situation has made me sick at heart, and I hate to look at the paper each day, but at the same time can't wait for it to arrive. I do hope you are giving that grand masculine trio of yours a proper horror of war and an appreciation of the sordidness that invariably lies behind them,—sordidness and greed. I am really so peeved with the world. It is really astonishing when one thinks how decent people seem individually,—and in the mass how cruel and grasping and unintelligent. Intensely anti-Franco, Natalie was bitterly disappointed by the world's apathy towards the Spanish Civil War, the Fascist uprising supported by Hitler and Mussolini. She felt frustrated by the plight of Spain's Republican Loyalists and proud of her friend Siqueiros, who joined the Loyalist army to fight Franco's forces while the Western democracies did nothing.[44]

As Franco gained the upper hand, Natalie found disgusting the world's acceptance of his repressive regime. *I am more and more confirmed in the deduction that the English 'classes' consider Fascism with complacency, if not definite sympathy. I have a mournful amusement in the irony of the poor little demonstration against the recognition of Franco: as tho the so-called non-intervention policy would have led to anything else! As for Franco's attitude toward the poor Loyalists, betrayed by all the world, they will surely also be betrayed by him. And you may imagine how many things will come under the heading of "crime" when his courts get busy!! I couldn't sleep all night after seeing in the movie in Mexico [City] pictures of the retreating refugees toiling into France thru bitter cold. It was worse than the French refugees, which heaven knows seared a lasting scar in my memory.* As though in defiance of Natalie's written worries, Hitler bloodlessly occupied Austria only days later.[45]

By late September 1938, Natalie was dreading the direction of world events, as Hitler's territorial demands escalated and the Western democracies remained inactive. Better to challenge the aggressors now than later, she reasoned. *It really makes me sick at heart to read about it all, many nights I have lain awake with the spectre of impending suffering, again to be offered up on the altar of greed. Old medieval devil-worship wasn't nearly so disastrous. Italy is much handicapped, as is Germany, with the aid they are giving Spain; and Italy is suffering from the drought besides, and has her troops busy in Abyssinia. Even Hitler does not say that Germany is quite ready for war now. Whereas it is obvious that if England and France yield in this, there will be other demands later, with Germany's power grown, and Italy's as well, and perhaps a Fascist dominated Spain to help them. When I slept last night, my dreams were all of those sickening memories of tortured human flesh. And one has to sit helpless!*

It seems incredible that we can pursue our daily little rounds, while in Spain and in China the daily martyrdoms go on; with the threat of expanding into all Europe. "Christ whose pale face on the Cross Sees only this after the passion of a thousand years."[46]

Natalie's fears proved prophetic. Only days later at Munich, British and French leaders conceded to Hitler's demands for the Sudetenland of neighboring Czechoslovakia. Natalie struggled for patience with the British prime minister, Neville Chamberlain, hopeful though skeptical that territorial concessions would end Hitler's aggression. *What a week that was! The Sunday night announcement absolutely sunk me: I couldn't close my eyes harassed of course by visions conjured up from memory.* As she wrote, Natalie was operating the Hotel Taxqueño temporarily while the Sutherlands were off on vacation. She glued herself to the shortwave radio there, gathering all news she could find from Europe. *How I hung over it at every possible moment! And sleep was simply impossible. When news of the conference came, it was a great relief of course. We got London daily, and Prague, also, with shudders, Berlin and Rome, and heard the Pope, Hitler and Mussolini. I heard Chamberlain, and Sir Anthony Eden.*

As for Chamberlain, I think that he is eminently conscientious, a very religious devout man, and I am sure that his every action had the highest motives. The only thing is that it is still doubtful as to whether or not war is simply put off. Hitler has got himself into the position of the Kaiser, having built up such a large war-machine that he must direct it against something, otherwise it will turn on him and devour him. I feel that he would never have given in but for Mussolini, who is cooler-headed and knows that they could not fight now. Mussolini saved himself in like situations by grabbing Abyssinia, but that was less of a problem than facing unified Europe. Italy would be negligible now: they are very short of rations after the drought; the people dislike the Germans anyway, and the army is much occupied in Spain and Abyssinia. So they would be little help to Germany.

Germany, for all her vaunted stores, still has no butter-fat, and many of her substitute foods are being shown to be inadequate. Moreover, she has no credit. So I do not think that at the last moment they would have fought. It would have been a terrific gamble, of course. But it does seem that Hitler is bent on war,—that seems certain. And if it is, now would be the best time to stop him, before he consolidates all his gains.

As for the Sudetans, they wanted to be joined with Austria before, not with Germany; obviously much propaganda has been at work there from Germany. The Czechs were tardily but fully offering them the same degree of self-government, the full extent of their original demands. With each concession, Hitler demanded more. The ultimate agreement giving Czecho-Slovakia's fortifications away, maiming their economic independence, does seem a frightful injustice. Were it a certain cure for the menace of war, it would be worth it, even tho the honor of two great nations goes with it, but it is so doubtful that it is the end! In March 1939, scarcely six months later, Hitler suddenly erased the rest of Czechoslovakia from the map.[47]

Weeks before Czechoslovakia's fall, Natalie took a New Orleans trip, during which she had struggled to calm her passions over world events. Attending a Tulane lecture of a New York newspaper editor, she stood during the question period and contested the speaker's pro-neutrality stance towards Hitler and Franco. In a second controversy, she spoke out in a letter to the Tulane Board of Supervisors, published in the *New Orleans Item-Tribune,* defending several Tulane faculty members who were accused of socialist leanings, then forced to resign. Hard feelings followed. *I heard I was a Communist, this being due to the fact that I wrote a letter of remonstrance in regard to members of the Faculty finding their positions made untenable because they had social-economic ideas distinct from those of the Faculty. Me 'n' liberty, you know: I can't see why a man should be forced to give up his convictions as to his obligations as a private citizen, just because he is on a Faculty. Odd how people take personally a divergence of opinion!*

In Taxco, divergences were everywhere. *Here, there are various opinions represented,—ultra capitalistic, of course, of the mining-men; liberals; an occasional (but rather rare) communist; bohemians, Roman Catholics, Protestants: yet we all get along quite easily, arguing for hours at a time, but still quite friendly. New Orleans is not that way, but I love it just the same. Actually, I am a much milder 'liberal' than was Christ! Thru the war and my life here, I have come in closer contact with the varied agonies of poverty than most so am more acutely aware of the vast miseries of the world. So much so, that I'd really rather be as poor as I am than very rich. The war, no doubt, did a lot to producing a different sense of values, breaking down barriers between individuals, the artificial social barriers. For instance, one of my persistent admirations is for an ex-dancer, a mick from Boston, with the oddest brogue and the highest sense of honor and decency I've almost ever met.*[48]

Also in September 1938, Natalie's ire was aroused by another issue closer to home, a controversy between the two lands she most loved, the United States and Mexico. Her response revealed powerful perspectives gained from life and travels among the humble, isolated people of primitive Mexico, where nationality had little meaning. That year, Mexican president Lázaro Cárdenas confronted American oil companies over the control of Mexican petroleum reserves. Cárdenas ordered the nationalization of domestic oil, dispossessing U.S. companies of their vast Mexican holdings. The American oil industry protested loudly, turning to Pres. Franklin Roosevelt for intervention.

Offended by condemnations of Cárdenas by the United States press, particularly an editorial in *The Atlantic Monthly* assailing the Mexican government as corrupt and high-handed, Natalie organized a letter-writing campaign among her American cohorts in Mexico. A flurry of letters defending Mexico arrived at American newspapers and magazines, none more compelling than Natalie's response published in *The Atlantic Monthly*.

The cartoon you published synthesizes the whole question. It pictures foreign capital coming into Mexico as generosity, out of sheer kindness of heart, developing resources which Mexico could not develop, and then being ungratefully ejected. Now, an accurate cartoon would present, in like symbolism, a little boy without a spade in his yard where he has a pot of gold buried. A big boy with a fine spade comes along and says, "Here, son, here's ten cents: I'll dig up your gold". Whereupon he digs it up, begins handing it by fistfuls into his own pot, occasionally giving the little boy a small piece. And that bad little boy isn't grateful!

The usual retort is, of course, that some general here was reimbursed. There is some graft here, of course; but that should hardly startle a citizen of the Louisiana of Huey Long and his successors, nor of many other states in our Union (Nor do I mean to criticize harshly my own country, but, when it is used as a house from which to throw rocks, its glass panels stand out.) You point with horror at the strikes here: are there none in the United States? As for what the present Government is doing for the people as a whole, quite as large a proportion of its small resources are going to the raising of living conditions as in our own enlightened country,—and Mexico started from infinitely farther back.

Riding-trips of two or three months duration each, over a period of more than eight years in remote and primitive sections have given me a proof. Innumerable are the villages and the sections where a pre-Conquest language is the current, sometimes, the only language spoken. People in one village cannot understand those from another four hours away. The Government has established schools in all these regions. The children speak Spanish. Inter-village school contests take place, so that the children come to know each other. Hygiene is introduced: in a Oaxaca village eight days away from Oaxaca City on horseback, I found the teacher giving serum against whooping-cough. The ravages of small-pox, formerly hardly combated, are reduced to a minimum, as sanitary units travel through the country inoculating the natives. Free clinics are being scattered increasingly through the country. Among the most primitive Indians, you may find a trained district nurse. There are free Government boarding schools for the Indians in the most remote regions, where the children are given decent living-conditions, taught trades, and go back to their homes as culture-carriers, full of faith and hope in their nation.

Yet, talking even in dollars and of laziness as well, which, you imply to be a Mexican trait,—I stood on the porch of one of the creators of the Citrus Fruit industry in the famous Texas valley. "This would have been impossible", he said thoughtfully, "without Mexican labor". And is it laziness and lack of enterprise to work one's farm from earliest light daily during planting and harvest season, and do eight hours work in the mines besides, as do some of my humble acquaintances here?

Such things are beside the point in your general indictment of Mexico. That the Cárdenas regime has made mistakes and may make more is not to be denied; but that the general direction of it is for the steady betterment of the people no impartial observer would deny. The controversy did not go away, though FDR chose not to take sides.[49]

The fall of Czechoslovakia ended any patience Natalie could muster for Chamberlain. She wrote to Martha Robinson, appalled by the Western paralysis that enabled, even encouraged, Hitler's actions. *Every day's news seems worse than the last. My own hunch has been increasingly that Chamberlain is Fascist in sympathy, very strongly,—that he has put class above empire and is afraid of England's own labor class. And that he has been able to fool them, and now realizes that he can no longer fool them, so is making the pretense of putting up a bold front. But the time may come when the rest of the country will not tolerate any more of his weak-kneed attitude.*

As for me, my mind refuses to keep away from the present situation in Europe, and all its horrible implications and potentialities, and, harassed by them all the time, has me nervous and jittery. I have been wondering what to do when the most amazing solution presents itself. Already, in April 1939, Natalie was thinking of rejoining the Red Cross, going to another world war, but this time almost at the age of fifty.[50]

When Martha's reply came, in Chamberlain's defense, Natalie volleyed back. *I don't see how you can have any faith in Chamberlain as being for the democracies. The French have him pat, I think, in speaking of him as 'J'aime-Berlin'. He is so afraid of the labor party, and of the privileged classes losing some of their privileges. It seems impossible that Germany and Italy would go up against the tremendous line-up that is set against them. Yet I suppose it is a case of self-preservation for Hitler and for Mussolini, preserving themselves for a time at the cost of millions of lives. And only assuredly to go down in the end. It is a nightmare to contemplate.*[51]

Then in May 1939, in another letter to Martha, Natalie wrote: *My cross is world conditions,—the low standard of integrity, individual and national; I deplore the prevailing materialistic standards, the abeyance of the spiritual values. The cynical betrayals, active and passive, of Abyssinia, Spain, Austria, Czecho-Slovakia, are an ever present anguish in my spirit. So, too, is the blindness, deliberate or unconscious, to the mass of poverty and suffering in our own country, with the resulting bitterness of opposition to any steps that might ameliorate it.*[52]

In the summer of 1939, as the French and British were busily negotiating with Moscow for a mutual-defense treaty that would contain Hitler, the Soviet Union astounded the world by signing, on August 23, a non-aggression treaty with Germany. This doomed Poland while also focusing Hitler's deadly aggression upon the Western democracies. Hitler immediately demanded from Poland a return of lands lost by Germany after World War I. Her worst fears confirmed, Natalie wrote to Martha. *It was bound to come, no doubt: dear old materialists like Mr. Chamberlain have sacrificed the idealist in vain. It's a sorry outlook in the world today. And I am sick at heart for so many in England and France. Of course the fate of Spain, delivered over to reactionaries and bigotry, is a constant haunt; but things as bad are to be added. The dark age is upon us.*[53]

Hitler marched his Nazi armies into Poland only days later, September 1, 1939. France and Britain, honoring their treaty commitments to Poland, promptly declared war on Germany. World War II had begun, with Poland falling in three weeks. In April 1940, Hitler attacked the West, overrunning Denmark, Norway, the Netherlands, Belgium, and finally France. France surrendered in June, leaving Britain standing alone against Hitler. Bombs began falling on London in August 1940. With Western Europe in his grip, a confident Hitler then turned on the Soviet Union, invading in June 1941. Meanwhile, the United States scrambled to prepare for war and materially assisted Britain, but remained officially neutral until Japan's attack on Pearl Harbor, December 7, 1941.

Chapter Nine

World War II (1940-44)

Portrait of Natalie Vivian Scott by New York painter Wayman Adams, an occasional Taxco resident (ca. 1940). *John W. Scott Collection*

Early in 1940 Natalie applied for readmission to the Red Cross for war service. While awaiting the reply, Natalie wrote to Martha Robinson regarding another idea for joining the war effort. *Heard over the radio that they are looking for hostesses for recreation camps for the new army. I'd hate to leave my dear Taxco, and the interesting life here; but at least the salary offered is very good,— $2100 a year and expenses. Maybe I could then save up something, and do a bit for the children. Do you know where one applies? Or can you find out? If so, do let me know. I think I could probably manage a recreation hut very well, what with my experience in the last war; I could get a lot of recommendations. So do try to get this information and let me know by Air Mail.[1]*

Thus began Natalie's campaign to find an overseas war job, an effort that would frustrate her over the next two years despite recommendation letters to the Red Cross and the assistance of Congressman Eddie Hebert of New Orleans (a former newspaperman who had been among Jack Scott's best friends until Jack's sudden death in 1937). Harry Hopkins, her old friend from his days as director of the New Orleans Red Cross in the early 1920s, was her best connection in the Roosevelt White House, and he advocated for her as well. By regulation, only persons thirty-five or younger were eligible; Natalie had reached age fifty. Her hopes depended upon a Red Cross waiver of the age restriction. The Washington bureaucracy proved frustratingly unresponsive. *I am going up to Mexico [City] Monday and Tuesday, and hope to go to see the man in charge of Cultural Relations and also the one in charge of propaganda here. I am also filling out a blank that Eddie Hebert sent me, for the Office of Emergency Management. If those two won't take me, or one of them in any case, I shan't know where else to turn to try to be useful.*[2]

Meanwhile, new American arrivals and prominent European refugees settled in Taxco. *I suppose I told you that we have a French countess refugee, Gilberte, Comtesse de Charenterray. She seems remarkably detached from all the horror . . . a great leader in getting up parties, and such. Her husband is in the French army, and writes her not to go back.*

Natalie on her Taxco porch with her dog, "Juby" or Jubal Early (ca. 1940). *Courtesy of the Historic New Orleans Collection*

Two of Natalie's favorites were Jane and Paul Bowles, the young couple (he was thirty, Jane twenty-three) having arrived in early 1940 to lease one of Natalie's houses. Both writers, neither had yet achieved literary fame, though Paul's music career was well under way. *Probably the most attractive of the recent acquisitions is Jane Bowles. She is small and slight, with very wavy hair combed up from a roguish face, with a turned-up nose and saucy eyes, and a wistful mouth. She writes poetry, and her husband, Paul, is a musician. Paul, however, had to go to New York for a long session, doing the music for the Theatre Guild's production of Twelfth Night. But Jane is a dear, and most amusing.*[3]

Jane and Paul Bowles lived in Taxco until 1943, their friendship with Natalie deepening. Here, Jane completed her important book, *Two Serious Women,* later judged by Tennessee

Williams to be the best novel ever written by an American woman. Natalie read the manuscript, offering encouragement as Jane made revisions. Paul's first major novel, *The Sheltering Sky,* would not appear until 1949. Others in their Taxco circle included painter Paul Cook; Clinton and Narcissa King; Fritz Henle of *Life* magazine; and New York literary agent Anne Kennedy, who played an important role in publishing Latin American authors during this period. Lyricist John La Touche was an occasional visitor for whom Natalie wrote a letter of introduction to Frances Toor in Mexico City and Martha Robinson in New Orleans. She told Toor: *Am sending you an extremely nice couple, the La Touches. He is the author of Ballad for Americans and one*

Author Jane Bowles. She and her husband, Paul, became Taxco friends of Natalie during Jane's writing of *Two Serious Women* (1940-43). *Courtesy of Special Collections, Tulane University Libraries of the best paid radio script writers in the States, I hear. Contract with National Broadcasting, and so on. Wife is the daughter of one of the important movie magnates. Touchey has a grand sense of humor, very witty; but also very intelligent, widely read and sensitive. They have been here for about three weeks. You'll like them, so I don't feel apologetic as I sometimes do when I give people letters,—which isn't often.*[4]

To overcome financial problems, Natalie sold in 1938 her interest in her only remaining French Quarter property, the Scott-McClure House, John McClure acquiring her interest while continuing to live there. Natalie used $600 of this money to send her niece and nephew, both new college graduates, on an extended tour of Europe. Finally the upkeep and mortgage on the Lowerline house became too much, so she sold this property in 1940, thereby eliminating her last financial tie to New Orleans. Meanwhile, she went on managing Taxco houses for friends such as Anne Kennedy and operating the Kitigawa House and her peasant school. Occasionally she leased out her own house and moved into her *pensión.*[5]

Natalie's cookbooks were another source of income, very modest but steady. Subsidizing her day school and addressing the various needs of peasant families left her perpetually without funds. In early 1942, three months after Pearl Harbor brought America into the war, she published another Mexican cookbook, *Cocina to You,* self-published in Mexico City and distributed through an American agent. When Natalie finally found her way into the war in 1943, the marginal proceeds of her cookbooks and rental properties, overseen by Alice Crouch, would be devoted to operating the peasant school during her long absence.

Natalie's passion over the war remained unrelenting, her commentary regularly taking the world's politicians, including American senators, to task. *As for Tom Connally and his asininity, he has all too many companions. That complete fool, Bob Reynolds, from North Carolina, who suggested that we should take over Baja California! What a lovely bit of news that made in the Mexican press, when all of the effort of the Nazi Fifth Columnists is now directed towards reviving old grudges in Mexican minds. Ay de mi, it's difficult to sit back and take.*[6] Pres. Franklin Roosevelt she held to be a major exception, both in his deviation from neutrality during the late 1930s and his anti-poverty programs. In one letter during his second term, Natalie described Roosevelt's performance as "magnificent." She blamed poverty and world economics for producing Hitler, Mussolini, and Franco, and advocated what she called economic democracy. *The millions in want endure, and endure: but bitterness builds up in their hearts, slowly and without expression. Till suddenly it erupts in hatred and violence and destruction. And one is aghast at the 'cruelty',—disregarding the years of unconscious cruelty that have made them what they are.*

Roosevelt has at least recognized the problem at intervals; but his attempts at solution have not gone very far so far. In fact, I sometimes wonder if he has formulated it clearly enough in his own mind. At least he is the only one who has suggested any recognition of it. Natalie hoped for his 1940 election to a third term.[7] The local American mining engineers were strongly pro-Wendell Willkie. *In August, before I was so broke, I took on about a hundred pesos worth of bets on Roosevelt. Paying them would be a real calamity for me.*

My only contribution to the forces that I advocate is to talk individually, with as much tact and tirelessness as I can muster, to the recalcitrant. And lend them books and articles. The engineering gang here is all Willkie. They are a good sort and good friends of mine: but yet very exasperated with me. They take no end of pains to tease me about Roosevelt. We meet on Wednesday (the day after election day) to settle the bets. I have vowed my winnings to de Gaulle. We are starting a de Gaulle Club here. Have about three hundred pesos pledged, which is a big sum for Taxco. I feel fairly sure I'll win my bets. I should just not pay if I lose. But of course I will, if I starve for it.[8] It all turned out well, FDR making her a winner a few days later.

In March 1942, Natalie sent word to Martha to look after three friends who were coming up to New Orleans, Jane and Paul Bowles and their companion. *These are such unusually intelligent and delightful people that my scruples are less than usual. They are: Mrs. Helvetia Orr Perkins, firstly. She has character, humor, intelligence, and independence. She flaunted a Roosevelt button in the last election, against every tradition of her ultra-conservative Chicago society background,—just as one example of her independence. There are plenty of others. With her will be Jane and Paul Bowles. Jane has just written an excellent novel, but hasn't sent it off yet. She's a slip of a thing, with bright black eyes that can twinkle impishly: widely read and excellent taste. Her husband Paul did the incidental music for Theatre Guild's Twelfth Night; the music for the Saroyan plays; a ballet that was tremendously successful, and various other things. He is down here on a Guggenheim Fellowship. He is very sensitive and keen, and quite charming, well up on modern trends of art in every field, literature and art as well as music. They are really all very close friends of mine, and I want them to see a cross-section of New Orleans.*[9] After enjoying New Orleans, Jane Bowles found her publisher in New York, then returned to Taxco.

After Pearl Harbor, with the U.S. finally in the fight against Japan, Germany, and their Axis partners, Natalie fought the war as best she could from Taxco. *I had a bit of a battle the other evening at the Bar Paco, where I was sitting sipping on innocent lemonade. Back of me was a table with the young artist (Antonio Álvarez) who did my cook-book illustrations: he is 21 but looks 17 and everybody treats him accordingly. He was between two American young women in their thirties, who know him well. And another, of the same age came in, patted his shoulder and caressed his cheek. Whereupon a gross-looking American man at the next table said, 'How would you like it if I threw you over the railing?' Antonio didn't know he was being spoken to, so the man said, 'Hey. YOU!' and repeated his remark.*

Knowing my Mexicans, I had a fear that Antonio, a third of the man's size, might feel called upon to take up the remark; so I riz up and stood between the tables. I spoke low and pleasantly to the old drunken bully: 'I beg your pardon, but just one American to another, do you think it is quite tactful to be so completely insulting to a Mexican in his own country? Especially when we are trying to get the friendship of the country just now?' He: 'He's nothing but a dirty Mexican.' Me: 'I beg your pardon. He is an exceptionally talented young artist with many American friends who admire his work.' 'Well, he ought to learn how to behave'. That last a good one. 'I'm not quite sure what you mean. Don't you think it would really be more tactful

if you went home now?' I turned to the two women who were
with him, and asked them if they didn't agree. They did hearti-
ly, and off they went. I was shaking with rage. I thought the peo-
ple were tourists of course. It turned out that the man is the
head of the Seven-up distribution down here in Mexico! I didn't
feel in the least repentant. That sort of person can knock
Cultural Relations into a cocked hat,—and there are all too
many of them, alas.[10]

With still no word from the Red Cross, Natalie did what she
could there in Taxco. She formed the de Gaulle Club to collect
monies and clothing for the Free French. She joined the Red
Cross Mexican fundraising drive, an effort that raised 300,000
pesos by March 1943. She formed the Silver Thimbles in Taxco
but searched for another leader, *as I have been associated with*
so many money-getting things,—constantly for the Day Nursery
and then for the Free French, I thought it better for them to get
somebody fresh. It hasn't been done yet. She was not able to find
anyone else.[11]

A young Mexican woman, Ana Brilanti, destined to become an
exceptional silver designer, moved to Taxco in 1941, just below
Natalie's door. She recalled first meeting Natalie Scott upon
entering the Bar Paco, she and her husband witnessing a most
unusual scene. All the men in the bar were knitting socks while
carrying on their normal socializing. Natalie had put them to
work, supplying needles and thread, teaching and coaxing the
weaving, all for the war effort to put good warm socks on soldiers
and refugees. Asked by Natalie to help, her husband took up the
knitting while Ana rolled bandages. Ana became a member of
Natalie's Silver Thimbles.[12]

In March 1942, a formal Red Cross rejection arrived. *The Red*
Cross turned me down with a very pleasant quite long person-
al letter,—but turned me down, none the less. And from my
other applications I heard nothing whatever. I fear my rare tal-
ents are not appreciated. Natalie joined a nurse training course
taught by Dr. Meana, and her classmates formed a civil defense-
medical emergency team. *I've forgotten all I ever knew about*
nursing, so I have to rush down and spend the entire afternoon
practicing bandages so that I won't disgrace myself. Taxco has
gradually roused itself to the war. Can you imagine that we
have a drum corps? Every morning, some sixty or a hundred

lads report for duty, have drill from six to seven; and again in the evening. There is an office for the 'Defensa' here, and I supply them with some propaganda, and of course I deliver propaganda to people in the Square every Sunday morning. There have been several balls for the benefit of the 'Defensa', and that is all to the good. There is no little apathy, if not direct pro-Axis sympathy in parts, and I think the activity of the really interested is the best propaganda we can have. The Defensa has organized our First Aid Group, and our Nurses Training was already organized before the Defensa got well under way. That's pretty good for a little town like Taxco, I think.

As a member of the Defensa Nurses Corps, Natalie was occasionally expected to march in military formation. *Our group has its uniforms. I am the only American who was invited to join, so I feel I must keep up.*[13] *In September 1942, the Defensa nurses were summoned to help a truckload of merrymakers injured in a dreadful accident. All the victims were of the working class, and, as one worked over the hideous wounds, one couldn't help thinking of the poor families for whom it would mean a heavy economic difficulty, as well as emotional distress. My Mexican companeras did beautifully. There were thirty wounded, parceled out among the four doctors, and four killed. One of our patients had not quite fifty percent chance of reaching Mexico [City] alive, with a big piece of bone caved in just over the temporal bone. It has been twenty-two years since I've done anything like that. I need the excellent training that Dr. Meana is giving us.*[14]

Natalie took the Defensa drilling and marching with good humor. *The girls insisted strongly, and Dr. Meana calmly said that I could take it. So I did. And I could. And actually I believe that it has done the old fallen arches good. The first two or three times, I was actually pale with the pain in my feet.* On one memorable day, in Iquala, former president Cárdenas, revered in Mexico, reviewed their ranks. *On the day of the march, we had all to wear tennis shoes. We had to report in the plaza here at six in the morning, lined up for inspection. Then we drove to Iquala and were marched all around the outskirts of town, saluting here and there, as Generals went by; then waited for formation while the regular army units went by, and were finally paraded all thru the town. We were drawn up in the new big Square, where a statue was unveiled, and many speeches.*

The privilege of surveying us was accorded to General Cardenas, General Padilla, the Governor of the State, and various others. Cardenas particularly made an excellent speech. It was very intriguing to see the Indians, who had emerged from their mountain fastnesses for the occasion, taking it all in and gradually registering the fact that the country was at war. We eeled thru the crowd, sitting in front on the grass. I had a good look at the dignitaries. Cardenas has a fine face, intelligent brow and head, and a most winning smile. The Governor remembered me. Quite flattering.[15]

A Time for Action

Though not directly involved in Russian war relief, Natalie was strongly supportive. Her Russian friend and cohort in the Defensa Nurses Corps, dancer Tamara Schee, was a leader in the Russian relief cause. *The Russians have been so magnificent. How I shudder to think of Stalingrad and the carnage and human anguish there. It seems the Russian Relief in Mexico is the first one to be formed outside of Russia. They had a cable of thanks from Moscow. It seems amazing that no Russian Relief had been started in the States, when that country has been holding out so superbly, a bulwark to the Allies. It seems to me that starting a few would be a fine measure, counteracting the anti-Russian feeling that appears here and there still in the States. If our own government is run ultimately so as to give the masses a fair chance, I don't see why we need ever fear communism, or any other -ism. Eh what? Only under-privileged and resentful peoples offer soil for growth of foreign ideologies.*

I went to Mexico [City] to see the Russian Benefit for two pressing reasons,—one, the Russians have done a magnificent job, and the other, that Tamara had directed several of the numbers. She was showered with adulation. They made 22,000 pesos, about $4500 dollars.[16]

Then they organized another project in Taxco. *We had a huge benefit party last week,—on December 5th. Tamara and I worked like dogs over it for three weeks beforehand and are still gathering together the loose ends,—and cash. Artistically and socially it was a success; but we don't know yet how we came out financially. It was for the benefit of the Defense Civil of Taxco and of the Russian Red Cross. The floor show was simply stunning and directed by Tamara. As good as anything you could have seen in New York.*[17]

War news dominated every letter Natalie wrote in 1942. She traced worldwide events while keeping track of Martha's, Hilda's, and Sidonie's sons and sons-in-law in military service. *Reading about the Solomon Islands depressed me so. We did well, it seems,—but it's a very solid beginning and so much has to happen before peace comes again. I still can't get myself to reading calmly, 'Casualties were reported at more than two hundred thousand', and such. Eyes look at me, voices call and beg, out of the cold figures. The only thing to do is to become absorbed in the present tasks at hand and not lift the eyes for more than a fleeting glance at all the panorama of horror. Only one can't always follow that recipe. Actually, I suppose that my little chores down here are just as worthwhile as any I could do, but the war compels me. I would rather have something more exacting. The chores I do here are scattered, unrelated, tumultuous: I'd rather have something more cohesive, and more definitely along the lines of war work. Time will tell.*[18]

The time for action had arrived. Natalie had been putting money aside for a bus trip to the States. She planned to tackle the bureaucracy in Washington in person, to confront the Red Cross and army and find her way into some form of overseas war service. *Am going to try to get a war job when I go up. I would prefer foreign service, of course, in the morale division if possible. There was a woman here who has a friend in one of the departments where foreign languages are necessary. Says the friend doesn't know as much French as I do, and not nearly as much Spanish. So I ought to fit in somewhere. Perhaps I'll try with the Free French, if the Americans won't take me.*[19]

Natalie's plans became specific by mid-December 1942, as America's entry in the war passed its first anniversary. *I plan to go up towards the end of January. My good friend, Helvetia Perkins, to whom you were very kind in New Orleans (thank you again) has bought a farm in Vermont and her gasoline rationing card will apparently accumulate sufficiently to let her take her station wagon back up. And she has invited me to go along.* A string of good fortune brought money into Natalie's hands. She collected commissions on two sales of Taxco houses; furthermore, the Kitigawa House was full, as were her rental properties.

Natalie's next letter was written on the road, traveling north through Laredo on January 23, 1943, with Helvetia Perkins and Jane Bowles. *Helvetia, Jane and I are driving to New York at the dizzying pace of thirty miles an hour. Very amusing. We didn't think the rationing board would permit us to go by way of New Orleans, but I adduced the argument that altho the mileage was more by that way, the mountains are fewer, so that gas would be about the same. Hope to make New Orleans Tuesday. We'll only be there a very few days, as Jane has to get on to New York to see about the next set of proofs on her book. I may have written you that Knopf accepted it for spring publication. I am taking the trip on a shoestring anyway, and am quite panicky about it; but it looked like now or never. I want to go to Washington to see if I can get a war job. Had the most wonderful piece of luck: rented my house for three months paid in advance at one o'clock of the day I was leaving. That was when I decided definitely on this trip. It seemed the hand of fate.[20]*

The visit in New Orleans was brief but productive. Natalie established direct contact with her friend Congressman Hebert and scheduled personal appointments in Washington with the Red Cross and the State Department. Gathering letters of recommendation in New Orleans, she recruited the help of her prominent Red Cross friends from World War I, particularly Dr. Hugh Young of Johns Hopkins, by then among America's best-known surgeons. Dr. Young's 1940 memoir, *Hugh Young: A Surgeon's Autobiography,* had told of his deep friendship with Natalie Scott, her heroism during Germany's bombing of Beauvais, and her Croix de Guerre.[21] Natalie had correctly judged that her aggressive presence in Washington was the missing ingredient necessary to find an overseas war job. She gained Red Cross and State Department approval, her World War I record and social work in Mexico offering formidable proof of her value.

Natalie went to work for the Red Cross in February, and she was soon assigned to North Africa, where the Allies were fighting the Axis forces commanded by German Gen. Erwin Rommel. Victory was crucial for control of the Mediterranean Sea. In late June, Natalie shipped out aboard a troop transport packed with

American soldiers. They crossed the dangerous, submarine-infested Atlantic as part of a large navy convoy. There were nine persons assigned to each cabin. Her room was packed with three-level bunk beds, and every porthole was closed tight day and night. The cabins were uncomfortably hot, so most slept on deck while sitting on their life preservers, as there were no chairs. All personnel ate twice per day. Natalie's meal schedule was 10:00 A.M. and 7:30 P.M.

Natalie was assigned the job of getting out a daily shipboard newspaper; she named her paper *The Bilgewater Bugle*. *There are all sorts of men of distinction in their lives on this ship. Some Rockefeller men. Some State Department people. Captain Andre Maurois, the French writer, who said he hoped to march into Paris with the American troops.* She wrote of the soldiers and their endless variety of stories. One had a brother shot down and hospitalized in North Africa; two other *brothers in the service who had not seen each other for 18 months found themselves bunked on this ship within 50 feet of each other.* Her paper offered stories about those aboard, daily schedules, war news, announcements from commanders, contests, puzzles, cartoons, and other forms of humor. The idea was to keep up interest and morale during the long hours at sea.[22]

North Africa

Martha Robinson shared with the *Times-Picayune* Natalie's first letter from North Africa. It would be the first of a series of Natalie Scott war diary reports the newspaper would publish, a fact Martha did not reveal to Natalie until the following year. Typically, her letters began with "Somewhere in North Africa" or, later, "Somewhere in Italy."

After ten days in the Moroccan town of Oujda, Natalie was assigned to a large general hospital in the Algerian coastal city of Oran, the Seventh Station Hospital. She served here for eleven months. She reported the same *quiet grit and triumph of the spirit* she had seen in American soldiers of the last war. *I am astounded, too, at the progress in surgery and in the treatment of burns. The suffering seems to have been cut down greatly. Of course there is a heart-breaking amount of it still.*

Nathalie Scott Tells About
Courage Among Wounded

Cheerfulness Is Paramount, Writes Orleanian

A poignant account of the courage and cheerfulness displayed by young American soldiers and sailors in a North African hospital is contained in a letter written to Mrs. Martha G. Robinson by Miss Nathalie Scott, former New Orleans writer, now American Red Cross hospital visitor in foreign duty.

In a style which seems typical, Miss Scott tells of the 19-year-old sailor, "With game, pitifully young chin, so stubbornly set." She tells of another lad, with great hazel eyes, who laughs aloud when she read him one of Kipling's Mulvaney stories. And she tells of a madcap parachutist, who turns up with amazing frequency as a patient and begs her to write letters for him to a Spanish girl friend.

Miss Scott calls her typewriter, "Penelope Typewriter Scott," tops her letter with, "Sumwheer in Africker," and interposes foolishness with serious facts.

"I live in a Red Cross villa," she writes, "which we call the Stork Club, because it was formerly a maternity hospital. My room is agreeable. I have five hangers and use my suit case for shelves. We have a shower that is sometimes hot in the mornings. It is salt water and sometimes I think only my conscience is clean, with soap that refuses to lather and is so completely uncongenial with salt.

Bounce About

"I rise about eight, watch my chance for a shower, sort laundry and clothes hectically then go downstairs to a small kitchen where we eat. The French domestics preside over a gas stove of sorts. We have two metal tables set together, with room for eight. Usually late-comers are hovering harpylike above one, waiting for a place and the nobly inclined (count me, of course, I bow) usually rise meekly and finish coffee standing to give room for others.

"We chip in about 10 cents apiece for fruit and are not charged for breakfast nor for laundry. I then bolt forth and walk three blocks to the dispensary, an annex to our hospital, which is about 25 blocks away.

MISS NATHALIE SCOTT

My gray hairs rate me front seat in the weapon carrier. As we ride, we discuss latest developments and bounce about. And gasp several hundred times, as we nearly kill languid civilians, who show all too much faith in providence and chauffeurs."

"We slow up for the grinning salute of a guard, who often calls a familiar greeting since most of them are Cajans from Louisiana. How we have discussed Lafayette and Broussard and St. Martinsville."

Recounting her many duties, Miss Scott says, "I write letters for the men who can't use their hands or lack hands. I even hold a cigarette for them to smoke. I have long talks with patients, which the doctor thinks is helpful. I distribute all the Red Cross graces of cigarettes and toilet articles; get news sheets and books and tote them about, read to helpless patients, make silly jokes.

"I have four wards, one surgical, one burns and two neuro-psychopathic. Instinctively all the old vitality rushes up. One needs it to face without a start the sights there—a young face above a cast enclosing all his torso. Another with a steel apparatus reaching to the knee in place of an arm, and so on. But the percentage of cheer is a marvel. Sometimes one is perforce all tears within. But reassurance has to appear on the surface and to be convincing.

Miss Scott said, "one could write reams about the different personalities." "'Baby' for instance, the little sailor, who swears he is 18, but doesn't act or think even 16."

"Next him is a tall lad, with enormous dark, intelligent eyes. A Christian Scientist. I've got the Christian Science chaplain for him, who 'treats' him. And there are the rough fellows from the merchant marine. One, who had his hands badly burned, is a tough saint, a great bear of a man, always thinking of some good turn he can do somebody.

"A great pet of mine is a Puerto Rican. He was badly burned, swathed in bandages. But always making jokes, singing rollicking Spanish songs, being a monkey to divert the other. 'I thought he was badly burned,' I said to the nurse. 'He is,' she said, 'Those burns are very bad indeed. We can't understand his gayety.' When I complimented him on his courage, he looked puzzled, 'But what do you expect?' he inquired, 'I am a man.' He is 23."

Initiate New Ones

"Another pet of mine is a young sailor, just 19, a stalwart the young body and a grave intelligent young face, with brown eyes that light up and a mouth that is a little boyish when he smiles. He has had a very bad time, with a bad leg wound. He's had to go through a lot of pain. But never a murmur from him.

"When new patients come in, it is amusing to see how the old-timers initiate them. When I appear they say to the new ones, 'Here she is,' and then to me, 'Miss Scott, here're some new fellows. They haven't got any cigarettes,' or 'they need a toothbrush. We told 'em you'd fix 'em up.'"

Miss Scott, who has lived in Taxco, Mexico, for the past 13 years, where she devoted her time to free-lance writing, was formerly a feature writer for the New Orleans States. She is a native New Orleanian and served with the American Red Cross for two years in the first World war, being decorated for bravery under fire.

This *New Orleans Times-Picayune* clipping is one of the series of Natalie Scott's war journal articles published by the newspaper during World War II. *Courtesy of Special Collections, Tulane University Libraries*

She performed light nursing duties and served as confidante, translator, activities organizer, and counselor for the wounded, dealing directly with the sorrows of the war.

Oran had been one of three Allied amphibious assault targets in the African invasion of November 1942. In the aftermath, the Germans were trapped in Tunisia between British (from the southeast) and American forces (from the west). Pushing the Germans out of North Africa was essential to launching the next phase of Allied operations: the invasion of Sicily and mainland Italy. This entire Mediterranean operation served as the prelude to the long-planned Normandy invasion. The Germans were defeated in Tunisia by May 20. Over 250,000 enemy prisoners were taken, and the remnants of Rommel's army escaped across the Mediterranean. Natalie was at work in Oran when the Sicilian invasion was launched on July 10, 1943.

The Seventh Station Hospital was packed in July and August with the wounded from the African and Sicilian campaigns. *Sometimes the men have other than physical afflictions to bear. One young fellow showed me the picture of his wife and told me so happily that she was going to have a baby. That afternoon came a cable saying she was dead, dying in childbirth.* Another soldier wounded in Sicily *told of running with a wounded friend half an hour to get to a Sicilian village, his friend badly shot in the forearm, his hand dangling loose. At a Sicilian house in the darkness he encountered a woman. 'En damned if the old lady didn't bust out crying when she seen his arm and get busy, pours some wine over it and in him, done up the bandages swell and fed him five raw eggs and fixed a whole supper for the four of us and then put us in the barn for fear of the Germans.' I am awed by the triumph of the spirit in these simple lads. Their cheery letters home go to one's heart, their pride in their girl and wife.*[23]

Natalie told of another soldier, with great hazel eyes, who laughed aloud when she read him one of Kipling's Mulvaney stories. And she wrote of a madcap parachutist who turned up frequently with fresh wounds, always asking her to write letters for him to a Spanish girlfriend. In her published *Times-Picayune* diary, she named her typewriter, which traveled with her, "Penelope Typewriter Scott." Topping one letter with

"Sumwheer in Africker," she interposed foolishness with serious facts. *I live in a Red Cross villa which we call the Stork Club because it was formerly a maternity hospital. My room is agreeable—five hangers and my suitcase for shelves. We have a shower. It is saltwater and sometimes I think only my conscience is clean. I rise about eight for breakfast. We have two metal tables, room for eight. Late-comers are hovering harpy-like, waiting for a place. I then bolt forth and walk three blocks to the dispensary, an annex to our hospital, which is about 25 blocks away. My gray hairs rate me front seat in the weapon carrier. As we ride, we discuss developments, bounce about, and gasp several hundred times, as we nearly kill languid civilians. We slow up for the grinning salute of a guard, who often calls a familiar greeting since most are Cajuns from Louisiana. How we have discussed Lafayette and Broussard and St. Martinville.*

I write letters for the men who can't use their hands or lack hands. Hold a cigarette for them to smoke. I have long talks with patients, which the doctor thinks is helpful. I distribute all the Red Cross graces of cigarettes and toilet articles; get news sheets and books and tote them about, read to helpless patients, making silly jokes.

I have four wards, one surgical, one burns and two neuro-psychopathic. Instinctively all the old vitality rushes up. One needs it to face without a start the sights there—a young face above a cast enclosing all his torso. Another with a steel apparatus reaching to the knee in place of an arm, and so on. But the percentage of cheer is a marvel. Sometimes one is perforce to hold all tears within. But reassurance has to appear on the surface and to be convincing. One could write reams about the different personalities. 'Baby' for instance, the little sailor, who swears he is 18, but doesn't act or think even 16. Next to him is a tall lad, with enormous dark, intelligent eyes. A Christian Scientist, I've got the Christian Science chaplain for him, who 'treats' him. And there are the rough fellows from the merchant marine. One, who had his hands badly burned, is a tough saint, a great bear of a man, always thinking of some good turn he can do somebody.

A great pet of mine is Puerto Rican. He was badly burned,

swathed in bandages. But also making jokes, singing rollicking Spanish songs, being a monkey to divert the others. 'I thought he was badly burned,' I said to the nurse. 'He is,' she said. 'Those burns are very bad indeed. We can't understand his gayety.' When I complimented him on his courage, he looked puzzled. 'But what do you expect?' he inquired. 'I am a man.' He is 23. Another pet of mine is a young sailor, just 19, a stalwart lithe young body and a grave intelligent young face. He had had a very bad time, with a bad leg wound. A lot of pain but never a murmur from him.

When new patients come in, it is amusing to see how the old-timers initiate them. 'Here she is,' and then to me, 'Miss Scott, here're some new fellows. They haven't got any cigarettes,' or 'they need a toothbrush. We told 'em you'd fix 'em up.'[24] Not surprisingly, Natalie's daily work often covered *a steady and harassed twelve to thirteen hours, dropping down to ten occasionally.* The interpreter for her unit, she was in charge of recreation and presided over the library, which she steadily improved, asking in her letters for books to be donated. *I love to work under high steam.*

Natalie's duties in Oran included bargaining in the marketplace for various supplies, fruit, and even candy for the wounded on Halloween and Armistice Day. *We went to the market, as we had done on Halloween, too, and found our Arab. He is crowned with a yellow turban, over a brown face which age has shrunk into fine little wrinkles, some for each of all the known emotions, but the result on the whole benevolent. When he saw us, he reached over the counter and took a hand of each of us and all the kindly wrinkles deepened. And the pandemonium began at once.* Natalie described the frenzy of bargaining as the wily old man and his assistants, *a lesser Arab and an old woman vixen,* upped the prices by claiming various expenses. *Our old Ali swept a lordly hand over slim crates shaped like a baby's cradle, brimming with yellow fruit, and chanted the excellence of the wares. In the midst of the clamor and gesticulations, the old boy weighted the crates and began to add to the bill. I managed to scream a demand that he subtract the weight of the crates. Finally we paid, and our wares were carried out by a ragged old Arab, a head habitually bent and eyes sad with toil that looked out and up like an English shepherd dog's. The market is like so many*

Mexican ones, and the whole transaction was like so many in Mexico, that a spasm of homesickness shook me.

On Armistice Day, November 11, Natalie attended services at a nearby cemetery. Before her New York departure, she had learned of the death of young Franklin White from Alexandria, the son of her brother's law-school classmate. They were Scott neighbors; Natalie had known Franklin as he grew to manhood. Now he was dead, a victim of the North African invasion, buried here in Algeria. Natalie searched out and visited the grave on Armistice Day. *It was bleak and chill and gray, but I had a very personal reason for wanting to go to the American Cemetery for the laying of the wreath there. We went to the flower-shop. The chrysanthemums now are glorious. I chose some lovely ones for the cemetery, great golden globules, mixed with some that had reddish purple on the inside of their petals and pale lavender without. When the charming little Frenchwoman who owns the shop saw my Croix de Guerre and learned that the flowers were for one of our soldiers, she promptly took off the price. The clouds parted gradually, and when I reached there the rows of white crosses were glinting with light, and in the chill wind the vast American flag lifted high on its pole, floated and dropped and floated again, brilliant and serene. Files of soldiers were lined motionless on either side of it, and beyond, in front of the little chapel, a small group of officers with much gold braid stood beside the two chaplains in their simple uniforms. Spectators, officers and nurses and a few WAACS, were lined up off to one side. I stood apart and looked on.*

The splendid MBS Band played Holy, Holy, Holy. Our own 7th Station Chaplain Trickett said some simple impressive prayers; another chaplain read the 24th psalm. And General Roosevelt, flanked by two other officers, laid a magnificent wreath at the foot of the flag-pole. A group of three, one carrying the flag, stepped forward, and a bugler blew taps, while from the foot of the slope another bugle responded like an echo. A shadowy throng seemed to gather about me: my buddies from the last war with that dear young lad at the foot of the very hill, their families, the crushing sense of the terrible cost of keeping that proud flag aloft; the folly, the greed, the blind selfishness, that has made it necessary to add again to that cost; the hospital beds that stretch endlessly from the last war into this, some to be emptied under just such white crosses; and other such groups of crosses, in Africa, Sicily, Italy, the East.

The ceremony ended with the playing of 'America the Beautiful' and a silent throng went down the road between the crosses, the slight shadows of which lay heavy on my spirit all through the day in spite of all my effort to throw it off, as we all do perforce.[25]

Back at the hospital the same day, Natalie adopted an entirely different attitude, joking, encouraging the soldiers, and arranging treats and entertainment for her wards. *We went thru all the wards with candy and mandarine for each patient. And at a little before three, the Garcia group of French actors and actresses came to entertain. Most amusing show, the hit of which was a middle-aged woman with several gold teeth but so much personality. Arab children peeped in among the legs of our men.*

Other celebrities made appearances in Natalie's hospital. Actress Anna Lee visited the ward, *a slender little young figure in officer's uniform, very trim; pan-cake make-up, and red hair—the roots not to be closely observed. She really 'gave', tho. My worst burned patients were there, then, and she was charming to them. Al Jolson came with a show one day. He was the show, in fact. He looked tired and old, but he made a great hit, and his impromptu wit, though by no means delicate, met enthusiastic response. Cab Calloway came with his complete show. They were most generous: when one group or another was not on the stage, they would dash up to one of the wards and put on an act for the bed-patients,—so moved by the plight of my burned patients that they came back twice, two singers and two guitarists, and played for them.*

The stories and troubles of patients filled the pages of every letter Natalie wrote home. *I went thru a ward with books one day (I take books every day, along with supplies). One lad with eleven wounds, asked for a Readers' Digest. 'Have you read this one?' I asked, giving him our latest, 2 months old. He looked at it, turning the pages experimentally and murmured, 'Hmm-mm, MMM. Yes. I think this is the one I was readin' when the boat went down'. Unique way of identification, I thought.*

All the countless personalities. What a pity not to be able to give innumerable vignettes. Charlie, eighteen, with a great wound in the back to which he refers petulantly some times as tho it were a blister on his foot. He has two teeth out in front, and the gap makes him look all the more little-boyish and appealing. He is getting on splendidly: yesterday (after nearly a month in bed) he was sitting on the steps when I came along, with mischievous expectancy of my surprise—like a child. Of course I made a tremendous to-do, and he was radiant. Then he glanced nervously back. 'They don't know I'm out. I'm not supposed to be. Just wanted to surprise you.' Such a time to get him on his feet and in again!

Yesterday another made his first appearance in the Rec Hall. So proud and pleased,—and every step a major problem still. He was looking at the books, and inadvertently knocked down half a shelf-full. His expression was so ludicrous and so pitiful, as he looked down at them helplessly, then started trying to bend slowly and painfully at the knees, in the hope of picking them up. One thinks one is accustomed to the wounds and suffering, but such trifles send a fresh stab of realization,—this helpless contrite 6-footer! 'Bad thing!' I scolded. 'Let them alone. I can pick them up, but I can't put you together again, if you pull apart.' He grinned sheepishly, as I led him to a chair and eased him into it, and dug up a precious 'Western' for him. . . .

One of my standbys is Pratty,—Pratt. He 'caught an 88 in his lap', as he says. Actually, it passed just over his legs and ripped them to ribbons. I don't know how many skin-grafts he had, done under spinal, while he looked on with keen interest, always describing the details to me afterwards! As soon as he could walk at all, he appeared to carry my baskets! I refused; but he took them anyway from me. One leg he couldn't bend at all, but along he went, beaming with pride, walking grotesquely with straight leg flung out sidewise. The first day he asked for a pass, he went 5 painful blocks, and had to hail an ambulance to come back. The first time he actually made it downtown, he came back with a little carved box as a present for me. We battle all the time about his chewing tobacco. He had me write his family when he was in bed, and tell them that he had given up chewing. So I razzed him unmercifully about beginning again. Now he has really given it up, and he is trying to make me stop smoking!

Several people from home have turned up at odd moments. The maid came up and told me there were two officers to see me. I was in a negligee, but went out to find Leon Labotz, Major, and Lawrence Williams, Captain, from N.O. awaiting me. We have no living room so we sat on a stiff bench in the hall and chatted. A few days later, Lucie Lee Kinsolving and I went out to their Replacement depot, where they gave us an elegant dinner, with excellent tender steaks. Trust Leon for comfort. In his neat tent, which, being a Major, he shares with only one other officer, he has N.O. drip coffee pots; a thermos jug; everything for comfort. Larry mixed the cocktails. We had a merry evening.

Afterward, they phoned me asking me to get some R.C. girls to go to a dance as dates for them and their officers,—Larry gallantly declared himself my date. I got a fairly attractive group: Miss Parsons, and two of the younger girls who are the prettiest here, and Elinor Glynn who studied at Newcomb. The dance was at the City Hall here, and was very elegant. I became mellowed sufficiently to be the last guest, chatting with their Colonel, who started picking on the R.C. so that I picked on the army—'good clean fun'. Larry gallantly danced with me and told jokes and paid compliments.

Christmas Is Coming

Hoping for a transfer to the Italian war zone, Natalie worked on her long-neglected Italian. She recruited as her teacher an Italian prisoner of war who was a supervised laborer in the hospital. *I am now studying Italian. My teacher is an exceptionally handsome young Italian officer. He comes from near Naples, but has none of the suavity of the Neopolitan. Tall and slender, with firm chiseled features, erect as a staff. He has dimples, but little sense of humor, alas. I pay him by teaching him English. My Italian returns in gushes at times, more than his English. We argued last evening. He says that Italy will be chopped to bits after the war, a piece for France; one for Jugo-Slavia and so on. I don't know that he is Fascist, but he is Fascist material, with scorn of 'the people', austerity, cynicism. And yet likable, for honesty. Very continental with the click and the bow, the brief kiss on the hand, et cet. I do about an hour a day of Italian. I am interpreter in general for our unit, as I am the only one who speaks foreign languages.*[26]

In December, Christmas gifts from home surprised Natalie,

adding to her already good spirits. *Meanwhile, much, much Xmas cheer in my life. I had no idea anybody would try to send me anything; but a box from Bé turned up first of all,—saved for Xmas. Grand box of candies from Longchamps, from ever-thoughtful Anne Kennedy; and such a beautiful red and silver box from Nieman-Marcus, sent by Matilda Gray and Top Noble, full of the first sort of leather things, all so beautiful and useful. Harnett Kane's new book, so pleasantly autographed, from Martha, a most enticing book from Burdette, a glorious fruit-cake from the Brazeales. Xmas for the hospital is much in the air, too.*

Natalie wrote of the hospital decorations, which required creativity since there was so little to work with. She recycled wrapping materials from the gifts she had received: white tissue paper for mounds of snow, ribbons for the tree, red paper for stars. *Moreover, I've asked the Mess officer to spare some tin cans for us and we're getting tin shears to cut their strips, and we—patients, too,—will make them into trees and stars and ornamental shapes as people do in Taxco.* They eventually made candle-holders, angels, also crepe paper for garlands and imitation holly wreaths. *The patients will have forgot their troubles in their effort.*

Natalie's patient Pratt remained hospitalized, in rehabilitation for his leg wounds suffered during an amphibious assault landing. *But he's my pet, and carries my basket every day. There was a horseshoe-curve of beach it seems, where they were to land. A smoke screen was thrown up, and the boats went in under its cover, except the boat Pratt was on. Their officer said, 'We'll go center and draw the fire.' They did. Both. An 88 tore over, took a big gob out of each of Pratty's legs, and did other damage. "En my buddy sez, 'Jump, Pratt'. En I sez, 'Hell, I can't make it. Go ahead. Don't wait for me'. An' he sez, 'I'm not goin' without you.' An' the kid tried to pick me up. I couldn't move an inch, but that explosion caught the boat on fire and hell, before I knew it, I was overboard in a flash. I came up under the boat. I know I can't hold my breath much longer. Sure enough I came up in the clear. If I didn't have my knife, I wouldn't be here now. I carry my knife on my pants belt; you know most of the men hook 'em on their cartridge belt, and they flash that off quick, because it's heavy, and then there they are with their packs. But I cut my pack right off with my knife. An English fellow came up behind me and grabs me, and yells, help me! So I go under and push him off me. He's got his pack and heavy boots on, so I cut 'em off him. And we got hold o' life-preservers. And jes' then my buddy yells, 'Pratt, can you help me'. So I cut his pack off. Then a rescue ship comes up."*

He's really the ideal soldier. Everything's all right with Pratty.

Natalie wrote of the variety of the sick and wounded, some brave, some not so brave. *One, a spoiled boy who has never grown up, stole some money because he had heard that if a man stole money he was given six months and sent home. 'And I wanted to see my wife and baby,' he explained. 'You can understand that. Look at that baby.' And the baby really is beautiful. He always wants first attention; sulks like a small child; is gay like a 5 year old. The nervous cases, like our young parachutist shot down at the same time with his buddy, who was then torn by a shell, killed instantly. And our lad untouched, except that horror fills all the foreground for him. I eased out the fact that he likes poetry, Sandburg and Hart Crane, oddly enough. And his eyes lost their haunted look and became eager for awhile as I told him little homely details about Hart Crane.*

In mid-December, Natalie was again swamped with patients. She described the ships coming in, the ambulances arriving, the paperwork on admissions, and the distribution of cigarettes, toiletry items, and chewing gum to the wounded soldiers. They would keep the patients busy making dog tags, belts, and various crafts, not only for morale but as therapy for the hands of burn patients. *We are hoping to get some carpentry work going.* The problem was the shortage of materials: leather, wood, cord, cloth. Natalie solicited these in her letters home and searched locally in the marketplace, as the Red Cross could not meet the need.

Meanwhile, Natalie continued to offer humor and sympathy in her wards. *We had some trench-feet this time. Quite painful. They have to keep their feet out from under the covers. It's a funny effect to enter the ward and see all these feet sticking out! I suggested we decorate them, paint the toes green, and put red enamel on the nails (the ward was full of materials for Xmas trimmings). So we all laugh happily, while secretly I feel for them. Some of these lads, in fact most, had been in the line for*

75 days. Mountain heights; cold; rain. Lots of tales. 'Them Germans have regular rooms dug into the mountains. It's tough getting 'em, but we sure like 'em when we do. I got me a Czech prisoner one time; and he says, 'You don't have to hold that gun on me. I bin waiting for this chance for a year an' a half,' he tells me. 'Course I holds the gun on him anyhow, but I think he was tellin' the truth. Said he didn't want to surrender to the Russians.' 'That Goering Division has a lot of kids in it,' says another youngster. 'We got a boy wasn't more than 14. I coulda slapped him for bein' there tryin' to hold us back.'

Some of the men who were near the 8th Army [British] swear they saw Rome in the distance from the mountain tops. I hope they're right! I can't help hoping that Rome won't be too damaged: it belongs to the world. Two hotels where I stayed at one time or another in Naples have been destroyed,—among others.

During the Christmas preparations, the soldiers of each ward added their own creative touches. *We have a Xmas box for each one. Xmas eve we are having 125 French orphans, our neighbors, in. We've had little stockings made for them and dolls made of washcloth tied over soap for a head, with red ribbon. Some of the patients have made toys for them,—simple wagons, and so on. Lots of candies. Xmas day we plan to go thru the wards with carol singers—and in the afternoon will be the patients party. After the Xmas Eve party, I am going to a dance with Larry Williams; then to midnight Service at the Officer's Club, then to a turkey supper at Mme. Veaux's (Terese Kohn's sister-in-law). And am still getting in 11 to 12 hours daily,—tho that includes an Italian lesson.*[27]

Christmas and New Year's preparations proved an enormous success in the hospital. *The lads were apathetic at first, but gradually became feverishly alive, till at last every few minutes there was somebody dashing in, with child-like eagerness to ask, 'Kin we have more o' that red crepe paper?' Or, 'Have you got any crayons?' Or, 'Is there any drawing paper we could have in our d?' Xmas spirit is as violent as N.O. Mardi Gras, and more universal.*

Of course I felt sentimental. I careened among my wards, applauding and egging-on, and whooping it up. Had a lot of men fresh back from over 2 months in tough action. Their morale was marvelous, now having a spot of spoiling. We'd been saving mirrors, wash-cloths, and handkerchiefs, three things highly prized and difficult to get, for ages, up for every patient, in addition to his ARC box. For New Year's, Natalie had arranged music and bingo for the patients. Each of her three Christmas seasons during these war years would be spent in army hospital wards on three different continents: 1943 in Africa, 1944 in Europe, 1945 in Asia.

Natalie had gotten to know her young Italian officer better, the POW who was helping her improve her Italian. *He is quite thrilled to find somebody he can talk to. 'Do you know,' said he earnestly in Italian, 'that you are the first woman I have talked to since March, 1941?' 'Too bad I had to be an old lady', I told him. 'But perhaps better to become readjusted gently'. Of course he was very poised, Italians being so civil. He's helped me quite a lot, and I've got back enough Italian to tell anecdotes.* His name was Fernando; they became friends as Natalie gained his trust and found cracks in his formal facade. *I am now giving my Italian lessons in democracy. He now admits that its theory is much better than fascism,—but says European character won't take it. I explained that European character is formed of a thousand years of fear and the hate that springs therefrom; and generations of security will change it. Heaven guide us to wise peace.*[28]

Natalie even tried to help Fernando make other friends in the hospital. *Poor dear. Actually he speaks just a bit of French, school French and nothing else except Italian, so he has no contact. I've tried my best to be a go-between, finding some charming young thing for a mild flirt. But alas, none of the charmers can speak anything but English.* Suddenly, just before New Year's Eve, he was gone. *Fernando, my Italian officer teacher, has been ordered off, much to my distress, and to his. But he has given me a start, so that if I can manage to study a bit each day and talk with the workmen a bit, I feel I can still make progress.*[29] A month passed before she heard again from Fernando. She received a letter in which the prisoner expressed his appreciation for her kindnesses and friendship during his stay in Oran.

Five days into the New Year, 100 wounded were delivered to the hospital. Natalie and her co-workers were the first friendly faces each soldier encountered. *Drivers obligingly opened the doors of each ambulance for us, and even the most drawn faces mustered a smile. 'Red Cross sure is right on the job.' We have a colored patient, badly burned. And so patient, poor thing. He's had a really hard time and never complains. Nearly a month now. And a skin-graft and a new pressure bandage that is very painful. 'And how are you, Jo?' I asked him today. 'I'm sure you're having a pretty tough time just now; but you're a mighty good soldier and can really take it, can't you?'*

'Well'm, I rekkun hit be better termorrer mebee. Kina jes' startin' out agin now, cain' rightly expec' it to be easy jes' yet.' He's old fashioned and loveable and has taken his 'misry' so bravely. He does us proud.

Martha Robinson, responding in New Orleans to Natalie's written appeals for help, regularly sent boxes of much-desired items for the wounded, such as books, issues of *Reader's Digest, Time,* and *Life,* thread, cord, Plasticine, and cigarette lighters and holders. Many patients were unable to handle matches; they needed lighters to smoke. Natalie quoted her burn patient, Jo, thanking her for the supplies: *'Cause I sho can't smoke without dat holder.*[30]

Pvt. Clayton Pratt, Natalie's patient who had been wounded during the amphibious landings, was shipped home in early January. Natalie received a letter from him in mid-February, written from his Atlantic City home on January 24. It certainly pleased her, as he was doing well, though he was scheduled to return to the hospital for more therapy on his legs.

My folks thought it was wonderful that I could walk. They kept telling me to rest all the time, but there's too many interesting things to do. I've had many friends to visit and I've made three or four speeches for war bond drives since I've been home. You ought to see the girls' eyes "pop out" when I tell them about it. They think I'm wonderful, but I think I'm darned lucky to be alive. Remember, I told you I'd be a "big shot" when I got home. Well, the Mayor of our city was one of my callers and I also had a talk with the ex-governor of the State. It made me feel sort of like a visiting celebrity. I've told everybody what a wonderful job you and the girls are doing "over there" with the Red Cross. And thanks a lot for the letter that you wrote to the Red Cross in Bristol. Mother and Dad thought it was very nice of you and think you must be a wonderful woman. I told them you were the grandest lady on earth. You were personally swell to me and I'll never forget you as long as I live. Please give the whole gang in Ward 61 my regards. With lots of love from your best beau, Clayton.

The Natalie Scott Fund

Natalie did not learn until early 1944 that Martha had been turning her letters over to the *Times-Picayune* for publishing periodically as a Natalie Scott war diary. Though at first concerned over military regulations, Natalie acquiesced. *We are not to write anything for the public press unless okayed, but apparently they don't mind anything as informal as these letters, because one turned up in the club here, the Regional Director happened to see it, and liked it. I was on the verge of writing a veto about any further such procedure. But as the Regional Director here didn't seem to think it out of line, I refrained. Had a letter from head of publicity, N.O. Chapter, asking me to do an article for her publicity, and intend to write her to apologize. But simply haven't time for a formal article. Anne Kennedy who's been acting as authors' agent for Latin American writers, most successfully, wrote me that she felt sure she could get an article in the Sat. Evening Post, if I would write one; but even such bait hasn't made me able to clear enough 'time-space' to rise to it. Wish I could: the shekels would be welcome!*[31]

Simultaneously, Natalie learned from Martha Robinson that the Newcomb Alumnae Association had met in late January and adopted as its new project "assisting Natalie Scott in her wonderful work with wounded soldiers in Africa." They approved Martha's proposal to establish the Natalie Scott Fund. The association magazine explained Natalie's Seventh Station Hospital assignment and noted, "Louisianians who have been sent back to this country report that she is known all over North Africa as 'Old Scottie.'" The fund's purpose was to obtain and send materials that Natalie had specifically asked for: "twine for making belts, modeling clay, weaving materials, books, pasteboard, airplane and boat models, games, books, Western detective stories, current magazines, cigarette holders for those with bandaged hands."

The association magazine published Natalie's appeal. *You know lots of burned cases and many of the surgical ones, too, need something to make them stretch shortened muscles. It seems impossible to get foot-lathes or looms, but we haven't even any cord now. There are two kinds of cord that we use: one regular old fuzzy white cotton wrapping cord. One of the patients and I have concocted a frame, and I got the last of such* cord anywhere in these parts. It is nearly gone. The other is a slick, very strong cord that comes in various colors, used for making belts and so on. I've actually learned how to do it, so that I might teach the boys. And another thing is modeling clay.

Just to show you how useful it can be: we have a patient whose hands are very badly burned. They are healed now, but the skin is as thin as the thinnest tissue paper, and the least makes a new blister on it. He couldn't gain confidence to try to force the muscles at all. I started him off on a dog-tag chain. He couldn't touch his thumb to his fingers. I said easily, 'Well, that's all right: just pull the knots with your finger only.' So he started off. I went back a bit later and found him absorbed, pulling the knots with his thumb and fingers! The doctor came along a moment later and was charmed. In the physiotherapy room, the man had declared himself completely unable to touch thumb to fingers. So you see there is quite a practical aspect to that sort of thing. All the bed-patients, except the medical ones, of course, love doing that sort of work, and it is a tremendous help to them for passing the time. But with some, as with the above-named, it has a very definite therapeutic value.[32]

Martha organized and became chairman of the Natalie Scott Fund, spearheading solicitations and continuing the newspaper publicity with Natalie's diary articles, which attracted donations. Meanwhile, Natalie learned how to use a loom. *Kmarf, you should see my latest development: a 16 pointed picture frame made of crochet thread! A clever Merchant Marine taught me. He has had one of the worst cases of jaundice imaginable, was on the seriously ill list just a little over a week ago. But he made a grand come-back. He was crotchety at first, but we became the greatest buddies. He was sent out yesterday, as were a number of long-timers, and I do miss them.*

The cig-holders haven't come yet, but I'm expecting them happily. Leila Williams sent some, and who are the others? We got some cord from ARC, but it wasn't Belfast, and so the dye comes off! However, we're making belts out of it happily, none the less. Perhaps there is no more Belfast to be had. It's grand about the Newcomb Alumnae: I feel sure you drove them to it! But I am flattered that they let you. Is there any possibility of even the humblest portable radio. Each ward can only have one only 1 day a week. And they do love them so. Do send one if humanly possible. I know they're almost impossible to buy now. You've been simply a Rock of Gibraltar plus, and it means more than I can say.[33]

On March 17, 1944, Natalie replied to literary agent Anne Kennedy's request for an article on the war for the *Saturday Evening Post*. The two were old friends. Natalie had managed Anne's house in Taxco for years, and before the war, Anne had placed Natalie's articles with various magazines. *Dearest Anne: I do so much enjoy your letters. It's a lovely thought, that of my doing an article for the Sat. Eve. Post; but alas, my outpourings are just that,—done at top speed, with never time for reconsideration nor even for a rereading and correction. So how could I ever do anything of formal sort? There really isn't any time. Your suggestion is most tantalizing, none the less. Perhaps only if I had copies of my various outpourings, perhaps I could consign them to a 'ghost' to string together. It just occurs to me that a friend of mine to whom I send one each time, she was keeping them. You could cast an agent's eye over the ghost's efforts. The suggestion is a wild one; but if you think anything of it, could write Mrs. R. G. Robinson.*

Anne immediately did so, writing Martha, "I know you will agree with me that the letters she [Natalie] writes are the most human and interesting news of the Red Cross that has come out of the war over seas. I have found a very fine writer to ghost the article, a Genevieve Parkhurst, a well known writer for all magazines, she knows Natalie and admires her and says she might find material for a small book." Martha promptly sent the letters, Natalie's "outpourings"; Genevieve Parkhurst immediately began to work on the project.[34]

At this time, Natalie and Martha's exchange of letters dealt with their hopes and fears for Martha's sons and Natalie's nephews in the war. Of Natalie's two nephews, only Nauman then served in the army, though Bino (Albin, the youngest of Nauman Scott's five children) would become a paratrooper in the Pacific in late 1944. Much of Natalie's news came through an Alexandria soldier named Frank Brame, a well-connected logistics officer who invited her out for officer parties in Oran on several occasions.[35]

Supplies sent by the Natalie Scott Fund streamed into the hospital. *Your packages arrived day before yesterday and were the causes of the greatest rejoicing. The 'models' didn't last the day.*

I reserved most of them for bed patients, but over and over again walking patients came up eager-eyed asking for one. Suffering over saying no, I gave out two before the others managed to restrain me. As it is, one model entertains a whole ward. Everybody looks on, helps, gives advice. You would really feel well-rewarded if you could see the pleasure they give.

I expect to get at weaving next. We have some looms like the one you sent, but the material is scant, in fact, non-existent, until yours arrived. Of course, the ARC ships as much as rapidly as possible, but there is such a tremendous territory to cover, so little shipping space. Craft materials have to await their turn. These are simply invaluable to us. The cig. holders are ever useful, not only for the burned cases but for various types of facial injuries, and have meant solace to any number of patients who couldn't have had cheer of cigarettes in any other way.[36]

A fundamental task was writing letters to patients' families. Many were written for patients, while others were direct correspondence from Natalie giving serious news to information-starved relatives. One such letter that went to the family of a critically wounded soldier, Roy Korbin of Milwaukee, brought replies from both his sister and mother. Said the sister:

> We can't thank you enough for letting us know of Roy's condition. We all hope and pray that it isn't as serious as it sounds. Your letter is the first news we heard of Roy. Mother, Dad and family feel so badly and we tried so hard to get news of Roy ever since his letters ceased. We checked with the American Red Cross here and they advised us to send Cablegrams which we did but as yet we haven't received an answer.

Natalie had arranged for a local artist to sketch Roy. She sent the portrait to his family, who liked it very much. Roy's mother sought more news, "for I miss him so much and not to hear a word is hard to take." She continued, "He is my only son I got and he means so much to me. Roy was gone in the Army 25 months, gone from home is hard to take for him and never got a furlough so I know if we could see him and he see us would mean lots to both of us. It was in your letter that you are good to him which makes me feel good for he is a good boy." Thus one letter brought multiple replies, and then Natalie's responses. In this way, she kept up correspondence on behalf of her four wards. Her typewriter, Penelope, was kept very busy, often late into the night, leaving little time for answering the dozens of letters from Natalie's own friends. She told Martha, *If once anything gets into that stack of unanswereds, it's the devil to extract it again. I get no farther than writing to Scotts or Provostys, or to you or Whildo; and rarely to the Herb Mullers in Washington who spoil me a lot with letters. I do take time to answer letters from ex-patients and often their families, ex-patients especially if they are 'at the front.' I had one recently, headed brazenly, Anzio Beachhead, which surprised me.*[37]

The arrival of a package of books from Martha for Natalie's library elicited new words of thanks, plus further insight into Natalie's Oran world. *It was certainly good to get them. We have rather a lot of paper-bounds, but they go to pieces so easily. Ole Momma pads along with a big basket full everyday, together with other supplies. I have lost all taste for conventional 'social life', and can hardly prod myself on the occasions when I sally forth. Went to a huge dinner-party at the Schotts last week. He is the American consul here, and I had met them both in Mexico casually several times. The party was very swagger, bristling with stars and eagles, only four women, including the hostess, and about a dozen or more officers. As luck would have it, a cough medicine I have been taking had made me 'constricted' to put it delicately; so I took Ep. that morning. It didn't work, and I was petrified when I remembered the dinner. So I took a big enema! And did I feel wan when I arrived at dinner! Would that happen to anybody but me?*

By early April, Natalie felt too far away from the front lines, where she believed she would be most effective with wounded soldiers. *I have begged and pleaded for a transfer to a more forward zone, but it hasn't worked out that way. The odd thing about the 'set-up' is that those who 'do their job' simply stay put, no matter what their wishes are; and the only ones who get transferred according to their desire are those who 'make a stew'. Kay Parsons, our Assistant Field Director (therefore the head of our unit) also wants to move. We are patted gently and told that we are doing a good job where we are. This is a Social Service Workers set-up. Only those with formal training are allowed to be AFDs. My two years hospital experience in the last war and all the successful S.S. organizing that I've done in Taxco count for nothing over here. However, little do I care, as I am charmed with the work I am doing. In fact, we all do practically the same thing, and you could hardly tell us apart, except for title. I look after the library; Cunningham after Recreation. But I do recreation and crafts on my own wards,— nobody else does. And I do all correspondence regarding any patient in my wards. This is not orthodox, but it works. Results count![38]*

Natalie learned a week later that she was indeed being transferred, though the date was uncertain. *I practically burst with the news. I am going to be transferred very soon and in the direction that I want to go.* She added a note to Martha on April 27 regarding the "ghost writing" of a book or magazine article based on her letters. *Incidentally, suppose you've had Anne Kennedy's letter. She is a grand soul and such a good friend. Don't think that my old friend Genevieve Parkhurst will be able to make a book or magazine article of the outpourings, tho; there are too many gaps.[39]*

Natalie had applied for transfer in December 1943, seeking assignment to an evacuation or field hospital at the front lines. In late May, she realized that *its coming thru now may land me in what may soon be a backwater, or at least a 'side issue'. Ay de mi! However, it's a large-scale war, and I shall try to be duly philosophical about any place I have in it. It's all worth doing.*

Natalie had been in North Africa for almost eleven months. She had made many interesting friends in Oran, often passing on to Martha local character sketches. *I think I've written about my friend, the Abbé Thierry. He was anti-Vichy from the start, had meetings at least weekly at his house, was advised in advance of our landing, and told to tell his followers the evening before. But the evening before, the authorities sent at ten to search the house. He seated their chief on a box containing the signal flares to be used to help us. After midnight, he notified his men of the approaching landing. And did not return to his house. Fortunately, for the next day, the police went to arrest him,—the afternoon of the landing.*

He is delightful, short, with a puckish face, rather round with humorous wrinkles. He always kisses me on both cheeks and calls me 'me fille'. He lives at the house of Mme. Ribeton. I dined with them Sunday evening. We had a glorious gigot and we sang and were merry.

There were other good times as Natalie's departure approached, including the chore of packing her overstuffed bags. *Had a most amusing time packing. Frank Brame (Lt.) from Alex and his buddy, Bill Condon, came in to pack my bed-roll, as did also an ex-patient, awfully nice, Bob Connolly, and another enlisted man, Jack Fullilove, who is charming, well-read and intelligent, 6 ft. four! I had some eau de vie and Coca-cola and Vermouth; Frank had some, too. So in between efforts, they sipped and laughed and made a party out of it.*

On May 24, Natalie wrote a letter from the deck of the ship taking her to her new assignment in southern Italy. Her new medical unit supported the Allied forces pushing towards Rome. Natalie described how, on her last day in her Oran hospital wards, many patients and visitors had come to say goodbye. Then, the ship set sail for Naples, accompanied by *destroyers, troop-ships, sub-chasers, and planes swirling about, and swooping and droning over us. The first night at sail the French sang and a British officer played the bag-pipes. Everybody listened quite sentimentally, because, I suppose one felt so strongly his feeling for his country that each of us were thrown back to our own. The Americans after the French songs were inspired to answer back with some of ours. The paratroopers have a most gory song, which they sing very gaily,—the devil-may-care of the old romantic spirit. Dear me, they sang the songs that were sung when I went over in August 1917. It made me weak, I could see the old Touraine, with faces so young, demanding life as eagerly. And there they were again,—here they were! Seated for this mass death,—when they might have so much to give as well as to get.*

But all night long in my sleep I made speeches to the Congressmen! And I had stretchers brought in, with one maimed young body after another on them, and kept saying, "You did that". And I became very impassioned. "If I were vengeful, I'd have your son like that. And have you know you put him there." But no, they go on, blythely oblivious. Some few statesmen, no; but even the statesmen must compromise and make deals. And so we won the last war at what a cost, and lost the peace for what ends? And spoiled to a degree the simple faith of our people. And all of that stays with me all the time, yet when I try to speak of it, I end by sounding merely puny and sentimental.[40]

Italy

The invasion of mainland Italy had started eight months earlier, September 1943, with British general Sir Bernard Montgomery leading his forces across the Strait of Messina into Italy's southern toe. The major attack brought American-British forces to Salerno, on Italy's west coast below Naples (half of the large American strike force had sailed from Oran). Maj. Gen. Mark Clark's forces triumphantly entered Naples on October 1, 1943. Its harbor was then resurrected from ruin—an engineering miracle—and became the logistical base of operations for the Italian war.[41]

Natalie stepped off her ship in Naples into a busy port scene of tank carriers and heavy trucks disgorging armaments and heavy equipment of all sorts. *We were a large number of women, all set into a gigantic room with high ceilings, walls pock-marked with bullet holes, windows out, but replaced with burlap. Kay [Parsons] and I dug in quite nicely. My suit-case made a good night-table and my musette bags served as drawers.* Simultaneously, D-Day was unfolding to their west.

After four days in the staging area, Natalie and Kay were loaded into an open truck for transfer to the hospital. *We roared sweetly about, to innumerable hospitals, at each one we coughed up a worker. We spent 3 hours under a blazing sun in this interesting tour.* Finally Natalie and Kay, with two others, were deposited at their Naples hospital. *I find myself assigned to a hospital ensconced in a vast dingy museum in the heart of the city. There are lots of hospitals in this area full of French patients with nobody who speaks French. In this one, not one French patient!*

As the weeks passed, Natalie also became displeased with the leisurely pace of the work and the poor attitude of the supervising staff. *My personal disappointment I could bear, if I felt I were in a place where the work was fresh and vigorous. But no: the present AFD believes in leisure. We have an 8 hour schedule; but she to date has never arrived less than half an hour*

*late, usually an hour and her chum yet later, but they leave on
time. These Social Service workers! Ay de mi. Every time (this
is confidential!) I've talked to my chiefs, I've been made to feel
an aged infant. The air of patient determined tolerance, as tho
to a mild lunatic. That page-twenty-four-of-the-text-book smile!
It is infuriating. They mention my age as against Evac hospitals, but I discover that the other 2 veterans of the last war over
here are both in Evacs. And they can't be more than a year
younger than I. What most gets me down is that never since I
have been here have I heard a word from the Higher ups, jack-
ing up the workers. Nothing to show any awareness that this is
a time more full of profound and lasting tragedy than any other
in the world's history. Any comment of the sort is considered
sentimental. There are, however, frequent reminders that we
'mustn't do too much for the men'.*

*My criticism is chiefly a question of emphasis. How I resent
that Social Service probing regardless of pride or sensitiveness.
I find out a man's situation quite well, in a comradely fashion.
But the complete unawareness of my AFD as to the men's feelings makes me die several deaths daily. As yesterday, when she
and I were discussing some trivial question in the inner office,
and a patient put his head in the door with an eager friendly
smile, asking, "Could I have a piece of soap?" She answered
with that infuriating S.S. smile of conscious patience, "Will you
wait outside, please? You see, we are busy just now". The soap
was within 10 inches of her hand. And of course the patient
didn't wait.*

*In the morning at 9:30 a nurse passed me a new patient
badly wounded, who had nothing. Would I take him toilet articles? I sent up and prepared a bag for him. "Whom is that for?"
asked my AFD. (She checks up on me often, to see that I do not
give to the undeserving.) I explained. "But he's in Maureen's
ward," she objected sweetly. "Maureen can take it to him when
she comes". "I have to pass just by the door to that ward", I
offered casually. "Maureen won't be here till noon or later, and
the patient might want to brush his teeth". "He can wait," she
replied severely. And of course the patient, in that desolating
endurance of pain, did wait. Until two o'clock.*

*I did all of the ward visiting,—500 patients—for all the week.
I found at the start some badly wounded patients who had been*

there for 2 days without being seen by us and without toilet articles. "My only fear" says my AFD sweetly, "Miss Scott, is that you do too much for the men". "I appreciate your criticism," I answered pleasantly. "But would you give an example, so that I can understand exactly what you mean." She couldn't. I was smiling inwardly, because I knew what she meant. I treat the men as individuals, and never use the Text-book smile.

As the weeks passed, Natalie's frustration grew to the point that she considered resigning and going home. *Wrote a formal request seeking release from service, saying that "I am constantly and increasingly aware that there is no place for the non-professional in the present ARC hospital set-up". Then didn't send it, deciding that I'd all the more stick it out, even though no amount of experience is supposed to equal a bit of professional training! Shall stay till they kick me out!*

Then Natalie relented a bit, putting her discontent in perspective. *Fortunately, the larger percentage of the workers do have a sense of obligation, a genuine devotion to their work; an unfailing sympathy directed intelligently and devotedly. So my criticism of the 'authorities' does not mean that a good job is not being done. In most places there is really good work going on. But my own unit is depressing. The patients are my consolation. Their wit, their appreciation, their funny comments; their teasing; and their serious discussions; their loyalties, worries, and problems. Far from being soft with them, I razz them mercilessly. If any of them says anything such as 'I want to go home', for instance. "Yes, you'd make a fine 4-F, something for that little boy whose picture you showed me to brag about." Then they always crawl out of it, poor fellows. "I mean, I wish the war was over". One did better still. "Where do you think home is?" he demanded. "Where? I'll bite". "Home", he answered proudly. "That's where my outfit is and that's home to me."*

Natalie fumed on about her AFD's attitude and practices, giving multiple examples of her patients' endurance, courage, and tragic plights. *But of course it would be sentimental and not in the S.S. text-book to admire his pluck,* she wrote of one terribly wounded Texan, all limbs splinted and casted. He was eager to rejoin his combat unit, yet joked, *"But I'd be in a fix if a fly lighted on my nose now, wouldn't I?"* Still, the AFD would ask, much to Natalie's resentment, *"But are you sure you are not writing letters for any of the men who can write for themselves, Miss Scott?"*[42]

There was much in Naples that pleased Natalie, particularly the effective occupational therapy and the social clubs for GIs. *We've quite a lot of plastic glass here, and the men make most attractive things of it,—picture frames, rings of every sort, lockets. The set-up is excellent in many ways. The Special Services officer is doing an excellent job. There is a magnificent club for the enlisted men here,—five stories high, with everything imaginable,—a man who will draw your picture, a steady schedule of entertainment. Some very attractive and capable girls there, too,—delightfully unprofessional and doing simply a swell job. It's a pleasure to go in there.* She wrote of patients who struggled with their fears and their memories of companions in combat who had lost their lives gallantly. *The death of a comrade seems to get the men down more than any personal danger or hardship. So I manage to bring out at times the fact that mortal wounds are almost never felt; that a man may scream and scream in such a case, but, if he lives, will say later that he felt no pain. The men listen with an eagerness that is significant. "Is that right?" they will say anxiously. And by the way they say it, one knows that they are not thinking of themselves but are looking back on dreadful memories.*

The psychology is endlessly interesting. One man has told me twice the same story. "You know the two times I was most scared? Once at barely dawn we were half out of our holes, and here comes a German tank. We dived in, believe you me. And this fellow calls out, 'Come out of there and give yourselves up, or we'll blow you off the map'. Perfectly good English too. None of us said anything, and he let loose with everything he had. And I was clawing at that hole and trying to dig with my head, too. Our fellows came up just then and he beat it. But I was sure scared. And the other time, I'd just gone into a house. The Capt. was downstairs and he sent me up. And just as I got to the top of the stairs, a bunch of Jerries came in. I dived into the room where the other fellow was, and we barricaded the door. And they banged on it, and yelled, 'Come out.' And they kept firing thru it. And they'd have had it open in another minute, but one of their fellows gave an alarm, and they beat it. I was sure scared".

Something in his way of telling the story, as tho to himself and not to me, made me know that he is still scared. And scared of being scared. He is going back to combat, so I thought probably it was a good idea to let him talk it out. What unbearable things these men have to bear,—for whom we mustn't do too much!

Natalie found solace in her Naples living quarters, *a long climb to the 7th floor atop a "tenement-ish" building directly facing across the street another tall building housing officers. Looks out over blue waters with shipping, and a svelte peak beyond. The height makes for coolness, and the view releases the soul. My soul today, is far away, sailing a certain well-known bay!* It was the Bay of Naples. Kay Parsons shared her quarters, and they were soon joined by Jane Connor, a young nurse who had once traveled with Natalie during leave in Oran.

Have just finished an elegant supper of K-rations, supper unit. Not bad: bouillon, and a can of ham-ish stuff with white of egg, or so it says. My landlady (manager of this dingy R.C. Transients Hotel) warmed everything for me regardless. My bed might as well be in the middle of Canal St. because of the number of heavy trucks, tank-carriers,—every known combination of metallic noise at its maximum and unremitting, night and day. Everything from the Port comes by here. I discovered an electric heater in the store-room: we turn it on its side and cook on it! One evening, one of the girls brought steaks (source, a military secret) and Mrs. Kummler, fellow-occupant, broiled them. She made a marvelous salad, potatoes and peas, onions, and a marvelous egg-dressing made with powdered eggs, a cooked dressing. Delicious. Kay and I supplied preliminary Martinis, some passable army gin and ditto white Vermouth, with a twist of lemon peel. We sat on the terrace looking over the bay,—luxurious. I feel ashamed to occupy such comfortable quarters,—but enjoy them anyway.[43]

Kay is like a squirrel: she always has a little nest of edibles. Also, she keeps useful Colonels on tap here and there, tho her heart-interests run usually to Captains. Her local Col. did well by us: fished us from our remote spot, whirled us about, took us to dinner to his mess, which is arranged like a good restaurant, with a bar and little tables at the entrance. Certain parts of this city that were once the most beautiful are sad to see now.

Actual damage has been cleaned neatly up; but there is an air of desolate dinginess in places that once were proudly gleaming. A glance shows the facade of a haughty building; a 2nd, shows that the facade is a shell only. What horror this city has known: bombed by both sides alternately. Recently met a Major from N.O. who is working with the Italians on public health: they've really done a magnificent job in battling disease and starvation. Kay's Col. is head of CC [Civilian Corps] here,—looks just like General Pershing and is rather like him in many ways.

During the course of June, Natalie gradually gained independence from the AFD whose interference had troubled her. She even established a friendship with Maureen, the AFD's usual companion. The pair organized two parties for the patients. *One party was a birthday party for everybody whose birthday came in June. I did the decorations.* Natalie described the repainting of the dayroom as *wild-looking but gay. I suggested, "Happy Birthday June Babies" for the announcement, and the decorations followed this theme. Patients did the work. From each letter dangled a baby, each one in a helmet, while above June was a Sad Sack (what the babies grew up into).*

Yesterday was the 4th of July party. This time, I had a Liberty Bell, large size, complete with a "God We Trust" band, and a large V surrounded by Liberty Bells. Maureen is really good at planning parties. I was afraid that the entertainment— games—proposed, would seem too childish. Two did, but the third made up for that. The ping-pong table was the center of it; two teams of 4 each. They had to kneel, two of a team at the end, and one on either side. The object was to blow the ping-pong ball off the opponents' side. The men had to keep their hands behind them. Maureen and I had to hold the 2 halves of the table together, so we were in between the players. These grown men blowing looked so ridiculous that I laughed till tears literally ran down my cheeks, and the audience did the same. The players actually grew intense about it, at the same time they couldn't help laughing, too, and their efforts to blow while laughing were killingly funny.

We had ice-cream and cake afterwards, Ole Mamma cutting those huge cakes. Reminding me of when I used to try to help the Sutherlands out when they started the Hotel Tasqueno! The hospital is beautifully cooperative. They have a band, the Sad

Sacks, headed by an officer. One member is a wonderful clown. They insisted on 'entering' in the ping-pong contest, and of course turned it into comedy by breaking rules and doing antics. One man played serum bottles!—very well. The officer of the Sad Sacks played the mouth organ. The feature of the evening was a last minute discovery: two negroes who were awfully good at jitter-bug. We dressed them up as George and Martha Washington. The effects of their abandoned jitter-bugging in that stately costume was irresistibly funny and our audience of well over two hundred went into one long roar of laughter.

Memorable Occasions

Preparations for the July 4 festivities were complicated by the sudden arrival of more wounded. Natalie felt closer to the war for the first time since she came to Naples. *Yesterday was the first day that I worked until I was tired. Going to the ground floor for supplies, I saw ambulances coming in: new patients flown down from the front. Poor fellows, so pitifully glad to be at the end of their trip in clean restful beds. Then Agnes told me that more had come in. Again toured the wards. There was a large proportion of quite serious cases. We have some excellent nurses who are genuinely devoted, for which I am most deeply and consciously grateful. I've come to know them fairly well, which is a great help in the work. The wardmen, too, are a good lot. They were all working top speed last evening.*

At that point, Agnes and I sallied forth on the wards with our Italian, Caprino, to serve ice-cream to the bed patients. It was the most thankful operation! Pineapple ice-cream. I dished at breakneck speed, first to the wards where were most of the new patients, and those men just back from the tough life of the front combat lines were so thrilled that it did one good to see it. Sometimes another patient would have to feed it to one or another. One man with both eyes bandaged insisted he could manage his own and did. "One of 'em's gone", he said about his eyes. "But before they put these bandages on, I could see outa the other; and believe me, am I glad of that."

Natalie was given responsibility at the hospital for organizing Sunday-evening lectures on current events, world problems, *and so on. I was a little uncertain about it, but they've gone beautifully. The first talk, very anecdotal, was given by a young Lt. Hart on 'Our Entry into Rome'. The Lt. inadvertently got up with the shock troops, who were stopped there. But saw great sights, machine-gunning as correspondents crouched in ditches pounding typewriters madly; a wedding going on in the village at the same time with the machine-gunning! The next lecture was on Russia, a very fair picture, given by Mr. Trowbridge. I was most happily surprised at the reaction of the men to these talks. We began with about 65 men, and the last 3 lectures have been over a hundred each time. We've had a talk on What Sort of Peace Terms Should We Make; and another on Amgot (American Military Govt). This coming Sunday will be Jugo-Slavia.*

I do a build-up for the talks during the week, remind the men of how we lost the peace after the last war; that their words as veterans will be listened to; and it's their obligation to learn as much as they can so that their words may make sense, just as much an obligation as it is to fight for our 'way of life', I tell them. As we do a lot of joking and joshing, too, all the time, they are willing to listen to me when I lapse into seriousness at intervals. Lots of them ask quite intelligent questions. Mr. Trowbridge is brilliantly educated, partly at Oxford, very cultured. I was a bit worried for fear the men would find him 'high-brow'; but they seemed to like him very much.

The Amgot lecture was interesting by a Major who used to be a Congressman. Amgot operated civil governments in captured (liberated) communities. *Quite a job Amgot has done and is doing. ACC (Allied Control Commission) takes over after them: they go in with the troops and they first freeze funds; inspect and take over utilities; survey hospital possibilities, civilian relief organizations, and so on.*

Each day Natalie walked eighteen blocks from her billet to the hospital for work, then back. She encountered soldiers and locals of all ages as she walked, and she shared vignettes about them in her letters. Once she became lost taking a shortcut and found herself *in a tenement district at dusk. A woman sent her little boy, a clean bright little 12 year old to escort me. I offered him ten lire when we arrived. He wouldn't take it. So some candy; likewise refused. "It was a pleasure to go with you, Signora," he said. Incidentally, I've had to come around to calling our soldiers 'G.I.'s' as they speak of themselves. All foreigners call them Jo, of course. In the last war, it was Sammy. Any children they spoil hopelessly. The children beg 'caramelos' constantly. In another instance two young enlisted men asked me a trumped-up question, if I was in a hurry, because they never got a chance to talk to American women. "Why not the Club?" I asked. "Oh, well, there are so many fellows there, you can just get a word in; you can't really talk." So I stood for nearly an hour discussing and chattering with them. And they thanked me most warmly and said, "It sure had been swell."*

Three in a jeep turned back from their direction and took me to the hospital one hot day. A few days later they dropped in to see me, bringing me roses! I've seen quite a few that I knew at the 7th Station, and one comes in regularly once a week on his day off, as he's stationed near here. All of which is very nice indeed. Natalie supervised the craft work in the dayroom during afternoons, but the AFD would not allow her to initiate a craft program with the bed patients. In the dayroom, *we can never get more than 17 to 18 at most to work in spite of my efforts. So then I pick out the forlorn or shy and engage them in casino or such.*

As for the Newcomb Alumnae work of sending supplies for crafts and occupational therapy, Natalie wrote Martha to hold new shipments because the Naples hospital had greater resources. *There is a good supply of plastic glass, some clay has come in; we have some string; and are even promised some leather. You would be charmed to see the 'Craft Corner', with always eight or ten men about, much absorbed in their work. At present, one is making a band for my wrist watch. To this old Momma they look a lot like a bunch of little boys.*

In June, Natalie learned her nephew Bino would soon complete his army basic training, just as Martha Robinson's youngest son was entering the service. *What a bad time to start out in Army life, which is no picnic at best. They'll make the grade, tho.* Natalie celebrated her July 18 birthday in Naples with candy from Martha and two dresses from Sidonie. *Can't wear civies so much here as I could before, but do love putting them on 'at home',—makes a different woman out of me, and somehow makes me really feel the war may be over some day. One good-looking quite sophisticated seeming navy patient, tall and forty-ish, has got flirtatious with me, if you please! He came in the office to-day when I was alone, advancing upon me as I was looking at files saying, "I must hold you in my arms!" I batted him playfully with a file, not too gently, and said, "You're going to hold your sassy tongue in your mouth", stepping around him into view of the hall. I played acie-ducie with him peacefully afterwards. I hadn't expected to have that sort of trouble this war!*[44]

Anyway, the war news in general is certainly heartened at present. I do wish we could do something to stimulate the revolt among the German people,—may it grow and expand! Have talked to various ones who were in on the Normandy invasion. Their reports, first-hand, were really encouraging, as they all seem to think that it was a magnificent piece of work, in coordination, timing, and so on. Some of my informants had been in on most of the other 'invasions' and they most of all were impressed by the brilliance of this one. I remind myself that we took years 'last time' fighting over a much smaller section of France. On the other hand, this is a blitzkrieg,—as the Germans set the pace, perhaps we can surpass them in it in the end. And how I hope so. The Russians are doing wonders still.[45]

Amidst the turmoil of work in the late-summer heat, Natalie managed quiet diversions: cooking, reading Eve Curie's *Journey Among Warriors*, then rereading *War and Peace, which I haven't read since I was in my teens and how I am enjoying it! I really hate for it to end. It seems so incredibly alive, after all these years. Do read it again, if you haven't done so.* She began tending and watering the neglected plants on their terrace, *and now they are brightening. Yesterday evening, hot and soggy as I was, I set to work, weeding them all, transplanting a few, trimmed and cut, and altogether had a wonderful time, loving the smell of the earth and the feel of it,—here in the midst of a noisy city.*[46]

Natalie heard from Genevieve Parkhurst, the author who had undertaken the task of converting her letters into a small book. *Genevieve Parkhurst turned down a thousand dollars for my edited letters,—she says she can do better! Heaven knows what she has done to them! But it would be just that much falling into my lap, so I'd be charmed.* However, Natalie noted that Genevieve would be required to submit the book to the American Red Cross publicity committee, *which is quite capable of putting a crimp in the whole affair. Alas.*[47]

A sudden opportunity came Natalie's way in mid-September: a chance to visit war-weary, liberated Rome. *I'm going on a jaunt to-morrow to a far-famed capital, riding for several hours in an open jeep in the sun! Everybody kept saying, "O, but you must go to Rome". I didn't want to go to Rome, having my own memories of it in the old days. I finally said ungraciously, "All Right". Was offered a sub-rosa ride in a plane; but stiffened my spine and managed to hold to my resolve which I kept all thru the last war, that is, not to break any regulations during war time. Of course, after the war is a different matter! What a lovely AWOL I had after the last war!*[48]

So I set forth in a jeep. Lovely picture. It was an open jeep. The wind and sun gave me pink freckles. So I put on a light straw helmet from Capri, and entwined myself in yards of white cheese-cloth. Quite a picture I presented, and a little dangerous to traffic, as cars meeting us would sometimes wobble, drivers gaped and stared, a truckload of GIs stopped just opposite us. We exchanged persiflage, and they kept saying, "Lift up your drapes, Red Cross, and let's see your face".

"Things are better as they are", I called back. "Just take my word for it: I'm a dazzling blonde and only came over here to get away from Hollywood". "Hollywood?" "Yes. They were just about to start a little war there over me, so I came away. If I have to have a war, I might as well take a big one. Like you all". The truck started, their driver grinning. They still called, "Lift up the veil, Hollywood". I waved, and bowed, and flaunted the 'veil'.

It was a glorious day, windy but sunny. But the face of it was full of tragedy which all the sunshine could not brighten. Whole villages were tumbled into heaps of desolate ruins, just single gutted pock-marked walls rising starkly out of heaps of rubble. Yet the people had come back. They would choose the least damaged room, rig up some sort of overhead. Some were working patiently among the stones; others in the fields. Little stands of fruit and some few vegetables stood along the cleared streets. And on the roads we would meet little family groups trudging along behind a wobbly cart piled with forlorn household objects, all too few. Sometimes there was no cart, and the people themselves would creep along, bending under loads. And how, how in the world will it ever get right again?

Yet the fields were bright, tho many were devastated or

unplanted, the trees were fresh and buoyant and surprisingly few were damaged. On the way back, we took a different road and went thru Cassino. It was starker than the landscape of Childe Harold to the Dark Tower Came. There was not even a skeleton wall left standing. Marshy land on one side; and up what seemed an immeasurable stretch of terrifically steep straight slope was the remains of the famous monastery that dominated everything. An officer who had fought there was in the car with us. How our men ever faced that place is more than I can see. It was agonizing to think what that struggle must have been.

We reached Rome in the early afternoon. Our road took us in past the Colosseum, the old ruined arches, the Forum. The ARC has a fine hotel there, on the ground floor a very attractive officers' club. Rome was amazing itself, in all its old majesty and splendor. I took the Red Cross sight seeing bus, just to renew my acquaintance. I would have been somewhat bewildered, if the places visited had not already been familiar to me, Sta. Maria Maggiore, San Juan de Letran, the various "ruins", the Catacombs, and St. Peter's! At the Catacombs, I purchased some rosaries for my Mexican Roman Catholic friends. They are made of beads from the bush from which the crown of thorns were made. Several of the young club girls who were buddies of mine at the Stark Club (her Oran lodgings) were there, and were charming to me, Celia Senney from St. Louis who is a special pet of mine, also Sally Steinman. They invited me to the opera.

The shop windows were full of things alluring; but the prices were formidable. I've always had an affection for the Piazza di Spagna, I can't remember just why; but I found myself going back there several times, and ending for a Vermouth in the little bar reportedly frequented by Keats and Shelley and Mark Twain, and others. And I went again to the Keats-Shelley memorial. It's presided over by a quiet young woman, of very definite charm. Russian extraction, and a student, with a hush in her voice and manner that suits the place. I wondered whether she was naturally that way, or whether the place had molded her.

A hearty amiable woman had come up in the jeep with me. I told her that I was going to renew my acquaintance with Michelangelo's Moses, which I heard had been 'uncovered'. She asked if she might come along. It was good, incidentally, on approaching, to note Mussolini's famous balcony and to realize that his figure would nevermore appear upon it. AND I went to see the Pope. Now, he receives the Allied Forces every day at twelve-thirty. As a preliminary, I had inquired about best places to buy rosaries near St. Peter's, there are innumerable vendors who sell tawdry rosaries at huge prices. I finally found a tiny shop near the Pantheon, and bought some twenty rosaries. The shop was small and all four of the family who ran it clustered to help me in my choice. Two sergeants overtook me when I was nearby there. They were chagrined when they saw my rosaries so I gave them one apiece.

We climbed the various series of steps in the magnificent building, and finally after proper turns, reached the chapel for the audience. GIs were crowded solidly on either side and in the back. The guards, in their resplendent uniforms designed by Michelangelo, the black satin with the full sleeves of red and yellow stripes with one great slash of orange, looked especially resplendent. To my surprise, the guards at the entrance lowered their halberds between my companions and me, and waved me toward the empty aisle. Officers and nurses were put up front, I discovered.

I looked back at my chagrined sgts. and grinned. "Like Peacocks' Alley", I whispered, "only it's about fifty years late for me to be going up one". I only wanted to gloss over their being left behind; but they laughed out as did the GIs around them, so I hurried off up the aisle. And heard a raucous whisper, "Miss SCOTT! Miss SCOTT!" And there was one of my ex-patients leaning out from the side. I stopped and spoke to him. And as I turned to go on, murmured, "I feel like a bride. But where's the groom?" Which caused some more GI laughter, so I streaked up the aisle in my demurest manner, fearing I'd be put out.

There were guards at intervals all the way up. I was shepherded up a low dais richly carpeted in red. There were seats on each side, on the left, officers, on the right, nurses and a very few ARC workers; and some French WACs. They pleasantly made a place for me. It was an effective setting. In the center, under a crimson canopy, the throne chair, a heavy red brocaded background. We waited over half an hour, and finally the Pope was carried in on the shoulders of (I suppose) the Papal noblemen. They lowered the chair at the dais, and he descended. He had a really royal manner, and was at the same time a most impressive figure, slight and ascetic looking, scholarly and kindly. His face is very thin, skin drawn up tightly over the fine bone structure. He faced us with serene dignity. He sat and spoke a few words in perfect English, the gist of which was the necessity for Christian love. Then he spoke in French with more emotion and warmth. Understandable, as the French have really suffered more than any of the rest of us. And he blessed all of us.

Then he descended to our level on this dais and made a round, starting with the officers. I had had the luck, being late, to be on the front row. And I had my hands literally dripping with rosaries, and my St. Christopher medal. I resolved for the sake of the Roman Catholics in my family, I would kiss the Pope's ring, and planned to do so with great dignity. When he came to me, he put his hand on all my rosaries and my medals, and asked if I was with the Red Cross. I said, "Yes, Holy Father". Only at the last moment a doubt assailed me as to whether Holy Father was the correct form of address, so I gulped it, school-boy style. And instead of kissing the ring with dignity, I fear I pecked at it. So I didn't come out so well in that interview. Anyway he said, "They are doing a great work". It was a memorable occasion none the less.[49]

Chapter Ten

World War II (1944-46)

Natalie received orders on October 12, 1944, to board ship in Naples and sail for Marseilles, France, where she would be reassigned. She hoped for an evacuation hospital assignment. First she was encamped in a recent battlefield in southern France, awaiting instructions. *And now here I sit, on one bare Army cot, with Penelope perched on another before me, in an empty tent. We left our former station about a week ago, so delightful a trip in a comfortable ship. Some fifty of us were in a 'ward' in double-deckers. We are in pyramidal tents, four to a tent meant for six. Two empty cots for parking things, which together with a stout rope across for hanging things gives us plenty of room. It is quite rustic: underfoot are grass and scattered pine-cones. The walkways are a morass, but we found some stacked corrugated tin and have laid it along, with one piece at the entrance of our tent.*

The location is perfectly lovely, surrounded by Corot-esque trees, chestnut and beeches, dark cedars, and sober Lombardy poplars. We were told we wouldn't need a guard as the fields all around us are heavily mined. We are glad not to have a guard: they are so inclined to flash inquiring lights at embarrassing moments! We have two latrines, one quite eloquent twelve holer, in its own little house, and one that reminds me of my early days in Taxco, as it has no roof at all. It consists of one long canvas strip wrapped around poles. They are only about a hundred yards along from our tent.

Water we get from a perfectly charming well, a block away, with a tripod of heavy old chains, most decorative; but a modern pipe has been set onto the side of it. We bathe quite successfully in our helmets; and we can even get hot water after each meal; tho I prefer cold myself even in the cold weather. We eat at two long green tables set in the open. Two of our own hospital boys, and another from the staging area preside over some prisoners, who serve us from enormous 'cauldrons'. The food is sent over from the main kitchen and heated here. Afterwards, we scrub our mess gear in a huge cauldron of soapy water. Idle talk and laughter drifts in to me here, as I sit in a empty tent with its sides rolled up, my rather soggy and chill field boots are in the sun.

It seems impossible that so short a time ago this was a 'front line'. Under the tall trees is a huge gun emplacement, and several well-constructed fox-holes. It commands a stretch of rolling country below.[1]

Prime Minister Churchill and General Eisenhower had differed sharply over the priority of a southern France invasion through Marseilles that would advance northward to align near the German border with Gen. George Patton's Third Army, forming the southern end of the Allied front lines that would invade Germany. Churchill had preferred devoting these forces, the U.S. Seventh Army commanded by Lt. Gen. Alexander Patch, to the Italian campaign. Eisenhower prevailed. He recognized that German forces had been drawn northward by the Normandy invasion. An invasion through Marseilles would open a more efficient and quick route to Metz, up the Rhone valley, than was possible from the French west coast. The Allies captured Marseilles on August 28, six weeks before Natalie's arrival.[2]

Her camp was located ten miles beyond Marseilles, towards Avignon. *You may imagine with what a swelling of the old cardiac I saw the coast I love so much and have not seen for so many years. But the town had been piteously harried. A little French woman in a restaurant told me that if the Germans had not had to leave hurriedly there would not have been one stone left on another, as they mined and blew up everything they had time for. That, on top of our own heavy raids. In the States, we will never, I hope, know what war is. These unfortunate people have felt its full impact. They tell me of towns near here which the Germans burned, not allowing the inhabitants to leave when they were set fire to. It seems incredible that human beings could become so brutalized. Food is presently very scarce. The FFI is being very vigilant, on the watch for Germans still about in civilian clothes. The old French lady on the boat told me that they had a tragic time in her native Nice,—were using poppy stalks, boiled, as a vegetable, and that she lost fifty pounds.*

The morning after we docked, they routed us out at five in the morning. We changed our sheets and pillow slips, threw our things together, breakfast at six-thirty, and were off the ship at seven-thirty. Pretty picture, of course, with each of us with her 'pistol-belt' with canteen and first-aid kit, gas-mask, helmet, huge bulging musette-bags, field-jacket and rain-coat.

We stood around in the deserted dock and waited. Ambulances drove up and I chatted with the waiting patients. There were some ruined little buildings across the street. Made myself a nice 'bench' of a door sustained by some fallen masonry, and relaxed. One of our ship's officers stopped to chat with me, and later sent me four sandwiches; so I cut them each in four and passed them around our truck. Off we went. The drivers were very vague about our destination and finally turned in at a recently installed hospital. I believe it was formerly an insane-asylum. There was much activity everywhere, stretches of tents on the grounds, trucks grunting to and fro, groups of men digging, and mud wherever the stretches of lawn were interrupted.

A pleasant very talkative head nurse received us, and installed us in big ward-tents. We were a block from the mess-hall and at least two from the latrine. We of the Red Cross were in our chief nurse's tent. Fruit-juice and bread and marmalade turned up. It rained most of the first few days, but it wasn't bad, except that we froze at night, all right except for feet and fanny. I now sleep on my opened bed-roll, and am very snug and warm. When some of the girls started griping the first day, I said pertly, "Well, think of the infantry". There was a moment's silence, and I was afraid I'd been too exasperating; but some of the other girls took it up. So since then, "think of the Infantry" is a sort of a watchword.

Natalie described her companions. *That pretty young anaesthetist Judy Pollock, Miss Ludovico, the chief nurse, a thinfaced little Brooklyn girl, with a most typical accent. Micky,—really a character, the typical heart of gold. Her pal is a slight pretty girl of Italian extraction, from Jersey, Couma, quiet, gentle and sweet. They are very light-hearted and gay, and keep me amused. I am informally general interpreter, and am always being called to help with shopping and so on. We are on a road between a large port (Marseilles) and a fairly important town, a lot of traffic. A tram passes to town, but we always hitchhike and get there more quickly. A Lt. Col. picked us up, and was very pleasant. He said, "Would you girls like to go to my room and freshen up? I've a pleasant room and good bath in a hotel in town". I started to refuse, but glanced at my hand and saw it was almost covered with mud on the back and a big splotch of mud was on my skirt (I refuse to wear ODs to town). He went out while we 'freshened', returned and invited us to luncheon with a Major and himself at an excellent mess. GI food with a French magic touch which transformed it past recognition. I could hardly believe it was GI, until the Col. explained the basis of each dish!*

Quite a sociable place all in all. Too sociable. But pleasant. Frank Brame (Lt.) from La. is stationed in the city, and I went out for luncheon and dinner at his place in a former merchant marine school. When the Germans came, the French owner took out all the doors and frames, and windows, to make the place uninhabitable,—but when we came, produced them. It will be very nice when they get finished. It is a much better set-up than they had in Oran. Beds, even a few clothes-closets. Frank has an inner-spring mattress! I relaxed on Frank's bed, while he and several other officers (I know them all) sat around and chatted. Frank gave me shelter halves because our tent leaks, unfortunately, and the only half I had we are using to cover the leaks over Judy's and my bed.

Natalie described the *transient officer's mess in town, where one sees all nationalities,—Poles, British, American officers, nurses, Red Cross. Almost as good a French touch as the Colonel's mess. Nurses and officers pay only ten cents a meal. There is an Enlisted Men's Club, too, with a Snack Bar,—a long line of GIs. It's a nice set-up. As for me, all sorts of ex-patients from Oran and Italy turned up, and I could hardly get out of the place,—had a very gay time there. There's a Red Cross theatre, too, with good movies. My old pal, Em Cunningham, who was with me at the 7th, and was transferred to another hospital, is just ten miles away, and I plan to see her if we stick around here much longer. We heard to-day that our officers and men and equipment have arrived and that the equipment is being unloaded.*

One sees and gradually comes to accept, all sorts of dramas. For instance, a couple of days ago, French troops from Italy were being landed, on the dock, behind the barrier of 'chicken wire'. Across the street was gathered all day a silent crowd, their eyes fixed on the incoming soldiers, watching hopefully to see some loved one among them. Old people were there, women, young mothers with babies. Our patients have told me that it was a sight to see the first French who landed. Many were shaking as with a chill; many had tears in their eyes. Some picked up a handful of sand, raised it to their lips and kissed it. The old lady on the boat told me that she almost dreaded coming back, as friends had returned to find parents dead, a husband missing, and many tragedies. The French journalist was very competent, interesting. "And soon you'll be in Paris", I said the last evening. "I don't look forward to it" she said briefly. Her eyes filled with tears, and she drew a deep breath.

Then Natalie updated events from a new assignment in Marseilles. On October 21, a Saturday, *orders came for us to move. Some of us were sent to a hospital in the city on DS, some to Cunningham's general hospital; and Judy, Micky, Couma, two other nurses, and my ARC gang were sent here. I miss so much my out-of-door life. This is clean but not alluring, iron beds, four single and one double bed as close together as they can be. This is the nurses quarters for a large Gen. hospital, which has taken over another (the largest) hotel in the town, a University and several villas. It is just setting-up, but already had a good number of patients. Red Cross has a whole villa to itself. It was so good to be chatting with patients again. These were mostly NPs (neuro-psychiatric) of mild but obvious sort. One very good-looking boy was simply sitting, staring at nothing. I wanted to start him talking, so asked if he was the one who had asked me if I played chess (I knew he wasn't). He's been over 26 months, in all our major offenses. "I got a few scratches; but nothing much; just an aid station would fix me up". But recently he was with two buddies and one stepped on a mine. One was killed; the other had both legs blown off, and he himself was momentarily knocked out. When he came to, he put tourniquets on his buddy's legs.*

He frowned painfully telling about it; so I assured him that his buddy probably felt no pain. He said, "You know, I guess that's right. He talked to me right long. He said, 'You always told me I was too careless about mines. Now it happened, just like you said'. But my nerve's gone, just the same. You'd know, if you could have seen me up there. I'm thru. I won't be any good any more".

I smiled at him. "That's what they all say, you know. There are so many who have gone thru the same sort of thing. It's just like twanging on a guitar string: it keeps quivering some time after. And that's the way your nerves are after a big shock. Besides, you see, you've been under a strain for a long time; and even machinery has to be oiled, you know, after you use it for a long time. So you'll have your nerves oiled with a good rest; and you'll be all fresh again."

So finally I started teaching him Rook solitaire. Several gathered around, and we all became quite animated. The villa is a fresh clean building, with no architectural charm, but it is quite roomy, three stories. A library and a game room, and a writing room. To my complete amazement, Kay Parsons, who was my AFD in the 7th Station, turned up here, just returned from leave in the States. She had new things, including a bottle of Gilby's gin, with which yesterday evening we celebrated our reunion. She has a sense of humour and is sympathetic, so she'll brighten the atmosphere notably.

The AFD here would like me to be assigned here, too. Things are in an uncertain state. Our hospital may be made a POW hospital in which case there will be only one ARC worker. Miss Ludovico said, "If that's so, you stay, Scottie. We want you." Which is flattering; but of course I want to be moving further on (towards the front). So I shall probably be assigned here. The work is interesting anywhere, so I'll bear up. But I would so like an Evac hospital![3]

Natalie's hospital in Marseilles was the Third General Hospital, a branch of the main institution. Her work sometimes took her into the other hospitals in a nearby converted hotel and university. At one of these hospitals, *patients from my former stations kept appearing. I kept the day-room, gave out supplies, started games, and got up a Halloween party. A patient from the 7th helped a lot in that,—Foster. Foster had trench feet before, a quiet pleasant-looking young man, with serious brown eyes and a shy smile. He'd long been back in combat, but a shell killed a buddy and knocked him out. "I came to in the Aid Station. I told the Doc I'd be all right, if I could rest a little. They have me down as a nervous case; but I'm all right." Meanwhile, he made witches and black cats and pumpkins for me. And was sent out the day before the party!*[4]

Determined to make the Halloween party a special event, Natalie managed to overcome the problem of no refreshments. *Much drama, with my phoning loyal officer friends, getting materials for—what a treat!—chocolate éclairs! The old French chef, who looks 100, and is called Pápá by everybody, was a-twitter with sympathy. And we had our éclairs, with hot choco-late, and the patients were wildly enthusiastic. A patient as a ghost handed out fortunes (typed by N. Scott). There was a dunking for apples; biting apples on a string; pinning the broom on a witch; and the absurd "hot-air ping-pong". A Hawaiian patient made a marvelous Hula costume and lovely leis, and danced the Hula while another patient accompanied him on the ukulele. The MC was an officer-patient who had been on a national radio hook-up: he sang, too. A huge success! When we opened the doors at 6:30 to let the patients in, they swept in endlessly. But I stood on the steps and roared laugh-ing directions, and steered some to the games upstairs.*[5]

Moving North

In November, Natalie was transferred again, this time farther north in Provence to a large, brand-new hospital. *I had orders to leave for the North. Cunningham went over for dinner with us the evening before I left. She, Kay, and I went to a gay little bar in town. Americans and French civilians crowded the bar; the drinks were $1.00 a cocktail (but big cocktails, and potent). Kay saw me into a six-by-six with my bags the next morning. Then a cloud-burst! We took our enlisted men, dripping, into the ambulances with us. The truck turned over on its side in a deep ditch! But the road was like glass; the main road was blocked by accidents, and we had to take a détour, and one of our ambulances nearly went into a ditch, too. We arrived* *shivering and damp,—to see a line of ambulances drawn up and patients being admitted! We dashed at once to work.*

An enormous variety of practical problems hampered operations. This new hospital had been filled with patients even before supplies arrived or were unpacked. Its two buildings were *part of a huge new French hospital set-up. I was the only one of our unit here, and there were no supplies. I dashed down the long walk, to the road, to hitch-hike into town. Hailed a jeep, which stopped at once, and I was greeted with, "have you a kiss for me?" Which annoyed me, till I saw that it was a Captain who had come over on the boat with me and whom I'd seen in Naples! Nobody was in ARC Hq to Okay my requisition for supplies. But I went to the Warehouse (having cajoled Bradshaw, of ARC Transportation, a grand GI whom I'd known in Oran, to drive me the miles out to the Warehouse!). There, I talked our supply man into filling my un-okayed requisition, as an emergency.*

Here Natalie briefly encountered a celebrity turned volunteer worker. *Madeline Carroll was there. She had come down on the train with the patients we had just received, and they had been enthusiastic, not only over her status as a movie star, but over her tirelessness in looking after them, and her friendliness. We chatted as we waited for respective supplies, and I told her of the men's approval, which pleased her very much. She sent them her love. The message pleased them a lot. She is quite pleasant, natural manner, and any artifice is not apparent. She seems very interested in her work. . . .*

I was out of bed before seven in the morning, having to be ready to receive the supplies which were to be sent at eight. What a morning! Supplies had to be dumped, as I had no storage space. Finally got loan of a room. Finally got things unpacked and that afternoon took all the needed things thru the wards! Very welcome. For days, I was the only ARC here. Then Sylvia came, but had to be hospitalized for her cold. I am still doing two-thirds of the hospital,—and like it!

Our quarters are bleak, but improving. The house is old, tall and ungainly, splotchy looking. Somebody called it, Wuthering Heights. Which I corrected to Withering Heights. Alias, the Haunted House. No furniture but an army cot; but we are gradually making things of the packing boxes. The patients came in the day after the hospital was acquired, practically nothing unpacked; bedlam ever since. Hammering, building, moving. But the management is good, so things are going smoothly. Very capable and quick. No dayroom as yet,—only hopes! The Px was several days setting up, so I had to give out rations and all toilet articles. And so it goes. I enjoyed the excitement.[6]

Here Natalie and Martha Robinson resumed their Newcomb Alumnae supply program for the patients. Prior to the transfer, Natalie told her, *Those air-plane models are always the greatest treat. Also, if you could find any articles that we could include in the Xmas boxes that the ARC provides for the patients, I'd simply love that. I don't know that you'd have enough money, tho, because we'd have to allow for 1,000. Perhaps you could get something wholesale, in that quantity. I thought about white pocket-handkerchiefs. Or, failing that, perhaps a sturdy little note-book or address-book. The men love those. ARC used to give out little note-books but we haven't had any for ages. Maybe you could send us some things for Xmas decorations,— little Santa Clauses, and red candles. If none of that is possible, that Belfast cord is always tremendously welcome, as is the cro-chet cord, too, which latter is used for making picture-frames.*[7]

A reply from Martha assured her that notebooks would be forthcoming. Natalie wrote back in mid-November that *we are so thrilled over the prospect of the note-books! They'll be a grand addition to the Xmas box. Do you think that you could wrangle a bolt or two of dark blue denim out of our old friend, Jo Haspel? Our patients long for ditty-bags. As it is, the poor stretcher cases when they go out, simply can't take care of their belongings, tossed loose on the stretcher with them. Even for the ambulatory, it's very hard. Nothing to put their things in. Hate to ask anything else when you've done so much! Am going to write to Christ Church Guild to-night. The cig. holders are a constant help.*[8]

The 1944 letters between Natalie and Martha consistently exchanged concerned news about Martha's four sons, Hilda's son Arthur (a marine veteran of Guadalcanal, Rendova, Munda, and later Okinawa), the sons of their friends, and Natalie's two nephews, all in the war. Sidonie's youngest son Bino had gone into the paratroopers and would be going to the Pacific. In late October, the news had arrived that July Waters' son Peter was downed over German territory, feared dead. *Then the news about Peter Waters distressed me so much, coming just on top of that that Bino is being sent to the Pacific. As for Bino, I know that often paratroopers are held in their own theatre of operations and given quite a bit of training there. On the other hand, one never knows whether or not at some critical moment that they may not be sent right in. And it's by no means cheering. As for that darling young Peter, I am hoping so much that July is going to get word that he is in a German prison camp. Do let me know.* Martha had been fearful due to no word in weeks from her boys Jack and Bobby. *Am so glad that you've heard from Jack. But as to Bobby, if he were missing or injured, you would surely have some word.*[9]

The two also discussed the political fortunes of President Roosevelt, who was then seeking election to an unprecedented fourth term. Both were unshakeable advocates for FDR, Martha assuring Natalie that the president would prevail. Natalie replied, *Was so relieved over the election. An amazing percentage of the men were, too. Of course it happened just when our radios were still not unpacked, and they hounded me hourly for news. You couldn't find an isolationist with a magnifying glass! And they certainly put the international question first of all. And think R. is the man for it. May inspiration not be lacking to him!*[10]

Airplane models and crossword puzzles arrived from Martha in early December. *They are wonderful, the best you've sent. The note-books have all arrived. I know what a labor it was to get all those packages done, the buying, the primary labor of getting the money. Everybody is simply thrilled over all the things for the patients. Even my lethargic AFD and Recreation Director have been fired into life. Our ARC Xmas packages have not yet arrived, and it looks as tho they may not come for Xmas so it's especially nice to have these.* Natalie also shared pleasant news of the AFD giving her a flattering appraisal report, *while Mary Terry, the Sec. and I were nominated from the ARC for the House Committee of the Officers Club; lots of nurses too. A nurse and I were elected, as woman members. Nice, as it shows a certain affection for me in the unit, and I like that. Went to a very swagger party last evening, Staff Dinner, given by a one-star Gen. with lots of eagles around. Wonderful food, and quite agreeable. The only time I've stepped out in ages. I've been invited, but haven't really felt inclined.*

Natalie closed her early December letter with a brief war assessment. *The news is discouraging to-day. The picture of our grimly struggling men in the frightful cold up there is too much with me, alas.*[11] The Battle of the Bulge would soon break out in the frigid north.

One Christmas gift that Martha sent, at Natalie's request, was Homer's *Iliad*, Natalie's favorite classic of the ancient world. *I came back from the wards at ten the evening it arrived, very worn more in spirit than in body, and I began to read it. And its vigor and freshness and fullness of life breathed new life into me. I read some of it every night. In the last war, it was Keats. I happened to know so much of Keats by memory; Keats is so easy to memorize. But there is something about these things that are for 'all times': they give the confidence and strength. Keats is softer by far, in comparison with Homer, but both are of the eternal good of life. And one needs reassurance these times. Sometimes I wonder how people at home would feel, used to strength and wholeness, if they suddenly walked thru just one of our wards. A 19-year-older, on his face, both legs in plaster, knees bent unnaturally and feet in the air, legs held apart by a plaster bar; in another bed, a boy 22, paralyzed from the neck down; arms gone; legs gone. And one tries to produce hope, and faith in life. And tries to have it.*

You may read all you like but the actuality is different. And day by day I go, and try to find the ray for this one, and for that one,—and to hold one for myself. And then sometimes at the end of the day I feel myself done. You know, it isn't so much for just now. But I saw the last war. Just now, there is fresh sympathy for these boys; ready understanding. They have faith in young wives who have loved them, who will receive them with anguished sympathy. But I look ahead into the years. How many will keep the sympathy fresh, the understanding fresh? They themselves are sustained now by the drama, by their 'buddies', who 'know how it is'. But there are the years ahead. How many of them and of those in their circle will stand the test? How many love them adequately?

Sometimes I wish that I were like two of my fellow-workers who are untroubled by a spark, to whom all the patients appear in a lump as 'cases'. Yet I don't really; for I know that just thru the 'suffering with them' (the literal translation of sympathy) I have been able to give some of them a bit of solid help. So little, to so few.

This must all sound very discouraging. I've had a very strenuous week, in fact, weeks. But it's really part of saying what a perfect Xmas gift was Homer. It made me remember so freshly my old friend, Dr. Smith. You know, he used to send me pages at intervals, of his translation, after I was in Taxco. The last one I received was of Achilles' address to his horse. And it is not only the Homer itself, but old Dr. Smith's really admirable conception of life, his faith in life, his vast scope of vision. He was a fine old fellow, and gave me a solid treasure of thought; and added no little to my appreciation of Homer.

Meanwhile, package after package from practically all of the directory of New Orleans, has been arriving, with those nice little note-books, which will make a grand addition to our Xmas packages. You have a lot of value, Kmarfoonie, with your realization of what the little things can mean. When Xmas comes, and our packages have these little books, there'll be a grin of pleasure on so many young faces, and requests for addresses; and a satisfied air in producing the book. So good to find something, any little thing, that brings a bright look.[12]

Notes from a Hospital

Following this letter, the Germans mounted their *ghastly Nazi drive,* the Battle of the Bulge, which made this Christmastime a very troubled one. Two of Martha's sons were in the midst of it, one on the ground, the other a pilot. The words and cooperative action of these two old friends, Natalie and Martha, reveal their strong work ethic, their deep mutual affection, and their invincible determination as patriots to win their private war to defeat Germany.

Natalie wrote too of the plight of the French civilians. *There is little to buy here. Everything sky-high. It is incredible. I feel so sorry for the people. I don't know how they manage to live. Quite impossible to buy any underwear, any sheets, or tablecloths, or any wash-cloths. There was a ration of fish made available this past week, a certain weight was allocated each person. Naturally, all goods go up in price in proportion to the cost of food-stuffs, so that all prices are really formidable. There is no wool of any sort to be had, of course, and I do hate to see these poor people shivering along in this cold. Well. The French have an unquenchable vitality, and they will make a come- back ultimately. It's quite cold, but by no means so cold as it is farther north; and I suffer thinking of our men out in fox-holes, and feel ashamed of the comparative comfort in which we live. After which I got up and put on some woolen GI socks over my silk ones, and now expect to be yet more comfortable.*[13]

Natalie would later reflect on her work in Provence. *We became a ZI hospital (for very seriously wounded soldiers who likely would be sent home upon discharge) for the most part. I loved my work there. I had all of the most serious surgical cases, both the officers' wards (Med. and Surg.), the EENT patients (including of course the pitiable blind, of whom there were not many, fortunately) and four large medical wards. It was a large order, and meant being on my feet the entire time. I had seven of the eleven wards in the hospital. Each ward con- sists of two or more large long rooms, together with small rooms for the most serious cases. My only lament was that, with so many patients to see, I could not give as much time as I would have wished to certain patients. Of course each patient who is ZI'ed (you know, I suppose, that that means Zone of the Interior) has a handicap more or less grave. There were lots and lots of amputations; colostomies, a condition that somehow seems to demand a difficult psychological readjustment; the blind; some paralyzed from the waist down; and some few par- alyzed from the neck down. The pity of it, the tragedy of it,— sometimes it seems a sensible weight one is carrying around inside somewhere.*[14]

There was a young Hawaiian, an only son, paralyzed from the neck down. He lay quiet always, with his large dark eyes infinitely sad. I always managed a chat with him; and one day, as the doctor was passing, Harold (the Hawaiian) laughed aloud. "How did you manage to make Harold laugh?" the doc- tor asked me curiously, later. "I'd be ashamed to tell you", I smiled. "It was so silly." "Good for him, tho", he answered. "Don't forget to give some time to my colostomies, will you?" I was already doing that, of course. Another case was a blind sol- dier named Schultz. *Schultzie, I called him. He was not gloomy;*

but he simply lay on his bed, or sat on it. His buddy, who had lost one eye, fed him, and led him to the latrine. I stopped and chatted with him. "Have some beechies [gum]", I said, and put some in his hand. He took them, but handed the package back to me to open.

"Sonny", I said cheerily, "I'd love to do anything for you that you couldn't do for yourself. That's what I'm here for. But you're a big old husky boy; and after awhile you wouldn't like being waited on. You'd hate it, really. For instance, you can open those beechies all right". It hurt me to say it: one's impulse is to forestall those pathetic groping hands, to do everything for them; and one actually suffers with the effort to refrain. But I felt it was the only thing to do. My line was something like this: "You've lost something important: It's terribly hard to get used to that. But after all you can't do anything with what you've lost. So the thing to do is to concentrate on what you have left. And you have a lot. Why, you can get around this ward by yourself; you can come to know who's in which bed, and go around and chat with them. You would finally get around in any case to getting a lot from hearing that you used to get from sight; but you can do it more quickly if you make a definite effort. You can get to recognize one person from another by the footsteps, even before they speak. That sort of thing. How would you like to learn to type?"

Not all that in one breath, naturally, but by degrees. And that red-headed Schultzie was soon all over the place. He learned in ten days to type, so that slowly and laboriously he wrote a readable letter to his mother. It began with deer-hunting, and saving him some venison, and some sassy messages to his brothers; and then, in a new paragraph, "And by the way, I don't think I told you that I was hit in the eyes. I lost both of them. But I get around all right. And I have learned to typewrite. I am writing this. So you see I am all right. And don't worry."

One wants to 'bus right out crying' on reading such a letter. But there was no sham about Schultzie's cheer. One day I found him downstairs: he had got there by himself. Another day, he called to me as I entered the door, "How are you, Scottie?" and grinned delightedly, because he had recognized me by my footsteps. Schultzie would help new blind patients. I told him of one who was desperately sad. Schultzie found his bed by my directions, and joshed him into cheeriness.

Capt. Baisinger, the doctor, was interested in such results, that these blind boys be started at the earliest possible moment in developing initiative and self-confidence. I started Schultzie to eating unaided, and now all of them are made to do that.

There's a story in every personality. I could go on and on. There was Nollen! He had lost his eyesight, and one leg, which was paining him terribly, and two fingers. Just after he left, someone was speaking of him. A new patient sat up. "Why, those Medics were attached to us. You shoulda seen him the day of the Invasion. We ran into mortar fire and Nollen was hit pretty bad, but he went right on taking care of the fellows that were hit, and wouldn't turn in himself. He's a swell guy". He had belonged to the detachment of a hospital near us, but had volunteered for combat service. When he came in, he asked hesitantly if it would be too much trouble to phone his old outfit. "I think some of the fellows would come over", he said, anxiously. "I'll go this minute", I said. And did. In no time a group of Nollen's friends were there. Poor fellows: they could hardly muster a word, because they were so shocked to see the shape he was in. They managed some throaty greetings. It was Nollen who made the visit gay.

One day, he was having an especially bad time with his leg. I saw him gripping the side of his mattress at intervals convulsively with the fingers of his good hand. I spoke to him and he had his one weak moment. "Oh, Scottie", he whispered. "Why couldn't they have finished me off, why did they have to just leave a piece of me, like this?" It seems almost insolent for the healthy to try to offer consolation in such a case. But what can one do? "Hank, old boy, you have the most valuable thing of all: a strong spirit and the gumption to face things. But you surely have a right to a weak moment. I know you're having an awfully tough time and lots of pain; but I heard they are to change the dressing this afternoon, and you'll feel easier. And that wonderful old backbone of yours will stiffen up again. And think of that pretty little wife of yours, how deeply thankful she'll be to have you back again, and how proud she will be over how you're seeing this thru". He held onto my hand, squeezed it without a word. I simply stood there and stroked his forehead with my other hand. And soon they came and took him off for the dressing.

That evening, Hank had his visitors in gales of laughter

again. The night before he left, the order came thru for a Silver Star for him. The OD was determined to make a proper ceremony of it, somehow. The C.O. was out, but he got Col. Fitz, the Executive Officer. There weren't many patients able to stand, but those that could, and the wardmen were all called to attention. Col. Fitz spoke impressively, and Hank had his Silver Star.

Ward after Ward of these boys. Yet the general spirit in the surgical wards is gay and bright. They tease each other unmercifully, make jokes of their afflictions. "I already have one foot in the grave", is a favorite with the amputations. Or two feet! Then they have bragging contests as to what they are going to do when they get their new plastic legs.

The more fortunate patients are taken in by this show. Before one group was leaving, a patient who was to go back to combat was standing joking with the "amputations". "You guys are lucky", he said, suddenly serious. "I'd swap places with any one of you". A sudden shocked silence fell. Then one of the amputations said grimly, "Guy, you don't know what you're saying. I'd swap with you right now and take my chances on what might happen up there, to have that leg back again". The others looked a shy assent, then, suddenly shame-faced, began hastily joking again.

One 19-year old had lost both legs between the knee and ankle. He had been given the Silver Star incidentally. He was a Medic, and had gone deliberately into a mined terrain to help the wounded. He was a monkey in his wheel-chair, all over the place. He managed to attach combat boots to his stumps, setting the soles of the boots on the chair base. He wheeled himself around the ward, saying to other patients, "Gee! We sure got a swell doc: Look, he's made my legs grow out again".

This little Friedman was responsible for quite an achievement of ours. A play, Junior Miss, was in town, and I was getting up a list of patients able to go. We sent even men with one leg, since they could go on crutches to the trucks and be hauled up and down by comrades. But Friedie couldn't go on crutches, naturally. Just for fun, he bounced himself up and down on his bed like a five year old, saying teasingly, "I want to go, Miss Scottie. Can't I go, Miss Scottie?" I went to the doctor. "What about Friedman, Captain? He's so light. If some of the husky patients would carry him, might he go to the show?" "Sure", said the Captain, heartily. So off he went. It gave me a thought. If we could get long cars, seven-passenger, for instance, what about double amputations, and even the stiff cast patients, who could sit up? The other workers fell for the idea. Maureen and Sylvia, who have many 'contacts', acquired the cars. We got a 'strong-arm squad' and such a to-do! Making the lists, getting doctors' permissions, and so on. And then getting those crippled boys into the cars! We had four rows of front seats roped off for them at the show. And off they went. What a kick those boys got out of that expedition! We got forty-nine of them off finally. They talked of it for days.[15]

I failed to boast of my contrivance of a reading-board for the paralyzed. Sylvia wanted to wait until the craft shop for our patients was opened; but I couldn't bear it: why should they wait! One morning, I was along with our POW, so I aired my German (language, not POW); we discussed, and drew pictures. Finally we evolved a reading-board that can be moved to hold the book in proper position, even with the patient flat on his back. The only help he needs is when he has read the two open pages,—then a comrade will turn the page for him. Boys who have lost one arm, I set to writing with their left hands, pinning a sheet of paper to a reading-board with thumb tacks. Always something new: one day I heard a guitar in pain. I walked in the ward, and there were two boys, one with a right arm gone, one with a left one missing, trying to get together on the guitar, all the ward grinning at them. They finally managed fairly well, after a few trying days!

One quiet young patient and several of his comrades were wounded, and their company had to push ahead. They were left there for four days; he had a bad head-wound, but tried to crawl around and help the others; but they all died, one by one, except him. He would spot a K-ration can, crawl, open it with his teeth, and eat the contents. Only remembers things in spots. A burial squad came along finally, and found him. Meanwhile, with the terrible cold, he had trench feet so badly that both feet had to be amputated.

Such an experience would seem enough to scar him for life, psychically; and surely it will leave its mark. He is rather quiet, but responsive. It is remarkable how cheery are the amputation cases. They razz each other, and talk cheerfully about the merits *of artificial legs. I tied red ribbons on all the traction cases on Xmas day. As I was trying to affix a bow on one, the others watched, and finally one said, impatiently, "Go on: hold your nub up better, so she can get at it". The surgery is so vastly superior to that of the last war, that one can only be intensely thankful,—even tho there is still so terribly much pain. You know, of course, that the wounds are thoroughly cleaned, then closed up in plaster, and left for days. Naturally, after a few days, they begin to smell, more and more strongly. It's quite trying till one gets used to it, and some of the more sensitive patients feel humiliated about it, and find it revolting. The other day, one of the boys said, anxiously, "Miss Scottie, do you think you could buy me some cheap perfume?" He wanted it to overcome the smell of his cast! So I lent him a bottle of my Lenthéric toilet water. The combination, I must say, was worse. But he felt better about it, so we all humored him.*

All of these men are so anxious about their wives,—longing for them so, yet half-apologetic to go back in such shape. What a test it will be of the women! For a few days, a few weeks, a few months,—the drama will uphold them. But will they have the backbone to hold up thru the years? There is too much over here to be faced for one to face that, too; but it keeps haunting me. As for the men here who get letters that their wives or girl-friends 'can't wait for them any longer',—that's another matter. It's as cruel a thing as can happen. Poor girls who bare such paltry values—but more pitiful the men who have been counting on them, finding the sustainment they so much need in the thought of them. I feel that such women should have their heads shaved, as was done with the Collaborationist women over here![16]

When I took the patients to the show, I took them behind the scenes, and all the cast chatted with them, autographed programs, and made them have a wonderful time. A new blind patient hadn't wanted to go. He was tall and angular, with copper-colored hair, a quiet sort and rather older than the others. "What's the use?" he said bitterly. "I can't see anything". "But you're not deaf", I remonstrated gently. "Just go to please me", I finally coaxed. "And afterwards you be perfectly honest with me, about whether or not you enjoyed it".

One of the girls in the cast devoted herself to him behind the scenes. When I went back on the wards that evening, the first thing I heard was a throaty chuckle from Adler. Before, he had retreated into a hurt corner of his mind; but from that time on, he was like Schultzie, visiting around.

The other patients are so kind to the blind,—in the bluff hearty man-like way that is so truly tender. "Gee", said one of the patients in hangman's row (traction cases) when I came back from leading Greenie (one of the more recent blind patients) to a band-concert. "I sure feel sorry for that guy." The speaker had an arm and leg in traction, and a head wound besides! Daily little vignettes multiplied,—such as a slender young patient busily scrubbing away at the big paw of his buddy, who was minus one arm, cleaning him up! They are always taking care of each other in so many ways; and have such a brisk, matter-of-fact way of doing it,—and accepting it. For instance, a little group playing cards looked around and saw that one of the blind boys was alone. They glanced at each other, and by mutual consent, moved over.

"Mind if a couple of us sit on your bed, fellow? Too many things on mine", and they swept him into the card talk. "This monkey thinks he can play pinochle, see?" And so on.

I must mention the Hawaiian boys, a fine group, one we can be proud of. The other men say they are marvelous fighters. One—Abis—was a carpenter, the leading hand in building my furniture,—entirely their own idea. One, Oseki, was ill a long while, threatened with TB, so gentle and uncomplaining. His nurse told me that he has the Congressional Medal of Honor. I can't vouch for that: he never spoke of it certainly. We've had lots of Puerto Ricans,—nice boys, too. I used to get them together calling them the 'Club Puertorriqueño', and we all prattled Spanish happily together. Another happy reunion was of several La. negroes,—I found several, 2 from N.O. They enjoyed each other hugely. Here was one big fellow from Acadia,—I think it was. He had lost both legs above the knees, poor fellow, and was as good a patient as possible. I paid him all possible attention. And one day I explained the rehabilitation program to him. He brightened up noticeably after that: he had been worried over what would happen to him.

Our hospital has hit a very good note. On the whole, it manages a good mean between the GI attitude and laxness,—a genuinely friendly atmosphere. All the staff, doctors, nurses, and wardmen, seem genuinely concerned. For instance, when we took the stiff-cast patients to the show, two of the doctors stopped Sylvia and me to thank us! I laughed, and said, "We wanted to thank you for letting them go. So we're all happy". Sylvia, Natalie's cohort, had been the AFD in Naples with whom Natalie had been so displeased, a situation by then behind these two war-hospital veterans.

A Wish Granted

Ironically, in January 1945, as Natalie was deeply absorbed in her satisfying work in Provence, she received approval for an evacuation hospital position. *It is possible that I may get an Evac Hospital at last. I have been approved for such by the HQ of ARC. The unit does not at all want me to leave, and argues with me until it becomes embarrassing. But I really want to go. I have to wait until there is an opening.*[17] This long-awaited reassignment suddenly became official on February 1, 1945. Natalie would join the Ninth Evacuation Hospital in northern France. *My heart is really torn at leaving here, however. But I have asked for Evac work ever since I've been over, and now when it is offered me, I feel I can't refuse. The excitement part of it appeals to me so much,—that, of course is why I asked in the first place. But now I am debating whether it is not a selfish view-point, since even the ARC supervisors stress the point strongly that I get a long way with patients, working with them over long periods (three weeks to three months) as we have them here.*

I could have turned down the offer; but I didn't. I was released from duty here as of Sunday; but of course have been going to the wards anyway. My patients, who are having such a bleak spot in their poor young lives just now, at best, reproach me; the doctors reproach me; the nurses reproach me. And the Red Cross staff has argued itself at me endlessly. They've all been so kind in the hospital here, so over-appreciative. And perhaps I may be making a most awful error! The old heart has hung like a heavy weight within me. So many people have given me little presents, affectionate and flattering speeches to me. I could practically bust out crying.

My reasoning was—and is—so many people have said, "Oh,

you can only give out tooth-brushes in an Evac". Whereas in the last war, I didn't even have tooth-brushes, but I know that I got somewhere with the patients; and tho it is true that I did nursing then (with the French) I could have been very busy without ever doing any nursing. After all, it is there that patients often have to learn for the first time of the extent of their wounds, the loss of a limb, or of eyesight, perhaps,—with such difficult adjustment to be made. They come in worn with combat, and often have to face an adjustment to a lifelong handicap. I feel that they need and could be given much more than 'tooth-brushes'. I've asked for a transfer to the Pacific area (since Bino is over there) after the war is over here. This would be a good time to try out the Evac work, so that if I get to the Pacific, I would then know where I felt most useful.

As you may guess, I feel a strong twinge of homesickness for the unit and shall always have an affection for it. That's probably why I'm not in a more humorous vein.

You know, I love the feel of adventure, a little spice of danger, movement, change, and such. But I'd feel a complete heel if I let such a personal motive influence me. You can see where I must distrust myself. The die is cast now, so off I go. Strictly entre nous, I gather that my assignment has something to do with a personnel problem,—one fellow worker, well-intentioned, but difficult to work with; but that mustn't be mentioned in these parts.[18]

Only a week later Natalie was at work in northern France, on duty in her Seventh Army Ninth Evacuation Hospital. *And plenty of mud. The Red Crossers tell me that often one hears the artillery from the front. I must admit I haven't. But then in Marseilles, I always thought the ack-ack at the beginning of an alert was somebody moving furniture overhead. The thing had to get really in full swing before I realized its true nature. Planes zoom in fairish numbers overhead. The officers and men are wearing helmets. I passed a couple of tanks riding along quite royally on their enormous carriers. It all looks more business-like than my former station.*

Then Natalie, in a letter to Martha, retraced the events that brought her to this new assignment with the U.S. Seventh Army, by then aligning on the southern flank of Patton's Third Army.[19] Her departure had begun with a visit to Kay Parsons and Em

Cunningham at the Third General Hospital, and a farewell party. *That evening, officers appeared in force, and a party was on! Whiskey appeared, and things were very merry.* Kay returned with Natalie the next day for another party, this one with Natalie's patients, one that Natalie herself had planned by starting a rumor in the hospital that Roosevelt was in town.

We fostered the rumor. Meanwhile, we had planned a birthday party for all patients whose birthday was in January. They had a special table, decorated, with places for each one, and a present with his name on it. All the other patients were invited, too. Maureen is good at make-up. And the feature of the party was Visiting Celebrities. She borrowed a large Cadillac; the MPs lent themselves complete with motorcycles and sirens as escort. And one of the patients was dressed up as Pres. Roosevelt, and swept in in state, sirens screaming. The Hoax made a great hit. A 'fireside' had been rigged up in the Day Room, and the 'President' gave an amusing fireside chat. After that, there were various other celebrities. Ice-cream and cake afterwards, the first we've had since we've been in France, so it was ardently appreciated.

Those last few days! There is something more poignant in leaving a group formed by the turbulence of war. I understood that I could take only a bedding-roll and valise, and my musette-bag and of course that most undramatic panoply of modern warfare with which we always go encumbered: the 'pistol-belt' that never knows a pistol, the first-aid kit (the contents of which, I blush to say, I have never investigated), a canteen, the gas-mask complete with cover (some kind soul had packed mine full of cigarette packages) and the helmet. There was one last farewell party for Natalie, given by the nurses and doctors, in a tiny bar just completed beside the Officers' Mess. *The walls are red and decorated with all our signatures in white, copied in large with startling accuracy. Everybody gathered including the Colonel. Everybody scolded me for leaving, and I was much toasted, and scolded,—and kissed.*

Natalie traveled by train to Lyon. Her friend Em Cunningham, also being transferred, met her at the station. *The good soul had risen early, borrowed a Cadillac from a General whom we used to know in Oran and come to meet me. Style!*

Natalie had one day to enjoy the city, staying in a hotel, the

Cloche, *where I had stayed years ago. C. was installed in one of those vast pleasantly stuffy old-fashioned French rooms. Besides the radiator, there was an open fire! We dashed in for breakfast just under the line.* Natalie was invited to lunch by a French Red Cross woman, *chic and charming,* who knew young Supervielle, son of the writer, Jacques, *whom I had the pleasure of knowing, with his beautiful wife, in Granada, and Paris, years back.*

Tony, the general's driver, remained at their disposal, driving them about *in our grandeur. It was altogether the first day of real complete leisure I've had since I've been overseas. We (with Em) relaxed after luncheon in front of the fire, in kimonos; had a couple of leisurely high-balls, and chatted at random. Festivities started around five-thirty, then went into the very comfortable quarters of the General for a high-ball; and contin-ued, in the apartment of the Colonel, who was giving a large and very gay party,—uniformed figures standing about with high-balls in their hands, nurses and a WAC Lt. and lots of Army officers.*

Tony and the Cadillac whisked me in final grandeur to the billeting office the next morning at 8:30. Here Natalie encoun-tered various routing and bureaucratic obstacles, but a *kind young corporal dug up a friend who was being transferred up the line, in a jeep, with all his chattels in the rear.* "He doesn't go to your place either", said the Corporal aloud. "But he might make a detour", he added under his breath. He did. *Such a nice man, Meyer. A bus driver from Seattle, 47 years old. But no gripes about being here. He and the Corporal did twin Tarzans on that bedding-roll and somehow squeezed it in. We passed thru many villages. It was not cold, in spite of the wastes of snow. The road was bad in the home stretch. But we bounced jauntily into this very long town, about five o'clock and finally located a large building, the EM (Enlisted Men's) Club, of the ARC. Card-tables, ping-pong tables, dart-boards, in full swing; radios blaring out, all the gay pandemonium that our men like. It's good to think that they have such gathering places.*

Natalie had arrived in Lunéville, where she remained for two days of ARC paperwork before finally joining her new unit. She briefly lodged in a boardinghouse, *the Grey Horse, as the Americans call the Cheval Gris. It was Old Home week. Ran plump into nice old Blanche De Clerq who crossed from the States with me. She steered me into my large gaunt room, and then down to the transient mess. Afterwards saw Pope'y, also of the old Stork Club. She yelped cheerily to me, shrieked surprise and invited me for high-balls with several officers who were about. I meant to make it brief, so that I might come in to write letters. But all the lights went out; so I lingered in the candle light, and absorbed shrimp, and some Wisconsin cheese, both smoked and fresh, and finally took an icy sponge bath and fell into bed. Malcolm Lowe and some other Red Cross I had met before were there, too. Some of them were "Field Men", out with the troops, absorbed in their work.*

The morning went to making my status formal. The ARC office, a billeting office marooned in another of these mud-oceans. The supervisor was Mary Mock, whom I knew in Oran. I had seen her in Marseilles, and she told me that she had been asking for me for this job, for some time.[20]

The Invasion of Germany

Several days passed before Natalie finally reached the Ninth Evacuation Hospital, unceremoniously delivered *on the mail truck, driven by the Sergeant-Major in person, who is very nice indeed.* Her temporary room *was not so cute. There are four of us in it, three nurses and I. And they are grand girls, and have been angelic to me. And yesterday afternoon, a very nice officer sent me a bottle of champagne! Am planning a bingo game for to-morrow evening, and a Valentine party. Enough ambulants to make it worthwhile. Also a number of quite serious cases, very interesting, and I already know a lot of the patients quite well, and have them helping me—notably wrapping Purple Hearts.*[21]

This evacuation hospital was a mobile unit, moving forward with the Seventh Army as the battlefront moved. Personnel usually lived and worked in tents. Natalie shipped most possessions to Martha in New Orleans *to get rid of extra impediments as Evac Hospitals are given to moving without notice.* It was March before the opportunity came to write. *I have about 250 un-answered letters. There are several ex-patients to whom I continue to write for special reasons,—usually because they have very few people who write to them, and seem to count so much on my letters. I give them preference over my old friends.*

Still no more news of Bino, though Natalie knew he was in combat. Martha's son Jack, a marine, had recovered from wounds received in the bloody Pacific battle for Pelchiu Island and had returned to war. Martha's other three sons were also at risk: Bobby, an engineer in Belgium after the Battle of the Bulge, was putting in airfields and bridges; Tar, a pilot flying raids over Germany, had just been awarded the Air Medal; Tizo was serving aboard a merchant marine tanker in the Atlantic, location and destination unknown. Natalie learned that July Waters' son Peter remained missing behind enemy lines and that the sons of several of their friends had been wounded or killed in combat.[22]

Natalie wrote Martha: *At any rate, the war news is really most encouraging now, from the East as well as over here. And, as I had guessed, there is really infinitely more to be done for the men in Evac hospitals. One of the things that has developed, believe it or not, is that I am interpreting in German. Of course, I haven't spoken it for 18 years, except quite briefly to the POWs we had at the 70th* (in Provence); *and I was very brief with them. However, it seems to come back, enough at least to get across the necessary things. The hitch comes when encouraged, the Jerries sometimes start telling me their life histories at top speed.*

Our men are incorrigibly kind. They will say, in their best hard-boiled manner, "Oh, you ought just to let him die",—of some German patient. And the next thing you know, they are splitting a candy-bar with him. We are quite beautifully located in the midst of rolling fields, with a dark line of slender forest way off on each side of us. Have run across two New Orleans boys. One is named Walker, and his father has a butcher shop, on St. Claude near Canal. Not very ill, and was out before we left our last place. And he came back to see me,—an awfully nice boy. Another boy was such a youngster, Joe Salvatore, whose family lives at 1532 Dumaine Street, a mere infant, really, very appealing. If they have a phone, you might tell them that I saw him several times daily while he was here, just the sweetest and most loveable little fellow imaginable. Do let them understand that I couldn't give details even if I knew all the diagnosis. They will be given all that by the War

Department. I just want them to know that I took very special interest in him.

In March, word arrived that Martha's son Jack had survived the fighting at Iwo Jima, though the news was sketchy. Bino had also written Natalie from the Pacific, his exact location unknown. He had been wounded but not seriously. Natalie told Martha: *But O dear me, how I shrink from his going back into combat! I'm an awful weakling, I know; but paratroopers seem so terribly vulnerable. And of dear old Jacko, after that terrible Iwo Jima? It sounded an inferno, and I've been very much concerned about him. I was tremendously relieved to know that there is hope of Peter Waters being a POW. Do be sure to tell me details. I have always hoped that he was a POW, or was being concealed by some sympathizers somewhere. Am so eager to know what are the new developments that give 'hope'.*[23] *Am terribly eager for news of Bino. I want so much to be near where he is.*

Natalie's rapidly moving Ninth Evacuation Hospital plunged into Germany, advancing with the American Seventh Army as it invaded Bavaria in late March. *Things have been and are tremendously interesting at present. We get the news really fresh, and with so many graphic incidents described first-hand, that we feel finally as tho we've been right on the spot. We read the Stars and Stripes (when we get it) and speak of the news, whereupon a patient will pipe up, and say, "Oh, but that's all changed now: I just left there this morning". And forthwith enlightens us. Easter Eve and Easter day, we saw an unending procession of tanks go by. In fact, Easter morning the chaplain's sermon was blotted out at regular intervals by the tremendous din of their passing. We watched the tanks for long intervals. The men's faces were like gray masks, so thick with dust; but their teeth flashed white in smiles, when we waved. It was a stirring sight, I can tell you.*

We get about you know. One convoy of ours missed out as to the road, and we were told afterwards that we went thru a couple of towns before the infantry! The tanks had taken it, but the infantry hadn't come up. We were none the wiser. What queer people are these Germans! Do you know that lots of times they smiled at us. I was sitting in the very back of a 2 and a half ton truck, and the nurse next to me said to me, "Look: he's waving!" I thought she meant a GI, so I waved away merrily,—only to note with dismay that a German man was waving, and redoubled his waves delightedly on seeing mine. Some GIs in a town tossed us a few boxes of rations. We stopped there for a few minutes, and they came racing down with a whole pot of hot coffee. Nothing ever tasted better. Our tents came after we did, and our officers were most gallant, putting them up for us. One of them managed to find a couple of Army cots for me, after I had scouted in vain. A very dusty trip indeed. I might as well join the tanks. We're in a most picturesque spot. Sometimes I wonder if the Army hadn't gone aesthetic on us: we've been in such beautiful places. This one is a shallow valley, with a soft rolling green slope leading up to a narrow low ridge along which runs a road: we see every sort of vehicle silhouetted against the sky there. Off to the left is a lovely-looking town, with red tile roofs that remind me of my little Taxco. A slender toy spire rises, red, too, in the midst of it.

The roads are morasses of mud,—not the main roads, but those in our area. The trick is to go crab-style, sidewise, stepping in the ruts left by the ambulances and trucks. And often the mud on the sides of the rut is knee-deep! And the only overshoes I have are a pair of Arctics, two sizes too big for me, and a pair of galoshes that have been patched and have now come open, sole parting from body; but I wear them anyway. Going around in those Arctics was a trial, and I felt like Charlie Chaplin,—following my shoes around![24]

My present hospital is a very crack outfit, from the Roosevelt Hospital in N.Y. It was recently cited for Meritorious Service. They have not been too fortunate in their Red Cross workers. The one I am with has been here constantly, is a good soul, but ineffectual and concentrated on trifles,—goes her way with a worried glance over the shoulder at myriads of bugaboo regulations, and so on. It's difficult to do constructive work with her, but I'm having a go at it. I've been here two months. At least, I've been able to see the sudden flares on the horizon, presaging the muted roar of the artillery; have seen our men and their great engines of war on the road. In one place, we saw at least a hundred tanks go by, singly. A memorable spectacle, the men's heads rising above the turrets. We passed an artillery outfit on the move,—that particular outfit was based on our old Washington Artillery! They were eating spaghetti and meat-balls out of tins, *laughing and cracking jokes. They had innumerable pets whom they coddled shamelessly,—lots of puppies. And some baby wild boars! What élan they have.*

And to think I've actually crossed the Siegfried Line! We saw the green swell of it coming closer, we saw the low lift of those trim and deadly innumerable pill-boxes, rising out of the spring-green grass. Back of them were the rows of dragons' teeth, squat thick wedges, grotesque, reaching as far as we could see on either side. Behind them ran the 'tank trap',—or another tank trap, a canal. There it was,—somehow not at all like what I expected. Only I don't know what I had expected. And I had a sudden still sick feeling to think of our men facing all that. But they did,—and overcame it.

There were great splotches of destruction in the villages beyond. The first few were quite charming in architecture, chiefly half-timbered houses, with roofs steeper than our tents,—fairy-tale houses. Almost all of them displayed the white flag. Two tremendous factories had become vast tumbled masses of mortar and stone and twisted frame-work. A railroad ran parallel torn in many places. Lots of dead horses lay in the fields, and wrecks of every sort of vehicle. The surviving houses were all neat and trim, primly arranged immaculate curtains, and flower boxes. Lots of flowers in the gardens, masses of forsythia, apple-trees looking so ethereal in their virginal white blossoms, jonquils, narcissus, daffodils, pansies, violets. And somehow all of that made it the most shocking that these people could applaud, aid, and abet a Hitler! I promptly thought of knitting at the guillotine. Just the type.

We are in a quite lovely place at present, the Top of the World it seems. The land drops off in front of our area into a blooming green valley, with brown dots of villages set about. We can see seven of them from one point. We have a tent set-up, of course, two in a tent wide enough for our two cots. We all have bedding-rolls and sleeping bags, and are quite comfortable. We have a little kerosene stove that gives off a lot of smell and some heat. The food is plentiful and good, if not particularly delicate.

As for me, I've been working away to the full limit. Very heart-breaking and at the same time, most satisfying work. I can't tell you the admiration I have for our Enlisted Men. They have restored my faith in the country, actually. Their invincible endurance of pain, the complete simplicity of their courage, their ready keen wit, their sound common sense, their warm sympathy and sweetness, their acceptance of cruel handicaps, covering their dismay so completely with jokes and quirks, that lots of people are taken in by it. But Ole Mommer knows what's underneath. I'll go to bat for those lads any day.

As it is, I trot my fat (not quite so fat as when I left the States, I may say) self around hour after hour, day in and day out, and any time I feel I've done anything constructive for them, that's my big moment. It's really deeply satisfying to work with them. Reflecting on the enormity of the war machine and the human drama, Natalie added that *the thing that worries me about the sophisticated among our people is that they seem to have lost their wonder of life. They see only 'things' and how sad that is,—when there at hand is all the intricacy of relationships, the complex network of significances, the wild disorder and the fundamental awe-inspiring order beneath and thru it all. If I should lose my sense of all that, I'd go and graze with the other cattle!*[25]

In mid-April, Natalie was dispatched on a quick trip to Paris on ARC business—a two-day journey by artillery carrier, then train. The unexpected death of Franklin D. Roosevelt on April 12 had thrown the city into mourning. *The City was in its sweetest mood, the most benign and gracious of cities. Due to that most lamentable and tragic event, the death of President Roosevelt, everything was closed on Saturday. Monday was horribly hectic. In spite of that, I managed to have luncheon with Gene Jolas, the former editor of Transition. He had a 'friend' who served us a most delicious meal, in real old Parisian style,—an unbelievable treat.*

Natalie also had lunch with her old friend Fanny Ventadour, a New Orleans artist. Natalie was her maid of honor in her 1923 Parisian wedding—Natalie had written up the event for the front page of the *New Orleans States*. Her husband now dead, Fanny had struggled, trapped in Paris through the war with her two children. Her broadcasts over French radio were gaining in popularity, but her earnings remained meager and the French employed a strict rationing program. Still, Natalie found her optimistic, as she reported to Martha. *Had a luncheon with Fanny Ventadour, too. Food is so awfully scarce and so horribly dear. She served* *luncheon,—a can she had been saving for eight months. Her son Giles is a darling boy, very tall, about six feet, thin,—only 15. His trousers were really so shabby, but clothing is absolutely prohibitive in price. I felt really sad about it. They have a charming apartment, tho, and Fanny is really gallant in the way she faces things. She does a broadcast to the States. You should listen for it. It comes every day, it keeps them going. Jacqueline was there, so pretty and attractive. Incidentally, if you have a pair of cast-off trousers of one of your boys, do send it over to me.*²⁶ Natalie would see much of Fanny during her Parisian visits that summer.

On the Move

By the time Natalie returned to her unit, the hospital had moved sixty miles deeper into Germany. While traveling, Natalie composed a narrative of the people, places, and events since Lunéville, retracing her experience with the evac hospital. *The acting AFD received me cordially, she's in the good old forties, less than five-feet tall, amiable but meticulous. She formerly taught in a private school, very regulation conscious, and her first reaction to any idea is, 'They wouldn't like it', or, 'that's against a regulation'. She is well-disposed and agreeable.* Her name was Edith.

I learned that there had been practically no entertainment for the patients. So Monday, I had a Bingo night,—in fact, set up a schedule for one Bingo night, and one card-tournament night a week. And there was the Valentine party, just that week, so it had to be done in a hurry. It was a great success; I had at least 15 patients up there all day, cutting out hearts from some gold-foil and russet-foil paper (it comes as lining in certain ration boxes) and each patient in the hospital given one to send home to his girl. We acquired an accordionist from a neighboring engineering outfit. We had contests. But the greatest hit was the heart-pinning contest. We had a Varga girl on a dartboard. Roars of laughter greeted their blind-folded efforts. There was chocolate and heart-shaped cookies afterward.

Everybody had said that one never got to know the patients in Evac Hospitals but by the second day, I found myself facing the usual affectionate razzing and calls. The Valentine party was a wonderful introduction. Several of the nurses volunteered comments their patients had reported, 'Well, I never expected to get a kick out of kid games, but that really was a swell party last night". For Washington's birthday, I had a Whopper (Biggest Liars) Contest, some very amusing entries. The first prize was won by a patient with very bad trench-feet: he managed to attend the party because his buddy carried him up pick-a-back. For that occasion, I acquired a perfectly priceless negro band and quintet. They had a 'bass fiddle' made of a long round tin can, painted up extravagantly, and the music that black boy got from that extraordinary instrument was simply incredible.[27]

Written at Easter, Natalie's narrative was interrupted repeatedly by artillery barrages. *Thought I heard thunder, but it's grown into what is unmistakably a very big hearty barrage, artillery. We heard a barrage last night, and could see the soft sudden flare of light, followed at once by the sound, the loudest we've heard yet, tho, really business. 'Roar' never seems the right word for the sound,—it begins like a roar, full and heavy, but abruptly deadened; in a barrage, as now, the roars overlap and rumble and crash together. It's odd to hear it, and near at hand the girls in the other tents laughing and chatting,—and I clanking away with Penelope.*

In this unit, the ARC had abandoned the idea of taking supplies around to the patients. Edith simply left supplies on each ward. I'm agin that. For one thing, it seems an imposition on the nurses and ward man. For another, the patients often don't know that the supplies are available and so go on meekly doing without. When people at home give so liberally to the Red Cross, I feel they rate the satisfaction that comes with knowing that supplies which mean a bit of comfort to the soldier-patients are delivered. Edith made no objections to my taking supplies around. I found numbers of patients lacking tooth-brushes, paste, and so on. And I definitely feel that they like the little warmth of a personal presentation of these important objects. At our last set-up, Edith fell in line a few times and took supplies around, too. Red Cross work is full-time, if one is interested, and if there are not so many patients, it merely means that one can give more time to those that are there.

Their first move was a *great to-do. Our tents were set up in a stretch of rolling green fields. A damaged chateau was not far away. A few days later, they were setting off mines among the trees,—very martial sound, and columns of smoke rising. An officer gave me a treasure, a big piece of tarpaulin, and we put this on the floor, on top of the sturdy grass; then laid a blanket . . . which Edith had acquired, atop. And so we had a nice rug. A stool makes a night table for two. I have an oil-skin toilet case with generous pockets, and it hangs along side of the tent. My suit-case on a box holds a candle when we don't have electric lights. But the lights are always connected early in the game. In two days, our bath unit was up. Showers between 6 and 7:30 in the evening. I was busy every night until nine or ten at night. So I bathed in my helmet. The showers are in a tent, too,— everything is in a tent. We had to pass ward tents and all to get to them, duck-boards underneath them, and a bench for our clothes. Communal, of course. The ward-tents were set in rows. At first, they were all mud underfoot but in a few days, gravel was put in. The patients were on cots, except in Post-Op and Shock, where they had beds.*

Natalie organized a library and dayroom at the first location, her supplies then moving with them. *ARC has a very long tent, hard to make look attractive. The grass rapidly degenerated into mud. But the men came along anyhow, and sat around the stove. Our tables and the screen added a little gaiety, the books looked inviting, and there were always the piano, the radio, and a ping-pong table and other games to give allure. And many magazines. Patients came in rapidly, and I was constantly on the go, pattering about from tent to tent. At night the black-out demanded that the flaps be closed. We weren't there long. The men are often terribly tired when they come in, a long fatigue, aside from wounds. It is more unusual for them than for patients farther back, to see a woman,—American. They lend themselves readily to any sort of 'leading'. As for me, I lead them away from war-talk as soon as possible, once they've got recent (and always so vividly interesting) experiences off their chests. Their talk is great drama but I know it's better for them to be away on more tranquil topics.*

When they are suffering, a phrase always comes into my head, 'that strange world of pain'—suffering does make the normal ease of body seem remote, I know. Towards the end of War and Peace, that feeling is remarkably made present,—only there it is connected with approaching death. I sense it in the patients in great pain,—and I try to get them to see out of it, as it were, into our comfortable normal world of bodily ease,—to look ahead, to think of pain in terms of days and hours. We had an officer patient, headed for ultimate recovery; but he looked like a skeleton, had suffered a great deal, and his vitality was so low that he was mentally depressed, too. I spent quite a lot of time with him in snatches. One afternoon, I was in to see him for the third or fourth time that day. The nurse happened to come over. "Why, you're smiling! I didn't know you could do it", she said to him. Deviously, never once directly, but by suggestion, I had got it into his head as a conviction that he would really get well.

I worked the same thing on one of our GI patients. His attitude really changed remarkably. The afternoon before he was to leave, I went in to see him, and stopped a few minutes. "Will you come back after supper to see me?" he asked me. "Surely will", I said. "You know nothing sets up an old lady so much as to have a date with a good-looking boy". The others promptly razzed him and called him "Wolf". I went back duly, thinking he wanted me to write a letter for him. Not at all: he merely wanted me to visit! One of his buddies escorted me out, when they finally let me leave, at ten o'clock. "Sure am glad you came", he told me confidentially. "You know, he says you did more for him than a tonic." Which remark was of course an excellent tonic for me. Actually, of course, anybody can get the same results,—anybody who is interested and sees the problem. The French were wonderful about such insight.

Such intangible "services" occupy a lot of time,—the time best spent I feel. Wrote a great many letters for patients, in that set-up. "Don't worry; everything's okay; I'm feeling fine" even if their lips are stiff with pain. I've written the words endlessly— and always find them moving!

We had a number of German patients,—even a few civilians. There was one civilian woman. She was not in one of 'my' wards, but the nurse asked me to talk to her. She said, pitifully, "But civilians! Why should I be hurt?" I said, "It is hard, I know. But remember that thousands, probably by now millions of civilians have suffered as you are now suffering, or worse, in

Spain, in Poland, in Austria, Russia, England, Italy,—all of Europe!" She looked astonished, as tho the idea were quite strange! Two other German patients asked me if I had been in Germany since I spoke German. When I said, yes, they asked me where. As I named each town they said, sadly and reproachfully, "Alle weg,—all gone. Isn't it sad?" "Very sad," I agreed, "that not only those towns are gone, but so many others so fine and beautiful all over Europe. And worse still, so many human lives." They readily agreed!

In our tent set-up, we received some Russian patients, too,— ex POWs. Poor things: you have never seen such emaciation. One of our officers took pictures of them. Some of them had trench feet, simply frightfully. One had a terrible infection of his feet which had never been treated. Several had been prisoners in Germany at forced labor for a long time. They had some pretty awful tales to tell.

On May 1, they arrived at another new site, once again reestablishing their hospital of tents, *a tremendous high flat knoll with valleys around, the summits of low dark mountains. The minute I step out, I am aware of a soft flash of color. And the soft quick flush of light from the artillery rose up below and to the left, as I watched the moon climbing. I turned back, traversed our camp again, and followed a dirt road on beyond. And walked away from war. The orchards stretched on every side. Two birds were answering each other, Tcha-tcha-tcha-tcha-tcha. Twee. Twah. The air was fresh, everything clean and sweet from the soft rain. It was very soothing and lovely. No war was there. There might be mines there. I sighed, and turned back towards camp. So completely mad it all is.*

So many little incidents recur to me often. Returning to the long-deserted negro-band,—after the party that evening,—One of the patients was a little red-head from a small southern country town, with that fine voice and very flat 'a's' we all know,— and I enjoy. He had seven abdominal wounds, three colostomies, and was no more than a frame-work of a human form, worn and nervous. A miracle that they were pulling him thru. The little band, with the ready sympathy of negroes, was moved by the sight of the patients and they really 'gave'. Finally they started out. Van, the southern lad I spoke of, beckoned anxiously. "Cain't you ask 'em to play one more? En make it hot". It was so funny, and so pathetic. They played one more,—two more. And made 'em hot. I teased Van about it the next morning, and he smiled repeatedly. "Yes'm. I sure like music; looks like I like it more ennything else. That was sure good last night". He was so weak that his eyes would fill with tears at any emotion.

The surgery here is simply incredible, literally: you would never believe it possible that a human agency could draw men thru some of the desperate and heart-rending conditions in which they reach us. Sometimes, alas, in some few cases, it would almost seem better to let them go. But that is very rare.

Natalie wrote of the many stories she learned of the German people and the bewildering mass approval they had given Hitler. On one occasion in May 1945, she pondered differences in the behavior of German patients. *We had one Jerry medic who had been shot by his own men for going out to take care of a wounded American Captain. In many cases, they machine-gun their own prisoners. A 17-year old 'soldier' of the Wehrmacht looked up one of our men to surrender to. "They turned artillery on my town", he kept saying bitterly. The GI thought he meant that we had; but it turned out that the SS troops had done it when the little village, completely unable to hold out, had hung out white flags. The SS troops have made a cult of brutality,—devil's brood, like the Gestapo.*

Yet the supermen are not anything like so brave under pain as our men. With the same wounds that our men bear quietly, they groan, constantly, even scream, and call on a nurse every minute. A certain percentage of that may be ascribed, I suppose, to the fact that they do not know our language and have a subconscious fear that nobody knows of their pain. Whatever the reason, the fact remains that they are weaklings under pain compared with our men. Isn't that often true of cruel men?

I can't say that I hate them: in fact, I am quite kind to them. But I can't understand the stories of parties being given for German POWs in the States. With millions killed, suffering, tortured, starved and half-starved, homeless, maimed, and wrecked, because of this benighted people, I do feel each able-bodied one should be made to feel the guilt of his nation, not by our wreaking cruelty on them, since that would brutalize us; but by being kept apart, aware of the black stigma of their nationality, until they have shown a wish to redeem it. They are hypocritical. Nine-tenths of them claim that they were never for

Hitler; or that they are Poles; or anything else you like. As POWs, they kotow, salute everything and everybody. And all the while, most of them hate us and despise us. But their fawning endears them even to many of our people. They have none of the invincible self-respect of the Latin Peoples, who, as POWs, would be obedient and manageable, but never servile,—not even the Italians. The soldiers here are bitter over the parties given POWs: they themselves are fined $65 if they speak to Germans socially, 'fraternize'. Yet people at home entertain them!

Natalie noticed occasions when the Germans were truly pleased, or relieved, to see the Americans. *There are times when one evinces a real pleasure in seeing us. I suppose that they are so worn by war that they are glad to get it over at any cost. It is remarkable that every one of those European nations has a touching faith in our sense of justice, and in our decency. I must say we haven't let them down in that, and it's a good feeling. Even the Germans have faith in us.*

In the one area where I spoke of the orchards, we were merely bivouaqed. The next area was pretty, too—we were in a rolling valley just below the road, and that is where there were so many wild-flowers, including wild violets. They always make me think of Muddie, my mother, for when my brothers and I were children, we always had contests in the spring, riding out to the woods to see who could find the first wild violets for Muddie. Blue ones and white ones. She loved them. So long a time ago. That, too, is where I saw Bed-Check Charlie (we could actually see him in the dusk, he came in so low) machine-gun the truck. We had the patients in the hospital for treatment within seven minutes, no bad wounds except one. An extra gasoline tank had caught fire. The driver had shown great presence of mind, brought the truck to a stop, unhooked the flaming gasoline tin, and put out the blazing gasoline that had spilled with blankets.

Surrender

As they penetrated deep into Germany's interior, across the Rhine towards Munich, Natalie attentively observed *the scenery which was incredibly lovely,—one of the beauty spots of Europe blighted in so many spots by destruction. On one trip, we passed miles and miles of an abandoned ammunition dump. They, our men, were tranquilly and casually in occupation in a number of towns. In one, a GI was looking out of a second story window as tho he had lived there all his life. "How long have you been here?" I called to him. "Three days." "What's the name of the town?" He looked startled and exclaimed, "Heck, I don't know. Wait a minute: maybe some of the other guys know." He dived in, but reappeared shortly. "Nope. None of them know. But we're on our way."*[28]

About five we stopped in a village to see if we could get information. I looked up and saw some GIs drinking coffee on a balcony above us. They were calling down to us. "Is that coffee?" I exclaimed. "Sure. You want some?" "We won't be here long enough", I cried sadly. But down he came and soon all of us were drinking steaming hot coffee. The others were tossing rations boxes down to us, so we gobbled rations happily and arrived in a grand mood.

Natalie wrote more about her April ARC trip to Paris. *The news of Pres. Roosevelt's death seemed incredible. I heard it just before I left for Paris—a very long trip—on business, and I felt as tho I were moving thru black mists. Had to drive from nine o'clock until five in a weapons carrier to get to a station. There was a German city on the way, a vast industrial center; it was in utter and complete ruin, so that it seemed absolutely uncanny. The city was Mannheim. Yet people were moving thru its streets, rather dismally, but still purposefully. While our driver was asking directions, a German civilian came up. "Your president is dead". "Yes" I said, "I know". "I just heard it on the radio", he went on. "It is a great loss for you". "It is a great loss for all the world", I answered, "for he was a rare and a great man, with a great sense of justice. But our country, unlike yours, never depends on the will of one man alone. We'll carry on". He hesitated, bowed, and left. His face was impassive, and I never knew how he actually felt about it.*

Next day I went to Notre Dame for the Mass for Pres. R. I couldn't get near the church because of the tremendous crowds. General de Gaulle, our Ambassador, and lots of other distinguished people were there, and Fanny had offered me a card for the church. I was glad to be with the crowd. When they found I could speak English, they surrounded me after the ceremony and held me there for over half an hour talking. Lots of them had tears

*in their eyes when they spoke of the Pres. "A great hope for all
the world is gone", was the gist of their comment. The French
trusted him implicitly. I assured them that we would carry
on,—and wished I felt as much conviction as I tried to imply.
He had the international savoir-faire which few of our statesmen possess. What a great utter catastrophe that his death
should come at this time!*

*Only those who know the scene from that spot in front of
Notre Dame can realize how strikingly beautiful it was. I
inspected it lovingly as I talked to the French people. The crowd
was varied. All invited me to their houses.* Natalie wrote more
of time spent in Paris with Fanny Ventadour and Eugene Jolas,
an old friend who used to be editor of the *Transition*, now with
Psychological Warfare. Her walks through the city took her
thoughts back to the first war and her long residences there during the 1920s. She attended to her work in the Red Cross headquarters within the Normandy Hotel, where she had lived during
the summer of 1919. *I went to Pouquete to meet Fanny. I was
early and sat at a table alone, watching the passers-by on the
Champs Elysees, looking up often to the Arch of Triumph not far
away,—and slipped back in time years and years. Jacqueline*
(Fanny's daughter) *and I ranged the Left Bank later. I went by
my old Hotel Danube,* where Natalie had lived in 1927 as a journalist. *There were servants who had been there when I was
there, but my old friend, the 'patron', M. Jeantot, was dead.
Poor fellow: he had been a soldier in the last war, and when the
Germans came in he was informed that they had requisitioned
his hotel. He died of a heart attack! Another war victim.*

I can't tell you how I loved it! Every minute of being there (in
Paris). *It has always been for me a personality, and a personal attitude. I felt as tho it were saying to me, 'Welcome back,
my child. My dear child.' We sat in front of Deux Magots and
looked out at the familiar old church of St. Germain des Pres
and its little garden.* Twenty years earlier, Natalie had often sat
here, one of her favorite quiet spots in Paris, writing her "Peggy
Passe Partout" column as French children played about her. *A
young American soldier-photographer started talking to me,—
turned out he knew Peggy Guggenheim and daughter Pegeon.
Told us of seeing Gertrude Stein still about the Quarter. It was
so restful and so relaxing to slip back into the old atmosphere,*

to go into 'homes', and feel the quality of intimacy which war relationships usually lack. Fanny and Jacqueline and my good friend, Lucie Lee Kinsolving, and I dined at the Red Cross mess. We stayed chatting in the Hotel till nearly eleven.

When Natalie returned to her hospital site, it had moved forward. *Most of it had gone! All my things had gone. I spent one of the coldest nights in history, then bounced five hours* on another weapons carrier to catch up with the evac hospital.

And what a month it has been,—our armies struggling so bitterly at first, but moving steadily forward, and now sweeping so magnificently on. And to think that our great President has died, but also Mussolini and reputedly Hitler as well. When I heard that last news, I said at once it was a trick. The Russians seem to agree with me. It's an interesting psychological problem,—it's equally almost conceivable that he and Goering committed suicide, to leave a 'glorious' memory to the German people.

You can't imagine how exciting it was to receive the released prisoners. Their stories held us all entranced. We received prisoners with 'nutritional edema' I suppose it's called: their legs horribly swollen with thin-skinned blisters everywhere. One could poke the flesh with a finger and the dent would remain. A thousand or so French POWs were working in a city not far from the border. They were marched in forced marches over 200 kilometers, sleeping in the woods with no blankets and on that entire march had had only bowls of thin meatless soup to sustain them. They heard our guns. 100 or so of them managed to hide out as the order was instantly given to move on. The one who told me of it said that the next morning they started down to find 'the Americans', but he fell on the way. Others made it, and the Americans sent back to get the fallen ones. Another was so weak that he whispered to me, 'I'm too tired: I don't want to live. I truly want to die and rest'. I told him that in four days he would be smiling and reading the French book that I was leaving for him; and that in four weeks he would be back in France with a busy future in helping his great country get back on her feet. The first part of the prophecy certainly came true,—and I hope that the last may, as well.

Our own men had been prisoners for a short time,—none that we had for more than a year, and most for only a month or two; but they were so utterly happy to be with us. I've seen men tho who saw those concentration camps,—depths of depraved cruelty unimaginable. It's all been in the papers, so the censor shouldn't mind my saying that a Lt. Col. told me of seeing those 30,000 bodies starved to death: and the remnants of others who had unfortunately not been lucky enough to be quite dead, so were put into a building and burned. Beyond conception. And the SS troops fire on their own people. One patient, German, asked me eagerly, "Do the Americans have Nuremburg yet?" I said, "No, but they are near." "Got so i dank," he muttered to himself. That puzzled me, until he explained, "My parents are there. And Hitler has ordered that if we were taken prisoner, even wounded, some member of our family is to be shot."

But the end is near here, for Europe at least. I can hardly believe that Italy is ours! That grand 5th Army which has been so overshadowed in the news, but has fought so steadily and so splendidly can now rest on laurels. May ours soon follow suit up here. And then,—the Pacific! Everybody talks of getting tight when the news comes: my instinct is to beat a retreat and in quietness cherish the thought of safety at last for our men; comfort for those young bodies that have been put to the uttermost test of endurance,—and ease to the hearts at home that have been suffering for them.

So dull, so drab, all this stretch of words in the face of what they should convey. Excuse.

Germany's complete unconditional surrender occurred on May 7, 1945. As Churchill wrote in his memoir of the war, "The unconditional surrender of our enemies was the signal for the greatest outburst of joy in the history of mankind."[29] This held true a few miles from Landsberg, Germany, in a former German training center where Natalie's field hospital had been installed. *Have I written you since VE Day?* Natalie asked Martha. *I don't know. I've had so little chance to write. For me, the big moment was the surrender in North Germany, for I knew that meant the end was a matter of days only. I was so glad that I was away from a center, with the hysterical celebrating. As it was, Katie, a happy-hearted young nurse who lived in the tent across from me, came over and told me at once. We sat and stared at each other. I really just wanted to be alone, but perhaps it's just as well that Katie dragged me over to hers, and six of us finally gathered there, and we all sang and had a few drinks. We were in candlelight as we were leaving the next morning to come here.*

Natalie Scott celebrating the surrender of Germany (three miles outside of Landsberg, Germany, May 7, 1945). *Courtesy of Special Collections, Tulane University Libraries*

VE Day gave me no time to think of anything but scrambling up a party for our patients. I was wild-eyed over it. But suddenly I bethought me: we had gathered in for help a number of those unfortunate DPs (Displaced Persons!), chiefly Russians and Polish. I got hold of them and arranged that they do their dances. One of the Russians was a wonderful concertina player. Our Italians agreed to sing some of their songs. The party finally went off wonderfully. I ran my feet off the whole day. We sang the Star-Spangled Banner first (and got thru with it, all the patients in their funny Kimonos standing rigidly at attention). Then I announced God Save the King; but of course most of them promptly sang My Country Tis of Thee to the music. Then the Russians came on. Nobody had a better time. There were fewer Poles, and they were less madly hilarious,—poor things, how they have all suffered! The Russians sang their national anthem, too. And our men were perfectly charmed. MacGowen of the NY Sun wrote it up. Our officers and nurses had a party, but it had almost ended when I arrived. I was glad that I could not think on that VE Day, and that on the next, I had to go on working quite busily. Leisure gives perspective and that is so painful. There has been little of the San Francisco Conference over here and the little not too encouraging. People talk lightly of 'another war in twenty years': My blood runs cold. I feel I'll have to go on working at something.[30]

Germany's surrender brought forth from Natalie conflicting emotions: joy and anguish, elation and weariness, relief and anger, fear of what would come next. She was happy to help the war's victims yet resented that the victims were abruptly forgotten in the victory celebrations. A nagging loneliness weighed upon her. For Natalie, the war was not over. She informed Martha: *The really drastic happening in my own little orbit is that I have asked for a release from the ARC. If you ever waded thru that dreary array of pages in my last letter, I mention the opposition to my giving comfort articles to the German patients. I feel quite strongly about this. Each hospital has a large Red Cross outside it, indicating that the little spot is 'neutral territory' and thereby claiming exception from the perils of war. My first childish impressions of the Red Cross were of its humanitarianism, and the motto that 'the sick and wounded have no nationality'. Our ARC—which is affiliated with the*

International Red Cross—has taken the stand that each CO in a hospital shall determine whether or not comfort articles shall be given to German patients. Our own CO does not approve their being given even tooth-brushes and tooth-paste!

He is from Missouri and so is Edith. She practically does obeisance when he speaks. And she is against the German patients receiving any comfort articles, so I am sure she inspired his decision. However that may be, the fact that the Red Cross does not take its stand and insist that its humanitarian spirit be preserved is something I cannot accept. I didn't want to act hastily, so I waited some time before coming to a decision. I feel it would be dishonest to remain.

You'll probably tell me how wrong I am. I've carried on the work steadily and been quite agreeable to my trying co-worker (my two predecessors left because of her). But the organization according to my own conviction, is betraying the ideals for which it stands. Constructive punishment is essential. I thoroughly approve of the war criminals being brought to justice. Many of the German people themselves were as terrified of the SS troops and of the Gestapo as anybody could be. Patients have told me (ex-POWs) of SS troops' acts towards civilians; for example, when a civilian was in the way, drawing a pistol and shooting him, or her! Of seeing an SS trooper kick a 3 year old child. Of their shooting their own men who had surrendered. God knows the stories of the camps—and I know many eye-witnesses of the horrors of one not far from here,—makes one sick with dismay not only at the anguish of the victims, but at the spectacle of a human being sunk to such depths of barbarism as to be able to inflict such misery. To punish the criminals is constructive: a deterrent, a lesson, a protective measure. But why would we take even one fraction of an inch of a motion in their direction, by inflicting little deprivations on little people, worst of all, on the sick and wounded?

Beyond *this little immediate problem of mine*, Natalie's work went on. One patient who's been having a mighty tough battle to survive has been longing to get certain belongings from his outfit, and I tried many times to reach them. Finally heard that our own Transportation was going down in that direction so I hot-footed it over to the Transportation office. The boys were angelic as they always are, and so completely willing to help.

But there they sat, with a great treat,—some vermouth and sour wine. Nothing for it but Momma must have a drink with them. There were eight or ten of them. If I hadn't taken a drink, they would have thought I was 'high-hat'. As it was, I sat around and chatted with them for half an hour and took two drinks, warding off a third. And it's so sweet of them. They're so much fun.[31]

The small controversy over Natalie's protest resignation did not go away, despite the diplomatic visit of the regional supervisor. She wrote to Martha: *Did I tell you that Bea Eckerson, our supervisor, turned up, and assured me that the ARC policy remains unchanged, that 'patients have no nationality'. She says, however, that they feel that they cannot sacrifice the work for our men by withdrawing a unit from a hospital where the CO does not conform,—as here. That being the case, I am bowing my way out a week from to-day. Funny thing is that the CO wants very little said about it! He knows that my departure is most resented by the unit. But so it goes. And I go. I have asked every returned POW I've seen if he has ever heard of 'Peter Waters', but no news ever. I wonder if July has ever heard. To know nothing is the hardest thing of all.[32]*

Returning to Paris, Natalie contemplated whether or not to abandon her plans to serve in the Pacific Theater. She reconsidered her resignation during the weeks spent in the Red Cross headquarters processing out of the service. As she made new friends there, her attitude softened. *I sat around, and chatted, and now I find I know practically everybody in the place, and that's saying a lot. Anyhow, I went on record officially as being not in accord with the policy (or lack of it) in regard to POW patients. But the head of all Hospital Services in this area looked down her long thin nose with the wintry smile of the social worker and assured me that I just didn't understand it all.*

I put in for the Pacific. I had decided not to, but the more I thought about our nice high-hearted lads being so frequently exposed to that Social Service atmosphere, the more I thought I'd brave it all and go and chum around with them some more. So I put in for the Phillippines (I must learn to spell it before I go there), that is, for the Pacific area. Meanwhile, my old outfit, the 70th (Provence), which was wonderful to me, put in officially an urgent request to have me reassigned to them. That seemed a good bet. There was the little item that everybody over thirty-five is supposed to be ineligible. But I had a heart-to-heart with the doctor on the subject of tropical diseases and insect pests and such, so he decided to pull for me. Besides, I have a flawless health record in spite of having taken only a sixth of the leave due me. So it was finally agreed.

On June 5, Natalie learned more details. *And then to-day, the very nice personnel lady spoke to me, asked me if I would be willing to join up with the field hospital which has never had a Red Cross worker. I agreed with the greatest alacrity. Field Hospitals often have no ARC worker, are very small units and even closer to the front than Evacs. They are reserved usually for the very young and exceptionally fit.*[33]

Voyage to the Philippines

Natalie's return to Paris in early June was accompanied by fearful news that her nephew Bino had been badly wounded in the Philippines, the victim of a Japanese guerilla's homemade grenade stuffed with nails and other deadly shrapnel. She shared her grief in an otherwise joyful reunion with her nephew Nauman, an army officer stationed in London, *the greatest shock I've had in years: a letter telling me that Bino had been wounded in both the arms and both legs. He expected to be sent back to the States. A Sergeant wrote the letter for him. I still can't bear to think of it. And at the same time, I am relieved to think that he will be in safety. A heavenly thought. The two emotions, of anguish and relief, about pulling me to pieces. I can hardly wait to hear more, and plan to cable Sidonie from London.*[34]

Nauman had visited Natalie that week, the first family she had seen since early 1943. Upon receipt of her wire, Nauman immediately obtained a thirty-six-hour leave from his London duties. He reached Natalie's Paris hotel at eleven o'clock at night, and the two stayed up in conversation until three in the morning. The next day, they spent hours together on the Left Bank until Nauman's departure. Then Natalie made a London trip to celebrate Nauman's mid-June birthday. *The week in London was perfect for five days. Then late one afternoon Nauman received orders telling him he must go to Naples for fifteen days! I tried nobly not to repine, but it was really a blow. I had arranged to have birthday cake for him and a tiny party. We then went for a long quiet stroll thru the old parts of London. Nauman reminds me so much of his father, in the pleasure he has in quiet tranquil lovely things. It seemed so wonderful to be with him, and at the same time hurt so to think that I wouldn't see him for so very, very long. Somehow, he reminds me more of his father than ever before, so that at times I would start to refer to childhood memories as tho he had shared them! It was very poignant, somehow.*[35]

En route back to Paris, Natalie toured the French coastline to walk the D-Day battle sites and cemeteries. In Sainte-Mère Eglise, she met a young artist named Paul Renaud and his father, the town's mayor, who were pleased to learn she was a writer. During her stay, she agreed to the task of translating into English a well-written eighty-two-page book, *Sainte-Mère Eglise: First American Bridge Head in France,* the eye-witness account by the artist's father of the D-Day invasion. Their hope was that this dramatic story could be published in America. She began the project immediately.

Natalie did not receive a fuller explanation about Bino's condition until late June, finally learning that he was hospitalized in Memphis for a series of surgeries. Though "badly maimed," he was walking, using his left arm, and in good spirits.[36] While in transit to Marseilles in preparation for shipping out to the Pacific war, Natalie encountered Martha's son Bob in a chance meeting in Dijon. She wrote Martha immediately. *Bobby told me about Jack's being wounded. He said it was "slight" but it was bad news to have none the less. I thought of him so often during the Iwo Jima intensity. Alas, we are in the midst of times when we must be grateful that things are 'not worse'!*

I haven't left the staging area but once since I came here (Marseilles), and that was to go out for dinner at Frank Brame's mess. That was very pleasant. I know all the icers (officers) there, and they welcomed me back like an old friend; and after dinner, we sat under a huge tree and watched the late twilight come, and the light explode noiselessly into view on the harbor. Quiet and peaceful. I have had no news of Bino for ten days now. I worry a lot over that nerve suture, and do so hope that there is a really good surgeon. It distresses me constantly about Peter Waters. If only July could hear something definite.[37]

Then, unexpectedly, the Red Cross sent Natalie for several days to a leisurely spot on the Mediterranean coast, as she explained in a July 25 letter, a final respite before shipping out to the Pacific Theater. *Am writing this hastily, in the midst of the most theatrically lovely surroundings: our Mediterranean is asserting all her glamor at a stone's throw from my window. I've been sent to the Riviera, to my surprise and great delight, for several days. But am working devotedly (when allowed) on the translation. Have been dancing in the evenings! And the moon is full, and there's light-heartedness and gaiety all about. Wonderful for those who've been thru the mill of this war, but there's always the tug of the needs of those who are still in the horror of the Pacific. So I hope we may leave soon.*[38]

The "translation" referred to the Sainte-Mère Église project. Meanwhile, the Genevieve Parkhurst book of Natalie's letters would soon succumb to a different fate, the generous offers to publish evaporating at the war's end.[39] However, in late July 1945, the translation project kept her busy. *No more to-day, because I want to get off the first installment of my translation. Wish I had time to let it wait, so that I might have perspective on the English thereof. But that's impossible. Nothing will come of it probably, but it's been fun to do.*[40]

Natalie returned to Marseilles to board the SS *General Richardson* for the Philippines, finally sailing on August 5.[41] The two atomic bombs dropped that historic week on Japan changed the course of human history, bringing forth the Japanese surrender on August 14. It also abruptly changed the destination of Natalie's ship. *Most peculiar, most peculiar! We were really somewhat prepared for the announcement of the end of the war with Japan, tho we were also prepared for the possibility of going in for a final invasion. What none of us really expected was that we would be turned aside in the middle of the trip and sent to the U.S.A. But here we are, bearing down on old Boston. We haven't the vaguest idea what is to happen to us there.* She later described to a New Orleans newspaperman the response when the news of Japanese surrender reached the 5,000 soldiers and hospital units on her ship. *The boys almost broke up the ship. They shot off $10,000 worth of ammunition in salutes.*[42]

Thus the war ended for Natalie, her ship reaching Boston on August 19 with her immediate future uncertain. *My unit is having a month's leave. I am overdue a month's leave, and about thirty-one days besides, which I was entitled to overseas but never took. I am thinking vaguely of going on to the Pacific if there is any need over there, to work with the occupation troops over there. Shall probably have to go to Washington before anything else. If I'm held up in Boston, may run up for 2 days to Montpelier to see Helvetia (Perkins) and friends. Can't wait to see you and Whilda, and family.*[43]

In December, Natalie was finally on her way to the Philippines. During the long voyage across the Pacific, she was able to answer her enormous backlog of war letters. One response to an old Newcomb classmate offered a perspective on the final victory and what followed, her memories vivid.

We went in with the 7th Army. We moved four times in less than a month, and to do that with a 700 bed hospital is quite a feat. But we loved it! And it was thrilling to feel that we were riding the crest of Victory with a very large V. Alas for the buoyancy of those days! How exquisitely lovely was Bavaria. And then the stark horror of the vast silent cities lying in ruin. I had to go to Paris (heavenly obligation!) for three days in April. To get there, we had to ride from six in the morning till five that afternoon in a six-by-six to Saarbourg, where at seven we got a train. On the way we passed thru Mannheim. It's simply impossible to make anyone imagine it: that great industrial city had hardly one wall standing ten feet high. Yet the streets had been cleared for traffic,—which somehow made the desolation all the more stark and terrible.

We celebrated VE Day about three miles from Landsberg, in a former center for Air Cadet Training. Natalie described Munich. *It has been much damaged, but there were still magnificent houses there. And one small party I attended was in Hitler's former Munich apartment! We got lost in our jeep on the way home,—got onto the magnificent Autobahn and couldn't get off it. Afterwards it struck us as strange that we should be bowling along in a carefree manner, lost on a road that two nights before had been strafed constantly by Bed Check Charlie, as the boys called these night marauders. We had them coming over the hospital every night. Perhaps I told you that one machine gunned a truck 200 yards from me one night. And we had all the wounded on the operating tables in seven minutes after they were hit. We were proud of that.*

Natalie wrote of her return to France, then the preparations for the Pacific. *I spent the time in translating Sainte-Mère Eglise, our first American bridgehead in France,—written by the Mayor of the village and a good piece of journalism. And I wanted very much to have it appear in America for the sake of our men who went through that terrific ordeal for France, for it was suffered with that French feeling of tolerance in severity, and quiet unself-conscious strength. Also, I had a heavenly six day 'rest period' (during which I still worked on the translation) in Juan les Pins, which had been taken over for nurses and Red Cross as a rest area. The officers had Cannes, and it was all full of the light-hearted gaiety of relaxation after a stiff job. The GIs had Nice. The contrast was interesting.*

There was a minimum of restrictions in all these places. So officers and nurses appeared in any old clothes, their insignia worn somewhere. But the GIs—whom I had last seen in such cruelly hard conditions, were poured into the finest hotels in the world there at Nice—looked smart and clean and trim the whole time. And there was very little drinking. We sailed at last in August. And VJ Day caught us two days this side of Gibraltar! So we were re-deployed to Boston, landing there on August 19th. Three days there, then Washington, yet again assigned to the Pacific, this time with Clubs. (I could no longer face the Social Worker set-up that prevails in hospitals; I took it during the war, but could not face it in peace time.)

From there to Charleston for five days, to visit my niece (Bé Scott Thomas), *whose young husband was head of the Navy Radar School there. Sidonie joined me there, with Natie, my namesake niece, and Bino, my younger nephew, my wounded paratrooper. He was hideously wounded the second time, in both arms and both legs, last April 29th. His legs had healed nicely, and he had the use of three fingers of his left hand; but his right arm was held down in a body cast. He had six nerve injuries in it, and they had operated, hoping to restore at least some movement. It is too soon to know as yet. He had lost sixty pounds, having had 105 days of straight combat, and two combat jumps.*

From there I went to N.Y. to leave my translation with an agent. Dashed up to Conn. for a short visit, then back to Charleston, whence we set out for N.O. via Florida. A heavenly trip. N.O. a day; then 36 hours in Alex; then N.O. for five days.

Once again Natalie's commentary turned to the peace, the politics, and the perceptions of the American people. Would it all be different from the last war? *The States almost broke my heart. I had misgivings, but still I could not help but feel that surely this time I would find an awareness of the horror and extent of the tragedy of war; that there would be a violent insistent demand, not to be denied, for a way to peace, for tolerance, and understanding. Instead, I found everything interpreted in personal terms, 'my loss', my son's handicap, and so on. And a carping, carping,—against Russia, against France, against England,— always against. I quite literally could not take it, so I fled to Mexico for five days in Taxco.*

My welcome there was so deep and so warm that it helped a lot. I had no more than three hours sleep any night that I was there, but I was showered, not tired. Every time I went back to the house, there would be a former workman, or a former servant, or some other humble friend, waiting to greet me. One former maid walked ten miles to bring me flowers. The villagers and the Day Nursery Board of Directors *had a testimonial banquet for me, to which all the Americans were welcomed too. And the doctor made me a simple, very moving speech,—all of which made me very happy—and the children were so charming. So I drew a breath and went back to Alex. and New Orleans.*

Here I worked on re-editing the cook-book for a tenth edition. My leave was to last until November 30th. The Newcomb Alumnae were to have a mammoth reception for me. And there were parties galore ahead. When, on Nov. 13th, came a long distance call from Washington, ARC, asking me to take the train that night in order to catch this ship. Of course, it was 'right down my alley' to get off so madly. And there was a day and a half in Washington; then a four day train trip in two special cars, with a group of 39 ARC workers. Then Camp Stoneman (California) for a few days. And now (we're here at last!) this small new transport, bound for Manila.[44]

In San Francisco, Natalie boarded her new ship, the SS *Marine Shark*, as she described in a letter to Martha Robinson. *I've already written two letters to you and two to Whilda. Came on board yesterday. We were still loading. We've just had a tempest in a tea-pot. I had been asked in Washington to be Group Leader in charge of Women Personnel. (We have five men with us, and the Group Leader is a man.) I said, Thank you. But please no. Whereupon the very martinet lady who was appointed got into a squabble with the main ARC who is leading the whole gang and she resigned. Whereupon the group was asked to elect its own leader, and they elected me. So I'm it, willy-nilly. And DON'T LIKE IT! Still, it seemed rather an obligation, since this rather good group was getting restrictive under the somewhat too GI and autocratic ruling of the former leader. But what a bore it is, and a lot of details, to ruin my pleasant life.*

They say that this boat makes the trip in twelve to fourteen days. I wish it were even longer. However, I imagine that there will be quite a spot of sea-sickness aboard, for the little craft seems to rock and roll on the slightest provocation! Heaven help me from being nursemaid to a lot of vomiting damsels, but it promises to be my fate![45]

In a letter to Lyle Saxon written on the voyage to the Philippines, Natalie told of "hot poker games" and tending her seasick flock of Red Cross workers *while the ship is rolling so. Just at the end of dinner there came a huge swell and a tremendous crashing as all the dishes hurtled off the serving tables.* Natalie tried to explain to Saxon why she was not ready for civilian life. *There are quite a lot of officers, a good many of whom have seen a fairish amount of combat service and who, like me, found it difficult to plunge too suddenly from combat areas back into a civilian life in which the war as such seems to have made no impression. It seems to count only personal trials, losses, and inconveniences gallantly endured. But the great mass tragedy seems to have gone unobserved, seems not to have shaken our national spirit into any great urge for a new order. There is no such vast invincible demand for tolerance and international cooperation as one piteously hoped for.*

With me it was hope against hope, after the bitter disillusion following the last war, when the League of Nations was scrapped: So here we all are,—escapists in our own fashion. And so off I go, vaguely, on another 'treasure hunt', trying to prove something for my own satisfaction, and sometimes I think I know what, and sometimes I'm not quite so sure. Anyway, there are more ways than one of getting to know America, and my trail is one of them. And I'm very intrigued over seeing the Far East.[46]

Chapter Eleven

The Grande Dame of Taxco

By Christmas 1945, Natalie had settled into her new responsibilities in Manila, Philippines. Postwar conditions presented vastly different demands than had the war hospitals of Europe, as she wrote in a letter to Bé Scott Thomas. *You may picture me as Cupid. The one celebration I had planned for myself for Xmas was to go with the carol-singers to the hospitals. This afternoon (Christmas eve), in walked Ruth Davey, a girl of twenty-nine, a gentle soul—slender with tranquil face and steady grey eyes. Said grey eyes were all starry-looking as she announced blythely that she and Paul were to be married to-morrow afternoon! (Paul is a pleasant young officer she met on shipboard.) Everything, upon questioning, but Red Cross permission! And she was planning to go on with her work as tho nothing had happened.*

Leisure was shattered. I spent ages on the wire contacting some Red Cross official. The girl is to be married to-morrow afternoon, GI and the Red Cross permitting, so I stayed home for the phone message,—which never came. All the girls were out. Several have come in since,—it's twelve-thirty now—have told me of their various adventures and excitements.

I went to town for the Protestant Service. The United Protestant Church. The audience was largely Filipino. Many of the men wore white suits, some of the charming native women's costumes, of bright colors. Sprinkled thickly among them were GIs. The minister was a Filipino, graduate of an American university. He offered a Xmas prayer that was deeply moving, unmistakably from the heart, referring to the tragic years they had endured, the losses material and emotional, He must have lost some who were very close to him,—and begging that a lasting peace may be here in which they may work out their destiny and follow ever more closely the Christmas Star.

Got back in time for the most phenomenal Xmas dinner, with turkey, a rich stuffing, 'live' [very fresh] potatoes, Irish, and sweet asparagus, nuts, relish, cranberry sauce, mince and pumpkin pie! Alas, I had to race thru it, as I had to try again to get news for Ruth and Paul. I went thru the ordeal by telephone. And the answer was 'yes'.

I announced the glad tidings by walking into our 'street' chanting 'Here Comes the Bride' in my cigarette husky voice. And of course there was pandemonium. They leaped up. I caught Ruth and off we went to invite the CO, the Chief Nurse, and so on while I dispatched others to get nuts and pretzels at the Px and to do what they could about decorating and refreshments. Sent Ruth back to dress, and in half an hour I had arranged for a room in the Officers' Club for a 'reception', got the CO to agree to give the bride away, fixed up with the Chaplain,—then dashed back to dress. The wedding came off quite charmingly. One of the ARC girls played the organ, another was bridesmaid. Most impressive and dignified. All the girls were there, a number of WACs, officers from the boat and those of the Post. Afterwards the group gathered in the reserved room and the girls had made it look most attractive, including a 'wedding cake' made of a cold cream can 'iced' over with cream. People kept wanting to cut it. Immediately after the wedding, we went down to the Roosevelt Club to the GI Xmas dance. One of the girls had agonized cramps and the doctor thought it might be appendicitis, so we hustled her to the hospital. What a day![1]

A little later, Natalie wrote to Martha. *The picture out here has been in a most confusing state, what with soldiers being shipped home by the thousands. I've become attached to Manila now. The main street is the Avenue Rizal, which formerly had some sizeable business establishments on it. Practically all of them were damaged, if not annihilated but they have been patched up, the place has been cleaned out, and little mushroom shops have sprung up, with little businesses in them. Quezon Street parallels it, and there are a few extensive buildings remaining, notably the one that has been taken over by our headquarters—AFWESPAC (whole new batch of alphabet). The Americans have rebuilt, or built, in most instances, new bridges across the river that winds about the edge of the new city. There are seven in all, strongly built and not too ugly, a great boon to the mangled city. From the edge of the town, south, two long avenues run parallel, Taft*

Avenue and Dewey Blvd. (where are the Democrats in all this? I inquired in my rebel way). Dewey Ave. is my weakness. The all pervading soft brilliance of the sunset, liquefying the air in gentle radiance in which the hundreds of ships are scattered over the shimmering color-tinged water.

This country reminds me so much of Mexico. There are many of the same sorts of fruits. We have a papaya in our garden. And there is rosa montana, cocoanut, and so on. And also there are innumerable 'languages'. The one spoken generally here is Tagalog (accent on the second syllable). Most of them speak some English, but the simpler people speak little. Naturally I've started picking up phrases, and it amuses the Filipinos to no end. If I stay here any longer, I shall really try seriously to pick up a certain amount of the language. It is a very strange one, related to almost nothing else I ever heard. They say that it is related to Malay. Certain Spanish words have strayed into it; but not many of the people speak Spanish, only the older people and some few of the native aristocrats.

Natalie encountered one surprise that struck close to home, a remarkable coincidence. *The most extraordinary thing happened to-day. A Filipino (mestizo, really) Major came in. He was quite young and nice-looking. We started chatting, and he told me that he was present when Bino was wounded. He told me to tell Bino that Maj. Bob Reese (O dear, I hope that was the name) sent him greetings. I could hardly believe it, but he described Bino, and said he was 'tough to take it'. He also spoke of Sgt. Turner. Isn't that amazing. He said he would be in again.* Natalie learned from the young major that Bino had a companion with him when the Japanese grenade blew up, a young Filipino who was killed.[2]

In Manila until March 1946, Natalie worked in the hospitals and among the soldiers as a counselor-problem solver, resolving the infinite personal difficulties that trouble young soldiers stationed overseas. She was involved in the massive task of shipping over thirty thousand soldiers back to the States by March, making certain those in greatest need went home first. When this was completed, the Red Cross transferred Natalie to Japan, to work among American occupation forces commanded by Gen. Douglas MacArthur.[3] Natalie would remain in Asia for three years, serving in Japan and Korea. In December 1946, the Red Cross magazine published a two-page feature story on her career.[4]

On New Year's Eve, 1946, Natalie dined with a party at Tokyo's

Dai Iti Hotel, the field grade officers' billet. A few days later she summarized her first Asian year in a letter to Newcomb classmate Virginia Withers. *All during the war, I had feared After the War. And it has been so much worse than had anticipated.*

After the first days of "Realization," in New Orleans, I thought I had got my balance. So gradually my defenses went down; and insensibly the horror, the bitterness, the resentment, mounted. Remembering the human tragedies in war hospitals, Natalie contemplated her own war struggle. *And all day, I talked, and teased, listened and laughed, with the lads,—and all the while I saw them with doom upon them. And at night with the warmth of personal encounters gone, the Doom overshadowed everything.* Natalie wrote of having had a *Black Spring,* a period of depression she worked through in Manila and Yokohama. She struggled to brighten her letter. *It was an illness. A madness, quite near to being literally so. I can't even fix on what mental boot-strap it was by which I finally pulled myself out of it. I've accepted it now. So I look no farther, and rock along.*

So let's become factual. There was Manila, delectable Luzon: the vegetation reminded me so of Mexico. But many types and kinds of natural beauty have I seen in these last years with a start of pleasure only to be lost abruptly in a rush of horror at what happened there. A hilltop would suddenly show a dot that was Bino's young six feet so pitifully vulnerable.

Dear, dear, this will never do. You see why it is a good idea to go on working, and on working, and don't dare loosen your hold. But don't worry. I'll get along to the point where it is safe to stop, and everything will be under control.

Should I leap back to Manila? I was there during the bad time, of the hysterical demobilization. I was at the Repple Depot, which of course was a fever spot. It was pitiful to find so many lads there with Emergencies, urgent cases, and no plane transportation possible in the mad bottle-neck. I did get one thing done that helped. There was a transocean phone service run by a Spanish Filipino. I used all my Spanish, not only language but feeling. Calls and reservations normally had to be made days in advance. I 'put thru a deal' with him so that he would run in calls for my Emergency boys, in between the priority calls.

Never reaped such a harvest: it meant everything to those poor worried lads to get the latest news. There was one heavy-set warmhearted Italian. His little 4-year old boy had spinal meningitis. He was half-crazy. His call came thru. He never could tell me the whole story consecutively, because he would always start crying so copiously. As the news was good, it was really a comedy. The GIs, roused with tears of sympathy in their eyes, were twisted with laughter, too. The little boy was better; the hospital plugged in a phone, and his little boy talked to him. "Daddy, I love you. I help you drive the car."

But our 29th 'folded'. And I was assigned to Japan. Our first glimpse of this country was forbidding: great needles of rock, russet in the cold gray air, rose abruptly from a storming crash of angry waves. But at last there was a vast harbor and within all was mockingly serene. Home base of the Japanese fleet and of its submarines.

So I came to Yokohama. And there I stayed from early March until October. Loved the work I did, Service Bureau for GIs. Information, advice, tours, a Bulletin, little cultural squibs, travel items. All sorts of things. Though Natalie was scheduled to return to the States in October, a friend in Kyoto needed to rush home for a family emergency, so Natalie took on her work and let the friend go home in her place. Natalie took the job of personnel counselor and manager of the two women's billets there.

So I spent two months in Kyoto, the 'cultural center of Japan'. The country around Fuji is movingly beautiful. Fuji itself is everything you can imagine, such grace and such power! And the country about, well, as like Austria, I suppose. Such a variety of lakes. Innumerable shrines and temples. Some of the old pagodas are quite exquisite, with a strange feel of lift and lightness. The gardens are the top reach of Japanese creativeness, tho, for me: shrubs and trees, the interplay of texture and size, the use of mossy old natural boulders. And imagination![5]

Natalie described Japan to Martha also. *Here are made the finest porcelains and potteries, cloisonne and the finest silks. Have been introduced to various cultured Japanese here. I still feel quite strange with most of them. The people readily make gestures of friendship.* She befriended the Japanese liaison officer, Mr. Yamagida, owner of a chemical manufacturing company, who took her on numerous outings. They attended a cooking-school together, *packed to capacity by young Japanese girls, many of them very pretty. Some in European dress, but many*

Natalie in Yokohama, Japan, directing Red Cross services during the postwar occupation (1946). *John W. Scott Collection*

in charming kimonos and obis. All had notebooks and pencils out. The chef was a natural comic. He often tossed off explosive remarks that sent his pupils into musical peals of laughter. Natalie was ceremoniously honored by her hosts with an elaborate meal, a product of their cooking that day. *We duly removed our shoes before stepping onto the silken-fine padded straw matting that covered the floor. There we were all seated on cushions around a round lacquer table about ten inches high. We were served hot saki from entrancing old pottery saki bottles. And then the procession of dishes began.*

Our chemist sang some modern Japanese songs which were very strange, always a lavish use of falsetto. Then the chef sang a very old drinking song. "Drink saki, and you will be the greatest man in Japan" was the general sentiment. I suppose you may feel you are at any rate. Later on he and his brother 'sang a song' from a Noh play, the two men performing as they sang. Subsequently, we were entertained by the dancing of a geisha girl and her geisha duenna. The younger was a 'maiko', a child-dancer, one of the best in Kyoto. Her piquant little face was dead white with powder, so that her eyes looked like obsidian, all surface and no depth, glinting dark lights of demure coquetry. And her hair! Such a coiffure as had been construct-ed of her own ink-black hair.

Mr. Yamagida also took Natalie to Osaka, formerly an impor-tant business city and *the center of the puppet plays for which Japan was famous. The town was very widely damaged by the air raids.* Another outing with her chemist friend took Natalie and a friend to a Sunday ceremonial tea at an ancient Buddhist monastery with a well-known tea-master. *Our host, the chemist, had been dressed in quite decent European clothes, but for the Tea Ceremony he had donned a long dark man's kimono, which made him look very dignified. He is deeply religious as a Buddhist, from the comments he made.*[6]

Natalie befriended two older American ladies who had spent most of their lives in Japan. One was Miss Clapp, a concert pianist forced out of Europe in 1915 by the First World War. She had accepted a position as head of the Music College at the University of Kyoto. *She's a great old girl. In 1941, she and her closest friend, a Ph.D. head of the English Dept. decided they should resign. They were asked to take, instead, an indefinite leave of absence. No sooner was the war over, than they were requested to return. She thinks that the intellectuals quite sin-cerely think that, even tho the price was so tragically high, it is a godsend to have the country free at last of the military. I asked her if she felt the Japanese thought the war crimes trials harsh and unjust, in condemning key figures for the crimes of subor-dinates. "Not at all", she answered in her brisk assured tone. "That's the one thing they really understand and accept,—the responsibility of the leader."* The second lady, a Miss Denton, also in the university, was too old to leave when the war broke out. *She is known all over Japan. The only restriction placed on her was that she could not leave the grounds of her house but she felt hurt at that! She is being cared for devotedly by a Japanese family. Americans had arranged to get food for her. I*

*managed to get her some sheets, which was a major triumph,
as they are a critical item. And copies of LIFE.*[7]

The Seoul Club

By January 12, 1947, when she arrived by C-47 in Seoul,
Korea, Natalie had read all she could about the history of Korea,
particularly its twentieth-century hardships under the Japanese.
The temperature usually hovered around zero. The Japanese
were gone, the American troops the only military presence in a
rapidly deteriorating political atmosphere. *The country really
did look like the moon as seen thru a powerful telescope, endless wasteland, white barren snow with striations of the pushing mountains dark-etched in it.* The explosive turmoil and
Communist threat persisted throughout Natalie's fourteen
months here. In 1950, Korea would become the cold war's first
real battlefield, when the Soviet-supported North Korean army
invaded south across the thirty-eighth parallel.

When World War II drew to a close in 1945, the Soviet army
had accepted the Japanese surrender in Korea north of the thirty-eighth parallel, the Americans south of that line. Rival regimes
were established by the opposing superpowers north and south
of the parallel. *We are only an hour and a half from the parallel
by jeep and bad roads. It's rather a hodge-podge as to architecture. The mountains rise directly from the outskirts, and call
the gaze from the unlovely works of man. The mountains completely encircle the city, low jagged mountains they are.* Natalie
offered Martha a succinct summary of the foreign dominance of
Korea. *China, an all-too-powerful neighbor for centuries. Japan
growled on the other side, reaching out an eager paw; and
Russia from the north did the same. Unhappy Korea!*

*Did you read anything about our 'Independence Day' over
here, and the riots?* Independence Day celebrated Korea's passive resistance to the Japanese in 1919, a challenge inspired by
America's Declaration of Independence. *Fired by our noble
words, a group of 33 of the most prominent citizens signed a
declaration of independence here in the heart of Seoul. They
sent out many copies of it, then took themselves to a good
restaurant, sent for the Jap chief of police to arrest them. The*

proclamation circulated everywhere. They (the Japanese) clamped down. Their estimate is 20,000 killed in punishment; the Korean, 50,000. Between lies the sorry truth. Some of the victims were literally crucified. In other cases, whole classes were imprisoned with their teachers, and some were left to starve to death.

By March 1947, the Communists were using the symbol of Independence Day as propaganda for a new uprising. *Our men had been informed confidentially (and some of them confided to me) that the Russians were arming the Communists in the North and that they were to come down to attack us on that day. There was actually some scattered trouble over the country; and some here in Seoul.*[8]

Our building is about three blocks from the old South Gate. We heard shots from down that way, in the afternoon, and saw people running. But it died down. Shortly after we heard shots from the other direction.

I had to go to a large reception given by a group of Koreans for General Larch of M.G. [Military Government] at the Capitol, that afternoon. On the intersecting st. there was an orderly parade with banners. I was surprised, as the Communists had been told there would be no parade. So they contented themselves with a meeting on Shrine Hill (which one reaches from the South Gate). What should they find descending but an orderly large parade of rightest faction! They were infuriated, and a fight began. Some on both sides had got guns (mysteriously!) after the Korean police (and a few of ours) had broken up the riot, shooting over the heads of the people and crowding into them, several wounded were left on the ground. One was a woman with a baby on her back on the ground on her face, pulling herself along by her arms.

The alert went on very markedly for 2 weeks. We had to have an armed guard with us in our jeep; and all GIs had to be armed. We were not allowed to go on the streets alone, even in broad daylight. I didn't know this and walked happily to the Club on Independence Day itself. Had a very good time, too, taking pictures, all the way! And no difficulties. As for our own men, it is really quite rough, beyond a doubt, and not so good as it was towards the latter part of the combat period. High-ranking officers have told me that hundreds of them are living in non-winterized quarters. A man from engineers told me that when he went to inspect a ceiling that threatened to cave in in a barracks, he glanced into the men's shower room: the water was frozen on the floor.

Indicative incident: One evening a GI asked me in a throaty voice, "You think there's any way I could spend the night here on one of those long sofas?" "But why, sonny?" (I thought he might be drinking.) "I came up on a medical pass to have my eyes examined. Long trip, 15 hours in that unheated train. And I get tonsillitis." "Let me take you to the dispensary, next door", I suggested. "I've been there", he said wearily. "They told me I had fever 102 and something, and I'd better have the doctor look at my throat too when he looked at my eyes. They gave me a gargle."

I led him to a warm seat, gave him an aspirin dissolved in water to hold back in his throat, and phoned the hospital. I told of the boy's condition, his temperature, adding (untruthfully), "I'm sure they couldn't have realized he was a transient." The captain at the other end demurred, "We have very few beds, you know." I was so furious that my voice was positively sweet. "I'm rather new here," I said. "But I'd hate to see a soldier go out to the transient area in that condition. You know it's a 20 minute bus ride in the cold, and then they must walk at least three blocks in the bitter wind. And that transient area is tough even for well men." There was a long pause. Then, resignedly, "Well, see if you can get him over here and we'll see what we can do." "Thank you Captain", I said still sweetly. "I'll ask your driver to wait to see what the verdict is." They took him in.

If your teeth are bad, you may be able to get an appointment in two months. And then may quite probably be told, "I think they'll last another few months till you get home." One GI I know has terrible headaches from his eyes. His Bn. [Battalion] Medication Officer has been trying to get his eyes examined since Nov. They say now they may be able to take him around the 15th of April. Old rebel that I am, suggested to him that he speak to the I.G. about it (Inspector General). Officers here say that the trouble is that GHQ [general headquarters] in Japan grabs off the cream of supplies and of officers for themselves,— to have something to show when the IPs turn up! Certainly it is pretty awful for the men here.

Natalie commanded one of two GI clubs in the Seoul area. The newer one, the Bankers Club, was far better equipped than hers. *As for our club, we are really out of luck. We are under HQ. COMNDT. Just between us, it is the most mixed-up organization I know. The Bankers Club in town has a Sp. Service officer that visits daily. It took me six weeks to find out who my supply officer was. He has never set foot in our club. I have to buy playing cards for our game room myself. And the only way we manage to keep our ping-pong room going is for us to scrounge supplies out of channels.*

The extreme of absurdity is the broom situation. It's a huge building. We are scattered over 4 floors, and our place swarms with GIs. Needless to say, they fling cigarettes, butts and ashes, etc. We try to keep the place clean. We now have a broom and a half,—both looking like toothless old hags, with the straw worn down to the binding. We serve coffee and donuts, and sandwiches. Sunday, we served over 1600 cups of coffee. And now we can get no paper cups!

'Have no' is the favorite reply in Korea. I have suggested it as a motto for the Army of Occupation here. You asked for an article. Beaming smile (that's apology). "Have no." "Have no?" you question sadly. Wider smile. "Yes, have no." "Yes, we have no bananas!" A bright side of the picture is that the ARC set-up is very agreeable. The atmosphere is about the pleasantest I've met. Some new ARC girls, just arrived, tell me that their friends assigned in the Tokyo-Yokohama area write that they are coldly received and are unhappy; so the girls here feel fortunate.

I was sent for here to set up an information service in the Seoul Club, and to run the Club, which is a "lounge operation", in contrast to the Bankers Club, which runs many programs. I was appalled when I saw the set-up. The building is handsome on the exterior. The furniture is hardly worthy of a junk-heap. Springs broken and sagging. And the place was awfully dirty and messy.

We have cleaned it up to the nth degree, and by unremitting effort keep it that way. We acquired some canvas on wood chairs from ARC warehouse, which are gay in color tho not imposing; and some bridge-tables. And some very good books. My girls are all new to ARC, and I have started them out in the way I like. "Just feel that you are hostesses at a mammoth house-party", I tell them, "and you know you want your guests to be happy." Our place is a center for transients. GIs from all over the country make a bee-line for it as soon as they land in Seoul. And boys from outlying outfits. We do everything we can for those from the notoriously wretched spots, such as On Yang, Chong Ju, Kunson, and so on. How they appreciate it.

One Sunday morning, a group of 35 turned up, with their officer. They had been riding 15 hours in an unheated train. The poor lads were really rigid with cold,—and burdened with rifles and bags. We had them stack their rifles and sent upstairs for hot coffee and doughnuts. You should have seen their faces! Then we arranged for them to have chow nearby. Their officer, a young 2nd Lt. was much concerned about the 2 men he had left

Natalie (alone on top row) in the Seoul Club with Red Cross women under her command (Seoul, Korea, ca. 1948). *Courtesy of Special Collections, Tulane University Libraries*

Natalie in Korea, sitting in her Seoul Club bedroom with family photographs pinned to her wall (ca. 1948). *John W. Scott Collection*

*guarding heavy luggage at the train; so we turned ourselves into
a clubmobile and sent them a big pot of coffee and doughnuts.*

*Japan has been improved, its roads improved, its train service
improved. Nothing of that sort here. We stay open 0900 to 2200.
At best, I stay the whole time thru, in order to keep things going.
I have to be Club Director, take care of all paper-work, official
contacts, et cet; help in the programming; check on the Koreans;
and be staff assistant too. The last-named is the most fun! But I
enjoy it, and am bearing up wonderfully. We have a huge ping-
pong room with 8 tables going most of the time; that's the third
floor. On the second, we have a music room, a library, writing
room, and quiet game room; and an office; on the first floor, we
have an Information Desk and a Service Center (package wrapping and sewing). And in the basement, we have our corner for
making coffee. I have a room on the 4th floor with a window the
full width of the wall. Japanese style, very pleasant.*[9]

*Our Club is very ratty but we keep it quite clean. The Bankers
Club has all new furniture and had been done completely over. A
group of GIs told me happily that the ARC Director for Korea was
in the B. Club the other evening where they had stopped to pick
up a buddy. They told him that they were just there by accident,
because they mostly hung out at the Seoul Club. The Powers feel
that after they have spent so much money on the Bankers, the
boys should like it better. Our dancing class and our Camera
Club have more members than the other clubs combined, and
we're the only club that has been able to make a go of a Korean
class. But our misguided powers insist on fitting that square peg
into the round hole: instead of observing what the men like and
emphasizing that, they construct what they think the men ought
to like, and, when they don't react as intended, must now remove
what they do like; so they'll take the other or nothing.*[10]

The interesting, unorthodox tours organized by Natalie set her
Seoul Club apart. She ventured into the countryside, discovering
new travel ideas for the soldiers. One example was her Sou Wahn
tour, which she described to Martha. *It was a rough jeep trip, I
have a Greek American driver named Jimmy Vozotis, who is a
darling to me. We went thru a purely Korean section,—interesting to see the real native shops, with tin objects and some copper. The country was rolling, and we went for some miles along
a high ridge,—waiting for ox-carts often.*

I have made Opal (capable, warm-hearted and balanced Staff Assistant) head of the Tours, so I took her along and a boy who had tried to find our objective, got most of the way, then missed it in the end. He was a help in the first part of the trip. And Take-it-E, as we call a little Korean boy who works for us (really Tai Kai Hil). He says he is sixteen, but doesn't look twelve, and he has an open nature rare in the Koreans and a ready grin. And has learned so much English that he often interprets for our evening interpreter, Mr. Chong (whom I call Lord Beau Brummel Chesterfield).

The road grew worse and worse. Jimmy hurtled us over bumps. Poor little Take-It-E hit the ceiling with his shaved head repeatedly. I advised him to keep one hand against the top, and to hang on to the seat. But all the while there was lots to see. First the mountains that guard Seoul, bleak and rugged. Then the land grew more level, and there were patches of garden— most often what looked like garlic. And always people on the road, the women in brilliant colors. Lots of old men, with white or gray or black robes. Most of them wore the small versions of the Mad Hatter hat so often seen, of black horsehair weave. Take-it-E says they have their hair long and wear it tucked under the hat. Lots of them had long slender canes. Their pipes vary in length with their age, the older, the longer the pipe.

Younger men carried every sort of burden. The women carry everything on their heads, and have the graceful carriage which that custom imparts. Some of the men were carrying clustered twigs closely bound, and often the burden was twice as tall as the man. One man had a whole steel plow (of which he was obviously proud) strapped on his back, and at the same time, led an ox!

The people were very friendly, increasingly so. Cities certainly seem to kill, or drive under cover, natural human sociability. In the country, the people have the feeling that it is their home, and they are "hosts" in the sense, and that apparently does away with the sense of inferiority which the contrasts of station so obvious in the cities produce.

Rice paddies became more and more numerous. There were runways built out into them. There were tiny tracks laid along them and on them run out little 'cars' of fertilizer! Which makes me think of the famous (or infamous) 'honey-carts'. 'Fertilizer' of human origins! Hold your lunch. Still, one of the specialists in SCAF told me that tests had shown that it was not a disease carrier. It is put in containers (often of cement) open in the ground, and decomposition plus sunlight produces such intense heat as to kill bacteria,—so my friend told me. But that doesn't help the smell. Just like the GIs to christen these deplorable objects 'honey-carts'.

Finally came to Sou Wahn, an old walled village. Only 25 miles from here, but one would have sworn it was a hundred,— probably was, if the vertical motions were counted in. Jimmy stopped the vehicle abruptly before a charming pagoda, not high, but with that quality of soaring which the uptilt of the corners so often imparts. It was truly medieval in appearance,— the emplacements of the crude cannons used to repel the Manchus (I think it was) in 1592. Moreover, thru it came as in a slow-motion picture, a succession of individuals, groups, or animals, that were out of our world. Oxen, old men, slender women gaudily gowned, children in brilliant Joseph's coats.

We stood fascinated.

We passed thru Sou Wahn. Not an American of any description along the way. We saw no sign of Americans in the village. It looked clean, and there was an air of cheer about it that I suddenly realized one doesn't find in Seoul. Near to old Mother Earth, they are. We went straight thru the bustling little town to another gate at the far end. Along thru another village and between rice paddies, to yet another. Take-it-E asked questions all the way. We turned abruptly onto a clay road that was muddy and rutted, sleek as glass, built up thru rice paddies. The jeep slithered so alarmingly and we bumped so violently, that we all feared we'd go off the road; but Jimmy drove stubbornly on.

Then there was a wooded rise of ground, the road as slippery and as torturingly rutted as ever, but at least without the alarming drop on both sides. Wonderful to smell the pines. Most of the trees were twisted, or at the best, bent; but they were cutting out timber from them. The Japs, they say, almost cleared this country of its timber, so it is a rare treat to see a stretch of forest. And how wonderful was that pine smell! Then right again thru the woods, and we came to find the lair of peace. A knoll that rose up easily, a tremendous open space completely surrounded by pines, thick dried yellow grass underfoot, and all of it in utter stillness, pervaded with the soft spring sunlight. It was a benediction of a place.

Into the gentle slope had been set a beautiful pagoda, the rich color of old brick, gracefully proportioned, and it was flanked far out on either side by tiny square ones. The hill sloped up behind it very sharply. We climbed up slowly, stopped to look often at the pagoda and the grotesquely charming little flat stone figures that follow the curve of the roof lines. The turf was thick with centuries, with the soft resistance of piled silk. Low deep purple flowers studded it profusely,—they smelled like mayhaws.

At the top of the slope, we came amazingly upon a great semi-circle, paved and partly walled with stone. Around it were tall figures of rough-grained stone, with an animal between each pair. The figures were warriors, in suits of armor: the chain of the mail on the upper part was carefully worked, as were the 'scales' on the lower. There were two of these figures on either side, and the animals beside them were like particularly svelte cows! (but calf-size!) Farther in were other animals, versions of lions et cet, which faced outward while the little cows face inward like their human masters.

In the center of the semi-circle set on massive stone supports was a giant slab of marble, sleek as glass, and about eight feet long, warm gray in color. The contrast in texture with the stone was most effective. It looked like an altar. Behind it was set a circle of stone tablets, very tall, probably to the dead. The altar serves to receive food offerings to the dead. We would have loved to linger indefinitely, but as usual, had to rush,—most reluctantly away. Some Koreans came up, and talked to us quite friendlily, thru Take-It-E, and told us there is a similar tomb just a short way thru the woods.

Plan to take a picnic to this place next Sunday, with sandwiches and doughnuts, also baseballs, gloves and bats. It should be good. Very dull account of a fascinating trip. But stir your imagination: it was good.

Thus, a tour was added to the opportunities that Natalie's Seoul Club provided to the soldiers. She described how the following week's excursion to this new place turned out. *We sent the tour in three truck loads. One truck caught on fire, but that was stifled, so it proceeded; another lost two wheels, but it had six so proceeded; another on the return trip, slid over into the rice paddies and lay pitifully with its big paws in the air on one side. The boys thought this great fun, and were charmed with the expedition.*

To-morrow we send a tour to the Tomb of the eastern kings. Friday, I am sending out a small experimental tour to a fine monastery up in the mountains,—hiking for most of the way. I have a hunch the men are going to like the hiking jaunts I've planned. We always send out a tour of the city on Saturdays and Sundays.[11]

Natalie worked on, cheerfully, through the summer. However, the political strife persisted, as she wrote in her annual August birthday letter to Martha Robinson. *The Stars and Stripes carried a rather lurid article predicting troubles this coming Sunday, and the two to follow it. You doubtless read of the murder of one of the national leaders. And that we refuse to admit that the young man held as the murderer by the Korean police is actually the guilty one, since it hasn't been possible to find any affiliation with a political party. There is high feeling over the matter. There was to have been a meeting last Sunday, apparently Communistic in trend. And it was said that General Brown had been asked to speak. Everybody was uneasy. But a downpour came and prevented it. Everybody breathed a sigh of relief. Only to find that the meeting had merely been postponed. We can hardly expect to have rain for 52 Sundays! I feel it is a pity that the week went by: there will be more time for the Koreans to get stirred up, poor things. I feel so sorry for all of them, all parties. Their history has been so full of invasions and oppression. And yet their spirit is unbroken.*

Meanwhile, mad and bad as the world is, it has its points,—such as your being in it,—to express my gratitude for which fact, the present is blessed with hopes of much happiness for that day and all days. Much love, Knat[12]

Return to Taxco

In 1948, after her long wartime absence, Natalie stepped off the old Mexican bus in the *zócalo* of Taxco, with the Church de la Santa Prisca on one side and the popular, second-story Bar

Paco on the other. As she stood beside the bus gathering her baggage, loud applause and friendly cheers broke forth from above her. The Bar Paco patrons, her old friends, all stood along the balcony's iron railing, looking down upon her, smiling, clapping, and welcoming her home after more than five years on overseas duty.

The horror and pressures of the world war had been softened by her transitional years in the Philippines, Japan, and Korea. Finally at ease, Natalie resumed her life in Taxco. While most war veterans returned home to a spouse or family, Natalie returned to the peasant children of her Guardería. Though she resumed her property management business and her gracious, sometimes raucous, but always interesting social life, Natalie focused the final decade of her life on her school for the most impoverished children of Taxco.

Natalie had returned to America in April 1948, her first stops the Red Cross headquarters in Washington, D.C., and then Alexandria and New Orleans. There she reunited with family and old friends and tended to business in revising and republishing her cookbooks. Then she went home to Taxco.[13] Bill Spratling's Taxco house became one of many she began managing, a challenging task as he had allowed the place to fall into disrepair since moving into his Taxco Viejo hacienda several miles outside of town. *Bill Spratling rented his 'town house' to some very good friends of mine. It had been robbed some months before. So I devotedly moved in to try to get it in shape for my friends. It was so damp and musty that I felt water-logged all the time. And the grippe bugs loved it.*

The watchman meanwhile had been sleeping alternately in two rooms and had over-supplied both with a vast horde of bed-bugs. The Battle of the Bed-Bugs was epic. I thought I had them vanquished, and Charlie Durieux came to visit me. I put him in one of the rooms, and the next morning was quite astonished to find him sleeping in the living room wrapped in his sleeping bag! He explained—all too clearly.[14]

Natalie described for Martha a busy life filled with *many missions and chores,* including acting as hostess to a steady stream of Taxco visitors. *Helen Stevenson, the daughter of 'Bill', who was head of ARC in N. Africa and Italy turned up with a letter to me. I invited her to come on up. And she did,—with six companions, and they stayed until three A.M. It was all very wild.*

The day before my birthday, I had visitors beginning at nine A.M. and continuing on until four-thirty P.M. I was invited to a cocktail party which sounded promising, and then a Mr. Sullivan, who has bought a fine old hacienda (up above the aqueduct under which the road passes into Taxco), was going to have a birthday party for his wife and me that evening.

Usually, I take the Day Nursery children out on an all-day picnic, complete with chicken and other treats, on my birthday and had everything ready for same. The morning dawned in downpour and my throat was worse than ever. So I sent the 'treats' down to the Nursery. Then the children came and begged me to go down to eat chicken with them. So I mournfully riz and did same and went back to bed.

My cunning little cook, Ofelia, was none the less determined that I have a birthday dinner, so she invited my two great friends, a pair of young Yale boys, for dinner, and paid for the dinner herself. Poor thing, I could hardly swallow anything. But she insisted on serving the three of us in my bed-room! And brought me presents. My Yale lads have been bright spots all the while. One of them is John Kurten, whom I knew in Korea, an amazingly mature, intelligent, and sensitive as well as talented young man. He did the most remarkable things in the Soldier Show in Korea. He is now only 22! His friend, Phil Stone, is a tall handsome merry soul. Another friend of theirs, Alger Beal, has joined them. And Alger's sister, who is an especially ravishing young blonde. They include me on everything they plan.

Suffering with her throat infection, Natalie went to a German physician in Mexico City. *He filled my life with medicines and treatments. Fortunately, I was staying with Chiltipin Sutherland, who cared for me wonderfully. And I still had to rat around, trying to arrange to get a little deaf-mute from our Nursery into a home for same in Mexico [City] where he will be taught. And I did arrange it. And the next week I had to take him up. It was an ordeal. The poor little monkey (who is very bright and intelligent) is only six years old and tiny for his age. I had such horrid qualms that I ended by taking his mother and little brother to whom he is devoted up with us the day before; took them all to an amusement park and gave them a big afternoon and evening. But the next evening when I had to leave that tiny little thing alone with strangers,—I really felt as tho a steam-roller had run over me.*[15]

Natalie managed to restore Spratling's house nicely. *My good friends, John and Clare Evans, are here now with their two children, aged 11 and 13, a girl and a boy respectively, plus a couple, Eletha and Martin Swenson. They have taken Bill's house. John is Mable Dodge Luhan's son; moreover in his own right, he wrote a successful and well-written but morbid novel once, and Clare wrote an excellent one, Gallow's Orchard, which was spectacularly successful. They rather plan to write this autumn. Martin is to tutor the children.*

The family that has my casa rented for the summer (while I live in the casita) are the Herbert Mullers with their two little boys aged seven and nine. They are really delightful and Herb is a profoundly scholarly person: his book, SCIENCE AND CRITICISM, which came out while I was still overseas, made a tremendous sensation. It took me, I may say, about two months to read it, but it is more than worthwhile. In it, he surveys the advance in all the modern sciences and appraises them, and analyzes their passage into popular thought, with its corresponding effect on literature and criticism. Quite an order. And written with quiet brilliance and force. But he is completely 'unscholarly' to talk to, with an exceptionally strong 'human interest' in people. Muller, then professor of English at Purdue University, had long spent his summers in Taxco, writing his many books as one of Natalie's favorite lodgers.[16]

In the spring of 1949 Natalie attended the fortieth reunion of her Newcomb class of 1909, wisecracking her way through a series of luncheons and parties with her two great friends, Hilda Phelps Hammond and Martha Robinson. Hilda had gained lasting renown as Huey Long's most implacable foe during the early 1930s. She organized the Louisiana Women's Committee to fight corruption, petitioning and appearing before Senate committees as Long sought the national spotlight. She traveled behind him to America's major cities, speaking before audiences and doing newspaper interviews. Long attempted to quiet her, even making racist accusations that she was of black ancestry. Hilda's book, *Let Freedom Ring*, appeared in 1936, shortly after Long's assassination but before the corruption scandals in Louisiana that sent his cronies, including the new governor, to jail. Through the 1940s, Hilda maintained a New Orleans radio program and prolifically wrote short stories and magazine articles.

Fortieth anniversary of the Newcomb Class of 1909. Natalie is in the center (fifth from left). Hilda Phelps Hammond and Martha Robinson are third and fourth from left, respectively (New Orleans, 1949). *Courtesy of Special Collections, Tulane University Libraries*

Though the threesome of Natalie, Hilda, and Martha enjoyed a frivolous, happy time throughout Natalie's reunion visit, Natalie later confided some concerns to Martha. *I am rather worried about Whilda. I didn't think she looked too well while I was there. Not that she hinted a thing. I do wish she could have some prosperity and security for awhile.* Natalie's own finances remained modest but not strained. In a 1953 interview with *Dixie* magazine, Natalie explained that she had long ago accepted semi-poverty as a worthwhile exchange for her satisfying, invigorating life in Mexico. *Taxco is like a peaceful oasis, to which I always return.*[17]

In August 1949, Natalie received word from Martha that Newcomb College wished to retain her services to lead a major fundraising campaign to build new dormitories on campus. They would pay her travel expenses to New Orleans plus several hundred dollars in fees. Natalie accepted immediately. *If it should really turn out to be a few hundred I'll be a changed woman. There is something grim-making about being constantly on the ragged edge. Do tell the Dean he can count on me, quite definitely. As for the expenses of*

*the trip up, I will go in my usual plebian manner, sitting all the
way in bus and train. Sorry I am too broke to contribute to the
dormitory fund. Maybe I can give a little something.*[18] The dean at
first planned for Natalie to campaign for Newcomb only in
Louisiana. By January 1950, when Natalie moved into a Newcomb
dormitory room for a seven-month stay, the plan had changed.
She became director of Newcomb's national campaign, her face
gracing the cover of the March 1950 edition of *The Tulanian* magazine. The feature story announced Natalie's leadership.

> Miss Natalie Vivian Scott, '09 Newcomb, has been named direc-
> tor of alumnae activities to raise $200,000. . . . The appointment
> was announced by Miss Marian Nash, national president of the
> Newcomb Alumnae Association. The appointment of Miss Scott
> will be hailed by Newcomb graduates in all sections of the country.
> She is known personally to hundreds of them, while many others
> are equally familiar with her record of dynamic accomplishment.
>
> She will stay in New Orleans while working on the dormitory
> campaign. The Newcomb alumnae rooms are headquarters for the
> work. Miss Nash stressed the need. . . . Since three-quarters of the
> out-of-town applicants are being turned down solely because of lack
> of dormitory facilities, something must be done at once. Newcomb
> in 1918 was the most highly endowed college for women in America.
> Today, it ranks twelfth. Agnes Scott, in Decatur, Ga., which had only
> $186,000 at that time, today is richer than Newcomb. New dormito-
> ries will relieve the strain on its limited earnings. An extra 100
> tuition-paying students will give Newcomb an additional income of
> $40,000 annually, equivalent to the income from about $1,000,000
> endowment. At the same time, it will enable another 100 of the
> brightest young women to gain a Newcomb education.[19]

Natalie had recruited a staff of volunteers, many her old
friends from the New Orleans area. Her speaking engagements
began with appearances in Jackson, Birmingham, and Houston.
The Newcomb alumnae chapters advertised Natalie's Mexican
work and her reputation as a world traveler, war heroine, and
writer. The fundraising functions were a success in each city. On
May 2, a *Times-Picayune* article headlined "NAT'S BACK" more
fully explained her work.

Natalie's uncovered hundreds of friends she'd misplaced in her traveling benefit parties. She revels in the hectic atmosphere at the "campaign" headquarters on campus. 'We expect to raise at least $200,000. We're hoping the total will be nearer $400,000.' Under Natalie's direction, more than a dozen alumnae sorority groups have banded together to raise funds. Kappa Kappa Gamma sponsored a dramatic reading, the Phi Mu a puppet show.

The Newcomb Alumnae Club gave a rummage sale and the Pan-Hellenic Council put on skit night. In Baton Rouge, Newcomb alumnae put on a "Vanities of the '20s" show, and local Chi Omega alumnae gave a dramatic reading and tea. Saturday the

Natalie at work, chain-smoking, as chairman of the Newcomb College fundraising campaign (New Orleans, 1950). *Courtesy of Special Collections, Tulane University Libraries*

New Orleans Alumnae Club sponsored a rummage sale, and Sunday the Delta Zeta alumnae presented a jazz afternoon at the Parisian Room. Things to come include an Old New Orleans Night, sponsored by Beta Sigma Omicron on May 5; a soft-bar-maid booth conducted by Alpha Omicron Pi on May 6; a student carnival on May 13, and a Newcomb Jamboree on June 3.

Miss Scott has contacted 17 alumnae groups across the country and organized another group in the Mississippi Delta. Out-of-state groups plan their own entertainments and send the money to the Newcomb headquarters. An average of 40 checks a week pour in from other individual alumnae.

By the end of 1950, the fundraising campaign passed the $400,000 mark, Newcomb's fondest hopes achieved.[20]

Upon her return to Taxco, Natalie devoted her fundraising efforts to her peasant school. Perhaps inspired by the success of her Newcomb campaign—as well as a rent hike imposed by her small school's landlord—Natalie began a new drive to gain financial independence for the Guardería. Her goal was to construct a larger, permanent building.

Between 1948 and 1951, Natalie encountered difficulties regaining her permanent "resident" status in Mexico, which had been lost due to her five years' absence for wartime service. Her tourist visa forced her to leave Mexico and apply for renewal every six months. Mexico City newspapers publicized Natalie's plight, pressuring the government to remedy the injustice. These articles, aside from recalling her war service and peasant school, spoke of her other civic works: "She got the town its first doctor by getting the 10 Americans there to okay a group plan, augmented by the post of coroner which she arranged for. There's a hospital now, Rotary and Lions Clubs are busy with school improvements, and the American colony pitches in vigorously."

One appeal was made by a Mexico City columnist named Chisme.

To those of us who have been living here for at least ten years, Natalie is Taxco. . . . Natalie came to Taxco in 1930—over the old road built by Don José de la Borda (circa 1740). It took a full day in a decrepit Studebaker loaded with nine people, bundles and a few chickens. Natalie described it as 100 miles horizontal and 600 vertical. She was the first American woman to settle. There was no doctor in town . . . she established the "Associación de Salud,"—a successful experiment in group medicine. In 1938 she organized the "Guardería de Ninos." . . . Her good works for the native Tasqueños expanded to the young and eager tourists like myself who flocked down to Taxco. Who can ever forget her "pensión" Casa Kitigawa where for a few pesos a day we were able to live comfortably and in an intellectual atmosphere. Her Mexican cookbook introduced many visitors to the favorite recipes of Mexico families in Taxco. It was illustrated by the two local youngsters, Amador Lugo and Delfino García, who were then beginning their careers. Both these young men have since had exhibitions in Mexico City and the traveling Mexican Art Show in the United States. . . . Recently she has been lecturing in the United States through the mediums of radio and Women's Clubs. Her topic? "Mexico."

Another newspaper told the story of Natalie's Guardería, much of that history taken from an earlier illustrated article in the *Mexico City News.*

Since 1938 the nursery has thrived, helping hundreds of children get a better start in life. . . . The holiday which the children love best is Miss Scott's birthday, July 18. On that day, the town declares a fiesta. Two local silversmiths donate piñatas filled with sweets and nuts for the day nursery's party, ingenious displays in fireworks—St. Michael beating the Devil, or a Satan with rolling eyes and a protruding tongue—are shot into the sky. On the ground a mechanical "fireworks bull" shoots sparkles out of his mouth. But life is not all fiestas. . . . Poor conditions in their homes have left many toddlers with vitamin deficiencies, tuberculosis and parasites. . . . Medical care is given those who need it and Natalie has made special efforts for children with extreme handicaps. One was a small boy with a club foot and tuberculosis. She went to Mexico City and practically shadowed a prominent surgeon until she could get him to listen to her story about the boy. He agreed to operate. A year later, after a successful operation and . . . care for his tubercular condition, the child returned to Taxco, a happier, healthier youngster.[21]

Rest in Peace

By Christmas 1950, Natalie's residency was finally being restored, as her friend Mary Louise Doherty reported in a letter to novelist Katherine Anne Porter. Ms. Doherty also wrote of a social function in Natalie's small hilltop home, a very lively party during the Christmas season. "There is a party at her place for some 15 people Sat. at 9 pm. The place is charming . . . tho she's other side of the hill and way to highest point again. Just can't imagine serving drinks at her place and expecting guests to get down her hill safely . . . the mining crowd is coming." Then she added, "We may go." Subsequently, Ms. Doherty wrote that the party did not break up until five o'clock in the morning.[22]

Most of Natalie's social gatherings were more sedate, typically intended for her visitors or lodgers to meet the locals. Her hospitality often featured a Mexican band, and the magnificent view from her porch put all at ease. Her guests often contributed to the *Guardería.* Natalie had found peace in Taxco, as she wrote to Sam Gilmore in November 1950: *the weather is perfectly heavenly, and altogether, if the bank account didn't keep hounding me with its plaintive appeals for sustenance, I could be completely happy.*[23]

Taxco, Mexico (by Antonio Gallegos, 1997). *Courtesy of the Antonio Gallegos Collection*

In 1951, Natalie accelerated her campaign to build a much larger school for Taxco's children. Her efforts attracted press support in Mexico, Texas, and Louisiana, such as this article by a Mexico City columnist describing his visit to the school.

> Today, a thriving nursery takes care of thirty children between the ages two and six. They arrive at 8 in the morning and leave around 6 . . . three good nourishing meals a day. They go to kindergarten in the morning, then return for lunch, a siesta, and hours of play and dance. . . . It is fun to visit the school. If you drop in around 1 you will probably find Miss Scott or Miss Crouch with the children. . . . Everyone was singing London Bridge to music from the victrola, and with appropriate gestures. Late comers showed beautiful manners as they came in, shook Miss Scott's hand, then mine, saluted us, and joined in the singing. They performed with a great glee the dance of the Bunito and are learning all kinds of native dances, the Jarabe, and the Chapanecos, the dance of Guerrero.
>
> They showed me their beautiful toys, their victrola, and their books in English and Spanish. The Treasure Chest, an organization in New York, which sends children's books to foreign countries, had just sent a fine supply. Miss Scott was prepared to translate the Wizard of Oz for them. As I was leaving, one three year old girl stood up and asked to do a dance all by herself, a charming little number which she calls La Cucaracha.
>
> The school keeps going on the help of townspeople, and the interest of passing travelers. One woman was interested enough to include the school in her lectures in the States and now receives contributions for it. Many of the stores in town, Mexican and American, give money. The mothers themselves are charged 2.50 pesos per month. Mr. Nibbi (of the Hotel Victoria) helps. All of the students are given thorough physical examinations, have their lungs x-rayed, are given vitamins and any kind of special treatment they require.[24]

In Laredo, the Pan American Student Forum of Martin High School became a steady source of clothes and toys, making Natalie's Guardería its international project. Another club at the school, the Future Homemakers of America, began in 1952 sending toys made by the members.[25] Another high school in Sacramento, California adopted Natalie's Guardería as its sister school, annually sending donations, clothes, and toys. Natalie initiated this relationship by hosting some California tourists, who then made arrangements with the Sacramento school.[26]

In October 1951, the sudden death of Hilda Phelps Hammond in New Orleans brought Natalie shock and grief comparable only to the losses of her parents and brother in the 1920s. Hilda suffered a fatal stroke while typing a letter to Natalie. Godmother to two Hammond children, one of them by then the wife of her nephew Nauman, Natalie flew to New Orleans to join the family for the funeral, remaining in Louisiana through Christmas.[27]

During the course of the 1950s, several books characterized Natalie's role in Taxco, including a novel, *Stuffed Shirt in Taxco* by Leslie Cortes de Figueroa, and another book written by American humorist H. Allen Smith. The novel, written shortly after Natalie's death, tells the story of a New York workaholic whose wife drags him away from his business for an extended Taxco vacation. Unhappy to be there, the "Stuffed Shirt" resents Natalie's "effervescence" and her offers to introduce them around. He instead isolates himself within the refuge of the Bar Paco, refusing any interest in Taxco or its inhabitants.

Natalie (left) camping out with friends on Acapulco beach (ca. 1952). *John W. Scott Collection*

Figueroa, who with her husband had owned the Bar Paco and founded the Taxco School of Art, featured prominent Taxco figures such as Natalie, Spratling, and Carlos Nibbi in her book. In parallel plots, the eyes of the workaholic are gradually opened to the significance of both Taxco and Natalie, his indifference transforming into genuine affection. From his vantage point in the Bar Paco, he notices Natalie each day surrounded by peasant children in the *zócalo* as she gives them refreshments and organizes games and art activities. From an acquaintance in the bar, the "Stuffed Shirt" learns of her social work in Taxco.

> "The children are well fed and dressed and the mothers call for them at night when this work is over. Naturally they come from the poorest homes and some have parents in the jail. Three of them sleep in the jail and go to school by day."
>
> "Very interesting," I remarked. "I had no idea that Miss Scott did such serious work. Thought she was just an incurable land-lady."
>
> Jeff smiled in his quiet way. "She does a lot for Taxco. Was the first American woman to live here. She loved the place and seeing few houses suitable for Americans, she leased a few at very low rents, fixed them up and re-rented them to tourists. That brought a lot of money into Taxco, for Americans keep servants and pay better than the average Mexican family. Natalie introduces them to other Americans and the first thing you know they are so happy here and sold on Taxco that they keep on coming back year after year. Have you met Prof. Müller yet? No? Well, he is one of her tenants who comes back every chance he gets."
>
> "About Miss Scott—" I began, but Jeff went right on as though I had not spoken.
>
> "The Day Nursery idea was hers and took hold at once. Not only are the children fed and dressed, but those with physical defects are taken to doctors and dentists and many times she takes children to famous surgeons in Mexico City who operate on them for nothing, Hare lips, crossed eyes, crooked limbs—all are taken care of by this big-hearted woman. . . .
>
> "That's wonderful," I agreed. "Am afraid I misjudged her at first. . . ."[28]

In another conversation, this one between the "Stuffed Shirt"'s wife and a local, the reader learns that Natalie manages twenty houses. "She advertises in New York publications and many come and take houses sight unseen." In another passage,

Bill Spratling explains more about Natalie and her hospitality to visitors such as the "Stuffed Shirt" and his wife. "Mr. Spratling said he had known her for many years and that she had done so much good in the community, not only for the children in her Day Nursery, but for strangers in town. Any tenants she had were introduced and given a party or two to orient them and she never tired of helping them regulate their servants, learn 'Kitchen Spanish' or surmount any problem which came up. This made people feel at home and many of her tenants returned time and again."[29]

The book by New York author H. Allen Smith offered a diary of his fun-filled travels through Mexico, focusing on Taxco in 1955 and his new friends there, particularly Natalie Scott. His book, *The Pig in the Barber Shop,* took its name from a humorous Taxco controversy about whether or not pigs should be banned from the *zócalo.* "In the plaza today we met Natalie Scott. If Spratling is the King of Taxco, then Miss Scott is surely the Queen." He writes on about her sense of humor, her newspaper work in New Orleans, her horseback explorations, her cookbooks, and her Guardería de Niños. He is entertained at parties at Natalie's house on the hill, crowning her "the grande dame of Taxco." Her local stories gave him more material for his book. After that first 1955 visit, H. Allen Smith returned annually to Taxco, writing the introduction to Figueroa's novel two years later.[30]

Among those enjoying Natalie's hospitality were three young men from Harvard who arrived in 1957. David Read, a young writer and teacher, had driven down to Taxco in an old convertible to join two of his friends for the summer. Forty years later, holding forth in the dining room of Taxco's Hotel Victoria, he spoke vividly of his first encounter with Natalie, sixty-seven years old when he met her.

> I had been driving for a week, and I was so relieved to get to Taxco. I couldn't wait to collapse! But my friends were just getting dressed to go to a party at Natalie Scott's when I arrived with a huge suitcase and typewriter. That was the summer I was going to write the Great American novel.
>
> We were all on foot. I was supposed to be in shape after coaching track, but it seemed like a real climb up to Natalie's—and dangerous. They hadn't filled the *barranca* [ravine] below Natalie's yet—now it's mostly hotel—and there was no wall on the *barranca* side. The stone walk couldn't have been more than a yard wide.

I had only just met Natalie and had been given a martini, but Natalie made me feel as if I had always known her. And the house was so simple and yet so sophisticated! Books galore, wonderful Mexican curios, and unforgettable paintings of the Virgin de Guadalupe! Most of us were sitting on the wall of the corridor [the front porch], between geraniums and more exotic plants, and behind us the view of the faraway mountains and of course the towers of Santa Prisca all lit up.

Since I was quite near Natalie, sort of on the edge of her group, I had become aware that she kept having another martini. I must have had several, but for some reason I kept counting Natalie's! And suddenly Natalie said to me, "David Read, would you make me another martini?" And of course I was delighted to, and headed for the kitchen, where probably Rosario was making plates full of *tostaditos*.

But all the time I was thinking, what kind of martini do you make for someone who had already had six martinis? Very proper Bostonian kind of thoughts. The Last Puritan. So I put in not very much gin and more vermouth than I should have, and a big squeeze of a very juicy lime right out of Natalie's garden, and some ice. It looked like a martini.

I was naive enough to think that Natalie might even think it was one! But no such luck! Natalie made the most wonderful face when she tasted it. Her whole face somehow screwed itself up and you could just tell that it was the most dreadful tasting thing she had ever tasted in her life! Of course, she was sitting on the corridor wall with a very beautiful *rebozo* around her shoulders—and she just turned toward the garden, spit out that mouthful, and emptied her glass in the garden. And then she turned back to me and handed me the empty glass and said, "David Read, when I want a lemonade, I will tell you!"

And then I went back to the kitchen and filled the glass with gin and just looked at the vermouth and did not bother with the lime, a piece of ice, and I went back to Natalie. She sipped it very delicately and approved it. So that was my initiation into Natalie's friendship![31]

David Read spoke humorously of the challenge every time they had to negotiate their way back down the long winding walkway, essentially a stone staircase, to the town below.

It was scary! We used to think it was terribly funny. Herb Muller had the worst accident. Poor Janet would usually wait for him at the bottom of the path where it was easier to climb down. And that *barranca* was rushing with water in the rainy season. There would be little cries for help as people slithered home. But you know, Herb turned out a tremendous amount of work while he was here . . . *The Uses of the Past.* I think they still use it in college courses. Hard to think of the author struggling to climb out of Natalie's *barranca!*[32]

Another of David Read's Harvard threesome, Walter Foulke, only eighteen at the time and an aspiring concert pianist, described Natalie as a "vivid presence in Taxco" and "the acknowledged leader of the American community."

What I remember most was her ability to talk to anyone of any age as a complete equal, an intriguing person, interested in everything.

I explained to Natalie that I was anxious to keep up the momentum playing the piano. I had been taking lessons in Philadelphia with a great classical piano teacher, Gordon Stanley. Among other pieces, Mr. Stanley had taught me Rachmaninoff's Prelude in C-sharp Minor, a rather showy piece that revolves around three distinctive notes—A, G-sharp, C-sharp. The three loud initial notes starting the piece are quite unforgettable.

And, as I was telling all this to Natalie, she took my hands in hers and examined them very thoroughly. My hands are rather square and my fingers very stubby and wide. Natalie said, "What perfect hands for the piano!" I was thrilled at this comment coming from someone older who looked so wise and knowledgeable. Many people wrongly suppose that piano players should have long slender fingers.

I asked her why she thought my hands were good for the piano and she said, "Rubinstein has hands like yours." I do not know if she ever met Rubinstein but I suppose she might have. I had met Rubinstein once. His hands *were* square and his fingers *were* blunt and strong. I was very impressed.

The problem, as I explained it, was that there was no piano I could play except a small electric one located on the second floor of Bar Paco. Taxco was a town more dedicated to guitars than pianos. Fortunately, a woman friend of Natalie's owned what must have been the only good-size acoustic piano in the town.

Natalie took me over to her friend's house and introduced me. Instead of leaving, however, Natalie sat down and asked me to play Rachmaninoff's C-sharp Minor Prelude. I played the piece with great flourish and when I finished Natalie was very complimentary. She said she thought if I wanted to do it I could become a concert pianist. I was greatly flattered, but then she added that she thought it was unlikely I would follow this career path. When I asked why, she said, "Because you have too many other interests." She was, of course, quite right. I did have many other interests and, as things turned out, I never did take up serious classical music again after that summer. Instead, I branched out into jazz, which I still play and love.[33]

David Read moved into Natalie's casita for the summer of 1957, where he worked away on his novel and spent much time in long talks with Natalie. Taxco became for him a permanent second home. Before returning to Boston after that first visit, he wrote a poem for her, "Portrait of Natalie," that was a collage of the many stories she had shared with him. It was among Natalie's possessions donated to the Tulane Archives after her death. Seeing the poem again after four decades, Read sent a newly handwritten version inscribed to my wife and me, "who are discovering how alive the memory of Natalie Scott still is, in Taxco and elsewhere, in the minds and hearts of her friends and admirers. Cheers, David Read, Taxco—July '96."

Portrait of Natalie

do you know how a carriage wheel spins, Natalie?
do you know how a carriage wheel spins?
the wheels roll forward
and
the spokes spin backward
that is the way a carriage wheel spins:
   forward and backward but on and on
   until the roads end or the horses are done.

I.

The spokes spin backward
to when you were your Father's daughter
moving southward and toward a golden fleece
that no Medea guarded, only a serpent plumed

Natalie Scott, the year before her death (New Orleans, 1956). *Courtesy of Special Collections, Tulane University Libraries*

and coiled, but not for striking, to whom
you fed your heart; whom your laughter
moved to motions of love long hidden
but poured upon you as you rode
through time and the hot land,
through words corroded by the same wind
the feathers fanned for your lover
whose bones waited for you
under the sacred altar
upon whose red steps
you found your heart.

II.

The wheels roll forward
from the time you first moved
onward, voyaging in circles toward
Colchis and the frightening sea, through
love and turmoil and every landed tongue,
their dust echoing in your heart between
silence and the guns, the battles, jokes, puns
of voyagers all on the same ship, or from the same
home, or for the same port at some time or place:
oh the wind blowing, plumed and feathered fan,
oh Cuahtemoc! oh Colua my brothers! gold and gold!
and in the jungle your Father and Mother,
their voices, action, love; as rich a pattern
as the screened green jungle through which you rode
to peaks as distant as Olympus before dawn,
between dawn and dark; and the wood-smoke,
the long voices of men, the robed motions
of their women, the gestures, the laughter
of their children, yours, become yours in that ascent
through the red dust to the bones
whose power moves your words, eyes, hands,
and your heart and mind make incantation
where the fleece hangs, and shines.

envoi

now you know how a carriage wheel spins, Natalie,
now you know how a carriage wheel spins,

the wheels roll forward
and
the spokes spin backward
that is the way a carriage wheel spins:
 forward and backward but on and on
 until the roads end or the horses are done.

DWR To Natalie—with love and admiration—August, 1957[34]

Natalie died unexpectedly a few months later, on November 18, 1957, two days following a painful attack of uremic poisoning. There had been no hint earlier in November that anything was amiss. Natalie had just returned from an October visit to Louisiana, and several of her lively, playful November letters survive today. When she fell ill, her devoted neighbors, Héctor and Lois Aguilar, rushed her in their station wagon to the French Hospital in Mexico City. They immediately notified her sister-in-law, Sidonie Scott, in Louisiana, who flew to Mexico City with her daughter, Bé Scott Thomas. Sidonie wrote afterwards of Natalie's greeting from her hospital bed. "She apologized to my daughter and me for receiving us in 'so boring' a manner." She suffered severe and unremitting pain. The nurses refused her a cigarette, but Bè and Sidonie let her smoke once they were alone. An old Taxco friend, Carl Pappe, a fine artist and the husband of author Bernice Goodspeed, also came to her just before the surgery that was meant to save her life. Natalie prepared for the operation by applying lipstick and combing her hair, the modest behavior of a Victorian lady facing death—and reminiscent of British nurse Edith Cavell, whose heroism had inspired Natalie in 1915.[35]

Natalie died quietly before dawn. A funeral service was held in the small hospital chapel. Her body was then taken to Taxco for the burial, the road into the *zócalo* lined with children holding flowers, among hundreds of mourners. Here is one newspaper's account.

> The casket was placed in a balcony room of the famous Borda Palace which opens wide upon the Plaza so that all might share in the touching tribute. . . . These devoted, grieving people placed the precious old crucifix, removed for the first time from its niche in the beautiful Santa Prisca Church, at the head of her bier. The

local priests offered their prayers. The large sala was a bower of beautiful blossoms in containers completely surrounding the coffin, the most magnificent being the giant wreath fashioned by the mothers of the Nursery children. A guard of eight men changed shifts the whole night through.[36]

In the morning, a two-mile procession of children and friends followed the hand-carried casket on the long walk to the cemetery below town. The inscription on her tombstone read simply:

Natalie Scott

1890-1957

"Rest in Peace Near the Little Ones You Loved"

The donations that flowed in afterwards completed Natalie's fundraising campaign to construct the new building for her school. She had acquired the land and approved the architectural plans, complete with patios, a large garden (*"jardin de niños"*), offices, *sala,* dining room, and kitchen, among other facilities.[37] The new school building was finished, opened, and dedicated with a large ceremony on the one-year anniversary of Natalie's death. Its name was changed to Pro-Infancia Natalie Scott. Along with contributions came letters, including one from an old friend, Vera Von Meysenburg O'Leary, a German-American who had worked for the German cause in the First World War. She remembered the ostracism she had felt in New Orleans in 1919 and Natalie's perceptive, helpful role, as well as their many good times whenever Natalie visited New Orleans in the decades that followed:

"Hi Verily! What gives?" were the cheery words that greeted me as I picked up the receiver of my phone. The words, the voice, quickly dispelled the gloom that had settled over me that morning. Instead a warm glow of gladness. It was Natalie. And it was a surprise.

Natalie. Natalie Scott. Her name alone set off a welter of thoughts and memories. There was bustling and commotion always when Natalie came to town!

Our phone chat,—tid-bits of spicy gossip and swept along by gales of laughter, for Nat was a wit and could make anyone laugh. Yet, with her wit went profundity too.

It was shortly after World War I had ended. It was a harrowing time for me as it was for most of us. I would like very much to skip this part of my story but I cannot, for it was this that really brought Nat and me together and tied the knots of our friendship.

We met in a Tea Room in a downtown section of our city, a Tea Room which, because of its German flavor and name, was destined to die.

I was leaning over the glass counter trying to decide which of a long row of appetizing tarts I should choose—when I felt a tap upon my shoulder, followed by a cheery voice which I did not recognize at first. Nor did I even recognize Natalie whom I had known only slightly and had not seen in years.

"Hi, Verily!" she greeted me. "It's been a long time." The smile that accompanied her friendly greeting warmed my heart starved as it was from so much unfriendliness! Indeed, it was a treat, for heretofore, during those early post-war days, only frowns or jeers had greeted me everywhere, from old and new friends alike, who were now my enemies! I was wary of course, for I had been too deeply hurt too often, not to watch for signs of insincerity. But Natalie seemed genuinely sincere,—and interested!

Amenities over, during which I observed her every expression, she cordially insisted that I lunch with her. She who had won the Croix de Guerre for her bravery requested that I relate a few of my own experiences in Germany, which hesitantly, I did! The ice was broken; a bond established. Urged on by her deep understanding that was so fundamentally a part of Natalie, I even went so far as to confide in her the taunts, the jibes and all the insults I had suffered after my return from Germany in 1917, even though the re-telling hurt and only opened afresh, my wounds. She had heard them all before—their injustice, their untruthfulness had infuriated her and was the reason why she was determined to look me up had we not met by chance.

She even offered me a job that was vacant in the same newspaper office where she was working which I gladly accepted. Thus for several years we were thrown often together while our friendship deepened and grew.

She had only recently returned when I met her, but I knew that the whole city was acclaiming her a heroine.

It astonished me therefore, yet flattered me too, that she should seek me out and want me for a friend at a time when she was being lionized, when I was more or less an outcast! Now, many years later, I appreciate more than ever what she did for me: She restored my trust in humanity and gave me back the faith I had lost!

Is it any wonder that through the years since her death, I have carried, and shall always carry in my heart, the notes of her clarion clear voice, and whenever my telephone rings, hear her cheery greeting:

"Hi Verily! It's been so long—what gives?"[38]

Notes

Chapter 1

1. Luis Reyes, interview by author, Taxco, Mexico, July 30-31, 1996. Carl Pappe, interview by author, Taxco, Mexico, August 9, 1996. Sidonie Scott Thomas (Bé Scott Thomas), interview by author, May 17, 1996. *Mexico City News*, November 19-21, 1957. Natalie Vivian Scott Collection (N.V.S. Collection), Tulane University, Howard-Tilton Library (Box 13, Folder 18). Sidonie Provosty Scott, "Two Unforgettable Pilgrimages" (Essay in Scott Family Collection, 1959). Nauman S. Scott, Jr., interview by author, February 17, 1996.

2. Charles Lawrence Dyer, *Along the Gulf* (1895; reprint, Pass Christian, Miss.: Pass Christian Historical Society, 1971), 13-20. N.V.S. Collection (Box 8, Folder 3), Natalie Vivian Scott, "A Comparison of Certain Plays of Euripides with Later Plays on the Same Subject" (master's thesis, Newcomb College, 1914), biographical note, 1. The Bay St. Louis *Seacoast Echo.* , 1896-1903. John Wilds, *Afternoon Story: The History of the New Orleans* States-Item (Baton Rouge: Louisiana State University Press, 1976), 41-42, 64-68. Charles Gray, Hancock County Historical Society Archives, Bay St. Louis, Mississippi.

3. John Wyeth Scott was born in Sheffield, Alabama on February 1, 1887; Nauman Steele Scott was born in Cave Springs, Georgia on October 3, 1888; Natalie Vivian Scott was born in Bristol, Tennessee on July 18, 1890. The Bay St. Louis property was owned then and now by the Swoop family; it was destroyed in 2005 by Hurricane Katrina. A circa-1896 photo of the home has Muddie's handwritten inscription. An October 22, 1907, letter by Muddie Scott states that the Swoops were again using the house. N.V.S. Collection (Box 7, Folder 11; Box 8, Folder 3; Box 11, Folder 11; Box 10, Folder 1; Box 12, Folders 3, 8, 9, 12; Box 3, Folder 5). Henry F. Chambers, *A History of Louisiana* (Chicago: American Historical Society, 1925), 2:209-10, 3:347. Laverne Thomas III, *LeDoux* (New Orleans: Polyanthos, 1982), 313. N.V.S. thesis, 1. John Smith Kendall, *History of New Orleans,* vol. 2 (Chicago: Lewis, 1922). The Boyd County Public Library, Ashland, Ky. Census records, Hancock County, 267A. Hancock County Clerk of Court. Hancock County Public School Records (1897-1900). *Seacoast Echo,* June 13, 1896; February 13, 27; March 20, 27; April-June 1897; July 3, 17; August 14, 1897. Dyer, 24. *The Hancock Historian,* Hancock County Historical Society, May 1996.

4. John W. Scott, "Yellow Fever Strikes Bay St. Louis: The Epidemic of 1897," *Journal of Mississippi History* 63, no. 2 (summer 2000). *Seacoast Echo,* July 17; August-December 1897. Dyer, 21-22. N.V.S. Collection (Box 6, Folder 1). N.V.S. Collection (Box 7, Folder 8; Box 13, Folder 1; Box 11, Folder 5) contains an October 23, 1987, telegram from Ashland friends and a newspaper clipping

regarding Muddie's illness. Box 6, Folder 2, contains a short story by N.V.S. citing Mrs. Scott's illness in 1903, which required a friend to stay with her at home. Natalie's World War I letters make numerous references to her mother's health, such as those dated February 4, 1918, and October 7, 1920.

5. *Confederate Veteran* (May 1912): 205-8. Thomas, *LeDoux*, 313. Chambers, 2:208. N.V.S. Collection (Box 1, Folder 5), letter of February 6, 1918. N.V.S. Collection (Box 6, Folder 3; Box 7, Folders 1-3; Box 10, Folder 1) contains early family material that Nathaniel Graves Scott gathered while researching his genealogy. John Allan Wyeth, *Life of General Nathan Bedford Forrest*, vols. 5-8 (New York: Harper and Brothers, 1908, republished as *That Devil Forest*, vols. 12-14, 23-25, Baton Rouge: LSU Press, 1989). Forrest scattered his recruiting agents during the summer of 1861 through northern Alabama, middle and west Tennessee, and northern Mississippi, while he personally recruited in southern Kentucky. Two of his original eight companies in his mounted battalion in October 1861 were Company B, commanded by Captain Bacot from southern Alabama, and Company H, commanded by Captain Milner of Marshall County, Alabama, where Guntersville was located. Wyeth also wrote an autobiography, *With Sabre and Scalpel*. Sidonie Scott Thomas and Albin P. Scott, interview, October 19, 1982, Friends of the Cabildo Collection, New Orleans Public Library, 313. Laverne Thomas III, interview by author, Easter 1996. Kendall, vol. 2. According to Kendall's biographical summary, Boss went from the Selma, Rome, and Dalton Railroad to the Birmingham Bridge Company, then was employed by Chicago's American Bridge Company in Little Rock, Arkansas. He probably worked with John Allan Wyeth on the White and Red rivers between 1869 and 1872 (Wyeth, *That Devil Forest*, vol. 13). Boss was the Texas and Pacific's superintendent in building the Dallas and Wichita railroad to Denton, then built the T & P line from New Orleans to Shreveport and the Yazoo and Mississippi Valley railroad between Baton Rouge and Port Gibson. He was then in charge of constructing the trestle across Lake Pontchartrain, bringing him to New Orleans in 1879. For the next thirty-five years, he did contract work for many firms across the South. Rev. Pike Thomas and Kay Lee Wrage Gunn, *The Scotts of Southwest Virginia* (Marion, Va.: Tucker, 1999).

6. *Biographical and Historical Memories of Louisiana* (Chicago: Goodspeed, 1892), 1:235. Silliman College was established in 1852, chiefly through the benevolence of William Silliman, "to give to the public an institution of learning to which all may send their children, without interfering with the religious prejudices of any." It was located in the same terrain that John James Audubon had explored and made famous. Thomas, *LeDoux*, 313. Sidonie Scott Thomas, interview. Scott, interview. N.V.S. Collection (Box 2, Folder 4) contains her letter of June 6, 1918, which discusses Muddie's health. Box 3, Folder 5, contains Natalie's letter to Martha Gilmore Robinson, October 22, 1942. Box 7, Folders 2, 8; Box 10, Folder 1; and Box 2, Folder 1, contain Natalie's letters to Nauman dated September 8, 1918, and October 27, 1917. Box 12 contains family photographs. Census records, Hancock County. Census, L. W. Anderson Genealogical Library, Bay St. Louis (1890). Hancock County Tax Records (1898).

7. *Seacoast Echo*, 1896-1903. N.V.S. Collection (Box 7, Folders 7, 8, 11, 14; Box 8, Folders 1, 2, 7; Box 9, Folders 2, 3, 4, 13; Box 10, Folders 1, 2; Box 13, Folders 2, 9, Oversized Folders 1, 2; Folders 3, 9; Oversized Folders 1, 2). Box 10, Folder 1, contains scrapbook of Martha Fauver Scott, with *Seacoast Echo* clipping referring to her charity work and Natalie's assistance. Hancock County Public School records, 1897-1900. Census, L. W. Anderson Genealogical Library (1900). Hancock County Tax Records (1898). Thomas, *LeDoux*, 313-15. Sidonie Scott Thomas, interview. Nauman S. Scott, Jr., interview. Christ Episcopal Church records, Bay St. Louis (April 12, 1896).

8. *Seacoast Echo,* April 26, June 7, 28, July 12, 1902. N.V.S. Collection (Box 10, Folder 1). R. M. DuBose (The University of the South—Sewanee) to Mrs. N. G. Scott, June 14, 1901. Hancock County Public School Records (1896-1905). George W. Engelhardt, *The City of New Orleans: The Book of the Chamber of Commerce and Industry of Louisiana* (New Orleans: 1894). Ferrell School photograph of Nauman and Wyeth Scott, Albin P. Scott Collection, Covington, Louisiana. New Orleans City Directory, New Orleans Public Library (1901-4).

9. Brandt V. B. Dixon, *A Brief History of H. Sophie Newcomb Memorial College, 1887-1919* (1928; reprint, Gretna, La.: Pelican, 1998), 44-50, 66, 88, 132, 185, 191. Tulane University and Newcomb College Transcripts of John Wyeth Scott, Nauman Steele Scott, and Natalie Vivian Scott. N.V.S. Collection (Box 6, Folder 2; Box 7, Folders 6, 7; Box 8, Folder 3). Chambers, 2:209, 3:346-47. N.V.S. thesis, biographical note.

10. Hilda Phelps Hammond, *Let Freedom Ring* (New York: Farrar & Rinehart, 1936), 23-24.

11. Edith J. R. Isaacs, ed., *Plays of American Life and Fantasy* (New York: Coward-McCann, 1929), 309-28. Inscription on title page of volume in Tulane Library.

12. N.V.S. Collection (Boxes 1-3, 7-8, Folders 1, 2, 3, 7; Box 9, Folders 1-4; Box 10, Folders 1-4; Box 12, Folder 2; Box 13, Folders 18, 22). *New Orleans Times-Picayune,* September-December 1909. Newcomb College Records of Faculty Meetings (March 19, 1906). Tulane *Jambalaya,* 1905-9. A comparison between the 1908 *Jambalaya* and 1909 *Jambalaya* of the organizations and the positions held by Newcomb College students demonstrates a radical change. Martha Robinson, interview by Dorothy Schlesinger, Friends of the Cabildo Oral History Project, New Orleans. Martha Robinson Collection (Box 2, Folder 10-F), Tulane University. New Orleans *Times-Democrat,* May 18, 1909. New Orleans *Daily Picayune,* February 26, May 18, 23, 1909. Dixon, 46-48, 66-72, 84-88, 96-104, 108-17, 115-28, 132-54. Natalie Vivian Scott, "The Forest Primeval," *The Newcomb Arcade* 1, no. 1 (January 1909). *The Newcomb Arcade* (June 1909). *The Newcomb Arcade* was named for the large three-storied edifice, the Arcade, built in 1896 to connect each floor of the school's College Hall to the Academy building, Newcomb's two largest classroom buildings. *Tulane Weekly,* October-January 1909-10, October 8, 14, 21, 1909.

13. Newcomb College Transcripts of Natalie Vivian Scott. N.V.S. Collection (Box 1; Box 9, Folder 1). Dr. J. N. Irey letter to Mrs. N. G. Scott, June 26, 1908.

14. N.V.S. Collection (Box 2, Folder 2; Box 3, Folder 4; Box 8, Folder 3; Box 11, Folder 9; Box 13, Folder 22). H. P. Caemmener, *Washington: The National Capital,* 1932, S. Doc. 322, 544. W.P.A. Writers Project Publications (Washington, D.C.: Government Printing Office, 1935), 170, 684-85. Laverne Thomas III, interview by author, Alexandria, Louisiana, June 28, 1996. New Orleans *Times-Democrat,* December 8, 1909; May 25, June 2, 1910. Mrs. Ramsey and her husband, Mr. Arthur Ramsey, operated the school.

15. N.V.S. Collection (Box 1, Folders 1-5; Box 6, Folder 6; Box 8, Folders 3, 6; Box 11, Folder 9; Box 12, Folders 1-11; Box 15, Folder 7). *The Newcomb Arcade* 1, no. 7; 3, no. 2, 4; 6, no. 4; 7, no. 1, 2, 4; 8, no. 4. Tulane University Transcripts of Nauman Scott. Hammond, 24-26. Natalie Vivian Scott, "Small Talk," a short story found in Hilda Phelps Hammond's belongings, New Orleans, Louisiana. Thomas, *LeDoux,* 297-300, 312-15. Chambers, 2:209. Pointe Coupee *Banner,* November 18, 1914. Tulane Graduate School Transcripts of Natalie Vivian Scott. Newcomb College Archives, Newcomb Center for Research on Women, Minutes of Newcomb High School Faculty, June 4, 1914, 104-8. Newcomb College Records, Employment Registration records of Hilda Phelps (September 18, 1913. Natalie began the master's program during the fall of 1910, majoring in English

and minoring in philosophy and French. In 1913, she changed her major to Greek studies, and her minors were in philosophy and English. Hilda began the graduate program in 1912; they graduated together in 1914.

16. N.V.S. Collection (Box 8, Folder 3; Box 9, Folder 12; Box 10, Folder 1; Box 12, Folder 1; Box 13, Folder 4), letter of February 13, 1918. N.V.S. Collection (Box 2) contains her June 13, 1918, letter to her mother referring to both the Guatemala trip and Hilda and Blanche Moulton Phelps in Estes Park, Colorado. "Peggy Passe Partout" column, *New Orleans States*, August 23, 1925. *New Orleans Item*, October 13, 1915. The Lyons Historical Society, *Lyons and Surrounding Area: Double Gateway to the Rockies* (Lyons, Colo., 1977). Enos A. Mills, *Early Estes Park* (Estes Park, 1996), 47-52.

Chapter 2

1. Martin Gilbert, *The First World War: A Complete History* (New York: Henry Holt, 1994), 1-54. Between August and November 1914, the German armies conquered neutral Belgium, battered the French in Alsace, battled the British Expeditionary Force and the French army at the French-Belgian border, then spread its assault above and east of Paris, close enough to see the top of the Eiffel Tower, where the Allies finally achieved a defensive victory on the Marne River. By December 1914, shortly after Sidonie and Nauman Scott's November marriage, the Germans and French had each already suffered almost one million casualties. N.V.S. Collection (Box 13, Folder 5; Box 14, Folder 5; Box 15, Folder 1). *New Orleans Item*, August 10, 15, 16, 18, 21, 22, 1914.

2. *New Orleans Item*, November 21, 1914. N.V.S. Collection (Box 13, Folder 4). *New Orleans States*, October 19, 1919. *The Newcomb Arcade* 10, no. 2 and 3 (February and March 1918). Gilbert, 230-46, 289-324.

3. N.V.S Collection (Box 1, Folder 5; Box 6, Folder 6; Box 13, Folder 5; Box 8, Folders 5, 8; Box 14, Folder 6). Loyola University Archives. Tulane University Transcripts. American Red CrossArchives, Washington, D.C.

4. David M. Kennedy, *Over Here: The First World War and American Society* (Oxford: Oxford University Press, 1980), 17-18, 31, 33-37, 73, 83, 88, 114-17, 126-32, 145-47, 286. N.V.S. Collection (Box 13, Folder 5; Box 14, Folder 10). *New Orleans Daily States*, August 4, 5, 12, 15, 16, 19, 20, 22, 25, 26, 1917. *Alexandria Daily Town Talk*, July 7, 23; August 6-11, 13, 15, 18, 23, 25, 27, 1917. *New Orleans Item*, August 14, 16, 18-22, 24-26, 30, 31; September 2, 1917. *New Orleans Times-Picayune*, August 5, 6, 9, 10, 12, 14, 16, 1917. The cited newspaper articles for July-August are replete with reports of draft resistance, objections, and controversial draft board meetings in New Orleans and elsewhere.

5. *New Orleans Times-Picayune*, July 26-31; August 1-12, 14, 16-20, 1917. *New Orleans Item*, July 12, 28-31; August 4-12, 14-22, 26, 1917. *New Orleans States*, August 15-21, 26, 1917. In New Orleans, the second district draft exemption board certified in mid-August that eighty-one men that day failed to answer their call to report. Federal officers were directed to "hunt them up." The local exemption boards, working their way through long case dockets, held meetings before volatile, disruptive crowds threatening to riot. The district attorneys of surrounding parishes gathered in New Orleans to devise a strategy with federal officials to deal with the draft resistance problem.

6. *Alexandria Daily Town Talk*, August 12-14, 1917. N.V.S. Collection (Box 1, Folders 6, 7; Box 7, Folders 11, 13; Box 12, Folder 2; Box 13, Folder 5). Chambers, 2:209. *New Orleans Item*, August 15, 19, 20, 22, 26, 1917. Thomas, *LeDoux*, 313. N.V.S. war letters, September-October 1917.

7. *New Orleans Daily States*, August 26, 1917. *New Orleans Item*, August

15, 19, 20, 22, 26, 1917. The newspaper of August 22, 1917, states Nauman Scott is leaving for officer's training camp by train from Alexandria on August 24, 1917. Natalie left New Orleans by train for her ship in New York on September 4, 1917. Details of the party and railroad station departure appear in Natalie's letters. N.V.S. letter to her mother, September 4-13, 1917. Natalie awoke early and wrote her first letter to Muddie as they passed through Montgomery, Alabama.

8. N.V.S. Collection (Box 13, Folder 5).

Chapter 3

1. N.V.S. Collection, N.V.S. letter to her mother, September 25, 1917.

2. Lambert's friendship with President Roosevelt went beyond their physician-patient relationship. He had often been Roosevelt's companion on hunting and fishing trips long before T.R.'s White House days. Roosevelt valued his knowledge and judgment, and made at least one very important presidential decision, overruling William H. Taft, based upon his trust of Lambert. Yellow fever had been a major obstacle to construction of the Panama Canal, for the disease was prevalent year round in the mosquito-infested jungles. Dr. William C. Gorgas, a colleague of Dr. Walter Reed in fighting this plague, had been placed in charge of sanitary work. Canal officials questioned Gorgas's heavy emphasis on mosquito control, as it seemed to delay the project. Taft, then secretary of war, joined the political chorus urging his recall. Roosevelt asked Lambert for his opinion and received a terse written reply: "Keep Gorgas or there will be no canal." Roosevelt complied. N.V.S. Collection, N.V.S. letter to her mother, September 26, 28, October 1, 3, 1917. *The National Encyclopedia of American Biography,* vol. D (New York: James T. White, 1934). *American Medical Association Journal* 112, no. 20 (April-June 1939). Morris Fishbein, *A History of the A.M.A.: 1847 to 1947* (Philadelphia: W. B. Sanders, 1969), 744.

3. N.V.S. Collection, N.V.S. letter to her mother, September 26, 28, 1917.

4. N.V.S. Collection, N.V.S. letter to her mother, September 30, 1917.

5. N.V.S. Collection, N.V.S. letter to her mother, September 27, October 1, 5, 8, 1917.

6. N.V.S. Collection, N.V.S. letter to her mother, October 1, 8, 12, 17, 1917.

7. N.V.S. Collection, N.V.S. letter to her mother, September 26, 1917 (entry of Sunday, September 30, 1917), October 5, 8, 1917. Another trip to observe the techniques and apparatus of the English Red Cross is described in N.V.S. letter to her mother, October 20, 27, 1917.

8. N.V.S. Collection, N.V.S. letter to her mother, October 10, 23, 1917. *Before I forget it, tho, I want to tell you a foolish little incident, but worth telling as it is enlightening. This afternoon, after it had grown dark,—as it does at 5:30 (or 17 h 30 to be very French)—I was still typing busily away, in the fairly good light that the office ceiling-light affords. It had been a terribly busy day, with people, and letters, and phones for Major Lambert and he had been continually occupied and still was beset. I glanced up and saw him doing something with his desk-light. In a moment, he was at my desk with it, and had connected it for me! Dr. Ward and Dr. Burlingame were overcome. He had done it all in a second, and said to Dr. Burlingame, "It's extraordinary that there is no light on Miss Scott's desk anyway. Take it up, please," and was going to a nurse who was waiting for him in the reception room. He is never too busy to be nice.* N.V.S. Collection, N.V.S. letter to her mother, October 17, 20, 1917.

9. N.V.S. Collection, N.V.S. letter to her mother, October 20, 23, Nov. 18, 1917. Her letter also said: *I have just come in from the Chinese Umbrella,*

where I had the most American meal ever known in Paris. Mr. Matheson took me. He is a Cornell man. He hadn't finished college when he enlisted in the Navy. He was business manager of the Widow. *He is an ensign now. He is just about 23, I should judge from that; but looks much older. He is engaged, it seems, and while we were at dinner he told me all about it, as a strict secret. My old trade as confidante!*

They are a clean, straight crowd,—I love to claim them for America. No one who hasn't been here can realize what a real and strong impulse towards the "worst things" there is in Paris. The "jolies Parisians" are simply ubiquitous, and everywhere, quite openly, you see them accosting the men, following them, wheedling and cajoling them . . . it takes character not to be persuaded to "just one drink in the café"—as they say one of the pet phrases goes.

10. N.V.S. Collection, N.V.S. letter to her mother, October 23, 1917. Natalie had a similar day the second Sunday of November. This time she shared the day with a succession of six men, beginning with a long horseback ride in the Fontainebleau forest. N.V.S. letter to her mother, November 12, 1917.

11. N.V.S. Collection, N.V.S. letter to her mother, November 12, 13, 17, 18, 1917.

12. N.V.S. Collection, N.V.S. letter to her mother, October 1, November 13, 1917. Natalie's letter also spoke of other war-workers who were her friends. *Madame Felix, an attractive little French woman in our office, is a widow, and so, too, are her two sisters. . . . Last night she worked till 10:30 on a translation. "I love my war-work," she says (she has a quaint little French purr to her words), "and eet ees go-ood that I do. So I do not think. And that ees good, you know. We must not think too much. That's ba-ahd. My seesters, they can not work. And eet ees ba-ahd for them." Every male member of their family has been killed. And she is a brave, cheery little soul, always friendly and eager to help. And quite alone here. But she hates war . . . "It ees terr-orr-eeble," she says. "I would die rather than that I leeve again through such a time."* N.V.S. Collection, N.V.S. letter to her mother, November 17, 1917.

13. N.V.S. Collection, N.V.S. letter to her mother, November 18, 28, December 2, 15, 1917. She also wrote: *I thought of you all the time as I rushed desperately about, with the hurried, desperate feeling that you know so well,—the Xmas eve feeling! Most of the stores close at 6:30, but some few stay open till 7. I entered the Metro with my arms distended to encompass quantities of bundles of every size and shape, breathless, exhausted, dreadfully late for dinner, somewhat chilled, but with the triumphant, exhilarated feeling which always goes with Xmas shopping . . . it seemed that you must be somewhere in the jostling and pushing crowd that thronged the Metro,—the circumstances were so like the old familiar, well-loved ones! I could imagine you saying, "I'll go to Miss Stella's, and you run and get the things from Holmes—meet me at Adler's right away to see if he has that (blank-blank). Ready yet? . . . And, O I just must get something for so-and-so. Can't you think of anything?" And Canal Street and the Boulevard seemed very close akin.*

14. N.V.S. Collection, N.V.S. letter to her mother, November 8, December 8, 13, 1917; January 8, 30, February 4, March 4, 5, 1918. Dr. Cabot, of the well-known Boston family, was born in Brookline, Massachusetts, the son of James Elliott Cabot and Elizabeth Dwight Cabot, on May 21, 1868. His father was the biographer of Ralph Waldo Emerson. Dr. Cabot graduated from Harvard Medical School in 1892 and remained a professor there throughout his career, becoming professor emeritus in 1933. He was president of the National Conference of Social Work in 1931 and consultant to many hospitals and social organizations. Dr. Cabot was best known for his books and academic articles, especially in the field of social welfare. Particularly important were these books: *Clinical Examination of the Blood* (1896), *Physical Diagnosis* (1901), *Social Work*

(1919), *Case Teaching in Medicine* (1906), *Differential Diagnosis* (1911). *The National Encyclopedia of American Biography,* D:219.

15. N.V.S. Collection, N.V.S. letter to her mother, December 13, 1917.

16. N.V.S. Collection, N.V.S. letter to her mother, October 23, November 28, December 8, 13, 15, 18-24, 1917.

17. N.V.S. Collection, N.V.S. letter to her mother, December 18-24, 1917.

18. N.V.S. Collection, N.V.S. letter to her mother, December 25-30, 1917.

19. N.V.S. Collection, N.V.S. letter to her mother, December 18-24, 1917.

20. N.V.S. Collection, N.V.S. letter to her mother, December 18-24, 25-30, 1917.

21. N.V.S. Collection, N.V.S. letter to her mother, January 8, 15, 23, February 12, 1918. Natalie wrote: *Yesterday morning, the Military Affairs Dept. had a meeting. Mr. Patton, the Director, made us a little address. He told us that 500 additional people had been ordered for our department,—a tremendous expansion, and one, he said, that was so great that, if we didn't take care, it would be not merely an expansion but an explosion! . . . The Red Cross is to divide its work along the same line as the army,—i.e., the zone of the Advance, the Intermediate Zone, Base Section #1, and Base Section #2, and each of those will have an organization which will duplicate in miniature that of our central organization. We have built 8 new warehouses in the last six weeks. And we have all this new personnel to educate and set to work tooty-arooty (as the new Americans say . . .). He remarked, too, that Civil Affairs was doing great work, and doing it well; but theirs was a work whose failure or success could vary much without the variation being crucial,— with our department, anything but great success was equal to failure (here endeth the speech). And that is true. Their work is rebuilding,—ours is new building, and it is to be seen (and prayed and hoped for, and worked for!) if it is to be successful. There is a certain significant filing-clerk who does try! "Dumps is doin' de bes' she kin."*

22. N.V.S. Collection, N.V.S. letter to her mother, January 30, February 3, 1918.

23. N.V.S. Collection, N.V.S. letter to her mother, January 23, February 4, 1918.

24. N.V.S. Collection, N.V.S. letter to her mother, February 19, 1918. Natalie also wrote: *Mr. Fowler gave me some interesting descriptions of Rheims and a very good one of a fight between three French planes and a Boche, in which the Boche, when close-pressed, played a very pretty and difficult trick. He let go his control, so that his wings flapped and he fell turning and twisting as tho hit. Two of the French planes continued to circle up above, only one following the descent, and he in a most leisurely fashion. When the Boche had fallen half the distance from his former height to the ground, he suddenly recovered, and shot out clear of his adversaries, and straight for his lines. Mr. Fowler said that they, as they watched him fall, were saying, "they got him. Poor devil." Then, when they saw his trick and saw him dart to safety, they all gasped indignantly, and one said, "The d——d scoundrel!"*

25. N.V.S. Collection, N.V.S. letter to her mother, February 19, 23, 1918.

26. N.V.S. Collection, N.V.S. letter to her mother, February 25, 1918.

27. N.V.S. Collection, N.V.S. letter to her mother, March 3-4, 1918.

28. N.V.S. Collection, N.V.S. letter to her mother, February 25, March 1, 3, 1918. Natalie also wrote: *Paris at night now is a dismal sight. At twilight, it is wonderful, for the streets are simply thronged with the interesting, heterogeneous Parisian crowd, and lamp-lighters trot to and fro, reminding me of the twelfth century or so, and everything is interesting. But later! It is desolate-looking. Not a light shows from the window of a house. Or, at least, it is to be hoped not, for there is a 25 franc fine, payable at once, at the first offense; fine and imprisonment for the second, and so on. The few lights that make the darkness visible are all blue, and give an uneasy color, truly ghostly. And every little*

while, a cluster of the spectral blue glows indicates a "shelter", in case of a raid. Even in the Metro the lights are blue. The reason is, of course, that blue lights do not show so much, and so we won't be such a good target for the Boches.

29. N.V.S. Collection, N.V.S. letter to her mother, March 4, 17, 1918.

30. N.V.S. Collection, N.V.S. letter to her mother, March 4, 1918.

31. N.V.S. Collection, N.V.S. letter to her mother, March 11, 1918. Natalie also wrote: *Of course, everyone has a tale. It is interesting to get their point of view. Mme. Brin and Mme. De Valori think they will go south . . . more than 35,000 people have left Paris. One little girl, an American at school here, 14 years old, sagely remarks that the rich should stay to give example to the poor, who have to stay! This is Mme. Brin's niece. Her father is governor of the Philippines.*

32. Ibid.

33. N.V.S. Collection, N.V.S. letter to her mother, March 19, 1918. Lewis L. Gould, *The Presidency of Theodore Roosevelt* (Lawrence: University of Kansas Press, 1991), 5, 103, 226, 297. Quentin was the youngest of former president Theodore Roosevelt's five children, born 1897. Archie (Archibald) was the fourth child. Natalie wrote of incidents during the late-night bombings: *Léontine is just as faithful and good as she can be. She took Madame down long ago, after helping her dress. Yesterday evening, it was very funny. I came in. The house was black and I didn't have my "glim". I "mountain"ed in that dark. Last night and the night before, the concierge was not there because of the raids, but even if she had been there, I couldn't have had the electric light turned on, for it is not permitted after 10:30. There is quite an art in going up . . . in the dark. Last night, I found the downstairs door open, no concierge, and not a soul in the building. Then I thought that I had better go down to the cellar and tell the concierge to lock the door if she was going to stick in the cellar. So down I went and nearly broke my neck in the darkness. I found "tout le monde" assembled in the cave, for the most part sitting. I passed thru this group to the cave of the baker next door, where Madame had been installed. The baker, a thin, wiry little man, barefoot in slippers, stood at a table, with his back turned to us, and deftly, busily and unceasingly grasped, one after another, dabs of dough from one end, and with quick dexterity pulled and patted them out in a second, into long thin shapes, and laid them in long wicker baskets. The grocer's wife stood hospitably up to receive me, and trotted about; Mlle. Alice ran to meet me, remonstrating with me for coming thru the streets . . . and,—the dearest picture,—Madame, sitting stately on the kitchen chair as tho it were a throne, lifted her old hand in welcome, and smiled at me indulgently. The "baker's boys", two fine brown-eyed, rosy-cheeked little fellows about seven and nine, with their soldier caps jauntily awry and their big eyes bigger and bright with excitement, ran to tell us that one could hear the "corps de cannons" quite plainly still. Surely a picture I'll never forget. And so the baker baked, and Madame waited, quiescent. And so I left them.*

34. N.V.S. Collection, N.V.S. letter to her mother, March 11, 25, 1918.

35. N.V.S. Collection, N.V.S. letter to her mother, March 11, 19, 24, 25, 1918. Gilbert, 406.

36. N.V.S. Collection, N.V.S. letter to her mother, March 25, 1918. Postscripts of March 29, April 1, 1918.

Chapter 4

1. N.V.S. Collection, N.V.S. letter to her mother, April 1, 1918.

2. Ibid.

3. N.V.S. Collection, N.V.S. letter to her mother, April 4, 9, 1918.

4. N.V.S. Collection, N.V.S. letter to her mother, April 11, 1918.

5. N.V.S. Collection, N.V.S. letter to her mother, April 15, 1918.

6. N.V.S. Collection, Evelyn Preston letter to N.V.S., undated, received on April 15 or 16, 1918.

7. N.V.S. Collection, N.V.S. letter to her mother, April 15, 1918.

8. N.V.S. Collection, N.V.S. letter to her mother, April 16, 1918.

9. N.V.S. Collection, N.V.S. letter to her mother, April 16, 23, 25, 1918. A separate office for Natalie had become necessary due to her being given administrative responsibility for all of the American and English patients.

10. N.V.S. Collection, N.V.S. letter to her mother, April 25, 1918.

11. N.V.S. Collection, Dr. Lambert letter to N.V.S., April 23, 1918; Dorothy Cheney letter to N.V.S., April 23, 1918.

12. N.V.S. Collection, N.V.S. letter to her mother, April 25, 1918.

13. N.V.S. Collection, N.V.S. letter to her mother, May 2, 1918.

14. N.V.S. Collection. Evelyn Preston letter to N.V.S., April 27, 1918.

15. N.V.S. Collection, N.V.S. letter to her mother, May 5-6, 1918.

16. N.V.S. Collection, N.V.S. letter to her mother, May 10, 13, 1918.

17. N.V.S. Collection, N.V.S. letter to her mother, May 16, 1918.

18. N.V.S. Collection, N.V.S. letter to her mother, May 17, 1918.

19. N.V.S. Collection, Harold Ober letter to N.V.S., May 11, 1918.

20. N.V.S. Collection, N.V.S. letter to her mother, May 27-28, 1918.

21. N.V.S. Collection, N.V.S. letter to her mother, May 27-29, 1918. Gilbert, 422-27. On May 27, German commander Erich Ludendorff unleashed another offensive wave aimed at reaching Paris. The Third Battle of the Aisne began with 4,000 guns opening fire on a twenty-four-mile front. By the end of May 28, a forty-mile-wide, fifteen-mile-deep wedge had been driven through the Allied lines. But the Allies were not everywhere driven back, and in the first sustained American offensive of the war, advances were actually made by the 4,000 Americans, a full brigade, in action at Cantigny. The French provided air cover, as well as 368 heavy guns, trench mortars, flame-thrower teams, and twelve French tanks. Though Cantigny was taken, German counterattacks over the next three days were murderous. But the Americans held Cantigny, depriving the Germans of an important observation point and giving the first clear evidence to the Germans that the infusion of fresh American troops on the front would be a vital factor in the war. Despite Cantigny, the German advance proceeded into Soissons and, by the end of the third day of the onslaught, more than 50,000 French soldiers had been taken prisoner with heavy arms. On May 30 the Germans reached the Marne near Château-Thierry. By June 2, the French government was preparing to leave Paris for safety farther south. Tens of thousands of civilians were fleeing the capital as more waves of refugees were on their way to Paris. On the Paris-Metz road, at the closest point to Paris of the German advance and where the French troops were in disorganized retreat, the Americans established a new line of defense that finally stopped the furious six days of German advances. General Pershing reinforced the French during June with 170,000 American troops on the front line. The Germans were prevented from crossing the Marne.

22. N.V.S. Collection, N.V.S. letter to her mother, May 28-29, 1918.

23. N.V.S. Collection, N.V.S. letter to her mother, May 31, 1918. "L.C.'s" referred to the "Lover's Cross" gesture that the two often exchanged when they parted.

Chapter 5

1. Hugh H. Young, *Hugh Young: A Surgeon's Autobiography* (New York: Harcourt, Brace, 1940), 351-52. American Red Cross Archives, Washington, D.C.

2. *New Orleans States,* May 31, 1918. Newspaper reports identified other American nurses in the hospital, including Mary McCandish of Atlanta, Helen Spaulding of Brooklyn, Blanche Gilbert of Cleveland, and Constance Cook of San Francisco. Articles also mentioned that Natalie had recently headed a delegation at the funeral of "gassed" American soldier Pvt. H. B. Mashburn of Unadillo, Georgia.

3. N.V.S. Collection, N.V.S. letter to her mother, June 6, 9, 1918.
4. N.V.S. Collection, N.V.S. letter to her mother, June 9, 1918.
5. N.V.S. Collection, N.V.S. letter to her mother, June 12, 1918.
6. N.V.S. Collection, N.V.S. letter to her mother, June 15, 1918.
7. N.V.S. Collection, N.V.S. letter to her mother, June 17, 1918.
8. N.V.S. Collection, N.V.S. letter to her mother, June 15, 1918. Natalie also wrote: *I think I told you that he* (Mr. Telstead) *was a twice golf-champion of Australia and his partner, who was killed a few months ago, was also champion at one time.*
9. N.V.S. Collection, N.V.S. letter to her mother, June 23, 25, 29-30, 1918.
10. N.V.S. Collection, N.V.S. letter to her mother, July 1, 3, 1918.
11. N.V.S. Collection, N.V.S. letter to her mother, July 17, 1918.
12. N.V.S. Collection, N.V.S. letter to her mother, July 17, 19-20, 1918.
13. N.V.S. Collection, N.V.S. letter to her mother, July 21, August 14, 1918.
14. N.V.S. Collection, N.V.S. letter to her mother, July 26, 1918.
15. N.V.S. Collection, N.V.S. letter to her mother, July 26, 28, 31, 1918.
16. N.V.S. Collection, N.V.S. letter to her mother, July 31, August 18, 1918.
17. N.V.S. Collection, N.V.S. letter to her mother, July 31, 1918.
18. N.V.S. Collection, N.V.S. letter to her mother, August 11-12, 1918.
19. N.V.S. Collection, N.V.S. letter to her mother, July 28, August 4, 1918.
20. N.V.S. Collection, N.V.S. letter to her mother, August 26, 1918.
21. N.V.S. Collection, N.V.S. letter to her mother, August 21, 1918.
22. N.V.S. Collection, N.V.S. letter to her mother, August 17, 21, 1918.
23. N.V.S. Collection, N.V.S. letter to her mother, July 21, 25, 1918.
24. N.V.S. Collection, N.V.S. letter to her mother, August 27, 1918.
25. N.V.S. Collection, N.V.S. letter to her mother, August 18, 1918.

Chapter 6

1. N.V.S. Collection, N.V.S. letter to her mother, September 2, 6, 1918.
2. N.V.S. Collection, N.V.S. letter to her mother, September 8, 1918.
3. N.V.S. Collection, N.V.S. letter to her mother, September 9, 1918.
4. N.V.S. Collection, N.V.S. letter to Nauman Scott, September 8, 1918.
5. N.V.S. Collection, N.V.S. letter to her mother, September 13, 15, 1918.
6. N.V.S. Collection, N.V.S. letter to her mother, September 19, 24, 1918.
7. N.V.S. Collection, N.V.S. letter to her mother, September 19, 25; October 4, 1918.
8. N.V.S. Collection, N.V.S. letter to her mother, October 4-5, 12, 1918; to Wyeth, October 5, 1918.
9. N.V.S. Collection, N.V.S. letter to her mother, October 13-14, 23, 1918.
10. N.V.S. Collection, N.V.S. letter to her mother, October 23, 25, 1918.
11. N.V.S. Collection, N.V.S. letter to her mother, October 26, 1918.
12. N.V.S. Collection, N.V.S. letter to her mother, November 3-4, 7, 1918.
13. N.V.S. Collection, N.V.S. letter to her mother, November 4, 11, 22, 1918. Gilbert, 500-504.
14. N.V.S. Collection, N.V.S. letter to her mother, November 22, 1918. Rosalie had been the social columnist Cynthia St. Charles (pen name) for the *New Orleans States* newspaper. Natalie wrote about one reunion: *I walked into*

the Café to meet Sadie for luncheon and someone called my name. I looked around, and there at a table were Peter O'Donnell, Omer Villere (I think that it was Omer—I never can remember which is Omer and which is Pierre), old Avegne, and several other New Orleans boys. They all stood up and talked and we had quite a nice reunion. They all looked so well and clean and strong. I was glad to know them and proud to have them represent New Orleans. Afterwards, I saw Omer(?) again at the bank, and we had a long, long talk. He is too disappointed for anything that he never got into action . . . they were turned into a school after they arrived. This boy can hardly speak of it; he is so disappointed. I told him that after the war the question will be not whether a man was in the line or not, but whether he did his part in joining or trying to join the army. He said that Gus Westfeldt had been in and that he had been in a busy part of the line, and looked very well. I imagine that he would make a good soldier.

15. N.V.S. Collection, N.V.S. letter to her mother, December 10, 1918. N.V.S. Collection (Box 14, Folder 14), church service program.

16. N.V.S. Collection, N.V.S. letter to her mother, November 22, December 3, 1918.

17. N.V.S. Collection, N.V.S. letter to her mother, November 22, 1918; N.V.S. letter to her father, November 24, 1918.

18. N.V.S. Collection (Box 6, Folder 9), report on the American Red Cross Evacuation Hospital 34, written by N.V.S.

19. N.V.S. Collection, N.V.S. letter to her mother, November 22, December 20, 1918.

20. N.V.S. Collection, N.V.S. letter to her mother, December 10, 13, 20, 23-24, 1918.

21. N.V.S. Collection, N.V.S. to her mother, December 26, 1918.

22. N.V.S. Collection, N.V.S. letter to her mother, January-July 9, 16, 1919.

23. N.V.S. Collection, N.V.S. letter to her mother, July 16, 1919.

24. World War I Records of the French Military, Croix de Guerre, Paris. N.V.S. Collection, N.V.S. letter to her mother, September-October 1919. The Parisian actress wearing her "dress only" was in just her undergarment. "Jimmy," Natalie's dinner host in Biarritz, is Jimmy Stouse, an old friend from New Orleans.

25. *New Orleans States,* October 26, 1919.

Chapter 7

1. *New Orleans States,* November 4-5, 8, 10-11, 1919; March 22, 1920.

2. Robert Tallant, *The Romantic New Orleanians* (New York: E. P. Dutton, 1950). 307-10. Lyle Saxon, *Fabulous New Orleans* (1928, 1950; reprint, Gretna, La.: Pelican, 1988), 273. The Historic New Orleans Collection, French Quarter Survey (Era Photographs). Harnett T. Kane, *Queen New Orleans* (New York: William Morrow, 1949), 357. John G. Clark, *New Orleans, 1718-1812: An Economic History* (Baton Rouge: LSU Press, 1970), 21-46, 221-40, 275-90. James W. Thomas, *Lyle Saxon: A Critical Biography* (Birmingham, Ala.: Summa, 1991), 18. *New Orleans States,* October 7, 1919. *New Orleans Illustrated News,* May, December 1922. *New Orleans Item,* November 3, 1918; January 19, 26, 1919.

3. In 1920, Mrs. Oscar Nixon was awarded the Times-Picayune Loving Cup for civic achievement for establishing Le Petit Théâtre du Vieux Carré. Her father, Benjamin Jonas, was a nineteenth-century U.S. senator from Louisiana (1879-85). An organizer of the *New Orleans Illustrated News,* Mrs. Nixon also organized the Club Lecture Course, which brought to the city lecturers in art, music, drama, and economics. Starting in 1917, she hosted plays performed by the Drawing Room Players, often in French, in her home and was a leader of

the Drama League. Dedicated to preserving the French language in Louisiana, she was awarded the Palmes Académiques by the French government in 1922. For her preservationist work, particularly in the French Quarter, she received special tribute and a loving cup from the Louisiana Historical Society. Despite her advanced age, Mrs. Nixon performed in numerous Le Petit Théâtre productions, including *Two Crooks and a Lady,* by Eugene Pillot, in which she and Natalie played lead roles (March 1920). Helen Schertz was prominent in New Orleans society. Her novel *An Angel by Brevet* appeared in 1904; she wrote a guidebook for the French Quarter during the 1920s. She founded the New Orleans Spring Fiesta. Schertz played the lead role in the May 1921 production of *What, Again?,* written by Natalie Scott and Sam Gilmore. Her home was among the city's oldest, a small plantation house on Bayou St. John built in the 1730s where she hosted prominent visitors, including playwright Maurice Maeterlinck and Bertrand Russell. Her home was among those featured in Natalie's book (illustrated by William Spratling), *Old Plantation Houses in Louisiana* (New York: William Helburn, 1927). Tallant, 259-61, 302, 304, 307-11, 320. Thomas, *Lyle Saxon,* 27, 30. *New Orleans States,* October 7, 26, November 2, 1919; February 1, 1922; "Peggy Passe Partout" columns, 1920-28. *New Orleans Times-Picayune,* November 16, 1919. *New Orleans Item,* October 26, 1919; May 7, 1922. Le Petit Théâtre du Vieux Carré Archives, New Orleans. *The Double Dealer* (July 1921), Hill Memorial Library, LSU. John W. Scott, "The Origins, People and Times of the French Quarter Renaissance (1920-1930)" (dissertation, LSU, May 1999), 44-48.

4. *New Orleans States,* November 2, 30, December 4-7, 1919; January-April 1923. *New Orleans Times-Picayune,* November 12, 30, December 4-7, 1919. Scott, "The French Quarter Renaissance," 48-51. Thomas, *Lyle Saxon,* 21-23. Tallant, 119-22.

5. Le Petit Théâtre Archives. Scott, "The French Quarter Renaissance," 52-53, 320-21. *New Orleans States,* December 1919; May 16-30, 1920; October 16, 1926. *New Orleans Times-Picayune,* May 16, 1930.

6. *New Orleans Times-Picayune,* May 16, 1920; January 23, 1921. *New Orleans States,* February 5, 29, March 21, April 28, May 3, 23, 16-30, June 13, 20, September 26, November 7, 21, 28, December 20, 1920. *The Double Dealer* (February 1920; February, March 1922). Scott, "The French Quarter Renaissance," 53-55.

7. Scott, "The French Quarter Renaissance," 30-33, 66-70, 454. N.V.S. Collection, correspondence 1920-30. "Peggy Passe Partout" columns, *New Orleans States,* 1920-28.

8. Martha Robinson Collection, N.V.S. letter to Martha Gilmore Robinson, October 7, 1920. *New Orleans States,* August 22, September 5, December 12, 1920. Thomas, interview. Scott, "The French Quarter Renaissance," 67-68.

9. *New Orleans States,* April 25, 1920. Scott, "The French Quarter Renaissance," 73-77.

10. *New Orleans States,* January 2, 1921. Scott, "The French Quarter Renaissance," 79-80. *New Orleans Times-Picayune,* May 29, 1921. *New Orleans Item,* May 29, 1921. Le Petit Théâtre Archives. Samuel Gilmore Collection, Tulane University, Howard-Tilton Library.

11. *New Orleans States,* November 21, 28, 1920.

12. Ibid., May 22, 1921; January 29, 1922. William Spratling, *Picturesque New Orleans* (New Orleans: Tulane University Press, 1923), 3. Scott, "The French Quarter Renaissance," 81-82.

13. *New Orleans States,* June 22, 1921. *The Double Dealer* (February 1922). Orleans Parish Conveyance Records (book 340, 469). The Scott-McClure house, 626 Orleans Alley, provided a home for artists and writers throughout

the decade. Natalie and McClure would be co-owners until 1937. William Spratling, *File on Spratling: An Autobiography* (Boston: Little, Brown, 1967). Scott, "The French Quarter Renaissance," 82-83.

14. *The Double Dealer* (January, August 1921). The Historic New Orleans Collection, *The Double Dealer* Archives. Scott, "The French Quarter Renaissance," 83-110. Frances Jean Bowen, "*The Double Dealer,* 1921-May, 1926" (dissertation, Vanderbilt University, 1954, 3-20). Julius Friend, "*The Double Dealer:* Career of a 'Little' Magazine," *Mississippi Quarterly* 31 (fall-winter 1977-78): 589-604. Frances Jean Bowen, "The New Orleans *Double Dealer,* 1921-26," *The Louisiana Historical Quarterly* 39, no. 4 (October 1956): 447. The *New Orleans Illustrated News,* December 1920, announced that *The Double Dealer's* first issue would be forthcoming in January and that its motto would be "a plague on both your houses." This motto would change. The covers were drawn by artist Olive Leonhardt until June 1922, when she left for an extended European trip. Beginning in August 1922, an enlarged double-faced Roman coin appeared on each cover. According to the *Illustrated News* in December 1920, *The Double Dealer* editors would be Julius Friend, Basil Thompson, Paul Godchaux, Jr., and Albert Goldstein; its advisory council would include John McClure, Sam Gilmore, Olive Lyons, Gideon Stanton, W. Weeks Hall, and Marguerite Samuels. However, Weeks Hall's name never appeared in any capacity. Lyle Saxon was initially listed as a staff member but his name quickly disappeared from the monthly publications. Natalie published reviews of each *Double Dealer* issue, from its 1921 beginning until its 1926 demise. Examples: *New Orleans States,* February 13, April 3, May 15, June 12, 26, 1921. Natalie's name first appeared in the staff list in the August-September 1921 *Double Dealer* issue.

15. Julius Friend eventually wrote numerous books, including *Science and the Spirit of Man, The Unlimited Community, What Science Really Means,* and *The Odyssey of the Idea. Dixie* (April 30, 1950). Basil Thompson's poetry was featured in a 1918 anthology, *Estrays*; then his book *Auguries* appeared in 1919. Another book of his poems, *The Grey Men and Other Rhymes,* appeared after his death. Thompson's work, including essays, was published in many periodicals, notably *The Century Magazine, The Bookman, The Nation, Republic, The Forum, The Lyric, Contemporary Verse, Pearson's Magazine, Smart Set, The Wave,* and *The Poetry Review (London).* Thompson's father was T. P. Thompson, president of the Board of Curators of the Louisiana State Museum. The elder Thompson had authored an article in *The Double Dealer* in February 1922, "The Renaissance of the Vieux Carre."

16. John McClure's poetry credits included a book of verse, *Airs and Ballads* (1918), and an anthology, *The Stag's Hornbook* (1919). He published prolifically in periodicals throughout the country and in *The Double Dealer.* He was the *Times-Picayune's* news editor for over twenty-five years and wrote his literary review column, "Literature and Less," from the 1920s to the 1950s. Scott, "The French Quarter Renaissance," 83-110, 457-61.

17. Natalie was listed as the fifth stockholder in *The Double Dealer* issues prior to the death of Basil Thompson, then fourth through the publication's last 1926 issue. Since the quarterly stockholder listings are not in alphabetical order, and the listings change, it is likely that stockholders were listed by the amount of their accumulated contributions. The number of stockholders owning at least 1 percent was usually around thirty. A different list of all guarantors appeared on the back cover of the magazine, in alphabetical order. Faulkner's work, a poem, was first published in *The Double Dealer* in its June 1922 issue; Faulkner later appeared often in the magazine in 1925 and 1926 when he lived in the French Quarter.

18. Flo Field was the daughter of Louisiana author Catherine Cole (Martha Field). Flo authored several plays, including *A La Creole,* a three-act production

performed by Le Petit Théâtre in February 1928 in which she played the lead role. The play was produced professionally, and widely, in 1929. An expert on French Quarter history and architecture, she provided French Quarter tours. Olive Boullemet Lyons was a poet, the wife of a New Orleans merchant, and a French Quarter resident. She was very close to Lyle Saxon, who, according to 2one of his biographers, was in love with her. Thomas, *Lyle Saxon,* 50; Tallant, 227. Gideon Stanton was a New Orleans artist and served on the board of directors of the Delgado Museum; he was a vital leader of the Arts and Crafts Club of the 1920s and 1930s. *New Orleans States,* September-October 1923; November 8, 1928. Scott, "The French Quarter Renaissance," 83-84, 105-110, 458. Le Petit Théâtre Archives.

19. *The Double Dealer* (January 1921-December 1922). Walter B. Rideout, "The Most Civilized Spot in America: Sherwood Anderson in New Orleans," in *Literary New Orleans in the Modern World,* ed. Richard S. Kennedy (Baton Rouge: LSU Press, 1998), 2-5. Mr. Rideout suggests that Anderson may have seen the Hart Crane review for the first time during this first visit to *The Double Dealer* office, when a copy of the May issue was given to him as a gift. Natalie wrote that week that Anderson had been in touch with *The Double Dealer* for some time; *The Double Dealer's* favorable treatment of his work explains Anderson's interest and eagerness to visit the magazine's office. *New Orleans States,* January 22, 1922; March 4, 1923; July 13, 1924. In 1924, Anderson married Elizabeth in Las Vegas, then came to New Orleans ahead of his wife to find an apartment. He was reported to have "taken the Danziger apartment in the upper row of the Pontalba buildings." Scott, "The French Quarter Renaissance," 101-6, 180-81; Kim Townsend, *Sherwood Anderson* (Boston: Houghton Mifflin, 1987), 203-15. The "Danziger apartment" refers to artist Alfred Danziger. Anderson stayed briefly in this three-room apartment at the corner of St. Peter facing the river levee and Jackson Square; the Andersons soon moved into a two-story apartment at the opposite end of the St. Peter Street Pontalba building.

20. *New Orleans States,* January 22, 1922. "Books Abroad," *The Arts and Letters in Mexico, New York Herald Tribune,* June 8, 1930. Anderson's quote also appears elsewhere. Taylor Littleton, *The Color of Silver: William Spratling, His Life and Art* (Baton Rouge: LSU Press, 2000), 290-91.

21. Martha Fauver Scott death certificate dated January 23, 1922, Orleans Parish death records (book 183, 836). N.V.S. Collection (Boxes 1 and 2; Box 3, Folder 3; Box 6, Folder 22; Box 7, Folder 5; Box 14, Folder 1). Thomas, *LeDoux,* 313. "Peggy Passe Partout" columns and N.V.S. features, *New Orleans States,* January 1920-30. Natalie spent months traveling each year: the summers in Europe in 1922 and 1923, in New York the last four months of 1924, New York and Europe again in 1925, Mexico for three months in 1926, then almost the entirety of 1927 based in Paris for the Associated Press, writing feature articles as she traveled throughout Europe, North Africa, and England. Scott, "The French Quarter Renaissance," 111-12, 120-23, 127-34. Orleans Parish Conveyance Records (book 347, 384). D'Arcy McNickle, *Indian Man: A Life of Oliver La Farge* (Bloomington: Indiana University Press, 1971), 53. *Preservation Magazine* (New Orleans, February 1996): 23. *New Orleans Illustrated News,* May 13, 27, 1922.

22. *New Orleans States,* May 21, June 11, 18, 25, 30, July 30, August 6, 13, 20, 27, September 12, 1922.

23. Spratling, *File on Spratling,* 16-17. John W. Scott, "William Spratling and the French Quarter Renaissance," *Louisiana History* (summer 2004). John W. Scott, "William Spratling in New Orleans" in *William Spratling and the Mexican Silver Renaissance,* ed. Penny Morrill (San Antonio: San Antonio Museum of Art, 2002). Scott, "The French Quarter Renaissance," 159-65, 169-76. Penny Chittim Morrill, *Mexican Silver: Twentieth Century Handwrought*

Jewelry and Metalwork (Washington, D.C.: Schiffer, 1994), 17-19. Sandraline Cederwall and Hal Riney, *Spratling Silver* (San Francisco: Chronicle, 1990), 11-13. Spratling elaborately designed Le Petit Théâtre's program for the March 1927 production of *A La Creole*, written by Flo Field; Spratling and Ethel Crumb prepared the scene design. He drew a portrait of Jessie Tharp in her March 1928 performance in *The Adventurer* and also one of Flo Field in *A La Creole*. Both portraits now hang on the wall of Le Petit Théâtre's conference room. Spratling's roles included one of a crowd of people in *John Ferguson* by St. John Ervin, performed during November 1927; he played two roles, one of the clowns and one of the two witches, in *The Rose and the King* by William Makepeace Thackeray. *New Orleans States,* October 15, November 19, 21, 26, December 10, 17, 1922; March 4, 1923. Le Petit Théâtre Archives.

24. Scott, "William Spratling and the French Quarter Renaissance." Scott, "The French Quarter Renaissance," 165-67. *The Double Dealer* (January, February, March 1922). Littleton, 61. *New Orleans States,* March 6, 1921; January 27, October 1, 15, November 12, 19, 21, 26, December 3, 10, 17, 24, 1922; March 4, 1923.

25. *New Orleans States,* November 19, 21, 26, 1922; June 8, 13, 15, August 3, 1924. Le Petit Théâtre Archives. Scott, "The French Quarter Renaissance," 169-72, 174-76, 181. Scott, "Spratling in New Orleans." Spratling, *Picturesque New Orleans.* William P. Spratling, *Pencil Drawing* (New Orleans: Searcy and Pfaff, 1923). Spratling, *File on Spratling,* 30.

26. *The Double Dealer* (April 1924). Basil Thompson death certificate, 1013, Office of Secretary of State, La. *New Orleans States,* May 18, 1924, wherein Natalie reviewed the April 1924 issue of *The Double Dealer,* which she had helped produce: "Remarkably, poignantly noteworthy is the latest issue of the Double Dealer, which is devoted wholly to Basil Thompson . . . a man sensitively meticulous as to words, poems, where an elfin imaginativeness glints through musical, lilting rhythm, shot through at times with a Byronic melancholy of a more than Byronic virility and sincerity. And again the awareness of life, sometimes delicious, sometimes a pain, sometimes just transcendently itself, is keen in them as a knife edge. There is brilliant promise in the work, and noteworthy achievement beside. . . . " *New Orleans States,* July 13, 1924, in which Natalie describes Anderson's return to the French Quarter. *New Orleans States,* August 17, 24, September 28, December 21, 1924. The inscribed book is in the possession of the Scott family. Sherwood Anderson Collection, The Historic New Orleans Collection. Sherwood Anderson Collection and Archives, Smyth County Library, Marion, Va.

27. In New York, Natalie's regular companions included her closest friend from World War I, Evelyn Preston. N.V.S. Collection, exchange of correspondence from New York with her father, October 1924. *New Orleans States,* August 3, September 7, October 5, 26, November 9, 16, December 7, 14, 21, 28, 1925; January 4, 18, February 8, 1926. Scott, "The French Quarter Renaissance," 194-202.

28. William Faulkner was twenty-seven years old when he moved in with Spratling. Spratling, *File on Spratling,* 21-22. Malcolm Cowley, ed., *The Portable Faulkner* (New York: Penguin, 1977), viii. Townsend, 203-19. James C. Watson, ed., *Thinking of Home: William Faulkner's Letters to His Mother and Father 1918-1925* (New York: W. W. Norton, 1992), 167-69, 176-77, 186-89. Carvel Collins, ed., *William Faulkner: New Orleans Sketches* (New York: Random House, 1958), xviii.

29. Scott, "The French Quarter Renaissance," 238-44. *New Orleans States,* March 15, 22, 1925. William Faulkner, *Mosquitoes* (New York: Liveright, 1926), 1-7. Spratling, *File on Spratling,* 29. Cowley, ix. Townsend, 222-23. Elizabeth Anderson and Gerald R. Kelly, *Miss Elizabeth: A Memoir* (Boston: Little,

Brown, 1969), 117-21. The guests on Anderson's yacht named by Natalie included Virginia Parker, the Marc Antonys, Mrs. Kahn, Bill Faulkner, Bill Spratling, Sam Gilmore, and Hamilton Basso. Faulkner wrote to his mother many more details in late March, noting there were about twelve on board (perhaps including the crew). Watson, 181, 187-88.

30. *New Orleans States,* February 17, 22, March 8, 1925. McNickle, 32-35, 39-42, 44-59. Anderson and Kelly, 195, 205. Scott, "The French Quarter Renaissance," 203-15.

31. *New Orleans States,* March 8, 1925. Esther Dupuy Breckinridge, interview by author, New Orleans, April 7, 15, 1997.

32. *New Orleans States,* February 17, April 21, July 5, August 23, 1925. N.V.S. Collection (Box 15, Folder 3). Preliminary report entitled "Archeological and Ethnographic Expedition to Middle America," *Tulane News Bulletin* 6, no. 1 (October 1925). *Preservation Magazine* 23, no. 1 (February 1996). Esther Dupuy Breckinridge, interview by author, New Orleans, April 7, 15, August 24, 1997. Enrique Alferez, interview by author, New Orleans, June 20, 1996, which confirmed location of Blom's Pontalba apartment. Scott, "The French Quarter Renaissance," 203-15, 284, 318, 323. McNickle, 32-35, 39-42, 44-59. *New Orleans States,* February 17, 22, March 8, 1925. The fact that La Farge came to New Orleans before going to Mexico is established by cited newspaper accounts.

33. Scott, "William Spratling in New Orleans," 8-16, 21-23. *New Orleans States,* July 12, August 23, October 18, 1925. Watson, 217. Breckinridge, interview, April 15, 1997. McNickle, 39-52. Spratling, *File on Spratling,* 17-19. Morrill, *Mexican Silver,* ix-21. Scott, "The French Quarter Renaissance," 213-15, 234-37, 254-57, 260-62, 264-65.

34. Ibid. Frans Blom and Oliver La Farge, *Tribes and Temples,* 2 vols. (New Orleans: Tulane University Press, 1926). *New Orleans States,* March 8, 15, 20-22, June 8, 1925; December 3, 1926; July 15, 1928; February 24, 1929; May 18, 1930. La Farge's short stories, based upon Indian topics and characters, were published by *Scribner's* in 1926 and *Dial* in January and February 1927. Edmund Wilson, *The Twenties* (New York: Farrar, Straus and Giroux, 1975). Littleton, 50, 28, 133, 137. Scott, "The French Quarter Renaissance," 235, 240, 242, 318-19, 323, 344-45, 350-52, 360, 369-74, 405-10. *New Orleans Times-Picayune,* March 7, 20-22, 1925. Spratling, *File on Spratling,* 29-30. William Faulkner, "Sherwood Anderson: An Appreciation," *The Atlantic Monthly* 1991 (June 1953): 27, 28. Townsend, 213-32, 302-4. Thomas, *Lyle Saxon,* viii-ix, 52-58, 101-31, 133-52, 177-82. Tallant, 307-28. Richard S. Kennedy, *Literary New Orleans in the Modern World,* 83, 102, 123, 136. Richard S. Kennedy, *Literary New Orleans: Essays and Meditations* (Baton Rouge: LSU Press, 1992), 51-60, 83-88. *The Double Dealer* (January-February, April, June 1925). Spratling, *New Orleans Sketches,* v-3, 132-39.

35. The Historic New Orleans Collection, French Quarter Survey. Orleans Parish Conveyance Records (book 423, 31). Natalie purchased the Court of Two Sisters, 613-15 Royal Street, on July 14, 1925, from the heirs of Emile B. Angaud, a boot and shoe merchant. She resold the property at a profit to Anthony Denapolis on August 16, 1926. *New Orleans States,* September 27, October 4, 1925. Orleans Parish Conveyance Records (book 398, 125; book 403, 73) confirm Natalie's acquisition of 621 St. Peter Street. *New Orleans States,* December 6, 1925; Natalie purchased the building for $3,000 on April 2, 1925; she sold it on August 27, 1926, for $9,000. Scott, "The French Quarter Renaissance," 249-50, 258, 260, 265.

36. Sidonie Scott Thomas, interviews by author, January 19, May 15, June 15, 1996. Nauman S. Scott, Jr., interview. Scott, "The French Quarter Renaissance," 270-84. *Alexandria Daily Town Talk,* June 15, 1926. *New Orleans States,* June 6, 15, 27, October 17, 1926. Nauman S. Scott death certificate dated June 15,

1926, 7709, La. Bureau of Vital Statistics. Nathaniel G. Scott death certificate, dated July 6, 1926, Orleans Parish death records (book 192, 1681). *New Orleans Times-Picayune,* October 25, 1925. Littleton, 90. N.V.S. Collection (Box 12, Folder 8).

37. Scott, "William Spratling and the French Quarter Renaissance." Bowen, "The *Double Dealer,*" 20-34. Bowen, "The New Orleans *Double Dealer,*" 454. Ms. Bowen wrote: "Although McClure and Friend insist today that lack of time on the part of the staff was the sole cause of their discontinuance, one [Ms. Bowen] is forced to conclude this was merely the apparent reason."

38. Scott, "The French Quarter Renaissance," 286-303. N.V.S. Collection (Box 3, Folder 3), postcard to her niece (Sidonie Scott Thomas), October 1926. *New Orleans States,* November 2, 14, 20-21, December 12, 16, 1926. Charles W. Durieux, interview by author, April 18, 1997. *Mexican Folkways* 3, et seq. (1927). Natalie would resume her literary work for *Mexican Folkways* in 1929 and 1930 upon her return to Mexico. Frances Toor, a young Californian, had come to Mexico two years earlier when writing her master's thesis (University of California); she stayed and began publishing her magazine in 1925.

39. *New Orleans States,* December 12, 1926.

40. Sherwood Anderson Collection, Smyth County Library. Townsend, 218-27. Spratling, *File on Spratling,* 21-30. Anderson and Kelly, 98-102, 150-55. William P. Spratling, "Chronicle of a Friendship," *University of Texas Quarterly* (1966). William Spratling, *Sherwood Anderson and Other Famous Creoles* (reprint, Austin: University of Texas Press, 1966), 11-16.

41. Scott, "William Spratling and the French Quarter Renaissance." Spratling, "Chronicle of a Friendship," 12-13. Scott, "The French Quarter Renaissance," 303-14, sets forth a detailed history and analysis of Spratling and Faulkner's little book, *Sherwood Anderson and Other Famous Creoles.* Its caricatures offered a Who's Who of the New Orleans art and literary world. Though the publication was Spratling's idea, by December it had become a joint enterprise with Faulkner, "with a neatly turned introduction in Sherwood Anderson's own style, done by Bill Faulkner," Natalie noted. "Sherwood's own massive head looks out of the front page . . . concludes with a caricature of the author and the artist." The slim volume provides glimpses of life within their inner circle: inside jokes and settings. The frontispiece, entitled "The Locale," was Spratling's drawing of the St. Peter-Cabildo Alley-Orleans Alley neighborhood. Spratling is shown climbing onto the roof of his attic apartment, while Faulkner leans out a window. Also portrayed were other characters and studio locations of artists, writers, and creative people living there: artist Alberta Kinsey is painting before her easel; Flo Field is leading a tourists tour through the alley; decorator Mark Antony is at work in his apartment with his Leonardo Studio on the corner; the anonymous young priest from St. Louis Cathedral who supplied their illegal alcohol is drawn at their door; the apartment of Conrad Albrizio is identified with the initials "C.A.A."; and the Scott-McClure House is noted as "Literature and Less," the name of McClure's popular *Times-Picayune* column. The anonymous priest dealing in the illegal alcohol trade is identified in the Faulkner biography by Joel Williamson, *Faulkner and Southern History* (Oxford: Oxford University Press, 1993), 199.

42. Spratling's leading biographer is Penny Chittim Morrill. Williamson, *Faulkner,* 202, 215. Breckinridge, interview, April 15, 1997.

43. Scott and Spratling, *Old Plantation Houses in Louisiana. New Orleans States,* October 16, December 26, 1926; March 6, May 22, June 18, July 10, August 7, 15, December 12, 1927; February 26, April 29, 1928. Scott, "The French Quarter Renaissance," 320-34. An analysis, with prolific quotations from *Zombi,* appears in Scott, "The French Quarter Renaissance," 337-43. Isaacs, 309-28. *New Orleans Item,* April 1943; May 2, 1950. *New Orleans*

Times-Picayune, December 18, 1927; January 1, 1928; April 10, 1943; May 2, 1950. Breckinridge interview, April 7, 15, 1997. Natalie Scott postcards, April 25, August 18, November 15, 1927 (Scott Family Collection). N.V.S. Collection (Box 3, Folders 3, 15; Box 13, Folders 11, 15, 17; Box 14, Folder 4). *Mexico City News,* July 29, 1950; June 27, 1955. Sidonie Scott Thomas interview. Nauman S. Scott, Jr., interview. *Dixie* (May 31, 1953). *The Tulanian* (March 1935).

44. Orleans Parish Conveyance Records on each N.V.S. property: 626 Orleans Alley, 1921 (book 340, 469 and 1937 (book 449, 54); 714 St. Peter Street, 1922 (book 347, 384) and 1925 (book 396, 274); 621 St. Peter Street, 1925 (book 396, 125; book 403, 42); Court of Two Sisters, 1925 (book 394, 489) and 1926 (book 423, 30); St. Ann and Royal Street, 1925 (book 403, 47) and 1926 (book 408, 364); Carondelet-Baronne-Clio-Calliope streets property acquired with Samuel L. Gilmore, 1926 (book 417, 407) and 1930 (book 444, 435); 439 Lowerline Street, May 29, 1928 (book 434, 565). Celeste Lyons Frierson, interview by author, New Orleans, February 10, March 2-3, 1996. N.V.S. Collection (Box 2, Folder 9). N.V.S. Collection, N.V.S. letter to Lyle Saxon, February 19, 1929, confirms N.V.S. and Spratling contemplation in December 1928 of residing in Mexico. Scott, "The French Quarter Renaissance," 334-38. John P. Hammond and Arthur B. Hammond, interview by author, New Orleans, March 18, 1997.

45. See note 34. *New Orleans States,* May 27, June 1, 1928. Littleton, 130-32.

46. Townsend, 218-27, 249. Welford Dunaway Taylor and Charles E. Modlin, ed., *Southern Odyssey: Selected Writings by Sherwood Anderson* (Athens: University of Georgia Press, 1997), 186-89. Anderson and Kelly, 188-95. Elizabeth Anderson's memoirs explain that she had received an invitation (1935) from Natalie Scott to visit her in Taxco. This is confirmed in Natalie's correspondence from Taxco, 1935-36 (N.V.S. Collection). Natalie's 1928 visit for several days with Sherwood Anderson in Marion, Virginia, was reported in New Orleans newspapers. Sherwood wrote of his friend's visit and their long talks the next week in the *Marion Democrat. New Orleans States,* August 26, 1928.

47. Hammond and Hammond, interview. Scott, "The French Quarter Renaissance," 344, 356-59. Lillian Hammond Waterhouse, interview by author, Naples, Fla., June 23, 1998. *New Orleans Illustrated News,* 1929-30. Hilda was social editor of this New Orleans magazine. Blanche Scott, interview by Pamela Tyler, October 24, 1984. Hilda Phelps Hammond, *Pierre and Ninette in Old New Orleans* (New Orleans: Hauser Press, 1946). Oliver La Farge married in New York in 1929; Natalie hosted an elaborate dinner party for the couple in her Lowerline home. *New Orleans States,* May 26, November 3, 10, 1929. Also see Scott, "The French Quarter Renaissance," 362-64; Breckinridge, interview, April 7, 15, August 24, 1997. Natalie V. Scott, *Mandy's Favorite Louisiana Recipes* (Gretna, La.: Pelican, 1978, et seq.). This book was originally privately printed in New Orleans in 1929 as *Mirations and Miracles of Mandy.* Natalie published numerous subsequent editions *Mexican Folkways* (January 1930).

48. Scott, *Mandy's.* Natalie V. Scott, *200 Years of New Orleans Cooking* (New York: Cape and Smith, 1931; reprint, Gretna, La.: Pelican, 1999). Natalie Vivian Scott, *Your Mexican Kitchen* (New York: G. P. Putnam's Sons, 1935). Natalie Vivian Scott, *Mexican Cookbook* (Mexico City: n.p., 1939). Natalie Vivian Scott and Caroline Merrick Jones, *Gourmet's Guide to New Orleans: Creole Cookbook* (New Orleans: Scott and Jones, 1933, with 20 printings by 1957; reprint, Gretna, La.: Pelican, 1975). Conchita Castrejón, interview by author, Taxco, Mexico, August 1997.

49. Le Petit Théâtre Archives. *New Orleans States,* November 3, 10, 24, December 15, 1929. *New Orleans Times-Picayune,* November 24, December 1, 1929. Martha Robinson Collection (Box 2, Folder 9). N.V.S. Collection, N.V.S. letter to *Atlantic Monthly* magazine, September 23, 1938.

50. Scott, "The French Quarter Renaissance," 344-45, 350-52, 360, 369-74. Scott, "William Spratling in New Orleans," 20-21, 25-30. Littleton, 130-36, 139, 159, 166. *New Orleans States,* November 11, December 16, 1928; March 24, September 15, 1929. Esther Dupuy Breckinridge, interview by author, New Orleans, August 29, 1997. Morrill, *Mexican Silver,* 119-21. Spratling, *File on Spratling,* 36-38. William Spratling, *Lienzo de Noxtepec,* Latin American Library Collection, Tulane University. Spratling, *Sherwood Anderson and Other Famous Creoles,* 73-80. Lesley Byrd Simpson, foreword to *A Small Mexican World* (Boston: Little, Brown, 1964); this is a reprint of the original *Little Mexico.*

51. *New Orleans States,* July 6, 1930. *Mexican Folkways* (January 1930). Natalie departed from New Orleans by ship on May 8, 1930, proceeding by the same ship and train route to Mexico City as on her 1926 trip. She continued by collectivo to Cuernavaca via the ancient cobblestone road built by Cortez's army in the sixteenth century then on to Taxco. N.V.S. Collection (Box 3, Folder 3), letter to her niece (Sidonie Scott Thomas), April 29, 1930.

Chapter 8

1. *New Orleans States,* August 18, 1929. Alma Gutierrez, *Taxco* (Mexico City: n.p., 1996). Margarita Dominguez Islas, *Tasco: Histories, Biográfico, Anecdotico y Legendario* (Mexico City: n.p., 1996). Leslie C. De Figueroa, *Taxco: The Enchanted Hill Town,* 3rd ed. (Mexico City: n.p., 1965).

2. *New Orleans States,* July 6, 29, 1930. *Mexican Folkways* (March-April 1930): 80-83; (May-June 1930): 132, 146. *Mexico City News,* July 29, 1950, p. 12. Alice Crouch letter to Sidonie Scott Thomas, February 12, 1976 (Scott Family Collection). *Mexico City Herald,* May 31, 1949, p. 4.

3. N.V.S. Collection, correspondence 1930. Luis Reyes, interview by author, Taxco, Mexico, July 16, 1996. William Spratling, *Little Mexico* (New York: Jonathan Cape and Harrison Smith, 1932), 23-68. Spratling letter to Carl Zigrosser, September 24, 1931, Carl Zigrosser Papers, Archives of American Art; originals at University of Pennsylvania, Van Pelt Library. Spratling willed much of his collection to the town of Taxco; it is now housed there in the William Spratling Museum. Ambassador Morrow had entrusted him with the task of gathering an authentic pre-Columbian art collection for Morrow's Cuernavaca home, providing funds he had badly needed and an opportunity to acquaint himself with the variations of tribal groups and obscure sources of valuable collectibles. Spratling gradually acquired a valuable collection of his own, also bringing items back to New Orleans for Frans Blom to market to museums or include in the Tulane collection.

4. Spratling, *Little Mexico,* 18-23 .

5. Natalie Scott, "Don Guillermo of Taxco," *The New Orleanian* (November 15, 1930). N.V.S. Collection, correspondence 1930. Martha Robinson Collection, correspondence 1930. Ernie Pyle, *The Story of a Girl Who Was Afraid* (Bloomington: Indiana University Press, 1936).

6. N.V.S. Collection, correspondence 1930-43. *Mexican Folkways* (1930-35). Charles Nibbi records, Hotel Victoria, Taxco, Mexico. Reyes, interview, July 16, 1996. Spratling, *File on Spratling,* 19-69, 97-107, 188-205. Conchita Castrejón, interview by author, Taxco, Mexico, July 15, 1996. Antonio Castillo, interview by author, Taxco, Mexico, August 1996.

7. David Alfaro Siqueiros, *13 Grabados* (Taxco: n.p., 1931). Philip Stein, *Siqueiros: His Life and Works* (New York: International, 1994), 155-58. Spratling, *File on Spratling,* 19-69, 97-107. The address of the Durieux house renovated by Natalie Scott was Chava Rietta 9. Reyes, interview, July 16, 1996.

8. July (Mrs. Arthur) Waters, interview by Dorothy Schlesinger, Friends of the Cabildo Oral History Project, New Orleans, October 6, 1982.

9. Reyes, interview, July 16, 1996. Reyes was the telegraph-postal delivery boy in Taxco during 1928-32; he knew the location of every home in the village. Museo Nacional de Arte, *David Alfaro Siqueiros: Portrait of a Decade, 1930-1940* (Mexico City: Patronado del Museo Nacional de Arte, 1997), 32-33, 37-39, 41, 43, 45, 76, 118, 139, 141. *New Orleans Item Tribune,* February 14, 1932. The Historic New Orleans Collection, Arts and Crafts Club Archives. N.V.S. Collection (Box 3).

10. En route, Natalie and Blanca Luz were delayed by a flat tire, Natalie finding the moment humorous enough to take photographs (now in the N.V.S. Collection). An international audience, including Hart Crane and Russian filmmaker Sergei Eisenstein, attended the Siqueiros exhibit.

11. Carl Zigrosser Papers, N.V.S. letter to Zigrosser, May 3, 1933. Stein, 68-73.

12. See note 11. Littleton, 231. Carl Zigrosser Papers, Spratling letter to Zigrosser, March 15, 1934. Spratling, *Little Mexico. New Orleans Times-Picayune,* May 22, 1938. Scott, "Don Guillermo of Taxco," Natalie leased her Callejón de la Luz house to another American, John Evans, then to artist Howard Cook and his wife.

13. Spratling, *File on Spratling,* 98-102. John Unterecker, *Voyager: A Life of Hart Crane* (1969; reprint, New York: Liveright, 1987), 712-35. Katherine Anne Porter Collection, University of Maryland, N.V.S. letter to Porter, November 5, 1935.

14. Thomas S. W. Lewis, *Letters of Hart Crane and His Family* (New York: Columbia University Press, 1947), 649. Unterecker, 714, 728, 732. Hart Crane letter to his mother, January 9, 1932, quoted in Unterecker.

15. Spratling, *File on Spratling,* 58-59.

16. Reyes, interview, July 16, 1996. Spratling, *File on Spratling,* 58, 60. Katherine Anne Porter Collection.

17. H. Allen Smith, *The Pig in the Barber Shop* (Boston: Little, Brown, 1958), 165. Anderson and Kelly, 216-17. Katherine Anne Porter Collection. *New Orleans States,* July 29, 1934. Alferez, June 20, 1996. A 1989 letter from Austin Boyle in the possession of the Alferez family contains fond reminiscences of his week on the horseback journey led by Natalie Scott. David Read, interview by author, Taxco, Mexico, July 20, 1996. Lois Boyle, interview by author, Cleveland, Ohio, July 1996.

18. See note 17. Dorothy Sutherland Chittim, interview by author, June 15, 1996. Sidonie Scott Thomas, interview, New Orleans and Alexandria, La., January 19, May 17, June 15, 1996. N.V.S. Collection (Box 3, Folder 3), postcard to Martha Gilmore Robinson. Pyle. Morrill, *Mexican Silver,* 20-21.

19. The *retablo* is owned by Natalie's great-niece, Natalie Vivian Scott, daughter of Albin P. Scott.

20. See note 17. Chittim, interview.

21. Anderson and Kelly, 216-17.

22. Katherine Anne Porter Collection, University of Maryland, Porter letter to N.V.S., December 1, 1935; N.V.S. letter to Porter, April 10, 1936.

23. Martha Robinson Collection (Box 2, Folder 7), N.V.S. letter to Robinson, March 19, 1936. Donald Cordry Collection, Benson Latin American Collection, University of Texas at Austin. The Heye Foundation is now the Museum of the American Indian.

24. Frierson, interview.

25. Katherine Anne Porter Collection, N.V.S. letter to Porter, November 5, 1935.

26. Pyle.

27. Natalie Vivian Scott, "WWL Interview: Viva Mexico" (New Orleans: Tulane Latin American Studies Special Collection, November 11, 1936).

28. Frans Blom Collection, Tulane Middle American Research Institute, N.V.S. letter to Blom, July 4, 1937.

29. Frans Blom Collection, Blom letter to N.V.S., July 8, 1937.

30. Frans Blom Collection, N.V.S. letter to Blom, July 4, August 26, 1937; Blom letter to N.V.S., July 8, September 3-4, 1937.

31. Martha Robinson Collection, N.V.S. letter to Robinson, September 21, 1938. Natalie V. Scott, *Book of Verses for the Dance of the Companions of Santiago* (New Orleans: Tulane Latin American Library, 1938).

32. Martha Robinson Collection, N.V.S. letter to Robinson, July 6, 1939.

33. "Foreigners in Taxco," *Modern Mexico* (May 1938). *New Orleans Times-Picayune,* May 22, 1938.

34. Amador Lugo, interview by author, Taxco, Mexico, July 16, 1996. MacKinley Helm, *Mexico Painters: Rivera, Orozco, Siqueiros and Other Artists of the Social Realist School* (1941; reprint, New York: Dover, 1989), 187-88. Taxco Municipal Archives, C.E.P.E., Universidad National Autonoma de Mexico, Taxco, Gro. Kitigawa, a protégé of Picasso, taught in Díaz de León's school, then became the director in Taxco of the last of the government-supported open-air art schools. Helm wrote that Kitigawa, more than any other visitor from a different culture, accurately painted the spirit of Mexico.

35. Martha Robinson Collection, N.V.S. letter to Robinson, October 4, 1938. Read, interview. Board of Directors, the Guardería de Niños de Natalie Scott, interview by author, Taxco, Mexico, July 18, 1996. Guardería de Niños de Natalie Scott (Guardería de Niños Sor Juana Inez de la Cruz de Taxco, Gro.) Archives, Taxco, Mexico.

36. Castrejón, interview, July 15, 1996. Señora Castrejón's husband owned the Coca-Cola franchise in the state of Guerrero. She attended Natalie's first meeting to organize the Guardería de Niños in December 1938. Guardería de Niños Archives.

37. Guardería de Niños Archives. The other original board members (Mesa Directiva) were leading Taxco women: Sra. Angela Selana (vice-president), Sra. Consuela L. de Cardenas (secretary), Sra. Lois C. de Aguilar (pro-secretária), Sra. María Luisa L. de Curiel (treasurer), Srta. Secorro Guerreros, Sra. Felisa Mastachi, and Sra. Sofía G. de Alba. Martha Robinson Collection, N.V.S. letter to Robinson, August 26, 1939.

38. See note 37. N.V.S. to Robinson, November 30, 1939. Guardería de Niños Archives.

39. Martha Robinson Collection, N.V.S. letter to Robinson, March 19, 1936; July 6, 1939. Katherine Anne Porter Collection, N.V.S. letter to Porter, November 5, 1935; April 10, 1936.

40. Martha Robinson Collection, N.V.S. letter to Robinson, April 1, 1939.

41. Martha Robinson Collection, N.V.S. letter to Robinson, April 17, 1939.

42. Martha Robinson Collection, N.V.S. letter to Robinson, July 19, 1938.

43. Martha Robinson Collection, N.V.S. letter to Robinson, August 26, 1939. Sidonie Scott Thomas letter to her mother, Sidonie P. Scott, August 26, 1939 (Scott Family Collection). Sidonie Scott Thomas, interview by author, November 18, 2001.

44. Martha Robinson Collection, N.V.S. letter to Robinson, March 19, 1936.

45. Martha Robinson Collection, N.V.S. letter to Robinson, March 1, 1938.

46. Martha Robinson Collection, N.V.S. letter to Robinson, September 21, 1938.

47. Martha Robinson Collection, N.V.S. letter to Robinson, October 4, 1938.

48. N.V.S. Collection, N.V.S. letter to Agnes George Hardie, March 6, 1939.

49. N.V.S. Collection, N.V.S. letter to the editor, *Atlantic Monthly* (September 23, 1938).

50. Martha Robinson Collection, N.V.S. letter to Robinson, April 1, 1939.

51. Martha Robinson Collection, N.V.S. letter to Robinson, April 17, 1939.

52. Martha Robinson Collection, N.V.S. letter to Robinson, May 16, 1939.

53. Martha Robinson Collection, N.V.S. letter to Robinson, August 26, 1939.

Chapter 9

1. N.V.S. Collection, N.V.S. letter to Robinson, April 9, 1940.

2. N.V.S. Collection, N.V.S. letter to Robinson, March 23, 1942.

3. N.V.S. Collection, N.V.S. letter to Robinson, March 16, November 3, 1940. Natalie and Paul Bowles shared mutual literary friends in New York and Paris. Eugene Jolas, editor of *Transition* in Paris, with whom Natalie worked in 1927, had published a short story by Bowles in the early 1930s. This influential periodical published the words of leading thinkers of the day, James Joyce, Gertrude Stein, H. L. Mencken, Franz Kafka, Ezra Pound, William Carlos Williams, and David Alfaro Siqueiros among them. Natalie would reunite with Jolas in Paris when it was liberated in 1944.

4. N.V.S. Collection, N.V.S. letter to Frances Toor, November 23, 1940.

5. N.V.S. Collection, N.V.S. letter to Robinson, April 9, 1940.

6. N.V.S. Collection, N.V.S. letter to Robinson, March 23, 1942.

7. N.V.S. Collection, N.V.S. letter to Robinson, November 3, 1940.

8. Ibid.

9. N.V.S. Collection, N.V.S. letter to Robinson, March 23, 1942.

10. Ibid.

11. Ibid. Ana Brilanti, interview by author, Taxco, Mexico, July 20, 1996.

12. Brilanti, interview.

13. N.V.S. Collection, N.V.S. letter to Robinson, August 13, 1942.

14. N.V.S. Collection, N.V.S. letter to Robinson, September 1, 1942.

15. N.V.S. Collection, N.V.S. letter to Robinson, September 21, 1942.

16. N.V.S. Collection, N.V.S. letter to Robinson, Spetember 1, 21, 1942.

17. N.V.S. Collection, N.V.S. letter to Robinson, December 16, 1942.

18. N.V.S. Collection, N.V.S. letter to Robinson, August 13, 1942.

19. N.V.S. Collection, N.V.S. letter to Robinson, October 22, 1942.

20. N.V.S. Collection, N.V.S. letter to Robinson, December 16, 1942; January 23, 1943. Natalie had left the Guardería in the managerial care of her friend Alice Crouch, María Estrada, and the board. Monthly financial pledges from donors and the government stipend were adequate to cover overhead for the immediate future. Her plan was that if she failed to get a war job, she would resume her work in Taxco. If the war job came through as hoped, Natalie's cookbook and house-rental income, together with a portion of her new salary, would be devoted to the peasant school. The Kitigawa House would be sold. These financial details would be tended to by reliable Taxco friend Alice Crouch. Guardería de Niños Archives.

21. Young, 351-52.

22. *New Orleans Times-Picayune,* July 29, 1943. N.V.S. Collection (Box 13, Folder 11). Informed she would ship out from New York in June, Natalie decided she had time for a quick trip to Colorado Springs, where her niece and godchild, Bé Scott Thomas, was hospitalized with tuberculosis. Her husband was on duty with the navy, and her mother, Sidonie, was attending her. In late April, on her return trip, Natalie made a stopover in New Orleans to see her two-week-old great-niece, the infant's parents being Natalie's godchild Blanche Hammond Scott (Hilda Hammond's daughter) and Natalie's nephew Nauman Scott, Jr.; the couple had married in January 1942.

23. *New Orleans Times-Picayune,* August 11, 1943. N.V.S. Collection (Box 13,

Folder 11). Dwight D. Eisenhower, *Crusade in Europe* (New York: Doubleday, 1948), 156-58.

24. *New Orleans Times-Picayune,* September 26, 1943.

25. N.V.S. Collection, N.V.S. letter to Martha Gilmore Robinson, October 28, November 12, 1943.

26. N.V.S. Collection, N.V.S. letter to Robinson, November 12, 1943.

27. N.V.S. Collection, N.V.S. letter to Robinson, December 3, 15, 1943.

28. Ibid.

29. N.V.S. Collection, N.V.S. letter to Robinson, December 30, 1943.

30. N.V.S. Collection, N.V.S. letter to Robinson, January 5, 1944.

31. N.V.S. Collection, N.V.S. letter to Robinson, March 5, 1944.

32. Martha Robinson Collection, *Newcomb Alumnae News* (March 1944).

33. N.V.S. Collection, N.V.S. to Robinson, March 5, 1944.

34. N.V.S. Collection, N.V.S. letter to Anne Kennedy of All-Americas Literary Agency, March 17, 1944; Anne Kennedy letter to Martha Robinson, March 29, 1944; Martha Robinson letter to Anne Kennedy, April 11, 1944.

35. N.V.S. Collection, N.V.S. letter to Robinson, March 5, 17, 1944.

36. N.V.S. Collection, N.V.S. letter to Robinson, March 17, 1944.

37. N.V.S. Collection, Roy Korbin family letters, March 23, 29, 1944; N.V.S. letter to Robinson, March 25, April 7, 1944.

38. N.V.S. Collection, N.V.S. letter to Robinson, April 7, 1944.

39. N.V.S. Collection, N.V.S. letter to Robinson, April 27, 1944.

40. N.V.S. Collection, N.V.S. letter to Robinson, Hilda Phelps Hammond, and Sidonie P. Scott, May 24, 1944.

41. Eisenhower, 174-86, 190. Eisenhower's headquarters were in Algiers, where he directed the Italy campaign until Christmas 1943, when he turned his full attention to D-Day planning.

42. N.V.S. Collection, N.V.S. letter to Robinson, Hammond, and Scott, June 17, 1944.

43. Ibid.

44. N.V.S. Collection, N.V.S. letter to Robinson, June 23, undated July, July 18, 1944. Kay Parsons and Emily Cunningham, co-workers in Oran, were with her for her birthday. Natalie wrote to Martha: *It was a surprise to have her [Cunningham] turn up on DS [Detached Service] with us, when the AFD and her pal, Maureen, the Rec-Director, went off together on leave. . . . A Col. and 2 nice Lts. severally asking me to dinner this evening but I already made a date,—going out for the sole reason that I want my new white dress to be seen. I can see you sniff.*

45. N.V.S. Collection, N.V.S. letter to Robinson, August 1, 1944.

46. N.V.S. Collection, N.V.S. letter to Robinson, August 1, September 11, 1944.

47. N.V.S. Collection, N.V.S. letter to Robinson, September 11, 27, 1944.

48. N.V.S. Collection, N.V.S. letter to Robinson, September 11, 1944. Eisenhower, 213, 264. The steady military advance up the Italian peninsula demanded a succession of outflanking operations by sea, as the mountainous frontiers rendered a head-on approach slow and costly. The Anzio operations in 1944 became the most important of these, providing a vital step north towards Rome. The move also convinced Hitler that the Allies intended a major push in the Italian campaign, causing him to shift eight divisions to Italy and weakening his defenses in France and elsewhere. American troops had entered Rome during June 1944, almost simultaneous with D-Day and Natalie's arrival in Naples. Winston S. Churchill, *Closing the Ring* (New York: Houghton Mifflin, 1951), 523.

49. N.V.S. Collection, N.V.S. letter to Robinson, September 27, 1944. The pope during World War II was Pope Pius XII.

Chapter 10

1. N.V.S. Collection, N.V.S. letter to Martha Gilmore Robinson, October 18, 1944.

2. Eisenhower, 282, 304.

3. N.V.S. Collection, N.V.S. letter to Robinson, October 18, 1944 (entry of October 21, 1944).

4. N.V.S. Collection, N.V.S. letter to Robinson, October 18, 1944 (entry of November 14, 1944).

5. Ibid.

6. Ibid..

7. N.V.S. Collection, N.V.S. to Robinson, September 27, October 18, 1944.

8. N.V.S. Collection, N.V.S. to Robinson, October 18, 1944 (entry of November 14, 1944).

9. Martha Robinson's four sons were in the war: Bobby in France with the Engineers Corps, Jack in the Pacific with the Marines, Charles ("Tar") in Europe as a pilot, and Tizo with the merchant marines. N.V.S. Collection, N.V.S. letter to Robinson, October 30, November 14, 1944.

10. N.V.S. Collection, N.V.S. letter to Robinson, November 14, 1944.

11. N.V.S. Collection, N.V.S. letter to Robinson, December 2, 1944.

12. N.V.S. Collection, N.V.S. letter to Robinson, December 9, 1944.

13. N.V.S. Collection, N.V.S. letter to Robinson, January 14, 1945.

14. N.V.S. Collection, N.V.S. letter to Robinson, Hilda Phelps Hammond, and Sidonie P. Scott, February 6, 1945.

15. Ibid.

16. Ibid.

17. N.V.S. Collection, N.V.S. letter to Robinson, January 14, 1945.

18. N.V.S. Collection, N.V.S. letter to Robinson, February 1, 1945.

19. Eisenhower, 320-22, 392-94, 418-19.

20. N.V.S. Collection, N.V.S. letter to Robinson, February 1, 1945.

21. N.V.S. Collection, N.V.S. letter to friends at 70th Hospital, Southern France, early February 1945.

22. N.V.S. Collection, N.V.S. letter to Robinson, March 14, 1945.

23. N.V.S. Collection, N.V.S. letter to Robinson, March 22, 1945.

24. N.V.S. Collection, N.V.S. letter to Robinson, April 7, 1945.

25. N.V.S. Collection, N.V.S. letter to Virginia Reese-Withers, March 1945.

26. N.V.S. Collection, N.V.S. letter to Robinson, April 17, 1945.

27. N.V.S. Collection, N.V.S. letter to Robinson, Hammond, and Scott, Easter 1945.

28. Ibid. (entry of May 3, 1945).

29. Winston S. Churchill, *The Second World War: Triumph and Tragedy* (New York: Houghton Mifflin, 1953), 469.

30. N.V.S. Collection, N.V.S. letter to Robinson, May 16, 1945.

31. Ibid.

32. N.V.S. Collection, N.V.S. letter to Robinson, May 19, 1945.

33. N.V.S. Collection, N.V.S. letter to Robinson, June 5, 1945.

34. Ibid.

35. N.V.S. Collection, N.V.S. letter to Robinson, June 20, 1945. Natalie had seen old friends in London, took Nauman to the country for a weekend and attended a play, *Mr. Jacobsky and the Colonel. It was not too clever, but pleased me in that it was an understanding and sympathetic treatment of the Jewish question. I am finding my worst fears confirmed by England's contin-ued imperialistic incurable ways, in international politics. And we follow meekly in her train! One advantage of going to the Pacific is that I shan't have*

time to stew over it all. And certainly there is nothing I can do. The high-hand-ed insulting attitude they've taken towards the French in Syria makes me boil. And their objecting to our ideas as to bases in the Pacific for fear that the natives there might get kicked about! This, from England! Of course she has always been jealous of the favorable understanding France had in Syria and the famous pipe-line. And now as always, she uses her power,—with our tacit backing.

Mr. Churchill was the grand old man of the war; but I do hope he gets defeat-ed. The difficulty is that the less reactionary forces have been cleverly divided by those astute politicians. It looks as tho Mr. Churchill will be 'returned'. This time Natalie was wrong. Churchill's Conservative party met defeat that summer, a loss that, according to Dwight D. Eisenhower, gave the British leader the oppor-tunity for a much-needed short vacation from great responsibilities. Churchill assumed the role of leader of the opposition in the House of Commons, also writ-ing his six-volume memoirs of the war. He returned to power in 1951.

36. Henri Jean Renaud, interview by author, Sainte-Mère Eglise, France, May 30, 2005. N.V.S. Collection, Martha Robinson letter to N.V.S., July 18, 1945; N.V.S. letter to Robinson, June 20, July 25, 1945.

37. N.V.S. Collection, N.V.S. letter to Robinson, July 3, 1945.

38. N.V.S. Collection, N.V.S. letter to Robinson, July 25, 1945.

39.Ibid.; Martha Robinson letter to N.V.S., July 18, 1945. Martha Robinson Collection (Box 11, Folder 1).

40. N.V.S. Collection, N.V.S. letter to Robinson, July 25, 1945.

41. N.V.S. Collection, N.V.S. letter to Robinson, August 5, 1945.

42. New Orleans *Times-Picayune,* September 20, 1945.

43. N.V.S. Collection, N.V.S. letter to Robinson, August 18, 25, 1945.

44. N.V.S. Collection (Box 11, Folder 1), N.V.S. letter to Virginia Reese-Withers, December 1, 1945. The cookbook was probably *Gourmet's Guide to New Orleans.*

45. Ibid.; N.V.S. letter to Robinson, November 26, 1945.

46. N.V.S. Collection, N.V.S. letter to Lyle Saxon, December 1, 1945.

Chapter 11

1. N.V.S. Collection, N.V.S. letter to Bé Scott Thomas, December 24-25, 1945.

2. N.V.S. Collection, N.V.S. letter to Robinson, January 4, 21, 1946. Turner was the soldier in Bino's unit who wrote Bino's letter home about being wounded.

3. N.V.S. Collection, N.V.S. letter to Robinson, June 20, 1946.

4. *Boomerang,* (December 1946).

5. N.V.S. Collection, N.V.S. letter to Virginia Reese-Withers, January 4, 1947.

6. N.V.S. Collection, N.V.S. letter to Robinson, October 30, 1946.

7. N.V.S. Collection, N.V.S. letter to Virginia Reese-Withers, January 4, 1947.

8. N.V.S. Collection, N.V.S. letter to Robinson, March 24, 1947.

9. Ibid.

10. N.V.S. Collection, N.V.S. letter to Robinson, April 15, 1947.

11. Ibid.

12. N.V.S. Collection, N.V.S. letter to Robinson, August 11, 1947.

13. N.V.S. Collection, Willie B. Wisdom letter to N.V.S., April 17, 1948; N.V.S. letter to Pike Thomas, June 11, 1948.

14. N.V.S. Collection, N.V.S. letter to Robinson, August 8, 1949. *Dixie* (May 31, 1953).

15. N.V.S. Collection, N.V.S. letter to Robinson, August 8, 1949.

16. N.V.S. Collection, N.V.S. letter to Robinson, August 13, 1949. Prof. Herbert J. Muller was fifteen years younger than Natalie. He and his family were

regular summer residents of Taxco and Natalie's guests since the 1930s, his children referring to her in letters as Aunt Natalie. Muller, a Cornell Ph.D., taught literature at Purdue University until 1956, then Indiana University, having served with the State Department and the War Production Board during the war. An avid traveler and prolific writer, he twice served as visiting professor at the University of Istanbul as a Fulbright Fellow. Most of his writing in Taxco was in the fields of literary criticism and history, *The Uses of the Past* (1952) being his best known. Some of his other prominent works were *Modern Fiction* (1937), *Science and Criticism* (1943), *Thomas Wolfe* (1947), and *The Spirit of Tragedy* (1956). In his inscribed copy to Natalie of *The Spirit of Tragedy,* which dealt in part with the topics she had tackled in her master's thesis at Tulane in 1914, Muller wrote: "Still another book for Natalie, still with love—Herb."

17. N.V.S. Collection, N.V.S. letter to Robinson, August 13, 1949. *Mexico City News,* May 20, 1949; July 29, 1950. *New Orleans Item,* January 24, 1957. *Dixie* (May 31, 1953).

18. N.V.S. Collection, N.V.S. letter to Robinson, August 15, 1949.

19. *The Tulanian* (March 1950).

20. New Orleans *Times-Picayune,* May 2, 1950. *The Tulanian* (December 1950). *Houston Post,* May 10, 1950. N.V.S. Collection (Box 13, Folder 15).

21. *Mexico City News, July 29, 1950; February 26, 1951. Dixie* (May 31, 1953). Board of Directors, the Guardería de Niños de Natalie Scott, interview. *Mexico City Herald,* May 31, 1949.

22. Mary Louise Doherty Collection, Mary Louise Doherty letters to Katherine Anne Porter, December 27, 1950 and May 10, 15, 1951 (University of Maryland Libraries, McKeldin Library, College Park, Maryland).

23. N.V.S. Collection, N.V.S. letter to Sam Gilmore, November 26, 1950.

24. *Mexico City News,* February 26, 1951.

25. *Laredo Times,* December 9, 1952.

26. Guardería de Niños Archives.

27. N.V.S. Collection (Box 13, Folder 16). *New Orleans Times-Picayune,* October 17, 1951. Hammond and Hammond, interview.

28. Leslie Cortes de Figueroa, *Stuffed Shirt in Taxco* (Taxco: Taxco School of Art, 1962), 66, 98, 131.

29. Ibid.

30. Smith.

31. Read, interview.

32. Ibid.

33. Walter Foulke letter to author, November 10, 1996.

34. Read, interview. N.V.S. Collection, Tulane University.

35. Sidonie Scott Thomas, interview. Carl Pappe, interview by author, Taxco, Mexico, August 9, 1996. *Mexico City News,* November 19-21, 1957. N.V.S. Collection (Box 13, Folder 18). Sidonie Provosty Scott. Nauman S. Scott, Jr., interview. Natalie's nephew, Nauman S. Scott, Jr., arrived in time for the funeral. He served as a pallbearer, carrying Natalie's casket through the streets of Taxco to the cemetery below town.

36. American Foreign Service, "Report of the Death of an American Citizen" (Mexico City, November 29, 1957; No. 10451 [342053]). The death report declared the cause of Natalie's death to be "coronary thrombosis and mesenteric—hypertension, arterial-sclerosis, emphysema pulmonary." Death recorded in Book 13, p. 21, of the Civil Registry of the Federal District of Mexico. Guardería de NiñosArchives.

37. Guardería de Niños Archives.

38. N.V.S. Collection, Vera Von Meysenburg O'Leary, "Hi Verily! What Gives?" (unpublished essay, 1958).

Index